HILLSBOROUGH COUNTY
NEW HAMPSHIRE
COURT RECORDS
1772-1799

Pauline J. Oesterlin

HERITAGE BOOKS
2010

HERITAGE BOOKS

AN IMPRINT OF HERITAGE BOOKS, INC.

Books, CDs, and more—Worldwide

For our listing of thousands of titles see our website
at
www.HeritageBooks.com

Published 2010 by
HERITAGE BOOKS, INC.
Publishing Division
100 Railroad Ave. #104
Westminster, Maryland 21157

Other books by the author:

Hopkinton, New Hampshire Vital Records: Volumes 1 and 2
New Hampshire 1742 Estate List
New Hampshire Marriage Licenses and Intentions, 1709–1961
Rockingham County, New Hampshire Paupers
Surname Guide to Massachusetts Town Histories
Pauline J. Oesterlin and Phyllis O. Longver

International Standard Book Numbers
Paperbound: 978-0-7884-0449-8
Clothbound: 978-0-7884-8561-9

TABLE OF CONTENTS

PREFACE

All the information found in this book was taken from old Hillsborough County court cases. The boxes had been filed away for many years, and the records were in bundles which had to be opened up, cleaned, flattened and filed in acid-free folders and new boxes, before the list could be put on my computer to work with. Land deeds were in a separate bundle. In some cases the amount of time between a transaction and its recording spanned many years.

In this book, there is much information for the genealogist, the land surveyor and anyone interested in what was going on from 1772 to 1799. There is a case involving President Wheelock of Dartmouth College, who had problems acquiring some land in about 1785. You can also find where Paul Revere gave a deposition on the selling of some black powder.

The information found in these records gives the surnames of the main parties, what their occupations were at the time, and where they were living. Judging by the dates that I found on the paperwork, some of the cases were carried on for a few years.

Most of the cases were for a debit, or a judgment for a debit, but also there are fornication cases, land disputes, road layouts, stealing of cattle, tavern license appointments, liquor licenses, and a few cases that the state was involved with. This is a small sample of what you might find; many of the larger cases have many depositions of people, but due to the volume (8,314 names) only a few have been listed here. There also were listed on most deed records a vol and fol number, but due to the fact that the volumes cannot be found this information has been left off in these abstracts.

In many of the land dispute cases that involve deeds, you can find a number of names; one case even gives the relationship of the plaintiff to the landowner. Some of the cases have more than one deed, and of course many of the deeds have the mark or the signature of both the owner and his wife.

The purpose of this book was to give researchers a place where they might find information, and at the same time to help preserve these records.

Pauline Johnson Oesterlin
Genealogist

INTRODUCTION

On April 29, 1769, the New Hampshire General Court, consisting of only a single house, voted to pass "An Act For Dividing This Province into Counties, and for the More Easy Administration of Justice" [Laws of New Hampshire, vol. 3, p.524]. Because such acts required approval by the King, the act was carried to London where it was confirmed on March 19, 1771. By the time notice of confirmation could be returned to New Hampshire it was late 1771 and establishment of county administration became effective only in 1772.. [For a more elaborate treatment see John W. Durel, "Dividing the Province of New Hampshire into Counties," Historical New Hampshire, XXXII (Spring/Summer 1977), 28.] Until then, all records of the province had been maintained by the colonial/provincial secretary, the equivalent of today's secretary of state. Today those colonial/provincial land, court, and probate records are housed at the State Archives in Concord. Upon establishment of five counties—Rockingham, Strafford, Hillsborough, Grafton, and Cheshire—records of land transactions, courts, and probate offices began to be kept by each of the counties at their respective sites.

The Hillsborough County court case records addressed by this index were created at the county seat in Amherst, New Hampshire, and maintained there until a new courthouse was built in the late 20th century in the city of Manchester. In the 1970s these early records were stored in the basement of the Manchester courthouse. The records had been folded into thirds and docketed on the outside, in traditional filing mode, and bundled according to court sessions which occurred four times per year according to law. The case records back up the docket books kept by the clerks of the court.

In the late 1980s these records, dating from 1772 to about 1860 (in terms of sessions in which decisions were made), including the docket books, were physically moved once again, this time to the state archives in Concord where, through the voluntary efforts of Pauline Oesterlin, they have been flat-filed and indexed. They are important not only for purposes of genealogical research and as a history of litigation, but also as a record source for the development of trades and commerce as depicted in the information contained in the documentation.

The publication of this index will only enhance the accessibility of these court records, and hence their value. While the state applauds the efforts of Mrs. Oesterlin and Heritage Books, Inc., users must understand that this index has not been reviewed by the Archives staff, and hence is not an official publication of the State of New Hampshire.

February 22, 1995   Frank C. Mevers
                                     New Hampshire State Archivist

HOW TO USE THIS BOOK

Over 8,000 court records, spanning 1772 to 1799, make up this text. The book is divided into several sections (Individuals, Institutions and Other Assorted Records, and Warnings Out); within each, records have been abstracted in index form, alphabetically by plaintiff name.

The order of elements within these records is: plaintiff's name, occupation/title and residence; defendant's name, occupation/title and residence; document date; date of recording; cause of action; file number (a reference to the original archives); and notations. Not all records contain all this information. In some cases, when the record is of a judgment or court order, there is no *plaintiff;* thus, the indexed name is the first or only name given.

The last section of the book is an index of buried surnames (e.g., those of defendants).

Because some of the terminology found in these records may be unfamiliar, below is a glossary of titles and occupations, followed by brief explanations of several legal processes.

Titles & Occupations

Apothecary — a shopkeeper or person who sells drugs or compounds for medical purposes

Cabinetmaker — a skilled worker who makes fine furniture

Cooper — one who makes and repairs wooden barrels, casks and tubs

Cordwainer — one who makes shoes, boots and wallets from leather; a shoemaker

Distiller — one who distills, esp. alcoholic liquors

Esquire — a landed proprietor; the rank below knight; the title given (in England) to the younger sons of noblemen, to justices

of the peace, sheriffs, landed proprietors, to almost any man of respectable standing

Gentleman — in English law, a man of noble birth; a man of good family or good social position; a farmer of noble birth; one belonging to the landed gentry; a man whose education, occupation or income gives him superior social position and wealth

Gentlewoman — a woman of good family or good social position

Hatter — one who makes, sells, cleans and repairs hats

Husbandman — one who plows and cultivates the land; a farmer

Joiner — a person who constructs furniture by joining pieces of wood together, and has vast knowledge of wood and wood properties; a carpenter or cabinetmaker

Miller — one who operates or owns a mill, especially a grain mill

Planter — one who cultivates plants; also, one who settles or founds a plantation or place, especially a new colony

Shipwright — a carpenter skilled in ship construction and repair

Tinsmith — one who makes articles and utensils out of tin

Turner —one skilled in wood shaping who make furniture parts with a lathe; also, a performer of gymnastic exercises

Victualler — in English law, an innkeeper or person authorized to serve food or drink prepared for consumption on the premises; also, a grocer, food seller or food supplier, usually of unprepared food

Wheelwright — a maker and repairer of wheels and wheeled vehicles

Whitesmith — one who polishes; a tinsmith

Wiggmaker — one who makes wigs for heads

Yeoman — in English law, a commoner; a lesser official or assistant of a royal or noble household; the rank just below gentleman; an independent farmer or landowner of a small amount of land

Legal Processes

Deposition — written testimony given under oath, usually a statement made in response to court questions

Doom • Doomage — a judgment, especially an adverse judgment, penalty or condemnation

"When a person neglects to make a return on his taxable property to the assessors of a town, those officers doom him; that is, judge upon, and fix his tax according to their discretion." – *J. Pickering (1816)*

"If any person refuses to give an invoice of his taxable estate, it is in the power of the selectman, to set down to such a person as much as they judge equitable, by way of doomage; from which there is no appeal." – *J. Belknap (1792)*

Execution — action taken to enforce a court order or judgment

Indictment — a statement written by a prosecuting attorney which charges a party with committing a crime or other offense

Presentment — a statement concerning an offense written by a grand jury, from their own observation and knowledge without any bill of indictment

INDIVIDUALS

ABBOT Darius, gentleman, of Amherst, vs KARR James, gentleman, of Goffstown, rec date 1783, judgment, debt, file #3795

ABBOT Jacob, esquire, of Wilton, vs BEVINS Edward, husbandman, of Lyndeborough, rec date 1783, judgment, debt, file #2857

ABBOT Jacob, esquire, of Wilton, vs ASTEN Timothy, husbandman, of Temple, rec date 1783, judgment, debt, file #2864

ABBOT Jacob, esquire, of Wilton, vs HUTCHINSON George, yeoman, of Wilton, rec date 1782, appeal, debt, file #4031

ABBOT Jacob, esquire, of Andover MA, vs PERRY Obadiah, yeoman, of Wilton, rec date 1784, appeal, debt, file #4141

ABBOT Jacob, esquire, of Andover MA, vs WILKINS Archalous, yeoman, of Wilton, rec date 1784, appeal, debt, file #4141

ABBOT Jacob, esquire, of Andover MA, vs PARKER Henry, yeoman, of Lyndeborough, rec date 1784, appeal, debt, file #4132

ABBOT Jacob, esquire, of Wilton, vs BARKER Phineas, husbandman, of Lyndeborough, rec date 1782, execution, debt, file #5728

ABBOT Nathan, husbandman, of Danvers MA, vs BLANCHARD Jothan, merchant, of Peterborough, rec date 1785, various, debt, file #5250

ABBOT Thomas, clerk, of Brookline, vs CHANDLER Zechariah, of Bedford, rec date 1785, deed, land transfer, file #5612

ABBOT William, esquire, of Wilton, vs BLANCHARD Caleb, husbandman, of Andover MA, rec date 1785, judgment, debt, file #5176

ABBOT William, esquire, of Wilton, vs BLANCHARD Samuel, husbandman, of Andover MA, rec date 1785, judgment, debt, file #5176

ABBOTT Benjamin, of Hollis, doc date 1784, petition, various judgments, file #30

ABBOTT Benjamin, yeoman, of Hollis, vs McLAUGHLIN John, innkeeper, of New Boston, rec date 1783, writ, debt, file #3102

ABBOTT Benjamin, yeoman, of Hollis, vs CONANT John, husbandman, of Townsend MA, rec date 1783, writ, debt, file #3117

ABBOTT Benjamin, husbandman, of Hollis, vs DOUGLAS Samuel, husbandman, of Raby, rec date 1783, writ, debt, file #3434

ABBOTT Benjamin, yeoman, of Hollis, vs HUNT Elizabeth, widow, of Hollis, rec date 1783, writ, debt, file #3918

ABBOTT Benjamin, yeoman, of Hollis, vs ATWELL John, innkeeper, of Hollis, rec date 1784, writ, debt, file #4615

ABBOTT Benjamin, yeoman, of Hollis, vs ATWELL John, innkeeper, of Hollis, rec date 1785, various, debt, file #4842, fragile

ABBOTT Benjamin, husbandman, of Hollis, vs HUNT Elizabeth, yeoman, of Hollis, rec date 1785, writ, debt, file #2402

ABBOTT Daniel, husbandman, of Lyndeborough, vs HILDRETH Ephraim, gentleman, of Amherst, rec date 1786, writ, debt, file #6875

ABBOTT Darius, gentleman, of Amherst, vs BISHOP George, yeoman, of Hillsborough, doc date 1784, execution, debt, file #1519

ABBOTT Darius, gentleman, of Amherst, vs CLARK Timothy, yeoman, of Amherst, rec date 1782, execution, debt, file #3478

ABBOTT Darius, gentleman, yeoman, rec date 1783, execution, debt, file #3884, faded and hard to read

ABBOTT Darius, gentleman, of Amherst, vs TAGGART Archibald, gentleman, of Hillsborough, rec date 1786, writ, debt, file #6336

ABBOTT Darwin, innkeeper, of Amherst, vs CHAMPNEY Ebenezer, esquire, of Groton MA, rec date 1785, judgment, debt, file #5366

ABBOTT Ephraim, bill, file #7055

ABBOTT Jacob, esquire, of Andover MA, vs MURDOUGH Thomas, yeoman, of Hillsborough, rec date 1785, judgment, debt, file #5517

ABBOTT Jacob, esquire, of Andover MA, vs GOODRIDGE Sewall, clerk, of Lyndeborough, doc date 1784, execution, debt, file #1798

ABBOTT Jacob, esquire, of Wilton, vs HOLT Litchfield Jr (sic), of Wilton, doc date 1784, deed, land transfer, file #2007

ABBOTT Jacob, yeoman, of Wilton, vs BROWN James, gentleman, of Moultonborough, rec date 1776, writ, debt, file #2198

ABBOTT Jacob, esquire, of Wilton, vs HUTCHINSON George, yeoman, of Wilton, rec date 1783, judgment, debt, file #2856

ABBOTT Jacob, esquire, of Wilton, vs BEVIN Edward, husbandman, of Lyndeborough, rec date 1783, execution, debt, file #2886

ABBOTT Jacob, esquire, of Wilton, vs ASTEN Timothy, husbandman, of Temple, rec date 1782, appeal, debt, file #4028

ABBOTT Jacob, esquire, of Wilton, vs BEVINS Edward, husbandman, of Lyndeborough, rec date 1782, appeal, debt, file #4020

ABBOTT Jacob, esquire, of Wilton, vs RICHARDSON Joseph, yeoman, of Temple, rec date 1782, appeal, debt, file #4021

ABBOTT Jacob, esquire, of Andover MA, vs GOODRIDGE Sewall, clerk, of Lyndeborough, rec date 1784, judgment, debt, file #4365

ABBOTT Jacob, esquire, of Andover MA, vs PERRY Obadiah, yeoman, of Wilton, rec date 1784, judgment, debt, file #4296

ABBOTT Jacob, esquire, of Andover MA, vs CRAM Benjamin, husbandman, of Lyndeborough, rec date 1784, judgment, debt, file #4297

ABBOTT Jacob, esquire, of Andover MA, vs CRAM Benjamin, husbandman, of Lyndeborough, rec date 1784, appeal, debt, file #4137

ABBOTT Jacob, esquire, of Andover MA, vs GREELE Jonathan, yeoman, of Wilton, rec date 1784, judgment, debt, file #4397

ABBOTT Jacob, esquire, of Andover MA, vs PARKER Henry, yeoman, of Lyndeborough, rec date 1784, judgment, debt, file #4393

ABBOTT Jacob, esquire, of Andover MA, vs WILKINS Archelaus, yeoman, of Wilton, rec date 1784, judgment, debt, file #4296

ABBOTT Jacob, esquire, of Andover MA, vs GREEN David, yeoman, of Hillsborough, rec date 1785, judgment, debt, file #4947

ABBOTT Jacob, esquire, of Andover MA, vs PEARSON Nathan, yeoman, of Lyndeborough, rec date 1785, judgment, debt, file #4945

ABBOTT Jacob, esquire, of Andover MA, vs HUTCHINSON John Jr, cordwainer, of Weare, rec date 1784, judgment, debt, file #5306

ABBOTT Jacob, esquire, of Andover MA, vs BOYES William, of New Boston, rec date 1786, judgment, debt, file #5754

ABBOTT Jacob, esquire, of Wilton, vs LUND Phineas, yeoman, of Lyndeborough, rec date 1782, execution, debt, file #5723

ABBOTT Jacob, esquire, of Andover MA, vs SPAULDING Levi, gentleman, of Lyndeborough, rec date 1785, execution, debt, file #5924

ABBOTT Jacob, esquire, of Andover MA, vs WALLACE Matthew, esquire, of Peterborough, rec date 1786, judgment, debt, file #5768

ABBOTT Jacob, esquire, of Andover MA, vs SPAULDING Levi, gentleman, of Lyndeborough, rec date 1785, writ, debt, file #6032

ABBOTT Jacob, esquire, of Andover MA, vs DANA William, gentleman, of Amherst, rec date 1785, writ, debt, file #6674

ABBOTT Jacob, esquire, of Andover MA, vs WALLACE Matthew, esquire, of Peterborough, rec date 1786, writ, debt, file #6887

ABBOTT Jacob, esquire, of Andover MA, vs BOYES William, esquire, of New Boston, rec date 1786, writ, debt, file #6888

ABBOTT Jacob, esquire, of Andover MA, vs WYMAN Timothy, yeoman, of Deering, rec date 1786, writ, debt, file #6867

ABBOTT Jacob, esquire, of Wilton, vs CHASE Samuel, esquire, of Litchfield, rec date 1788, writ, debt, file #6915

ABBOTT Jacob Jr, gentleman, of Wilton, vs ABBOTT Joseph, esquire, of Wilton, rec date 1787, various, debt, file #6591

ABBOTT Jesse, yeoman, of Concord, vs YOUNG Daniel, yeoman, of Hopkinton, doc date 1799, judgment, debt, file #561

ABBOTT Joel, trader, of Westford MA, vs STEVENS John, yeoman, of Mason, rec date 1784, writ, debt, file #4865

ABBOTT Joseph, gentleman, of Wilton, vs BLANCHARD Jacob, husbandman, of Mile Slip, rec date 1785, judgment, debt, file #5518

ABBOTT Joseph, gentleman, of Wilton, vs BATCHELDER Archelus, gentleman, of Wilton, doc date 1778, rec date 1779, deed, land transfer, file #2120

ABBOTT Joseph, gentleman, of Wilton, vs CROSBY William, yeoman, of Amherst, rec date 1783, writ, debt, file #3974

ABBOTT Joseph, gentleman, of Wilton, vs RIDEOUT Nathaniel, yeoman, of Hollis, rec date 1785, judgment, debt, file #5099

ABBOTT Joseph, shopkeeper, of Wilton, vs HOLT Jeremiah, husbandman, of Wilton, rec date 1785, writ, debt, file #6041

ABBOTT Joseph, innholder, of Wilton, vs HOPKINS Benjamin, husbandman, of Westmoreland, rec date 1785, writ, debt, file #6142

ABBOTT Joseph, gentleman, of Wilton, vs RIDEOUT Nathaniel, yeoman, of Hollis, rec date 1785, judgment, debt, file #6485

ABBOTT Joseph, gentleman, of Wilton, vs DICKINSON Jesse, blacksmith, of Strafford, rec date 1788, various, horse ownership, file #6596, see also folder 6590

ABBOTT Josiah, yeoman, of Lyndeborough, vs CUTTLER Zacheus, esquire, of Amherst, doc date 1774, writ, debt, file #1095

ABBOTT Josiah, yeoman, of New Boston, vs JONES James, yeoman, of Hillsborough, doc date 1784, execution, debt, file #1882

ABBOTT Josiah, blacksmith, of Amherst, vs GRAHAM Alexander, yeoman, of Amherst, doc date 1766, rec date 1778, deed, land transfer, file #2115

ABBOTT Nathan, husbandman, of Danvers MA, vs BLANCHARD Jotham, merchant, of Peterborough, rec date 1785, judgment, debt, file #4799

ABBOTT Samuel, of Hollis, vs WEBSTER Grant, merchant, of Boston MA, doc date 1795, petition, release from jail, file #48

ABBOTT Samuel, yeoman, of Hollis, vs BURGE Ephraim, gentleman, of Hollis, rec date 1778, recognizance, debt, file #2245

ABBOTT Samuel, yeoman, of Hollis, vs AMOS Jeremiah, gentleman, of Hollis, rec date 1778, recognizance, debt, file #2245

ABBOTT Samuel, yeoman, of Hollis, vs WESTON Ebenezer, gentleman, of Amherst, rec date 1782, recognizance, debt, file #2614

ABBOTT Samuel, yeoman, of Hollis, vs LAWRENCE Ephraim, physician, of Pepperell MA, rec date 1782, appeal, debt, file #3983

ABBOTT Samuel, husbandman, of Hollis, vs GIBSON Simeon, gentleman, of Pepperell MA, rec date 1782, appeal, debt, file #3980

ABBOTT Samuel, yeoman, of Bedford, vs BALDWIN Nahum, esquire, of Amherst, rec date 1785, judgment, debt, file #4971, estate of Thomas BOUTELL

ABBOTT Samuel, husbandman, of Bedford, vs UNDERWOOD James, esquire, of Goffstown, rec date 1785, judgment, debt, file #5040

ABBOTT Samuel, husbandman, of Hollis, vs WEBSTER Grant, merchant, of Boston MA, rec date 1784, writ, debt, file #4743

ABBOTT Samuel, yeoman, of Bedford, vs BOUTELL Thomas, deceased, of Amherst, rec date 1785, judgment, debt, file #6417

ABBOTT William, esquire, of Wilton, vs BLANCHARD Samuel/Caleb, husbandman, of Andover MA, rec date 1786, judgment, debt, file #6478

ADAMS Aaron, yeoman, of Henniker, vs ROSS Jonathan, yeoman, of Henniker, rec date 1786, judgment, debt, file #6201

ADAMS Benjamin, physician, of Lynnfield MA, vs DRESSER Asa, yeoman, of Campbells Gore, rec date 1786, judgment, debt, file #2300

ADAMS Benjamin, physician, of Lynnfield MA, vs DRESSER Asa, yeoman, of Campbells Gore, rec date 1784, appeal, debt, file #4120

ADAMS Benjamin, physician, of Lynnfield MA, vs DRESSER Asa, yeoman, of Campbells Gore, rec date 1784, judgment, debt, file #4419

ADAMS Enoch, innholder, of Andover MA, vs POLLARD Timothy, husbandman, of Nottingham-West, rec date 1783, judgment, debt, file #2852

ADAMS Enoch, innholder, of Andover MA, vs FOSTER David, husbandman, of Nottingham-West, rec date 1783, judgment, debt, file #2852

ADAMS Enoch, innholder, of Andover MA, vs PORTER David Foster, husbandman, of Nottingham-West, rec date 1782, appeal, debt, file #4030

ADAMS Enoch, innholder, of Andover MA, vs POLLARD Timothy, husbandman, of Nottingham-West, rec date 1782, appeal, debt, file #4030

ADAMS Ephraim, yeoman, of New Ipswich, vs HOSMER Nathaniel, yeoman, of Mason, doc date 1772, civil litigations, debt, file #642

ADAMS Ephraim, husbandman, of New Ipswich, vs WIER Robert, gentleman, of Walpole, rec date 1782, execution, debt, file #5735

ADAMS Ephraim, yeoman, of New Ipswich, vs ADAMS Ephraim Jr, of New Ipswich, doc date 1771, rec date 1772, deed, land transfer, file #6842

ADAMS Gideon, trader, of Henniker, vs STRATHAM John, cooper, of Henniker, doc date 1799, debt, file #210

ADAMS Gideon, trader, of Henniker, vs HOWE William, husbandman, of Henniker, doc date 1798, judgment, debt, file #561

ADAMS Gideon, trader, of Henniker, vs HOWE William, husbandman, of Henniker, doc date 1799, various, fraud, file #526, deposition by Col Paul REVERE

ADAMS Gideon, trader, of Henniker, vs HOWE Ebenezer, saddler, of Henniker, doc date 1799, various, fraud, file #526, deposition by Col Paul REVERE

ADAMS Gideon, trader, of Henniker, vs ARNOLD Joseph, husbandman, of Henniker, doc date 1799, debt, file #472

ADAMS Gideon, trader, of Henniker, vs BEAN David, husbandman, of Springfield, doc date 1798, judgment, debt, file #561

ADAMS Gideon, trader, of Henniker, vs SMART Nathaniel, husbandman, of Henniker, doc date 1799, debt, file #463

ADAMS James, trader, of Cambridge MA, vs AUSTIN Stephen, trader, of Temple, doc date 1799, debt, file #443

ADAMS James, trader, of Cambridge, vs AUSTIN Stephen, trader, of Temple, doc date 1798, judgment, debt, file #561

ADAMS James, husbandman, of Charlotte NY, vs MOULTON William, husbandman, of Londonderry, rec date 1784, judgment, debt, file #4403

ADAMS James & Robert, husbandman, of Sheensboro NY, vs MOOERS Edmond, esquire, of Hampstead, rec date 1784, appeal, debt, file #4099

ADAMS James & Robert, husbandman, of Sheensboro NY, vs BOND John, physician, of Hampstead, rec date 1784, appeal, debt, file #4099

ADAMS James & Robert, husbandman, of Sheensboro NY, vs MOULTON William, husbandman, of Londonderry, rec date 1784, appeal, debt, file #4099

ADAMS Joseph, surgeon, of Liskeard England, vs HOSMER Nathaniel, yeoman, of Mason, rec date 1784, judgment, debt, file #4380

ADAMS Lydia, of Temple, vs DENSMORE Zebidiah, husbandman, of Temple, rec date 1788, various, debt, file #6717

ADAMS Nichols, yeoman, of Antrim, vs MARTIN Jesse, yeoman, of Francestown, rec date 1783, execution, debt, file #3815

ADAMS Robert, husbandman, of Charlotte NY, vs BOND John, physician, of Hampstead, rec date 1784, judgment, debt, file #4403

ADAMS Robert, husbandman, of Charlotte NY, vs MOORS Edmund, esquire, of Hampstead, rec date 1784, judgment, debt, file #4403

ADAMS Robert, husbandman, of Charlotte NY, vs MOULTON William, husbandman, of Londonderry, rec date 1784, judgment, debt, file #4403

ADAMS Samuel, yeoman, of Jaffrey, vs WHEELER Richard, laborer, of New Ipswich, doc date 1784, execution, debt, file #1689

ADAMS Samuel, yeoman, of Jaffrey, vs WHEELER Richard, laborer, of New Ipswich, rec date 1783, writ, debt, file #3453

ADAMS William, yeoman, of Andover MA, vs MORROW James, yeoman, of Winham, doc date 1772, writ, debt, file #1408

ADDISON George, yeoman, of Goffstown, vs MOORE James, husbandman, of Goffstown, rec date 1783, judgment, debt, file #3732

AFTEN Timothy, cordwainer, of Temple, vs CONANT John, miller, of Townsend MA, doc date 1773, writ, debt, file #1448

AFTEN Timothy, yeoman, of Temple, vs ROBINS Josiah, yeoman, of Pepperell MA, doc date 1773, writ, debt, file #1449

AIKEN James, yeoman, of Antrim, vs HOTINS William, sawyer, of Dunbarton, doc date 1782, rec date 1788, deed, land transfer, file #6837

AIKEN Thomas, yeoman, of Wilton, vs MILLER Thomas, yeoman, of Society Land, doc date 1777, rec date 1779, deed, land transfer, file #2147

AIKEN William, yeoman, of Society Land, vs BRADFORD Samuel, esquire, of Hillsborough, doc date 1773, judgment, debt, file #1293

AIKEN William, yeoman, of Deering, vs GRIMES James, yeoman, of Deering, doc date 1777, rec date 1786, deed, land transfer, file #5026

AKIN James, yeoman, of Chester, vs FRAZIER Nathan, merchant, of Boston MA, doc date 1772, writ, debt, file #1060

ALBREE Samuel, trader, of Amherst, vs MUNROE Josiah, gentleman, of Amherst, rec date 1786, writ, debt, file #6268

ALCOCK Robert, gentleman, of Deering, vs GRIMES James, gentleman, of Deering, doc date 1784, execution, debt, file #1514

ALCOOK Robert, gentleman, of Deering, vs GRIMES James, gentleman, of Deering, rec date 1783, civil litigious, debt, file #2943

ALD William, gentleman, of Peterborough, vs JONES Timothy, husbandman, of Lyndeborough, rec date 1788, writ, debt, file #6726

ALDRICH Andrew, husbandman, of Grafton, vs BOWEN Elenor, of Salisbury, doc date 1782, execution, file #1027

ALDRICH Eddie, vs CONCORD & Montreal Railroad, doc date 1892, defendants brief, supreme court, file #645

ALEXANDER Jabez, of Henniker, vs BARNS Elisha, yeoman, of Henniker, rec date 1785, various, assault, file #4571, black man called LONDON

ALEXANDER Jabez, of Henniker, vs CAMPBELL Jesse, yeoman, of Henniker, rec date 1785, various, assault, file #4571

ALEXANDER Jabez, of Henniker, vs KEMP Elisah, yeoman, of Henniker, rec date 1785, various, assault, file #4571

ALEXANDER Jabez, of Henniker, vs HOW Eliakim Jr, laborer, of Henniker, rec date 1785, various, assault, file #4571

ALEXANDER Jabez, of Henniker, vs HATHORN Nathaniel, yeoman, of Henniker, rec date 1785, various, assault, file #4571

ALEXANDER Jabez, of Henniker, vs BOWMAN Jonas Jr, yeoman, of Henniker, rec date 1785, various, assault, file #4571

ALEXANDER John, yeoman, of Londonderry, vs HARDY Daniel, gentleman, of Nottingham-West, rec date 1783, writ, debt, file #2765

ALEXANDER John, husbandman, of Manchester VT, vs MOORE John, gentleman, of Peterborough, rec date 1787, various, debt, file #6972

ALEXANDER Robert, selectmen, of Milford, doc date 1773, writ, tax collection, file #1177

ALEXANDER Robert, husbandman, of Merrimack, vs CHAMBERLIN John, husbandman, of Merrimack, rec date 1783, execution, debt, file #2866

ALEXANDER Robert, husbandman, of Merrimack, vs BLANCHARD Augustus, husbandman, of Merrimack, rec date 1783, execution, debt, file #2866

ALEXANDER Robert, husbandman, of Merrimack, vs NICHOLS Ebenezer, husbandman, of Merrimack, rec date 1783, execution, debt, file #2866

ALLD James, yeoman, of Francestown, vs WILKINS John, gentleman, of Francestown, rec date 1783, writ, debt, file #3023, fragile

ALLD John, yeoman, of Merrimack, vs BURNS John, yeoman, of New Boston, rec date 1784, judgment, debt, file #4611

ALLD John Jr, yeoman, of Merrimack, vs MOOR John, yeoman, of Bedford, rec date 1784, appeal, debt, file #4125

ALLD Samuel, gentleman, of Peterborough, vs CARLTON Samuel, yeoman, of Greenfield, doc date 1798, execution, debt, file #145

ALLD William, gentleman, of Peterborough, vs GREEN David, yeoman, of Hillsborough, rec date 1783, civil litigious, debt, file #2953

ALLD William, gentleman, of Peterborough, vs GREEN David, yeoman, of Hillsborough, rec date 1783, execution, debt, file #3680

ALLD William, gentleman, of Peterborough, vs GREEN David, yeoman, of Hillsborough, rec date 1782, execution, debt, file #3490

ALLD William, gentleman, of Peterborough, vs ADAMS John, yeoman, of Packersfield, rec date 1783, writ, debt, file #4047

ALLD William, gentleman, of Peterborough, vs KIDDER Thomas, yeoman, of Packersfield, rec date 1783, writ, debt, file #4047

ALLD William, gentleman, of Peterborough, vs PATTERSON James, gentleman, of Bedford, rec date 1783, judgment, debt, file #4303

ALLD William, gentleman, of Peterborough, vs GRAY Robert, gentleman, of Peterborough, rec date 1784, judgment, debt, file #4650

ALLD William, gentleman, of Peterborough, vs GRAY Robert, gentleman, of Peterborough, rec date 1785, judgment, debt, file #5122

ALLEN Eliah & John, yeoman, of Fitzwilliam, vs MILLS Luke, yeoman, of Needham MA, rec date 1785, judgment, debt, file #5364

ALLEN Timothy, husbandman, of Temple, vs HOOD Samuel, yeoman, doc date 1783, petition, release of debit, file #10

ALLINGFORD David, gentleman, of Hollis, vs CLARK Samuel, yeoman, of Andover MA, rec date 1786, judgment, debt, file #5552

ALLISON Samuel, husbandman, of Dunbarton, vs HARDY Dudley, husbandman, of Dunbarton, doc date 1798, judgment, debt, file #561

ALLISON Samuel, yeoman, of Dunbarton, vs MORSE Benjamin, husbandman, of Francestown, doc date 1799, debt, file #483

ALLISON Samuel, yeoman, of Dunbarton, vs HOW Benjamin, husbandman, of Francestown, doc date 1799, execution, debt, file #214

AMANS Sarah, wife, of Peterborough, vs AMANS David, of Peterborough, doc date 1799, various, divorce, file #543

AMBROSE Samuel, clerk, of Sutton, vs BOWEN John, husbandman, of Salisbury, rec date 1784, writ, debt, file #4856

AMES Burpee, husbandman, of Hollis, vs KENNEY Israel, of Hollis, rec date 1788, writ, debt, file #2433

AMES Burpee, yeoman, of Hollis, vs STATE of NH, rec date 1782, recognizance, debt, file #2610

AMES David, yeoman, of Hollis, vs WARREN Josiah, yeoman, of Groton MA, doc date 1784, execution, debt, file #1455

AMES David, husbandman, of Dublin, vs PARKER Lemuel, yeoman, of Groton MA, rec date 1783, writ, debt, file #3435

AMES David, yeoman, of Peterborough, vs MORRISON Moses, gentleman, of Hancock, rec date 1783, writ, debt, file #3911

AMES David, yeoman, of Peterborough, vs MORRISON Moses, gentleman, of Hancock, rec date 1784, judgment, debt, file #4612

AMES Eli, husbandman, of Sharon, vs BIGELOW Timothy, esquire, of Groton MA, doc date 1799, writ, debt, file #404

AMES Jacob, husbandman, of Hancock, vs BARRETT Moses, yeoman, of Wilton, rec date 1785, judgment, debt, file #5187

AMES Jeremiah, gentleman, of Hollis, vs STATE of NH, rec date 1782, recognizance, debt, file #2610

AMES Jeremiah, gentleman, of Hollis, vs HOWE Steven, yeoman, of Amherst, rec date 1782, execution, debt, file #5729

AMES Jonathan, yeoman, of Dublin, vs KENNY Israel, husbandman, of Hollis, rec date 1788, writ, debt, file #6931

AMES Nathan & Sarah, yeoman, of Goffstown, vs BOYD Samuel, gentleman, of Derryfield, doc date 1780, deed, land transfer, file #6831

AMES Phineas, yeoman, of Pembroke, vs ATKINSON Samuel, yeoman, of Boscawen, rec date 1785, judgment, debt, file #5161

AMES Phinehas, yeoman, of Pembroke, vs ATKINSON Samuel, gentleman, of Boscawen, rec date 1785, judgment, debt, file #6437

AMES Robert, yeoman, of Groton MA, vs FOSTER Simeon, husbandman, of Hollis, rec date 1784, judgment, debt, file #4660

AMES Robert, yeoman, of Groton MA, vs FOSTER Simeon, husbandman, of Hollis, rec date 1785, judgment, debt, file #5441

AMES Samuel, yeoman, of Hancock, vs AMES James, innkeeper, of Oakham MA, rec date 1783, writ, debt, file #3324

AMES Stephen, yeoman, of Raby, vs WARREN Josiah, yeoman, of Groton MA, doc date 1772, writ, debt, file #1046

AMES Stephen, yeoman, of Dublin, vs PATTEN Matthew, esquire, of Bedford, rec date 1783, writ, debt, file #3107

AMES Stephen, husbandman, of Dublin, vs THORTON Matthew, esquire, of Merrimack, rec date 1783, writ, debt, file #3170

AMES Stephen, yeoman, of Dublin, vs KILLICUT Reuben, husbandman, of Dunstable, rec date 1785, judgment, debt, file #5060

AMES Stephen, esquire, of Dublin, rec date 1788, various, land dispute, file #6586, 2 folders

AMORY Jonathan & John, merchants, of Boston MA, vs FISK Amos, gentleman, of Amherst, doc date 1774, judgment, debt, file #724

ANDERSON David, yeoman, of Manchester VT, vs GREGG David, wheelwright, of Francestown, rec date 1785, judgment, debt, file #6484

ANDERSON John, husbandman, of Corinth NY, vs LANE John Jr, gentleman, of Chester, rec date 1784, judgment, debt, file #4402

ANDREW Ammi, gentleman, of Hillsborough, vs ATHERTON Joshua, esquire, of Amherst, rec date 1784, writ, debt, file #4741

ANDREW Elliot, laborer, of Amherst, vs LOVEJOY Francis, feltmaker, of Amherst, rec date 1785, judgment, debt, file #5759

ANDREW Isaac, administrator of estate, of Hillsborough, vs KELLEY Moses, esquire, of Goffstown, rec date 1785, summons, debt, file #6220

ANDREW James, gentleman, of Boston MA, vs STEARNS Samuel, yeoman, of Lyndeborough, doc date 1772, execution, debt, file #1210

ANDREWS Ammi, vs JONES Sam, doc date 1781, bill, file #1281

ANDREWS Ammi, gentleman, of Hillsborough, vs JONES James, husbandman, of Hillsborough, doc date 1784, execution, debt, file #1883

ANDREWS Ammi, gentleman, of Hillsborough, vs COOLIDGE Silas, husbandman, of Hillsborough, doc date 1779, execution, debt, file #1883

ANDREWS Ammi, gentleman, of Hillsborough, vs WYMAN Timothy, innkeeper, of Deering, doc date 1784, execution, debt, file #1892

ANDREWS Ammi, gentleman, of Hillsborough, vs GRIMES Francis Jr, gentleman, of Deering, rec date 1783, writ, debt, file #3046

ANDREWS Ammi, gentleman, of Hillsborough, vs ATHERTON Joshua, esquire, of Amherst, rec date 1783, writ, debt, file #3045

ANDREWS Ammi, gentleman, of Hillsborough, vs INHABITANTS of Deering, rec date 1783, writ, debt, file #4542

ANDREWS Ammi, gentleman, of Littleton MA, vs GRIMES Francis, husbandman, of Deering, rec date 1784, writ, debt, file #4745

ANDREWS Ammi, gentleman, of Littleton MA, vs DOWN Evan, husbandman, of Hillsborough, rec date 1784, writ, debt, file #4744

ANDREWS Asa, husbandman, of Londonderry, vs REA Caleb, physician, of Windham MA, rec date 1784, judgment, debt, file #4246

ANDREWS Irking?, laborer, of Hillsborough, vs POPE William, esquire, of Hillsborough, rec date 1787, hearing request, file #6516

ANDREWS Isaac, esquire, of Hillsborough, vs WILKINS Bray, yeoman, of Hollis, doc date 1775, writ, debt, file #958

ANDREWS Isaac, yeoman, of Hillsborough, vs McCLENTOCK John, husbandman, of Hillsborough, rec date 1783, execution, debt, file #2999

ANDREWS Isaac, esquire, of Hillsborough, vs JONES Samuel, yeoman, of Hillsborough, rec date 1783, civil litigation, debt, file #3881

ANDREWS Isaac, esquire, of Hillsborough, vs CORSON John, gentleman, of Francestown, rec date 1783, judgment, debt, file #4441

ANDREWS Isaac, esquire, of Hillsborough, vs GRAHAM John, husbandman, of Halifax VT, rec date 1785, writ, debt, file #6229

ANDREWS Isaac, esquire, of Hillsborough, vs BIXBE Andrew, esquire, of Hillsborough, rec date 1785, writ, debt, file #6246

ANDREWS James, gentleman, of Boxford MA, vs STEVENS Samuel, yeoman, of Lyndeborough, doc date 1772, various, breaking & entry, file #879

ANDREWS James, vs STEVENS Samuel, rec date 1772, bill, file #6961

ANDREWS John, merchant, of Boston MA, vs BALL Nathaniel, husbandman, of Temple, rec date 1785, writ, debt, file #6221

ANDREWS Molly, widow, vs BLACKMAN Called London, rec date 1785, capias, assault, file #4571

ANDREWS Molly, widow, of Henniker, vs HOW Eliakim Jr, laborer, of Henniker, rec date 1785, various, assault, file #4571

ANDREWS Perkins, laborer minor, of Hillsborough, vs POPE William, esquire, of Hillsborough, rec date 1783, court case, slander, file #2875, PERKINS kinships

ANDREWS Solomon, esquire, of Windsor, vs McCLINTOCK Archibald, husbandman, of Windsor, doc date 1807, rec date 1807, deed, land transfer, file #5689

APPLETON Isaac, gentleman, of New Ipswich, vs TAGGART John, gentleman, of Peterborough Slip, doc date 1784, ejectment, land dispute, file #1600

APPLETON Isaac, gentleman, of New Ipswich, vs MINOT Jinas, gentleman, of MA, doc date 1784, writ, debt, file #1623

APPLETON Isaac, gentleman, of New Ipswich, vs TAGGART John, gentleman, of Peterborough Slip, rec date 1785, writ, debt, file #4682

APPLETON Isaac, of Ipswich MA, vs PAGE Nathan, blacksmith, of Bedford, doc date 1771, rec date 1773, deed, land transfer, file #6548

APPLETON Samuel, merchant, of Boston MA, vs CUTTER John, yeoman, of New Ipswich, doc date 1798, judgment, debt, file #561

ARCHER Michael, husbandman, of Henniker, vs NOYES Nathaniel, of Henniker, doc date 1799, petition, release of debit, file #25

ARMOR Garven, trader, of Claremont, vs WYMAN Henry, yeoman, of Society Land, doc date 1798, judgment, debt, file #561

ARNOLD John, deceased, of Henniker, vs STATE of NH, rec date 1773, inquisition, death inquiry, file #2257

ARNUM Stephen, husbandman, of Lyndeborough, vs BETTEY William, yeoman, of New Boston, rec date 1785, various, debt, file #4698

ASH John, yeoman, of Hopkinton, vs ATKINSON Samuel, gentleman, of Boscawen, rec date 1784, judgment, debt, file #4221

ASTEN Timothy, yeoman, of Temple, vs NICHOLS John, yeoman, of Billerica MA, rec date 1783, writ, debt, file #3122

ASTEN Timothy, husbandman, of Temple, vs WOOD Samuel, yeoman, of Mason, rec date 1783, writ, debt, file #3069

ASTEN Timothy, husbandman, of Temple, vs THORTON Matthew, esquire, of Merrimack, rec date 1783, writ, debt, file #3170

ASTIN Thomas, husbandman, of Raby, vs DICKEY James, gentleman, of Raby, rec date 1784, judgment, debt, file #4859

ATCKINSON Nathaniel, husbandman, of Boscawen, vs ATKINSON Samuel, esquire, of Boscawen, rec date 1787, writ, debt, file #6643

ATHERTON Israel, esquire, of Lancaster MA, vs SANDERS Joseph, gentleman, of Derryfield, rec date 1786, writ, debt, file #6313

ATHERTON Israel, gentleman, of Lancaster MA, vs SANDERS Joseph, gentleman, of Derryfield, rec date 1785, writ, debt, file #6145

ATHERTON John, vs HOLLAND Stephen, of Londonderry, doc date 1773, letter, file #785

ATHERTON John, esquire, of Amherst, vs HOW Theodore, yeoman, of Swansey, rec date 1785, judgment, debt, file #5130

ATHERTON Joseph, esquire, of Amherst, vs GOOLL Joseph, blacksmith, of Hollis, doc date 1773, execution, debt, file #1463

ATHERTON Joshua, esquire, of Amherst, vs BALDWIN Isaac, yeoman, of Hillsborough, doc date 1774, writ, debt, file #746

ATHERTON Joshua, esquire, of Amherst, vs TAGGART James, yeoman, of Hillsborough, doc date 1774, writ, debt, file #746

ATHERTON Joshua, esquire, of Amherst, vs COOLIDGE Nathaniel, husbandman, of Hillsborough, doc date 1798, execution, debt, file #93

ATHERTON Joshua, esquire, of Amherst, vs WHITE Robert, husbandman, of New Boston, rec date 1785, execution, debt, file #5480

ATHERTON Joshua, esquire, of Amherst, vs GAMELL William, yeoman, of Hillsborough, rec date 1785, execution, debt, file #5481

ATHERTON Joshua, esquire, of Amherst, vs GIBSON Matthew, yeoman, of Francestown, rec date 1785, execution, debt, file #5482

ATHERTON Joshua, esquire, of Amherst, vs BROWN Peter, yeoman, of Temple, rec date 1785, execution, debt, file #5489

ATHERTON Joshua, gentleman, of Merrimack, vs USHER Eleazar, yeoman, of Merrimack, doc date 1772, civil litigations, debt, file #638

ATHERTON Joshua, esquire, of Amherst, vs TAGGART Archibald, yeoman, of Hillsborough, doc date 1774, writ, debt, file #746

ATHERTON Joshua, gentleman, of Merrimack, vs McCLENCKE Joseph, yeoman, of Merrimack, doc date 1772, civil litigations, debt, file #638

ATHERTON Joshua, esquire, of Amherst, vs TAGGART Archibald, yeoman, of Hillsborough, doc date 1774, execution, file #981

ATHERTON Joshua, esquire, of Amherst, vs JOSLYN Nathaniel, yeoman, of Henniker, doc date 1774, judgment, debt, file #1156

ATHERTON Joshua, esquire, of Merrimack, vs LUND Phineas, yeoman, of Lyndeborough, doc date 1772, execution, debt, file #1205

ATHERTON Joshua, esquire, of Amherst, vs TAGGART Archibald, yeoman, of Hillsborough, doc date 1773, execution, debt, file #1216

ATHERTON Joshua, esquire, of Amherst, vs BATES Jonathan, yeoman, of Cockermouth, doc date 1784, execution, debt, file #1739

ATHERTON Joshua, esquire, of Amherst, vs HOW Nehemiah, yeoman, of Henniker, doc date 1784, execution, debt, file #1516

ATHERTON Joshua, esquire, of Amherst, vs ROBINSON William, yeoman, of Deering, doc date 1784, execution, debt, file #1723

ATHERTON Joshua, esquire, of Amherst, vs KIMBALL Henry, feltmaker, of Amherst, doc date 1784, execution, debt, file #1807

ATHERTON Joshua, yeoman, of Amherst, vs COCKRAN John, yeoman, of Amherst, doc date 1784, execution, debt, file #1825

ATHERTON Joshua, esquire, of Amherst, vs BRADFORD Samuel Jr, gentleman, of Hillsborough, doc date 1784, execution, debt, file #1921

ATHERTON Joshua, esquire, of Amherst, vs BOWTELL Amos, yeoman, of Amherst, doc date 1784, execution, debt, file #1984

ATHERTON Joshua, esquire, of Amherst, vs TAYLOR James, gentleman, of Merrimack, doc date 1784, execution, debt, file #1966

ATHERTON Joshua, esquire, of Amherst, vs BOSSEE Thomas, gentleman, of Lyndeborough, doc date 1784, execution, debt, file #1867

ATHERTON Joshua, esquire, of Amherst, vs ROBINSON William, yeoman, of Deering, doc date 1784, execution, debt, file #1957

ATHERTON Joshua, esquire, of Amherst, vs DODGE Samuel, yeoman, of Amherst, doc date 1784, civil litigation, debt, file #1833

ATHERTON Joshua, husbandman, of Amherst, vs STATE of NH, rec date 1777, recognizance, forgery, file #2211

ATHERTON Joshua, esquire, of Amherst, vs GOVE Jonathan, physician, of New Boston, rec date 1782, judgment, debt, file #2719

ATHERTON Joshua, esquire, of Amherst, vs PATTEN Matthew, esquire, of Bedford, rec date 1783, writ, debt, file #3107

ATHERTON Joshua, yeoman, of Amherst, vs CLARK Ephraim, yeoman, of Deering, rec date 1783, execution, debt, file #2991

ATHERTON Joshua, esquire, of Amherst, vs BATES Jonathan, yeoman, of Cockermouth, rec date 1783, civil litigious, debt, file #2921

ATHERTON Joshua, esquire, of Amherst, vs ROBINSON Joseph, yeoman, of Deering, rec date 1783, civil litigious, debt, file #2954

ATHERTON Joshua, esquire, of Amherst, vs BOUTWELL Amos, yeoman, of Amherst, rec date 1783, execution, debt, file #2988

ATHERTON Joshua, esquire, of Amherst, vs WILSON John, yeoman, of New Boston, rec date 1783, civil litigious, debt, file #2940

ATHERTON Joshua, esquire, of Amherst, vs BRADFORD Samuel Jr, gentleman, of Hillsborough, rec date 1783, execution, debt, file #3277

ATHERTON Joshua, esquire, of Amherst, vs WILSON John, yeoman, of New Boston, rec date 1783, execution, debt, file #3259

ATHERTON Joshua, esquire, of Amherst, vs BATES Jonathan, yeoman, of Cockermouth, rec date 1783, execution, debt, file #3268

ATHERTON Joshua, esquire, of Amherst, vs TAYLOR James, gentleman, of Cockermouth, rec date 1783, execution, debt, file #3269

ATHERTON Joshua, esquire, of Amherst, vs POLLARD Timothy, yeoman, of Nottingham-West, rec date 1783, judgment, debt, file #3731

ATHERTON Joshua, esquire, of Amherst, vs BARRET Moses, yeoman, of Nottingham-West, rec date 1783, judgment, debt, file #3731

ATHERTON Joshua, esquire, of Amherst, vs TAYLOR James, gentleman, of Merrimack, rec date 1783, execution, debt, file #3699

ATHERTON Joshua, esquire, of Amherst, vs BATES Jonathan, yeoman, of Cockermouth, rec date 1783, execution, debt, file #3495

ATHERTON Joshua, esquire, of Amherst, vs JONES Timothy, yeoman, of Amherst, rec date 1783, judgment, debt, file #3727

ATHERTON Joshua, esquire, of Amherst, vs CUMINGS Silas, blacksmith, of New Boston, rec date 1782, execution, debt, file #3522

ATHERTON Joshua, esquire, of Amherst, vs CUMMINGS Silas, blacksmith, of New Boston, rec date 1783, execution, debt, file #3664

ATHERTON Joshua, esquire, of Amherst, vs JOHNSON Zebadiah, yeoman, of Hillsborough, rec date 1782, execution, debt, file #3489

ATHERTON Joshua, esquire, of Amherst, vs BATES Jonathan, yeoman, of Cockermouth, rec date 1782, execution, debt, file #3483

ATHERTON Joshua, esquire, of Amherst, vs WYMAN Timothy, innkeeper, of Deering, rec date 1783, various, debt, file #3941

ATHERTON Joshua, esquire, of Amherst, vs BRADFORD Samuel Jr, yeoman, of Amherst, rec date 1784, appeal, debt, file #4118

ATHERTON Joshua, esquire, of Amherst, vs WILSON John, yeoman, of New Boston, rec date 1783, writ, debt, file #3887

ATHERTON Joshua, esquire, of Amherst, vs HOW Nehemiah, yeoman, of Henniker, rec date 1783, writ, debt, file #3929

ATHERTON Joshua, esquire, of Amherst, vs HOW Nehemiah, yeoman, of Henniker, rec date 1783, execution, debt, file #3853

ATHERTON Joshua, esquire, of Amherst, vs JONES Samuel, yeoman, of Hillsborough, rec date 1783, writ, debt, file #3901

ATHERTON Joshua, esquire, of Amherst, vs SMALL Joseph, yeoman, of Amherst, rec date 1784, judgment, debt, file #4273

ATHERTON Joshua, esquire, of Amherst, vs POLLARD Timothy, yeoman, of Nottingham-West, rec date 1784, judgment, debt, file #4392

ATHERTON Joshua, esquire, of Amherst, vs CUNNINGHAM Samuel, gentleman, of Peterborough, rec date 1784, judgment, debt, file #4334

ATHERTON Joshua, esquire, of Amherst, vs WYMAN Timothy, innkeeper, of Deering, rec date 1784, various, debt, file #4176

ATHERTON Joshua, esquire, of Amherst, vs BARRETT Moses, yeoman, of Nottingham-West, rec date 1784, judgment, debt, file #4392

ATHERTON Joshua, esquire, of Amherst, vs JEFTS Benjamin, yeoman, of Mason, rec date 1784, execution, debt, file #4251

ATHERTON Joshua, esquire, of Amherst, vs BRADFORD Samuel Jr, yeoman, of Hillsborough, rec date 1784, judgment, debt, file #4405

ATHERTON Joshua, esquire, of Amherst, vs TOWNE Bartholomew, yeoman, of Amherst, rec date 1784, appeal, debt, file #4130

ATHERTON Joshua, esquire, of Amherst, vs LITTLE Thomas, yeoman, of Peterborough, rec date 1784, writ, debt, file #4668

ATHERTON Joshua, esquire, of Amherst, vs STEELE Thomas, yeoman, of Peterborough, rec date 1784, writ, debt, file #4668

ATHERTON Joshua, esquire, of Amherst, vs KIMBALL Henry, feltmaker, of Amherst, rec date 1783, judgment, debt, file #4445

ATHERTON Joshua, esquire, of Amherst, vs HOW Theodore, yeoman, of Swansey, rec date 1784, judgment, debt, file #4643

ATHERTON Joshua, esquire, of Amherst, vs STEELE David Jr, yeoman, of Peterborough, rec date 1784, writ, debt, file #4668

ATHERTON Joshua, esquire, of Amherst, vs MESTES Benjamin, blacksmith, of Raby, rec date 1784, judgment, debt, file #4631

ATHERTON Joshua, esquire, of Amherst, vs MORREL Robert, weaver, of Bedford, rec date 1784, judgment, debt, file #4666

ATHERTON Joshua, esquire, of Amherst, vs HOLMES Oliver, gentleman, of Francestown, rec date 1785, judgment, debt, file #4946

ATHERTON Joshua, esquire, of Amherst, vs WILKINS Jonathan, yeoman, of Amherst, rec date 1785, judgment, debt, file #5558

ATHERTON Joshua, esquire, of Amherst, vs TOWNE Bartholomew, rec date 1785, petition, debt, file #4935

ATHERTON Joshua, esquire, of Amherst, vs TAYLOR John, yeoman, of Amherst, rec date 1785, judgment, debt, file #5558

ATHERTON Joshua, esquire, of Amherst, vs FULLER Jason, yeoman, of Francestown, rec date 1785, judgment, debt, file #4946

ATHERTON Joshua, esquire, of Amherst, vs STEEL Joseph, yeoman, of Nottingham-West, rec date 1785, judgment, debt, file #4954

ATHERTON Joshua, esquire, of Amherst, vs HUTCHINSON Stephen, yeoman, of Merrimack, rec date 1785, judgment, debt, file #5858

ATHERTON Joshua, esquire, of Amherst, vs STEARNS Samuel Jr, yeoman, of Amherst, rec date 1785, judgment, debt, file #5861

ATHERTON Joshua, esquire, of Amherst, vs GIBSON Timothy, esquire, of Henniker, rec date 1785, judgment, debt, file #5856

ATHERTON Joshua, esquire, of Amherst, vs WILKINS Daniel, yeoman, of Amherst, rec date 1785, judgment, debt, file #5862

ATHERTON Joshua, esquire, of Amherst, vs SMALL Simeon, yeoman, of Goffstown, rec date 1785, judgment, debt, file #5863

ATHERTON Joshua, esquire, of Amherst, vs McCLEARY David, yeoman, of Bedford, rec date 1785, judgment, debt, file #5869

ATHERTON Joshua, esquire, of Amherst, vs GOODELL David, yeoman, of Hillsborough, rec date 1785, judgment, debt, file #5864

ATHERTON Joshua, esquire, of Amherst, vs CUNNINGHAM Samuel, gentleman, of Peterborough, rec date 1785, judgment, debt, file #5803

ATHERTON Joshua, esquire, of Amherst, vs COOLEDGE Nathaniel, husbandman, of Hillsborough, rec date 1785, judgment, debt, file #5838

ATHERTON Joshua, esquire, of Amherst, vs BIXBE Andrew, husbandman, of Hillsborough, rec date 1785, execution, debt, file #5784

ATHERTON Joshua, esquire, of Amherst, vs WILKINS Daniel, yeoman, of Amherst, rec date 1785, execution, debt, file #5785

ATHERTON Joshua, esquire, of Amherst, vs CLEMENT Jesse, yeoman, of Weare, rec date 1785, judgment, debt, file #5870

ATHERTON Joshua, esquire, of Amherst, vs HILLS Stephen, yeoman, of Merrimack, rec date 1785, judgment, debt, file #5855

ATHERTON Joshua, esquire, of Amherst, vs COWAN Thomas Jr, husbandman, of Merrimack, rec date 1785, judgment, debt, file #5853

ATHERTON Joshua, esquire, of Amherst, vs BOYNTON Joshua, yeoman, of Hollis, rec date 1785, judgment, debt, file #5854

ATHERTON Joshua, esquire, of Amherst, vs BIXBE Andrew, husbandman, of Hillsborough, rec date 1785, judgment, debt, file #5848

ATHERTON Joshua, esquire, of Amherst, vs STEVENS Calvin, yeoman, of Hillsborough, rec date 1785, execution, debt, file #5913

ATHERTON Joshua, esquire, of Amherst, vs COWAN Thomas Jr, husbandman, of Merrimack, rec date 1785, execution, debt, file #5944

ATHERTON Joshua, esquire, of Amherst, vs COWEN Thomas Jr, husbandman, of Merrimack, rec date 1785, execution, debt, file #5929

ATHERTON Joshua, esquire, of Amherst, vs SPAULDING Stephen, husbandman, of Henniker, rec date 1785, execution, debt, file #5960

ATHERTON Joshua, esquire, of Amherst, vs SMALL Simeon, yeoman, of Goffstown, rec date 1785, execution, debt, file #5970

ATHERTON Joshua, esquire, of Amherst, vs STEVENS Calvin, yeoman, of Hillsborough, rec date 1785, judgment, debt, file #5867

ATHERTON Joshua, esquire, of Amherst, vs BENNETT Jonathan, gentleman, of Hancock, rec date 1785, execution, debt, file #5961

ATHERTON Joshua, esquire, of Amherst, vs BURNHAM Israel, yeoman, of Amherst, rec date 1785, execution, debt, file #5964

ATHERTON Joshua, esquire, of Amherst, vs STEARNS Samuel Jr, yeoman, of Amherst, rec date 1785, execution, debt, file #5912

ATHERTON Joshua, esquire, of Amherst, vs GREEN David, yeoman, of Hillsborough, rec date 1785, writ, debt, file #6222

ATHERTON Joshua, esquire, of Amherst, vs PIKE Joseph, yeoman, of Hollis, rec date 1785, writ, debt, file #6024

ATHERTON Joshua, esquire, of Amherst, vs LOVEJOY Francis, feltmaker, of Amherst, rec date 1785, writ, debt, file #6249

ATHERTON Joshua, esquire, of Amherst, vs COWAN Thomas Jr, husbandman, of Merrimack, rec date 1786, judgment, debt, file #6386

ATHERTON Joshua, esquire, of Amherst, vs WILKINS Daniel, yeoman, of Amherst, rec date 1786, judgment, debt, file #6379

ATHERTON Joshua, esquire, of Amherst, vs LOVEJOY Francis, feltmaker, of Amherst, rec date 1785, various, debt, file #6248

ATHERTON Joshua, esquire, of Amherst, vs FULLER Jason, gentleman, of Francestown, rec date 1786, judgment, debt, file #6380

ATHERTON Joshua, esquire, of Amherst, vs HOLMS Oliver, gentleman, of Francestown, rec date 1786, judgment, debt, file #6380

ATHERTON Joshua, esquire, of Amherst, vs ANDREWS Ammi, gentleman, of Hillsborough, rec date 1785, judgment, debt, file #6458

ATHERTON Joshua, esquire, of Amherst, vs PIKE Joseph, yeoman, of Hollis, rec date 1785, judgment, debt, file #6459

ATHERTON Joshua, esquire, of Amherst, vs SMALL Simon, yeoman, of Goffstown, rec date 1786, judgment, debt, file #6393

ATHERTON Joshua, esquire, of Amherst, vs HUTCHINSON Solomon, yeoman, of Merrimack, rec date 1786, judgment, debt, file #6470

ATHERTON Joshua, esquire, of Amherst, vs HUTCHINSON Solomon, yeoman, of Merrimack, rec date 1785, judgment, debt, file #6431

ATHERTON Joshua, esquire, of Amherst, vs CUMMINGS Samuel, gentleman, of Peterborough, rec date 1785, judgment, debt, file #6432

ATHERTON Joshua, esquire, of Amherst, vs CLEMENTS Jesse, yeoman, of Weare, rec date 1786, judgment, debt, file #6471

ATHERTON Joshua, esquire, of Amherst, vs ROWELL Abraham, of Hopkinton, rec date 1787, capias, information, file #6525

ATHERTON Joshua, esquire, of Amherst, vs HILLS Stephen, yeoman, of Merrimack, rec date 1785, judgment, debt, file #6433

ATHERTON Joshua, esquire, of Amherst, vs BRADFORD Samuel Jr, gentleman, of Hillsborough, rec date 1788, writ, debt, file #6723

ATHERTON Joshua, esquire, of Amherst, vs ROWELL Abraham, miller, of Hopkinton, rec date 1788, writ, bldg mill, file #6900

ATHERTON Joshua, esquire, of Amherst, vs EAGER George, surgeon, of Hanover, rec date 1787, writ, debt, file #6705

ATHERTON Joshua, esquire, of Amherst, vs MURDOUGH Thomas, yeoman, of Hill, rec date 1787, writ, debt, file #6695

ATHERTON Joshua (late), esquire, of Amherst, vs WOODBURY William, yeoman, of Amherst, rec date 1784, judgment, debt, file #4229

ATHERTON Joshua, esquire, of Amherst, vs MORRELL Robert, weaver, of Bedford, rec date 1785, judgment, debt, file #5128

ATHERTON Peter, gentleman, of Harvard MA, vs TAGGART Robert, yeoman, of Amherst, doc date 1774, judgment, debt, file #715

ATHERTON Peter, gentleman, of Harvard MA, vs TAGGART Robert, yeoman, of Amherst, doc date 1774, writ, debt, file #1089

ATHERTON Peter, gentleman, of Harvard MA, vs DODGE Thomas, pumpmaker, of Epping, rec date 1783, execution, debt, file #3644

ATHERTON Peter, gentleman, of Lancaster MA, vs SANDERS Joseph, gentleman, of Derryfield, rec date 1786, writ, debt, file #6313

ATKINSON Nathaniel, husbandman, of Boscawen, vs ATKINSON Joseph Jr, husbandman, of Boscawen, doc date 1801, various, debt, file #547

ATKINSON Samuel, husbandman, of Boscawen, vs HOBART Peter, husbandman, of Plymouth, doc date 1774, writ, debt, file #1184

ATKINSON Samuel, gentleman, of Boscawen, vs BURNHAM Josiah, husbandman, of Coventry, doc date 1784, court case, shooting of ox, file #1608

ATKINSON Samuel, gentleman, of Boscawen, vs ROLLINGS Reuben, of Sanborton, doc date 1784, execution, debt, file #1716

ATKINSON Samuel, gentleman, of Boscawen, vs NILES Barnabas, joiner, of Coventry, doc date 1784, execution, debt, file #1720

ATKINSON Samuel, gentleman, of Boscawen, vs CROSS Experience, husbandman, of Wentworth, doc date 1784, execution, debt, file #1721

ATKINSON Samuel, gentleman, of Boscawen, vs ROLLINGS Reuben, yeoman, of Sanbornton, doc date 1784, execution, debt, file #1913

ATKINSON Samuel, gentleman, of Boscawen, vs HAMBLET William, husbandman, of New Holderness, doc date 1784, execution, debt, file #1939

ATKINSON Samuel, gentleman, of Boscawen, vs JEWETT John, husbandman, of Bath, rec date 1782, writ, debt, file #2627

ATKINSON Samuel, gentleman, of Boscawen, vs NILES Barnabas, joiner, of Coventry, rec date 1783, writ, debt, file #2618

ATKINSON Samuel, gentleman, of Rumney, vs CHANDLER John, gentleman, of Boscawen, rec date 1782, writ, debt, file #2675

ATKINSON Samuel, gentleman, of Boscawen, vs BURNHAM Josiah, husbandman, of Coventry, rec date 1783, writ, killing ox, file #2617

ATKINSON Samuel, gentleman, of Boscawen, vs CROSS Ephraim, husbandman, of Wentworth, rec date 1783, civil litigious, debt, file #2915

ATKINSON Samuel, gentleman, of Boscawen, vs NILES Barnabas, joiner, of Coventry, rec date 1783, civil litigious, debt, file #2914

ATKINSON Samuel, gentleman, of Boscawen, vs CROSS Experience, husbandman, of Wentworth, rec date 1783, writ, debt, file #3383

ATKINSON Samuel, gentleman, of Boscawen, vs NILES Barnabas, joiner, of Coventry, rec date 1783, writ, debt, file #3380

ATKINSON Samuel, gentleman, of Boscawen, vs WEBSTER Benjamin, saddler, of Northfield, rec date 1783, writ, debt, file #3378

ATKINSON Samuel, gentleman, of Boscawen, vs HAMBLET William, of New Holderness, rec date 1782, execution, debt, file #3485

ATKINSON Samuel, gentleman, of Boscawen, vs ROLLINGS Reuben, of Sanbornton, rec date 1782, execution, debt, file #3486

ATKINSON Samuel, gentleman, of Boscawen, vs HALE John, husbandman, of Cockermouth, rec date 1783, judgment, debt, file #3702

ATKINSON Samuel, gentleman, of Boscawen, vs FENTON John, esquire, of Plymouth, rec date 1783, writ, debt, file #3809

ATKINSON Samuel, gentleman, of Boscawen, vs WEBSTER Benjamin, saddler, of Northfield, rec date 1782, execution, debt, file #4897

ATKINSON Samuel, gentleman, of Boscawen, vs CHAMABERLIN Richard, husbandman, of Newbury NY, rec date 1782, writ, debt, file #4851

ATKINSON Samuel, esquire, of Boscawen, vs BOWEN John, husbandman, of Salisbury, rec date 1785, writ, debt, file #4809

ATKINSON Samuel, gentleman, of Boscawen, vs ANNIS Thomas, husbandman, of Warner, rec date 1784, writ, debt, file #5297

ATKINSON Samuel, gentleman, of Boscawen, vs ANNIS Thomas, husbandman, of Warner, rec date 1785, judgment, debt, file #5137, very fragile

ATKINSON Samuel, gentleman, of Boscawen, vs BURNHAM Josiah, husbandman, of Coventry, rec date 1786, various, debt, file #6062

ATKINSON Samuel, gentleman, of Boscawen, vs SOUL Bildad, husbandman, of Goffstown, rec date 1787, writ, debt, file #6697

ATKINSON Samuel, esquire, of Boscawen, vs ATWOOD David, husbandman, of Alexandria, rec date 1786, writ, debt, file #6872

ATKINSON Samuel, esquire, of Boscawen, vs SMITH Robert Walker, husbandman, of Salisbury, rec date 1788, writ, debt, file #6948

ATKINSON Samuel, vs HOBART Jacob, rec date 1774, court bill, bill, file #7030

ATKINSON Samuel (Capt), gentleman, of Boscawen, vs BURNAM Josiah, husbandman, of Coventry, doc date 1784, civil litigation, debt, file #1657 B

ATKINSON Samuel (Capt), gentleman, of Boscawen, vs BURNAM Josiah, husbandman, of Coventry, doc date 1784, civil litigation, debt, file #1657 A

ATKINSON Theodore, esquire, of Portsmouth, vs WENTHWORTH Michael & Wife, esquire, of Portsmouth, doc date 1772, judgment, file #2093, Martha executrix of Benning WENTWORTH estate

ATTWELL John, joiner, of Hollis, vs SPAULDING Joseph, husbandman, of Henniker, rec date 1785, judgment, debt, file #5824

ATTWILL John, joiner, of Hollis, vs FARLEY Samuel, husbandman, of Plymouth, rec date 1785, various, debt, file #5568

ATWELL John, joiner, of Hollis, vs SPAULDING Stephen, husbandman, of Henniker, doc date 1784, execution, debt, file #1773

ATWELL John, innholder, of Hollis, vs SMITH David, yeoman, of Lyndeborough, rec date 1783, writ, debt, file #3034

ATWELL John, joiner, of Hollis, vs SPAULDING Stephen, husbandman, of Henniker, rec date 1784, judgment, debt, file #4378

ATWELL John, husbandman, of Groton, vs AMES Jeremiah, gentleman, of Hollis, doc date 1798, rec date 1799, deed, land transfer, file #5711

ATWELL John, joiner, of Hillsborough, vs SPAULDING Joseph, husbandman, of Henniker, rec date 1785, judgment, debt, file #6448

ATWELL John & Bridget, joiner, of Hollis, vs MERRILL Daniel, gentleman, of Dunstable, doc date 1778, rec date 1778, deed, land transfer, file #6566

ATWELL Samuel & John, of Hollis, doc date 1777, license, tavern license, file #858

ATWILL John, yeoman, of Hollis, vs FISK Amos, gentleman, of Hollis, doc date 1773, trial, assault, file #1285

ATWILL John, joiner, of Hollis, vs HUNT Elizabeth, widow, of Hollis, rec date 1784, judgment, debt, file #4986

ATWILL John, innholder, of Hollis, vs CARTER Edward, husbandman, of Hollis, rec date 1784, writ, debt, file #4973

ATWILL John, joiner, of Hollis, vs KENDALL Ebenezer, carpenter, of Hollis, rec date 1785, judgment, debt, file #5361

ATWOOD John, trader, of Atkinson, vs FLAGG Samuel, merchant, of Salem MA, doc date 1773, writ, debt, file #1332

ATWOOD Jonathan, gentleman, of Weare, vs McCLINTOCK Alexander, husbandman, of Hillsborough, rec date 1782, execution, debt, file #3514

ATWOOD Jonathan, gentleman, of Weare, vs McCLINTOCK Alexander, husbandman, of Hillsborough, rec date 1783, execution, debt, file #3654

ATWOOD Jonathan, gentleman, of Weare, vs McCLINTOCK Alexander, husbandman, of Hillsborough, rec date 1783, execution, debt, file #3846

AUSTIN Benjamin, cooper, of Hollis, vs LOVEJOY Samuel, husbandman, of Deering, doc date 1798, judgment, debt, file #561

AUSTIN Jacob, laborer, of Brookline, vs GORDON William, esquire, of Amherst, doc date 1799, writ, debt, file #378

AUSTIN John, husbandman, of Dunbarton, vs EATON Jothan, husbandman, of Weare, rec date 1783, writ, debt, file #3214

AUSTIN Phineas, husbandman, of Rochester VT, vs BARNS William, husbandman, of Antrim, doc date 1800, various, debt, file #544

AUSTIN Phineas, yeoman, of Antrim, vs BARNS William, trader, of Antrim, doc date 1800, rec date 1801, deed, land transfer, file #5672

AVERHILL Moses, vs PARKER Deborah, rec date 1785, deposition, file #7041

AVERILL Samuel, yeoman, of New Ipswich, vs SHATTUCK Peter, yeoman, of New Ipswich, doc date 1786, rec date 1786, deed, land transfer, file #5022

AYERS Simon, of Haverhill MA, vs LULL Simeon, yeoman, of Nottingham, doc date 1775, writ, debt, file #961

AYERS Simon, yeoman, of Nottingham-West, vs LULL Simon, yeoman, of Londonderry, doc date 1774, rec date 1776, deed, land transfer, file #4908, /39

BABSON Isaac, trader, of Hopkinton, vs CURRIER Sargent & Henry, husbandman, of Hopkinton, rec date 1784, judgment, debt, file #4605

BABSON Isaac, trader, of Hopkinton, vs HALL Ebenezer Jr, tanner, of Milford MA, doc date 1794, petition, debt, file #40

BACHELDER Phinehas, husbandman, of Fisherfield, vs HART Charles Walter, husbandman, of Bradford, doc date 1798, judgment, debt, file #561

BACON Daniel, yeoman, of Hillsborough, vs JEWELL Timothy, yeoman, of Hillsborough, rec date 1783, execution, debt, file #3651

BACON Daniel, husbandman, of Natick MA, vs BAYLES John, husbandman, of Deering, rec date 1785, execution, debt, file #5923

BACON Daniel, husbandman, of Natick MA, vs BAYLES John, husbandman, of Deering, rec date 1785, writ, debt, file #6019

BACON Daniel, yeoman, of Hillsborough, vs JEWELL Timothy, yeoman, of Hillsborough, rec date 1782, execution, debt, file #3530

BACON Peter, yeoman, of New Ipswich, vs WILSON Robert, gentleman, of New Ipswich, doc date 1770, writ, debt, file #831

BACON Retire, yeoman, of New Ipswich, vs DURY Zedekiah, yeoman, of Temple, doc date 1772, writ, debt, file #930

BACON Retire, yeoman, of New Ipswich, vs REED Frederick, innkeeper, of Surry, rec date 1782, judgment, debt, file #2733

BACON Retire, husbandman, of New Ipswich, vs PARKER Abel, husbandman, of Peterborough, rec date 1785, various, debt, file #4699

BACON Retire, yeoman, of New Ipswich, vs BOYNTON Caleb, yeoman, of Peterborough Slip, rec date 1785, judgment, debt, file #6454

BACON Retire, vs BOYNTON Caleb, rec date 1785, judgment, correction, file #6375

BACON Retire Jr, husbandman, of New Ipswich, vs KIDDER Reuben, esquire, of New Ipswich, rec date 1785, writ, debt, file #5436

BACROFT Benjamin, gentleman, of Groton MA, vs SWAN William & Alice, husbandman, of Peterborough, rec date 1788, writ, debt, file #2556

BADGER Melvin, vs PLATTS George W, doc date 1894, real estate mtg dispute, supreme court, file #585

BAGLEY David, gentleman, of Newtown, vs EMERY Amos, yeoman, of Dunbarton, doc date 1781, rec date 1785, deed, land transfer, file #5644

BAGLEY Jonathan, taylor, of Merrimack, vs FOSTER Samuel, blacksmith, of Merrimack, doc date 1779, rec date 1779, deed, land transfer, file #2146

BAGLEY Joseph, husbandman, of Hollis, vs TAYLOR Jacob, laborer, of Hopkinton, rec date 1788, writ, debt, file #2431

BAGLEY Phineas, gentleman, of Sanborton, vs NOYES Joseph, husbandman, of Weare, rec date 1785, writ, debt, file #6254

BAGLY William Jr, gentleman, of Lyndeborough, vs GILSON David, husbandman, of Dunstable, rec date 1787, writ, lost sheep, file #2366

BAILEY Abraham, blacksmith, of Tewksbury MA, vs MARBEL Nathaniel, laborer, of Pelham, rec date 1783, execution, debt, file #3661

BAILEY Abraham, blacksmith, of Tewksbury MA, vs MARBEL Nathaniel, laborer, of Pelham, rec date 1783, execution, debt, file #3843

BAILEY Abraham, blacksmith, of Tewksbury MA, vs KITTRIDGE Ebenezer, gentleman, of Goffstown, rec date 1782, judgment, debt, file #4035

BAILEY Abraham, blacksmith, of Tewksbury MA, vs WOOD Jonathan, yeoman, of Goffstown, rec date 1782, judgment, debt, file #4032

BAILEY Andrew, yeoman, of Peterborough, vs FRENCH John Jr, yeoman, of Packersfield, doc date 1784, execution, debt, file #1746

BAILEY Andrew, yeoman, of Peterborough, vs FRENCH John J, yeoman, of Packersfield, doc date 1784, execution, debt, file #1909

BAILEY Andrew, rec date 1779, deposition, land dispute, file #2236B

BAILEY Andrew, yeoman, of Peterborough, vs FRANCH John Jr, yeoman, of Packersfield, rec date 1783, civil litigious, debt, file #2935

BAILEY Daniel, carpenter, of Hollis, vs BALL John, yeoman, of Hollis, doc date 1784, execution, debt, file #1534

BAILEY Enoch, gentleman, of Hopkinton, vs STANLEY Samuel, husbandman, of Hopkinton, doc date 1799, execution, debt, file #204

BAILEY Enoch, trader, of Hopkinton, vs BARTLETT Edmund, yeoman, of Unity, doc date 1799, debt, file #500

BAILEY Enoch, gentleman, of Hopkinton, vs STANLEY Samuel, husbandman, of Hopkinton, doc date 1798, judgment, debt, file #561

BAILEY Isaac, trader, of Hopkinton, vs BARTLETT Edmund, yeoman, of Unity, doc date 1799, debt, file #500

BAILEY Isaac, husbandman, of Hopkinton, vs BALCH John, trader, of Newburyport MA, doc date 1798, execution, debt, file #181

BAILEY Isaac & Enoch, yeoman, of Hopkinton, vs PROCTOR Jonathan, husbandman, of Hopkinton, doc date 1798, execution, debt, file #161

BAILEY James, of Amesbury MA, vs HUTCHINSON Jonathan, hatter, of Pembroke, doc date 1798, judgment, debt, file #561

BAILEY John, cordwainer, of Hollis, vs SANDERSON David, husbandman, of Hollis, rec date 1785, judgment, debt, file #4695

BAILEY John, husbandman, of Hillsborough, vs JAMESON Thomas, yeoman, of Antrim, doc date 1799, debt, file #332

BAILEY Jonathan, yeoman, of Billerica MA, vs BLANCHARD Jeremiah, yeoman, of Wilton, doc date 1784, execution, debt, file #1501

BAILEY Jonathan, yeoman, of Billerica MA, vs BLANCHARD Jeremiah, yeoman, of Wilton, rec date 1783, judgment, debt, file #4448

BAILEY Noah, yeoman, of Dracut MA, vs WELLS John, yeoman, of New Boston, doc date 1784, civil litigation, debt, file #1832

BAILEY Timothy, yeoman, of Hollis, vs KILLICUT Reubin, yeoman, of Dunstable, rec date 1784, judgment, debt, file #4924

BAILEY Timothy, yeoman, of Hollis, vs KILLICUT Reuben, yeoman, of Dunstable, rec date 1785, judgment, debt, file #6438

BAILEY Timothy, husbandman, of Hollis, vs McGAA Robert, trader, of New Boston, rec date 1785, judgment, debt, file #6441

BAKER Amos, husbandman, of Nashua, vs SHANNON Richard Cutts, esquire, of Raby, rec date 1787, writ, debt, file #6762

BAKER Ephraim, housewright, of Amherst, vs WILKINS Benjamin, yeoman, of Amherst, rec date 1786, judgment, debt, file #6378

BAKER Jesse, husbandman, of Fisherfield, vs BAKER Nathaniel, husbandman, of Bedford, doc date 1782, rec date 1782, deed, land transfer, file #5660

BAKER Joseph, yeoman, of Wilton, vs WATSON John, yeoman, of Brookfield MA, rec date 1783, writ, debt, file #3075

BAKER Joseph, taylor, of New Ipswich, vs CLARK Isaac, gentleman, of New Ipswich, rec date 1785, writ, debt, file #6255

BALCH Israel, yeoman, of Francestown, vs BATTEN John, yeoman, of Francestown, doc date 1805, rec date 1806, deed, land transfer, file #5687

BALCH Israel, husbandman, of Francestown, vs CRESSEY Josiah, carpenter, of Marblehead MA, doc date 1814, rec date 1816, deed, land transfer, file #5701

BALCH Israel Jr, yeoman, of Francestown, vs BALCH Joshua, tanner, of Lyme, doc date 1802, rec date 1802, deed, land transfer, file #5675

BALCH Joseph, vs EPES Frances, doc date 1777, deed, land dispute, file #6702

BALCH Joshua, deceased, of Lyndeborough, vs CRESSEY Andrew, yeoman, of Lyndeborough, rec date 1787, various, land dispute, file #6702

BALCH Mary, widow, of Lyndeborough, vs CRESSEY Andrew, yeoman, of Lyndeborough, rec date 1787, various, land dispute, file #6702

BALCH Mary, widow, of Lyndeborough, vs BATTEN Richard, yeoman, of Francestown, rec date 1787, writ, land dispute, file #6667

BALCH Timothy, yeoman, of Keene, vs STEELE David, gentleman, of Peterborough, rec date 1785, writ, debt, file #5541

BALDDWIN Martha, widow, of Amherst, vs LUND Phineas, husbandman, of Lyndeborough, rec date 1790, judgment, debt, file #5466

BALDWIN Abel, yeoman, of Billerica MA, vs PERSON Thomas, yeoman, of Lyndeborough, doc date 1778, rec date 1780, deed, land transfer, file #6564

BALDWIN Isaac, blacksmith, of Antrim, vs MCFARALAND Moses, tanner, of Antrim, doc date 1799, execution, debt, file #156

BALDWIN Israel, yeoman, of Hillsborough, vs BRADFORD Samuel 3rd, yeoman, of Hillsborough, doc date 1772, writ, debt, file #1422

BALDWIN Israel, housewright, of Hillsborough, vs BRADFORD Samuel, yeoman, of Hillsborough, doc date 1772, writ, debt, file #1413

BALDWIN Jeremiah, yeoman, of Mile Slip, vs SLOAN David, yeoman, of Mason, rec date 1787, judgment, debt, file #5717

BALDWIN Jeremiah, yeoman, of Mile Slip, vs SLOAN David, yeoman, of Mason, rec date 1787, judgment, debt, file #6195

BALDWIN Jeremiah, yeoman, of Mile Slip, vs SLOAN David, yeoman, of Mason, rec date 1787, writ, debt, file #6896

BALDWIN Jesse, yeoman, of Amherst, vs SHEPARD John Jr, esquire, of Amherst, rec date 1783, writ, debt, file #3009, land deed

BALDWIN Jesse, yeoman, of Amherst, vs CRISTY James, yeoman, of Walpole, rec date 1783, writ, debt, file #3053

BALDWIN Jesse, yeoman, of Amherst, vs CLARK Timothy, yeoman, of Amherst, rec date 1783, writ, debt, file #3021

BALDWIN Jesse, husbandman, of Amherst, vs BARNARD Jeremiah, clerk, of Amherst, rec date 1783, writ, debt, file #3095

BALDWIN Jesse, yeoman, of Amherst, vs WHITWILL Mary, widow, of Roxbury MA, rec date 1783, execution, debt, file #3001

BALDWIN Jesse, yeoman, of Amherst, vs BROWN Jonathan, of Tewksbury MA, rec date 1782, debt, debt, file #3157

BALDWIN Joseph, executor, vs AYER Ann And Frank H, doc date 1890, defendants points, supreme court, file #610, will of Josephus BALDWIN

BALDWIN Nahaum, esquire, of Goffstown, vs GOULD Richard, yeoman, of Amherst, rec date 1785, judgment, debt, file #5974

BALDWIN Nahaum, esquire, of Amherst, vs McCLARY John, gentleman, of Hillsborough, rec date 1785, judgment, debt, file #5973

BALDWIN Nahaum, esquire, of Goffstown, vs MAXWELL Joel, yeoman, of Lyndeborough, rec date 1785, judgment, debt, file #5971

BALDWIN Nahaum, esquire, of Amherst, vs CRAM Benjamin, yeoman, of Lyndeborough, rec date 1785, judgment, debt, file #5972

BALDWIN Nahum, gentleman, of Amherst, vs FRYE Isaac, yeoman, of Wilton, doc date 1774, judgment, debt, file #714

BALDWIN Nahum, esquire, of Amherst, vs WHITE William, yeoman, of Peterborough, rec date 1785, execution, debt, file #5490

BALDWIN Nahum, gentleman, of Amherst, vs YOUNG John, physician, of Peterborough, doc date 1773, judgment, debt, file #1294

BALDWIN Nahum, esquire, of Amherst, vs HUTCHINSON John, yeoman, of Weare, doc date 1784, execution, debt, file #1749

BALDWIN Nahum, esquire, of Amherst, vs HUTCHINSON John, yeoman, of Weare, doc date 1784, execution, debt, file #1535

BALDWIN Nahum, esquire, of Amherst, vs JONES William, yeoman, of Hillsborough, doc date 1784, execution, debt, file #1785, trustees of Zacheus CUTLER

BALDWIN Nahum, esquire, of Amherst, vs DICKEY Joseph, yeoman, of Hollis, doc date 1784, execution, debt, file #1932

BALDWIN Nahum, esquire, of Amherst, vs SMALL Jonathan, husbandman, of Goffstown, doc date 1784, execution, debt, file #1861

BALDWIN Nahum, esquire, of Amherst, vs WILEY John, yeoman, of Deering, doc date 1784, execution, debt, file #1870

BALDWIN Nahum, esquire, of Amherst, vs WILSON Thomas, yeoman, of New Boston, doc date 1784, execution, debt, file #1931

BALDWIN Nahum, esquire, of Amherst, vs BRADFORD Samuel, gentleman, of Hillsborough, doc date 1784, execution, debt, file #1925

BALDWIN Nahum, esquire, of Amherst, vs JACK Andrew, blacksmith, of New Boston, doc date 1784, execution, debt, file #1933

BALDWIN Nahum, esquire, of Amherst, vs WHITE John, husbandman, of Peterborough, rec date 1785, writ, debt, file #2349

BALDWIN Nahum, esquire, of Amherst, vs WHITE William, husbandman, of Peterborough, rec date 1785, writ, debt, file #2345

BALDWIN Nahum, esquire, of Amherst, vs BRADFORD Samuel Jr, gentleman, of Hillsborough, rec date 1782, judgment, debt, file #2720, estate of Zacheus CUTLER

BALDWIN Nahum, esquire, of Amherst, vs GREGG James Jr, yeoman, of New Boston, rec date 1783, civil litigious, debt, file #2961, Zacheus CUTLER estate

BALDWIN Nahum, esquire, of Amherst, vs HITCHINS Josiah, cordwainer, of New Boston, rec date 1783, execution, debt, file #2869, Zacheus CUTLER estate

BALDWIN Nahum, esquire, of Amherst, vs GREGG Alexander, yeoman, of Deering, rec date 1783, court case, debt, file #2882, Zacheus CUTLER estate

BALDWIN Nahum, esquire, of Amherst, vs HITCHINS Josiah, cordwainer, of New Boston, rec date 1782, judgment, debt, file #3137

BALDWIN Nahum, esquire, of Amherst, vs FLANDERS John, yeoman, of Weare, rec date 1783, execution, debt, file #2873, Zacheus CUTLER estate

BALDWIN Nahum, esquire, of Amherst, vs COCKRAN John, yeoman, of New Boston, rec date 1783, civil litigious, debt, file #2970, Zacheus CUTLER estate

BALDWIN Nahum, esquire, of Amherst, vs PATTEN John, yeoman, of Merrimack, rec date 1783, execution, debt, file #2870

BALDWIN Nahum, esquire, of Amherst, vs SCOBY David, yeoman, of Francestown, rec date 1782, judgment, debt, file #3137

BALDWIN Nahum, esquire, of Amherst, vs PATTEN John, yeoman, of Merrimack, rec date 1782, judgment, debt, file #3137

BALDWIN Nahum, esquire, of Amherst, vs DICKEY Joseph, yeoman, of Hollis, rec date 1783, civil litigious, debt, file #2960, Zacheus CUTLER estate

BALDWIN Nahum, esquire, of Amherst, vs McMILLIAN Jr John, yeoman, of New Boston, rec date 1782, judgment, debt, file #3137

BALDWIN Nahum, esquire, of Amherst, vs FLANDERS John, yeoman, of Weare, rec date 1782, judgment, debt, file #3137

BALDWIN Nahum, esquire, of Amherst, vs SARGENT Archibald, gentleman, of Hillsborough, rec date 1782, judgment, debt, file #3137

BALDWIN Nahum, esquire, of Amherst, vs JONES William Jr, yeoman, of Hillsborough, rec date 1783, civil litigious, debt, file #2944, Zacheus CUTLER estate

BALDWIN Nahum, esquire, of Amherst, vs SCOBY David, yeoman, of Francestown, rec date 1783, execution, debt, file #3065, Zacheus CUTLER estate

BALDWIN Nahum, esquire, of Amherst, vs RAMSY Hugh, yeoman, of New Boston, rec date 1783, civil litigious, debt, file #2945, Zacheus CUTLER estate

BALDWIN Nahum, esquire, of Amherst, vs BURNS John, yeoman, of Antrim, rec date 1782, judgment, debt, file #3137

BALDWIN Nahum, esquire, of Amherst, vs LIVINGSTON William, gentleman, of New Boston, rec date 1783, judgment, debt, file #3736, estate of Zacheus CUTLER

BALDWIN Nahum, esquire, of Amherst, vs BLAIR William, yeoman, of New Boston, rec date 1783, judgment, debt, file #3737, estate of Zacheus CUTLER

BALDWIN Nahum, esquire, of Amherst, vs GREGG David, yeoman, of Francestown, rec date 1783, judgment, debt, file #3735, estate of Zacheus CUTLER

BALDWIN Nahum, esquire, of Amherst, vs GREGG James Jr, yeoman, of New Boston, rec date 1783, writ, debt, file #3890, estate of Zacheus CUTLER

BALDWIN Nahum, esquire, of Amherst, vs FLINT Jacob, yeoman, of Hillsborough, rec date 1783, execution, debt, file #3865

BALDWIN Nahum, esquire, of Amherst, vs BRADFORD Samuel Jr, yeoman, of Hillsborough, rec date 1783, execution, debt, file #3867

BALDWIN Nahum, esquire, of Amherst, vs HOLMS William, yeoman, of Francestown, rec date 1783, execution, debt, file #3866

BALDWIN Nahum, esquire, of Amherst, vs HOLMS William, yeoman, of Francestown, rec date 1783, writ, debt, file #3943, estate of Zacheus CUTLER

BALDWIN Nahum, esquire, of Amherst, vs GREGG James Jr, yeoman, of New Boston, rec date 1783, execution, debt, file #3864

BALDWIN Nahum, esquire, of Amherst, vs ABBOT Ephraim, yeoman, of Lyndeborough, rec date 1783, execution, debt, file #3863

BALDWIN Nahum, esquire, of Amherst, vs CHRISTY George, gentleman, of New Boston, rec date 1782, appeal, debt, file #4023, estate of Z CUTLER (Loyalist)

BALDWIN Nahum, esquire, of Amherst, vs SMITH Samuel, yeoman, of New Boston, rec date 1782, appeal, debt, file #4019, estate of Z CUTLER

BALDWIN Nahum, esquire, of Amherst, vs MILLER Thomas, yeoman, of Hancock, rec date 1784, judgment, debt, file #4210, estate of Z CUTLER

BALDWIN Nahum, esquire, of Amherst, vs ROBINSON Alexander, yeoman, of Deering, rec date 1785, writ, debt, file #4684

BALDWIN Nahum, esquire, of Amherst, vs BROWN James, gentleman, of Haverhill, rec date 1784, judgment, debt, file #4616

BALDWIN Nahum, esquire, of Amherst, vs HUTCHINSON John Jr, yeoman, of Weare, rec date 1783, judgment, debt, file #4449

BALDWIN Nahum, esquire, of Amherst, vs MILLER Charles, yeoman, of Francestown, rec date 1783, execution, debt, file #4919

BALDWIN Nahum, esquire, of Amherst, vs BRADFORD Samuel Jr, gentleman, of Hillsborough, rec date 1783, execution, debt, file #4907

BALDWIN Nahum, esquire, of Amherst, vs BRADFORD William, yeoman, of Hillsborough, rec date 1785, judgment, debt, file #4940, estate of Zacheus CUTLER

BALDWIN Nahum, esquire, of Amherst, vs RAMSEY Hugh, yeoman, of New Boston, rec date 1783, execution, debt, file #4910, estate of L CUTLER

BALDWIN Nahum, esquire, of Amherst, vs ROBINSON William, yeoman, of Deering, rec date 1785, judgment, debt, file #4937, estate of Zacheus CUTLER

BALDWIN Nahum, esquire, of Amherst, vs TUTTLE Stephen, yeoman, of Goffstown, rec date 1784, judgment, debt, file #5884

BALDWIN Nahum, esquire, of Amherst, vs KING William, laborer, of Hollis, rec date 1784, judgment, debt, file #5885

BALDWIN Nahum, esquire, of Amherst, vs GOULD Richard, yeoman, of Amherst, rec date 1785, writ, debt, file #6008

BALDWIN Nahum, esquire, of Amherst, vs CLARK Ephraim, yeoman, of Deering, rec date 1785, execution, debt, file #5777

BALDWIN Nahum, esquire, of Amherst, vs WOOD Jonathan, yeoman, of Goffstown, rec date 1786, judgment, debt, file #5766

BALDWIN Nahum, esquire, of Amherst, vs STEARNS Samuel Jr, yeoman, of Amherst, rec date 1785, writ, debt, file #6012

BALDWIN Nahum, esquire, of Amherst, vs GRIMES James, gentleman, of Deering, rec date 1786, execution, debt, file #6049

BALDWIN Nahum, esquire, of Amherst, vs GREEN David, yeoman, of Hillsborough, rec date 1785, various, debt, file #6044

BALDWIN Nahum, esquire, of Amherst, vs RICHARDSON Zechariah, yeoman, of Francestown, rec date 1785, writ, debt, file #6013

BALDWIN Nahum, esquire, of Amherst, vs GREEN David, yeoman, of Hillsborough, rec date 1785, judgment, debt, file #6447

BALDWIN Nahum, of Bedford, rec date 1777, application, tavern license, file #7034

BALDWIN Nathan, esquire, of Goffstown, vs Town of Goffstown, doc date 1783, treasury bond, bond for treasury, file #803

BALDWIN Nathan, esquire, of Amherst, vs MELLEN Charles, yeoman, of Francestown, doc date 1782, execution, debt, file #1169

BALDWIN Nathan, esquire, of Amherst, vs GOULD Richard, yeoman, of Amherst, rec date 1786, judgment, debt, file #6388

BALDWIN Nathaniel, esquire, of Amherst, vs GRAGG Samuel, of Peterborough, rec date 1783, execution, debt, file #2884, Zacheus CUTLER estate

BALDWIN Timothy, yeoman, of Amherst, vs BALDWIN Jesse, yeoman, of Amherst, rec date 1783, civil litigious, debt, file #2958

BALEY Andrew, yeoman, of Peterborough, vs FOX Timothy, yeoman, of New Ipswich, doc date 1772, civil litigation, debt, file #650

BALEY Andrew, yeoman, of Peterborough, vs HEALD Thomas, esquire, of New Ipswich, doc date 1784, writ, debt, file #1270

BALL Ebenezer, yeoman, of Hollis, vs STEVENS Joseph, yeoman, of Hollis, rec date 1784, recognizance, assault, file #4177

BALL Eleazer, husbandman, of Hollis, vs BROWN Joseph, joiner, of Hollis, doc date 1784, execution, debt, file #1683

BALL Eleazer, husbandman, of Hollis, vs BROWN Joseph, yeoman, of Hollis, doc date 1784, execution, debt, file #1543

BALL Eleazer, husbandman, of Mason, vs SIMS Stephen Jr, taylor, of Billerica MA, doc date 1784, execution, debt, file #1868

BALL Eleazer, yeoman, of Hollis, vs BRADLEY Ithmar, innkeeper, of Hollis, doc date 1784, execution, debt, file #1950

BALL Eleazer, husbandman, of Hollis, vs BLOOD Francis, esquire, of Temple, rec date 1782, writ, debt, file #2843

BALL Eleazer, husbandman, of Hollis, vs BROWN Joseph, joiner, of Hollis, rec date 1783, writ, debt, file #3426

BALL Eleazer, yeoman, of Hollis, vs BRODLEY Ithmar, innkeeper, of Hollis, rec date 1783, writ, debt, file #3406

BALL Eleazer, husbandman, of Mason, vs SIMS Stephen Jr, tailor, of Billerica MA, rec date 1784, judgment, debt, file #4271

BALL Eleazer, husbandman, of Mason, vs BROWN Isaac, husbandman, of Wilton, rec date 1784, judgment, debt, file #5003

BALL Eleazer, husbandman, of Mason, vs GREELE Jonathan, husbandman, of Wilton, rec date 1784, judgment, debt, file #5003

BALL Joseph, yeoman, of Hillsborough, vs BALL Jonathan & Silas, yeoman, of MA, doc date 1774, rec date 1778, deed, land transfer, file #2117

BALLARD John Osgood, gentleman, of Hopkinton, vs RUNNELLS Jonathan, clothier, of Concord, doc date 1799, debt, file #497

BALLARD Nathan, husbandman, of Wilton, vs PAINE Nathaniel, esquire, of Groton MA, rec date 1783, writ, debt, file #3162

BALLARD Uriah, yeoman, of Wilton, vs ABBOT Nehemiah, of Andover MA, doc date 1774, rec date 1774, deed, land transfer, file #6845

BALLARD Uriah Jr, yeoman, of Wilton, vs SMITH Jeremiah, yeoman, of Sanbornton, rec date 1785, judgment, debt, file #5198

BANCROFT Abel, deceased, of Groton MA, rec date 1788, writ, debt, file #6623

BANCROFT Ebenezer, yard brakeman, of Nashua, vs BOSTON & Maine Railroad, of Nashua, doc date 1893, defendants brief, supreme court, file #604

BANCROFT Ebenezer, esquire, of Dunstable MA, vs ESTERBROOK John, husbandman, of Packersfield, rec date 1782, execution, debt, file #3484

BANCROFT James, of Packersfield, vs SMITH John, yeoman, of Peterborough, doc date 1782, capias, recognizance, file #775

BANCROFT Sarah, widow, of Groton MA, vs HOSMER Nathaniel, yeoman, of Mason, rec date 1788, writ, debt, file #6623

BANCROFT Sarah, of Groton MA, vs STEWART Alexander, cordwainer, of Peterborough, rec date 1788, writ, debt, file #6946

BANCROFT Thomas, esquire, rec date 1794, recommendation, to become lawyer, file #4160

BANKS James, husbandman, of Packersfield, vs DAVIS Simon, husbandman, of Athens VT, rec date 1783, writ, debt, file #3963, fragile pieces

BARANS Silas, yeoman, of Henniker, vs CLOGSTONE Paul, yeoman, of Dunstable, doc date 1773, judgment, debt, file #1318

BARANS Silas, yeoman, of Henniker, vs CLOGSTONE Thomas, yeoman, of Dunstable, doc date 1773, judgment, debt, file #1318

BARBER Ephraim, joiner, of Amherst, vs WILKINS Jonathan, yeoman, of Amherst, doc date 1784, execution, debt, file #1889

BARBER Robert, gentleman, of Canaan, vs EASTMAN Moses, gentleman, of Salisbury, doc date 1799, judgment, debt, file #273

BARKER Daniel, husbandman, of Lyndeborough, vs FRYE Isaac, esquire, of Wilton, rec date 1784, writ, debt, file #4670

BARKER Ephraim, housewright, of Amherst, vs SOUL Bildad, yeoman, of Goffstown, rec date 1783, civil litigious, debt, file #2941

BARKER Ephraim, housewright, of Amherst, vs CLARK Joseph, yeoman, of Antrim, rec date 1783, civil litigious, debt, file #2942

BARKER Ephraim, housewright, of Amherst, vs JONES Samuel, yeoman, of Hillsborough, rec date 1783, civil litigious, debt, file #2910

BARKER Ephraim, housewright, of Amherst, vs SOUL Bildad, yeoman, of Goffstown, rec date 1783, writ, debt, file #3593

BARKER Ephraim, housewright, of Amherst, vs JONES Samuel, yeoman, of Hillsborough, rec date 1783, writ, debt, file #3596

BARKER Ephraim, housewright, of Amherst, vs CLERK Joseph, yeoman, of Antrim, rec date 1783, writ, debt, file #3594

BARKER Ephraim, housewright, of Amherst, vs WILKINS Benjamin, yeoman, of Amherst, rec date 1784, judgment, debt, file #4285

BARKER Ephraim, housewright, of Amherst, vs McMASTER Samuel, yeoman, of Lyndeborough, rec date 1785, judgment, debt, file #4961

BARKER Sarah, singlewoman, of Methuen MA, vs HILLS Ebenezer, minor, of Nottingham-West, rec date 1785, warrant, fornication, file #5532

BARKER William, physician, of Francestown, vs McGINNIS Barnabas, yeoman, of Nottingham-West, doc date 1784, execution, debt, file #1902

BARKER William, yeoman, of Packersfield, vs BREED Nathaniel, physician, of New Ipswich, rec date 1783, writ, debt, file #3585

BARKER William, physician, of Amherst, vs JONES Samuel, yeoman, of Hillsborough, rec date 1783, writ, debt, file #3891

BARKER William, physician, of Francestown, vs RICHARDSON Zachariah, husbandman, of Francestown, rec date 1785, judgment, debt, file #4686

BARN James, husbandman, of New Ipswich, vs PATTERSON Adam, husbandman, of Hancock, rec date 1786, writ, debt, file #6152, deed

BARNARD Jeremiah, clerk, of Amherst, vs BARNARD Joel, yeoman, of Mile Slip, doc date 1784, execution, debt, file #1537

BARNARD Jeremiah, clerk, of Amherst, vs BALDWIN Jesse, husbandman, of Amherst, rec date 1783, judgment, debt, file #3799

BARNARD Jeremiah, minister, of Amherst, vs INHABITANTS of Amherst, rec date 1784, writ, debt, file #4868

BARNARD Jeremiah, of Amherst, vs HOBART Joel, husbandman, of Mile Slip, rec date 1785, writ, land dispute, file #6416

BARNARD John, physician, of Bolton MA, vs HOW Nehemiah, yeoman, of Henniker, doc date 1784, execution, debt, file #1498

BARNARD John, physician, of Bolton MA, vs HOW Nehemiah, yeoman, of Henniker, rec date 1783, execution, debt, file #3854

BARNARD John, physician, of Bolton MA, vs HOW Nehemiah, yeoman, of Henniker, rec date 1783, writ, debt, file #3903

BARNARD John, gentleman, of Amesbury MA, vs PATTERSON William, husbandman, of Goffstown, rec date 1786, writ, debt, file #6311

BARNARD Samuel, husbandman, of Fitzwilliam, vs HOBART Joel, yeoman, of Miles Slip, rec date 1784, judgment, debt, file #4610

BARNES Joseph, physician, of Litchfield, vs McQUESTION William, gentleman, of Litchfield, doc date 1772, judgment, trespass, file #669

BARNES Joseph, physician, of Litchfield, vs KENDALL Daniel, gentleman, of Litchfield, doc date 1772, judgment, trespass, file #669

BARNES Joseph, physician, of Litchfield, vs CAMPBELL David, husbandman, of Litchfield, doc date 1772, judgment, file #669

BARNES Paul, yeoman, of Bradford, vs SHERMAN Miah, trader, of Marlborough MA, doc date 1799, writ, debt, file #353

BARNET Jonathan, husbandman, of Hancock, vs McFARLAND Moses, trader, of Antrim, doc date 1799, writ, debt, file #417

BARNET Jonathan, husbandman, of Hancock, vs MOOR Samuel, trader, of Antrim, doc date 1799, writ, debt, file #417

BARNET Nancy, widow, of Francestown, vs LICENSE Petition, of Francestown, doc date 1800, petition for license, debt, file #541

BARNETT Aaron, yeoman, of Concord MA, vs BAGLES John, rec date 1783, execution, debt, file #3878

BARNS Amos, yeoman, of Concord, vs ATKINSON Samuel, esquire, of Boscawen, rec date 1785, judgment, debt, file #5577

BARNS Elisha, husbandman, of Henniker, vs TEMPLE Jonathan, husbandman, of Marlborough MA, doc date 1799, various, debt, file #542

BARNS Henry, deceased, of Marlborough, rec date 1779, letter, about estate, file #7014

BARNS Jonathan, gentleman, of Antrim, vs BRADFORD Eliphalet, husbandman, of Hillsborough, doc date 1805, rec date 1805, deed, land transfer, file #5682

BARNS Joseph, housewright, of Peterborough, vs BROWN Ezekiel, esquire, of Concord MA, rec date 1784, judgment, debt, file #4364

BARNS Joseph, housewright, of Peterborough Slip, vs BARNS Joseph Jr, laborer, of Peterborough Slip, rec date 1785, deed, land transfer, file #5635

BARNS Joseph, husbandman, of Peterborough Slip, vs HOSMER Nathaniel, yeoman, of Peterborough Slip, rec date 1787, writ, debt, file #6712

BARNS Silas, yeoman, of Henniker, vs FOWLER Jeremiah, yeoman, of Hopkinton, doc date 1772, writ, debt, file #924

BARNS Silas, yeoman, of Newmarket, vs CUTLER Zacheus, esquire, of Amherst, doc date 1774, writ, debt, file #1104, fragile

BARNS Silas, yeoman, of Marlborough MA, vs KIMBALL William, yeoman, of Henniker, rec date 1783, various, killing of animal, file #3561

BARNS Silas, husbandman, of Henniker, vs BRADFORD Samuel, yeoman, of Hillsborough, doc date 1772, writ, file #1415

BARNS William, trader, of Antrim, vs ELLIOT Roger, husbandman, of Hillsborough, doc date 1800, rec date 1801, deed, land transfer, file #5673

BARNS William, trader, of Antrim, vs GIBSON Samuel, husbandman, of Hillsborough, doc date 1801, rec date 1801, deed, land transfer, file #6577

BARON William Capt, of Merrimack, doc date 1777, license, tavern license, file #857

BARR James, yeoman, of New Ipswich, vs INGALS Israel, gentleman, of Dunstable, rec date 1783, judgment, debt, file #3712

BARR James, yeoman, of New Ipswich, vs WARNER John, yeoman, of New Ipswich, rec date 1785, judgment, debt, file #5042

BARRET Charles, gentleman, of New Ipswich, vs CHAMBERLIN Aaron, gentleman, of Chelmsford MA, doc date 1775, rec date 1777, deed, land transfer, file #6556

BARRET Isaac, yeoman, of Chesterfield, vs BUTTERFIELD Joseph, gentleman, of Wilton, rec date 1782, writ, debt, file #2796

BARRET Joel, husbandman, of Chelmsford MA, vs RICHARDSON Zechariah, innkeeper, of Francestown, rec date 1784, judgment, debt, file #4410

BARRET Moses Jr, yeoman, of Nottingham-West, vs MELVEN Benjamin, yeoman, of Londonderry, rec date 1777, writ, debt, file #2185

BARRETT Amos, yeoman, of Concord MA, vs BAYLES John, husbandman, of Deering, rec date 1783, execution, debt, file #3659

BARRETT Amos, yeoman, of Concord MA, vs RAMSEY Hugh, husbandman, of New Boston, rec date 1782, execution, debt, file #5724

BARRETT Charles, esquire, of New Ipswich, vs BUSH David, yeoman, of Rindge, rec date 1788, judgment, debt, file #2558

BARRETT Charles, esquire, of New Ipswich, vs MELVIN John, yeoman, of New Ipswich, doc date 1784, rec date 1786, deed, land transfer, file #5036

BARRETT Charles, gentleman, of New Ipswich, vs RICHARDSON Zechariah, yeoman, of Francestown, doc date 1786, rec date 1786, deed, land transfer, file #5034

BARRETT Charles, gentleman, of New Ipswich, vs RICHARDSON Zechariah, innholder, of Francestown, doc date 1783, rec date 1785, deed, land transfer, file #5620

BARRETT Charles, esquire, of Hillsborough, vs PATTERSON Alexander, yeoman, of New Boston, rec date 1785, judgment, debt, file #5443

BARRETT Charles, gentleman, of New Ipswich, vs WHITTEMORE Peletiah, gentleman, of New Ipswich, doc date 1770, rec date 1785, deed, land transfer, file #5651

BARRETT Charles, esquire, of New Ipswich, vs HALE Enoch, esquire, of Walpole, rec date 1786, various, debt, file #6302

BARRETT Charles, esquire, of New Ipswich, vs BACON Retire, husbandman, of New Ipswich, rec date 1786, writ, debt, file #6289

BARRETT Charles, esquire, of Francestown, vs DEAN Benjamin, yeoman, of Francestown, doc date 1781, rec date 1788, deed, land transfer, file #6747

BARRETT Charles, esquire, of New Ipswich, vs RICHARDSON Zachariah, of Francestown, doc date 1787, rec date 1788, deed, land transfer, file #6749

BARRETT Charles (Capt), esquire, of New Ipswich, vs PATTERSON Alexander, yeoman, of New Boston, rec date 1784, judgment, debt, file #5312

BARRETT Isaac, husbandman, of Nottingham-West, vs MERRILL William, gentleman, of Warner, rec date 1786, writ, debt, file #6319

BARRETT Joel, husbandman, of Chelmsford MA, vs RICHARDSON Zachariah, innholder, of Francestown, rec date 1785, execution, debt, file #5471

BARRETT Joseph & Rebecca, husbandman, of Londonderry, vs KELLY Joseph, gentleman, of Nottingham-West, rec date 1772, various, assault, file #2175

BARRETT Moses, yeoman, of Nottingham-West, vs ELLENWOOD Rolandson, yeoman, of Amherst, rec date 1782, writ, debt, file #2817

BARRETT Samuel Jr, husbandman, of Concord MA, vs WYMAN Samuel, husbandman, of Jaffrey, doc date 1799, debt, file #476

BARRETT Zaccheus, yeoman, of Mason, vs BROWN Isaac, gentleman, of Mason, rec date 1783, various, debt, file #4300

BARRON Moses, husbandman, of Amherst, vs MORRISON John, husbandman, of Bedford, rec date 1785, execution, debt, file #5954

BARRON Moses, husbandman, of Amherst, vs MORRISON John, husbandman, of Bedford, rec date 1785, judgment, debt, file #5840

BARRON Timothy, gentleman, of Haverhill, vs BLANCHARD Joseph, esquire, of Amherst, doc date 1784, execution, debt, file #1706

BARRON Timothy, gentleman, of Haverhill, vs BLANCHARD Joseph, esquire, of Amherst, doc date 1784, execution, debt, file #1907

BARRON Timothy, gentleman, of Haverhill, vs BLANCHARD Joseph, esquire, of Amherst, rec date 1783, writ, debt, file #3376

BARROT Joel, husbandman, of Chelmsford MA, vs RICHARDSON Zechariah, innholder, of Francestown, rec date 1785, judgment, debt, file #5543

BARTLETT James Jr, vs BLAIR Henry W, doc date 1894, appeal of writ, supreme court, file #589

BARTLETT Stephen, yeoman, of Deering, vs BAXTER Jonathan, yeoman, of Amherst, doc date 1798, execution, debt, file #86

BASFORD Jonathan, husbandman, of Henniker, vs ALEXANDER Jabez Jr, husbandman, of Acworth, rec date 1786, writ, debt, file #6315

BASFORD Joseph, gentleman, of Chester, vs SMITH Reuben, husbandman, of New Boston, doc date 1777, rec date 1777, deed, land transfer, file #6560

BATCHELDER Archestous, gentleman, of Wilton, vs MORGAN Jonathan, clothier, of Wilton, rec date 1783, writ, debt, file #3567

BATCHELDER Bradbury, esquire, of Parkersfield, vs PIERCE Ephraim, husbandman, of Hollis, rec date 1776, civil litigation, indenture, file #2205

BATCHELDER Joseph, husbandman, of Mile Slip, vs LOVEJOY Jonathan, yeoman, of Amherst, doc date 1782, execution, file #1008

BATCHELDER Phinehas, yeoman, of Fisherfield, vs HART Charles Walter, yeoman, of Bradford, doc date 1798, judgment, debt, file #561

BAYLE William & Jr, yeoman, of Wilton, vs OSBOOD Phineas, husbandman, of Billerica MA, doc date 1784, rec date 1785, deed, land transfer, file #5663

BAYLE William, husbandman, of Wilton, vs BLANCHARD Lemuel, innkeeper, of Cambridge MA, doc date 1784, execution, debt, file #1728

BAYLEY Daniel, carpenter, of Hollis, vs BALL John, yeoman, of Hollis, rec date 1783, judgment, debt, file #4719

BAYLEY Elisah, yeoman, of Winsor VT, vs DARLING Josiah, trader, of Henniker, doc date 1798, execution, debt, file #196

BAYLEY Jacob, yeoman, rec date 1777, deposition, land dispute, file #2224

BAYLEY Joshua, esquire, of Hopkinton, vs CROSS Ephraim, yeoman, of Fishersfield, rec date 1785, judgment, debt, file #2291

BAYLEY Joshua, esquire, of Hopkinton, vs DODGE Nicholas, yeoman, of Londonderry, rec date 1785, judgment, debt, file #2291

BAYLEY Joshua, husbandman, of Newbury MA, vs THURSTON Enoch, yeoman, of Londonderry, rec date 1782, judgment, debt, file #2711

BAYLEY Phinehas, gentleman, of Dunbarton, vs LITTLE Moses, esquire, of Goffstown, doc date 1784, writ, debt, file #1586

BAYLEY Phinehas, husbandman, of Dunbarton, vs EATON Jothan, husbandman, of Weare, rec date 1783, writ, debt, file #3214

BEALS Thomas, yeoman, of Newton MA, vs ALLEN John, yeoman, of Fitzwilliam, rec date 1785, judgment, debt, file #4939

BEAN Beriah, carpenter, of Salsbury, vs SANBORN John, yeoman, of Epping, doc date 1765, rec date 1787, deed, land transfer, file #2482

BEAN Cornelius, yeoman, of New Marlborough, vs GILE Ebenezer, yeoman, of New Marlborough, doc date 1767, rec date 1778, deed, land transfer, file #2108

BEAN Joseph, esquire, of Salsbury, vs CHOATE Simeon, joiner, of Salsbury, rec date 1783, writ, debt, file #4546

BEAN Joseph, yeoman, of Salsbury, vs INHABITANTS of Salsbury, rec date 1783, writ, debt, file #4541

BEAN Joseph, esquire, of Salsbury, vs MOSHER Michael, blacksmith, of New Chester, rec date 1788, writ, debt, file #6610

BEAN Joseph, esquire, of Salsbury, vs BONNEY Jabez Bozworth, gentleman, of New Chester, rec date 1788, writ, debt, file #6610

BEAN Joseph Jr, yeoman, of Salsbury, vs SELECTMEN of Salsbury, of Salsbury, rec date 1794, petition, public highway, file #4064

BEAN Nathaniel, yeoman, of Salsbury, vs EASTMAN Moses, gentleman, of Salsbury, doc date 1799, execution, debt, file #172

BEAN Nathaniel, yeoman, of Salsbury, vs MORRISON Samuel, gentleman, of Amherst, doc date 1799, writ, debt, file #397

BEAN Samuel, deceased, of Sandown, vs STATE of NH, rec date 1776, inquisition, death inquiry, file #2256

BEAN Samuel, husbandman, of Pembroke, vs CALDWELL William, husbandman, of Francestown, rec date 1785, writ, debt, file #6266

BEAN Samuel, of Pembroke, vs CALDWELL William, husbandman, of Francestown, rec date 1785, writ, debt, file #6147

BEAN Samuel, port rider, of Pembroke, vs CALDWELL William, husbandman, of Francestown, rec date 1785, various, debt, file #6362

BEARCE William, husbandman, of New Boston, vs CLAGETT Clifton, gentleman, of Litchfield, rec date 1785, writ, debt, file #5435, estate of Barnabas McGINIS

BEARD Elizabeth, singlewoman, of Pembroke, vs BUTTERFIELD Joseph, gentleman, of Wilton, writ, debt, file #2335

BEARD Joseph, laborer, of New Boston, vs WILKINS Andrew, yeoman, of Amherst, rec date 1782, judgment, debt, file #2739

BEARD Joseph, laborer, of New Boston, vs WILKINS Andrew, yeoman, of Amherst, rec date 1783, civil litigation, debt, file #3880

BEARD Joseph & William, husbandman, of New Boston, vs MORRILL Robert, yeoman, of New Boston, rec date 1785, writ, debt, file #4800, also note of James PATTERSON

BEARD William, yeoman, of New Boston, vs KELLEY Moses, esquire, of Goffstown, rec date 1782, writ, debt, file #2788

BEARD William, yeoman, of New Boston, vs STINSON William, gentleman, of Dunbarton, rec date 1782, writ, debt, file #2830

BEARD William, husbandman, of New Boston, vs McINTOSH John, husbandman, of Bedford, rec date 1783, writ, debt, file #3948

BEARD William, husbandman, of New Boston, vs WEBSTER Benjamin, husbandman, of Boscawen, rec date 1785, judgment, debt, file #5208

BEARD William, husbandman, of New Boston, vs WASON Samuel, husbandman, of Nottingham, rec date 1785, writ, debt, file #5421, estate of Barnabas McGINNIS

BEARD Wm & Joseph, husbandman, of New Boston, vs McINTOSH John, yeoman, of Bedford, rec date 1783, various, debt, file #3965

BECKFORD Benjamin, yeoman, of Salem MA, vs FELLOWS Adonijah, husbandman, of Derryfield, rec date 1785, writ, debt, file #6146

BECKFORD Benjamin, yeoman, of Salem MA, vs PAGE James, husbandman, of Derryfield, rec date 1785, writ, debt, file #6146

BECKWITH Jabeth, husbandman, of Lempster, vs BOYNTON Thomas, housewright, of Fitchburg MA, doc date 1784, writ, debt, file #1569

BEDFORD Joseph, husbandman, of Lyndeborough, vs ABBOTT Josiah, husbandman, of New Boston, rec date 1783, judgment, debt, file #4479

BEEMAN Noah, yeoman, of Marlborough MA, vs BRADFORD Samuel Jr, gentleman, of Hillsborough, rec date 1785, judgment, debt, file #5186

BELCHER Larson, gentleman, of Boston MA, vs BLANCHARD Jotham, gentleman, of Peterborough, rec date 1783, land dispute, court case, file #3285

BELCHER Larson, gentleman, of Boston MA, vs GREEN David, yeoman, of Hillsborough, rec date 1784, judgment, debt, file #4225

BELCHER Larson, feltmaker, of Boston MA, vs TAGGART James, husbandman, of Hillsborough, rec date 1783, judgment, debt, file #4438, note of John HILL

BELCHER Larson, feltmaker, of Boston MA, vs TAGGART Archibald, husbandman, of Hillsborough, rec date 1783, judgment, debt, file #4438, note of John HILL

BELCHER Larson, gentleman, of Boston MA, vs BLANCHARD Jotham, gentleman, of Peterborough, rec date 1784, judgment, debt, file #5296

BELCHER Larson, gentleman, of Boston MA, vs BLANCHARD Jothan, gentleman, of Peterborough, rec date 1785, various, debt, file #5230

BELCHER Larson, gentleman, of Boston MA, vs McCALLEY John, gentleman, of Hillsborough, rec date 1785, judgment, debt, file #5585, estate of John HILL

BELCHER Larson, gentleman, of Boston MA, vs McCALLEY John, gentleman, of Hillsborough, rec date 1785, judgment, debt, file #6396

BELIKER Larson, feltmaker, of Boston MA, vs TAGGART Archibald, gentleman, of Hillsborough, doc date 1784, civil litigation, debt, file #1853

BELIVEAU Edouardina, of Manchester, vs AMOSKEAG Manufacturing Co, of Manchester, doc date 1891, injuries to plaintiff, supreme court, file #592

BELL James, painter, of Bedford, vs BLANCHARD Augustus, gentleman, of Amherst, rec date 1783, execution, debt, file #2963

BELL James, yeoman, of Bedford, vs BELL Joseph, yeoman, of Bedford, rec date 1783, writ, debt, file #3316

BELL James, painter, of Merrimack, vs SAWTELL Obadiah, gentleman, of Shirley MA, rec date 1784, judgment, debt, file #4241

BELL James, painter, of Merrimack, vs DODGE Samuel, husbandman, of Amherst, rec date 1784, writ, debt, file #5294

BELL John, husbandman, of Bedford, vs BOIL Thomas, husbandman, of Bedford, doc date 1784, writ, debt, file #1587

BELL John, husbandman, of Bedford, vs HALL Benjamin, esquire, of Medford MA, rec date 1782, writ, debt, file #2835

BELL John, yeoman, of Bedford, vs SEARLE William Jr, yeoman, of Temple, rec date 1784, judgment, debt, file #4197

BELL John & James, of Hollis, vs BEARD Aaron, husbandman, of Dunstable, rec date 1789, writ, debt, file #2434, Alias BRADFORD

BELL Jonathan, yeoman, of Goffstown, vs ATHERTON Joshua, esquire, of Amherst, rec date 1783, writ, debt, file #3070

BELL Joseph, yeoman, of Bedford, vs BELL James, yeoman, of Merrimack, doc date 1784, civil litigation, debt, file #1855

BELL Joseph, yeoman, of Bedford, vs KENNEDY Jane, widow, of Goffstown, rec date 1783, writ, debt, file #3080, Matthew KENNEDY estate

BELL Joseph, yeoman, of Bedford, vs TOWNSEND Thomas, yeoman, of Bedford, rec date 1783, writ, debt, file #3207

BELL Joseph, yeoman, of Bedford, vs STEARNS Jothan, yeoman, of Goffstown, rec date 1785, execution, debt, file #5952

BELL Joseph, yeoman, of Bedford, vs STEARNS Jotham, yeoman, of Goffstown, rec date 1785, judgment, debt, file #5850

BELL Samuel, esquire, of Francestown, vs CROSS Nathan, miller, of Amherst, doc date 1803, rec date 1803, deed, land transfer, file #5680

BELL Samuel, esquire, of Francestown, vs WILSON James, trader, of Francestown, doc date 1805, rec date 1811, deed, land transfer, file #5693

BELL Samuel, esquire, of Francestown, vs HOLMES Ebenezer, cordwainer, of Francestown, doc date 1782, rec date 1802, deed, land transfer, file #5677

BELL William, yeoman, of Concord, vs ATHERTON Joshua, esquire, of Amherst, rec date 1783, writ, debt, file #3070

BENJAMIN George, yeoman, of Hillsborough, vs STEEL John, yeoman, of Hillsborough, doc date 1772, civil litigation, debt, file #662

BENNETT Aaron, cordwainer, of Paxton MA, rec date 1788, deed, land dispute, file #6583, 2 folders

BENNETT Benjamin, husbandman, of Amherst, vs WRIGHT David, cordwainer, of Hollis, rec date 1783, writ, debt, file #3112

BENNETT Benjamin, cordwainer, of Amherst, vs NUTTING William, husbandman, of Groton MA, rec date 1783, writ, debt, file #3958

BENNETT Jonathan, gentleman, of Hancock, vs TAYLOR Joseph, yeoman, of Winsor NY, rec date 1783, qudita/quereta, debt, file #3311

BENNETT Phinehas & Mary, yeoman, of Hollis, vs CHANDLER John, yeoman, of Winthrop MA, doc date 1775, deed, land transfer, file #842

BENNETT Phinehas Jr, husbandman, of Hollis, vs HALE David, husbandman, of Cockermouth, rec date 1783, writ, debt, file #3428

BENT Elijah, trader, of Amherst, vs BRADFORD Samuel Jr, gentleman, of Hillsborough, rec date 1782, judgment, debt, file #2740

BENT Elijah, trader, of Amherst, vs BISHOP George, innkeeper, of Hillsborough, rec date 1782, judgment, debt, file #2740

BENT Elijah, trader, of Amherst, vs BRADFORD Samuel Jr, gentleman, of Hillsborough, rec date 1783, execution, debt, file #3247

BENT Elijah, trader, of Amherst, vs BRADFORD Samuel Jr, gentleman, of Hillsborough, rec date 1783, execution, debt, file #3688

BERNARD Jeremiah, clerk, of Amherst, vs HOBART Joel, husbandman, of Miles Slip, rec date 1784, judgment, debt, file #4632

BERRY Isaac, yeoman, of Middleton MA, vs AVERILL John, yeoman, of Amherst, rec date 1785, deed, land transfer, file #5603

BICKFORD Daniel, vs EATON James, gentleman, of Hillsborough, doc date 1802, rec date 1805, deed, land transfer, file #5683

BIGELOW James, esquire, of Pepperell MA, vs SPAULDING Jacob, yeoman, of Hollis, doc date 1798, execution, debt, file #143

BIGELOW Timothy, esquire, of New Ipswich, vs PARKER Joseph, gentleman, of New Ipswich, doc date 1798, execution, debt, file #136

BIGELOW Timothy, esquire, of Groton, vs HEAIL Joseph, husbandman, of Dunstable, doc date 1798, execution, debt, file #141

BISBE Andrew, yeoman, of Hillsborough, vs JONES Samuel, yeoman, of Hillsborough, rec date 1782, appeal, debt, file #4010, kinship to JONES of MA

BISBE Andrew Sr, yeoman, of Hillsborough, vs Town of Hillsborough, rec date 1783, petition, abatement of tax, file #3502

BISHOP George, innholder, of Hillsborough, vs DODGE Samuel, yeoman, of Amherst, rec date 1783, writ, debt, file #3076

BISHOP George, innholder, of Hillsborough, vs GOVE Jonathan, physician, of New Boston, rec date 1783, writ, debt, file #3077

BISHOP George, innholder, of Hillsborough, vs JONES Samuel, yeoman, of Hillsborough, rec date 1783, writ, debt, file #3906

BISHOP George, innholder, of Hillsborough, vs JONES Samuel, yeoman, of Hillsborough, rec date 1783, execution, debt, file #3832

BISHOP George, yeoman, of Hillsborough, vs TAGGART Archibald, gentleman, of Hillsborough, rec date 1783, various, debt, file #4292

BISHOP George, yeoman, of Hillsborough, vs ABBOTT Darius, gentleman, of Amherst, rec date 1784, various, debt, file #4328

BISHOP George, yeoman, of Hillsborough, vs BRADFORD William, gentleman, of Deering, rec date 1783, judgment, debt, file #4327

BISHOP John, distiller, of Medford MA, vs McLAUGHLIN John, gentleman, of New Boston, doc date 1798, judgment, debt, file #561

BISHOP John, gentleman, of Medford MA, vs BARRETT Moses Jr, yeoman, of Nottingham-West, rec date 1783, execution, debt, file #3871

BISHOP John, gentleman, of Medford MA, vs BARRET Moses, yeoman, of Nottingham-West, rec date 1783, writ, debt, file #3892

BISHOP John, merchant, of Medford MA, vs BARRETT Moses Jr, yeoman, of Nottingham, rec date 1784, judgment, debt, file #4533

BIXBE Andrew, yeoman, of Hillsborough, vs JONES Samuel, yeoman, of Hillsborough, doc date 1782, execution, file #1015

BIXBE Andrew, yeoman, of Hillsborough, vs GORDON John, yeoman, of Campbells Gore, rec date 1785, judgment, debt, file #5542

BIXBE Andrew, husbandman, of Hillsborough, vs GOODELL David, husbandman, of Hillsborough, rec date 1786, writ, debt, file #6283

BIXBE Andrew, husbandman, of Amherst, vs BRADFORD Andrew, gentleman, of Amherst, doc date 1771, rec date 1772, deed, land transfer, file #6851

BIXBE Andrew, husbandman, of Amherst, vs TOWNE Archelaus, gentleman, of Amherst, doc date 1771, rec date 1772, deed, land transfer, file #6851

BIXBE Asa, husbandman, of Westford MA, vs BARRETT Moses, yeoman, of Wilton, rec date 1785, execution, debt, file #5933

BIXBE Daniel (Capt), gentleman, of Litchfield, vs CLARK Timothy, yeoman, of Amherst, rec date 1787, writ, debt, file #2370

BIXBEE Andrew, husbandman, of Hillsborough, vs GOODEL David, yeoman, of Amherst, rec date 1785, judgment, debt, file #5347

BIXBEE Andrew, husbandman, of Hillsborough, vs SHANNON Richard C, esquire, of Hollis, rec date 1784, writ, debt, file #5373

BIXBEE Andrew, yeoman, of Hillsborough, vs WOOD Jonathan, yeoman, of Hillsborough, rec date 1788, writ, debt, file #6624

BIXBY Andrew, yeoman, of Hillsborough, vs WARNER Daniel, gentleman, of Amherst, rec date 1783, writ, debt, file #3089

BIXBY Asa, yeoman, of Westford MA, vs BARRETT Moses, yeoman, of Wilton, rec date 1785, judgment, debt, file #5270

BIXBY Bixby, yeoman, of Litchfield, vs HADLEY Nehemiah, yeoman, of Dunstable, rec date 1783, writ, debt, file #3364

BIXBY Daniel, trader, of Litchfield, vs BLODGET Daniel Jr, yeoman, of Litchfield, doc date 1798, execution, debt, file #77

BIXBY Daniel, gentleman, of Litchfield, vs CLARK Timothy Jr, husbandman, of Amherst, doc date 1798, judgment, debt, file #561

BIXBY Daniel, gentleman, of Litchfield, vs SHED John, yeoman, of Hollis, doc date 1799, writ, debt, file #575

BIXBY Daniel, gentleman, of Litchfield, vs CLARK Timothy, husbandman, of Amherst, rec date 1787, judgment, debt, file #6186

BIXBY Daniel Jr, trader, of Litchfield, vs HUNTING Nathan, husbandman, of Chelmsford MA, doc date 1798, execution, debt, file #179

BIXBY Thomas, yeoman, of Francestown, vs MARDEN George, yeoman, of Francestown, rec date 1784, writ, debt, file #4667

BIXBY William, yeoman, of Litchfield, vs RICHARDSON Zechariah, husbandman, of Francestown, doc date 1784, civil litigation, debt, file #1640

BIXBY William, yeoman, of Litchfield, vs HADLEY Nehemiah, yeoman, of Dunstable, doc date 1784, execution, debt, file #1779

BIXBY William, yeoman, of Litchfield, vs RICHARDSON Zachariah, yeoman, of Francestown, rec date 1783, judgment, debt, file #4487

BIXBY William, yeoman, of Litchfield, vs WRIGHT Uriah, husbandman, of Hollis, rec date 1785, judgment, debt, file #5338

BIXSBEE Andrew & Susana, yeoman, of Amherst, vs SMITH Jonathan, of Amherst, doc date 1774, deed, land transfer, file #833

BLACH Joshua, deceased, of Lyndeborough, rec date 1787, writ, land dispute, file #6667

BLAIR (Rogers) Catherine, deceased, of Londonderry, of Dunbarton, doc date 1787, rec date 1788, deed, land transfer, file #6823

BLAIR Alexander, yeoman, of Londonderry, vs BEALY Phineas, gentleman, of Dunbarton, doc date 1787, rec date 1788, deed, land transfer, file #6823

BLAIR David, yeoman, of Londonderry, vs BEALY Phineas, gentleman, of Dunbarton, doc date 1787, rec date 1788, deed, land transfer, file #6823

BLAIR Hugh, husbandman, of New Boston, vs DICKEY James, joiner, of Francestown, doc date 1799, writ, debt, file #320

BLAIR James, yeoman, of Londonderry, vs BEALY Phineas, gentleman, of Dunbarton, doc date 1787, rec date 1788, deed, land transfer, file #6823

BLAIR Robert, yeoman, of Londonderry, vs BEALY Phineas, gentleman, of Dunbarton, doc date 1787, rec date 1788, deed, land transfer, file #6823

BLAIR William, yeoman, of New Boston, vs BALDWIN Nahum, esquire, of Amherst, rec date 1782, writ, debt, file #2792, estate of Zacheus CUTLER

BLAIR William, yeoman, of New Boston, vs GREGG Alexander, administrator of estate, of New Boston, rec date 1788, various, debt, file #6976

BLANCHARD Abigail, widow, of Dunstable, vs CLARK Thomas, husbandman, of Dunstable, rec date 1785, judgment, debt, file #5047

BLANCHARD Amos, yeoman, of Milford, vs CROSBY William, husbandman, of Milford, doc date 1799, judgment, debt, file #287

BLANCHARD Augustus, esquire, of Milford, vs SUMMER Porter, gentleman, of Milford, doc date 1798, execution, debt, file #102

BLANCHARD Augustus, gentleman, of Amherst, vs DANA William, gentleman, of Amherst, doc date 1784, execution, debt, file #1791

BLANCHARD Augustus, gentleman, of Amherst, vs KING William Jr, husbandman, of Londonderry, rec date 1783, judgment, debt, file #3765

BLANCHARD Augustus, gentleman, of Amherst, vs MOORE John Jr, yeoman, of Bedford, rec date 1783, execution, debt, file #3669

BLANCHARD Augustus, gentleman, of Amherst, vs TAYLOR James, husbandman, of Merrimack, rec date 1783, judgment, debt, file #3765

BLANCHARD Augustus, gentleman, of Amherst, vs McCLENCHE John, blacksmith, of Londonderry, rec date 1782, execution, debt, file #4888

BLANCHARD Augustus, gentleman, of Amherst, vs BLANCHARD Jothan, merchant, of Peterborough, rec date 1785, judgment, debt, file #5574

BLANCHARD Augustus, gentleman, of Amherst, vs BLANCHARD Jothan, merchant, of Peterborough, rec date 1785, judgment, debt, file #6395

BLANCHARD Benjamin, husbandman, of Canterbury, vs TRACY Patrick, esquire, of Newburyport MA, doc date 1774, writ, debt, file #1128, fragile

BLANCHARD David, husbandman, of Woburn MA, vs HUTCHINSON Solomon Jr, yeoman, of Merrimack, rec date 1788, writ, debt, file #2399

BLANCHARD James, of Merrimack, vs BLANCHARD Joseph, of Merrimack, doc date 1782, execution, to appraise estate, file #975

BLANCHARD Jonathan, trader, of Weare, vs EATON Timothy, esquire, of Haverhill MA, doc date 1799, writ, debt, file #408

BLANCHARD Jonathan, carpenter, of Hillsborough, vs CARR Nathan, gentleman, of Deering, doc date 1799, writ, debt, file #426

BLANCHARD Jonathan, esquire, of Dunstable, vs GRIMES Bartholomew, husbandman, of Keene, doc date 1782, execution, debt, file #967

BLANCHARD Jonathan, yeoman, of Peterborough, vs WHEAT Jonathan, joiner, of Amherst, doc date 1774, writ, debt, file #1138

BLANCHARD Jonathan, esquire, of Merrimack, vs BATCHELLOR Breed, esquire, of Packersfield, rec date 1777, writ, debt, file #2194

BLANCHARD Jonathan, gentleman, of Amherst, vs BLANCHARD Joseph, esquire, of Amherst, doc date 1787, rec date 1787, deed, land transfer, file #2509

BLANCHARD Jonathan, esquire, of Dunstable, vs TAYLOR Aaron, yeoman, of Jaffrey, rec date 1783, writ, debt, file #3165, estate of Rebecca BLANCHARD

BLANCHARD Jonathan, esquire, of Dunstable, vs SEARLES John, yeoman, of Dunstable, rec date 1786, judgment, debt, file #5751

BLANCHARD Jonathan, esquire, of Amherst, vs FARLEY Christopher, trader, of Hollis, rec date 1786, judgment, debt, file #6117

BLANCHARD Jonathan, esquire, of Amherst, vs JEWETT Jacob, trader, of Hollis, rec date 1786, judgment, debt, file #6117

BLANCHARD Jonathan, esquire, of Dunstable, vs TARBELL Cornelius, gentleman, of Merrimack, rec date 1785, writ, debt, file #6143

BLANCHARD Jonathan, yeoman, of Dunstable, vs LAWRENCE Richard, yeoman, of # 1 (Mason), doc date 1759, rec date 1780, deed, land transfer, file #6826

BLANCHARD Jonathan, esquire, of Dunstable, vs HOLMES Oliver, gentleman, of Francestown, rec date 1786, writ, debt, file #6691

BLANCHARD Jonathan, esquire, of Dunstable, vs BRADFORD Samuel, gentleman, of Hillsborough, rec date 1788, writ, debt, file #6691

BLANCHARD Jonathan, esquire, vs LAWRENCE Enos, rec date 1778, court bill, file #7035

BLANCHARD Jonathan, merchant, of Peterborough, vs SHERBURN Samuel, of Portsmouth, rec date 1788, deed, transfer of land, file #6722

BLANCHARD Joseph, esquire, of Thornton, vs SERGENT Paul Dudley, esquire, of Sullivan Me, doc date 1799, judgment, debt, file #243

BLANCHARD Joseph, esquire, of Merrimack, vs POWERS Peter, gentleman, of Hollis, doc date 1775, deed, land transfer, file #841

BLANCHARD Joseph, esquire, of Amherst, vs KELLEY Joseph, gentleman, of Nottingham-West, doc date 1782, rec date 1787, deed, land transfer, file #2483

BLANCHARD Joseph, esquire, of Amherst, vs YOUNG John, physician, of Peterborough, rec date 1785, writ, debt, file #5536

BLANCHARD Joseph, esquire, of Amherst, vs ROGERS Robert, deceased, of Portsmouth, rec date 1787, various, debt, file #2539

BLANCHARD Joseph, esquire, of Amherst, vs GROUT Jehosaphet, yeoman, of Charlestown, rec date 1782, appeal, debt, file #4005

BLANCHARD Joseph, esquire, of Amherst, vs BLANCHARD Jonathan, esquire, of Dunstable, rec date 1784, writ, debt, file #4672

BLANCHARD Joseph, esquire, of Amherst, vs WILKINS Jonathan, yeoman, of Amherst, rec date 1785, writ, debt, file #5253

BLANCHARD Joseph, esquire, of Amherst, vs PEABODY Ephraim, blacksmith, of Wilton, rec date 1782, writ, debt, file #5737

BLANCHARD Joseph, esquire, of Amherst, vs SCOTT William, yeoman, of Peterborough, rec date 1785, various, debt, file #6214

BLANCHARD Joseph, esquire, of Amherst, vs ROGERS Robert, major, of Portsmouth, rec date 1785, various, debt, file #6339

BLANCHARD Joseph, deceased, of Dunstable, vs LAWRENCE Enos, yeoman, of # 1 (Mason), doc date 1758, rec date 1779, deed, land transfer, file #6838

BLANCHARD Joshua, merchant, of Boston MA, vs USHER Robert, yeoman, of Merrimack, doc date 1772, judgment, debt, file #673

BLANCHARD Joshua, merchant, of Boston MA, vs HUTCHINSON Solomon, yeoman, of Merrimack, doc date 1772, judgment, debt, file #673

BLANCHARD Joshua, merchant, of Boston MA, vs USHER Robert, yeoman, of Merrimack, doc date 1772, judgment, debt, file #790

BLANCHARD Jotham, mariner, of Portsmouth, vs QUIGLEY John, gentleman, of New Boston, doc date 1772, writ, debt, file #1055

BLANCHARD Jotham, merchant, of Peterborough, vs HILDRETH James, yeoman, of Pepperell MA, rec date 1782, writ, debt, file #2802

BLANCHARD Jotham, merchant, of Peterborough, vs BELCHER Larson, gentleman, of Boston MA, rec date 1785, writ, debt, file #4786

BLANCHARD Jotham, merchant, of Peterborough, vs ABBOTT Nathan, esquire, of Danvers MA, rec date 1785, writ, debt, file #5374

BLANCHARD Jotham, merchant, of Peterborough, vs WARNER Daniel, gentleman, of Amherst, rec date 1785, writ, debt, file #5407

BLANCHARD Jotham, merchant, of Peterborough, vs BELCHER Larson, gentleman, of Boston MA, rec date 1785, various, debt, file #6063

BLANCHARD Jotham, merchant, of Peterborough, vs HOLT Nehemiah, husbandman, of Wilton, rec date 1787, various, land dispute, file #6807

BLANCHARD Jotham, merchant, of Peterborough, vs ABBOTT Nathan 3rd, husbandman, of Danvers MA, rec date 1787, deed/various, land dispute, file #6807

BLANCHARD Jothan, yeoman, of Peterborough, vs CLARK Bunker, yeoman, of New Ipswich, doc date 1774, writ, debt, file #1137

BLANCHARD Nathan, cordwainer, of Mile Slip, vs BATCHELDER Hart, yeoman, of Mile Slip, doc date 1773, rec date 1779, deed, land transfer, file #2123

BLANCHARD Rebecca, widow, of Dunstable, vs BLANCHARD Joseph, of Dunstable, doc date 1776, deed, land transfer, file #1164

BLANCHARD Rebecca, widow, of Dunstable, vs TARBELL Thomas, of Mason, doc date 1769, rec date 1779, deed, land transfer, file #2140

BLANCHARD Rebecca, widow, of Dunstable, vs COLBURN Nathan, husbandman, of Dracut MA, doc date 1766, rec date 1779, deed, land transfer, file #2127

BLANCHARD Rebecca, widow, of Dunstable, vs FOSTER Joshua, of Peterborough Slip, doc date 1765, rec date 1778, deed, land transfer, file #2110

BLANCHARD Rebecca, of Dunstable, vs LAWRENCE Enos, yeoman, of # 1 (Mason), doc date 1758, rec date 1779, deed, land transfer, file #6838

BLANCHARD Rebecca, widow, of Dunstable, vs FARROW Isaac, husbandman, of Townsend MA, doc date 1758, rec date 1787, deed, land transfer, file #6791

BLANCHARD Rebeccah, of Dunstable, vs CONEK James, gentleman, of Raby, doc date 1772, execution, debt, file #1197

BLANCHARD Samuel, yeoman, of Andover MA, vs ABBOTT William, yeoman, of Andover MA, rec date 1785, deed, land transfer, file #5605

BLANCHARD Stephen, husbandman, of Duxbury Mile Slip, vs PATTEN John, husbandman, of Merrimack, rec date 1783, judgment, debt, file #3802

BLANCHARD W I, physician, of Nashua, doc date 1888, medical society certification, supreme court, file #636

BLANCHARD William, yeoman, of Raby, vs SPAULDING William, yeoman, of Groton, doc date 1771, rec date 1779, deed, land transfer, file #2135

BLANCHARD William, gentleman, of Wilmington MA, vs ELLINGWOOD Samuel, yeoman, of Hillsborough, rec date 1786, execution, debt, file #5459

BLANCHARD William, yeoman, of Raby, vs BLANCHARD Simion, yeoman, of Raby, doc date 1772, rec date 1772, deed, land transfer, file #6848

BLANEY William & Ruth, estate of, of Hollis, vs RIDEOUT James, husbandman, of Hollis, doc date 1799, execution, debt, file #165

BLANEY Wm & Ruth, estate, of Lyndeborough, vs DOW Joseph, gentleman, of Kensington, doc date 1799, execution, debt, file #166

BLASDEL Henry, yeoman, of Goffstown, vs KITTRIDGE Nathaniel, yeoman, of Goffstown, doc date 1781, rec date 1785, deed, land transfer, file #5633

BLASDEL Nathaniel, esquire, of Newburyport MA, vs VANCE William, tailor, of Chester, doc date 1774, judgment, debt, file #725

BLASDELL Henry, of Kingstown, vs PRENTICE William, yeoman, of Marblehead MA, doc date 1772, writ, debt, file #1050

BLASDELL Samuel, yeoman, of Lyndeborough, vs FAY William, gentleman, of Woburn MA, rec date 1783, writ, debt, file #3043

BLASEDELL William, shop owner, of Dunstable, vs SPAULDING Lot, husbandman, of Pelham, rec date 1787, writ, debt, file #6664

BLODGET Asahel, husbandman, of Nottingham-West, vs MERRILL Roger & Nathaniel, husbandman, of Goffstown, rec date 1783, writ, debt, file #3398

BLODGET Benjamin, husbandman, of Goffstown, vs STEARNS Elijah, husbandman, of Goffstown, doc date 1798, judgment, debt, file #561

BLODGET Benjamin, innholder, of Goffstown, vs EAYERS William, husbandman, of Goffstown, doc date 1798, judgment, debt, file #561

BLODGET Daniel, yeoman, of Mason, vs CHAMPNEY Ebenezer, gentleman, of New Ipswich, rec date 1773, writ, debt, file #2176

BLODGET Ebenezer, housewright, of Nottingham-West, vs DAKIN Justus, husbandman, of Nottingham-West, doc date 1767, rec date 1784, deed, land transfer, file #5007, 598

BLODGET Jonathan Jr, yeoman, of Nottingham-West, vs LUND Jesse, yeoman, of Lyndeborough, rec date 1784, judgment, debt, file #4204

BLODGET Josiah, husbandman, of Dunstable MA, vs MOSHER James, husbandman, of Hollis, rec date 1785, writ, debt, file #5278

BLODGET Samuel, esquire, of Goffstown, vs BLANCHARD Joseph, esquire, of Amherst, doc date 1798, execution, debt, file #123

BLODGET Samuel, esquire, of Goffstown, vs McCLEARY Andrew, gentleman, of Epsom, doc date 1773, execution, debt, file #1489

BLODGET Samuel, esquire, of Goffstown, vs BEAN Benjamin, husbandman, of Raymond, doc date 1771, writ, debt, file #1385

BLODGET Samuel, esquire, of Goffstown, vs HALL John, gentleman, of Derryfield, doc date 1773, judgment, debt, file #1315

BLODGET Samuel, esquire, of Goffstown, vs WOOD Jonathan, husbandman, of Goffstown, rec date 1783, judgment, debt, file #3742

BLODGETT Benjamin, merchant, of Goffstown, vs STEARNS Nathan, husbandman, of Goffstown, doc date 1798, judgment, debt, file #561

BLODGETT David, husbandman, of Mason, vs KIDDER Reuben, esquire, of New Ipswich, rec date 1783, writ, debt, file #3313

BLODGETT Nathan, merchant, of Boston MA, vs MILLER Thomas, husbandman, of Goffstown, rec date 1782, execution, debt, file #5743

BLODGETT Samuel, esquire, of Goffstown, vs GREGG David, wheelwright, of Goffstown, doc date 1774, judgment, debt, file #779

BLODGETT Samuel, esquire, vs PROVINCE of NH, rec date 1771, justices appointment, by j WENTWORTH, file #3542

BLOOD Abel, husbandman, of Hollis, vs JEWETT John, tanner, of Hollis, doc date 1798, writ, debt, file #574

BLOOD Abel, yeoman, of Wilton, vs DASCOMB Jacob, gentleman, of Lyndeborough, doc date 1799, execution, debt, file #173

BLOOD Abigail Jr, spinster, of Hollis, vs MORSE Benjamin, of Hollis, rec date 1785, warrant, fornication, file #5533

BLOOD Abigail, vs HALE Samuel, rec date 1781, note, debt, file #7036

BLOOD Abner, husbandman, of Groton MA, vs KILLICUT Reuben, husbandman, of Dunstable, rec date 1787, writ, debt, file #2420

BLOOD Daniel, husbandman, of Hollis, vs WARNER Daniel, gentleman, of Dunstable, rec date 1783, execution, debt, file #2888

BLOOD Daniel, husbandman, of Chelmsford MA, vs WARNER Daniel, gentleman, of Amherst, rec date 1784, writ, debt, file #6853

BLOOD Elnathan, yeoman, of Merrimack, vs SIMPSON William, sheriff, of Plymouth, doc date 1774, judgment, debt, file #723

BLOOD Elnathan, yeoman, of Merrimack, vs BLOOD Solomon, yeoman, of Cockermouth, doc date 1774, writ, debt, file #1103, fragile

BLOOD Elnathan, yeoman, of Merrimack, vs JOHNSON William?, of Plymouth, rec date 1782, execution, debt, file #4890

BLOOD Elnathan, yeoman, of Hollis, vs BLOOD Solomon, yeoman, of Hollis, rec date 1783, writ, debt, file #3171

BLOOD Elnathan Jr, yeoman, of Hollis, vs EMERSON Samuel, esquire, of Plymouth, rec date 1783, various, debt, file #3123

BLOOD Elnathan Jr, yeoman, of Hollis, vs EMERSON Samuel, esquire, of Plymouth, rec date 1782, appeal, debt, file #4024

BLOOD Francis, esquire, of Temple, vs SMITH Emerson, yeoman, of Hollis, rec date 1785, judgment, debt, file #4589

BLOOD Francis, husbandman, of Hollis, vs HOLT Nathaniel, husbandman, of Merrimack, doc date 1784, execution, debt, file #1712

BLOOD Francis, esquire, of Temple, vs PUTNAM Jacob, husbandman, of Temple, doc date 1784, execution, debt, file #1768

BLOOD Francis, yeoman, of Hollis, vs BLOOD Timothy, of Hollis, doc date 1782, rec date 1783, deed, land transfer, file #2659

BLOOD Francis, husbandman, of Hollis, vs HOLT Nathaniel, husbandman, of Merrimack, rec date 1783, writ, debt, file #3418

BLOOD Francis, esquire, of Temple, vs BALL Eleazer, husbandman, of Hollis, rec date 1783, judgment, debt, file #3711

BLOOD Francis, esquire, of Temple, vs PUTNAM Jacob, husbandman, of Temple, rec date 1783, judgment, debt, file #4095

BLOOD Francis, esquire, of Temple, vs DAVIS Josiah, yeoman, of New Ipswich, rec date 1784, judgment, debt, file #4345

BLOOD Francis, esquire, of Temple, vs BRADLEY Ithmar, yeoman, of Hollis, rec date 1785, judgment, debt, file #4589

BLOOD Francis, esquire, of Temple, vs SMITH Emerson, yeoman, of Hillsborough, rec date 1785, judgment, debt, file #5134

BLOOD Francis, esquire, of Temple, vs BRADLEY Ithmar, yeoman, of Hillsborough, rec date 1785, judgment, debt, file #5134

BLOOD Francis, of Temple, vs WHITNEY Oliver, gentleman, of Temple, rec date 1788, writ, debt, file #6607

BLOOD Francis, esquire, of Temple, vs SHATTUCK Nehemiah, husbandman, of Mason, rec date 1788, writ, debt, file #6990

BLOOD Francis, esquire, of Temple, vs WRIGHT Josiah, laborer, of Raby, rec date 1788, writ, debt, file #6990

BLOOD Josiah, yeoman, of Hollis, vs KENNEY Israel, yeoman, of Hollis, doc date 1774, writ, debt, file #1109, fragile

BLOOD Josiah, yeoman, of Hollis, vs WILKINS Israel, yeoman, of Hollis, doc date 1774, writ, debt, file #1109, fragile

BLOOD Josiah, yeoman, of Hollis, vs RIDEOUT James & Nathaniel, yeoman, of Hollis, doc date 1773, writ, debt, file #1340

BLOOD Josiah, yeoman, of Hollis, vs WILKINS Israel, yeoman, of Hollis, doc date 1774, judgment, debt, file #711

BLOOD Jotham, husbandman, of Concord MA, vs COBURN Edward, yeoman, of Pelham, rec date 1784, various, debt, file #4186, kinship included

BLOOD Nathaniel, husbandman, of Hollis, vs STATE of NH, rec date 1783, coroners report, inquisition, file #2596

BLOOD Robert, yeoman, of Peterborough, vs ADAMS Asa, yeoman, of Hancock, rec date 1784, judgment, debt, file #4333

BLOOD Robert, yeoman, of Peterborough, vs BENNETT Jonathan, yeoman, of Hancock, rec date 1784, judgment, debt, file #4333

BLOOD Robert, yeoman, of Peterborough, vs GOSS Ebenezer, esquire, of Concord, rec date 1784, writ, debt, file #4629

BLOOD Robert, vs HALE Samuel, rec date 1781, note, debt, file #7036

BLOOD Royal, gentleman, of Temple, vs BROWN Isaac, yeoman, of Lemester, doc date 1798, execution, debt, file #81

BLOOD Samuel, feltmaker, of Littleton MA, vs JOHNSON Jonathan, feltmaker, of Hollis, doc date 1772, judgment, debt, file #672

BLOOD Simeon Jr, yeoman, of Carlisle MA, vs HOSMER Reuben, husbandman, of Mason, rec date 1788, writ, debt, file #6625

BLOOD Simeon Jr, yeoman, of Carlisle MA, vs HOSMER Reuben, husbandman, of Mason, rec date 1788, writ, debt, file #6914

BLOOD Solomon, yeoman, of Hollis, vs HUNT Josiah, yeoman, of Hollis, doc date 1773, judgment, debt, file #1313

BLOOD Solomon, yeoman, of Hollis, vs HOW Joseph, yeoman, of Hollis, doc date 1772, writ, debt, file #1418

BLOOD William, yeoman, of Dunstable, vs POWERS Jonas, laborer, of Hollis, doc date 1802, judgment, debt, file #568

BLUNT Isaac, yeoman, of Andover MA, vs SHURTLEFF Jonathan, husbandman, of Merrimack, rec date 1784, appeal, debt, file #4116

BLUNT Isaac, yeoman, of Andover MA, vs SHURTLEFF Jonathan, husbandman, of Merrimack, rec date 1784, judgment, debt, file #4407

BLY James Jr, yeoman, of Plaistow, vs HADLEY George, husbandman, of Goffstown, doc date 1772, civil litigation, debt, file #661

BOARD William, husbandman, of New Boston, vs McGINNIS Barnabas, of Nottingham-West, rec date 1784, writ, debt, file #5380, estate of Barnabas McGINNIS

BODMAN Peter, carpenter, of Hillsborough, vs CARR Nathan, gentleman, of Deering, doc date 1799, writ, debt, file #426

BODWELL ----, of Amherst, vs ----, doc date 1791, petition, release of debit, file #18, no Christian name given

BODWELL Eliphalet, yeoman, of Unity, vs DODGE Jonathan, yeoman, of Osippee, doc date 1799, writ, debt, file #424

BODWELL John, husbandman, of Merrimack, vs BRAGG Thomas, deceased, of Andover, doc date 1791, petition, release of debit, file #24

BODWELLL William, yeoman, of Antrim, deed, land transfer, file #6794

BOFFE John, yeoman, of Lyndeborough, vs ROWE John, yeoman, of Lyndeborough, doc date 1781, rec date 1785, deed, land transfer, file #5607

BOFFE Melchisedcek, gentleman, of Lyndeborough, vs BOFFE Thomas, gentleman, of Lyndeborough, doc date 1783, rec date 1785, deed, land transfer, file #5613

BOFFE Thomas, gentleman, of Lyndeborough, vs HOWARD William, husbandman, of Amherst, rec date 1783, writ, debt, file #3014

BOICE Thomas, husbandman, of Bedford, vs MCGINNIS Barnabas, yeoman, of Nottingham-West, rec date 1783, judgment, debt, file #3760

BOICE Thomas, husbandman, of Bedford, vs RAND John, gentleman, of Bedford, rec date 1785, various, debt, file #4599

BOIES Thomas, husbandman, of Bedford, vs RAND John, esquire, of Bedford, rec date 1785, various, debt, file #5243

BOIS Thomas, yeoman, of Bedford, vs CURRIER Jonathan, yeoman, of Bedford, rec date 1772, various, debt, file #4880

BOND Little, husbandman, of Deering, vs CLOUGH David, husbandman, of Dracut MA, doc date 1784, execution, debt, file #1824

BONNER Samuel, gentleman, of Boscawen, vs PINGREE Aquilla, husbandman, of Salisbury, rec date 1788, writ, debt, file #6761

BONTEL Joseph, gentleman, of Amherst, vs HINCHMAN Nathaniel, physician, of Amherst, doc date 1799, writ, debt, file #574

BOOTMAN Benjamin, yeoman, of New Boston, vs McNEIL John Caldwell, yeoman, of New Boston, rec date 1783, judgment, debt, file #3720

BOOWERS Josiah Jr, innholder, of Billerica MA, vs WILKINS Jonathan, yeoman, of Amherst, rec date 1786, judgment, debt, file #6181

BOSSE Thomas, gentleman, of Lyndeborough, vs RICHARDSON Able, yeoman, of Woburn MA, doc date 1783, rec date 1783, deed, land transfer, file #2640

BOSSEE Thomas, gentleman, of Lyndeborough, vs STEVENS Samuel, yeoman, of Lyndeborough, rec date 1784, judgment, debt, file #4361

BOUTEL James, husbandman, of Lyndeborough, vs LEWIS Benjamin, yeoman, of Lyndeborough, doc date 1784, deed, land transfer, file #2006

BOUTELL James, yeoman, of Lyndeborough, vs MARSH Samuel Jr, of Nottingham-West, rec date 1786, judgment, debt, file #5761

BOUTELL Joseph, gentleman, of Amherst, vs HINCHMAN Nathaniel, physician, of Amherst, doc date 1799, writ, debt, file #574

BOUTELL M James, yeoman, of Lyndeborough, vs MARCH Samuel J, yeoman, of Nottingham-West, rec date 1786, judgment, debt, file #6209

BOUTELL Samuel, yeoman, of Wilmington MA, vs STEARNS Samuel Jr, yeoman, of Amherst, rec date 1784, judgment, debt, file #4646

BOUTELL Samuel, yeoman, of Wilmington MA, vs STEARNS Samuel Jr, yeoman, of Amherst, rec date 1785, judgment, debt, file #5146

BOUTWELL Amos, yeoman, of Amherst, vs STEVENS Daniel, yeoman, of Amherst, rec date 1783, execution, debt, file #2996

BOUTWELL Amos, yeoman, of Amherst, vs ATHERTON Joshua, esquire, of Amherst, rec date 1783, writ, debt, file #3020

BOUTWELL Amos, yeoman, of Amherst, vs NICHOLS Moses, esquire, of Amherst, rec date 1785, writ, debt, file #5427

BOUTWELL James, yeoman, of Lyndeborough, vs LEWIS Aaron, yeoman, of Lyndeborough, rec date 1785, judgment, debt, file #5516

BOUTWELL James, yeoman, of Lyndeborough, vs LEWIS Aaron, yeoman, of Lyndeborough, rec date 1785, judgment, debt, file #5997

BOUTWELL James, yeoman, of Lyndeborough, vs MARSH Samuel, yeoman, of Nottingham-West, rec date 1785, writ, debt, file #6864

BOUTWELL Joseph, husbandman, of Amherst, vs STEARNS Jotham, yeoman, of Goffstown, rec date 1785, writ, debt, file #6148

BOUTWELL Joseph 3rd, cordwainer, of Amherst, vs TRUELE Amos, yeoman, of Amherst, rec date 1782, writ, debt, file #2826

BOUTWELL Judith, single, of Amherst, vs TALBURT Philo, husbandman, of Amherst, rec date 1787, petition, fornication, file #6526

BOUTWELL Kendale, husbandman, of Amherst, vs TRUELE Amos, yeoman, of Amherst, rec date 1782, writ, debt, file #2826

BOWEN Elanor, singlewoman, of Salisbury, vs ALDRICH Andrew, husbandman, of Grafton, rec date 1783, execution, debt, file #3828

BOWEN Eleanor, singlewoman, of Salisbury, vs ALDRICH Andrew, husbandman, of Goffstown, rec date 1783, civil litigious, debt, file #2924

BOWEN John, yeoman, of Salisbury, vs FOLSOM John, yeoman, of Concord, rec date 1786, writ, debt, file #6312

BOWER William, gentleman, of Billerica MA, vs BARRETT Charles, esquire, of New Ipswich, rec date 1786, writ, debt, file #6278

BOWERS Andrew, esquire, of Salisbury, vs ELKINS Abel, innkeeper, of Salisbury, doc date 1798, judgment, debt, file #561

BOWERS Andrew, esquire, of Salisbury, vs ELKINS Mel, innkeeper, of Salisbury, doc date 1798, judgment, debt, file #561

BOWERS Andrew, esquire, of Salisbury, vs ELKINS Abel, innkeeper, of Salisbury, doc date 1799, debt, file #449

BOWERS Elisha, gentleman, of East Sudbury m, vs BRADFORD Samuel Jr, gentleman, of Hillsborough, rec date 1785, execution, debt, file #5959

BOWERS Ephraim, yeoman/minor, of Merrimack, vs DARRAH James, yeoman, of Merrimack, rec date 1783, writ, debt, file #4521, kinship Eliz BOWERS mother

BOWERS Isaac, yeoman, of Groton MA, vs SHED Jonas, yeoman, of Raby, rec date 1785, judgment, debt, file #5445

BOWERS John, blacksmith, of Amherst, vs HILLS Stephen, husbandman, of Merrimack, doc date 1799, writ, debt, file #394

BOWERS John, blacksmith, of Amherst, vs FARRAR Caleb, hatter, of Amherst, doc date 1799, writ, debt, file #393

BOWERS John, blacksmith, of Amherst, vs CLARK Robert Jr, merchant, of New Boston, doc date 1799, writ, debt, file #392

BOWERS Josiah Jr, innholder, of Billerica MA, vs WILKINS Jonathan, yeoman, of Amherst, rec date 1785, execution, debt, file #5478

BOWIN Jeremiah, yeoman, of Dunbarton, vs MOORE Samuel, esquire, of Canterbury, doc date 1773, writ, debt, file #1335

BOYD Ebenezer S, trader, of Boston MA, vs TILTON Joel, husbandman, of Lebanon, doc date 1798, judgment, debt, file #561

BOYD Samuel, husbandman, of New Boston, vs STARK John Jr, esquire, of Deerfield, doc date 1798, various, debt, file #540

BOYD Samuel, husbandman, of New Boston, vs STARK John Jr, esquire, of Derryfield, doc date 1798, judgment, debt, file #561

BOYD Samuel, husbandman, of New Boston, vs PERKINS Samuel, innkeeper, of Londonderry, doc date 1772, writ, debt, file #1051

BOYES James, yeoman, of Londonderry, vs PIERCE James, yeoman, of Deerfield, rec date 1783, execution, debt, file #3257

BOYLE William, husbandman, of Wilton, vs BLANCHARD Lemuel, innkeeper, of Cambridge MA, rec date 1783, judgment, debt, file #4517

BOYNTON Abel, trader, of Westford MA, vs PARKER Samuel, yeoman, of Rindge, rec date 1786, writ, debt, file #6116

BOYNTON Abraham, cordwainer, of Hollis, vs TARBOX James, yeoman, of Dunstable MA, doc date 1784, execution, debt, file #1927

BOYNTON Abraham, cordwainer, of Hollis, vs TARBOX James, yeoman, of Dunstable MA, rec date 1783, writ, debt, file #3422

BOYNTON Caleb, yeoman, of Peterborough Slip, vs BACON Retire, yeoman, of New Ipswich, doc date 1784, writ, debt, file #1595

BOYNTON Isaac, yeoman, of Groton MA, vs MOORE Samuel, yeoman, of Antrim, rec date 1784, appeal, debt, file #4111

BOYNTON Isaac, cordwainer, of Groton MA, vs MOSHER James, husbandman, of Hollis, rec date 1784, judgment, debt, file #4997

BOYNTON Isaac, cordwainer, of Groton MA, vs GOULD James, gentleman, of Hanover, rec date 1784, judgment, debt, file #5325

BOYNTON Jeremiah, minor, of Amherst, vs EVANS Zord?, husbandman, of Chesterfield, rec date 1786, writ, debt, file #6300

BOYNTON John, yeoman, of Hollis, vs BOYNTON Isaac, yeoman, of Hollis, rec date 1782, recognizance, debt, file #2612

BOYNTON Joshua, bricklayer, of Hollis, vs WOODS David, cooper, of Hollis, doc date 1799, writ, debt, file #362

BOYNTON Joshua, clockmaker, of Hollis, vs BUTTERFIELD Mary (widow), of Wilton, doc date 1792, petition, release from jail, file #38

BOYNTON Joshua, clockmaker, of Hollis, vs STATE of NH, rec date 1776, recognizance, counterfeiting, file #2255

BOYNTON Joshua, clockmaker, of Hollis, vs ROGERS Solomon, trader, of Hollis, rec date 1783, writ, debt, file #3115

BOYNTON Richard, husbandman, of Packersfield, vs GORDON Cosmo, rec date 1785, judgment, debt, file #4936

BOYNTON Richard, husbandman, of Packersfield, vs GORDON Cosmo, husbandman, of Dunstable MA, rec date 1785, judgment, debt, file #5978

BOYNTON Thomas, husbandman, of Hollis, vs LUTWYCHE Edward, esquire, of Merrimack, doc date 1772, writ, debt, file #878

BOYNTON Thomas, husbandman, of Hollis, vs MACK Robert Jr, blacksmith, of Londonderry, doc date 1772, writ, debt, file #1057

BOYNTON Thomas, yeoman, of Ashby MA, vs WILKINSON Daniel, clerk, of Amherst, doc date 1774, writ, debt, file #978

BOYNTON Thomas, yeoman, of Ashby MA, vs WILKINS Daniel, clerk, of Amherst, doc date 1775, writ, debt, file #2039

BOYNTON Thomas, guardian, of Amherst, vs EVANS Zord?, husbandman, of Chester, rec date 1786, writ, debt, file #6300, Thomas BOYNTON, guardian

BOYNTON Thomas, joiner, of Hollis, vs ELIOTT Jeremiah, husbandman, of Pepperell MA, doc date 1772, rec date 1772, deed, land transfer, file #6844

BOYTON Thomas, yeoman, of Hollis, vs TYNG James, merchant, of Dunstable MA, doc date 1772, writ, debt, file #1421

BRABROOK Joseph, hatter, of Chelmsford MA, vs PARSONS Kendal, yeoman, of Jaffrey, rec date 1783, execution, debt, file #3662

BRADBROOD Joseph, hatter, of Chelmsford MA, vs PARSON Kendal, yeoman, of Jaffrey, rec date 1783, execution, debt, file #3238

BRADBURY Joseph, of Bradford, vs WHITEMORE Reuben, yeoman, of Bradford, doc date 1791, deed, land transfer, file #1994

BRADFORD Andrew, gentleman, of Amherst, vs TAGGART Archibald, gentleman, of Hillsborough, doc date 1783, rec date 1783, deed, land transfer, file #2635

BRADFORD Andrew, gentleman, of Amherst, vs MEANS Robert, trader, of Amherst, rec date 1783, writ, debt, file #3010

BRADFORD Andrew, yeoman, of Hillsborough, vs HEYWOOD Nathaniel, yeoman, of Hillsborough, rec date 1783, writ, debt, file #3079

BRADFORD Andrew, gentleman, of Amherst, vs ATHERTON Joshua, esquire, of Amherst, rec date 1783, writ, debt, file #3055

BRADFORD Andrew, gentleman, of Amherst, vs KIMBALL Samuel, husbandman, of Henniker, rec date 1783, judgment, debt, file #4455

BRADFORD Andrew, esquire, of Amherst, vs BRADFORD John, esquire, of Amherst, doc date 1784, rec date 1785, deed, land transfer, file #5637

BRADFORD Andrew, gentleman, of Amherst, vs HOWARD William, of Amherst, rec date 1786, writ, debt, file #6882

BRADFORD Greenleaf Lydia, singlewoman, of Amherst, vs BOYNTON Jeremiah, laborer, of Amherst, rec date 1785, writ, fornication, file #5794

BRADFORD John, gentleman, of Amherst, vs BOWERS Ephraim, yeoman, of Merrimack, rec date 1785, execution, debt, file #5474

BRADFORD John, gentleman, of Hillsborough, vs BOWERS Ephraim, yeoman, of Merrimack, rec date 1785, writ, debt pasturing, file #2344

BRADFORD John, gentleman, of Amherst, vs BOWERS Ephraim, yeoman, of Merrimack, rec date 1785, judgment, debt, file #5779

BRADFORD Mary, widow, of Hillsborough, vs ATHERTON Joshua, esquire, of Amherst, rec date 1783, writ, debt, file #3357, estate of Samuel BRADFORD

BRADFORD Mary, widow, of Hillsborough, vs DODGE Samuel, yeoman, of Amherst, rec date 1783, writ, debt, file #3357, estate of Samuel DODGE

BRADFORD Samuel, husbandman, of Antrim, vs TOWAN John, yeoman, of Hillsborough, doc date 1799, judgment, debt, file #260

BRADFORD Samuel, husbandman, of Hillsborough, vs HOWE Nathan, husbandman, of Hillsborough, doc date 1799, debt, file #488

BRADFORD Samuel, yeoman, of Hillsborough, vs MILLS John, yeoman, of Amherst, doc date 1772, writ, debt, file #1424

BRADFORD Samuel, esquire, of Hillsborough, vs AIKEN William, yeoman, of Society Land, doc date 1773, writ, debt, file #1361

BRADFORD Samuel, yeoman, of Hillsborough, vs STEEL John, yeoman, of Hillsborough, doc date 1773, writ, debt, file #1347

BRADFORD Samuel, yeoman, of Hillsborough, vs WILLIAMS William, yeoman, of Hillsborough, doc date 1773, writ, debt, file #1348

BRADFORD Samuel, gentleman, of Hillsborough, vs WILLEY John, yeoman, of Hillsborough, rec date 1782, execution, debt, file #3529

BRADFORD Samuel, gentleman, of Hillsborough, vs WILLEY John, yeoman, of Hillsborough, rec date 1783, execution, debt, file #3677

BRADFORD Samuel, gentleman, of Hillsborough, vs SERVICE Robert, merchant, of Boston MA, rec date 1785, writ, debt, file #5424

BRADFORD Samuel, husbandman, of Amherst, vs CLARK Thomas, husbandman, of Dunstable, rec date 1786, writ, debt, file #6124

BRADFORD Samuel, gentleman, of Hillsborough, vs McCLINTOCK John, husbandman, of Hillsborough, rec date 1785, judgment, debt, file #6430

BRADFORD Timothy, yeoman, of Hill, vs DRESSER Asa, yeoman, of Campbells Gore, rec date 1783, writ, debt, file #3028

BRADFORD Timothy, gentleman, of Hillsborough, vs BRADFORD Mary, widow, of Hillsborough, rec date 1785, deed, land transfer, file #5646

BRADFORD William, gentleman, of Deering, vs BISHOP George, yeoman, of Hillsborough, doc date 1784, execution, debt, file #1517

BRADFORD William, husbandman, of Deering, vs KIDDER John Jr, yeoman, of Lyndeborough, rec date 1782, writ, debt, file #2798

BRADFORD William, yeoman, of Deering, vs BALDWIN Nathaniel, esquire, of Amherst, rec date 1782, writ, debt, file #2671, estate of Zacheus CUTLER

BRADFORD William, gentleman, of Deering, vs BRADFORD Samuel, gentleman, of Fitchburg MA, rec date 1783, writ, debt, file #3003

BRADFORD William, gentleman, of Deering, vs MEANS Robert, trader, of Amherst, rec date 1783, writ, debt, file #3051

BRADFORD William, yeoman, of Deering, vs CLEAVES Nathan, yeoman, of Amherst, rec date 1782, writ, debt, file #2824

BRADFORD William, husbandman, of Deering, vs BAYLES William, husbandman, of Wilton, rec date 1783, writ, debt, file #3348

BRADLEY Stephen, of Westminster NY, vs MITCHEL Isaac, husbandman, of Peterborough, rec date 1786, judgment, debt, file #6465

BRADLEY Stephen R, esquire, of Westminster MA, vs MITCHEL Isaac, husbandman, of Peterborough, rec date 1785, judgment, debt, file #6407

BRADLEY Stephen Roe, esquire, of Westminster VT, vs LOVEJOY Francis, feltmaker, of Amherst, rec date 1786, writ, debt, file #6295

BREWER Elisha, gentleman, of E Sudbury ma, vs BRADFORD Samuel Jr, gentleman, of Hillsborough, rec date 1785, judgment, debt, file #4964

BREWSTER Isaac, yeoman, of Francestown, vs BARKER William, physician, of Francestown, rec date 1785, judgment, debt, file #5781

BRIDGE Ebenezer, esquire, of Chelmsford MA, vs KEMP Jason, husbandman, of Henniker, rec date 1785, judgment, debt, file #5495

BROADSTREET Elijah, blacksmith, of Greenfield, vs GOULD Mary, widow, of Greenfield, doc date 1798, judgment, land dispute, file #561

BROOKS Abner, husbandman, of Conway MA, vs HOW John, yeoman, of
    Dunbarton, rec date 1788, writ, debt, file #2388
BROOKS Abner, husbandman, of Conway, vs HOW John, yeoman, of Dunbarton,
    rec date 1786, writ, debt, file #5897
BROOKS Isaac, esquire, of Amherst, vs WESTON Jesse & Daniel, of Amherst,
    doc date 1814, rec date 1814, deed, land transfer, file #6580
BROOKS John, blacksmith, of New Ipswich, vs HILL David, trader, of New
    Ipswich, doc date 1778, rec date 1787, deed, land transfer, file #2488
BROOKS Silas, yeoman, of Mason, vs MOORE Benjamin, yeoman, of Rindge,
    rec date 1783, judgment, debt, file #3302
BROOKS Solomon, yeoman, of New Ipswich, vs WILLARD Joshua, husbandman,
    of Fitzwilliam, rec date 1783, judgment, debt, file #3296
BROOKS Thomas, esquire, of Medford MA, vs STEVENS Samuel, deceased, of
    Amherst, rec date 1786, judgment, debt, file #2306, inventory of property
BROOKS William, gentleman, of Hancock, vs SMITH James, esquire, of
    Cavindish VT, doc date 1799, judgment, debt, file #297
BROOKS William, gentleman, of Hollis, vs WIER Robert, husbandman, of
    Walpole, rec date 1784, various, debt, file #4182
BROWN Aaron, yeoman, of Groton, vs BENNETT Phinehas, yeoman, of Roby,
    doc date 1798, execution, debt, file #82
BROWN Aaron, esquire, of Groton, vs HITCHER Henry, yeoman, of New
    Ipswich, doc date 1798, judgment, debt, file #561
BROWN Aaron, vs LAWRENCE Stephen, doc date 1772, deposition, file #1168
BROWN Aaron, shopkeeper, of Groton MA, vs WHEELER Uriah, husbandman,
    of Packersfield, doc date 1784, execution, debt, file #1680
BROWN Aaron, shopkeeper, of Groton MA, vs GRAGG Samuel, yeoman, of
    Peterborough Slip, doc date 1784, execution, debt, file #1710
BROWN Aaron, trader, of Groton MA, vs SMITH John, husbandman, of
    Peterborough, doc date 1784, execution, debt, file #1688
BROWN Aaron, shopkeeper, of Groton MA, vs AMES David, miller, of
    Peterborough, doc date 1784, execution, debt, file #1952
BROWN Aaron, trader, of Groton MA, vs CUTTER John, yeoman, of New
    Ipswich, rec date 1783, writ, debt, file #3451
BROWN Aaron, shopkeeper, of Groton MA, vs GRAGG Samuel, yeoman, of
    Peterborough Slip, rec date 1783, writ, debt, file #3626
BROWN Aaron, shopkeeper, of Groton MA, vs PRATT John, husbandman, of
    New Ipswich, rec date 1783, judgment, debt, file #3708
BROWN Aaron, shopkeeper, of Groton MA, vs TOWNE Edmond, yeoman, of
    New Ipswich, rec date 1783, writ, debt, file #3460
BROWN Aaron, shopkeeper, of Groton MA, vs AMEO David, miller, of
    Peterborough, rec date 1783, writ, debt, file #3628
BROWN Aaron, shopkeeper, of New Ipswich, vs WHEELER Uriah, husbandman,
    of Packersfield, rec date 1783, judgment, debt, file #4499
BROWN Aaron, trader, of Groton MA, vs SMITH John, husbandman, of
    Peterborough, rec date 1783, judgment, debt, file #4437
BROWN Aaron, shopkeeper, of Groton MA, vs ALLEN Abijah, yeoman, of
    Mason, rec date 1785, judgment, debt, file #5061

BROWN Aaron, shopkeeper, of Goshen MA, vs HALE John, esquire, of Hollis, rec date 1785, various, debt, file #6258

BROWN Aaron, shopkeeper, of Groton MA, vs BACON Retire, yeoman, of New Ipswich, rec date 1785, writ, debt, file #6038

BROWN Adam, yeoman, of Plymouth, vs HALE David, of Hollis, doc date 1782, execution, debt, file #973

BROWN Albert O, vs MERRIMACK River Savings Bank, bank, doc date 1893, defendants brief, supreme court, file #603

BROWN Alexander, trader, of Amherst, vs BROWN Timothy, innkeeper, of Tewksbury MA, doc date 1775, writ, debt, file #955

BROWN Aaron, trader, of Groton MA, vs TARBELL John, husbandman, of MA, rec date 1787, writ, debt, file #6707

BROWN Benjamin, husbandman, of Moultonborough MA, vs STEVENS Asa, blacksmith, of Deighton MA, rec date 1786, judgment, debt, file #6498

BROWN Elijah, cordwainer, of Weare, vs COLLINS Benjamin, husbandman, of Weare, doc date 1774, execution, debt, file #752

BROWN Elijah, cordwainer, of Weare, vs COLLINS Benjamin, husbandman, of Weare, doc date 1774, execution, file #942

BROWN Elijah, cordwainer, of Weare, vs COLLINS Benjamin, husbandman, of Weare, doc date 1774, execution, file #998

BROWN Eliphalet, minor, of New Boston, vs SMITH Timothy, husbandman, of Nottingham-West, rec date 1785, writ, debt, file #6245

BROWN Eliphalet, minor, of New Boston, vs HILLS Ezekiel, gentleman, of Nottingham-West, rec date 1785, writ, debt, file #6245

BROWN Eliphalet, minor, of New Boston, vs CUMMINGS David, gentleman, of Nottingham-West, rec date 1785, writ, debt, file #6245

BROWN Eliphalet, minor, of New Boston, vs MARSH Samuel, gentleman, of Nottingham-West, rec date 1785, writ, debt, file #6245

BROWN Eliphalet, minor, of New Boston, vs MARSHALL Daniel, yeoman, of Nottingham-West, rec date 1785, writ, debt, file #6245

BROWN Elisha Jr, husbandman, of Ipswich MA, vs PERKINS Philemon, husbandman, of New Boston, rec date 1785, judgment, debt, file #5847

BROWN Ezekiel, esquire, of Concord MA, vs SHANNON Richard Cutts, esquire, of Raby, rec date 1787, writ, debt, file #2375

BROWN Hannah, widow, of Dunstable, vs BROWN James 5th, yeoman, of Hanover, rec date 1784, writ, debt, file #4578

BROWN Isaac, gentleman, of Mason, vs INHABITANTS of Mason, doc date 1784, execution, debt, file #1724

BROWN Isaac, yeoman, of Wilton, vs BROWN Hannah & James, widow, of Dunstable, rec date 1787, judgment, debt, file #2541

BROWN Isaac, yeoman, of Wilton, vs BROWN James 5th, yeoman, of Hanover, rec date 1784, writ, debt, file #4578

BROWN Isaac & Hannah, yeoman, of Wilton, vs BROWN James, gentleman, of Hanover, rec date 1785, various, debt, file #5251, estate of James BROWN

BROWN James, vs TARBELL Edmund, of Mason, doc date 1774, summons to court, file #720

BROWN James, yeoman, of Wilton, vs HUTCHINSON Alexander, innkeeper, of Wilton, doc date 1774, writ, debt, file #1080

BROWN James, yeoman, of Wilton, vs BALLARD Joseph, husbandman, of Andover MA, doc date 1774, writ, debt, file #1094, fragile

BROWN James, vs TARBELL Edmund, doc date 1774, court cost, file #1148

BROWN James, yeoman, of Dunstable, vs PROPRIETORS of Wilton, of Wilton, doc date 1773, summons, debt, file #1234

BROWN James, yeoman, of Moultonborough, vs TARBELL Edmund, yeoman, of Mason, rec date 1783, writ, debt, file #3944

BROWN James, gentleman, of Plymouth, vs BUTTERFIELD Joseph, gentleman, of Wilton, rec date 1782, appeal, debt, file #4000

BROWN James, husbandman, of Hanover, vs FRY Isaac, esquire, of Wilton, rec date 1784, judgment, debt, file #4248

BROWN John, laborer, of Amherst, vs BLANCHARD John, yeoman, of Amherst, rec date 1785, writ, debt, file #2352

BROWN Jonathan, vs STRAW Abel, laborer, of Hopkinton, rec date 1785, writ, debt, file #52

BROWN Jonathan, esquire, of Tewksbury MA, vs BALDWIN Jesse, yeoman, of Amherst, rec date 1783, judgment, debt, file #3764

BROWN Jonathan, of Henniker, vs GOODENOW Ebenezer, yeoman, of Henniker, rec date 1785, capias, assault, file #4569

BROWN Jonathan, of Henniker, vs GOODENOW John, yeoman, of Henniker, rec date 1785, capias, assault, file #4569

BROWN Jonathan, of Henniker, vs GORDEN Abell, yeoman, of Hopkinton, rec date 1785, capias, assault, file #4569

BROWN Jonathan, of Henniker, vs GOULD John, laborer, of Henniker, rec date 1785, capias, assault, file #4569

BROWN Jonathan, of Henniker, vs HOW Eliakim, gentleman, of Henniker, rec date 1785, capias, assault, file #4569

BROWN Jonathan, of Henniker, vs HOW Eliakim Jr, laborer, of Henniker, rec date 1785, capias, assault, file #4569

BROWN Jonathan, of Henniker, vs KIMBALL Samuel, yeoman, of Henniker, rec date 1785, capias, assault, file #4569

BROWN Jonathan, of Henniker, vs PUTNEY Nathaniel, yeoman, of Henniker, rec date 1785, capias, assault, file #4569

BROWN Jonathan, of Henniker, vs PUTNEY Isaac, yeoman, of Henniker, rec date 1785, capias, assault, file #4569

BROWN Jonathan, of Henniker, vs STRAW Jacob, laborer, of Hopkinton, rec date 1785, capias, assault, file #4569

BROWN Jonathan Hillard, cordwainer, of Weare, vs SMITH Richard, yeoman, of Northfield, rec date 1788, deed, land transfer, file #6741

BROWN Joseph, yeoman, of Hollis, vs FLAGG Samuel, esquire, of Salem MA, rec date 1783, writ, debt, file #3044

BROWN Joseph, yeoman, of Andover, vs WADLEIGH Simeon D, tanner, of Salisbury, rec date 1783, writ, debt, file #3066

BROWN Moses, merchant, of Beverly MA, vs MITCHELL John, yeoman, of Hancock, rec date 1782, execution, debt, file #5725

BROWN Rachel, single, of Marlborough MA, vs POWELL Benjamin, of Marlborough MA, rec date 1787, complaint, fornication, file #6169, part of Samuel CURTIS file

BROWN Reuben, saddler, of Concord, vs SMITH Edward, gentleman, of Sharon, doc date 1799, debt, file #459

BROWN Reuben, saddler, of Concord MA, vs SMITH Thadius, yeoman, of Fitzwilliam, doc date 1799, debt, file #479

BROWN Reuben, saddler, of Concord, vs WHEAT Joseph Jr, laborer, of Amherst, doc date 1798, judgment, debt, file #561

BROWN Reuben, saddler, of Concord MA, vs AMES David, miller, of Peterborough, rec date 1783, writ, debt, file #3458

BROWN Reuben, gentleman, of Concord MA, vs DODGE Sussana, widow/administrator of estate, of Amherst, rec date 1787, writ, debt, file #6958, Samuel DODGE (deceased)

BROWN Samuel, husbandman, of Nottingham, vs GREELEY Noah, husbandman, of Nottingham, doc date 1798, execution, debt, file #192

BROWN Samuel, shipwright, of Nottingham-West, vs McGINNIS Barnabas, yeoman, of Nottingham-West, doc date 1784, execution, debt, file #1740

BROWN Samuel, husbandman, of New Boston, vs READ Zadock, husbandman, of New Boston, rec date 1788, writ, debt, file #2378

BROWN Samuel, shipwright, of New Boston, vs KELLEY Joseph, gentleman, of Nottingham-West, rec date 1787, judgment, land dispute, file #2542

BROWN Samuel, gentleman, of Nottingham-West, vs ROGERS Solomon, trader, of Hollis, rec date 1783, writ, debt, file #3202

BROWN Samuel, shipwright, of Nottingham-West, vs McGINNIS Barnabas, yeoman, of Nottingham-West, rec date 1783, writ, debt, file #4067

BROWN Samuel, shipwright, of New BOSTON, vs KELLY Joseph Jr, gentleman, of Nottingham-West, rec date 1785, writ, land dispute, file #4788

BROWN Sharon, gentleman, of Groton MA, vs ROBE William Jr, yeoman, of Peterborough, rec date 1788, writ, debt, file #6918

BROWN Silas, cordwainer, of Temple, vs GRIMES Thaddeus, yeoman, of Amherst, rec date 1783, judgment, debt, file #4535

BROWN Silas, yeoman, of Temple, vs WHITING Oliver, yeoman, of Temple, doc date 1784, rec date 1785, deed, land transfer, file #5636

BROWN Timothy, trader, of Tewksbury MA, vs CODMAN Henry, physician, of Amherst, rec date 1782, execution, debt, file #3528

BROWN Timothy, trader, of Tewksbury MA, vs CODMAN Henry, physician, of Amherst, rec date 1783, execution, debt, file #3656

BROWN Timothy, gentleman, of Tewksbury MA, vs COFFIN John, yeoman, of Amherst, rec date 1784, judgment, debt, file #4414

BROWN Timothy, gentleman, of Tewksbury MA, vs COFFIN John, yeoman, of Amherst, rec date 1784, appeal, debt, file #4122

BROWN Timothy, gentleman, of Tewksbury MA, vs McCLEARY William, yeoman, of Antrim, rec date 1784, appeal, debt, file #4126

BROWN Timothy, gentleman, of Tewksbury MA, vs WILLEY John, yeoman, of Amherst, rec date 1784, judgment, debt, file #4414

BROWN Timothy, gentleman, of Tewksbury MA, vs WILLEY John, yeoman, of Amherst, rec date 1784, appeal, debt, file #4122

BROWN Timothy, gentleman, of Tewksbury MA, vs WILKINS Jonathan, yeoman, of Amherst, rec date 1783, judgment, debt, file #4444

BROWN William, physician, of Hancock, vs WHIPPLE Oliver, esquire, of Portsmouth, doc date 1792, petition, release of debit, file #20

BROWN William, esquire, of Hollis, vs BLANCHARD Jonathan, of Hollis, doc date 1775, writ, land dispute, file #758, deed to land near Flint Hill

BROWN William, yeoman, of Sudbury MA, vs JONES Samuel, yeoman, of Hillsborough, rec date 1783, writ, debt, file #3893

BROWNING Joseph, yeoman, of Rutland MA, vs CUTTER John, yeoman, of New Ipswich, rec date 1787, writ, debt, file #6892

BRUCE Isaiah, yeoman, of Bolton MA, vs BRADFORD Samuel Jr, gentleman, of Deering, rec date 1784, judgment, debt, file #4196

BRUCE Isaiah, of Bolton MA, vs TAGGART Archibald, gentleman, of Hillsborough, rec date 1785, writ, debt, file #5966

BRUCE Josiah, of Bolton MA, vs BRADFORD Samuel, gentleman, of Hillsborough, rec date 1785, judgment, debt, file #5070

BUCKEY William, gentleman, of Hillsborough, vs WATSON John, saddler, of Amherst, doc date 1799, writ, debt, file #385

BUCKLEY John, gentleman, of Groton MA, vs SMITH Nathaniel, cooper, of Mason, doc date 1784, civil litigation, debt, file #1857

BUCKMAN John, yeoman, of Mason, vs PINKMAN Samuel, merchant, of Boston MA, doc date 1799, judgment, debt, file #221

BUEL Samuel, gentleman, of Milford, vs ABBOTT George, tanner, of Wilton, doc date 1798, execution, debt, file #83

BULKLEY John, gentleman, of Groton MA, vs KIDDLER Joseph, gentleman, of Temple, doc date 1774, execution, file #995

BULKLEY Mary, widow, of Groton MA, vs SLOAN David, yeoman, of Mason, rec date 1785, judgment, debt, file #4953

BULLARD Benjamin, yeoman, of Hillsborough, vs BACON Daniel, gentleman, of MA, rec date 1784, judgment, debt, file #4239

BULLARD John, clerk, of Pepperell MA, vs HOBART Joel, yeoman, of Mile Slip, doc date 1784, deed, land transfer, file #5037

BURBAND Moses, husbandman, of Boscawen, vs BOWIN John, husbandman, of Salisbury, rec date 1785, judgment, debt, file #5397

BURBANK Abner, yeoman, of Brentwood, vs BROWN Francis, husbandman, of Boscawen, doc date 1799, execution, debt, file #216

BURBANK Ebenezer, yeoman, of Boscawen, vs DEARBORN John, yeoman, of Hampton, doc date 1799, various, debt, file #518

BURBANK Jacob, yeoman, of Washington, vs JONES Samuel, yeoman, of Hillsborough, rec date 1782, judgment, debt, file #2736

BURBANK Jacob, yeoman, of Washington, vs JONES Samuel, yeoman, of Hillsborough, rec date 1783, execution, debt, file #3837

BURBANK Josiah, yeoman, of Boscawen, vs BURBANK Wells, yeoman, of Boscawen, rec date 1785, judgment, debt, file #5071

BURBANK Moses, husbandman, of Boscawen, vs BOWIN John, husbandman, of Salisbury, rec date 1784, judgment, debt, file #4665

BURBANK Moses, husbandman, of Boscawen, vs CORSER Samuel, gentleman, of Boscawen, rec date 1786, writ, debt, file #6693

BURBANK Moses Jr, husbandman, of Boscawen, vs HALL John, physician, of Warner, doc date 1784, execution, debt, file #1985

BURBANK Moses Jr, husbandman, of Boscawen, vs HALL John, physician, of Warner, rec date 1783, writ, debt, file #3393

BURBANK Moses Jr, yeoman, of Boscawen, vs WEBSTER Benjamin, saddler, of Northfield, rec date 1783, writ, debt, file #3388

BURBANK Moses Jr, yeoman, of Boscawen, vs ATKINSON Samuel, gentleman, of Boscawen, rec date 1783, writ, debt, file #3373

BURBANK Moses Jr, husbandman, of Boscawen, vs SEVERANCE Peter, husbandman, of Salisbury, rec date 1784, judgment, debt, file #4404

BURBANK Moses Jr, husbandman, of Boscawen, vs CHENEY Moses, clothier, of Brentwood, rec date 1786, writ, debt, file #6277

BURBANK Wells, carpenter, of Sanbornton, vs CALL John, yeoman, of Andover, doc date 1798, execution, debt, file #119

BURBANK Wells, husbandman, of Boscawen, vs ATKINSON Joseph, husbandman, of Boscawen, doc date 1784, writ, debt, file #1567

BURGE Moses, of Westford MA, rec date 1788, various, land dispute, file #6583

BURMAN Stephen, of Lyndeborough, vs Town of Lyndeborough, doc date 1787, license, tavern license, file #866

BURNAM Jonathan, gentleman, of Amherst, vs HOLT Valentine, husbandman, of Wilton, rec date 1788, writ, debt, file #6606

BURNAM Stephen, yeoman, of Lyndeborough, vs BLANEY William, husbandman, of Lyndeborough, rec date 1782, writ, debt, file #2701

BURNHAM David, husbandman, of One Mile Slip, vs BLANCHARD Jacob, husbandman, of One Mile Slip, rec date 1783, judgment, debt, file #2594

BURNHAM David, husbandman, of One Mile Slip, vs BLANCHARD Jacob, husbandman, of One Mile Slip, rec date 1783, execution, debt, file #2872

BURNHAM Josiah, husbandman, of Coventry, vs ATKINSON Samuel, captain, of Coventry, rec date 1783, various, appeal, file #2747, destroying house

BURNHAM Josiah, husbandman, of Coventry, vs ATKINSON Samuel, gentleman, of Boscawen, rec date 1785, judgment, debt, file #5362

BURNHAM Nathan, gentleman, of Dunbarton, vs WHITE Samuel Gilman, husbandman, of Hillsborough, rec date 1787, writ, debt, file #6657

BURNS John, gentleman, of Fisherfield, vs FULLER Jason, trader, of Francestown, doc date 1799, writ, debt, file #415

BURNS John, yeoman, of Antrim, vs BALDWIN Nahum, esquire, of Amherst, rec date 1782, appeal, debt, file #3992

BURNS John, husbandman, of Bedford, vs CROWN John, husbandman, of New Boston, rec date 1786, judgment, debt, file #6504

BURNS John, yeoman, of New Boston, vs GOODWIN Matthew, of Francestown, doc date 1786, rec date 1788, deed, land transfer, file #6755

BURNS John, husbandman, of Bedford, vs GAGE Phineas, husbandman, of Merrimack, rec date 1788, writ, debt, file #6992

BURNS John Jr, yeoman, of Bedford, vs McLAUGHLIN John Jr, husbandman, of New Boston, rec date 1784, judgment, debt, file #5457

BURNS Samuel, yeoman, of Washington, vs SHATTUCK William, yeoman, of Bradford, doc date 1798, judgment, debt, file #561

BURNS Samuel, yeoman, of Washington, vs WEBSTER Stephen, yeoman, of Boscawen, doc date 1798, judgment, debt, file #561

BURNS Thomas, gentleman, of Amherst, vs DODGE Samuel, yeoman, of Amherst, doc date 1784, execution, debt, file #1765

BURNS Thomas, gentleman, of Amherst, vs GRIMES James, gentleman, of Deering, doc date 1784, execution, debt, file #1765

BURTON Jonathan, gentleman, of Wilton, vs BROWN James, gentleman, of Moultonborough, rec date 1776, writ, debt, file #2197

BURUTT Benjamin, husbandman, of Wilmington MA, vs ATWELL John, husbandman, of Hollis, rec date 1787, writ, debt, file #2428

BUSCTON Benjamin, yeoman, of Merrimack, vs McCORICHE John, yeoman, of Merrimack, rec date 1783, writ, debt, file #3341

BUSWELL David, yeoman, of Dunbarton, vs ROBERTSON Peter, schoolmaster, of Amherst, rec date 1785, judgment, debt, file #5203

BUTERFIELD Isaac, of Temple, vs BARRETT Amos, gentleman, of Concord MA, rec date 1785, writ, debt, file #4760

BUTLER Elizabeth, single, of Peterborough, vs WHITE William Jr, husbandman, of Peterborough, rec date 1788, recognizance, debt, file #6538

BUTLER Elizabeth, single, of Peterborough, vs McCOY Thomas & William, husbandman, of Peterborough, rec date 1788, recognizance, debt, file #6538

BUTMAN Asa, yeoman, of Greenfield, vs WILSON James, esquire, doc date 1799, judgment, debt, file #298

BUTTERFIELD Abel, husbandman, of Dunstable, vs TAYLOR Timothy, of Merrimack, doc date 1799, judgment, debt, file #310

BUTTERFIELD Charles, yeoman, of Dunstable, vs STEARNS Samuel, yeoman, of Amherst, doc date 1773, judgment, debt, file #1298

BUTTERFIELD Ephraim, gentleman, of Wilton, vs BRIDGE John, yeoman, of Wilton, doc date 1778, rec date 1779, deed, land transfer, file #2139

BUTTERFIELD Ephraim, gentleman, of Wilton, vs STEVENS Samuel, husbandman, of Stoddard, rec date 1788, various, land dispute, file #6583, 2 folders

BUTTERFIELD Isaac, rec date 1788, deposition, debt, file #6583

BUTTERFIELD Jonathan, yeoman, of Dunstable, vs BOWERS Ephraim, yeoman, of Merrimack, rec date 1785, writ, debt, file #2357

BUTTERFIELD Jonathan, yeoman, of Dunstable, vs JAQUITH William, yeoman, of Dunstable, rec date 1783, writ, debt, file #3084

BUTTERFIELD Jonathan, yeoman, of Dunstable, vs HAIL Israel, yeoman, of Francestown, rec date 1785, execution, debt, file #5905

BUTTERFIELD Jonathan, yeoman, of Dunstable, vs BOWERS Ephraim, of Merrimack, rec date 1785, judgment, debt, file #6205

BUTTERFIELD Joseph, gentleman, of Wilton, vs FRENCH Joseph, gentleman, of Dunstable, doc date 1778, rec date 1779, deed, land transfer, file #2119

BUTTERFIELD Joseph, gentleman, of Wilton, vs BROWN James, gentleman, of Plymouth, rec date 1782, judgment, debt, file #3135

BUTTERFIELD Joseph, gentleman, of Wilton, vs BROWN James, gentleman, of Plymouth, rec date 1783, execution, debt, file #2902

BUTTERFIELD Joseph, gentleman, of Wilton, vs BARREL Isaac, yeoman, of Chesterfield, rec date 1783, judgment, debt, file #3715

BUTTERFIELD Joseph, gentleman, of Wilton, vs DAVIS Amos, gentleman, of Chesterfield, rec date 1783, judgment, debt, file #3710

BUTTERFIELD Joseph, gentleman, of Wilton, vs MOOR John, yeoman, of Francestown, rec date 1785, various, debt, file #5255

BUTTERFIELD Joseph, gentleman, of Wilton, vs MARCH Samuel, yeoman, of Nottingham-West, rec date 1786, judgment, debt, file #5760

BUTTERFIELD Joseph, gentleman, of Wilton, vs BEACON Philip, yeoman, of Lyndeborough, rec date 1787, judgment, debt, file #6193

BUTTERFIELD Joseph, innholder, of Wilton, vs DAVIS Samuel, gentleman, of Chesterfield, rec date 1785, writ, debt, file #6641

BUTTERFIELD Philip, cordwainer, of Dunstable MA, vs CHAMBERS William, yeoman, of Chelmsford MA, doc date 1780, rec date 1788, deed, land transfer, file #6822, land in Hollis

BUTTERFIELD Sewall, cordwainer, of Hollis, vs BOWERS John, esquire, of Pepperell MA, doc date 1799, writ, debt, file #357

BUTTERFIELD Simeon, yeoman, of Dunstable, vs HARDY Moses, yeoman, of Dunstable MA, rec date 1783, writ, debt, file #4046

BUTTERFIELD Simeon, yeoman, of Dunstable, vs CUNNINGHAM Robert, yeoman, of Merrimack, rec date 1783, judgment, debt, file #4321, proof of Revolutionary War Service

BUTTERFIELD Simeon, yeoman, of Dunstable, vs GORDON James & Cosmo, gentleman, of Dunstable, rec date 1784, writ, debt, file #5386

BUTTERFIELD Simeon, yeoman, of Dunstable, vs CUNNINGHAM Robert, yeoman, of Merrimack, rec date 1784, various, debt, file #4169

BUTTERFIELD William, husbandman, of Francestown, vs BIXBY Daniel, husbandman, of Litchfield, doc date 1799, judgment, debt, file #256

BUTTERFIELD William, husbandman, of Dunstable, vs BLOOD William, husbandman, of Dunstable, doc date 1798, judgment, debt, file #561

BUTTERFIELD William, husbandman, of Dunstable, vs BLOOD William, husbandman, of Dunstable, doc date 1798, judgment, debt, file #561

BUTTERFIELD William, yeoman, of Merrimack, vs KILLICUT Reuben, yeoman, of Dunstable, rec date 1684, judgment, debt, file #4383

BUTTERFIELD William, yeoman, of Dunstable, vs KELLICUTT Reuben, yeoman, of Dunstable, rec date 1787, writ, debt, file #6646

BUTTERFILED Jonathan, yeoman, of Dunstable, vs NEWMAN Jonathan, yeoman, of Deering, rec date 1785, execution, debt, file #5477

BUTTERFILED William Jr, husbandman, of Dunstable, vs SHERLE Abel, of Hollis, doc date 1800, judgment, debt, file #568

BUTTRICK Tilly, miller, of Westford MA, vs DAVIS Joseph, laborer, of New Ipswich, rec date 1785, judgment, debt, file #5223

BUXSTONE Benjamin, of Merrimack, vs BALEY Nathan, gentleman, of Andover MA, doc date 1785, petition, release of debit, file #11

BUXTON Benjamin, yeoman, of Merrimack, vs FURBUSH Charles Jr, yeoman, of Andover MA, rec date 1782, writ, debt, file #2815

BUXTON John, husbandman, of Wilton, vs CRAM John, husbandman, of Wilton, rec date 1784, appeal, debt, file #4144

BUXTON John, husbandman, of Wilton, vs CRAM John, husbandman, of Wilton, rec date 1784, judgment, debt, file #4395

BUXTON Jonathan, blacksmith, of Milford, vs BURNHAM Joshua, gentleman, of Milford, doc date 1799, writ, debt, file #368

BUXTON Jonathan, blacksmith, of Amherst, vs GEARFIELD Nathaniel, gentleman, of Merrimack, rec date 1785, writ, debt, file #6861

BYAM Benjamin, gentleman, of Temple, vs FURBUSH Charles, yeoman, of Andover MA, doc date 1772, writ, debt, file #1044

CALDWELL James, yeoman, of Middleton MA, vs CRAM John, yeoman, of Wilton, doc date 1773, execution, debt, file #1482

CALDWELL James, husbandman, of New Boston, vs BRADFORD Benjamin, husbandman, of Deering, doc date 1784, civil litigation, debt, file #1846

CALDWELL James, husbandman, of New Boston, vs PATTEN John, husbandman, of Merrimack, doc date 1784, civil litigation, debt, file #1847

CALDWELL James, husbandman, of New Boston, vs RUSSELL James, gentleman, of Goffstown, rec date 1787, judgment, debt, file #2320

CALDWELL James, husbandman, of New Boston, vs McMELLEN Archibald, husbandman, of New Boston, rec date 1783, judgment, debt, file #3791

CALDWELL James, husbandman, of New Boston, vs BRADFORD Benjamin, husbandman, of Deering, rec date 1783, judgment, debt, file #4462

CALDWELL James, husbandman, of New Boston, vs LIVINGSTON William, gentleman, of New Boston, rec date 1782, execution, debt, file #4905

CALDWELL James, husbandman, of Litchfield, vs GEARFIELD Nathaniel, yeoman, of Merrimack, rec date 1785, judgment, debt, file #5163

CALDWELL John, husbandman, of Nottingham, vs EMERSON Dearborn, stage driver, of Amherst, doc date 1799, writ, debt, file #379

CALDWELL John, cordwainer, of Nottingham-West, vs HILDRETH Ephraim, esquire, of Amherst, doc date 1784, writ, debt, file #1581

CALDWELL John, cordwainer, of Nottingham-West, vs KELLY Joseph, gentleman, of Nottingham-West, rec date 1787, judgment, debt, file #2311

CALDWELL John, yeoman, of Nottingham-West, vs SEAVEY John, cordwainer, of Nottingham-West, rec date 1783, writ, debt, file #3189

CALDWELL Joseph, tanner, of Nottingham-West, vs WILKINS Jonathan, yeoman, of Amherst, rec date 1783, execution, debt, file #3271

CALDWELL Joseph, yeoman, of Nottingham-West, vs CALDWELL John, cordwainer, of Nottingham-West, rec date 1785, judgment, debt, file #5593

CALDWELL Joseph, yeoman, of Nottingham-West, vs CALDWELL John, cordwainer, of Nottingham-West, rec date 1788, writ, debt, file #6953

CALDWELL Samuel, husbandman, of Antrim, vs STIMSON David, gentleman, of New Boston, doc date 1799, writ, debt, file #419

CALDWELL Samuel, husbandman, of Weare, vs WILSON Thomas, husbandman, of Henniker, rec date 1784, judgment, debt, file #4339

CALDWELL Thomas, of Nottingham-West, rec date 1777, petition, road lay out, file #2240

CALDWELL Thomas, yeoman, of Dunbarton, vs McGINNIS Barnabas, yeoman, of New Boston, rec date 1782, writ, debt, file #2786

CALDWELL William, husbandman, of Bedford, vs VOSE James, husbandman, of Bedford, doc date VAR, rec date 1778, land dispute, land & road, file #2086, on Bedford & Merrimack town road

CALDWELL William, yeoman, of Bedford, rec date 1778, judgment, land dispute, file #2232

CALDWELL William, yeoman, of Bedford, vs CLAGGETT William, rec date 1779, recognizance, debt, file #2239

CALDWELL William, yeoman, of Francestown, vs McCLEARY William, gentleman, of Antrim, rec date 1785, judgment, debt, file #5066

CALDWELL William, husbandman, of Francestown, vs BEAN Samuel, of Pembroke, rec date 1786, judgment, debt, file #6482

CALL David, yeoman, of Boscawen, vs BENNET Tilton, yeoman, of Sanbornton, doc date 1799, debt, file #464

CALL David, husbandman, of Boscawen, vs FOOTE Samuel, esquire, of Boscawen, rec date 1788, writ, debt, file #6936

CALL Hannah, widow, of Salisbury, vs NEWMAN Thomas, yeoman, of Concord, rec date 1783, judgment, debt, file #4085

CALLEY John W, yeoman, of Hillsborough, vs SARGENT Paul Dudley, merchant, of Amherst, doc date 1773, writ, debt, file #1349

CALLWELL William, yeoman, of Bedford, vs VOSE James, of Bedford, doc date 1778, various, land/road dispute, file #2046

CALVERY John M, yeoman, of Merrimack, vs BELL Joseph, husbandman, of Bedford, rec date 1785, various, debt, file #5236

CALWELL James, husbandman, of New Boston, vs PATTEN John, husbandman, of New Boston, rec date 1783, judgment, debt, file #4460

CALWELL John, yeoman, of New Boston, vs BOOTMAN Benjamin, yeoman, of New Boston, rec date 1782, writ, debt, file #3002

CALWELL John, yeoman, of Nottingham-West, vs HARWOOD Thomas, gentleman, of Dunstable, rec date 1782, writ, debt, file #2827

CALWELL William, yeoman, of Goffstown, vs PARKER Jonathan, physician, of Litchfield, rec date 1783, writ, debt, file #3330

CAMBELL Daniel, gentleman, of Amherst, vs STANLEY Jacob & Jr, yeoman, of Amherst, rec date 1785, execution, debt, file #5953

CAMBELL Isaac, husbandman, of Londonderry, vs WOODMAN John, husbandman, of New London, doc date 1799, debt, file #331

CAMBRIDGE Charles, printer, of Boston MA, vs CUSHING John, physician, of Goffstown, rec date 1788, writ, debt, file #6903

CAMPBELL Daniel, gentleman, of Amherst, vs KENDAL Daniel Jr, yeoman, of Litchfield, rec date 1785, judgment, debt, file #5564

CAMPBELL Daniel, gentleman, of Amherst, vs KENDAL Daniel, yeoman, of Litchfield, rec date 1785, judgment, debt, file #5564

CAMPBELL Daniel, gentleman, of Amherst, vs KENDAL Jacob, yeoman, of Litchfield, rec date 1785, judgment, debt, file #5564

CAMPBELL Daniel, gentleman, of Amherst, vs STANLEY Jacob & Jacob Jr, yeoman, of Amherst, rec date 1785, judgment, debt, file #5839

CAMPBELL David, gentleman, of Henniker, vs STANLEY Samuel, yeoman, of Hopkinton, doc date 1774, writ, debt, file #744

CAMPBELL David, husbandman, of Litchfield, vs BARNES Joseph, physician, of Litchfield, doc date 1772, writ, debt, file #1047, fragile

CAMPBELL David, yeoman, of Amherst, vs BRADFORD Joseph, husbandman, of Amherst, doc date 1771, rec date 1779, deed, land transfer, file #2125

CAMPBELL David, deacon, of Litchfield, vs STATE of NH, rec date 1777, jurors decision, death inquiry, file #2210

CAMPBELL Henry, trader, of Antrim, vs ELSWORTH Thomas, cordwainer, of Deering, doc date 1798, judgment, debt, file #561

CAMPBELL Henry, trader, of Antrim, vs ELSWORTH Thomas, cordwainer, of Deering, doc date 1799, debt, file #471

CAMPBELL Isaac, husbandman, of Londonderry, vs McFARLAND James, trader, of New London, doc date 1799, debt, file #330

CAMPBELL James, yeoman, of Bedford, vs GORDON William, esquire, of Amherst, doc date 1799, debt, file #349

CAMPBELL James, gentleman, of Raby, vs BOYNTON Joshua, yeoman, of Hollis, doc date 1784, civil litigation, debt, file #1647

CAMPBELL James, gentleman, of Raby, vs BOYNTON Joshua, yeoman, of Hollis, rec date 1783, judgment, debt, file #4077

CAMPBELL James, husbandman, of Lyndeborough, vs GOODRIDGE Sewall, clerk, of Lyndeborough, rec date 1783, judgment, debt, file #4478

CAMPBELL John, yeoman, of Henniker, vs HOYT Moses, cordwainer, of Society Land, doc date 1784, deed, land transfer, file #2004

CAMPBELL Robert, yeoman, of New Ipswich, vs GRAGG Samuel, innkeeper, of Peterborough Slip, rec date 1784, judgment, debt, file #4607

CAMPBELL Robert, yeoman, of New Ipswich, vs GRAGG Samuel, innholder, of Peterborough Slip, rec date 1785, judgment, debt, file #6451

CAMPBELL William, cordwainer, of New Boston, vs DODGE Ebenezer, joiner, of Peterborough, rec date 1783, writ, debt, file #3969

CAMPBELL William Jr, carpenter, of Francestown, vs CRAM Joseph, yeoman, of Francestown, doc date 1813, rec date 1813, deed, land transfer, file #5696

CAMPELL David, gentleman, of Henniker, vs DOW Oliver, gentleman, of Hopkinton, rec date 1784, appeal, debt, file #4098

CARLETON Jesse, clothier, of Wilton, vs SAWYER Nathaniel, trader, of Wilton, doc date 1799, writ, debt, file #575

CARLTON Benjamin, cordwainer, of Sutton MA, vs LAKE Daniel, esquire, of Rindge, rec date 1783, various, debt, file #3937

CARLTON Henry, husbandman, of Reading NY, vs JOHNSON Moses, husbandman, of Peterborough, rec date 1783, judgment, debt, file #3717

CARLTON Thomas, husbandman, of Amherst, vs FLETCHER Jonathan, of Dunstable MA, doc date 1772, writ, debt, file #905

CARLTON Thomas, yeoman, of Newtown, vs HOITE Thomas, yeoman, of Dunbarton, doc date 1772, writ, debt, file #1426

CARLTON Thomas, yeoman, of Newtown, vs HOIT Thomas, of Dunbarton, doc date 1773, judgment, debt, file #1326

CARLTON Thomas & Thomas Jr, yeoman, of Greenfield, vs GOULD Richard, yeoman, of Greenfield, rec date 1793, recognizance, debt, file #4153

CARNES James, yeoman, of New Boston, vs DUSTON Paul, yeoman, of New Boston, rec date 1782, execution, debt, file #5732

CARNES James & Agnes, yeoman, of New Boston, vs BUTTERFIELD John, yeoman, of Goffstown, rec date 1785, writ, debt, file #6244

CARR David, trader, of Boscawen, vs CATE Elisha, husbandman, of Sanbornton, rec date 1785, judgment, debt, file #5826

CARR David, trader, of Boscawen, vs GIBSON Enoch, yeoman, of Sanbornton, rec date 1785, judgment, debt, file #5575

CARR John, yeoman, of Londonderry, vs CULMORE John, yeoman, of Pembroke, doc date 1767, writ, debt, file #810

CARR John, yeoman, of Londonderry, vs KNOX Hannah, spinster, of Pembroke, doc date 1766, judgment, debt, file #788

CARSON John, yeoman, of Francestown, vs WILLEY John, gentleman, of Deering, rec date 1777, writ, debt, file #2184

CARSON John, yeoman, of Francestown, vs WILLSON John, gentleman, of Deering, rec date 1777, writ, debt, file #2184

CARSON John, gentleman, of Francestown, vs LOVEWELL Noah, of Dunstable, rec date 1783, writ, debt, file #2755

CARSON John, gentleman, of Francestown, vs NICHOLS Samuel, yeoman, of Francestown, rec date 1783, judgment, debt, file #4326

CARSON William, husbandman, of Lyndeborough, vs KENNY Israel, yeoman, of Hollis, doc date 1773, judgment, debt, file #1305

CARSON William, husbandman, of Lyndeborough, vs HUTCHAN Samuel, yeoman, of Lyndeborough, rec date 1787, writ, debt, file #6973

CARTER Edward, husbandman, of Hollis, vs JEWET Jacob Jr, trader, of Hollis, doc date 1773, writ, debt, file #1357

CARTER Hubbard, blacksmith, of Hopkinton, vs LIVERMORE Daniel, esquire, of Concord, doc date 1784, writ, debt, file #1568

CARTER Hubbard, gentleman, of Hopkinton, vs NEWCOMB Daniel, esquire, of Keene, rec date 1783, writ, debt, file #3432

CARTER Jacob, cordwainer, of Concord, vs BALDWIN Jesse, of Amherst, rec date 1783, writ, debt, file #3182

CARTER Oliver, trader, of Peterborough, vs PERRY Joseph, yeoman, of Greenfield, doc date 1798, execution, debt, file #72

CARTER Oliver Jr, trader, of Peterborough, vs BLASDELL Samuel, yeoman, of Greenfield, doc date 1798, judgment, debt, file #562

CARTER Thomas, labourer, vs STATE of NH, rec date 1782, recognizance, debt, file #2611

CARTER Thomas, husbandman, of Hollis, vs SANDERSON David, husbandman, of Hollis, rec date 1784, judgment, debt, file #5450

CASS Sherburne D, vs STEARNS Byron, plaintiffs brief, supreme court, file #611

CATE Benjamin, yeoman, of Amherst, vs COLE Benjamin, yeoman, of Society Land, doc date 1773, writ, debt, file #1233

CATE Melvin, housewright, of Andover MA, rec date 1788, writ, debt, file #6730

CATE Samuel Stephen, physician, of Amherst, vs CHAMBERS Matthew, gentleman, of Nottingham-West, rec date 1787, writ, debt, file #2373

CATE William, husbandman, of Salisbury, vs ADAMS Joseph, husbandman, of Salisbury, doc date 1799, judgment, debt, file #275

CELNDENION William C, yeoman, of Greenfield, vs NEWTON Silas, yeoman, of Francestown, doc date 1799, writ, debt, file #422

CHADWICK John, shopkeeper, of Medford MA, vs BRADFORD Mary, widow, of Hillsborough, rec date 1785, judgment, debt, file #5592

CHADWICK John, shopkeeper, of Medford MA, vs BRADFORD Mary, widow, of Hillsborough, rec date 1786, judgment, debt, file #6381

CHADWICK John, of Medford MA, vs CRISTY George, gentleman, of New Boston, rec date 1788, writ, debt, file #6981

CHAFFIN John, laborer, of Amherst, vs FOSTER Samuel, watchmaker, of Amherst, doc date 1799, writ, debt, file #365

CHALLIS William, husbandman, of Kingston, vs CHADWICK Thomas, esquire, of Boxford MA, doc date 1772, writ, debt, file #1059

CHAMBERLAIN Isaac, innholder, of Westmoreland, vs PATCH Benjamin, yeoman, of Groton MA, doc date 1774, writ, debt, file #1135

CHAMBERLAIN John, yeoman, of Lyndeborough, vs WOODMAN John, yeoman, of New London, doc date 1799, writ, debt, file #414

CHAMBERLAIN Samuel, husbandman, of Merrimack, vs BELL Samuel, gentleman, of Francestown, doc date 1799, judgment, debt, file #245

CHAMBERLAIN Samuel, husbandman, of Merrimack, vs PROCTOR Samuel, husbandman, of Amherst, doc date 1799, writ, debt, file #381

CHAMBERLIN Elijah, trader, of Dunstable, vs MARSHALL Richard, yeoman, of Nottingham, doc date 1798, execution, debt, file #56

CHAMBERS Margaret, spinster, of Nottingham-West, vs DAVIS Nathaniel, of Nottingham-West, rec date 1785, writ, stealing, file #6342

CHAMBERS William, gentleman, of Mason, vs SARTELL Ephraim, gentleman, of Townsend MA, rec date 1782, writ, debt, file #2685

CHAMBERS William, minor, of Mason, vs SCOTT William, yeoman, of Mason, doc date 1788, rec date 1788, deed, land transfer, file #6834

CHAMBERS William, husbandman, of Henniker, vs GREGG William, gentleman, of Londonderry, rec date 1787, writ, debt, file #6672

CHAMBERS William, gentleman, of Mason, vs SARTELL Ephraim, gentleman, of Raby, rec date 1787, writ, debt, file #6656

CHAMBERS William, gentleman, of Mason, vs SARTELL Ephraim, gentleman, of Raby, rec date 1788, writ, debt, file #6727

CHAMPERS William, husbandman, of Mason, vs HALL Benjamin, distiller, of Medford MA, rec date 1785, writ, debt, file #5414

CHAMPNEY Ebenezar, gentleman, of New Ipswich, vs TAGGART John, yeoman, of Peterborough Slip, doc date 1774, execution, file #989

CHAMPNEY Ebenezar, gentleman, of New Ipswich, vs WHITCOMB Jonathan, gentleman, of Swansey, doc date 1774, execution, file #992

CHAMPNEY Ebenezer, esquire, of New Ipswich, vs DOWNY William, yeoman, of Temple, doc date 1798, execution, debt, file #74

CHAMPNEY Ebenezer, esquire, of Groton MA, vs RUSSELL Nathaniel, gentleman, of Rindge, rec date 1785, judgment, debt, file #5499

CHAMPNEY Ebenezer, esquire, of New Ipswich, vs HOSMER Reuben, yeoman, of New Ipswich, doc date 1798, judgment, debt, file #562

CHAMPNEY Ebenezer, esquire, of New Ipswich, vs YOUNG John, physician, of Peterborough, doc date 1774, judgment, debt, file #707

CHAMPNEY Ebenezer, gentleman, of New Ipswich, vs SPAULDIN Stephen, husbandman, of Lyndeborough, doc date 1772, judgment, debt, file #679

CHAMPNEY Ebenezer, gentleman, of New Ipswich, vs DASCOMBE James, yeoman, of Wilton, doc date 1772, civil litigations, debt, file #641

CHAMPNEY Ebenezer, gentleman, of New Ipswich, vs LARKIN William, yeoman, of Peterborough, doc date 1772, civil litigations, debt, file #643

CHAMPNEY Ebenezer, gentleman, of New Ipswich, vs INGALLS Ebenezer, yeoman, of Rindge, doc date 1772, civil litigations, debt, file #644

CHAMPNEY Ebenezer, esquire, of New Ipswich, vs WILSON John, husbandman, of Peterborough, doc date 1774, judgment, debt, file #707

CHAMPNEY Ebenezer, gentleman, of New Ipswich, vs INGALLS Josiah, yeoman, of Rindge, doc date 1772, civil litigations, debt, file #644

CHAMPNEY Ebenezer, esquire, of New Ipswich, vs ABBOTT Samuel, yeoman, of Hollis, doc date 1782, execution, file #1019

CHAMPNEY Ebenezer, gentleman, of New Ipswich, vs CROSBY Jasaniah, yeoman, of Peterborough, doc date 1772, writ, debt, file #909

CHAMPNEY Ebenezer, esquire, of New Ipswich, vs WILLSON John, yeoman, of Peterborough, doc date 1774, writ, debt, file #976

CHAMPNEY Ebenezer, esquire, of New Ipswich, vs MITCHELL Isaac, yeoman, of Peterborough, doc date 1774, writ, debt, file #977

CHAMPNEY Ebenezer, gentleman, of New Ipswich, vs McCLENCHE John, yeoman, of Amherst, doc date 1772, writ, debt, file #923

CHAMPNEY Ebenezer, esquire, of New Ipswich, vs LAKE Daniel, yeoman, of Rindge, doc date 1774, writ, debt, file #1038

CHAMPNEY Ebenezer, gentleman, of New Ipswich, vs WILKINS John, yeoman, of Amherst, doc date 1772, writ, debt, file #923

CHAMPNEY Ebenezer, esquire, of Groton MA, vs REED James, esquire, of Keene, rec date 1785, judgment, debt, file #5509

CHAMPNEY Ebenezer, gentleman, of New Ipswich, vs HONEY Peter, yeoman, of Mason, doc date 1773, execution, debt, file #1492

CHAMPNEY Ebenezer, gentleman, of Hillsborough, vs CROSBY Jasaniah, yeoman, of Peterborough, doc date 1773, execution, debt, file #1450

CHAMPNEY Ebenezer, gentleman, of New Ipswich, vs SMITH Nathaniel, yeoman, of Mason, doc date 1773, execution, debt, file #1491

CHAMPNEY Ebenezer, vs McCOY William, doc date 1774, note & cost papers, file #1142

CHAMPNEY Ebenezer, esquire, of New Ipswich, vs McCOY William, yeoman, of Peterborough, doc date 1774, writ, debt, file #1145

CHAMPNEY Ebenezer, of New Ipswich, vs CROSBY Jasaniah, yeoman, of Peterborough, doc date 1773, execution, debt, file #1481

CHAMPNEY Ebenezer, gentleman, of New Ipswich, vs COBURN Robert, gentleman, of Hollis, doc date 1773, judgment, debt, file #1325

CHAMPNEY Ebenezer, esquire, of Groton MA, vs HALE Paul, yeoman, of Peterborough, doc date 1784, execution, debt, file #1518

CHAMPNEY Ebenezer, esquire, of Groton MA, vs TAYLOR Isaiah, yeoman, of Peterborough, doc date 1784, execution, debt, file #1777

CHAMPNEY Ebenezer, gentleman, of New Ipswich, vs McKILLIPS David, yeoman, of Henniker, doc date 1773, execution, debt, file #1493

CHAMPNEY Ebenezer, esquire, of Groton MA, vs TAYLOR Jonathan, husbandman, of Jaffrey, doc date 1784, execution, debt, file #1665

CHAMPNEY Ebenezer, esquire, of Groton MA, vs TAGGART John, gentleman, of Peterborough Slip, doc date 1784, ejectment, land dispute, file #1600

CHAMPNEY Ebenezer, esquire, of Groton MA, vs MINOT Jinas, gentleman, of MA, doc date 1784, writ, debt, file #1623

CHAMPNEY Ebenezer, esquire, of New Ipswich, vs McCAY William, yeoman, of Peterborough, doc date 1777, judgment, debt, file #2040

CHAMPNEY Ebenezer, esquire, of Groton MA, vs COBB Stephen, husbandman, of Packersfield, doc date 1784, execution, debt, file #1923

CHAMPNEY Ebenezer, esquire, of New Ipswich, vs WILSON John, husbandman, of Peterborough, doc date 1775, judgment, debt, file #2038

CHAMPNEY Ebenezer, esquire, of New Ipswich, vs YOUNG John, husbandman, of Peterborough, doc date 1775, judgment, debt, file #2038

CHAMPNEY Ebenezer, esquire, of Groton MA, vs TAYLOR Isaiah, yeoman, of Peterborough, doc date 1784, execution, debt, file #1924

CHAMPNEY Ebenezer, esquire, of Groton MA, vs WILKINS Jonathan, husbandman, of Amherst, doc date 1784, execution, debt, file #1943

CHAMPNEY Ebenezer, esquire, of Groton MA, vs HERRICK Joseph, yeoman, of Mason, rec date 1785, judgment, debt, file #5521

CHAMPNEY Ebenezer, esquire, of Groton MA, vs KIMBALL Stephen, gentleman, of Concord, rec date 1786, judgment, debt, file #2294

CHAMPNEY Ebenezer, esquire, of Groton MA, vs SCRIPTURE Samuel, yeoman, of Mason, rec date 1785, judgment, debt, file #5526

CHAMPNEY Ebenezer, esquire, of Groton MA, vs FRYE Isaac, gentleman, of Wilton, rec date 1788, writ, debt, file #2550

CHAMPNEY Ebenezer, esquire, of Groton MA, vs GRAY Robert, innkeeper, of Peterborough, rec date 1783, execution, debt, file #2986

CHAMPNEY Ebenezer, esquire, of Groton MA, vs WILKINS Jonathan, husbandman, of Amherst, rec date 1783, execution, debt, file #2985

CHAMPNEY Ebenezer, esquire, of Groton MA, vs TAYLOR Josiah, yeoman, of Peterborough, rec date 1783, execution, debt, file #2993

CHAMPNEY Ebenezer, esquire, of Groton MA, vs CUNNINGHAM Thomas, yeoman, of Peterborough, rec date 1783, writ, debt, file #3436

CHAMPNEY Ebenezer, esquire, of New Ipswich, vs SANDERS Joseph, gentleman, of Derryfield, rec date 1783, writ, debt, file #3287

CHAMPNEY Ebenezer, esquire, of Groton MA, vs CUMINGS Prudence, widow, of Peterborough, rec date 1783, writ, debt, file #3437

CHAMPNEY Ebenezer, esquire, of Groton MA, vs TAYLOR Isaiah, yeoman, of Peterborough, rec date 1783, writ, debt, file #3456

CHAMPNEY Ebenezer, esquire, of Groton MA, vs HAYWOOD James, yeoman, of Jaffrey, rec date 1783, writ, debt, file #3438

CHAMPNEY Ebenezer, esquire, of Groton MA, vs GRAY Robert, innkeeper, of Peterborough, rec date 1783, writ, debt, file #3454

CHAMPNEY Ebenezer, esquire, of New Ipswich, vs COBB Stephen, husbandman, of Packersfield, rec date 1783, writ, debt, file #3443

CHAMPNEY Ebenezer, esquire, of Groton MA, vs POWERS Whitcomb, yeoman, of Jaffrey, rec date 1783, writ, debt, file #3438

CHAMPNEY Ebenezer, esquire, of New Ipswich, vs ABBOTT Samuel, yeoman, of Hollis, rec date 1783, execution, debt, file #3663

CHAMPNEY Ebenezer, esquire, of Groton MA, vs AMES David, yeoman, of Peterborough, rec date 1783, execution, debt, file #3685

CHAMPNEY Ebenezer, esquire, of Groton MA, vs MACK Daniel, husbandman, of Acworth, rec date 1783, writ, debt, file #3462

CHAMPNEY Ebenezer, esquire, of Groton MA, vs AMES David, yeoman, of Peterborough, rec date 1783, writ, debt, file #3457

CHAMPNEY Ebenezer, esquire, of Groton MA, vs WILKINS Jonathan, husbandman, of Amherst, rec date 1783, writ, debt, file #3461

CHAMPNEY Ebenezer, esquire, of New Ipswich, vs BROWN Peter, yeoman, of Temple, rec date 1783, execution, debt, file #3839

CHAMPNEY Ebenezer, esquire, of Groton MA, vs BACON Retire, yeoman, of New Ipswich, rec date 1783, writ, debt, file #4069

CHAMPNEY Ebenezer, of New Ipswich, vs BROWN Peter, yeoman, of Temple, rec date 1783, writ, debt, file #3930

CHAMPNEY Ebenezer, esquire, of Groton MA, vs FELT Benjamin, blacksmith, of Temple, rec date 1784, judgment, debt, file #4379

CHAMPNEY Ebenezer, esquire, of Groton MA, vs STEARNS Samuel & Samuel Jr, husbandman, of Amherst, rec date 1784, judgment, debt, file #4406

CHAMPNEY Ebenezer, esquire, of Groton MA, vs SMITH John M, husbandman, of Newmarket, rec date 1784, judgment, debt, file #4341

CHAMPNEY Ebenezer, esquire, of Groton MA, vs WALLACE Matthew, gentleman, of Peterborough, rec date 1783, writ, debt, file #4552

CHAMPNEY Ebenezer, esquire, of Groton MA, vs SMITH William, esquire, of Peterborough, rec date 1783, writ, debt, file #4552

CHAMPNEY Ebenezer, esquire, of Groton MA, vs RUSSELL James, gentleman, of Litchfield, rec date 1783, writ, debt, file #4531

CHAMPNEY Ebenezer, esquire, of Groton MA, vs HALE Paul, yeoman, of Peterborough, rec date 1783, judgment, debt, file #4506

CHAMPNEY Ebenezer, esquire, of Groton MA, vs DWINNELL John, husbandman, of Londonderry, rec date 1783, judgment, debt, file #4492

CHAMPNEY Ebenezer, esquire, of Groton MA, vs TAGGART John, gentleman, of Peterborough Slip, rec date 1785, writ, debt, file #4682

CHAMPNEY Ebenezer, esquire, of Groton MA, vs TAYLOR Jonathan, husbandman, of Jaffrey, rec date 1783, judgment, debt, file #4495

CHAMPNEY Ebenezer, esquire, of New Ipswich, vs SANDERS Joseph, gentleman, of Derryfield, rec date 1785, various, debt, file #4847, fragile

CHAMPNEY Ebenezer, esquire, of Groton MA, vs BURLEY Stephen, husbandman, of Sanbornton, rec date 1785, writ, debt, file #4808

CHAMPNEY Ebenezer, esquire, of Groton MA, vs SLOAN David, husbandman, of Mason, rec date 1785, judgment, debt, file #5225

CHAMPNEY Ebenezer, esquire, of Groton MA, vs TAGGART John, gentleman, of Peterborough Slip, rec date 1784, judgment, debt, file #5314

CHAMPNEY Ebenezer, esquire, of Groton MA, vs ROGERS John, esquire, of Plymouth, rec date 1785, judgment, debt, file #5046

CHAMPNEY Ebenezer, esquire, of Groton MA, vs TARBELL Thomas, esquire, of Mason, rec date 1785, judgment, debt, file #5560

CHAMPNEY Ebenezer, esquire, of Groton MA, vs DINSMOOR Abraham, husbandman, of Lyndeborough, rec date 1785, judgment, debt, file #5507

CHAMPNEY Ebenezer, esquire, of Groton MA, vs SHEPARD John Jr, esquire, of Amherst, rec date 1785, judgment, debt, file #5566

CHAMPNEY Ebenezer, esquire, of Groton MA, vs REED Robert, esquire, of Amherst, rec date 1785, judgment, debt, file #5566

CHAMPNEY Ebenezer, esquire, of Groton MA, vs NICHOLS Moses, esquire, of Amherst, rec date 1785, judgment, debt, file #5566

CHAMPNEY Ebenezer, esquire, of Groton MA, vs GARLAND Jacob, yeoman, of Sanbornton, rec date 1785, judgment, debt, file #5841

CHAMPNEY Ebenezer, esquire, of Groton MA, vs CARRIGAIN Philip, physician, of Concord, rec date 1785, judgment, debt, file #5825

CHAMPNEY Ebenezer, esquire, of Groton MA, vs GARLAND Jacob, yeoman, of Sanbornton, rec date 1785, execution, debt, file #5787

CHAMPNEY Ebenezer, esquire, of Groton MA, vs HERRICK Joseph, yeoman, of Mason, rec date 1785, execution, debt, file #5955

CHAMPNEY Ebenezer, esquire, of Groton MA, vs COPLAND Jacob, esquire, of Stoddard, rec date 1785, writ, debt, file #6035

CHAMPNEY Ebenezer, esquire, of Groton MA, vs ELKINS Jonathan, yeoman, of Nottingham, rec date 1786, various, debt, file #6211

CHAMPNEY Ebenezer, esquire, of Groton MA, vs NICHOLS Moses, esquire, of Amherst, rec date 1786, judgment, debt, file #6473

CHAMPNEY Ebenezer, esquire, of Groton MA, vs MAGOON Joseph & Ephraim, of Thornton, rec date 1785, judgment, debt, file #6406

CHAMPNEY Ebenezer, esquire, of Groton MA, vs SHEPPARD John, esquire, of Amherst, rec date 1786, judgment, debt, file #6473

CHAMPNEY Ebenezer, esquire, of Groton MA, vs BOYNTON Joshua, husbandman, of Hollis, rec date 1786, writ, debt, file #6327

CHAMPNEY Ebenezer, esquire, of Groton MA, vs READ Robert, esquire, of Amherst, rec date 1786, judgment, debt, file #6473

CHAMPNEY Ebenezer, esquire, of Groton MA, vs SCOTT David, husbandman, of Stoddard, rec date 1787, writ, debt, file #6661

CHAMPNEY Ebenezer, esquire, of Groton MA, vs COLBY Sargent, husbandman, of Dunbarton, rec date 1788, writ, debt, file #6619

CHAMPNEY Ebenezer, esquire, of Groton MA, vs MOULTON David, yeoman, of Weare, rec date 1788, writ, debt, file #6620

CHAMPNEY Ebenezer, esquire, of Groton MA, vs O'NEIL John, schoolmaster, of Goffstown, rec date 1788, writ, debt, file #6618

CHAMPNEY Ebenezer, esquire, of Groton MA, vs DAVIS Benjamin, husbandman, of Amherst, rec date 1787, writ, debt, file #6655

CHAMPNEY Ebenezer, esquire, of Groton MA, vs NUTTING Simeon, yeoman, of Jaffrey, rec date 1787, writ, debt, file #6891

CHAMPNEY Ebenezer, esquire, of Groton MA, vs CHAMBERLAIN John, husbandman, of Peterborough Slip, rec date 1788, writ, debt, file #6714

CHAMPNEY Ebenezer, esquire, of Groton MA, vs BALL Joseph, yeoman, of Mason, rec date 1788, writ, debt, file #6716

CHAMPNEY Ebenezer, esquire, of New Ipswich, vs SAUNDERS Joseph, gentleman, of Derryfield, doc date 1784, court case, debt, file #1613

CHANDLER John, yeoman, of Boscawen, vs EVERETT Edward, gentleman, of Rumney, rec date 1783, execution, debt, file #3684

CHANDLER John, yeoman, of Boscawen, vs ATKINSON Samuel, gentleman, of Boscawen, rec date 1783, execution, debt, file #3684

CHANDLER John, husbandman, of Boscawen, vs COSTELLOR John, yeoman, of Effingham, rec date 1784, judgment, debt, file #4218

CHANDLER John, gentleman, of Boscawen, vs PATTERSON William, yeoman, of Goffstown, rec date 1788, writ, debt, file #6989

CHANDLER Joseph, yeoman, of Andover, vs EATON Levi, yeoman, of Seabrook, rec date 1783, deed, land transfer, file #2628

CHANDLER Joseph, gentleman, of Andover, vs FOWLER Samuel, esquire, of Boscawen, rec date 1783, writ, debt, file #3104

CHANDLER Joseph, gentleman, of Andover, vs WARE Peter, gentleman, of Andover, rec date 1783, writ, debt, file #3221

CHANDLER Moses, minor (laborer), of Concord, vs PERHAM William, husbandman, of Derryfield, rec date 1786, writ, debt, file #6309

CHANDLER Moses, minor (laborer), of Concord, vs GOFFE John, husbandman, of Derryfield, rec date 1786, writ, debt, file #6309

CHANDLER Zachariah, of Bedford, rec date 1777, application, tavern license, file #7034

CHANDLER Zechariah, yeoman, of Bedford, vs BURNS John, yeoman, of Bedford, doc date 1778, rec date 1778, deed, land transfer, file #2114

CHANDLER Zechariah, yeoman, of Bedford, vs CALAUGHAN John, laborer, of Bedford, doc date 1773, rec date 1785, deed, land transfer, file #5654

CHANDLER Zechariah, yeoman, of Bedford, vs MURFEY Patrick, laborer, of Bedford, doc date 1773, rec date 1777, deed, land transfer, file #5654

CHANDLER Zechariah, yeoman, of Bedford, vs DOWR John, laborer, of Bedford, doc date 1773, rec date 1777, deed, land transfer, file #5654

CHANEY John, gentleman, of Dunstable MA, vs CHAMBERS William, yeoman, of Chelmsford MA, doc date 1780, rec date 1788, deed, land transfer, file #6822, land in Hollis

CHAPMAN ----, vs NEWMARKET Manufacturing Co, doc date 1892, defendants brief, supreme court, file #618

CHAPMAN Israel & Jeremiah, estate, of Hopkinton, vs PARKER Samuel, esquire, of Boston MA, doc date 1799, judgment, debt, file #280

CHAPMAN Susanna, of Newington, vs TRICKEY James, of Newington, doc date 1770, warrant, house damage, file #825

CHASE Abner, yeoman, of Almsbury, vs FITTS Isaac, blacksmith, of Boscawen, doc date 1772, writ, debt, file #1043, fragile

CHASE Abner, yeoman, of New Almsbury, vs EASTMAN Ebenezer Jr, yeoman, of Concord, doc date 1769, rec date 1772, deed, land transfer, file #6843

CHASE Dudley, husbandman, of Deering, vs ESTEY Jonathan, husbandman, of Hillsborough, doc date 1799, debt, file #342

CHASE Ebenezer, blacksmith, of Litchfield, vs CROSS Nathan, yeoman, of Amherst, rec date 1788, writ, debt, file #6908

CHASE Henry, husbandman, of Nottingham-West, vs BURN William, gentleman, of Nottingham-West, doc date 1787, rec date 1787, deed, land transfer, file #2491

CHASE Jonathan, esquire, of Cornish, vs MARCH Clement & Stephen, esquire, of Greenland, rec date 1789, writ, land dispute, file #2568

CHASE Joshua, yeoman, of Chesterfield, vs PRATT Thomas, feltmaker, of Hollis, rec date 1784, appeal, debt, file #4106

CHASE Joshua, yeoman, of Chesterfield, vs PRATT Thomas, feltmaker, of Hollis, rec date 1784, judgment, debt, file #4411

CHASE Samuel, esquire, of Litchfield, vs TAGGART Archibald, gentleman, of Hillsborough, rec date 1788, judgment, debt, file #2559

CHASE Simeon, yeoman, of Litchfield, vs GIBSON William, yeoman, of Nottingham-West, doc date 1779, various, debt, file #2089

CHASE Wells Jr, husbandman, of Hopkinton, vs STICKNEY Richard, husbandman, of Newbury MA, rec date 1782, debt, debt, file #3143

CHASE William, husbandman, of Hopkinton, vs STRAW Jonathan, gentleman, of Hopkinton, rec date 1782, debt, debt, file #3149

CHENEY John, gentleman, of Dunstable MA, vs LAWRENCE Zachariah, yeoman, of Hollis, doc date 1784, execution, debt, file #1964

CHENEY John, gentleman, of Dunstable MA, vs LAWRENCE Zachariah, yeoman, of Hollis, rec date 1783, civil litigious, debt, file #2934

CHICKERING Isaac, tanner, of Amherst, vs CLARK Joseph (Capt), gentleman, of Sanborntown, doc date 1799, petition, dispute over animal, file #516

CHILDS Elisha, yeoman, of Temple, vs FRYE Abiel, husbandman, of Wilton, doc date 1798, execution, debt, file #131

CHOAT Solomon, yeoman, of Ipswich MA, vs PROCTOR Jonathan, yeoman, of Hopkinton, doc date 1799, debt, file #477

CHOUTE Jacob, tanner, of Enfield, vs JOHNSON Jesse, of Plymouth, doc date 1795, petition, release from jail, file #41

CHRISTY George, gentleman, of New Boston, vs BALDWIN Nahum, esquire, of Boston MA, rec date 1784, various, debt, file #4164, Z CUTLER estate

CHRISTY James, saddler, of Amherst, vs JONES Samuel, yeoman, of Hillsborough, rec date 1783, execution, debt, file #3838

CHRISTY James, saddler, of Amherst, vs JONES Samuel, yeoman, of Hillsborough, rec date 1783, writ, debt, file #3907

CHRISTY James, saddler, of Skeensboro NY, vs GIBSON Matthew, husbandman, of Francestown, rec date 1785, judgment, debt, file #4967

CHRISTY Jesse, blacksmith, of New Boston, vs TUTTLE Stephen, yeoman, of Goffstown, rec date 1786, judgment, debt, file #5762

CHUBBUCH Ensign, yeoman, of Bedford, vs POLLARD Amaziah, husbandman, of Merrimack, rec date 1783, writ, debt, file #3322

CHURCH John, husbandman, of Dunbarton, vs UNDERWOOD James, gentleman, of Bedford, doc date 1784, execution, debt, file #1789

CHURCH John, yeoman, of Dunbarton, vs HACKET Ebenezer, husbandman, of Dunbarton, rec date 1783, judgment, debt, file #3704

CHURCH John, yeoman, of Dunbarton, vs CLEMENT James, husbandman, of Dunbarton, rec date 1783, judgment, debt, file #3704

CHURCH John, husbandman, of Dunbarton, vs UNDERWOOD James, gentleman, of Bedford, rec date 1784, judgment, debt, file #4350

CILLEY Benjamin, of Andover, doc date 1787, license, tavern license, file #865

CLAGAETT Wyseman, esquire, of Litchfield, vs BARRETT Moses, gentleman, of Nottingham-West, rec date 1782, execution, debt, file #4896

CLAGET Clifton, gentleman, of Litchfield, vs HOBBS Joseph, yeoman, of Nottingham-West, rec date 1785, judgment, debt, file #5534

CLAGET Clifton, gentleman, of Litchfield, vs SENTER John, husbandman, of Hollis, rec date 1785, judgment, debt, file #5535

CLAGET Clifton, gentleman, of Litchfield, vs CALDWELL John, cordwainer, of Nottingham-West, rec date 1785, writ, debt, file #5583

CLAGETT Clifton, esquire, of Litchfield, vs CUSHING John, physician, of Goffstown, doc date 1799, execution, debt, file #209

CLAGETT Clifton, gentleman, of Litchfield, vs McQUAID Jacob, husbandman, of Bedford, rec date 1785, judgment, debt, file #4689

CLAGETT Clifton, gentleman, of Litchfield, vs HONEY Parmenter, husbandman, of Dunstable, rec date 1785, judgment, debt, file #5265

CLAGETT Clifton, gentleman, of Litchfield, vs FOSTER David, husbandman, of Bedford, rec date 1785, judgment, debt, file #5264

CLAGETT Clifton, gentleman, of Litchfield, vs McQUAID Jacob, husbandman, of Bedford, rec date 1785, judgment, debt, file #6456

CLAGETT Clifton, gentleman, of Litchfield, vs COTTON Samuel, clerk, of Litchfield, rec date 1788, writ, debt, file #6601

CLAGETT Clifton, esquire, of Litchfield, vs LITTLE John, gentleman, of Derryfield, rec date 1788, writ, debt, file #6983

CLAGETT Clifton, gentleman, of Litchfield, vs MAXWELL Thomas, gentleman, of Shruesbury MA, rec date 1788, writ, debt, file #6984

CLAGETT Lettice, widow, of Litchfield, vs CALDWELL John, cordwainer, of Nottingham-West, rec date 1785, writ, debt, file #5580

CLAGETT Lettice, widow, of Litchfield, vs PEMBERTON James, husbandman, of Nottingham-West, rec date 1785, execution, debt, file #5937

CLAGETT Lettice, gentleman, of Litchfield, vs MAXWELL Thomas, gentleman, of Shruesbury MA, rec date 1788, writ, debt, file #6984

CLAGETT Lettice & Clifton, widow, of Litchfield, vs PEMBERTON James, husbandman, of Nottingham-West, rec date 1785, judgment, debt, file #5851

CLAGETT Lettice, widow, of Litchfield, vs SAUNDERS James, husbandman, of Salem, rec date 1788, writ, debt, file #6600

CLAGETT Waseman, rec date 1788, note, file #7028

CLAGETT Wentworth, husbandman, of Litchfield, vs SMITH Edward, innkeeper, of Boston MA, rec date 1785, judgment, animal dispute, file #5357

CLAGETT Wentworth, husbandman, of Litchfield, vs KARR James & Samuel, husbandman, of Hanover, rec date 1788, writ, debt, file #6938

CLAGETT Wyecomon, esquire, of Litchfield, vs MOULTON Josiah, gentleman, of Hampton, doc date 1784, execution, debt, file #1761

CLAGETT Wyman, of Litchfield, vs MACK Robert Jr, blacksmith, of Charlestown, doc date 1773, execution, debt, file #1475

CLAGETT Wyman, esquire, of Litchfield, vs SHURTLETT Jonathan, husbandman, of Merrimack, rec date 1784, judgment, debt, file #6413

CLAGETT Wyseman, esquire, of Litchfield, vs CUMINGS Samuel, esquire, of Hollis, rec date 1777, writ, debt, file #2190

CLAGETT Wyseman, esquire, of Litchfield, vs SHURTLEFF Jonathan, husbandman, of Merrimack, rec date 1784, appeal, debt, file #4117

CLAGETT Wyseman, esquire, of Litchfield, vs MOULTON Josiah Jr, gentleman, of Hampton, rec date 1783, execution, debt, file #4909

CLAGETT Wyseman, deceased, of Litchfield, rec date 1787, writ, debt, file #6701

CLAGETT Wyseman, deceased, of Litchfield, vs MAXWELL Thomas, gentleman, of Shruesbury MA, rec date 1788, writ, debt, file #6984

CLAGGETT Alfred, gentleman, of Litchfield, vs WARNER Jonathan, esquire, of Portsmouth, rec date 1788, various, debt, file #6584

CLAGGETT Lettice, widow, of Litchfield, vs WARNER Jonathan, esquire, of Portsmouth, rec date 1788, various, debt, file #6584

CLAGGETT Wyseman, deceased, rec date 1788, various, debt, file #6584

CLALGETT Clifton, gentleman, of Litchfield, vs WARNER Jonathan, esquire, of Portsmouth, rec date 1787, writ, debt, file #6701

CLALGETT Lettice, widow, of Litchfield, vs WARNER Jonathan, esquire, of Portsmouth, rec date 1787, writ, debt, file #6701

CLARK Abigail, single, of Boston MA, vs TYNG John, gentleman, of Dunstable, doc date 1753, rec date 1753, deed, land transfer, file #2171

CLARK Bunker, husbandman, of New Ipswich, vs INGALLS Solomon, yeoman, of Packersfield, rec date 1785, execution, debt, file #5917

CLARK Bunker, husbandman, of New Ipswich, vs INGELS Solomon, yeoman, of Packersfield, rec date 1785, judgment, debt, file #5830

CLARK Daniel, of Boscawen, doc date 1772, license, tavern license, file #853

CLARK Elijah, wheelwright, vs LAWRENCE Ephraim, of Pepperell MA, doc date 1791, petition, release of debit, file #19

CLARK Ephraim, husbandman, of Hillsborough, vs MURRY Ralph, esquire, of St Johnsbury VT, doc date 1799, petition, release from jail, file #37

CLARK Ephraim, yeoman, of Deering, vs DODGE Samuel, esquire, of Amherst, rec date 1783, writ, debt, file #3011

CLARK Ephraim, yeoman, of Deering, vs ATHERTON Joshua, esquire, of Amherst, rec date 1783, writ, debt, file #3011

CLARK Ephraim, yeoman, of Deering, vs STEELE Moses, yeoman, of Hillsborough, doc date 1799, writ, debt, file #430

CLARK Gilman Peter, esquire, of Lyndeborough, vs POLLARD Samuel, husbandman, of Nottingham-West, rec date 1785, writ, debt, file #6150

CLARK Hannah, of Ashby MA, rec date 1787, various, debt, file #6700

CLARK Isaac, gentleman, of New Ipswich, vs HARRIS Robert, merchant, of Boston MA, rec date 1785, writ, debt, file #5382

CLARK John, yeoman, of Londonderry, vs CLARK George, yeoman, of Londonderry, doc date 1765, judgment, debt, file #783

CLARK Joseph, husbandman, of Hillsborough, vs ELLINGWOOD Samuel, husbandman, of Hillsborough, doc date 1801, rec date 1801, deed, land transfer, file #5670

CLARK Joshua, yeoman, of Amherst, vs GAUT Thomas, yeoman, of Bedford, doc date 1784, execution, debt, file #1503

CLARK Joshua, yeoman, of Amherst, vs GAUT Thomas, yeoman, of Bedford, rec date 1783, judgment, debt, file #4454

CLARK Joshua, yeoman, of Amherst, vs FRENCH William, yeoman, of Hollis, rec date 1786, writ, debt, file #6269

CLARK Joshua Jr, husbandman, of Amherst, vs FRENCH Ephraim, yeoman, of Amherst, rec date 1785, writ, debt, file #2404

CLARK Josiah, husbandman, of Hillsborough, vs EATON Moses, husbandman, of Francestown, doc date 1799, judgment, debt, file #231

CLARK Josiah, esquire, of Nottingham, vs RAWLINS Philip, esquire, of Westford MA, doc date 1772, writ, debt, file #917

CLARK Lydia, widow, of Amherst, vs UNDERWOOD James, gentleman, of Goffstown, rec date 1785, judgment, debt, file #5802

CLARK Ninian, husbandman, of New Boston, vs RAMSEY Jonathan, yeoman, of New Boston, rec date 1784, judgment, debt, file #4925

CLARK Peter, esquire, of Lyndeborough, vs Town of Lyndeborough, doc date 1796, various, road dispute, file #506

CLARK Peter, esquire, of Lyndeborough, vs RICHARDSON Zachariah, innkeeper, of Francestown, rec date 1787, judgment, debt, file #2463

CLARK Peter, esquire, of Lyndeborough, vs CARSON John, gentleman, of Francestown, rec date 1787, judgment, debt, file #2463, Benjamin DODGE estate

CLARK Peter, esquire, of Lyndeborough, vs CARSON John, gentleman, of Francestown, rec date 1786, judgment, debt, file #2461

CLARK Peter, esquire, of Lyndeborough, vs BOSSEE Thomas, gentleman, of Lyndeborough, rec date 1784, judgment, debt, file #4351

CLARK Peter, esquire, of Lyndeborough, vs HUSTON Samuel, gentleman, of Lyndeborough, doc date 1808, rec date 1814, deed, land transfer, file #5697

CLARK Peter, esquire, of Lyndeborough, vs LEWIS Aaron, gentleman, of Lyndeborough, doc date 1808, rec date 1814, deed, land transfer, file #5697

CLARK Peter, esquire, of Lyndeborough, vs MURDOUGH Samuel & Thomas, husbandman, of Hillsborough, rec date 1785, writ, debt, file #6006

CLARK Peter, esquire, of Lyndeborough, vs JONES James, husbandman, of Hillsborough, rec date 1785, judgment, debt, file #5993

CLARK Peter, esquire, of Lyndeborough, vs MURDOUGH Thomas, husbandman, of Hillsborough, rec date 1785, judgment, debt, file #5993

CLARK Peter, esquire, of Lyndeborough, vs JONES James, husbandman, of Hillsborough, rec date 1785, writ, debt, file #6006

CLARK Peter, esquire, of Lyndeborough, vs KIDDER Jonas, gentleman, of Lyndeborough, doc date 1808, rec date 1814, deed, land transfer, file #5697

CLARK Peter, esquire, of Lyndeborough, vs EPES Joseph, gentleman, of Lyndeborough, doc date 1808, rec date 1814, deed, land transfer, file #5697

CLARK Peter, esquire, of Lyndeborough, vs CLARK John, yeoman, of Lyndeborough, doc date 1808, rec date 1814, deed, land transfer, file #5697

CLARK Peter, esquire, of Lyndeborough, vs CLARK John Jr, yeoman, of Lyndeborough, doc date 1808, rec date 1814, deed, land transfer, file #5697

CLARK Peter, esquire, of Lyndeborough, vs GADNER Daniel, yeoman, of Lyndeborough, doc date 1808, rec date 1814, deed, land transfer, file #5697

CLARK Peter, esquire, of Lyndeborough, vs JONES Benjamin, esquire, of Lyndeborough, doc date 1808, rec date 1814, deed, land transfer, file #5697

CLARK Peter, esquire, of Lyndeborough, vs CARION John, innholder, of Lyndeborough, rec date 1787, judgment, debt, file #6206

CLARK Peter, esquire, of Lyndeborough, vs RICHARDSON Zachariah, innholder, of Lyndeborough, rec date 1787, judgment, debt, file #6206

CLARK Samuel, physician, rec date 1785, loose paper, file #5493

CLARK Thomas, yeoman, of Amherst, vs SPRAGUE John, esquire, of Lancaster MA, doc date 1774, writ, debt, file #1083

CLARK Thomas, yeoman, of Dunstable, vs GORDON James, merchant, of Dunstable MA, rec date 1782, writ, debt, file #2785

CLARK Tim, yeoman, of Amherst, vs GORDON James, merchant, of Dunstable MA, rec date 1782, writ, debt, file #2785

CLARK Timothy, husbandman, of Amherst, vs WHEAT Joseph, cooper, of Amherst, doc date 1799, writ, debt, file #351

CLARK Timothy, husbandman, of Amherst, vs LUNT David, yeoman, of Amherst, doc date 1799, writ, debt, file #375

CLARK Timothy, husbandman, of Amherst, vs EMERSON Dearborn, stage driver, of Amherst, doc date 1799, writ, debt, file #351

CLARK Timothy, yeoman, of Amherst, vs SPRAGUE John, esquire, of Lancaster MA, doc date 1774, writ, debt, file #1083

CLARK Timothy, yeoman, of Pelham, vs FLANDERS Thomas, yeoman, of Candia, doc date 1772, writ, debt, file #1405

CLARK Timothy, yeoman, of Pelham, vs FLANDERS Benjamin, cordwainer, of Candia, doc date 1772, writ, debt, file #1405

CLARK Timothy, yeoman, of Amherst, vs McCLENCHE John, cordwainer, of Merrimack, doc date 1779, writ, trespass of land, file #2101

CLARK Timothy, yeoman, of Amherst, vs ALEXANDER John, yeoman, of Peterborough Slip, rec date 1785, writ, debt, file #2356

CLARK Timothy, yeoman, of Amherst, vs WILSON Thomas, gentleman, of New Boston, rec date 1783, writ, debt, file #3198

CLARKE Bunker, yeoman, of New Ipswich, vs READ Benjamin, yeoman, of Chelmsford MA, rec date 1784, judgment, debt, file #4236

CLEAVES Nathan, yeoman, of Amherst, vs BRADFORD William, yeoman, of Deering, rec date 1783, judgment, debt, file #3734

CLEMENT James, husbandman, of Dunbarton, vs CHURCH John, yeoman, of Dunbarton, rec date 1783, writ, debt, file #3100

CLEMENT James, husbandman, of Dunbarton, vs STEWART James (estate), gentleman, of Dunbarton, rec date 1782, debt, debt, file #3152

CLEMENT James, husbandman, of Dunbarton, vs STEWART James, gentleman, of Dunbarton, rec date 1783, judgment, debt, file #3705

CLEMENT Patrick, currier, of Bow, vs FRENCH Daniel, yeoman, of Hopkinton, doc date 1782, execution, file #1028

CLEMENT Samuel, husbandman, of Salem, vs AYER Peter, tanner, of Haverhill MA, doc date 1772, civil litigation, debt, file #655

CLEMENT Timothy, innholder, of Chester, vs HOW Peter, husbandman, of Hopkinton, doc date 1774, writ, debt, file #745

CLEMENTS Jesse, gentleman, of Weare, vs SARGENT Moses, husbandman, of Weare, rec date 1788, writ, debt, file #6934

CLEMENTS John, physician, of Hopkinton, vs HOW Theodore, husbandman, of Henniker, doc date 1773, judgment, debt, file #1288

CLEMENTS Jonathan, yeoman, of Weare, vs UNDERWOOD James, esquire, of Goffstown, rec date 1786, writ, debt, file #2362

CLEMENTS Jonathan, yeoman, of Weare, vs UNDERWOOD James, esquire, of Goffstown, rec date 1786, judgment, debt, file #5750

CLEWIS Jonathan Clark, deceased, of Groton, vs YOUNG John, physician, of Peterborough, rec date 1784, judgment, debt, file #4372

CLEWIS Jonathan Clark, deceased, of Groton, vs TAGGART James, yeoman, of N Y, rec date 1784, judgment, debt, file #4372

CLIFFORD Israel, innholder, of Dunbarton, vs DOW Oliver, gentleman, of Hopkinton, rec date 1784, judgment, debt, file #4195

CLOGETT Clifton, gentleman, of Litchfield, vs POPE William, husbandman, of Hillsborough, doc date 1784, execution, debt, file #1781

CLOGSTON John Jr, husbandman, of Goffstown, vs MARTIN Robert, laborer, of Goffstown, doc date 1783, rec date 1789, deed, land transfer, file #6570

CLOGSTONE John, yeoman, of Goffstown, vs GOSS John, esquire, of Deerfield, doc date 1772, writ, debt, file #896

CLOUGH Benjamin, husbandman, of Henniker, vs BRUCE Joseph, husbandman, of Washington, doc date 1784, execution, debt, file #1906

CLOUGH Benjamin, husbandman, of Henniker, vs BRUCE Joseph, husbandman, of Washington, rec date 1783, writ, debt, file #3374

CLOUGH David, husbandman, of Henniker, vs CAMPBELL David, esquire, of Henniker, doc date 1798, judgment, debt, file #562

CLOUGH David, husbandman, of Weare, vs MAXFIELD Joshua, husbandman, of Weare, rec date 1783, judgment, debt, file #4488

CLOUGH James, yeoman, of Hopkinton, vs WEST Mary, widow, of Haverhill MA, rec date 1783, writ, debt, file #3105, administrator of Thomas WEST estate

CLOUGH John, yeoman, of Henniker, vs SPAULDING Joseph, yeoman, of Henniker, rec date 1785, writ, debt, file #6225, deed copy

COBURN George, husbandman, of Wilton, vs BALLARD Nathan, gentleman, of Wilton, rec date 1785, judgment, debt, file #5598

COBURN Lydia, spinster, of Dracut MA, vs LEARY John, cordwainer, of Litchfield, doc date 1777, fornication, file #761

COBURN Nathan, yeoman, of Mason, vs AFTEN Timothy, yeoman, of Temple, doc date 1772, writ, debt, file #1432

COBURN Oliver, yeoman, of Dunstable MA, vs RUSSELL James, gentleman, of Goffstown, rec date 1785, writ, debt, file #5263

COBURN Peter, gentleman, of Dracut MA, vs DAKIN Justus, yeoman, of Nottingham-West, doc date 1784, execution, debt, file #1734

COBURN Robert, gentleman, of Hollis, vs JEWETT Jacob Jr, yeoman, of Hollis, doc date 1774, writ, debt, file #1085

COCHAM Isaac, husbandman, of Antrim, vs MOOR John, husbandman, of Francestown, rec date 1785, judgment, debt, file #6444

COCHRAN Isaac, husbandman, of Antrim, vs MOOR John, husbandman, of Francestown, rec date 1785, writ, debt, file #6010

COCHRAN James, yeoman, of Amherst, vs GILBERT Sanford, of Amherst, doc date 1777, deed, land transfer, file #2057

COCHRAN James, yeoman, of Andover MA, vs COCHRAN John, yeoman, of Amherst, rec date 1783, judgment, debt, file #4477

COCHRAN John, yeoman, vs BALDWIN Nahum, esquire, of Amherst, rec date 1782, writ, debt, file #2670, estate of Zacheus CUTLER

COCHRAN John, yeoman, of Amherst, vs HALE Paul, gentleman, of Peterborough, rec date 1783, writ, debt, file #3018

COCHRAN John, yeoman, of Amherst, vs STEVENS Samuel, yeoman, of Amherst, rec date 1783, writ, debt, file #3194

COCHRAN John, rec date 1783, work journal, file #3536

COCHRAN John, yeoman, of New Boston, vs JONES Samuel, yeoman, of Hillsborough, rec date 1783, writ, debt, file #3895

COCKRAN Jacob, husbandman, of Enfield, vs FIFIELD William, husbandman, of Salisbury, rec date 1785, judgment, debt, file #5201

COCKRAN John, yeoman, of New Boston, vs JONES Samuel, yeoman, of Hillsborough, rec date 1783, execution, debt, file #3284

COCKRAN Peter, husbandman, of New Boston, vs DICKERMAN Samuel, blacksmith, of Francestown, rec date 1784, judgment, debt, file #5157

CODMAN Henry, yeoman, of Amherst, vs MANN Robert, yeoman, of Camden, doc date 1774, execution, debt, file #751

CODMAN Henry, of Amherst, doc date 1772, license, tavern license, file #854

CODMAN Henry, yeoman, of Amherst, vs MANN Robert, yeoman, of Camden, doc date 1775, writ, debt, file #950

CODMAN Henry, trader, of Amherst, vs MILLS John, yeoman, of Amherst, doc date 1772, writ, debt, file #1424

CODMAN Henry, trader, of Amherst, vs SARGENT Paul Dudley, merchant, of Amherst, doc date 1773, writ, debt, file #1236

CODMAN Henry, yeoman, of Amherst, vs WILEY John, yeoman, of Amherst, doc date 1784, execution, debt, file #1752

CODMAN Henry, physician, of Amherst, vs WILKINS John, gentleman, of Francestown, rec date 1782, appeal, debt, file #4002

CODMAN Henry, physician, of Amherst, vs ROSS Jonathan, yeoman, of Henniker, rec date 1784, judgment, debt, file #4270

CODMAN Henry, physician, of Amherst, vs HAZELTINE Nathaniel, cordwainer, of Amherst, rec date 1787, judgment, debt, file #4661

CODMAN Henry, physician, of Amherst, vs HACKET Mary, widow, of Francestown, rec date 1785, judgment, debt, file #4942, Mary was Mary STEARNS in 1772

CODMAN Henry, husbandman, of Amherst, vs CONRAY John, husbandman, of Goffstown, rec date 1785, judgment, debt, file #5588

CODMAN Henry, physician, of Amherst, vs HACKET Mary, widow, of Francestown, rec date 1785, judgment, debt, file #6000

CODMAN Henry, physician, of Amherst, vs HASELTON Nathaniel, cordwainer, of Amherst, rec date 1787, judgment, debt, file #6184

CODMAN Peter, trader, of Hillsborough, vs WILSON David, yeoman, of New Boston, doc date 1799, writ, debt, file #429, fragile

COGGIN Joseph, blacksmith, of Amherst, vs WELLS John, yeoman, of New Boston, doc date 1784, execution, debt, file #1901

COGGIN Joseph, blacksmith, of Amherst, vs CHASE Ebenezer, blacksmith, of Litchfield, rec date 1788, judgment, debt, file #7053

COGIN Joseph, blacksmith, of Amherst, vs CHASE Ebenezer, blacksmith, of Litchfield, rec date 1788, writ, debt, file #2389

COGIN Joseph, blacksmith, of Amherst, vs WELLS John, yeoman, of New Boston, rec date 1783, writ, debt, file #3592

COGSWELL Emerson, feltmaker, of Concord MA, vs HOSMER William, yeoman, of Mason, rec date 1784, judgment, debt, file #4382

COGSWELL Nehemiah, husbandman, of Boscawen, vs MUZZEY Samuel, husbandman, of Boscawen, rec date 1783, judgment, debt, file #4482

COLBURN Benjamin, husbandman, of Hollis, vs GRIDLEY Samuel, gentleman, of Boston MA, rec date 1783, judgment, debt, file #4707, estate of Robert COLBURN

COLBURN George, husbandman, of Wilton, vs GRAY Robert, innholder, of Peterborough, rec date 1786, writ, debt, file #6054

COLBURN James, cordwainer, of Hollis, vs GOLD Jonas, yeoman, of Cockermouth, doc date 1774, execution, debt, file #1208

COLBURN James, wheelwright, of Concord MA, vs BARNS Joseph, housewright, of Concord MA, doc date 1779, rec date 1785, deed, land transfer, file #5618

COLBURN Oliver, gentleman, of Dunstable MA, vs McMASON Samuel, of Lyndeborough, rec date 1785, writ, debt, file #5403

COLBURN Peter, gentleman, of Dracut MA, vs FLETCHER Robert, esquire, of Dunstable, rec date 1788, writ, debt, file #6991

COLBURN Robert, yeoman, of Hollis, vs FRENCH William Jr, yeoman, of Hollis, doc date 1790, rec date 1790, deed, land transfer, file #6573

COLBY Benjamin, husbandman, of Hopkinton, vs PEASLEE Francis, gentleman, of Fisherfield, doc date 1799, debt, file #474

COLBY Ebenezer, husbandman, of Bradford, vs WHITCOMB Benjamin, yeoman, of Henniker, doc date 1799, debt, file #502

COLBY Elizabeth, singleman, of Boscawen, vs LITTLE Benjamin & Enoch, husbandman, of Boscawen, rec date 1782, writ, child support, file #4848

COLBY Ephraim, gentleman, of Concord, vs WEARE Peter, gentleman, of Andover, rec date 1788, various, ownership of horse, file #6588

COLBY Ephraim, gentleman, of Concord, vs WEARE Peter, gentleman, of Andover, rec date 1787, writ, debt, file #6786

COLBY Hezekiel, yeoman, of Boscawen, vs ATKINSON Samuel, gentleman, of Boscawen, rec date 1782, writ, debt, file #2626

COLBY Isaac, husbandman, of Weare, vs McGREGOR David, esquire, of Londonderry, rec date 1786, various, trespass, file #6080

COLBY Lamson, physician, of Hopkinton, vs COSTON Ebenezer, yeoman, of Wilton, doc date 1772, writ, debt, file #1067

COLBY Philbrick, yeoman, of Nottingham-West, vs STEEL William, husbandman, of Nottingham-West, rec date 1785, various, debt, file #5273

COLBY Samson, physician, of Hopkinton, vs HOMER John, trader, of Winchendon MA, doc date 1774, writ, debt, file #1152

COLLIDGE Silas, yeoman, of Hillsborough, vs DODGE Samuel, yeoman, of Amherst, rec date 1782, writ, debt, file #2820

COLLIDGE Silas, husbandman, of Hillsborough, vs ANDREWS Ammi, gentleman, of Hillsborough, rec date 1783, writ, debt, file #3205

COLLINS Moses, cordwainer, of Malden MA, vs WHITTERMORE Pelatiah, husbandman, of New Ipswich, rec date 1784, writ, debt, file #4228

COLLINS Moses, cordwainer, of Malden MA, vs HEALD Thomas, esquire, of New Ipswich, rec date 1782, judgment, debt, file #4511

COLLS Stephen, esquire, of Bedford, vs GADER John, yeoman, of Bedford, rec date 1783, various, stealing sheep, file #4062

COLMAN Aaron, yeoman, of Peterborough Slip, vs DELAP Robert, yeoman, of Jaffrey, rec date 1782, judgment, debt, file #2721, 102

COMBES Medad, yeoman, of Hollis, vs STATE of NH, rec date 1783, recognizance, debt, file #2608

COMICK John, yeoman, of Hollis, vs GALUSHA Daniel, yeoman, of Lynn MA, doc date 1784, petition, release of debit, file #5

CONANT John, miller, of Townsend MA, vs CUNNINGHAM James, yeoman, of Peterborough, doc date 1779, rec date 1783, deed, land transfer, file #2655

CONANT John, husbandman, of Townsend MA, vs ABBOT Benjamin, yeoman, of Hollis, rec date 1783, judgment, debt, file #3770

CONANT John, husbandman, of Townsend MA, vs WRIGHT Uriah, gentleman, of Hollis, rec date 1784, judgment, debt, file #4262

CONANT Josiah, joiner, of Hollis, vs MERRILL Daniel, gentleman, of Hollis, doc date 1782, rec date 1785, deed, land transfer, file #5642

CONAWAY John, mariner, of Marblehead MA, vs PIERCE James, yeoman, of Deerfield, doc date 1784, execution, debt, file #1799

CONEK James, gentleman, of Raby, vs BLANCHARD Rebecca, widow, of Dunstable, doc date 1772, writ, debt, file #901

CONEY John, yeoman, of Lyndeborough, vs ROBBE William, gentleman, of Peterborough, rec date 1783, writ, debt, file #3586

CONNER James, trader, of Lyndeborough, vs CARLTON Samuel, yeoman, of Greenfield, doc date 1798, execution, debt, file #146

CONNER Simeon, of Andover, vs SELECTMEN of Andover, doc date 1787, license, tavern license, file #864

CONNICK William, husbandman, of Hollis, vs NUTTING John, husbandman, of Hollis, rec date 1787, writ, debt, file #2427

CONNICK William, laborer, of Hollis, vs POOL Jonathan, physician, of Hollis, rec date 1786, judgment, debt, file #2457

CONOWAY John, mariner, of Marblehead MA, vs PIERCE James Jr, yeoman, of Deerfield, rec date 1783, judgment, debt, file #4712

CONRY John, yeoman, of Hollis, vs JEWET Jacob Jr, yeoman, of Hollis, doc date 1773, writ, debt, file #1368

COOK Noah, gentleman, of New Ipswich, vs STARK John, esquire, of Derryfield, rec date 1785, writ, debt, file #5376

COOLEDGE Uriah, yeoman, of Hillsborough, vs BRADFORD Eliphalet, yeoman, of Hillsborough, rec date 1786, judgment, debt, file #6203

COOLIDGE Nathaniel, yeoman, of Hillsborough, vs BARNES William, yeoman, of Antrim, doc date 1799, debt, file #346

COOLIDGE Nathaniel, husbandman, of Hillsborough, vs MINOTT Joseph, husbandman, of Hillsborough, doc date 1799, writ, debt, file #324

COOLIDGE Nathaniel, yeoman, of Hillsborough, vs JONES Nehemiah, trader, of Hillsborough, doc date 1799, debt, file #339

COOLIDGE Nathaniel Jr, yeoman, of Hillsborough, vs JONES Nehemiah, yeoman, of Hillsborough, doc date 1799, writ, debt, file #423

COOLIDGE Silas, yeoman, of Hillsborough, vs DOW Peter, clothier, of Goffstown, rec date 1782, writ, debt, file #2809

COOLIDGE Silas, yeoman, of Hillsborough, vs STEEL Moses, yeoman, of Hillsborough, rec date 1782, writ, debt, file #2829

COOLIDGE Silas, yeoman, of Hillsborough, vs DRESSER Asa, yeoman, of Campbells Gore, rec date 1783, writ, debt, file #3041

COOLIDGE Silas, yeoman, of Hillsborough, vs DRESSER Asa, yeoman, of Campbells Gore, rec date 1783, writ, debt, file #3027

COOLIDGE Silas, yeoman, of Hillsborough, vs DRESSER Asa, yeoman, of Campbells Gore, rec date 1783, writ, debt, file #4324

COOMBS John, gentleman, of Amherst, vs SHANNON Andrew, yeoman, of Amherst, doc date 1798, execution, debt, file #57

COPP Joshua, husbandman, of Hampstead, vs MANSIS Cornelius, merchant, of Haverhill MA, doc date 1772, writ, debt, file #1053

COPP Joshua, husbandman, of Hampstead, vs HADLEY Samuel, husbandman, of Newbury NY, doc date 1772, writ, debt, file #1056

CORLISS John, husbandman, of Haverhill MA, vs BROWN Adam, yeoman, of Tuxbury MA, doc date 1783, rec date 1783, deed, land transfer, file #2644

CORLISS Jonathan, plea, debt, file #781

CORLISS Jonathan, yeoman, of Salem, vs PINGRY Moses & Hannah, cordwainer, of Methuen MA, doc date 1770, various, debt, file #830

CORNISH Margaret, widow, of Weare, vs JACK Andrew, blacksmith, of Weare, doc date 1799, debt, file #465

CORSER David, husbandman, of Boscawen, vs CORSER Stephen, husbandman, of Boscawen, doc date 1798, judgment, debt, file #562

CORSER David, husbandman, of Boscawen, vs SWEAT John, gentleman, of Boscawen, rec date 1788, writ, debt, file #6612

CORSER Elicy, singlewoman, of Boscawen, vs CORSER David, yeoman, of Boscawen, doc date 1799, execution, debt, file #188

CORSER Samuel, gentleman, of Boscawen, vs DANA Anna, widow, of Amherst, doc date 1799, judgment, debt, file #242

CORSER Samuel, gentleman, of Boscawen, vs McGREGORE Robert, esquire, of Goffstown, doc date 1798, judgment, debt, file #562

CORSER Samuel, gentleman, of Boscawen, vs PARKER William, innkeeper, of Bedford, doc date 1798, judgment, debt, file #562

CORSER Samuel, gentleman, of Boscawen, vs MORRISON Samuel, gentleman, of Amherst, doc date 1799, writ, debt, file #396

CORSER Samuel, yeoman, of Boscawen, vs CORSER David, yeoman, of Boscawen, rec date 1783, writ, debt, file #2754

CORSER Samuel, husbandman, of Boscawen, vs CORSER David, yeoman, of Boscawen, rec date 1784, various, debt, file #4175

CORSER Samuel, husbandman, of Boscawen, vs ATKINSON Simeon, gentleman, of Boscawen, rec date 1783, various, debt, file #4566

CORSER Samuel, gentleman, of Boscawen, vs CARR Simeon, husbandman, of Chester, rec date 1788, writ, debt, file #2548

CORSER Samuel, yeoman, of Boscawen, vs BURBANK Moses Jr, husbandman, of Boscawen, rec date 1785, writ, debt, file #6243

CORSER Samuel, gentleman, of Boscawen, vs PARKHURST William, trader, of Boscawen, rec date 1788, writ, debt, file #6611

CORSER Samuel & Sarah, yeoman, of Boscawen, vs FLANDERS John J, yeoman, of Boscawen, rec date 1784, various, assault, file #4167 & #4167A, see also file 2749

CORTON Ebenezer, of Society Land, vs PARKER Robert Robert Jr, yeoman, of Amherst, doc date 1784, execution, debt, file #1940

COSER Samuel, yeoman, of Boscawen, vs MORRILL Ezekiel, gentleman, of Loudon, rec date 1783, writ, debt, file #2595

COSER Samuel, gentleman, of Boscawen, vs HAVEY John, gentleman, of Fisherfield, rec date 1788, writ, debt, file #6928

COSTELLOE John & Lydia, trader, of Berwick Me, vs COSER Samuel, yeoman, of Boscawen, doc date 1781, rec date 1785, deed, land transfer, file #5626

COSTELLOE John & Lydia, trader, of Berwick Me, vs COSER Samuel, yeoman, of Boscawen, doc date 1782, rec date 1785, deed, land transfer, file #5627
COSTELLOE John & Lydia, trader, of Danvers MA, vs COSER Samuel, yeoman, of Boscawen, doc date 1783, rec date 1785, deed, land transfer, file #5628
COSTELO John, trader, of Danvers MA, vs BURBANK Moses, husbandman, of Boscawen, rec date 1783, writ, debt, file #3371
COSTON Bishop, yeoman, of Derryfield, vs PARKINSON Henry, schoolmaster, of Concord, rec date 1785, deed, land transfer, file #5602
COSTON Bishop, yeoman, of Derryfield, vs MOOR Daniel, esquire, of Bedford, rec date 1785, judgment, debt, file #5852
COSTON Ebenezer, yeoman, of Wilton, vs COLBY Samson, physician, of Hopkinton, doc date 1772, judgment, debt, file #682
COSTON Ebenezer, yeoman, of Society Land, vs KITTREDGE James, husbandman, of Goffstown, doc date 1782, execution, debt, file #964
COSTON Ebenezer, yeoman, of Society Land, vs KITTRIDGE James, husbandman, of Goffstown, rec date 1783, execution, debt, file #3821
COSTON Ebenezer, yeoman, of Society Land, vs GRIMES James, gentleman, of Deering, rec date 1786, writ, debt, file #6108
COSTON Ebenezer, yeoman, of Francestown, vs CORY Ebenezer, yeoman, rec date 1786, writ, debt, file #6128
COTTON Benjamin, husbandman, of Gilmington, vs DICKEY Jesse, husbandman, of Goffstown, rec date 1785, writ, debt, file #4805
COTTON Benjamin, husbandman, of Gilmanton, vs DICKEY Jesse, husbandman, of Goffstown, rec date 1785, various, debt, file #5882
COTTON Roland, esquire, of Sandwich MA, vs MAN James, husbandman, of Mason, doc date 1774, writ, debt, file #1144
COTTON Samuel, clerk, of Litchfield, vs REED Joseph, yeoman, of Merrimack, rec date 1785, execution, debt, file #5485
COTTON Samuel, clerk, of Litchfield, vs INHABITANTS of Litchfield, rec date 1783, writ, debt, file #3584
COTTON Samuel, clerk, of Litchfield, vs LOWELL John & Rebecca, esquire, of Boston MA, rec date 1783, judgment, debt, file #4198
COUBURN ----, vs STORER ----, doc date 1891, defendants brief, supreme court, file #632, court arguments
COURSER David, husbandman, of Boscawen, vs WOODMAN Joshua, gentleman, of Meredith, rec date 1793, judgment, debt, file #2583
COWAN Margaret, spinster, of Merrimack, vs COWAN Thomas, of Merrimack, doc date 1781, summons, fornication, file #766
COWEN Thomas Jr, yeoman, of Merrimack, vs MEANS Robert Jr, trader, of Amherst, rec date 1783, writ, debt, file #3037
COX Charles, husbandman, of New Holderness, vs ORDWAY Joseph, husbandman, of Goffstown, doc date 1774, judgment, debt, file #734
COX Edward, weaver, of Dunstable, vs COX William, blacksmith, of Dunstable, doc date 1777, deed, land transfer, file #2064
CRAIGE Andrew, gentleman, of New Chester, vs CRAMBEE Hugh, husbandman, of Chester, doc date 1772, writ, debt, file #1393

CRAM Abigail, of Weare, vs FLANDERS Phebe, single, of Campbell Gore, rec date 1788, affidavit, death of child, file #6530

CRAM Benjamin, yeoman, of Lyndeborough, vs DASCOMB Jacob, gentleman, of Lyndeborough, doc date 1799, debt, file #335

CRAM Benjamin, yeoman, of Lyndeborough, vs GORDON William, merchant, of Dunstable MA, doc date 1774, writ, debt, file #1112

CRAM Benjamin, husbandman, of Lyndeborough, vs ASHTON Jacob, husbandman, of Salem MA, rec date 1789, writ, debt, file #2575

CRAM Benjamin, clerk, of Lyndeborough, vs BOFFE Thomas, gentleman, of Lyndeborough, doc date 1784, rec date 1785, deed, land transfer, file #5616

CRAM John, yeoman, vs CALDWELL James, yeoman, of Middleton, doc date 1772, writ, debt, file #903

CRAM John, miller, of Milford, vs PUTNAM Ephraim, yeoman, of Lyndeborough, doc date 1799, judgment, debt, file #293

CRAM Joseph, husbandman, of Society Land, vs HAWKINS William Adriun, gentleman, of Wilton, rec date 1785, writ, debt, file #5043

CRAM Nathan, yeoman, of Lyndeborough, vs LUMAN Nathaniel, yeoman, of Hollis, rec date 1786, judgment, debt, file #5755

CRAM Nathan, yeoman, of Lyndeborough, vs LEAMAN. Nathaniel, yeoman, of Hollis, rec date 1786, writ, debt, file #6097

CRAM Nathaniel, gentleman, of Boscawen, vs GILSON Enock, yeoman, of Canterbury, rec date 1788, writ, debt, file #6684

CRAM Solomon, husbandman, of Lyndeborough, vs OSGOOD Carlton, of New Ipswich, doc date 1772, writ, debt, file #940

CRAWFORD John, yeoman, of Hollis, vs BLOAD Seth, husbandman, of Temple, doc date 1799, writ, debt, file #437

CRAWFORD John, gentleman, of Francestown, vs DRUARY Benjamin, physician, of Spencer MA, doc date 1784, writ, debt, file #1593

CRISTY George, esquire, of New Boston, vs LEWIS Moses, yeoman, of Lyndeborough, rec date 1782, writ, debt, file #2667

CRISTY Jesse, yeoman, of New Boston, vs SMITH Reuben, yeoman, of New Boston, doc date 1777, deed, land transfer, file #2062

CRISTY William, yeoman, of Francestown, vs BALDWIN Nahum, esquire, of Amherst, rec date 1783, writ, debt, file #3024, Zacheus CUTLER estate

CROMBIE James, cordwainer, of New Boston, vs SPEER Samuel, cordwainer, of New Ipswich, rec date 1784, judgment, debt, file #5307

CROMBIE John, gentleman, of Londonderry, vs UNDERWOOD James, esquire, of Litchfield, rec date 1783, writ, debt, file #3339

CROSBY Hesekiah, yeoman, of Billerica MA, vs GIPSON Timothy, esquire, of Henniker, rec date 1785, deed, land transfer, file #5632

CROSBY Josiah, husbandman, of Amherst, vs CHAMPNEY Ebenezer, gentleman, of New Ipswich, doc date 1773, writ, debt, file #1225

CROSBY Josiah, yeoman, of Billerica MA, vs HEYWOOD Nathaniel, husbandman, of Hillsborough, rec date 1785, writ, debt, file #5073

CROSBY Stephen, yeoman, of Amherst, vs BUTTERFIELD Jonathan, yeoman, of Dunstable, rec date 1786, judgment, debt, file #2297

CROSBY William, husbandman, of Milford, vs PIERCE Merrill, husbandman, of Hillsborough, doc date 1799, debt, file #489

CROSBY William (Mr), of Amherst, vs SELECTMEN of Amherst, of Amherst, rec date 1788, appointments, tavern license, file #3539

CROSS Anna, singlewoman, of Hopkinton, vs DAVIS Aquilla, husbandman, of Warner, doc date 1783, recognizance, debt, file #812

CROSS Anna, singlewoman, of Hopkinton, vs DAVIS Francis Jr, husbandman, of Warner, doc date 1783, recognizance, debt, file #812

CROSS Anna, singlewoman, of Hopkinton, vs DAVIS Zebulon, husbandman, of Warner, doc date 1783, recognizance, debt, file #812

CROSS John, husbandman, of Litchfield, vs DUNBAR Asa, gentleman, of Harvard MA, rec date 1783, writ, debt, file #3017

CROSS Joseph, yeoman, of Swanzey, vs MARSH Samuel Jr, yeoman, of Nottingham-West, rec date 1785, judgment, debt, file #5102

CROSS Nathan, yeoman, of Antrim, vs TOLLBURT William, trader, of Antrim, doc date 1799, judgment, debt, file #269

CROSS Parker, yeoman, of Hillsborough, vs TUCKER Joseph, yeoman, of Andover, doc date 1783, rec date 1787, deed, land transfer, file #2505

CROSS Peter, husbandman, of Nottingham-West, vs DAVIS Asea, husbandman, of Nottingham-West, rec date 1771, writ, assault, file #2172, 2

CROSS Stephen & Ralph, shipwrights, of Newburyport MA, vs TILTON Joseph, trader, of Kingston, doc date 1772, judgment, debt, file #814

CROSS Thomas, trader, of Northfield, vs BOWEN John, husbandman, of Salisbury, doc date 1798, judgment, debt, file #562

CROWN John, husbandman, of Bedford, vs BURNS John, husbandman, of New Boston, rec date 1785, writ, debt, file #6261

CUDWORTH Samuel, yeoman, of Society Land, vs MORRISON Thomas, yeoman, of Peterborough, rec date 1783, various, debt, file #3936

CUDWORTH Samuel, yeoman, of Society Land, vs WHEELER Uriah, yeoman, of Packersfield, rec date 1783, various, debt, file #3936

CUDWORTH Samuel, yeoman, of Society Land, vs TAGGART James, yeoman, of Society Land, rec date 1784, writ, force and arms, file #6854

CUMING Prudence, widow, of Hollis, vs WHITTEMORE Samuel, gentleman, of Cambridge, rec date 1785, judgment, land dispute, file #5358

CUMINGS Eleazer, gentleman, of New Ipswich, vs PARKER Phineas, yeoman, of Groton MA, doc date 1784, writ, debt, file #1272

CUMINGS Eleazer, gentleman, of New Ipswich, vs GOLDSMITH Josiah, gentleman, of Walpole, rec date 1784, judgment, debt, file #4657

CUMINGS John, husbandman, of Dunstable MA, vs FLETCHER Joshua, yeoman, of Plymouth, rec date 1784, judgment, debt, file #4272

CUMINGS Samuel, esquire, of Hollis, vs TEMPLE Jonathan, yeoman, of Henniker, doc date 1774, judgment, debt, file #1035

CUMINGS Thomas, gentleman, of Hollis, vs STATE of NH, rec date 1776, recognizance, counterfeiting, file #2250

CUMINGS William, yeoman, of Hollis, vs HALE William, physician, of Hollis, rec date 1786, judgment, debt, file #2455

CUMINGS William, schoolmaster, of Hollis, vs CUMINGS Benjamin, gentleman, of Hollis, rec date 1783, judgment, debt, file #4446

CUMMINGS Benjamin, of Hollis, vs WRIGHT Uriah, gentleman, of Hollis, rec date 1785, various, debt, file #6264

CUMMINGS Benjamin Lt, of Hollis, doc date 1787, license, tavern license, file #871

CUMMINGS Ebenezer, yeoman, of Hollis, vs TYNG James, merchant, of Dunstable, doc date 1772, writ, debt, file #1425

CUMMINGS Eleaser, gentleman, of New Ipswich, vs GOLDSMITH Josiah, gentleman, of Walpole, rec date 1785, judgment, debt, file #5114

CUMMINGS Eleazer, gentleman, of New Ipswich, vs MILLS Philip, gentleman, of New Ipswich, doc date 1798, execution, debt, file #87

CUMMINGS Eleazer, gentleman, of New Ipswich, vs LAWRENCE Stephen, husbandman, of Mason, rec date 1785, writ, debt, file #5957

CUMMINGS Eleazer, gentleman, of New Ipswich, vs TOWNSWEND Samuel, husbandman, of Mason, rec date 1785, writ, debt, file #5957

CUMMINGS Philip, joiner, of Peterborough, vs SMITH Moses, husbandman, of Hollis, rec date 1784, judgment, debt, file #4352

CUMMINGS Samuel, yeoman, of New Ipswich, vs KEEP Jonathan, bloomer, of Westford MA, doc date 1774, writ, debt, file #1108, fragile

CUMMINGS Samuel, esquire, of Hollis, vs CURRIER Samuel & Moses, yeoman, of Bedford, doc date 1774, writ, debt, file #1087

CUMMINGS Samuel, esquire, of Hollis, vs STEARNS Samuel Jr, yeoman, of Hollis, doc date 1777, writ, debt, file #2023

CUMMINGS Samuel, esquire, of Amherst, vs BANCROFT Benjamin, husbandman, of Groton MA, doc date 1778, writ, debt, file #2049

CUMMINGS Samuel, esquire, of Hollis, vs STEARNS Joseph, yeoman, of Hollis, doc date 1778, writ, debt, file #2020

CUMMINGS Samuel, esquire, of Hollis, vs BANCROFT Benjamin, gentleman, of Groton MA, doc date 1777, writ, debt, file #2024

CUMMINGS Samuel, esquire, of Hollis, vs KEEP Jonathan, bloomer, of Harvard MA, doc date 1777, writ, debt, file #2022

CUMMINGS Samuel, esquire, of Hollis, vs GREENLEAF Enoch, merchant, of Newbury MA, rec date 1777, writ, debt, file #2183

CUMMINGS Samuel, esquire, of Hollis, vs PATTEN Matthew, esquire, of Bedford, rec date 1783, writ, debt, file #3107

CUMMINGS Samuel, gentleman, of Peterborough, vs WHITING Leonard, esquire, of Merrimack, rec date 1785, writ, debt, file #4764

CUMMINGS Samuel, gentleman, of Peterborough, vs KELLEY Moses, esquire, of Goffstown, rec date 1785, writ, debt, file #5348

CUMMINGS Silas, blacksmith, of New Boston, vs GOVE Jonathan, gentleman, of New Boston, doc date 1784, writ, debt, file #1617

CUMMINGS Silas, blacksmith, of New Boston, vs TARBOX James, yeoman, of Dunstable MA, doc date 1784, execution, debt, file #1969

CUMMINGS Simeon, gentleman, of Merrimack, vs SMITH James, esquire, of Cavindish VT, doc date 1799, judgment, debt, file #295

CUMMINGS Simeon, gentleman, of Dunstable MA, vs RIDEOUT Nathaniel, yeoman, of Hollis, doc date 1784, execution, debt, file #1980

CUMMINGS Simeon, esquire, of Merrimack, vs MOOR Joseph, gentleman, of Deerfield, doc date 1799, writ, debt, file #369

CUMMINGS Simon, esquire, of Merrimack, vs INHABITANTS of Merrimack, rec date 1788, writ, debits, file #6810

CUMMINGS Thomas, cordwainer, of Hollis, vs SHERLE Abel, yeoman, of Hollis, doc date 1802, judgment, debt, file #568

CUMMINGS Thomas, yeoman, of Hollis, vs KELLEY Joseph, gentleman, of Nottingham-West, doc date 1772, writ, assault, file #932

CUMMINGS William, schoolmaster, of Hollis, vs CUMMINGS Benjamin, gentleman, of Hollis, doc date 1784, civil litigation, debt, file #1829

CUMMINGS William, gentleman, of Dunstable, vs MERRILL Daniel, deed, land transfer, file #6566

CUNNINGHAM George, husbandman, of Goffstown, vs HOUSTON William, housewright, of Peterborough, rec date 1784, judgment, debt, file #4609

CUNNINGHAM George, husbandman, of Goffstown, vs HOUSTON William, housewright, of Peterborough, rec date 1785, judgment, debt, file #6421

CUNNINGHAM John, husbandman, of Merrimack, vs BUTTERFIELD Simeon, husbandman, of Dunstable, doc date 1782, execution, file #1026

CUNNINGHAM Moses, husbandman, of Peterborough, vs GRAGG Samuel, gentleman, of Peterborough, rec date 1785, judgment, debt, file #4798

CUNNINGHAM Robert, yeoman, of Merrimack, vs BUTTERFIELD Simeon, yeoman, of Dunstable, rec date 1785, judgment, debt, file #6356

CUNNINGHAM Samuel, yeoman, of Peterborough, vs SHANNON Richard Cutts, esquire, of Portsmouth, doc date 1799, judgment, debt, file #303

CUNNINGHAM Samuel, yeoman, of Peterborough, vs MANN Robert, husbandman, of Washington, rec date 1783, execution, debt, file #3499

CUNNINGHAM Samuel, vs POLLARD Thomas, yeoman, of Nottingham, rec date 1784, writ, debt, file #4975

CUNNINGHAM Samuel, gentleman, of Peterborough, vs LITTLE Thomas, husbandman, of Peterborough, doc date 15, rec date 1785, judgment, debt, file #5815

CUNNINGHAM Samuel & James, husbandman, of Peterborough, vs FOX Timothy, yeoman, of New Ipswich, rec date 1782, writ, debt, file #2841

CURDY John W, of Dunbarton, vs LESLEY Alexander, cordwainer, of Dunbarton, doc date 1799, execution, debt, file #207

CURRIER Jonathan, yeoman, of Bedford, vs WHITNEY James, yeoman, of Dunstable, doc date 1772, writ, debt, file #897

CURRIER Jonathan, yeoman, of Bedford, vs WARNER Daniel, yeoman, of Dunstable, doc date 1771, writ, debt, file #877

CURRIER Jonathan, yeoman, of Bradford, vs MORRILL Robert, yeoman, of Bedford, doc date 1773, execution, debt, file #1453

CURRIER Samuel, yeoman, of Bedford, vs ABBOTT Isaac, yeoman, of Exeter, doc date 1774, writ, debt, file #1105, fragile

CURTICE Isaac P, yeoman, of Amherst, vs INHABITANTS of Amherst, rec date 1783, execution, debt, file #3678

CURTICE Isaac Palmer, yeoman, of Amherst, vs INHABITANTS of Amherst, rec date 1782, execution, debt, file #3532

CURTICE Joseph, husbandman, of Londonderry, vs REA Caleb, physician, of Windham MA, rec date 1784, judgment, debt, file #4246

CURTICE Lemuel, yeoman, of Amherst, vs CODMAN Henry, physician, of Amherst, rec date 1783, execution, debt, file #3658

CURTICE Lemuel, yeoman, of Amherst, vs CODMAN Henry, physician, of Amherst, rec date 1782, execution, debt, file #3493

CURTIS Eli, husbandman, of Amherst, vs CURTIS Abigail, widow, of Wilton, doc date 1799, writ, debt, file #573

CURTIS John, yeoman, of Hillsborough, vs WILSON David, gentleman, of Deering, doc date 1799, writ, debt, file #319

CURTIS John, husbandman, of Hillsborough, vs JONES Nehemiah, trader, of Hillsborough, doc date 1799, execution, debt, file #155

CURTIS Joseph, in jail, of Londonderry, vs DWINNELL Elijah, doc date 1785, petition, release of debit, file #8

CURTIS Samuel, esquire, of Amherst, vs ELLSWORTH Norman Jr, tanner, of Deering, doc date 1799, writ, debt, file #350

CURTIS Samuel, physician, vs CODMAN Henry, physician, of Amherst, rec date 1796, judgment, debt, file #5467

CURTIS Samuel, physician, of Amherst, vs MICHIN John, trader, of Boston MA, doc date 1799, writ, debt, file #573

CURTIS Samuel, physician, of Amherst, vs KETCHUM Stephen, yeoman, of Albany NY, doc date 1784, various, debt, file #1565

CURTIS Samuel, yeoman, of Antrim, vs TAYLOR William, yeoman, of Antrim, doc date 1784, execution, debt, file #1553

CURTIS Samuel, justice peace, of Marlborough MA, rec date 1793, various, copies of cases, file #2590

CURTIS Samuel, esquire, of Worcester MA, vs DANA William, gentleman, of Amherst, rec date 1785, judgment, debt, file #5106

CURTIS Samuel, esquire, of Worcester MA, vs DANA William, gentleman, of Amherst, rec date 1784, judgment, debt, file #5293

CURTIS Samuel, vs MORSE Winsor, rec date 1787, loose papers, bill, file #5387

CURTIS Samuel, esquire, of Boston MA, vs GOOCH William, laborer, of Litchfield, rec date 1785, appointments, debt, file #6155, part of Samuel CURTIS file

CURTIS Samuel, physician, rec date 1779, various, debt, file #6153

CURTIS Samuel, esquire, of Marlborough MA, vs WHEELER Joshua, yeoman, of Bolton MA, rec date 1789, writ, debt, file #6176, part of Samuel CURTIS file

CURTIS Samuel, esquire, of Marlborough MA, vs BRUCE Isaiah, husbandman, of Marlborough MA, rec date 1785, writ, debt, file #6156, part of Samuel CURTIS file

CURTIS Samuel, esquire, of Marlborough MA, vs BRIGHAM Forunatus, laborer, of Watertown MA, rec date 1788, writ, debt, file #6164, part of Samuel CURTIS file

CURTIS Samuel, esquire, of Marlborough MA, vs WHITNEY Daniel, yeoman, of Marlborough MA, rec date 1787, writ, debt, file #6167, part of Samuel CURTIS file

CURTIS Samuel, esquire, of Marlborough MA, vs BRUCE Jonathan, yeoman, of Marlborough MA, rec date 1788, writ, debt, file #6165, part of Samuel CURTIS file

CURTIS Samuel, esquire, of Marlborough MA, vs MAYNARD Levinah, single, of Marlborough MA, rec date 1788, fornication, file #6163, part of Samuel CURTIS file

CURTIS Samuel, esquire, rec date 1788, signed notes, debt, file #6595

CURTIS Samuel, physician, of Boston MA, vs TEMPLE Jonathan, husbandman, of Henniker, rec date 1785, various, debt, file #6343

CURTIS Samuel, esquire, of Marlborough MA, vs LONGLEY Calvain Joshua, gentleman, of Shirley MA, rec date 1787, various, debt, file #6168, part of Samuel CURTIS file

CURTIS Samuel, of Durham, doc date 1789, misc, file #1213

CUSHING John, physician, of Goffstown, vs TODD Alexander, gentleman, of Goffstown, doc date 1799, execution, debt, file #159

CUSHING John, physician, of Goffstown, vs LITTLE George, blacksmith, of Goffstown, rec date 1782, writ, debt, file #2692

CUSHING John, physician, of Goffstown, vs KELLEY Moses, esquire, of Goffstown, rec date 1782, debt, debt, file #3156

CUSHING John, physician, of Goffstown, vs WRIGHT Abel, yeoman, of Goffstown, rec date 1786, judgment, debt, file #5772

CUTLER Jemima, widow, of Bradford, vs MOOR John, husbandman, of Bedford, doc date 1799, debt, file #442

CUTLER Jemima, widow, of Groton MA, vs SMITH Nathaniel, cooper, of Mason, rec date 1785, judgment, debt, file #5498

CUTLER Jemima, widow, of Groton MA, vs DAVIS Benjamin, cooper, of Amherst, doc date 1784, writ, debt, file #1267

CUTLER Jemima, shopkeeper, of Groton MA, vs COCHRAN John, yeoman, of Amherst, doc date 1784, execution, debt, file #1675

CUTLER Jemima, widow, of Groton MA, vs STEWART Henry, yeoman, of Dublin, doc date 1784, execution, debt, file #1674

CUTLER Jemima, widow, of Groton, vs WILLIAMS David, husbandman, of Amherst, rec date 1783, writ, debt, file #3445

CUTLER Jemima, widow, of Groton MA, vs COCHRAN John, yeoman, of Amherst, rec date 1783, writ, debt, file #3636

CUTLER Jemima, widow, of Groton MA, vs STEWART Henry, yeoman, of Dublin, rec date 1783, writ, debt, file #3622

CUTLER Jemima, widow, of Groton MA, vs WINCHESTER Lemuel, husbandman, of Amherst, rec date 1783, writ, debt, file #3635

CUTLER Jemima, widow, of Groton MA, vs FOSTER Simeon, laborer, of Hollis, rec date 1784, judgment, debt, file #4408, estate of Jonas CUTLER

CUTLER Jemima, widow, of Groton MA, vs ELLINWOOD Rolandson, yeoman, of Amherst, rec date 1783, judgment, debt, file #4498

CUTLER Jemima, widow, of Groton MA, vs FOSTER Simeon, laborer, of Hollis, rec date 1784, appeal, debt, file #4733, estate of Jonas CUTLER

CUTLER Jemima, of Groton MA, vs FOX Eliphalet, yeoman, of Walpole, rec date 1785, judgment, debt, file #5806, estate of Jonas CUTLER

CUTLER John, yeoman, of New Ipswich, vs WILSON Benjamin, yeoman, of Townsend MA, doc date 1779, rec date 1783, deed, land transfer, file #2643

CUTLER John, yeoman, of Fisherfield, vs BURNUM Asa, of Dunbarton, doc date 1784, rec date 1788, deed, land transfer, file #6754

CUTLER Jonas, shopkeeper, of Groton MA, vs CONCK (CONICK) James, gentleman, of Raby, doc date 1774, judgment, debt, file #1036

CUTLER Jonas, shopkeeper, of Groton MA, vs DICKEY Elias, yeoman, of Raby, rec date 1782, writ, debt, file #4852

CUTLER Jonas, shopkeepers, of Groton MA, vs FLETCHER Gersham, yeoman, of Westford MA, doc date 1767, rec date 1774, deed, land transfer, file #5653

CUTLER Jonas & Ebenezer, shopkeepers, of Groton MA, vs CONIK James, gentleman, of Raby, doc date 1774, judgment, debt, file #728

CUTLER Joseph, husbandman, of Nottingham-West, vs POLLARD Timothy, husbandman, of Nottingham-West, doc date 1781, rec date 1783, deed, land transfer, file #2660

CUTLER Nathan, physician, of Dunstable, vs PIKE Zachariah, husbandman, of Bedford, rec date 1783, judgment, debt, file #4075

CUTLER Nathan, physician, of Dunstable, vs LOVEJOY John, husbandman, of Amherst, rec date 1783, judgment, debt, file #4075

CUTLER Nathan, physician, of Dunstable, vs BURNS John, yeoman, of New Boston, rec date 1785, judgment, debt, file #5332

CUTLER Solomon, gentleman, of Rindge, vs HURD Benjamin, leather drop, of Billerica MA, rec date 1784, judgment, debt, file #4219

CUTLER Zacheus, esquire, of Amherst, vs STEARNS Samuel, yeoman, of Amherst, doc date 1774, judgment, debt, file #736

CUTLER Zacheus, esquire, of Amherst, vs CARLTON Thomas, yeoman, of Amherst, doc date 1774, execution, debt, file #754

CUTLER Zacheus, esquire, of Amherst, vs DIKE Benjamin, yeoman, of Amherst, doc date 1774, judgment, debt, file #736

CUTLER Zacheus, esquire, of Amherst, vs FRYE Isaac, yeoman, of Wilton, doc date 1773, judgment, debt, file #1308

CUTLER Zacheus, esquire, of Amherst, vs BARNS Silas, yeoman, of Henniker, doc date 1774, recognizance, debt, file #1151

CUTLER Zacheus, esquire, of Amherst, vs WILEY John, yeoman, of Deering, doc date 1784, execution, debt, file #1870

CUTLER Zacheus, of Amherst, rec date 1776, misc, file #2261

CUTLER Zachery, esquire, of Amherst, vs McGRATH Daniel, of Amherst, doc date 1775, deed, land transfer, file #835

CUTTER John, husbandman, of New Ipswich, vs MILLER Joseph, husbandman, of Peterborough Slip, rec date 1785, judgment, debt, file #2290

CUTTER John, yeoman, of New Ipswich, vs McDONALD James, husbandman, of Hollis, rec date 1785, judgment, debt, file #4692

CUTTER John, yeoman, of New Ipswich, vs LAWRENCE Thomas, husbandman, of Mason, rec date 1786, judgment, debt, file #6372

CUTTER John, husbandman, of New Ipswich, vs GRAHAM Arthur, husbandman, of Hancock, rec date 1788, writ, debt, file #6677

CUTTER Nathan, gentleman, of New Ipswich, vs DAVIS Jonathan, shopkeeper, of New Ipswich, doc date 1772, civil litigation, debt, file #652

CUTTER Nathan, gentleman, of New Ipswich, vs PARKER Joseph, yeoman, of New Ipswich, doc date 1772, civil litigations, debt, file #640, first case for Hillsborough county

CUTTER Nathan, housewright, of New Ipswich, vs KIDDER Reubin, esquire, of New Ipswich, doc date 1773, trial, land dispute, file #1284

CUTTER Nathan, yeoman, of New Ipswich, vs ATHERTON Joshua, esquire, of Merrimack, doc date 1772, writ, debt, file #891

CUTTER Nathan, gentleman, of New Ipswich, vs MINOT Jinas, gentleman, of MA, doc date 1784, writ, debt, file #1623

CUTTLER James, yeoman, of Jaffrey, vs DUNLAP Robert, yeoman, of New Ipswich, doc date 1782, execution, debt, file #966

DAKIN Amos, miller, of Mason, vs DODGE William, husbandman, of Mason, doc date 1784, civil litigation, debt, file #1642

DAKIN Amos, miller, of Mason, vs DODGE William, husbandman, of Mason, rec date 1783, judgment, debt, file #4501, kinship Lydia & Amos Jr

DAKIN Justrus, yeoman, of Nottingham-West, vs COBURN Peter, gentleman, of Dracut MA, rec date 1783, writ, debt, file #3208

DAKIN Justrus, husbandman, of Nottingham-West, vs BROWN Timothy, husbandman, of Tewksbury MA, rec date 1782, debt, debt, file #3155

DAKIN Justrus, husbandman, of Nottingham-West, vs BLODGET Jonathan, husbandman, of Nottingham-West, doc date 1766, rec date 1784, deed, land transfer, file #5008

DALE John Jr, yeoman, of Wilton, vs WHITTEMORE Samuel, potter, of Lyndeborough, rec date 1784, judgment, debt, file #4647

DALE John Jr, yeoman, of Wilton, vs WHITEMORE Samuel, potter, of Lyndeborough, rec date 1785, judgment, debt, file #5144

DANA Anna, widow, of Amherst, vs SEARLE William Jr, cordwainer, of Temple, doc date 1798, judgment, debt, file #562

DANA Anna, widow, of Amherst, vs ELSWORTH Thomas, cordwainer, of Deering, doc date 1798, judgment, debt, file #562

DANA Jonathan, innholder, of Keene, vs WEBSTER Daniel & Amos, trader, of Hampstead, doc date 1799, various, debt, file #517

DANA Luther, trader, of Amherst, vs STEARNS Samuel, yeoman, of Amherst, rec date 1785, execution, debt, file #5488

DANA Luther, trader, of Amherst, vs BARKER William, physician, of Francestown, rec date 1785, judgment, debt, file #5207

DANA Luther, trader, of Amherst, vs STEARNS Samuel, yeoman, of Amherst, rec date 1786, judgment, debt, file #6187

DANA Samuel, esquire, of Amherst, vs LOVEJOY Joshua L, gentleman, of Amherst, rec date 1786, various, breaking & entry, file #2531

DANA Samuel, esquire, of Amherst, vs GRAHAM Arthur, yeoman, of Hancock, rec date 1785, execution, debt, file #5473

DANA Samuel, esquire, of Amherst, vs GREEN David, yeoman, of Hillsborough, doc date 1784, execution, debt, file #1540

DANA Samuel, gentleman, of Amherst, vs ROBERTSON Peter, yeoman, of Amherst, doc date 1784, execution, debt, file #1709

DANA Samuel, esquire, of Amherst, vs STEARNS John & John Jr, yeoman, of Hollis, doc date 1784, execution, debt, file #1792

DANA Samuel, gentleman, of Amherst, vs WRIGHT David, cordwainer, of Hollis, doc date 1784, execution, debt, file #1547

DANA Samuel, esquire, of Amherst, vs McGINNIS Barnabas, trader, of Nottingham-West, doc date 1784, execution, debt, file #1546

DANA Samuel, gentleman, of Amherst, vs ROBERTSON Peter, yeoman, of Amherst, doc date 1784, execution, debt, file #1953

DANA Samuel, gentleman, of Amherst, vs SMITH Nathaniel, cooper, of Mason, doc date 1784, civil litigation, debt, file #1857

DANA Samuel, gentleman, of Amherst, vs WRIGHT David, cordwainer, of Hollis, doc date 1784, execution, debt, file #1893

DANA Samuel, esquire, of Amherst, vs HAYNES Joshua, yeoman, of Temple, rec date 1785, writ, debt, file #2342

DANA Samuel, esquire, of Amherst, vs DENNIS Arthur, cordwainer, of New Boston, rec date 1788, writ, debt, file #2384

DANA Samuel, esquire, of Amherst, vs RUSSELL James, gentleman, of Goffstown, rec date 1788, writ, debt, file #2383

DANA Samuel, esquire, of Amherst, vs DICKEY James, gentleman, of Raby, rec date 1788, writ, debt, file #2376

DANA Samuel, esquire, of Amherst, vs GOVE Obediah, husbandman, of Weare, rec date 1787, writ, debt, file #2369

DANA Samuel, esquire, of Amherst, vs GRIMES James, gentleman, of Deering, rec date 1787, writ, debt, file #2367

DANA Samuel, esquire, of Amherst, vs POLLARD Amaziah, husbandman, of New Boston, rec date 1787, writ, debt, file #2363

DANA Samuel, esquire, of Amherst, vs CUNNINGHAM Samuel, gentleman, of Peterborough, rec date 1788, writ, debt, file #2386

DANA Samuel, esquire, of Amherst, vs GRAHAM Arthur, yeoman, of Hancock, rec date 1785, writ, debt, file #2360

DANA Samuel, esquire, of Amherst, vs McLAUGHLIN Thomas, gentleman, of Bedford, rec date 1785, judgment, debt, file #2437

DANA Samuel, esquire, of Amherst, vs RICHARDSON Zachariah, husbandman, of Francestown, rec date 1785, judgment, debt, file #2440

DANA Samuel, esquire, of Amherst, vs DODGE Zebulon, husbandman, of Peterborough, rec date 1785, writ, debt, file #2353

DANA Samuel, esquire, of Amherst, vs GRIMES James, gentleman, of Deering, rec date 1785, writ, debt, file #2351

DANA Samuel, esquire, of Amherst, vs HOGG James, gentleman, of Francestown, rec date 1787, writ, debt, file #2367

DANA Samuel, esquire, of Amherst, vs WRIGHT Uriah, yeoman, of Hollis, rec date 1788, writ, debt, file #2392

DANA Samuel, esquire, of Amherst, vs HODGEMAN Joseph, yeoman, of Raby, rec date 1785, writ, debt, file #2359

DANA Samuel, esquire, of Amherst, vs WOOD Ebenezer, yeoman, of Goffstown, rec date 1788, writ, debt, file #2390

DANA Samuel, esquire, of Amherst, vs GRAY Robert, husbandman, of Peterborough, rec date 1788, writ, debt, file #2398

DANA Samuel, esquire, of Amherst, vs WAKEFIELD Thomas, housewright, of Amherst, rec date 1787, various, breaking & entry, file #2531

DANA Samuel, esquire, of Amherst, vs WAKEFIELD Thomas, gentleman, of Amherst, rec date 1786, various, breaking & entry, file #2531

DANA Samuel, gentleman, of Amherst, vs ROBART Peter, yeoman, of Amherst, rec date 1782, writ, debt, file #2702

DANA Samuel, esquire, of Amherst, vs ELLSWORTH Thomas, cordwainer, of Amherst, rec date 1787, various, breaking & entry, file #2531

DANA Samuel, gentleman, of Amherst, vs PARKER Abel, yeoman, of Peterborough, rec date 1783, civil litigious, debt, file #2918, estate of John BUCKLEY

DANA Samuel, gentleman, of Amherst, vs ROBERTSON Peter, yeoman, of Amherst, rec date 1783, execution, debt, file #3282

DANA Samuel, gentleman, of Amherst, vs WRIGHT David, cordwainer, of Hollis, rec date 1783, writ, debt, file #3599

DANA Samuel, gentleman, of Amherst, vs TAGGART Archibald, gentleman, of Hillsborough, rec date 1783, judgment, debt, file #3783

DANA Samuel, gentleman, of Amherst, vs LOWELL Stephen, yeoman, of Hollis, rec date 1783, writ, debt, file #3581

DANA Samuel, gentleman, of Amherst, vs JONES Samuel, yeoman, of Hillsborough, rec date 1783, writ, debt, file #3908

DANA Samuel, gentleman, of Amherst, vs SMITH Nathaniel, cooper, of Mason, rec date 1783, various, debt, file #4537

DANA Samuel, gentleman, of Amherst, vs JONES Samuel, yeoman, of Hillsborough, rec date 1783, execution, debt, file #3873

DANA Samuel, esquire, of Amherst, vs STEARNS John & John Jr, yeoman, of Hollis, rec date 1784, judgment, debt, file #4366

DANA Samuel, esquire, of Amherst, vs JONES James, yeoman, of Hillsborough, rec date 1784, judgment, debt, file #4287

DANA Samuel, esquire, of Amherst, vs BIXBE Andrew, husbandman, of Hillsborough, rec date 1784, judgment, debt, file #4290

DANA Samuel, esquire, of Amherst, vs PIKE Daniel, innkeeper, of Dunstable, rec date 1784, judgment, debt, file #4280

DANA Samuel, esquire, of Amherst, vs PIKE Zachariah, yeoman, of Bedford, rec date 1784, writ, debt, file #4295

DANA Samuel, esquire, of Amherst, vs GREEN David, yeoman, of Hillsborough, rec date 1784, judgment, debt, file #4291

DANA Samuel, esquire, of Amherst, vs RUSSELL Jason, husbandman, of Mason, rec date 1783, judgment, debt, file #4456

DANA Samuel, esquire, of Amherst, vs GREGG David, wheelwright, of Francestown, rec date 1784, judgment, debt, file #4664

DANA Samuel, esquire, of Amherst, vs SEARLE William Jr, husbandman, of Temple, rec date 1785, judgment, debt, file #5448

DANA Samuel, esquire, of Amherst, vs SCOTT James, yeoman, of Stoddard, rec date 1785, various, debt, file #4602

DANA Samuel, esquire, of Amherst, vs TARBELL John, husbandman, of Mason, rec date 1783, judgment, debt, file #4456

DANA Samuel, esquire, of Amherst, vs CHAMBERS William, innkeeper, of Mason, rec date 1785, judgment, debt, file #4965

DANA Samuel, esquire, of Amherst, vs LIVINGSTON William, gentleman, of New Boston, rec date 1785, judgment, debt, file #4966

DANA Samuel, esquire, of Amherst, vs STEWART Thomas, yeoman, of Antrim, rec date 1785, judgment, debt, file #5081

DANA Samuel, esquire, of Amherst, vs SCOTT James, yeoman, of Stoddard, rec date 1785, judgment, debt, file #5138

DANA Samuel, esquire, of Amherst, vs McCLEARY William, gentleman, of Antrim, rec date 1785, judgment, debt, file #5074

DANA Samuel, esquire, of Amherst, vs GRAGG John, yeoman, of Peterborough, rec date 1785, judgment, debt, file #5326

DANA Samuel, esquire, of Amherst, vs STUART Francis, yeoman, of Antrim, rec date 1785, judgment, debt, file #5081

DANA Samuel, esquire, of Amherst, vs RICHARDSON John, husbandman, of Peterborough, rec date 1790, judgment, debt, file #5260

DANA Samuel, esquire, of Amherst, vs GRAY Robert, innholder, of Peterborough, rec date 1785, judgment, debt, file #5591

DANA Samuel, esquire, of Amherst, vs ROLF Daniel, yeoman, of Hillsborough, rec date 1786, execution, debt, file #5461

DANA Samuel, esquire, of Amherst, vs LUND Phineas, husbandman, of Lyndeborough, rec date 1790, judgment, debt, file #5256

DANA Samuel, esquire, of Amherst, vs PARKER William, yeoman, of Hillsborough, rec date 1785, writ, debt, file #2343

DANA Samuel, esquire, of Amherst, vs GRAGG David, wheelwright, of Francestown, rec date 1785, judgment, debt, file #5400

DANA Samuel, esquire, of Amherst, vs MONTOGOMERY Hugh, husbandman, of Francestown, rec date 1788, writ, debt, file #5896

DANA Samuel, esquire, of Amherst, vs WHITE John, yeoman, of Peterborough, rec date 1787, execution, debt, file #5718

DANA Samuel, esquire, of Groton MA, vs CROSS Nathan, miller, of Amherst, doc date 1803, rec date 1803, deed, land transfer, file #5680

DANA Samuel, esquire, of Amherst, vs WHITE William, husbandman, of Peterborough, rec date 1787, judgment, debt, file #5720

DANA Samuel, esquire, of Amherst, vs STEWART Alexander, cordwainer, of Peterborough, rec date 1785, writ, debt, file #5975

DANA Samuel, esquire, of Amherst, vs McLAUGHLIN Thomas, of Bedford, rec date 1786, judgment, debt, file #5753

DANA Samuel, esquire, of Amherst, vs MOOR Daniel, esquire, of Bedford, rec date 1786, judgment, debt, file #5769

DANA Samuel, esquire, of Amherst, vs DICKERMAN Samuel, blacksmith, of Francestown, rec date 1786, judgment, debt, file #5767

DANA Samuel, esquire, of Amherst, vs MOOR Daniel, esquire, of Bedford, rec date 1786, writ, debt, file #6110

DANA Samuel, esquire, of Amherst, vs KELLEY Joseph, gentleman, of Nottingham-West, rec date 1786, writ, debt, file #6058

DANA Samuel, esquire, of Amherst, vs WALTON William, husbandman, of Amherst, rec date 1786, writ, debt, file #6096

DANA Samuel, esquire, of Amherst, vs MOOR Daniel, esquire, of Bedford, rec date 1786, writ, debt, file #6226

DANA Samuel, esquire, of Amherst, vs DICKERMAN Samuel, blacksmith, of Francestown, rec date 1786, writ, debt, file #6092

DANA Samuel, esquire, of Amherst, vs MONTGOMERY Hugh, yeoman, of Francestown, rec date 1786, writ, debt, file #6094

DANA Samuel, esquire, of Amherst, vs WHITE John, husbandman, of Peterborough, rec date 1786, writ, debt, file #6089

DANA Samuel, esquire, of Amherst, vs WALLINGSFORD David, gentleman, of Hollis, rec date 1786, writ, debt, file #6088

DANA Samuel, esquire, of Amherst, vs CRAM Nathan, yeoman, of Lyndeborough, rec date 1786, writ, debt, file #6091

DANA Samuel, esquire, of Amherst, vs WHITE William, husbandman, of Peterborough, rec date 1786, writ, debt, file #6090

DANA Samuel, esquire, of Amherst, vs WALLINGSFORD David, gentleman, of Hollis, rec date 1786, judgment, debt, file #6188

DANA Samuel, esquire, of Amherst, vs BEARD William, husbandman, of New Boston, rec date 1786, judgment, debt, file #6509

DANA Samuel, esquire, of Amherst, vs WOOD Samuel, yeoman, of Mason, rec date 1785, judgment, debt, file #4980

DANA Samuel, of Amherst, vs BROWN Silas, husbandman, of Dublin, rec date 1786, writ, debt, file #6330

DANA Samuel, esquire, of Amherst, vs STEWART Alexander, cordwainer, of Peterborough, rec date 1788, writ, debt, file #6629

DANA Samuel, esquire, of Amherst, vs FRENCH Isaac, yeoman, of Washington, rec date 1788, writ, debt, file #6952

DANA Samuel, esquire, of Amherst, vs WOOD Ebenezer, yeoman, of Goffstown, rec date 1788, writ, debt, file #7050

DANA Samuel, esquire, of Amherst, vs HAYNES Joshua, yeoman, of Temple, rec date 1785, judgment, debt, file #5813

DANA Samuel, esquire, of Amherst, vs BOFFE John, yeoman, of Lyndeborough, rec date 1786, judgment, debt, file #5807

DANA Samuel, esquire, of Amherst, vs GRIMES Thaddeus, yeoman, of Amherst, doc date 1784, execution, debt, file #1756

DANA Samuel, esquire, of Amherst, vs GREGG Lesley, yeoman, of New Boston, rec date 1785, judgment, debt, file #2436

DANA William, gentleman, of Amherst, vs ELLSWORTH Thomas, cordwainer, of Deering, rec date 1788, writ, debt, file #2397

DANA William, gentleman, of Amherst, vs DRESSER Asa, yeoman, of Campbells Gore, rec date 1788, writ, debt, file #2377

DANA William, gentleman, of Amherst, vs ELLSWORTH Thomas, cordwainer, of Amherst, doc date 1787, rec date 1787, deed, land transfer, file #2484

DANA William, esquire, of Amherst, vs BARNARD Samuel, yeoman, of Pepperell MA, rec date 1783, execution, debt, file #3676

DANA William, esquire, of Amherst, vs BARNARD Samuel, yeoman, of Pepperell MA, rec date 1783, execution, debt, file #3856

DANA William, gentleman, of Amherst, vs DRESSER Asa, husbandman, of Campbells Gore, rec date 1784, judgment, debt, file #4396

DANA William, gentleman, of Amherst, vs DRESSER Asa, husbandman, of Campbells Gore, rec date 1784, appeal, debt, file #4136

DANA William, esquire, of Amherst, vs BARNARD Samuel, yeoman, of Pepperell MA, rec date 1782, execution, debt, file #4895

DANA William, gentleman, of Amherst, vs DICKINSON Jesse, blacksmith, of Strafford, rec date 1785, writ, debt, file #5368

DANA William, gentleman, of Amherst, vs RICHARDSON Zachariah, innholder, of Francestown, rec date 1784, execution, debt, file #5715

DANA William, gentleman, of Amherst, vs HILDRETH John, husbandman, of Litchfield, rec date 1788, writ, debt, file #6993

DANE Samuel, gentleman, of Amherst, vs JONES James, husbandman, of Hillsborough, rec date 1783, writ, debt, file #3569

DANE Samuel, gentleman, of Amherst, vs COOLIDGE Silas, husbandman, of Hillsborough, rec date 1783, writ, debt, file #3569

DANFORD Nathaniel, husbandman, of Andover, vs GREEN Peter, esquire, of Concord, rec date 1783, writ, debt, file #3211

DANFORTH David, gentleman, of Amherst, vs JONES Nehemiah, trader, of Stoddard, doc date 1799, judgment, debt, file #253

DANFORTH David, gentleman, of Salem, vs BUTTERFEILD Abel, yeoman, of Dunstable, doc date 1798, judgment, debt, file #562

DANFORTH David, gentleman, of Salem, vs CARLTON Samuel, husbandman, of Greenfield, doc date 1799, debt, file #490

DANFORTH David, gentleman, of Salem, vs BUTTERFIELD Abel, yeoman, of Dunstable, doc date 1798, judgment, debt, file #562

DANFORTH David, of Amherst, license, tavern license, file #873

DANFORTH David, innholder, of Amherst, vs BOFFEE Thomas, gentleman, of Lyndeborough, rec date 1788, writ, debt, file #6715

DANFORTH Joseph, gentleman, of Dunstable MA, vs WALKER William, esquire, of Amherst, doc date 1784, civil litigation, debt, file #1840

DANFORTH Joseph, gentleman, of Dunstable MA, vs WALKER William, esquire, of Amherst, rec date 1783, judgment, debt, file #3300

DANFORTH Josiah, yeoman, of Billerica MA, vs THOMPSON James, husbandman, of Litchfield, doc date 1784, execution, debt, file #1524

DANFORTH Josiah, yeoman, of Billerica MA, vs THOMPSON James, husbandman, of Litchfield, rec date 1782, judgment, debt, file #4510

DANFORTH Nathaniel, of Andover, vs Town of Andover, doc date 1799, voucher of pauper, support of child, file #186

DANFORTH Samuel, yeoman, of Andover MA, vs McQUAID Jacob, yeoman, of Bedford, rec date 1783, judgment, debt, file #3738

DANFORTH Samuel, yeoman, of Fitchburg MA, vs HOLT Jonathan, yeoman, of Jaffrey, rec date 1783, writ, debt, file #3914

DANFORTH Samuel, yeoman, of Billerica MA, vs TUTTLE Stephen, yeoman, of Goffstown, rec date 1785, execution, debt, file #5939

DANFORTH Samuel, yeoman, of Billerica MA, vs TUTTLE Stephen, yeoman, of Goffstown, rec date 1785, writ, debt, file #6005

DARLING John, of Marlborough MA, vs JOSLYN Nathaniel, of Henniker, doc date 1771, rec date 1772, deed, land transfer, file #6840

DARLING Jonas, yeoman, of Marlborough MA, vs WHEELER Silas, yeoman, rec date 1786, summons, debt, file #6160, part of Samuel CURTIS file

DARLING Joshua, trader, of Henniker, vs CAMPBELL John, blacksmith, of Henniker, doc date 1798, various, debt, file #521

DARRAH David, yeoman, of Greenfield, vs STILES Jacob, yeoman, of Greenfield, rec date 1804, deed, land transfer, file #5681

DARRAH James, yeoman, of Merrimack, vs VICKERY John, yeoman, of Bedford, rec date 1783, writ, debt, file #3091

DARRAH William, yeoman, of Litchfield, vs HEYWOOD Samuel Smith, yeoman, of Nottingham-West, rec date 1784, various, debt, file #4922

DASCOMBE James, yeoman, of Wilton, vs HARRIS Robert, merchant, of Littleton MA, doc date 1772, writ, debt, file #1072

DAURY Thomas, vs STATE of NH, application, tavern license, file #874, poor quality

DAVIDSON David, yeoman, of Raby, vs STATE of NH, rec date 1782, recognizance, debt, file #2609

DAVIDSON Francis, yeoman, of Merrimack, vs POLLARD Timothy, yeoman, of Nottingham-West, rec date 1783, judgment, debt, file #2860

DAVIDSON Francis, yeoman, of Merrimack, vs MARSH Samuel, yeoman, of Nottingham-West, rec date 1783, execution, debt, file #2893

DAVIDSON Francis, yeoman, of Merrimack, vs POLLARD Timothy, yeoman, of Nottingham-West, rec date 1783, execution, debt, file #2893

DAVIDSON Francis, yeoman, of Merrimack, vs MARSH Samuel, yeoman, of Nottingham-West, rec date 1783, judgment, debt, file #2860

DAVIDSON Thomas, yeoman, of Peterborough, vs JOHNSON Moses, husbandman, of Peterborough, doc date 1784, execution, debt, file #1747

DAVINSON Thomas, yeoman, of Peterborough, vs JOHNSON Moses, husbandman, of Peterborough, doc date 1784, execution, debt, file #1794

DAVIS Abraham, cordwainer, of Hopkinton, vs EASTMAN John, yeoman, of Hopkinton, doc date 1774, rec date 1784, deed, land transfer, file #5009, ?

DAVIS Amos, gentleman, of Chesterfield, vs BUTTERFIELD Joseph, gentleman, of Wilton, rec date 1782, writ, debt, file #2838

DAVIS Asa, of Nottingham-West, doc date 1774, venire, file #1211

DAVIS Benjamin, yeoman, of Bedford, vs SPAULDING Reuben, gentleman, of Nottingham-West, rec date 1783, writ, debt, file #2767

DAVIS Benjamin, husbandman, of Amherst, vs KELLEY Moses, esquire, of Goffstown, rec date 1783, bond, debt, file #3358

DAVIS Daniel, yeoman, of Harvard MA, vs McALLISTER Peter, yeoman, of Peterborough, rec date 1783, execution, debt, file #3671

DAVIS David Jr & Amos, yeoman, of Chester, vs MORLIN William, rec date 1784, recognizance, counterfeiting, file #5458

DAVIS Ezekiel Jr, husbandman, of Acton MA, vs WETHERBEE Jacob, husbandman, of Mason, rec date 1784, appeal, debt, file #4107

DAVIS J Samuel, yeoman, of Carlisle MA, vs HAYWOOD James, yeoman, of Jaffrey, doc date 1782, rec date 1783, deed, land transfer, file #2629

DAVIS John Jr, yeoman, of Peterborough Slip, vs MANNING John Jr, physician, of Ipswich MA, doc date 1774, writ, debt, file #742

DAVIS Jonathan, gentleman, of Littleton MA, vs GRAGG Samuel, yeoman, of Peterborough, doc date 1784, execution, debt, file #1802

DAVIS Jonathan, yeoman, of New Ipswich, vs BAILEY Isaac, husbandman, of Jaffrey, doc date 1784, execution, debt, file #1542

DAVIS Jonathan, yeoman, of New Ipswich, vs BAILEY Isaac, husbandman, of Jaffrey, doc date 1784, execution, debt, file #1684

DAVIS Jonathan, gentleman, of Littleton MA, vs POLLARD Joseph, husbandman, of New Ipswich, rec date 1785, judgment, debt, file #5062

DAVIS Jonathan Jr, yeoman, of New Ipswich, vs BAILEY Isaac & Isaac Jr, husbandman, of Jaffrey, rec date 1783, writ, debt, file #4519

DAVIS Moses, husbandman, of Derryfield, vs DAVIS James, husbandman, of Pelham, rec date 1785, judgment, debt, file #5343

DAVIS Nathan, yeoman, of Boscawen, vs FOWLER Samuel, esquire, of Boscawen, rec date 1782, execution, debt, file #5731

DAVIS Nicholas & Mary, deceased, of Boscawen, vs CAR Joanna, widow, doc date 1784, deed, land transfer, file #2011

DAVIS Oliver, trader, of Boscawen, vs RAWLINGS Richard, joiner, of Warner, doc date 1784, deed, land transfer, file #1991

DAVIS Samuel, yeoman, of Nottingham-West, vs RIDEOUT Rowland, yeoman, of Nottingham-West, rec date 1776, recognizance, murder, file #2251

DAVIS Simon, husbandman, of Athens VT, vs BANKS James, husbandman, of Packersfield, rec date 1783, judgment, debt, file #3804

DAVISON Charles, cordwainer, of Peterborough, vs STEELE David Jr, husbandman, of Peterborough, rec date 1785, appeal, debt, file #5497

DAVISON Charles, cordwainer, of Peterborough, vs STEELE David Jr, husbandman, of Peterborough, rec date 1785, judgment, debt, file #5987

DAWSON Timothy, schoolmaster, of Lyndeborough, vs BOOTMAN Benjamin, husbandman, of Francestown, doc date 1784, court case, debt, file #1607

DAWSON Timothy, schoolmaster, of Lyndeborough, vs WILKINS John, gentleman, of Amherst, doc date 1784, court case, debt, file #1607

DAWSON Timothy, schoolmaster, of Lyndeborough, vs WILKINS John, gentleman, of Amherst, rec date 1783, judgment, ejectment, file #3298

DAWSON Timothy, schoolmaster, of Lyndeborough, vs BOOTMAN Benjamin, husbandman, of Francestown, rec date 1783, judgment, ejectment, file #3298

DAWSON Timothy, schoolmaster, of Francestown, vs WILKINS John, gentleman, of Amherst, rec date 1786, various, debt, file #6082

DAY John, gentleman, of Hillsborough, vs SHEPARD Isaac, yeoman, of Portsmouth, doc date 1798, judgment, debt, file #562

DAY Joseph, yeoman, of Pepperell MA, vs COMBS Midah Jr, husbandman, of Dunstable, rec date 1783, writ, debt, file #3401

DAYDE Susannah, of Peterborough, vs DAYDE James, of Peterborough, doc date 1799, petition, divorce, file #522

DEAN Supply, yeoman, of Woburn MA, vs POLLARD Timothy, yeoman, of Nottingham-West, rec date 1784, judgment, debt, file #4201

DEAN Supply, yeoman, of Woburn MA, vs BUTLER Jesse, yeoman, of Pelham, rec date 1785, writ, debt, file #5280

DEARBORN Simon & Dorothy, yeoman, of Epsom, vs DOW Oliver, gentleman, of Hopkinton, doc date 1776, rec date 1779, deed, land transfer, file #2132

DeBLOIS George, merchant, of Salem MA, vs GOODRIDGE Sewall, clerk, of Lyndeborough, rec date 1785, judgment, debt, file #5859

DeBLOIS George, merchant, of Salem MA, vs GOODRIDGE Sewall, clerk, of Lyndeborough, rec date 1785, judgment, debt, file #6434

DENIS Thomas, gentleman, of Ipswich MA, vs HOAR Benjamin, of New Ipswich, doc date 1775, deed, land transfer, file #846

DENNIS Ambrose, fisherman, of Marblehead MA, vs TAGGART Archibald, husbandman, of Hillsborough, rec date 1784, various, debt, file #4188

DENNIS Ambrose, fisherman, of Marblehead MA, vs TAGGART Archibald, husbandman, of Hillsborough, rec date 1783, writ, debt, file #4550

DENNIS Arthur, yeoman, of New Boston, vs WHITNEY Samuel, husbandman, of Amherst, doc date 1799, judgment, debt, file #265

DENNIS Arthur, cordwainer, of New Boston, vs MOREL Hugh, yeoman, of Francestown, doc date 1784, execution, debt, file #1929

DENNIS Arthur, cordwainer, of New Boston, vs MORRELL Hugh, yeoman, of Francestown, rec date 1783, execution, debt, file #3281

DENNIS Arthur, cordwainer, of New Boston, vs MORRIL Hugh, yeoman, of Francestown, rec date 1783, writ, debt, file #3899

DENNIS Arthur, cordwainer, of New Boston, vs HOLMS Robert, yeoman, of Peterborough, rec date 1786, execution, debt, file #5875

DENNIS Arthur, cordwainer, of New Boston, vs HOLMS Robert, yeoman, of Peterborough, rec date 1786, execution, debt, file #5892

DENNIS Arthur, cordwainer, of New Boston, vs FAIRFIELD Matthew, gentleman, of Windham, rec date 1785, writ, debt, file #6247

DENNIS Moses, yeoman, of Hancock, vs KIMBALL Richard, yeoman, of Rindge, doc date 1784, execution, debt, file #1669

DEOLPH Ezra, husbandman, of Hopkinton, vs WHEELOCK John, President Dartmouth College, of Lebanon, doc date 1785, various, land dispute, file #525, Landraff grantees listed also

DEXTER John, of Marlborough MA, vs COGSWELL William, trader, of Marlborough MA, rec date 1787, writ, debt, file #6171, part of Samuel CURTIS file

DICKANSON Jesse, blacksmith, of Strafford, vs ABBOTT Joseph, gentleman, of Wilton, rec date 1785, writ, taking of cow, file #4784

DICKERMAN Samuel, blacksmith, of Francestown, vs FORSAITH William, gentleman, of Deering, rec date 1783, writ, debt, file #3068

DICKERMAN Samuel, blacksmith, of Francestown, vs DEAN George, yeoman, of Francestown, rec date 1785, deed, land transfer, file #5652

DICKERMAN Samuel, yeoman, of Francestown, vs DEAN George, yeoman, of Francestown, doc date 1808, rec date 1808, deed, land transfer, file #5690

DICKEY Adam, husbandman, of Bedford, vs DICKEY James, gentleman, of Roby, doc date 1784, execution, debt, file #1552

DICKEY Adam, husbandman, of Bedford, vs MOORE Samuel, yeoman, of Bedford, doc date 1784, writ, debt, file #1602

DICKEY Adam, husbandman, of Bedford, vs DICKEY James, gentleman, of Raby, doc date 1784, execution, debt, file #1877

DICKEY Adam, husbandman, of Bedford, vs MOORE Samuel, miller, of Bedford, rec date 1783, summons, file #3172

DICKEY Adam, husbandman, of Bedford, vs DICKEY James, gentleman, of Raby, rec date 1783, writ, debt, file #3416

DICKEY Adam, yeoman, of Francestown, vs FELT Benjamin, blacksmith, of Temple, rec date 1785, execution, debt, file #5776

DICKEY Adam, husbandman, of Bedford, vs BELL James, yeoman, of Merrimack, rec date 1786, various, debt, file #6376

DICKEY Adam, husbandman, of Bedford, vs STEELE James, of Antrim, rec date 1785, judgment, debt, file #6357

DICKEY Adams, yeoman, of Bedford, vs BARNET John, yeoman, of Bedford, doc date 1782, execution, file #1016

DICKEY Agnes, widow, of Society Land, vs KELLEY Moses, esquire, of Goffstown, rec date 1785, judgment, debt, file #5494

DICKEY Agnes, widow, of Society Land, vs GREGG James, wheelwright, of Londonderry, rec date 1783, judgment, debt, file #3781

DICKEY Agnes, widow, of Society Land, vs GREGG James, wheelwright, of Londonderry, rec date 1783, writ, debt, file #3955

DICKEY Agnes, widow, of Society Land, vs DICKERMAN Samuel, blacksmith, of Litchfield, rec date 1784, judgment, debt, file #4338

DICKEY Agnes, widow, of Society Land, vs PALMER Jonathan, husbandman, of Litchfield, rec date 1784, judgment, debt, file #4338

DICKEY Agnes, widow, of Society Land, vs KELLEY Moses, esquire, of Goffstown, rec date 1785, execution, debt, file #5921

DICKEY Elias, husbandman, of Raby, vs DICKEY James, gentleman, of Raby, doc date 1783, warrant, assault, file #776

DICKEY Elias, yeoman, of Raby, vs CUTLER Jonas & Ebenezer, traders, of Groton MA, doc date 1773, judgment, debt, file #1181

DICKEY Elias, yeoman, of Hollis, vs WARREN Josiah, yeoman, of Groton MA, doc date 1773, execution, debt, file #1455

DICKEY Elias, yeoman, of Raby, vs STATE of NH, rec date 1782, recognizance, debt, file #2609

DICKEY Elias, yeoman, of Raby, vs KELLEY Moses, esquire, of Goffstown, rec date 1783, writ, debt, file #3184

DICKEY Elias, yeoman, of Raby, vs DICKEY James, gentleman, of Raby, rec date 1783, writ, debt, file #3355

DICKEY Elias, yeoman, of New Boston, vs AMES Stephen, gentleman, of Dublin, rec date 1784, various, land dispute, file #4173, kinships

DICKEY Elias, yeoman, of New Boston, vs NEWHALL Oliver, yeoman, of Hollis, rec date 1785, writ, debt, file #6217

DICKEY Elias, yeoman, of New Boston, vs SHANNON Richard Cutts, esquire, of Raby, rec date 1788, various, land dispute, file #6586, 2 folders

DICKEY Elias (minor), yeoman, of Raby, vs WARREN Josiah, yeoman, of Groton MA, doc date 1772, writ, debt, file #1046

DICKEY James, gentleman, of Raby, vs LAMSON Amos, husbandman, of Harvard MA, rec date 1785, judgment, debt, file #2446

DICKEY James, gentleman, of Raby, vs GOVE Jonathan, physician, of New Boston, rec date 1782, recognizance, debt, file #2607

DICKEY James, gentleman, of Raby, vs TARBELL Edmund, husbandman, of Mason, rec date 1782, writ, land dispute, file #2787

DICKEY James, gentleman, of Raby, vs GOVE Jonathan, physician, of New Boston, rec date 1782, recognizance, debt, file #2607

DICKEY James, gentleman, of Raby, vs COMBS Medad Jr, husbandman, of Dunstable, rec date 1783, civil litigious, debt, file #2917

DICKEY James, gentleman, of Raby, vs ROBY Samuel, cordwainer, of Dunstable MA, rec date 1782, writ, debt, file #3097

DICKEY James, gentleman, of Raby, vs HASELTON Stephen, husbandman, of Hollis, rec date 1783, writ, debt, file #3367

DICKEY James, gentleman, of Raby, vs PARKER Oliver, gentleman, of Groton MA, rec date 1783, writ, debt, file #3430

DICKEY James, gentleman, of Raby, vs FURBUSH Charles, gentleman, of Andover MA, rec date 1783, writ, debt, file #3217

DICKEY James, gentleman, of Raby, vs ABBOTT Samuel, husbandman, of Hollis, rec date 1783, writ, debt, file #3414

DICKEY James, gentleman, of Raby, vs FLETCHER Robert, esquire, of Dunstable, rec date 1783, writ, debt, file #3345

DICKEY James, gentleman, of Raby, vs COMBS Midad Jr, husbandman, of Dunstable, rec date 1783, writ, debt, file #3429

DICKEY James, gentleman, of Raby, vs ABBOTT Benjamin, yeoman, of Hollis, rec date 1784, judgment, debt, file #4640

DICKEY James, gentleman, of Raby, vs DICKEY Elias, husbandman, of Raby, rec date 1782, writ, debt, file #4853

DICKEY James, gentleman, of Raby, vs GREEN Peter, esquire, of Concord, rec date 1784, judgment, debt, file #5342

DICKEY James, gentleman, of Raby, vs SHANNON Richard C, esquire, of Hollis, rec date 1785, writ, debt, file #5430

DICKEY James, gentleman, of Raby, vs PARKER Samuel, yeoman, of Amherst, rec date 1786, writ, debt, file #6103

DICKEY James, of Hollis, rec date 1788, various, land dispute, file #6586, 2 folders

DICKEY John And Adam, husbandman, of Francestown, vs WILSON Thomas, husbandman, of New Boston, rec date 1783, writ, debt, file #3188

DICKEY Joseph, yeoman, of Hollis, vs BALDWIN Nahum, esquire, of Amherst, rec date 1782, writ, debt, file #2684, estate of Zacheus CUTLER

DICKEY Mary, widow, of Antrim, vs MITCHELL John, yeoman, of Francestown, rec date 1788, judgment, bad trade, file #2557

DICKEY Rosanna, widow, of Raby, rec date 1788, various, land dispute, file #6586, 2 folders

DICKINSON Jesse, blacksmith, of Strafford, vs ABBOTT Joseph, gentleman, of Wilton, rec date 1785, various, debt, file #5247

DICKINSON Jesse, blacksmith, of Strafford, vs DANA William, gentleman, of Amherst, rec date 1788, various, horse ownership, file #6597, see folder 6589

DICKSON Gilbert, innholder, of Acton MA, vs KING Samuel, physician, of Chesterfield, doc date 1784, execution, debt, file #1910

DICKSON Gilbert, innholder, of Acton MA, vs THING Samuel, physician, of Chesterfield, rec date 1783, writ, debt, file #3631

DIKE Benjamin, yeoman, of Amherst, vs CUTTER Zacheus, esquire, of Amherst, doc date 1774, writ, debt, file #1097

DIMOND Ephraim, husbandman, of Londonderry, vs GREER Daniel, yeoman, of Weare, rec date 1785, execution, debt, file #5916

DIX Benjamin, husbandman, of Hillsborough, vs GIBSON John, trader, of Francestown, doc date 1799, writ, debt, file #323

DIX Nathan, shopkeeper, of Peterborough, vs LAKIN William, yeoman, of Peterborough, rec date 1785, judgment, debt, file #5222

DIX Nathan, shopkeeper, of Peterborough, vs HOCKLEY James, husbandman, of Peterborough, rec date 1785, judgment, debt, file #5527

DIX Timothy, trader, of Boscawen, vs PETERSON Daniel, physician, of Boscawen, doc date 1798, judgment, debt, file #562

DIX Timothy, trader, of Boscawen, vs BOLTER Benjamin, yeoman, of Boscawen, doc date 1799, debt, file #441

DIX Timothy Jr, trader, of Boscawen, vs EMERSON Benjamin, husbandman, of Alexandria, doc date 1798, judgment, debt, file #562

DIX Timothy Jr, trader, of Boscawen, vs BOLTER Benjamin, yeoman, of Boscawen, doc date 1798, judgment, debt, file #562

DIX Timothy Jr, trader, of Boscawen, vs PETERSON Daniel, physician, of Boscawen, doc date 1799, execution, debt, file #99

DOCKMAN James, husbandman, of Meredith, vs TUCKER Joseph, husbandman, of Andover, rec date 1785, writ, debt, file #4780

DODGE Ammi, husbandman, of New Boston, vs HOGG Robert, husbandman, of Deering, doc date 1798, various, debt, file #523

DODGE Anna, administrator of estate, of Ipswich MA, vs TALBERT Philo, yeoman, of Amherst, rec date 1786, writ, debt, file #6267, estate of Ezekiel DODGE (trader)

DODGE Antipas, yeoman, of Goffstown, vs FERSON John & William, husbandman, of Goffstown, doc date 1798, execution, debt, file #108

DODGE Benjamin, of Lyndeborough, vs MURDOUGH Thomas, yeoman, of Hillsborough, doc date 1784, execution, debt, file #1823

DODGE Benjamin, yeoman, of New Boston, vs MURDOUGH Thomas, yeoman, of Hillsborough, doc date 1784, execution, debt, file #1678

DODGE Benjamin, yeoman, of New Boston, vs MURDOUGH Thomas, yeoman, of Hillsborough, doc date 1784, execution, debt, file #1707

DODGE Benjamin, yeoman, of Lyndeborough, vs DODGE Samuel, yeoman, of Amherst, rec date 1783, writ, debt, file #3057

DODGE Benjamin, yeoman, of New Boston, vs MURDOUGH Thomas, yeoman, of Hillsborough, rec date 1783, execution, debt, file #3256

DODGE Benjamin, yeoman, of New Boston, vs MURDOUGH Thomas, yeoman, of Hillsborough, rec date 1783, execution, debt, file #3825

DODGE Daniel, husbandman, of New Boston, vs MELVIN George, miller, of New Boston, doc date 1799, various, debt, file #524

DODGE Elishu, husbandman, of New Boston, vs SMITH Thomas, husbandman, of New Boston, doc date 1799, various, debt, file #520

DODGE Ezra, yeoman, of New Boston, vs CARTER John, husbandman, of Manchester MA, doc date 1777, deed, land transfer, file #2058

DODGE John Perkins, yeoman, of Mason, vs HUTCHINSON Charles, husbandman, of Keene, rec date 1782, appeal, debt, file #4006

DODGE Joseph, yeoman, of Stoddard, vs DUTTON Joseph, yeoman, of New Ipswich, doc date 1775, writ, debt, file #959

DODGE Robert, husbandman, of Peterborough, vs SPAFFORD Israel, physician, of Beverly MA, rec date 1785, writ, debt, file #5418

DODGE Ruth, widow, of Mason, vs WHITING Jona, cordwainer, of New Ipswich, rec date 1783, writ, animal dispute, file #4485

DODGE Samuel, husbandman, of Amherst, vs TAGGART Archibald, gentleman, of Hillsborough, doc date 1782, execution, debt, file #971

DODGE Samuel, husbandman, of Amherst, vs JONES William, yeoman, of Hillsborough, doc date 1782, execution, debt, file #971

DODGE Samuel, husbandman, of Amherst, vs ANDREWS Ammin, gentleman, of Hillsborough, doc date 1782, execution, debt, file #967

DODGE Samuel, husbandman, of Amherst, vs JOHNSON Zebediah, yeoman, of Hillsborough, doc date 1782, execution, debt, file #971

DODGE Samuel, yeoman, of Amherst, vs MURDOUGH Thomas, husbandman, of Hillsborough, doc date 1784, execution, debt, file #2070

DODGE Samuel, yeoman, of Amherst, vs JONES William Jr, yeoman, of Hillsborough, doc date 1784, execution, debt, file #1661

DODGE Samuel, yeoman, of Francestown, vs RICHARDSON Zachariah, innkeeper, of Francestown, doc date 1784, execution, debt, file #1815

DODGE Samuel, yeoman, of Amherst, vs WHITE Robert, yeoman, of New Boston, doc date 1784, execution, debt, file #1783

DODGE Samuel, yeoman, of Amherst, vs MURDOUGH Thomas, yeoman, of Hillsborough, doc date 1784, execution, debt, file #1754

DODGE Samuel, yeoman, of Amherst, vs HOUGHTON Israel, trader, of Keene, doc date 1784, execution, debt, file #1760

DODGE Samuel, yeoman, of Amherst, vs GRIMES James, gentleman, of Deering, doc date 1784, execution, debt, file #1782

DODGE Samuel, yeoman, of Amherst, vs MURDOUGH Thomas, yeoman, of Hillsborough, doc date 1784, execution, debt, file #1512

DODGE Samuel, yeoman, of Amherst, vs HUSTCHINSON Solomon, yeoman, of Merrimack, doc date 1784, execution, debt, file #1967

DODGE Samuel, yeoman, of Amherst, vs DODGE Benjamin, yeoman, of Lyndeborough, doc date 1784, execution, debt, file #1968

DODGE Samuel, yeoman, of Amherst, vs COCKRAN John, yeoman, of Amherst, doc date 1784, execution, debt, file #1986

DODGE Samuel, husbandman, of Amherst, vs STATE of NH, rec date 1777, writ, debt, file #2208

DODGE Samuel, husbandman, of Amherst, vs HOBART Jonathan Jr, husbandman, of Hollis, rec date 1785, writ, debt, file #2406

DODGE Samuel, yeoman, of Amherst, vs WILSON Jesse, yeoman, of Merrimack, rec date 1783, civil litigious, debt, file #2967

DODGE Samuel, husbandman, of Amherst, vs BIXBY Andrew, yeoman, of Hillsborough, rec date 1783, civil litigious, debt, file #2952

DODGE Samuel, yeoman, of Amherst, vs CLARK Ephraim, yeoman, of Deering, rec date 1783, execution, debt, file #2991

DODGE Samuel, yeoman, of Amherst, vs TAGGART James, yeoman, of Hillsborough, rec date 1783, execution, debt, file #3239

DODGE Samuel, yeoman, of Amherst, vs WILSON Jesse, yeoman, of Merrimack, rec date 1783, execution, debt, file #3261

DODGE Samuel, husbandman, of Amherst, vs BIXBY Andrew, yeoman, of Merrimack, rec date 1783, execution, debt, file #3262

DODGE Samuel, husbandman, of Amherst, vs MURDOUGH Thomas, husbandman, of Hillsborough, rec date 1783, execution, debt, file #3263

DODGE Samuel, yeoman, of Amherst, vs CUMMINGS Silas, blacksmith, of New Boston, rec date 1783, execution, debt, file #3638

DODGE Samuel, husbandman, of Amherst, vs BIXBY Andrew, yeoman, of Hillsborough, rec date 1783, execution, debt, file #3674

DODGE Samuel, yeoman, of Amherst, vs HASELTINE Nathaniel, yeoman, of Amherst, rec date 1782, execution, debt, file #3526

DODGE Samuel, yeoman, of Amherst, vs HAZELTINE Nathaniel, yeoman, of Amherst, rec date 1783, execution, debt, file #3675

DODGE Samuel, husbandman, of Hillsborough, vs MURDOUGH Thomas, husbandman, of Hillsborough, rec date 1783, execution, debt, file #3687

DODGE Samuel, yeoman, of Amherst, vs JONES James, yeoman, of Hillsborough, rec date 1783, judgment, debt, file #3743

DODGE Samuel, yeoman, of Amherst, vs CUMINGS Silas, blacksmith, of New Boston, rec date 1782, execution, debt, file #3511

DODGE Samuel, yeoman, of Amherst, vs WILSON Jesse, yeoman, of Merrimack, rec date 1783, writ, debt, file #3886

DODGE Samuel, yeoman, of Amherst, vs COOLEDGE Silas, yeoman, of Hillsborough, rec date 1783, judgment, debt, file #3743

DODGE Samuel, husbandman, of Amherst, vs MURDOUGH Thomas, husbandman, of Hillsborough, rec date 1782, execution, debt, file #3512

DODGE Samuel, yeoman, of Amherst, vs TAGGART Robert, physician, of Merrimack, rec date 1782, execution, debt, file #3510

DODGE Samuel, yeoman, of Amherst, vs HUTCHINSON Solomon, yeoman, of Merrimack, rec date 1783, execution, debt, file #3691

DODGE Samuel, innholder, of Amherst, vs HUSE Abel, husbandman, of Derryfield, rec date 1784, appeal, debt, file #4100

DODGE Samuel, yeoman, of Amherst, vs HASELTINE Nathaniel, yeoman, of Amherst, rec date 1783, execution, debt, file #3850

DODGE Samuel, yeoman, of Amherst, vs TAGGART Robert, yeoman, of Merrimack, rec date 1783, execution, debt, file #3845

DODGE Samuel, husbandman, of Amherst, vs FARWELL Abel, cooper, of Groton MA, rec date 1783, writ, debt, file #3973

DODGE Samuel, yeoman, of Amherst, vs BRADFORD Samuel Jr, yeoman, of Amherst, rec date 1784, appeal, debt, file #4118

DODGE Samuel, esquire, of Amherst, vs BRADFORD Samuel Jr, yeoman, of Hillsborough, rec date 1784, judgment, debt, file #4405, note of Henry CODMAN

DODGE Samuel, yeoman, of Hillsborough, vs SWEAT Josiah, husbandman, of Campbells Gore, rec date 1789, various, debt, file #5554

DODGE Samuel, innholder, of Amherst, vs GRIMES James, gentleman, of Deering, rec date 1785, judgment, debt, file #4685

DODGE Samuel, yeoman, of Amherst, vs ANDREWS Isaac, of Hillsborough, rec date 1783, writ, debt, file #4322, note of a Negro man

DODGE Samuel, yeoman, of Amherst, vs HOWARD Silas, yeoman, of Lyndeborough, rec date 1786, judgment, debt, file #5557

DODGE Samuel, yeoman, of Amherst, vs MOOR John, husbandman, of Bedford, rec date 1784, judgment, debt, file #4996

DODGE Samuel, innholder, of Amherst, vs BALDWIN Isaac, gentleman, of Hillsborough, rec date 1784, judgment, debt, file #4923, note of LEWIS a Negro

DODGE Samuel, innholder, of Amherst, vs GRIMES James, yeoman, of Deering, rec date 1785, judgment, debt, file #5125

DODGE Samuel, husbandman, of Amherst, vs BOYNTON Joshua, clockmaker, of Hollis, rec date 1785, judgment, debt, file #5079

DODGE Samuel, husbandman, of Amherst, vs TAGGART Archibald, gentleman, of Hillsborough, rec date 1785, execution, debt, file #5486

DODGE Samuel, husbandman, of Amherst, vs LUND John, gentleman, of Dunstable, rec date 1785, judgment, debt, file #5874

DODGE Samuel, yeoman, of Amherst, vs PRESTON Samuel, yeoman, of Deering, rec date 1783, execution, debt, file #5714

DODGE Samuel, yeoman, of Amherst, vs ALLD James, yeoman, of Hillsborough, rec date 1782, execution, debt, file #5747

DODGE Samuel, yeoman, of Amherst, vs ROFFE Benjamin, yeoman, of Deering, rec date 1783, execution, debt, file #5714

DODGE Samuel, innholder, of Amherst, vs DONOVAN John, yeoman, of New
Boston, rec date 1785, execution, debt, file #5793

DODGE Samuel, husbandman, of Hillsborough, vs SMALL Joseph, yeoman, of
Amherst, rec date 1785, judgment, debt, file #5989

DODGE Samuel, innholder, of Amherst, vs KITTREDGE James, yeoman, of
Goffstown, rec date 1785, execution, debt, file #5796

DODGE Samuel, husbandman, of Amherst, vs SMALL Joseph, yeoman, of
Amherst, rec date 1785, writ, debt, file #6029

DODGE Samuel, innholder, of Amherst, vs GRIMES James, gentleman, of
Deering, rec date 1785, execution, debt, file #6042

DODGE Samuel, esquire, of Amherst, vs EVERDEN John, yeoman, of Deering,
rec date 1785, judgment, debt, file #6462

DODGE Samuel, yeoman, of Amherst, vs DRESSER Asa, yeoman, of Campbells
Gore, rec date 1785, judgment, debt, file #6452

DODGE Samuel, husbandman, of Amherst, vs JONES Timothy, of Lyndeborough,
rec date 1785, judgment, debt, file #6359

DODGE Samuel, husbandman, of Amherst, vs CLARK Thomas, husbandman, of
Dunstable, rec date 1786, judgment, debt, file #6493

DODGE Samuel, husbandman, of Amherst, vs SMALL Joseph, yeoman, of
Amherst, rec date 1786, judgment, debt, file #6383

DODGE Samuel, innholder, of Amherst, vs SAWYER Jonathan, yeoman, of
Hancock, rec date 1785, judgment, debt, file #6429

DODGE Samuel, deceased, of Amherst, vs LOVEJOY Francis, feltmaker, of
Amherst, rec date 1785, various, debt, file #6248

DODGE Samuel, yeoman, of Amherst, vs NICHOLS William, yeoman, of
Lyndeborough, rec date 1785, judgment, debt, file #6453

DODGE Samuel, husbandman, of Hillsborough, vs ROBBINSON James, joiner,
of Boscawen, rec date 1788, writ, debt, file #6729

DODGE Solomon, yeoman, of New Boston, vs WHITE Robert, yeoman, of New
Boston, rec date 1785, execution, debt, file #5472

DODGE Solomon, yeoman, of New Boston, vs WHITE Robert, of New Boston,
rec date 1785, execution, debt, file #5792

DODGE Solomon, yeoman, of New Boston, vs WHITE Robert, yeoman, of New
Boston, rec date 1786, judgment, debt, file #6191

DODGE Susanna, widow, of Amherst, vs COLDWELL William, gentleman, of
Francestown, rec date 1785, judgment, debt, file #5545

DODGE Susanna, widow, of Amherst, vs HOWARD Silas, yeoman, of
Lyndeborough, rec date 1786, judgment, debt, file #5551, estate of Samuel
DODGE

DODGE Susanna, administrator of estate, of Amherst, vs BOYES William,
gentleman, of New Boston, rec date 1786, execution, debt, file #5894

DODGE Susanna, widow, of Amherst, vs WHITTAKER James, husbandman, of
Deering, rec date 1786, writ, debt, file #6291, estate of Samuel DODGE

DODGE Susanna, widow, of Amherst, vs ROBANSON Silas, husbandman, of
Bennington, rec date 1785, writ, debt, file #6257, widow of Samuel DODGE

DODGE Susanna, widow, of Amherst, vs DOW Evan, husbandman, of Deering,
rec date 1786, writ, debt, file #6291, estate of Samuel DODGE

DODGE Susannah, widow, of Amherst, vs HUTCHINSON Solomon, yeoman, of Merrimack, rec date 1788, judgment, debt, file #2563

DODGE Susannah, widow, of Amherst, vs LIVINGSTON William, gentleman, of New Boston, rec date 1785, execution, debt, file #5487, estate of William DODGE

DODGE Susannah, widow, of Amherst, vs MCCLENCHE Joseph, blacksmith, of Merrimack, rec date 1786, writ, debt, file #6126, estate of Samuel DODGE (see file 6125)

DODGE Susannah, widow, of Amherst, vs BRADFORD Andrew, husbandman, of Hillsborough, rec date 1786, writ, debt, file #6125, estate of Samuel DODGE

DODGE Susannah, widow, of Amherst, vs ROBINSON Silas, rec date 1786, judgment, debt, file #6505

DODGE Thomas, pumpmaker, of Epping, vs ATHERTON Peter, gentleman, of Harvard MA, rec date 1782, writ, debt, file #2803

DOKIN Justrus, husbandman, of Nottingham-West, vs SHANNON Richard Cutts, esquire, of Hollis, rec date 1782, debt, debt, file #3154

DOLE Stephen, husbandman, of Bedford, vs FLAGG Samuel, husbandman, of Worcester MA, rec date 1785, writ, debt, file #5392

DOLE Stephen, husbandman, of Bedford, vs FOWLER Samuel, of Boscawen, rec date 1784, judgment, debt, file #5038

DOLE Stephen, gentleman, of Bedford, vs MOOR John, yeoman, of Francestown, rec date 1786, execution, debt, file #5876

DONOVAN Matthew, gentleman, of Concord, vs ANDREWS Ephraim, of New Boston, rec date 1783, writ of possession, land dispute, file #3637, land deed

DOUGLAS Joseph & Mary, gentleman, of Landraff, vs HOW Peter, husbandman, of Henniker, rec date 1785, judgment, debt, file #5152

DOUGLAS Joseph & Mary, gentleman, of Landraff, vs EAGER Joseph, husbandman, of Henniker, rec date 1785, judgment, debt, file #5152

DOUGLAS Joseph & Mary, gentleman, of Landraff, vs EAGER Joseph, husbandman, of Henniker, rec date 1784, writ, debt, file #5321

DOUGLAS Joseph & Mary, gentleman, of Landraff, vs HOW Peter, husbandman, of Henniker, rec date 1785, writ, debt, file #5321

DOUGLAS Robert, husbandman, of Nottingham, vs SIMSON William, husbandman, of Windham, doc date 1798, execution, debt, file #132

DOUGLAS Samuel, yeoman, of Raby, vs ABBOT Benjamin, husbandman, of Hollis, rec date 1783, judgment, debt, file #3782

DOW Evan, yeoman, vs MARSHALL Samuel Jr, husbandman, of Nottingham-West, doc date 1782, execution, debt, file #972

DOW Evan, yeoman, of Deering, vs GRIMES James, gentleman, of Deering, rec date 1783, civil litigious, debt, file #2912

DOW Evan, husbandman, of Deering, vs ANDREWS Ammi, gentleman, of Littleton MA, rec date 1786, judgment, debt, file #6389

DOW James, yeoman, of Nottingham, vs WORSTER Noah, esquire, of Hollis, rec date 1785, judgment, debt, file #4257

DOW Job, esquire, of Goffstown, vs GREER David, husbandman, of Goffstown, rec date 1794, judgment, assault, file #4151

DOW Joseph Jr, yeoman, of Goffstown, vs GAGE John, joiner, of Lunenburg MA, doc date 1773, writ, debt, file #1334

DOW Nathaniel, blacksmith, vs McCLARY Andrew, doc date 1775, deposition, file #1167

DOW Oliver, husbandman, of Hopkinton, vs FARNUM Timothy, husbandman, of Hopkinton, rec date 1785, writ, debt, file #6025

DOW Perry, yeoman, of Nottingham-West, vs KELLEY Joseph, gentleman, of Nottingham-West, doc date 1784, writ, debt, file #1579

DOW Peter, clothier, of Goffstown, vs COOLIDGE Silas, yeoman, of Hillsborough, rec date 1783, execution, debt, file #3248

DOW Polly, spinster, of Goffstown, vs DOW Joseph, husbandman, of Deering, doc date 1814, rec date 1815, deed, land transfer, file #5700

DOW Samuel, yeoman, of Haverhill MA, vs CONNOR Jeremy, yeoman, of Allenstown, doc date 1784, execution, debt, file #1506

DOW Samuel, yeoman, of Haverhill MA, vs CONNOR Jeremy, yeoman, of Allenstown, rec date 1783, judgment, debt, file #4078

DOW Samuel, yeoman, of Nottingham, vs LAWRENCE Daniel, yeoman, of Hollis, rec date 1784, judgment, debt, file #4259

DOW Samuel, carpenter, of Pelham, vs MOSHER James, husbandman, of Hollis, rec date 1784, judgment, debt, file #4995

DOW Samuel, yeoman, of Haverhill MA, vs CONNER Jeremy, yeoman, of Allenstown, rec date 1785, judgment, debt, file #6455

DOW Samuel J, vs the ELECTRIC COMPANY, doc date 1893, petition for damages, supreme court, file #597

DOW ----, vs ELECTRIC COMPANY, doc date 1894, re hearing date, supreme court, file #584

DOWN Job, esquire, of Goffstown, vs JOHNSON Tim, rec date 1792, indictment, stealing, file #4055

DOWN Samuel, yeoman, of Haverhill MA, vs CONNOER Jeremy, yeoman, of Allenstown, doc date 1784, execution, debt, file #1692

DOWNS Amas, tanner, of Francestown, vs HOWE Abonijah, physician, of Jaffrey, doc date 1811, rec date 1811, deed, transfer of land, file #5694

DRESSER Asa, yeoman, of Campbells Gore, vs COOLIAGE Silas, yeoman, of Hillsborough, doc date 1784, execution, debt, file #1532

DRESSER Asa, yeoman, of Campbells Gore, vs COOLEGE Silas, yeoman, of Hillsborough, doc date 1784, execution, debt, file #1880

DRESSER Asa, yeoman, of Campbells Gore, vs RICHARDSON Zachariah, yeoman, of Francestown, rec date 1785, judgment, debt, file #2442

DRESSER Asa, yeoman, of Campbells Gore, vs COOLIDGE Silas, yeoman, of Hillsborough, rec date 1783, civil litigious, debt, file #2957

DRESSER Asa, yeoman, of Campbells Gore, vs TAGGART James, yeoman, of Bradford, rec date 1783, civil litigious, debt, file #2927

DRESSER Asa, yeoman, of Campbells Gore, vs BIXBY Andrew, of Hillsborough, rec date 1785, judgment, debt, file #5544

DRESSER Asa, husbandman, of Campbells Gore, vs GROUT William, husbandman, of Hillsborough, rec date 1785, judgment, debt, file #5185

DRESSER Asa, yeoman, of Campbells Gore, vs RICHARDSON Zachariah, yeoman, of Francestown, rec date 1785, execution, debt, file #5258

DRESSER Asa, yeoman, of Campbells Gore, vs RICHARDSON Zachariah, of Francestown, rec date 1785, judgment, debt, file #6182

DRUARY Benjamin, physician, of Spencer MA, vs WEATHERSPOON Alexander, yeoman, of Deering, doc date 1784, execution, debt, file #1918

DRUARY Zedekiah, gentleman, of Temple, vs DRUARY Daniel (heirs), of Temple, doc date 1777, deed, land transfer, file #2063

DRUARY Zedekiah, gentleman, of Alstead, vs BROWN Peter, yeoman, of Temple, rec date 1784, appeal, debt, file #4124

DRURY Benjamin, physician, of Spencer MA, vs HUTCHINSON John, yeoman, of Weare, doc date 1784, civil litigation, debt, file #1835

DRURY Benjamin, physician, of Spencer MA, vs BROWN William, yeoman, of Francestown, rec date 1783, writ, debt, file #4042

DRURY Benjamin, physician, of Spencer MA, vs DICKERMAN Samuel, yeoman, of Francestown, rec date 1783, judgment, debt, file #4439

DRURY Ebenezer, husbandman, of Temple, vs FOSTER Jacob, clerk, of Packersfield, rec date 1785, judgment, debt, file #5094

DRURY Zedikiah, gentleman, of Alstead, vs BROWN Peter, yeoman, of Temple, rec date 1785, judgment, debt, file #6358

DUDLEY Paul, merchant, of Amherst, vs FRYE Isaac, yeoman, of Wilton, doc date 1774, execution, file #946

DUGALL William, physician, of Dunbarton, vs WATT Hugh, husbandman, of Londonderry, rec date 1785, judgment, debt, file #5821

DUNBAR Asa, gentleman, of Harvard MA, vs CROSS John, husbandman, of Litchfield, doc date 1784, execution, debt, file #1736

DUNBAR Asa, yeoman, of Harvard MA, vs GREEN David, yeoman, of Hillsborough, doc date 1784, execution, debt, file #1538

DUNBAR Asa, gentleman, of Harvard MA, vs CROSS John, husbandman, of Litchfield, doc date 1784, execution, debt, file #1956

DUNBAR Asa, gentleman, of Harvard MA, vs GUN David, yeoman, of Hillsborough, doc date 1784, execution, debt, file #1873

DUNBAR Asa, gentleman, of Harvard MA, vs GREEN David, yeoman, of Hillsborough, rec date 1783, execution, debt, file #2979

DUNCAN Abraham, husbandman, of Londonderry, vs CLOUGH William, husbandman, of Salem, doc date 1772, writ, debt, file #1401

DUNCAN Abraham, husbandman, of Londonderry, vs CLOUGH James, husbandman, of Salem, doc date 1772, writ, debt, file #1401

DUNCAN George, yeoman, of Londonderry, vs CUMINGS Eleazer, of New Ipswich, rec date 1782, writ, land dispute, file #2677, land in Andover NY near CT river

DUNCAN George, yeoman, of Londonderry, vs WARNER John, yeoman, of New Ipswich, doc date 1782, rec date 1782, writ, land dispute, file #2677, land in Andover NY

DUNCAN George, yeoman, of Londonderry, vs ROGERS Josiah, yeoman, of New Ipswich, doc date 1782, rec date 1782, writ, land dispute, file #2677, land in Andover NY

DUNCAN George, yeoman, of Londonderry, vs HEYWOOD Samuel, gentleman, of New Ipswich, doc date 1782, rec date 1782, writ, land dispute, file #2677, land in Andover NY

DUNCAN J William, tax collector, of Antrim, vs DUNCAN John, gentleman, of Antrim, doc date 1793, rec date 1793, deed, land transfer, file #6794, pg 101 tax sale

DUNCAN James, husbandman, of Hancock, vs COSTEN Ebenezer, husbandman, of Francestown, rec date 1785, execution, debt, file #5922

DUNCAN James, husbandman, of Hancock, vs COSTEN Ebenezer, husbandman, of Francestown, rec date 1785, writ, debt, file #6022

DUNCAN John, husbandman, of Acworth, vs MOORE John, husbandman, of Francestown, rec date 1785, writ, debt, file #2355

DUNCAN John, husbandman, of Acworth, vs MOOR John, husbandman, of Francestown, rec date 1785, judgment, debt, file #5218

DUNCAN Robert, gentleman, of Hancock, vs HOYT Moses, cordwainer, of Henniker, rec date 1783, judgment, debt, file #4466

DUNCAN Robert, gentleman, of Hancock, vs PRESTON Abner, yeoman, of Hancock, rec date 1785, judgment, debt, file #5595

DUNCAN Robert, gentleman, of Hancock, vs CAMPBELL John, husbandman, of Deering, rec date 1787, execution, debt, file #5895

DUNCAN Samuel & Robert, traders, of Concord, vs CANN David, trader, of Boscawen, rec date 1785, writ, debt, file #4787

DUNCAN William, esquire, of Concord, vs FOWLER Samuel, esquire, of Boscawen, doc date 1798, judgment, debt, file #562

DUNKLE Joseph, yeoman, of Goffstown, vs LOWELL Stephen Jr, yeoman, of Dunstable, rec date 1784, judgment, debt, file #4282

DUNKLE Joseph, yeoman, of Goffstown, vs LOWELL Stephen, yeoman, of Dunstable, rec date 1784, judgment, debt, file #4282

DUNKLEE John, yeoman, of Amherst, vs HOPKINS Ebenezer, husbandman, of Amherst, rec date 1783, writ, debt, file #2771

DUNKLEE Joseph, yeoman, of Amherst, vs GOODRIDGE Sewall, clerk, of Lyndeborough, rec date 1783, writ, debt, file #3074

DUNLAP James, husbandman, of Antrim, vs EATON Thomas, physician, of Francestown, doc date 1799, judgment, debt, file #234

DUNLAP William, husbandman, of Henniker, vs ROSS Jonathan, husbandman, of Henniker, doc date 1784, execution, debt, file #1703

DUNLAP William, husbandman, of Henniker, vs ROSS Jonathan, husbandman, of Henniker, doc date 1784, execution, debt, file #1905

DUNLAP William, husbandman, of Henniker, vs ROSS Jonathan, husbandman, of Henniker, rec date 1783, writ, debt, file #3390

DUNLAP William, husbandman, of Henniker, vs ROSS Jonathan, husbandman, of Henniker, rec date 1785, judgment, debt, file #5212

DUNSHEE Hugh, weaver, of Londonderry, vs DUNOR John, weaver, of Londonderry, doc date 1771, writ, debt, file #1383, DUNOR John (deceased)

DUNSMOOR John, physician, of Lunenburg MA, vs BLOOD Robert, yeoman, of Peterborough, rec date 1783, judgment, debt, file #4496

DUNSMORE Abraham, yeoman, of Lyndeborough, vs RUSSELL Daniel, physician, of Lyndeborough, rec date 1788, writ, debt, file #6686

DURANT David, yeoman, of Nottingham, vs CUMMINGS Ephraim, yeoman, of Swansey, doc date 1784, writ, debt, file #1627

DURANT Jonathan, husbandman, of Henniker, vs ANDREWS Ammi, gentleman, of Hillsborough, rec date 1788, writ, debt, file #6940

DUREN Reuben, housewright, of Bedford MA, vs ANDREWS Ammi, gentleman, of Hillsborough, rec date 1782, judgment, debt, file #2717

DUREN Reuben, housewright, of Bedford MA, vs ANDREWS Ammi, gentleman, of Hillsborough, rec date 1783, execution, debt, file #3272

DUREN Reuben, housewright, of Bedford MA, vs ANDREWS Ammi, gentleman, of Hillsborough, rec date 1783, execution, debt, file #3668

DURKIN Moody, vs EDWARDS Thomas, rec date 1775, execution, file #7031

DURY Zedekiah, gentleman, of Temple, vs BACON Retire, yeoman, of New Ipswich, doc date 1772, writ, debt, file #939

DUSTER Jason, yeoman, of Mason, vs ADAMS Joseph, of Great Britain, rec date 1784, judgment, debt, file #4240

DUSTIN Eliphalet, husbandman, of Francestown, vs MURDOUGH Thomas, husbandman, of Hillsborough, rec date 1782, execution, debt, file #3477

DUSTIN Paul, yeoman, of New Boston, vs MELLEN Thomas, cordwainer, of Society Land, rec date 1783, judgment, debt, file #2853

DUSTIN Paul, yeoman, of New Boston, vs MELLIN Thomas, cordwainer, of Society Land, rec date 1783, execution, debt, file #2887

DUSTIN Paul, husbandman, of New Boston, vs BROWN James, gentleman, of Plymouth, rec date 1783, writ, debt, file #3372

DUSTIN Paul, yeoman, of New Boston, vs BROWN Adam, yeoman, of Plymouth, rec date 1782, execution, debt, file #5730

DUSTIN Paul, yeoman, of Goffstown, vs SHIRALA Thomas?, yeoman, of Goffstown, doc date 1778, rec date 1781, deed, land transfer, file #6565

DUSTIN Paul, yeoman, of New Boston, vs COSTER Ebenezer, yeoman, of Goffstown, rec date 1779, judgment, debt, file #7033

DUSTIN William, gentleman, of Weare, vs HOIT Philip, physician, of Weare, rec date 1782, execution, debt, file #3513

DUSTIN William, gentleman, of Weare, vs HOIT Philip, physician, of Weare, rec date 1783, execution, debt, file #3468

DUSTIN William, gentleman, of Weare, vs CUSHING John, physician, of Goffstown, rec date 1785, judgment, debt, file #5173

DUSTIN William, gentleman, of Weare, vs CUSHING John, physician, of Goffstown, rec date 1785, judgment, debt, file #6436

DUSTIN William, gentleman, of Weare, vs CUSHING John, physician, of Goffstown, rec date 1785, judgment, debt, file #6404

DUSTIN Zacheus, yeoman, of Society Land, vs LOVEJOY Francis Jr, yeoman, of Amherst, rec date 1787, judgment, debt, file #6197

DUSTIN Zacheus, yeoman, of Society Land, vs LOVEJOY Francis Jr, laborer, of Amherst, rec date 1787, writ, debt, file #2371

DUSTON Eliphalet, cordwainer, of New Boston, vs CALDWELL James, carpenter, doc date 1778, rec date 1779, deed, land transfer, file #2143

DUSTON Eliphalet, yeoman, of Francestown, vs BALDWIN Nahum, esquire, of Amherst, rec date 1782, appeal, debt, file #3991

DUSTON Paul, yeoman, of New Boston, vs COSTER Ebenezer, yeoman, of Goffstown, doc date 1779, writ, debt, file #2096

DUTTON Abigail, widow, of Amherst, vs STEARNS Nathan, yeoman, of Amherst, rec date 1787, judgment, debt, file #2467

DUTTON Asa, yeoman, of Greenfield, vs SMITH John, esquire, of Peterborough, doc date 1799, debt, file #438

DUTTON Jacob, yeoman, of Francestown, vs STICKNEY Abiel, yeoman, of New Boston, doc date 1798, execution, debt, file #105

DUTTON James, yeoman, of Hillsborough, vs GAMMEL William, yeoman, of Hillsborough, rec date 1783, execution, debt, file #3000

DUTTON James, blacksmith, of Hillsborough, vs DRESSER Asa, husbandman, of Campbells Gore, rec date 1783, writ, debt, file #3583

DUTTON James, blacksmith, of Hillsborough, vs GOODELL Job, trader, of Marlborough MA, rec date 1783, writ, debt, file #4313

DUTTON James, yeoman, of Hillsborough, vs GROUT William, yeoman, of Hillsborough, rec date 1786, writ, debt, file #6304

DUTTON Jesse, blacksmith, of Dunstable MA, vs ROLLINS Joseph, cooper, of Amherst, doc date 1778, writ, debt, file #2053

DUTTON John, yeoman, of Hillsborough, vs McCLENTOCK John, husbandman, of Hillsborough, rec date 1783, writ, debt, file #2999

DUTTON William, husbandman, of Stoddard, vs PARKER Oliver, gentleman, of Penobscott Me, doc date 1784, writ, debt, file #1629

DUTY Deborah, widow, of Beverly MA, vs STICKNEY Daniel, widow, of Hopkinton, doc date 1774, judgment, debt, file #780

DWINELL John, husbandman, of Londonderry, vs RICHARDS Samuel, gentleman, of Goffstown, doc date 1782, summons, debt, file #764

EAGER George, surgeon, of Groton MA, vs TARBEL Samuel, gentleman, of Amherst, doc date 1773, writ, debt, file #1237

EAGER George, surgeon, of Groton MA, vs BOND Thomas, yeoman, of Groton, doc date 1773, writ, debt, file #1243

EAGER Joseph, yeoman, of Henniker, vs DOUGLAS Joseph, yeoman, of Concord, doc date 1784, execution, debt, file #1697

EAGER Joseph, yeoman, of Henniker, vs DOUGLAS Joseph, yeoman, of Concord, rec date 1783, judgment, debt, file #4514

EAMES Jonathan, gentleman, of Newtown, vs LITTLE William & Joseph, silversmiths, of Newburyport MA, doc date 1769, summons, debt, file #809

EAMES Robert, yeoman, of Henniker, vs HOW Baxter, yeoman, of Hillsborough, doc date 1773, writ, debt, file #1229

EAMES Samuel, esquire, of Haverhill MA, vs FRYE Isaac, husbandman, of Wilton, doc date 1774, judgment, debt, file #705

EARTY Joshua, yeoman, of Hillsborough, vs ROBINSON William, yeoman, of Deering, doc date 1784, execution, debt, file #1803

EASTMAN Amos, blacksmith, of Hollis, vs FELT Benjamin, blacksmith, of Temple, doc date 1784, civil litigation, debt, file #1632

EASTMAN Amos, gentleman, of Hollis, vs CLOUGH James, husbandman, of Salem, doc date 1774, rec date 1785, deed, land transfer, file #5647

EASTMAN Amos Jr, blacksmith, of Hollis, vs STEARNS Samuel, husbandman, of Plymouth, rec date 1786, writ, debt, file #2419

EASTMAN Amos Jr, blacksmith, of Hollis, vs FELT Benjamin, blacksmith, of Temple, rec date 1783, judgment, debt, file #4718

EASTMAN Franklin J, vs PROVIDENT Mutual Relief Association, doc date 1889, plaintiff brief, supreme court, file #615

EASTMAN Ichabod, yeoman, of Nottingham-West, vs HADLEY Enos, yeoman, of Nottingham-West, rec date 1784, various, debt, file #4179

EASTMAN Jonathan, esquire, of Hollis, doc date 1786, license, tavern license, file #862

EASTMAN Joseph Fletcher, physician, of Hollis, vs ATWELL John, joiner, of Hollis, doc date 1799, judgment, debt, file #568

EASTMAN Moses, gentleman, of Salisbury, vs TUCKER Ebenezer, yeoman, of Andover, doc date 1798, execution, debt, file #69

EASTMAN Sarah, widow, of Brookline, vs PRATT Thomas, hatter, of Hollis, doc date 1799, judgment, debt, file #568

EASTMAN Sarah, widow, of Hollis, vs WARREN Benjamin, gentleman, of Hollis, doc date 1799, judgment, debt, file #568

EASTMAN Thomas, yeoman, of Hopkinton, vs CHASE Abner, husbandman, of Warner, rec date 1783, writ, debt, file #3805

EASTMAN Thomas, husbandman, of Hopkinton, vs CHASE Abner, husbandman, of Warner, rec date 1783, execution, debt, file #3830

EASTMAN William, husbandman, of Salisbury, vs BEAN Joseph, esquire, of Salisbury, rec date 1783, writ, debt, file #3210

EASTMAN Zachariah, yeoman, of Nottingham-West, vs HALL John, gentleman, of Deerfield, doc date 1784, writ, debt, file #1577

EASTON Benjamin, administrator of estate, of Reading MA, vs WILKINS Benjamin, yeoman, of Amherst, rec date 1786, various, debt, file #6366

EASTY Joshua, yeoman, of Hillsborough, vs COOLEDGE Silas, yeoman, of Hillsborough, rec date 1783, judgment, debt, file #4318

EASTY Joshua, yeoman, of Hillsborough, vs ROBINSON William, yeoman, of Deering, rec date 1783, judgment, debt, file #4447

EATON Abijah, of Walpole, rec date 1788, various, trespass/cattle, file #6585

EATON Benjamin, gentleman, of Woburn MA, vs NEWMAN Josiah, husbandman, of Deering, rec date 1788, writ, debt, file #2379

EATON Benjamin, husbandman, of Woburn MA, vs NICHOLS Moses, esquire, of Amherst, rec date 1785, writ, debt, file #6237

EATON Ebenezer, esquire, of Bradford, vs HILDRETH Simeon, husbandman, of Bradford, doc date 1799, various, debt, file #527

EATON Ebenezer, of Walpole, rec date 1788, various, trespass/cattle, file #6585

EATON Enoch, husbandman, of Acworth, vs ORDWAY Samuel, yeoman, of Goffstown, doc date 1784, execution, debt, file #1737

EATON Enoch, husbandman, of Atkinson, vs ORDWAY Samuel, of Goffstown, doc date 1784, execution, debt, file #1962

EATON Enoch, husbandman, of Atkinson, vs PALMER William, cooper, of Goffstown, rec date 1783, judgment, debt, file #3753

EATON James, yeoman, of Goffstown, vs WILSON David, yeoman, of Society Land, doc date 1772, writ, debt, file #920

EATON James, husbandman, of Goffstown, vs HADLEY George, gentleman, of Weare, rec date 1783, writ, debt, file #3343

EATON James, husbandman, of Goffstown, vs KELLY Moses, esquire, of Goffstown, rec date 1785, writ, debt, file #5429

EATON John, blacksmith, of Amherst, vs GRIMES Thaddeus, yeoman, of Amherst, doc date 1784, execution, debt, file #1755

EATON John, blacksmith, of Amherst, vs SERGEANT Moses, gentleman, of Londonderry, rec date 1782, writ, debt, file #2622

EATON John, blacksmith, of Amherst, vs CLARK Timothy, husbandman, of Amherst, rec date 1786, writ, debt, file #6087

EATON John, yeoman, of Amherst, vs CLARK Timothy, of Amherst, rec date 1786, summons, debt, file #6183

EATON Obadiah, husbandman, of Weare, vs LEVISTONE Isaac, husbandman, of Hillsborough, rec date 1783, various, debit on land, file #4564

EATON Samuel, yeoman, of Goffstown, vs BRIDGE John, gentleman, of Boston MA, doc date 1798, judgment, debt, file #562

EATON Thomas, husbandman, of Weare, vs STEWART James, husbandman, of Dunbarton, doc date 1784, execution, debt, file #1557

EATON Thomas, husbandman, of Weare, vs AUSTIN John, husbandman, of Dunbarton, doc date 1784, execution, debt, file #1557

EATON Thomas, physician, of Francestown, vs COGSWELL Henry F, gentleman, of Peterborough, doc date 1813, rec date 1820, deed, land transfer, file #5708

EAYERS Joseph, yeoman, of Merrimack, vs JONES Timothy, yeoman, of Amherst, rec date 1783, execution, debt, file #3649

EAYERS Joseph, yeoman, of Merrimack, vs BOYES William, gentleman, of New Boston, rec date 1783, judgment, debt, file #3777

EAYERS Joseph Jr, yeoman, of Merrimack, vs SCOTT James, yeoman, of Stoddard, rec date 1785, judgment, debt, file #5525

EAYERS Joseph Jr, yeoman, of Merrimack, vs SCOTT James, husbandman, of Stoddard, rec date 1785, execution, debt, file #5927

EAYRS Joseph, husbandman, of Merrimack, vs PIKE Daniel, innkeeper, of Dunstable, rec date 1783, writ, debt, file #3090

EAYRS Joseph, yeoman, of Merrimack, vs BOYES William, gentleman, of New Boston, rec date 1783, writ, debt, file #3953

EAYRS Joseph, yeoman, of Merrimack, vs JONES Timothy, yeoman, of Amherst, rec date 1783, execution, debt, file #3469

EAYRS Joseph, yeoman, of Merrimack, vs LAMBERT Thomas, yeoman, of Rowley MA, rec date 1784, judgment, debt, file #4363

EDWARDS Ebenezer, housewright, of Acton MA, vs PARKS Benjamin, husbandman, of Peterborough Slip, doc date 1777, deed, land transfer, file #2056

EDWARDS Thomas, gentleman, of Dunstable, vs KELLEY Joseph, gentleman, of Nottingham-West, doc date 1775, writ, debt, file #951

ELENWOOD Rolandson, yeoman, of Amherst, vs BARRET Moses, yeoman, of Nottingham-West, rec date 1783, judgment, debt, file #3740

ELIOT Andrew, laborer, of Amherst, vs LOVEJOY Francis, feltmaker, of Amherst, rec date 1785, execution, debt, file #5484

ELIOT John, yeoman, of Mason, vs BAGLEY Andrew, yeoman, of Peterborough Slip, doc date 1777, rec date 1777, deed, land transfer, file #5655

ELKINS Jonathan, yeoman, of Nottingham-West, vs CHAMPNEY Ebenezer, esquire, of Nottingham-West, rec date 1785, writ, debt, file #6345

ELKINS Richard, yeoman, of Salisbury, vs MERRILL Nehemiah, yeoman, of Pembroke, rec date 1788, writ, debt, file #6986

ELLENWOOD Joseph, yeoman, of Greenfield, vs HADLEY Seth, of Greenfield, doc date 1799, judgment, debt, file #307

ELLENWOOD Rowland, yeoman, of Amherst, vs HILLSBORO County, doc date 1772, deed for office, land transfer, file #801

ELLINGWOOD Benjamin, husbandman, of Amherst, vs WHITNEY James, yeoman, of Dunstable, doc date 1772, writ, debt, file #894

ELLINWOOD Samuel, yeoman, of Hillsborough, vs COOLIDGE Nathaniel Jr, yeoman, of Hillsborough, doc date 1798, various, debt, file #548

ELLIOT Andrew, laborer, of Amherst, vs LOVEJOY Francis, feltmaker, of Amherst, rec date 1785, execution, debt, file #5907

ELLIOT Jeremiah, husbandman, of Pepperell MA, vs BOYNTON Thomas, joiner, of Hollis, doc date 1772, rec date 1772, deed, land transfer, file #6850

ELLIOT John, husbandman, of Boscawen, vs LADD Nathaniel, husbandman, of Alexandria, rec date 1785, judgment, debt, file #5210

ELLIOT John Jr, yeoman, of Chelsea VT, vs PERKINS Robert, husbandman, of Northfield, doc date 1798, judgment, debt, file #562

ELLIOT Samuel, merchant, of Boston MA, vs DEXTER David, husbandman, of Hampstead, rec date 1786, judgment, debt, file #2295

ELLIS David, of Norton MA, yeoman, deed, land transfer, file #6797, signed on deed

ELLIS Hannah & Sheda, of Norton MA, yeoman, deed, land transfer, file #6797, signed on deed

ELLIS W E David, housewright, of Norton MA, vs CARR Thomas, yeoman, of Hillsborough, doc date 1793, rec date 1793, deed, land transfer, file #6797, pg 350

ELLSWORTH Jonathan, husbandman, of Deering, vs BELL Samuel, esquire, of Amherst, doc date 1811, rec date 1811, deed, land transfer, file #5695

ELLSWORTH Thomas, innholder, of Amherst, vs GRIMES James, gentleman, of Deering, rec date 1785, judgment, debt, file #5540

ELLSWORTH Thomas, innholder, of Amherst, vs GRIMES James, gentleman, of Deering, rec date 1785, judgment, debt, file #5174

ELLSWORTH Thomas, innkeeper, of Amherst, vs CHAMPNEY Ebenezer, esquire, of Groton MA, rec date 1785, writ, debt, file #5411

ELLSWORTH Thomas, cordwainer, of Amherst, vs PIKE Zachariah, husbandman, of Bedford, rec date 1784, writ, debt, file #5252

ELLSWORTH Thomas, innholder, of Amherst, vs GRIMES James, gentleman, of Deering, rec date 1785, judgment, debt, file #5262

ELLSWORTH Thomas, innholder, of Amherst, vs MOOR James, yeoman, of Goffstown, rec date 1786, judgment, debt, file #5765

ELLSWORTH Thomas, innholder, of Amherst, vs MOOR James, husbandman, of Goffstown, rec date 1786, writ, debt, file #6093

ELLSWORTH Thomas, yeoman, of Amherst, vs LUND Phineas, yeoman, of Lyndeborough, rec date 1786, writ, debt, file #6870

ELSWORTH Thomas, yeoman, of Amherst, vs CARLETON Thomas, yeoman, of Lyndeborough, rec date 1785, writ, debt, file #6863

EMERESON Daniel, gentleman, of Hollis, vs BOYNTON Joshua, clockmaker, of Hollis, rec date 1784, judgment, debt, file #4216

EMERSON Amos, esquire, of Chester, vs PRESSOTT James, yeoman, of Deering, rec date 1783, civil litigious, debt, file #2938

EMERSON Amos, esquire, of Chester, vs PRESCOTT James, yeoman, of Deering, rec date 1783, writ, debt, file #3315

EMERSON Charles, husbandman, of Fisherfield, vs WEBSTER Joseph, husbandman, of Fisherfield, rec date 1783, writ, debt, file #3220

EMERSON Charles, husbandman, of Fisherfield, vs LAIN John, husbandman, of Fisherfield, rec date 1783, writ, debt, file #3220

EMERSON Charles, husbandman, of Fisherfield, vs CUTLER John, husbandman, of Fisherfield, rec date 1785, judgment, debt, file #5197

EMERSON Daniel, gentleman, of Hollis, vs CUMINGS Samuel, esquire, of Hollis, rec date 1777, writ, debt, file #2187

EMERSON Daniel Jr, merchant, of Hollis, vs BUTTERFIELD William, yeoman, of Dunstable, doc date 1802, judgment, debt, file #568

EMERSON Dearborn, trader, of Amherst, vs LOVEJOY Lois, of Milford, doc date 1799, judgment, debt, file #386

EMERSON Dearborn, stage driver, of Amherst, vs STEVENS Charles, saddler, of Amherst, doc date 1799, writ, debt, file #575

EMERSON Dearborn, trader, of Amherst, vs NICHOLS Joseph, gentleman, of Amherst, doc date 1799, writ, debt, file #575

EMERSON Dearborn Jr, yeoman, of Amherst, vs HUMPHREY Charles, esquire, of Amherst, doc date 1799, judgment, debt, file #263

EMERSON Eleazar, husbandman, of Goffstown, vs EMERSON Nathan, yeoman, of Kingston, doc date 1773, writ, debt, file #1328

EMERSON George, yeoman, of Dunbarton, vs HOGG David, yeoman, of Dunbarton, rec date 1783, writ, debt, file #3219

EMERSON Hezikiah, yeoman, of Fisherfield, vs MOSES John, cordwainer, of Newbury MA, doc date 1784, deed, land transfer, file #2010

EMERSON Jonathan, yeoman, of Dunstable, vs ROBINSON James, yeoman, of Dunstable, doc date 1772, judgment, forgery, file #668

EMERSON Jonathan, yeoman, of Dunstable, vs EMERSON Nathaniel Jr, yeoman, of Dunstable, doc date 1772, judgment, forgery, file #668

EMERSON Oliver, husbandman, of Derryfield, vs EMERSON George, husbandman, of Dunbarton, doc date 1784, execution, debt, file #1696

EMERSON Parker, of Litchfield, doc date 1772, license, tavern license, file #852

EMERSON Parker, yeoman, of Litchfield, vs KITTRIDGE Thomas, husbandman, of Dunstable, doc date 1774, execution, file #944

EMERSON Parker, yeoman, of Litchfield, vs KILLICUT Thomas, husbandman, of Dunstable, doc date 1774, execution, file #994

EMERSON Peter, housewright, of Chelmsford MA, vs FREELAND John, cordwainer, of Chelmsford MA, doc date 1772, writ, debt, file #1045

EMERSON Samuel, esquire, of Plymouth, vs BLOOD Elnathan, yeoman, of Hollis, rec date 1783, execution, debt, file #2929

EMERSON Samuel Moody, mason, of Pepperell MA, vs GRIMES Jonathan, husbandman, of Amherst, rec date 1784, judgment, debt, file #4596

EMERSON Samuel Moody, of Pepperell MA, vs GRIMES Jonathan, husbandman, of Amherst, rec date 1785, judgment, debt, file #5155

EMERY Amos, husbandman, of Dunbarton, vs HOYT Thomas, gentleman, of Dunbarton, doc date 1784, rec date 1785, deed, land transfer, file #5638

EMERY Jonathan & John, merchants, of Boston MA, vs BLOOD Robert, yeoman, of Peterborough, rec date 1784, judgment, debt, file #4336

EMES Kelley (Hitty), singlewoman, of Peterborough, vs SCOTT William Jr, yeoman, of Peterborough, doc date 1782, summons, fornication, file #772

ENGLISH James, wheelwright, of Claremont, vs STEEL James Jr, husbandman, of Antrim, doc date 1799, rec date 1806, deed, land transfer, file #5686

ENGLISH James, wheelwright, of Claremont, vs TUTTLE Jacob, husbandman, of Antrim, doc date 1799, rec date 1806, deed, land transfer, file #5686

ENOCH Lawrence, gentleman, of Mason, vs RUSSELL George, yeoman, of Raby, doc date 1772, writ, debt, file #1048

EPES Benjamin, trader, of Tyngsboro, vs MARTIN Jesse, husbandman, of Francestown, doc date 1798, judgment, debt, file #562

EPES Benjamin, gentleman, of Manchester MA, vs GOULD Daniel, innkeeper, of Lyndeborough, rec date 1784, judgment, debt, file #4368

EPES Francis, gentleman, of Lyndeborough, vs PEARSON Amos, yeoman, of Lyndeborough, rec date 1788, writ, ejectment, file #2564

ERWIN Peter, husbandman, of Londonderry, vs WALLACE John, husbandman, of Bedford, doc date 1772, writ, debt, file #886

ESTEY Aaron, yeoman, of Rindge, vs HOW Isaac, yeoman, of New Ipswich, doc date 1772, writ, debt, file #938

EVANS Stephen, trader, of Dover, vs FRAZIER Nathaniel, of Boston MA, doc date 1772, writ, debt, file #937

EVANS Tappan, husbandman, of Warner, vs COLBY John, husbandman, of Warner, doc date 1799, judgment, debt, file #268

EVERDEN John, yeoman, of Amherst, vs WILKINS Jonathan, yeoman, of Amherst, doc date 1779, rec date 1779, deed, land transfer, file #2152

EVERETT Edward, gentleman, of Rumney, vs CHANDLER John, gentleman, of Boscawen, rec date 1782, writ, debt, file #2675

EVERETT William, yeoman, of Dedham MA, vs FELT Benjamin, blacksmith, of Temple, rec date 1785, judgment, debt, file #5120

EVERETT William, yeoman, of Dedham MA, vs FELT Benjamin, blacksmith, of Temple, rec date 1784, judgment, debt, file #5288

EWINS James, husbandman, of Londonderry, vs KELLEY Joseph, gentleman, of Nottingham, doc date 1772, writ, land dispute, file #882

EWINS James, husbandman, of Londonderry, vs SMALL Jonathan, husbandman, of Goffstown, rec date 1784, judgment, debt, file #4732

EWINS James, husbandman, of Londonderry, vs SMALL Jonathan, husbandman, of Goffstown, rec date 1786, judgment, debt, file #6469

EWINS James, deceased, of Londonderry, rec date 1785, debt, file #6998

EWINS James, of Londonderry, vs MOOR Samuel, esquire, of Nottingham-West, rec date 1786, writ, debt, file #6321, Mary MOOR widow

FABUSH Charles, esquire, of Plymouth MA, vs BROWN James, gentleman, of Plymouth, doc date 1784, writ, debt, file #1619

FAIRFIELD Hanna, spinster, of New Boston, vs FAIRFIELD Eunice, rec date 1794, various, assault, file #1794

FAIRFIELD Hanna, spinster, of New Boston, vs FAIRFIELD John, rec date 1794, various, assault, file #4155, kinship Brother John

FAIRFIELD Joseph, esquire, of Wenham MA, vs PERSON Daniel, husbandman, of Weare, rec date 1788, summons, debt, file #2400

FAIRFIELD Joseph, esquire, of Wenham MA, vs BABSON Isaac, innkeeper, of Hopkinton, rec date 1788, writ, debt, file #2552

FAIRFIELD Joseph, gentleman, of Wenham MA, vs TITCOMB Benjamin, yeoman, of Hopkinton, rec date 1785, judgment, debt, file #5214

FAIRFIELD Joseph, gentleman, of Wenham MA, vs TITCOMB Moses, tailor, of Wenham MA, rec date 1785, judgment, debt, file #5214

FAIRFIELD Matthew, gentleman, of New Boston, vs DENNIS Arthur, cordwainer, of New Boston, rec date 1788, writ, debt, file #6977

FAIRFIELD Matthew, gentleman, of New Boston, vs LUMMUS Porte, gentleman, of Milford, doc date 1798, judgment, debt, file #562

FALES Stephen, trader, of Boston MA, vs TODD Moses, trader, of Rindge NH, doc date 1798, debt, file #212

FALES Stephen, manufacturing trader, of Boston MA, vs RALSTON Alexander, esquire, of Keene, doc date 1799, various, debt, file #529

FARBUSH Charles, gentleman, of Andover MA, vs KEYES Daniel, yeoman, of Stoddard, rec date 1785, judgment, debt, file #4958

FARIFIELD Matthew, gentleman, of Wenham MA, vs RAMSEY Jonathan, yeoman, of New Boston, rec date 1784, writ, debt, file #4678

FARLEY Benjamin, esquire, of Brookline, vs PRATT Thomas, hatter, of Hollis, doc date 1799, judgment, debt, file #568

FARLEY Benjamin, esquire, of Hollis, vs WARREN Benjamin, gentleman, of Hollis, doc date 1799, judgment, debt, file #568

FARLEY Christopher, tanner, of Hollis, vs WHITE Robert, husbandman, of New Boston, rec date 1786, writ, debt, file #6051

FARLEY Ebenezer, husbandman, of Hollis, vs JEWET Jacob Jr, trader, of Hollis, doc date 1773, writ, debt, file #1358

FARLEY Hannah, singlewoman, of Hollis, vs WHITTEMORE Samuel, gentleman, of Cambridge, rec date 1785, judgment, land dispute, file #5358

FARLEY Samuel, gentleman, of Hollis, vs SEARLE William Jr, husbandman, of Temple, rec date 1784, judgment, debt, file #4988

FARMER Benjamin, cooper, of Hollis, vs HUNT Josiah, yeoman, of Hollis, doc date 1772, judgment, debt, file #673

FARMER Benjamin, cooper, of Hollis, vs JEWETT Jacob, shopkeeper, of Hollis, doc date 1772, writ, debt, file #888

FARMER Joseph, soldier minor, of Reading MA, vs STEVENS Caleb, cordwainer, of Merrimack, rec date 1782, judgment, debt, file #2737, kinship in file 63

FARMER Joseph, minor, of Reading MA, vs STEVENS Caleb, cordwainer, of Merrimack, rec date 1783, execution, debt, file #3225

FARMER Joseph & Hannah, husbandman, of Deerfield, vs INHABITANTS of Deerfield, doc date 1799, judgment, debt, file #314

FARNSWORTH David, yeoman, of Hollis, vs ABBOTT Elizabeth, widow, of Hollis, doc date 1771, writ, debt, file #798

FARNSWORTH David, yeoman, of Hollis, vs ABBOTT Benjamin (estate), widow, of Hollis, doc date 1771, writ, debt, file #798

FARNSWORTH David, yeoman, of Hollis, vs WILKINS Israel Jr, yeoman, of Hollis, doc date 1773, execution, debt, file #1484

FARNSWORTH Esther, widow, of Hollis, vs TUCKER Reuben, of MA, rec date 1782, various, debt, file #3610

FARNUM Stephen, yeoman, of Amherst, vs WESTON Isaac, yeoman, of Amherst, rec date 1778, judgment, assault, file #2262

FARRAR Oliver, husbandman, of Temple, vs DENSMORE Zebidiah, husbandman, of Temple, rec date 1788, various, debt, file #6717

FARRAR Rebeckah, of Temple, vs DENSMORE Zebidiah, husbandman, of Temple, rec date 1788, various, debt, file #6717

FARRAR Simeon, of Temple, vs DENSMORE Zebidiah, husbandman, of Temple, rec date 1788, various, debt, file #6717

FARRES Isaac, gentleman, of Townsend MA, vs ASTINS Beulah, widow, of Raby, doc date 1778, writ, debt, file #2033

FARROW Joseph & Samuel, clothier, of Pepperell MA, vs SHEPLE Abel, yeoman, of Hollis, doc date 1800, judgment, debt, file #568

FARTER David, husbandman, of Dunbarton, vs EMERSOON James, husbandman, of Hopkinton, rec date 1784, judgment, debt, file #4349

FARWELL Abel, cooper, of Groton MA, vs MITCHELL Isaac, husbandman, of Peterborough, doc date 1782, execution, debt, file #969

FARWELL Oliver, innholder, of Merrimack, vs BICKFORD Edmund, husbandman, of Lyndeborough, doc date 1784, writ, larceny, file #1566

FAUCHER Henry I, of Manchester, vs WILSON John W, trucking, of Manchester, doc date 1894, common carrier loss, supreme court, file #590

FAULKER Francis, trader, of Waterbury MA, vs PORTER Francis, trader, of Peterborough, rec date 1785, judgment, debt, file #6361

FAVOR David, yeoman, of Dunbarton, vs GORDON William, esquire, of Amherst, doc date 1799, writ, debt, file #401

FAY William, gentleman, of Wobury MA, vs BLASDELL Samuel, yeoman, of Lyndeborough, doc date 1784, execution, debt, file #1727

FAY William, yeoman, of Woburn MA, vs BLASDEL Samuel, yeoman, of Lyndeborough, rec date 1785, judgment, debt, file #5115

FAY William, yeoman, of Woburn MA, vs GOULD Richard, yeoman, of Amherst, rec date 1785, judgment, debt, file #5115

FELCH John, yeoman, of Francestown, vs COLEBY Ezekiel, yeoman, of Weare, doc date 1786, rec date 1787, deed, land transfer, file #2504

FELCH Joseph, husbandman, of Weare, vs McNEIL John Caldwell, yeoman, of New Boston, doc date 1784, execution, debt, file #1545

FELCH Joseph, husbandman, of Weare, vs McNEAL John Caldwell, husbandman, of Deerfield, rec date 1784, judgment, debt, file #4340

FELLOWS David, trader, of Bedford, vs BIXBY Daniel, trader, of Litchfield, doc date 1799, debt, file #49

FELLOWS Joseph, husbandman, of Andover, vs McMURPHY John, husbandman, of Alexandria, doc date 1784, execution, debt, file #1694

FELLOWS Joseph, husbandman, of Andover, vs McMURPHY John, husbandman, of Alexandria, rec date 1783, judgment, debt, file #4088

FELLOWS Joseph, husbandman, of Andover, vs TOLFORD Joshua, esquire, of Alexandria, rec date 1785, execution, debt, file #5790

FELLOWS Joseph, husbandman, of Andover, vs McMURPHY John, husbandman, of Alexandria, rec date 1785, execution, debt, file #5790

FELLOWS Joseph, husbandman, of Andover, vs McMURPHY John, husbandman, of Alexandria, rec date 1786, judgment, debt, file #6392

FELT Benjamin, blacksmith, of Temple, vs DICKEY John, husbandman, of Francestown, doc date 1784, execution, debt, file #1663

FELT Benjamin, blacksmith, of Temple, vs DICKEY John, husbandman, of Francestown, rec date 1783, writ, debt, file #3629

FELT Benjamin, blacksmith, of Temple, vs NUTT Samuel, husbandman, of Francestown, rec date 1783, writ, debt, file #3629

FELT Benjamin, yeoman, of Temple, vs WHITING Oliver, yeoman, of Temple, doc date 1786, rec date 1786, deed, land transfer, file #5027

FELT Peter, yeoman, of Temple, vs NORWOOD David, physician, of Londonderry, rec date 1783, execution, debt, file #2987

FERFIELD Nathaniel, gentleman, of Weare, vs WOOD Jonathan, husbandman, of Goffstown, rec date 1786, writ, debt, file #6310

FERFIELD Nathaniel, gentleman, of Weare, vs UNDERWOOD James, gentleman, of Goffstown, rec date 1786, writ, debt, file #6310

FERGUSEN John & James, yeoman, of Pelham, vs HARDY Levy, husbandman, of Pelham, doc date 1782, rec date 1783, deed, land transfer, file #2651

FERGUSON Henry, yeoman, of Peterborough, vs STEEL John, yeoman, of Campton, doc date 1772, writ, debt, file #935

FERGUSON James, weaver, of Goffstown, vs FERGERSON William, yeoman, of Goffstown, doc date 1775, deed, land transfer, file #845

FERGUSON John, husbandman, of Pelham, vs CHILDS Artemas, yeoman, of Wilton, doc date 1799, writ, debt, file #573

FERRIN Timothy, husbandman, of Goffstown, vs ORDWAY Joseph, husbandman, of Goffstown, doc date 1774, judgment, debt, file #733

FETCH John, husbandman, of Weare, vs McNEIL John Caldwell, yeoman, of New Boston, rec date 1783, writ, debt, file #4543

FEZZANDEN Thomas, saddler, of Framingham MA, vs HEMMENWAY Mary, widow, of Framingham MA, rec date 1788, writ, debt, file #6175, part of Samuel CURTIS file

FIELD John, currier, of Peterborough, vs EVINS Asa, trader, of Peterborough, doc date 1799, judgment, debt, file #296

FIELDS John, yeoman, of Merrimack, vs DAVIS Benjamin, yeoman, of Amherst, doc date 1782, execution, debt, file #970

FIELDS Joshua, yeoman, of Merrimack, vs GRAGG David, yeoman, of Francestown, rec date 1784, judgment, debt, file #4981

FIELDS Samuel, yeoman, of Amherst, vs LEWIS Samuel, yeoman, of Washington, rec date 1783, writ, debt, file #3096

FIFIELD Jonathan, husbandman, of Mile Slip, vs BETTEY William, husbandman, of Wilton, rec date 1785, judgment, debt, file #5209

FIFIELD Jonathan, yeoman, of Amherst, vs BETTEY William, yeoman, of Wilton, rec date 1786, writ, debt, file #6868

FIFIELD Nathaniel, gentleman, of Weare, vs STEVENS Thomas, blacksmith, of Amherst, rec date 1784, judgment, debt, file #4593

FIFIELD Nathaniel, gentleman, of Weare, vs STEVENS Thomas, blacksmith, of Amherst, rec date 1785, judgment, debt, file #5132

FIFIELD Nathaniel, gentleman, of Weare, vs PUFFER Matthew, blacksmith, of Weare, rec date 1788, various, debt, file #6592

FILCH Joseph, husbandman, of Weare, vs McNEIL John Caldwell, yeoman, of New Boston, doc date 1784, execution, debt, file #1695

FISH Amos, gentleman, of Amherst, vs AMORY Jonathan & John, merchants, of Boston MA, doc date 1774, writ, debt, file #1107

FISH Amos, tanner, of Haverhill, vs GILMORE David, yeoman, of Warner, doc date 1784, execution, debt, file #1914

FISH Eleazer, yeoman, of Mason, vs PARKER Samuel, yeoman, of New Ipswich, doc date 1782, judgment, debt, file #681

FISH Eleazer, husbandman, of Dunstable, vs INHABITANTS of Dunstable, rec date 1785, writ, debt, file #5428

FISH James, yeoman, of Hollis, vs JEWETT Jacob Jr, trader, of Hollis, doc date 1773, writ, debt, file #1362

FISH Patience, widow, of Mason, vs TARBELL Samuel, of Mason, doc date 1772, civil litigation, debt, file #663

FISH Patience, widow, of Mason, vs TARBELL Samuel, husbandman, of MA, doc date 1773, execution, debt, file #1477

FISH Patience, widow, of Mason, vs TARBELL Samuel, husbandman, of Mason, rec date 1771, writ, debt, file #4877

FISH Simeon, husbandman, of Mason, vs MUZZY Benjamin, husbandman, of Mason, rec date 1785, judgment, debt, file #5077

FISHER James, yeoman, of Francestown, vs DRURY Benjamin, physician, of Francestown, doc date 1781, rec date 1783, deed, land transfer, file #2650

FISHER James, yeoman, of Francestown, vs DONOVAN John, yeoman, of New Boston, rec date 1785, judgment, debt, file #4873

FISHER James S & Matthew, gentleman, of Francestown, vs EATERS Thomas, gentleman, of Francestown, doc date 1818, rec date 1819, deed, land transfer, file #5706

FISHER James S & Matthew, gentleman, of Francestown, vs WOODBURY Peter, gentleman, of Francestown, doc date 1818, rec date 1819, deed, land transfer, file #5706

FISHER James S & Matthew, gentleman, of Francestown, vs GIBSON John, gentleman, of Francestown, doc date 1818, rec date 1819, deed, land transfer, file #5706

FISHER James S & Matthew, gentleman, of Francestown, vs HOPKINS Ebenezer Jr, gentleman, of Francestown, doc date 1818, rec date 1819, deed, land transfer, file #5706

FISHER James S & Matthew, gentleman, of Francestown, vs LEWIS Daniel, gentleman, of Francestown, doc date 1818, rec date 1819, deed, land transfer, file #5706

FISHER John, esquire, of Salem MA, vs EMERY William Jr, yeoman, of Fisherfield, doc date 1775, rec date 1787, deed, land transfer, file #2486

FISHER John, esquire, of Salem MA, vs MacWILLIAM Thomas, husbandman, of Fisherfield, doc date 1775, rec date 1785, deed, land transfer, file #5640

FISK Amos, gentleman, of Hollis, vs ATWILL John, yeoman, of Hollis, doc date 1772, writ, debt, file #1427

FISK Amos, tanner, of Haverhill, vs GILMORE David, yeoman, of Warner, doc date 1784, execution, debt, file #1702

FISK Amos, gentleman, of Amherst, vs GRIMES Jonathan, yeoman, of Amherst, doc date 1774, judgment, debt, file #2035

FISK Amos, gentleman, of Plymouth, vs WILKINS Daniel, yeoman, of Amherst, rec date 1785, judgment, debt, file #6405

FISK Amos, gentleman, of Amherst, vs BLOOD Francis, yeoman, of Hollis, doc date 1773, rec date 1781, deed, land transfer, file #6552

FISK Eleazer, yeoman, of Dunstable, vs WARNER Daniel, gentleman, of Amherst, rec date 1783, judgment, debt, file #4486

FISK Eleazer Jr, husbandman, of Dunstable, vs GILSON Jeremiah, husbandman, of Dunstable, rec date 1785, judgment, debt, file #5837

FISK William, yeoman, of Wenham MA, vs SMITH Jonathan, yeoman, of Amherst, doc date 1773, deed, land transfer, file #832

FISKE Amos, tanner, of Plymouth, vs GILMORE David, yeoman, of Warner, rec date 1783, writ, debt, file #3375

FITCH Samuel & Abigail, husbandman, of Chelmsford MA, vs PARKER William, husbandman, of Hillsborough, rec date 1784, judgment, debt, file #4626

FITCH Samuel & Abiel, yeoman, of Acton MA, vs PARKER William, husbandman, of Hillsborough, rec date 1784, judgment, debt, file #4625

FITTS Isaac, blacksmith, of Boscawen, vs CHASE Abner, yeoman, of New Almsbury, doc date 1772, execution, debt, file #1199

FITZ Mark, manufacturing, of Henniker, vs PERKINS Daniel, yeoman, of Henniker, doc date 1798, execution, debt, file #92

FLADD Samuel, esquire, of Worcester MA, vs WOOD Jonathan & Edward, yeoman, of Goffstown, rec date 1785, judgment, debt, file #5866

FLAG Samuel, merchant, of MA, vs ATWOOD John, trader, of Atkinson, doc date 1774, execution, file #943

FLAG Samuel, merchant, of Salem, vs ATWOOD John, trader, of Atkinson, doc date 1773, execution, debt, file #1219

FLAGG Ebenezer, husbandman, of Mason, vs SWAIN John, cordwainer, of Redding MA, doc date 1799, execution, debt, file #178

FLAGG Eleazer, millwright, of Hollis, vs LAWRENCE Ephraim, physician, of Pepperell MA, rec date 1783, judgment, debt, file #4306

FLAGG Jonas, gentleman, of Hollis, vs LAWRENCE Zachariah Jr, trader, of Hollis, rec date 1783, execution, debt, file #3646

FLAGG Jonas, gentleman, of Hollis, vs LAWRENCE Zachariah Jr, husbandman, of Hollis, rec date 1782, execution, debt, file #3565

FLAGG Jonas, gentleman, of Hollis, vs LAWRENCE Zachariah, husbandman, of Hollis, rec date 1782, execution, debt, file #3565

FLAGG Jonas, gentleman, of Hollis, vs LAWRENCE Zachariah, husbandman, of Hollis, rec date 1783, execution, debt, file #3646

FLAGG Jonas, gentleman, of Hollis, vs BLOOD Francis, husbandman, of Hollis, rec date 1786, judgment, debt, file #5771

FLAGG Joseph, yeoman, of Hollis, vs WHEAT Joseph, husbandman, of Hollis, doc date 1793, rec date 1793, deed, land transfer, file #5667, ?

FLAGG Samuel, esquire, of Salem MA, vs BROWN Joseph, yeoman, of Hollis, doc date 1784, execution, debt, file #1668

FLAGG Samuel, esquire, of Salem MA, vs BROWN Joseph, yeoman, of Hollis, doc date 1784, execution, debt, file #1561

FLAGG Samuel, esquire, of Worcester MA, vs RIDEOUT James, yeoman, of Hollis, rec date 1787, various, debt, file #2536

FLAGG Samuel, esquire, of Worcester MA, vs JONES William, husbandman, of Hillsborough, rec date 1784, judgment, debt, file #4590

FLAGG Samuel, esquire, of Worcester MA, vs BLODGET Daniel, yeoman, of Litchfield, rec date 1784, writ, debt, file #4622, estate of Isaac STEVENS

FLAGG Samuel, esquire, of Worcester MA, vs GOODRIDGE Sewall, clerk, of Lyndeborough, rec date 1785, judgment, debt, file #4944

FLAGG Samuel, gentleman, of Salem MA, vs BAILS John, yeoman, of Deering, rec date 1785, judgment, debt, file #4941

FLAGG Samuel, merchant, of Salem MA, vs FRENCH James, yeoman, of Jaffrey, rec date 1784, judgment, debt, file #4857

FLAGG Samuel, esquire, of Worcester MA, vs JONES William, husbandman, of Hillsborough, rec date 1785, judgment, debt, file #5126

FLAGG Samuel, esquire, of Worcester MA, vs RIDEOUT James, yeoman, of Hollis, rec date 1785, writ, debt, file #5339

FLAGG Samuel, esquire, of Worcester MA, vs WRIGHT Uriah, gentleman, of Hollis, rec date 1785, judgment, debt, file #5092

FLAGG Samuel, esquire, of Worcester MA, vs LITTLE Moses, esquire, of Goffstown, rec date 1785, writ, debt, file #5408

FLAGG Samuel, esquire, of Worcester MA, vs RUSE Jonathan, yeoman, of Derryfield, rec date 1785, execution, debt, file #5941

FLAGG Samuel, esquire, of Worcester MA, vs BOYNTON Joshua, yeoman, of Hollis, rec date 1785, judgment, debt, file #5873

FLAGG Samuel, esquire, of Worcester MA, vs MOOR Samuel, gentleman, of Derryfield, rec date 1785, execution, debt, file #5941

FLAGG Samuel, esquire, of Worcester MA, vs McINTIRE Timothy, yeoman, of Mile Slip, rec date 1785, execution, debt, file #5932

FLAGG Samuel, esquire, of Worcester MA, vs BLODGETT Daniel, yeoman, of Litchfield, rec date 1785, judgment, debt, file #5857

FLAGG Samuel, esquire, of Worcester MA, vs LANDERS Joseph, husbandman, of Derryfield, rec date 1785, judgment, debt, file #5860

FLAGG Samuel, esquire, of Worcester MA, vs MOOR Samuel, gentleman, of Derryfield, rec date 1785, judgment, debt, file #5860

FLAGG Samuel, esquire, of Worcester MA, vs RUSS Jonathan, yeoman, of Derryfield, rec date 1785, judgment, debt, file #5860

FLAGG Samuel, gentleman, of Salem MA, vs HUTCHINSON Solomon, yeoman, of Merrimack, rec date 1785, execution, debt, file #5962

FLAGG Samuel, esquire, of Worcester MA, vs SANDERS Joseph, husbandman, of Derryfield, rec date 1785, execution, debt, file #5941

FLAGG Samuel, esquire, of Worcester MA, vs WOOD Jonathan & Edward, yeoman, of Goffstown, rec date 1785, execution, debt, file #5788

FLAGG Samuel, esquire, of Worcester MA, vs McINTIRE Timothy, yeoman, of Mile Slip, rec date 1785, judgment, debt, file #5804

FLAGG Samuel, esquire, of Worcester MA, vs DRURY Zedekiah, gentleman, of Alstead, rec date 1785, execution, debt, file #5931

FLAGG Samuel, esquire, of Worcester MA, vs DRURY Zedekiah, gentleman, of Alstead, rec date 1785, writ, debt, file #6262

FLAGG Samuel, esquire, of Worcester MA, vs DRURY Zedekiah, gentleman, of Alstead, rec date 1785, writ, debt, file #6034

FLAGG Samuel, esquire, of Worcester MA, vs DRURY Samuel, yeoman, of Alstead, rec date 1786, judgment, debt, file #6507

FLAGG Samuel, esquire, of Worcester MA, vs WHEELER William, yeoman, of Dunbarton, rec date 1785, judgment, debt, file #6398

FLAGG Samuel, esquire, of Worcester MA, vs McLAUGHLIN Thomas, gentleman, of Bedford, rec date 1785, judgment, debt, file #6399

FLAGG Samuel, esquire, of Worcester MA, vs GOODRIDGE Sewell, clerk, of Lyndeborough, rec date 1786, judgment, debt, file #5202

FLAGG Samuel, esquire, of Worcester MA, vs LITTLE Moses, esquire, of Goffstown, rec date 1785, judgment, debt, file #6397

FLAGG Samuel, gentleman, of Worcester MA, vs GOODRIDGE Sewall, clerk, of Lyndeborough, rec date 1788, various, land dispute, file #6598

FLAGG Samuel, gentleman, of Worcester MA, vs GOODRIDGE Sewall, of Lyndeborough, rec date 1788, power of attorney, file #6638

FLANDERS Betty, of Weare, vs FLANDERS Phebe, single, of Campbell Gore, rec date 1788, affidavit, death of child, file #6530

FLANDERS John, of Weare, vs BALDWIN Nahum, esquire, of Amherst, rec date 1782, appeal, debt, file #3990

FLANDERS John Jr, yeoman, of Boscawen, vs CORSER Samuel, yeoman, of Boscawen, rec date 1783, various, appeals assault, file #2749, see also 4167 & 4167A

FLANDERS Thomas, yeoman, of Deering, vs HEATH Asa, husbandman, doc date 1786, rec date 1787, deed, land transfer, file #2497

FLANDERS Thomas, husbandman, of Weare, vs BAILEY Moses, husbandman, of Deering, rec date 1787, writ, bldg damage, file #6704

FLANDERS Thomas, husbandman, of Weare, vs BARTLETT Jacob, husbandman, of Deering, rec date 1787, writ, bldg damage, file #6704

FLANDERS Thomas & Betsy, husbandman, of Weare, vs BAILEY Thomas, husbandman, of Deering, rec date 1793, various, assault, file #4703

FLANDERS Thomas & Betsy, husbandman, of Weare, vs GREGG John, husbandman, of Deering, rec date 1793, various, assault, file #4703

FLETCHER Adams, rec date 1799, journal, file #3543

FLETCHER Ebenezer, yeoman, of Westford MA, vs PARKER Samuel, yeoman, of New Ipswich, doc date 1772, civil litigations, debt, file #639

FLETCHER Ebenezer, yeoman, of Westford MA, vs PARKER Samuel, yeoman, of New Ipswich, doc date 1772, judgment, debt, file #681

FLETCHER Ebenezer, yeoman, of Westford MA, vs PARKER Samuel, yeoman, of New Ipswich, doc date 1773, execution, debt, file #1372

FLETCHER Gersham, gentleman, of Westford MA, vs JEWETT Jacob Jr, yeoman, of Hollis, doc date 1784, execution, debt, file #1758

FLETCHER Gershom, gentleman, of Westford MA, vs JEWET Jacob Jr, yeoman, of Hollis, rec date 1783, judgment, debt, file #4307

FLETCHER John, husbandman, of Dunstable, vs ADAMS David Jr, husbandman, of Dunstable, rec date 1784, judgment, debt, file #5309

FLETCHER John, husbandman, of Dunstable, vs LUND Phineas, husbandman, of Dunstable, rec date 1785, execution, debt, file #5951

FLETCHER John, husbandman, of Dunstable, vs LUND Phineas, husbandman, of Lyndeborough, rec date 1785, writ, debt, file #6031

FLETCHER Oliver, deceased, vs EDWARDS John, deed, land transfer, file #6571

FLETCHER Peter, yeoman, of New Ipswich, vs PARKER Samuel, yeoman, of Amherst, doc date 1773, writ, debt, file #1240

FLETCHER Peter, yeoman, of New Ipswich, vs PARKER Samuel, yeoman, of Amherst, rec date 1773, execution, file #1039

FLETCHER Robert, esquire, of Dunstable, vs STANLEY Joseph, husbandman, of Rindge, rec date 1785, judgment, debt, file #5513

FLETCHER Robert, surveyor, of Merrimack, vs WELDR'S (Mr), doc date 1783, survey, lot survey, file #1251

FLETCHER Robert, esquire, of Amherst, vs TAGGART Archibald, gentleman, of Hillsborough, rec date 1785, writ, debt, file #2348

FLETCHER Robert, esquire, of Amherst, vs WYMAN Timothy, husbandman, of Deering, rec date 1785, writ, debt, file #2350

FLETCHER Robert, esquire, of Amherst, vs CUMMINGS Benjamin, husbandman, of Hollis, rec date 1788, writ, debt, file #5553

FLETCHER Robert, esquire, of Dunstable, vs BLANCHARD Jonathan, esquire, of Dunstable, rec date 1785, writ, debt, file #4874

FLETCHER Robert, esquire, of Dunstable, vs TAYLOR David, husbandman, of Dunstable MA, rec date 1785, writ, debt, file #5377

FLETCHER Robert, esquire, of Amherst, vs BARKER William, physician, of Francestown, rec date 1785, judgment, debt, file #5207

FLETCHER Robert, esquire, of Dunstable, vs BUTTERFIELD Jonathan, laborer, of Merrimack, rec date 1788, writ, debt, file #4731

FLETCHER Robert, esquire, of Dunstable, vs STANLEY Joseph, husbandman, of Rindge, rec date 1785, execution, debt, file #5914

FLETCHER Robert, esquire, of Amherst, vs UNDERWOOD James, esquire, of Goffstown, rec date 1785, execution, debt, file #5891

FLETCHER Robert, esquire, of Amherst, vs SANDERS Joseph, yeoman, of Derryfield, rec date 1786, execution, debt, file #5958

FLETCHER Robert, esquire, of Amherst, vs SANDERS Joseph, gentleman, of Derryfield, rec date 1786, writ, debt, file #6057

FLETCHER Robert, esquire, of Dunstable, vs STANLEY Joseph, husbandman, of Rindge, rec date 1785, judgment, debt, file #6401

FLETCHER Robert, vs BUTTERFIELD Abraham, husbandman, of Wilton, rec date 1788, writ, debt, file #6604

FLETCHER Robert, deceased, of Dunstable, vs FLETCHER Robert, esquire, of Amherst, doc date 1787, rec date 1792, deed, land transfer, file #6795, f 506

FLETCHER Robert, esquire, of Dunstable, vs BLANCHARD Jotham, gentleman, of Amherst, rec date 1788, recognizance, debits, file #6809

FLETCHER Robert, esquire, of Dunstable, vs GOODELL David, husbandman, of Hillsborough, rec date 1788, writ, debt, file #6605

FLETCHER Robert & Sarah, of Dunstable, vs BLANCHARD Joseph, of Dunstable, doc date 1789, deed, land transfer, file #1253

FLETCHER Sarah, widow, of Dunstable, deed, land transfer, file #6795

FLETCHER Tabitha, widow, of Hollis, vs EDWARDS John, yeoman, of Haverhill MA, doc date 1784, rec date 1789, deed, land transfer, file #6571

FLETCHER Thomas, husbandman, of Dunstable MA, vs ATWILL John, joiner, of Hollis, rec date 1785, writ, debt, file #5345

FLETCHER Thomas, husbandman, of Dunstable MA, vs ATTWILL John, joiner, of Hollis, rec date 1786, various, debt, file #6076

FLETCHER William Jr, yeoman, of Westford MA, vs ABBOT Samuel, innkeeper, of Mason, doc date 1773, judgment, debt, file #1321

FLINT Amos, yeoman, of Amherst, vs CUTLER Jemima, widow, of Groton MA, doc date 1784, writ, debt, file #1266

FLINT Hutchinson, husbandman, of Antrim, vs HERRICK Josiah, yeoman, of Amherst, doc date 1798, execution, debt, file #91

FLINT Jacob, yeoman, of Hillsborough, vs RICHARDSON Zachariah, yeoman, of Francestown, rec date 1785, judgment, debt, file #2441

FLOOD Joseph, husbandman, of Weare, vs BLAISDELL Jonathan, blacksmith, of Weare, rec date 1783, judgment, debt, file #4074

FLOOD Richard, yeoman, of Boscawen, vs JACKMAN Samuel, blacksmith, of Boscawen, rec date 1775, judgment, debt, file #2181

FLOOD Richard, yeoman, of Boscawen, vs FOWLER Samuel, shipwright, of Newbury MA, rec date 1775, judgment, debt, file #2181

FLOOD Richard, yeoman, of Boscawen, vs HALE John, tailor, of Boscawen, rec date 1775, judgment, debt, file #2181

FLUCKER Thomas & Hannah, esquire, of Boston MA, vs KENDALL Ebenezer, of Dunstable, doc date 1768, rec date 1768, deed, land transfer, file #6839

FOLLANSBEE Moody, husbandman, of Newbury MA, vs CHASE Benjamin, husbandman, of Sandown, rec date 1783, writ, debt, file #4635

FOLLANSBEE Moses, husbandman, of Enfield, vs McLAUGHLIN John, yeoman, of New Boston, doc date 1784, writ, debt, file #1572

FOLLANSBEE William, yeoman, of New Boston, vs BOYES Robert, yeoman, of Londonderry, rec date 1786, writ, debt, file #6299

FOLLENSBE James, husbandman, of Dunstable, vs SMITH David, gentleman, of Amherst, doc date 1801, judgment, debt, file #568

FOLLENSBEE William, yeoman, of New Boston, vs WARREN Thomas, husbandman, of Francestown, rec date 1782, appeal, debt, file #4001

FOLSOM John, husbandman, of Salisbury, vs MARCH Moses, husbandman, of Sanbornton, rec date 1782, writ, debt, file #2676

FOLSOM John, yeoman, of Salisbury, vs CALLEY Samuel, carpenter, of Stratham, rec date 1783, execution, debt, file #3245

FOLSOM John, yeoman, of Salisbury, vs CALLEY Samuel, carpenter, of Stratham, rec date 1783, execution, debt, file #3690

FOLSOM Samuel, esquire, of Exeter, vs DAVIDSON David, husbandman, of Raby, rec date 1782, writ, debt, file #2696

FOOT Merriam, of Weare, vs FLANDERS Phebe, single, of Campbell Gore, rec date 1788, affidavit, death of child, file #6530

FOOTE Daniel, innholder, of Lyndeborough, vs TEMPLE Benjamin, husbandman, of Amherst, rec date 1786, judgment, debt, file #5371

FORBES David, esquire, of Keene, vs CODMAN Henry, physician, of Amherst, doc date 1799, debt, file #213

FORBUSH Charles, gentleman, of Andover MA, vs BROWN James, gentleman, of Plymouth, rec date 1782, judgment, debt, file #2707

FORD James, husbandman, of Nottingham, vs WHITNEY James, husbandman, of Dunstable, doc date 1772, writ, debt, file #895

FORD James, esquire, of Nottingham-West, vs MARSH Samuel Jr, yeoman, of Nottingham, doc date 1784, writ, debt, file #1591

FORD James, esquire, of Nottingham-West, vs ROGERS Solomon, trader, of Hollis, rec date 1783, writ, debt, file #3202

FORD James, esquire, of Nottingham-West, vs TUTTLE Stephen, yeoman, of Goffstown, rec date 1785, writ, debt, file #6040

FORLEY Benjamin, esquire, of Roby, vs AUSTIN Jacob, yeoman, of Roby, doc date 1798, judgment, debt, file #568

FORSAITH James, physician, of Deering, vs GAY Ichabod Jr, yeoman, of Francestown, doc date 1798, execution, debt, file #63

FORSITH William, gentleman, of Deering, vs WRIGHT Josiah, farmer, of Wilmington MA, rec date 1776, deed, land transfer, file #4886

FORSTER Ebenezer, yeoman, of Wilmington MA, vs JONES Samuel, yeoman, of Hillsborough, rec date 1783, writ, debt, file #3910

FORSYTHE David, yeoman, of Goffstown, vs TYLER John, yeoman, of Goffstown, doc date 1772, breach of Sabbath, file #1143

FORTIN David, yeoman, of Bedford, vs COFFIN Samuel, gentleman, rec date 1788, writ, debt, file #2549

FORTIN Stephen, trader, of Bradford MA, vs SESSIONS David, yeoman, of Derryfield, rec date 1788, writ, debt, file #6603

FOSS Peter, yeoman, of Littleton MA, vs KIDDER Joseph, gentleman, of Temple, doc date 1774, execution, file #987

FOSTER Daniel, yeoman, of Andover MA, vs BRAGG Thomas, innkeeper, of New Ipswich, doc date 1763, recognizance, debt, file #786

FOSTER David, yeoman, of Londonderry, vs KARR Thomas, yeoman, of New Boston, doc date 1774, recognizance, debt, file #1150

FOSTER David, yeoman, of Dunbarton, vs CLEMENT James, husbandman, of Dunbarton, rec date 1782, debt, debt, file #3150

FOSTER David, husbandman, of Dunbarton, vs PUTNEY Joseph, husbandman, of Hopkinton, rec date 1782, debt, debt, file #3151

FOSTER David, husbandman, of Dunbarton, vs PUDNEY James, husbandman, of Dunbarton, rec date 1784, judgment, debt, file #4194

FOSTER David, husbandman, of Bedford, vs PUTNEY James, yeoman, of Dunbarton, rec date 1785, writ, debt, file #5405

FOSTER Ebenezer, husbandman, of Wilmington MA, vs JONES James, husbandman, of Campbells Gore, doc date 1798, judgment, debt, file #562

FOSTER Ebenezer, yeoman, of Willington MA, vs JONES Samuel, yeoman, of Hillsborough, rec date 1783, execution, debt, file #3833

FOSTER Frederick, husbandman, of Pembroke, vs DOW Oliver, yeoman, of Hopkinton, rec date 1783, complaint, debt, file #3164

FOSTER James, of Boston MA, vs GILES John, yeoman, of Dorchester, doc date 1799, debt, file #462

FOSTER James, trader, of Boston MA, vs GILES John, yeoman, of Dorchester, doc date 1799, debt, file #462

FOSTER James, husbandman, of Hollis, vs DRURY Zedikiah, gentleman, of Hollis, doc date 1765, rec date 1788, deed, land transfer, file #6792

FOSTER Joseph, cabinetmaker, of Candia, vs ABBOTT Joshua, cordwainer, of Billerica MA, doc date 1799, writ, debt, file #435

FOSTER Joseph, yeoman, of Bow, vs STINSTON Agnes, of Dunbarton, doc date 1777, fraud, court case, file #2029

FOSTER Molly, singlewoman, of Mason, vs FISK Jonathan, doc date 1773, indictment, fornication, file #1190

FOSTER Samuel, yeoman, of New Ipswich, vs TON Timothy, yeoman, of New Ipswich, doc date 1772, writ, debt, file #904

FOWLE Daniel, gentleman, of Portsmouth, vs QUIGLEY John, gentleman, of New Boston, doc date 1772, writ, delivery dispute, file #933

FOWLE Robert, gentleman, of Portsmouth, vs QUIGLEY John, gentleman, of New Boston, doc date 1772, writ, delivery dispute, file #933

FOWLER David, husbandman, of Hopkinton, vs FLANDERS Stephen, husbandman, of Derryfield, doc date 1799, execution, debt, file #191

FOWLER Jeremiah, yeoman, of Hopkinton, vs BARNS Silas, yeoman, of Henniker, doc date 1772, judgment, debt, file #677

FOWLER John, gentleman, of Boscawen, vs GERRISH Joseph, husbandman, of Boscawen, rec date 1785, writ, debt, file #4810

FOWLER John, gentleman, of Boscawen, vs CORSER David, husbandman, of Boscawen, rec date 1785, writ, debt, file #4810

FOWLER John, gentleman, of Boscawen, vs JACKMAN George, esquire, of Boscawen, rec date 1785, writ, debt, file #4810

FOWLER Samuel, esquire, of Boscawen, vs CHANDLER Daniel, yeoman, of Concord, doc date 1784, execution, debt, file #1502

FOWLER Samuel, esquire, of Boscawen, vs CHANDLER Daniel, yeoman, of Concord, doc date 1784, execution, debt, file #1700

FOWLER Samuel, esquire, of Boscawen, vs NEWMAN Thomas, yeoman, of Concord, doc date 1784, execution, debt, file #1701

FOWLER Samuel, esquire, of Boscawen, vs NEWMAN Thomas, yeoman, of Concord, rec date 1783, judgment, debt, file #4083

FOWLER Samuel, esquire, of Boscawen, vs CHANDLER Daniel, yeoman, of Concord, rec date 1783, judgment, debt, file #4084

FOWLER Samuel, esquire, of Boscawen, vs Town of Boscawen, rec date 1794, petition, road and land dispute, file #4162

FOWLER Samuel, esquire, of Boscawen, vs PETERSON Willet, husbandman, of Boscawen, rec date 1788, writ, debt, file #6735

FOX Jonathan, yeoman, of Woburn MA, vs EAYERS Joseph, tanner, of Merrimack, rec date 1783, execution, debt, file #3641

FOX Jonathan, yeoman, of Woburn MA, vs EAYERS Joseph, tanner, of Merrimack, rec date 1782, execution, debt, file #3474

FOX Peter, yeoman, of Littleton MA, vs FARWELL Isaac, husbandman, of New Ipswich, rec date 1783, writ, debt, file #3627

FOX Peter, yeoman, of Littleton MA, vs DUDLEY Stephen, yeoman, of New Ipswich, rec date 1784, various, debt, file #4634

FOX Timothy, yeoman, of New Ipswich, vs REED James, gentleman, of Fitzwilliam, rec date 1782, judgment, debt, file #2735

FOX Timothy, yeoman, of New Ipswich, vs CONEY John, yeoman, of Lyndeborough, rec date 1783, execution, debt, file #3841

FOX Timothy, vs CONEY John, husbandman, of Lyndeborough, rec date 1783, writ, debt, file #3912

FOX Timothy, yeoman, of New Ipswich, vs ROBBE James, husbandman, of Peterborough, rec date 1783, judgment, debt, file #4071

FOX Timothy, yeoman, of New Ipswich, vs ROBBE Jane, widow, rec date 1784, writ, debt, file #4976, estate of John ROBBE

FOX Timothy, yeoman, of New Ipswich, vs CUNNINGHAM Samuel, gentleman, of Peterborough, rec date 1785, judgment, debt, file #5180

FOX Timothy, yeoman, of New Ipswich, vs PERRY James, saddler, of Temple, rec date 1788, writ, debt, file #6713

FRANCH William Jr, yeoman, of Hollis, vs ALLD William, gentleman, of Merrimack, doc date 1774, writ, debt, file #1091

FRANCIS Richard, husbandman, of Dunstable, vs SIMONDS Nathan, husbandman, of Dunstable, doc date 1779, various, debt, file #2104

FRAZIER Nathan, merchant, of Boston MA, vs HILL Isaac, trader, of Dover, doc date 1772, execution, debt, file #1202

FRAZIER Nathan, of Boston MA, vs HALE Enoch, esquire, of Walpole, rec date 1788, various, debt, file #6599

FREELAND John, cordwainer, of Chelmsford MA, vs EMERSON Parker, housewright, of Chelmsford MA, doc date 1772, execution, debt, file #1203

FRENCH Amos, yeoman, of Amherst, vs SPRAGUE John, esquire, of Lancaster MA, doc date 1774, writ, debt, file #1083

FRENCH Benjamin Capt, of Dunstable, doc date 1786, license, tavern license, file #859

FRENCH Daniel, husbandman, of Hopkinton, vs GILMORE David, husbandman, of Warner, rec date 1783, writ, debt, file #3806

FRENCH Ebenezer, husbandman, of Dunstable MA, vs SEARLES John, husbandman, of Dunstable NH, rec date 1788, writ, debt, file #2391

FRENCH Ephraim, husbandman, of Amherst, vs DINSMOOR William, husbandman, of Charlestown, doc date 1799, debt, file #337

FRENCH Ephraim, husbandman, of Amherst, vs MEANS Robert, esquire, of Amherst, doc date 1799, judgment, debt, file #286

FRENCH Ephraim, innholder, of Amherst, vs DANA Anna, widow, of Amherst, doc date 1799, writ, debt, file #574

FRENCH Ephraim, innholder, of Amherst, vs GREEN Peter, trader, of Milford, doc date 1799, writ, debt, file #574

FRENCH Ephraim, innholder, of Amherst, vs HINCHMAN Nathaniel, physician, of Amherst, doc date 1799, writ, debt, file #574

FRENCH Ephraim, yeoman, of Amherst, vs DODGE Benjamin, yeoman, of New Boston, rec date 1782, appeal, debt, file #3996

FRENCH John Jr, yeoman, of Packersfield, vs BAILEY Andrew, yeoman, of Peterborough, rec date 1782, writ, debt, file #2679

FRENCH Joseph, yeoman, of Westfield MA, vs KILLICUT Thomas, yeoman, of Dunstable, rec date 1783, writ, debt, file #3597

FRENCH Theodore, yeoman, of Dunstable, vs CONRAY Samuel, yeoman, of Hollis, rec date 1786, execution, debt, file #5893

FRENCH Theodore, yeoman, of Dunstable, vs CONRAY Samuel, yeoman, of Hollis, rec date 1786, writ, debt, file #6053

FRENCH Theodore, of Dunstable, vs HEAIL Joseph, yeoman, of Dunstable, rec date 1786, judgment, debt, file #6185

FRENCH Theodore, yeoman, of Dunstable, vs HEAIL Joseph, yeoman, of Dunstable, rec date 1786, judgment, debt, file #5808

FRENCH Thomas, yeoman, of Tewksbury MA, vs KITTREDGE Ebenezer, gentleman, of Goffstown, rec date 1783, judgment, debt, file #3758

FRENCH Todd, yeoman, of Hollis, vs JEWETT Jacob Jr, husbandman, of Hollis, doc date 1800, judgment, debt, file #568

FRENCH William, yeoman, of Billerica MA, vs DANFORTH Jonathan, blacksmith, of Hill, rec date 1786, writ, debt, file #6328

FRENCH William, cordwainer, of Dunstable MA, vs LOVEWELLL Noah, esquire, of Dunstable, rec date 1787, various, debits, file #6805

FRENCH William, cordwainer, of Dunstable MA, vs CHAMBERS William, yeoman, of Chelmsford MA, doc date 1780, rec date 1788, deed, land transfer, file #6822, land in Hollis

FRENCH William, cordwainer, of Dunstable MA, vs CUMMINGS Israel, husbandman, of Woodstock VT, rec date 1787, various, debits, file #6805

FRENCH William Jr, husbandman, of Hollis, vs PRIEST Timothy, husbandman, of Groton MA, rec date 1785, judgment, debt, file #5349

FRENCY Isaac, yeoman, of Hollis, vs JEWET Jacob, husbandman, of Hollis, doc date 1800, judgment, debt, file #568

FRESSENDEN Albert L, vs BARRETT Samuel N, doc date 1890, supreme court argument, land dispute, file #577

FRESSENDEN Albert L, vs SPALDING Edwin S, doc date 1892, supreme court argument, land dispute, file #577

FRIEND James, husbandman, of Wenham MA, vs RAMSEY William, husbandman, of Londonderry, rec date 1787, writ, debt, file #6648

FROST Joseph, yeoman, of Tewksbury MA, vs TRUEL David, tailor, of Litchfield, rec date 1783, judgment, debt, file #3793

FROST Samuel, laborer, of Wilmington MA, vs DIX Jonathan Jr, of Wilmington MA, doc date 1787, rec date 1788, deed, land transfer, file #6825, land Hillsborough

FROTHINGHAM Ebenezer, merchant, of Boston MA, vs McLAUGHLIN John, trader, of New Boston, doc date 1798, judgment, debt, file #562

FRYE Ebenezer, gentleman, of Pembroke, vs PARKER William, yeoman, of Bennington NY, doc date 1773, writ, debt, file #1333

FRYE Isaac, esquire, of Wilton, vs WILLIAMS Stephen, yeoman, of Wilton, rec date 1785, writ, debt, file #6235

FRYE Isaac, esquire, of Wilton, vs BROWN James, husbandman, of Hanover, rec date 1785, judgment, debt, file #6418

FRYE Isaac, esquire, of Wilton, vs BROWN James, husbandman, of Hanover, rec date 1785, judgment, debt, file #6443

FRYE Isaac, gentleman, of Wilton, vs HOLT Samuel, husbandman, of Peterborough, rec date 1788, writ, debt, file #6951

FULLER Jason, trader, of Francestown, vs SMITH Thomas, yeoman, of New Boston, doc date 1798, judgment, debt, file #562

FULLER Jason, trader, of Francestown, vs THOMPSON David Jr, yeoman, of New Boston, doc date 1798, judgment, debt, file #562

FULLER Timothy, gentleman, of Middleton MA, vs SMITH Jonathan Jr, yeoman, of Amherst, doc date 1784, rec date 1785, deed, land transfer, file #5609

FULTON Robert, yeoman, of Londonderry, vs SMITH Robert, yeoman, of Londonderry, doc date 1772, warrant, division of land, file #1398

FULTON Robert, yeoman, of Francestown, vs MONTGOMERY Hugh, yeoman, of Francestown, rec date 1785, various, debt, file #4696

FURBUSH Charles, gentleman, of Andover MA, vs BYAM Benjamin, gentleman, of Temple, doc date 1772, judgment, debt, file #685

FURBUSH Charles, gentleman, of Andover MA, vs DICKEY James, gentleman, of Raby, doc date 1784, civil litigation, debt, file #1834

FURBUSH Charles, yeoman, of Andover MA, vs TOLBERT William, yeoman, of Amherst, rec date 1782, writ, debt, file #2615, fragile

FURBUSH Charles, gentleman, of Andover MA, vs BROWN James, gentleman, of Plymouth, rec date 1783, execution, debt, file #3283

FURBUSH Charles, gentleman, of Andover MA, vs DUTTON Jonathan, yeoman, of Goffstown, rec date 1782, appeal, debt, file #4016

FURBUSH Charles, gentleman, of Andover MA, vs WILKINS Jonathan, yeoman, of Amherst, rec date 1784, writ, debt, file #4581

FURBUSH Charles, gentleman, of Andover MA, vs BROOKS Job, yeoman, of Stoddard, rec date 1784, judgment, debt, file #4586

FURBUSH Charles, gentleman, of Andover MA, vs WILKINS Jonathan, yeoman, of Amherst, rec date 1785, judgment, debt, file #5108

FURBUSH Charles, gentleman, of Andover MA, vs MUZZY Benjamin, yeoman, of Mason, rec date 1782, execution, debt, file #5740

FURBUSH Charles, gentleman, of Andover MA, vs KEYS Daniel, yeoman, of Stoddard, rec date 1785, judgment, debt, file #6420

FURBUSH Charles Jr, yeoman, of Andover MA, vs BUXTON Benjamin, yeoman, of Merrimack, rec date 1783, judgment, debt, file #3739

FURBUSH Charles Jr, husbandman, of Andover MA, vs BROOKS Job, husbandman, of Stoddard, rec date 1785, judgment, debt, file #5080

GAGE Joshua, yeoman, of Dunbarton, vs STARK William, of Dunbarton, rec date NONE, recognizance, debt, file #7048

GAGG John, yeoman, of Deering, vs McLAUGHLIN John Jr, innkeeper, of New Boston, rec date 1783, writ, debt, file #2773

GALE John Collins, husbandman, of Salisbury, vs BROWN Abby, of Andover, doc date 1782, execution, file #1014

GALE John Collins, yeoman, of Salisbury, vs WADLEIGH Benjamin, husbandman, of Salisbury, doc date 1784, execution, debt, file #1705

GALE John Collins, yeoman, of Salisbury, vs HOUSE John, esquire, of Hanover, doc date 1784, execution, debt, file #1719

GALE John Collins, yeoman, of Salisbury, vs WADLEIGH Benjamin, husbandman, of Salisbury, doc date 1784, execution, debt, file #1507

GALE John Collins, yeoman, of Salisbury, vs HOUSE John, esquire, of Hanover, rec date 1783, civil litigious, debt, file #2908

GALE John Collins, husbandman, of Salisbury, vs FARRAR Jonathan, gentleman, of Alexandria, rec date 1783, writ, debt, file #3386

GALE John Collins, husbandman, of Salisbury, vs TAYLOR Jonathan, husbandman, of Alexandria, rec date 1783, writ, debt, file #3387

GALE John Collins, yeoman, of Salisbury, vs HOUSE John, esquire, of Hanover, rec date 1783, writ, debt, file #3377

GALE John Collins, husbandman, of Salisbury, vs CHAMPNEY John, husbandman, of Alexandria, rec date 1783, writ, debt, file #3386

GALE John Collins, yeoman, of Salisbury, vs SMITH Robert Wadleigh, husbandman, of Protectworth, rec date 1783, judgment, debt, file #4082

GALE John Collins, yeoman, of Salisbury, vs WADLEIGH Benjamin, husbandman, of Salisbury, rec date 1783, judgment, debt, file #4081

GALE John Collins, blacksmith, of Salisbury, vs WEARE Peter, gentlemen, of Andover, rec date 1785, judgment, debt, file #6487

GALUSHA Daniel, yeoman, of Lynn MA, vs CONICK John, yeoman, of Hollis, rec date 1783, execution, debt, file #2889

GAMBEL William, yeoman, of Hillsborough, vs DUTTON James, blacksmith, of Hillsborough, doc date 1783, rec date 1783, deed, land transfer, file #2634

GARDNER Ezekiel, cordwainer, of Bedford, vs DOLE Stephen, esquire, of Bedford, doc date 1799, various, debt, file #534

GARDNER John, yeoman, of Bedford, vs HUTCHINSON Solomon Jr, husbandman, of Merrimack, rec date 1785, judgment, debt, file #5976

GARDONER John, yeoman, of Bedford, vs HUTCHINSON Solomon, husbandman, of Merrimack, rec date 1783, judgment, debt, file #4491

GARFIELD Aaron, yeoman, of Monadnock #1, vs WHITNEY Silas, yeoman, of Winchendon MA, doc date 1772, civil litigation, debt, file #653

GARFIELD Nathaniel, gentleman, of Merrimack, vs NUDD Samuel, esquire, of Epping, doc date 1773, writ, debt, file #824

GASHILL Silas, husbandman, of Richmond, vs PARKHURST Joseph, husbandman, of Dunstable MA, rec date 1784, judgment, debt, file #4252

GAY Ichabod, yeoman, of Francestown, vs CAMPBELL Henry, trader, of Antrim, doc date 1799, writ, debt, file #321

GAY Ichabod, husbandman, of Francestown, vs BULLARD Oliver, cordwainer, of Francestown, doc date 1799, writ, debt, file #428

GAY Ichabod, yeoman, of Francestown, vs KITTREDGE Asa, yeoman, of Deering, doc date 1799, writ, debt, file #427

GEAR James, yeoman, of Deering, vs McLAUGHLIN William, yeoman, of Londonderry, rec date 1788, writ, debt, file #6627

GEARFIELD Nathaniel, husbandman, of Merrimack, vs PARKER John Jr, husbandman, of Litchfield, doc date 1772, civil litigation, debt, file #660

GEARFIELD Nathaniel, husbandman, of Merrimack, vs BELL William, husbandman, of Goffstown, doc date 1771, execution, debt, file #1381

GEARFIELD Nathaniel, wigmaker, of Merrimack, vs CARTER Daniel, husbandman, of Concord, doc date 1772, writ, debt, file #1429

GEARFIELD Nathaniel, husbandman, of Merrimack, vs TYNG James, merchant, of Dunstable MA, doc date 1773, writ, debt, file #1230

GEARFIELD Nathaniel, gentleman, of Merrimack, vs BOYES James 3rd, yeoman, of Londonderry?, rec date 1782, writ, debt, file #2704

GEARFIELD Nathaniel, gentleman, of Merrimack, vs BOYES James Iii, yeoman, of Londonderry, rec date 1783, execution, debt, file #3249

GEARFIELD Nathaniel, husbandman, of Merrimack, vs PATTEN William, yeoman, of Amherst, rec date 1783, writ, debt, file #3568

GEARY John, yeoman, of Stoneham MA, vs WYMAN Timothy, yeoman, of Deering, rec date 1784, judgment, debt, file #4979

GEORGE Austin, husbandman, of Dunbarton, vs MOOR James, gentleman, of Goffstown, rec date 1783, writ, debt, file #3353

GEORGE Austin, husbandman, of Dunbarton, vs MOORE James, husbandman, of Goffstown, rec date 1783, judgment, debt, file #3749

GEORGE Bartholomew, yeoman, of Dublin, vs ROBBE John, yeoman, of Peterborough, doc date 1772, writ, debt, file #1065

GEORGE Joseph, yeoman, of Derryfield, vs SANDERS Joseph, gentleman, doc date 1778, rec date 1783, deed, land transfer, file #2639

GEORGE Joseph, husbandman, of Deering, vs CARR Nathan, yeoman, of Deering, doc date 1785, rec date 1788, deed, land transfer, file #6746

GERRISH Henry, esquire, of Boscawen, vs HAYES William, yeoman, of Sanbornton, doc date 1798, execution, debt, file #120

GERRISH Henry, esquire, of Boscawen, vs FLANDERS John, gentleman, of Boscawen, doc date 1798, judgment, debt, file #563

GERRISH Henry, esquire, of Boscawen, vs CLOUGH Gilman, yeoman, of Northfield, doc date 1799, debt, file #466

GERRISH Henry, esquire, of Boscawen, vs CALL John, cordwainer, of Andover, doc date 1798, judgment, debt, file #561

GERRISH Henry, esquire, of Boscawen, vs CALL Stephen, yeoman, of Sanbornton, doc date 1798, execution, debt, file #118

GERRISH Henry, esquire, of Boscawen, vs HOBART Peter, gentleman, of Plymouth, doc date 1773, writ, debt, file #1183

GERRISH Henry, esquire, of Boscawen, vs FENTON John (late), esquire, of Plymouth, rec date 1783, civil litigious, debt, file #2949

GERRISH Henry, esquire, of Boscawen, vs FENTON John, esquire, of Plymouth, rec date 1783, writ, debt, file #3392

GERRISH Henry, esquire, of Boscawen, vs SWEATT Benjamin, carpenter, of Boscawen, rec date 1785, judgment, debt, file #5045

GERRISH Henry & C Noyes, yeoman, of Boscawen, vs ROBINSON James, joiner, of Boscawen, doc date 1784, deed, land transfer, file #2002

GERRISH Joseph, esquire, of Boscawen, vs BOHANAN Andrew, gentleman, of Salisbury, doc date 1798, execution, debt, file #112

GERRISH Joseph, husbandman, of Boscawen, vs McMURPHY John, husbandman, of Alexandria, rec date 1783, civil litigious, debt, file #2916

GERRISH Joseph Jr, husbandman, of Boscawen, vs McMURPHY John, husbandman, of Alexandria, doc date 1784, execution, debt, file #1717

GERRISH Joseph Jr, husbandman, of Boscawen, vs McMURPHY John, husbandman, of Alexandria, rec date 1783, writ, debt, file #3385

GERRISH Joseph Jr, gentleman, of Boscawen, vs CARR David, yeoman, of Boscawen, rec date 1788, writ, debt, file #6927

GERRISH Moses, gentleman, of Canterbury, vs HALL John, taylor, of Boscawen, doc date 1773, execution, debt, file #1464

GIBSON Barnabas, esquire, of Pelham, vs MARSH Samuel Jr, husbandman, of Weare, doc date 1798, judgment, debt, file #563

GIBSON Daniel, yeoman, of Hillsborough, vs DICKERMAN Samuel, blacksmith, of Francestown, doc date 1784, writ, debt, file #1590

GIBSON Daniel, yeoman, of Hillsborough, vs GROUT William, yeoman, of Hillsborough, rec date 1785, judgment, debt, file #5175

GIBSON Daniel, yeoman, of Hillsborough, vs BARNES John, yeoman, of New Boston, doc date 1788, rec date 1788, deed, land transfer, file #6816

GIBSON Elizabeth, widow, of Pepperell MA, vs FLAGG Eleazer, housewright, of Hollis, rec date 1784, judgment, debt, file #4377

GIBSON Isaac, husbandman, of Fitchburg MA, vs FITCH John & Paul, yeoman, of Jaffrey, rec date 1783, writ, debt, file #4545

GIBSON James, yeoman, of Hillsborough, vs WILKINS Elijah, yeoman, of Middleton MA, doc date 1774, writ, debt, file #1078, very fragile

GIBSON James, husbandman, of Hillsborough, vs HILL John, esquire, of Boston MA, doc date 1773, writ, debt, file #1235

GIBSON John, trader, of Francestown, vs RICHARDSON Thomas, husbandman, of Deering, doc date 1798, judgment, debt, file #563

GIBSON John, trader, of Francestown, vs McALLESTER Archibald, yeoman, of Society Land, doc date 1799, various, debt, file #533

GIBSON John, cooper, of Pelham, vs KELLEY Joseph, gentleman, of Nottingham-West, rec date 1782, appeal, debt, file #3997

GIBSON John, gentleman, of Francestown, vs McCLINTOCK John, yeoman, of Hillsborough, doc date 1799, debt, file #532

GIBSON John, esquire, of Francestown, vs PEVEY Peter Jr, gentleman, of Greenfield, doc date 1816, rec date 1816, deed, land transfer, file #5703

GIBSON Samuel, yeoman, of Merrimack, vs MARSH Samuel Jr, yeoman, of Nottingham-West, doc date 1784, execution, debt, file #1926

GIBSON Samuel, yeoman, of Merrimack, vs MARSH Samuel Jr, yeoman, of Nottingham-West, rec date 1783, writ, debt, file #3580

GIBSON Samuel, yeoman, of Merrimack, vs BUTLER Jesse, yeoman, of Pelham, rec date 1783, writ, debt, file #3580

GIBSON Simon, gentleman, of Pepperell MA, vs WAIT John, husbandman, of Mason, rec date 1783, judgment, debt, file #4705

GIBSON Simon, gentleman, of Pepperell MA, vs SPAULDING Edward, husbandman, of Hollis, rec date 1784, judgment, debt, file #5310

GIBSON Timothy, esquire, of Henniker, vs KIMBALL William, husbandman, of Henniker, doc date 1779, various, debt, file #2401

GIBSON Timothy, esquire, of Henniker, vs BACON Daniel, husbandman, of Hillsborough, rec date 1783, judgment, debt, file #4708

GILBERT Peter Cummings, laborer, of Littleton MA, vs GRIMES James, husbandman, of Deering, rec date 1785, execution, debt, file #5945

GILBERT Peter Cummings, laborer, of Littleton MA, vs GRIMES Jonas, husbandman, of Deering, rec date 1785, writ, debt, file #6027

GILBERT Peter Cummings, of Littleton MA, vs GRIMES James, husbandman, of Deering, rec date 1786, judgment, debt, file #6496

GILCHRIST Alexander, yeoman, of Goffstown, vs ROSS Jonathan, yeoman, of Henniker, rec date 1783, civil litigious, debt, file #2922

GILCREST Alexander, husbandman, of Goffstown, vs THORNTON Matthew, esquire, of Londonderry, doc date 1774, writ, debt, file #1124

GILE Ebenezer, husbandman, of Henniker, vs HALL Daniel, husbandman, of Deerfield, doc date 1772, writ, debt, file #929

GILE Ebenezer, yeoman, of Henniker, vs GILE Johnson, yeoman, of Henniker, doc date 1772, rec date 1778, deed, land transfer, file #2111

GILE Ebenezer, husbandman, of Henniker, vs GILE Johnson, yeoman, of Henniker, doc date 1772, rec date 1778, deed, land transfer, file #2112

GILE Johnson, husbandman, of Hopkinton, vs WILLSON James, husbandman, of New Boston, doc date 1774, execution, debt, file #755

GILE Johnson, husbandman, of Hopkinton, vs WILLSON James & John, husbandman, of New Boston, doc date 1774, execution, file #997

GILES John, yeoman, of Londonderry, vs STUART Robert, husbandman, of Nottingham-West, rec date 1782, writ, debt, file #2833

GILL George, husbandman, of Milford, vs GAY Samuel, of Milford, doc date 1799, writ, debt, file #374

GILLINGHAM John, blacksmith, of Amherst, vs GRIMES Thaddeus, yeoman, of Amherst, rec date 1785, judgment, debt, file #5177

GILLINGHAM John, blacksmith, of Amherst, vs GRIMES Thaddeus, yeoman, of Amherst, rec date 1785, judgment, debt, file #6072

GILLIS Jonathan, husbandman, of Merrimack, vs SCOBY David, gentleman, of Francestown, rec date 1785, judgment, debt, file #6450

GILLIS Jotham, husbandman, of Merrimack, vs SCOBEY David, gentleman, of Francestown, rec date 1784, judgment, debt, file #5456

GILLSON Daniel, laborer, of Groton MA, vs CHAMBERLIN Isaac, gentleman, of Westmoreland, doc date 1774, writ, debt, file #1106

GILMAN Daniel, husbandman, of Springfield, vs PATCH Benjamin, yeoman, of Francestown, doc date 1799, writ, debt, file #411

GILMAN James, yeoman, of Amherst, vs GRIMES Thaddeus, yeoman, of Amherst, doc date 1784, civil litigation, debt, file #1841

GILMAN James, yeoman, of Amherst, vs PUTNAM Archelaus, yeoman, of Wilton, rec date 1786, writ, debt, file #6869

GILMORE James, yeoman, of Bedford, vs LYNCH Catherine, widow, of New Boston, rec date 1784, writ, debt, file #5375

GILMORE James, husbandman, of Merrimack, vs TAYLOR James, gentleman, of Merrimack, rec date 1785, writ, debt, file #5075

GILMORE James, husbandman, of Merrimack, vs BLOOD Elnathan Jr, husbandman, of Hollis, rec date 1785, writ, debt, file #5075

GILMORE James, husbandman, of Merrimack, vs MARSHALL John, yeoman, of Goffstown, rec date 1788, writ, land dispute, file #7001

GILMORE Mary, widow, of Goffstown, vs McCLEARY David, yeoman, of Bedford, doc date 1784, execution, debt, file #1510

GILMORE Mary, widow, of Goffstown, vs McCLEARY David, yeoman, of Bedford, rec date 1785, judgment, debt, file #6449

GILSOM Simon, gentleman, of Pepperell MA, vs WRIGHT David, cordwainer, of Pepperell MA, rec date 1793, various, theft trees, file #2581

GILSOM Simon, gentleman, of Pepperell MA, vs WRIGHT David, cordwainer, of Pepperell MA, rec date 1793, various, theft trees, file #2581 B

GILSOM Simon, gentleman, of Pepperell MA, vs WRIGHT David, cordwainer, of Pepperell MA, rec date 1793, various, theft trees, file #2581 C

GILSON David, yeoman, of Dunstable, vs STEPHENS Daniel, yeoman, of Amherst, rec date 1783, writ, debt, file #3049

GILSON Simon, gentleman, of Pepperell MA, vs SCOTT James, husbandman, of Stoddard, doc date 1784, execution, debt, file #1687

GILSON Simon, gentleman, of Pepperell MA, vs SCOTT James, husbandman, of Stoddard, rec date 1783, judgment, debt, file #4086

GILSON Simon, gentleman, of Pepperell MA, vs MOSHER James, husbandman, of Hollis, rec date 1784, judgment, debt, file #4990

GILSON Simon, gentleman, of Pepperell MA, vs GOLDSMITH Josiah, esquire, of Walpole, rec date 1788, writ, debt, file #6954

GLENWOOD Samuel, yeoman, of Hillsborough, vs CUMMINGS Peter & Gilbert, yeoman, of Littleton MA, rec date 1785, judgment, debt, file #4255

GLENWOOD Samuel, yeoman, of Hillsborough, vs BARTLETT Andrew, yeoman, of Littleton MA, rec date 1785, judgment, debt, file #4255

GLIDDON Levi, husbandman, of Unity, vs DODGE Jonathan, traders, of Ossipee, doc date 1798, debt, file #424

GLIDDON Levi, husbandman, of Unity, vs QUARLES Samuel, traders, of Ossipee, doc date 1798, debt, file #424

GLOVER Daniel, yeoman, of Marblehead MA, vs ROCH John, husbandman, of Campbells Gore, rec date 1783, execution, debt, file #3236

GLOVER Jonathan, esquire, of Marblehead MA, vs MITCHELL Francis, yeoman, of Dunbarton, doc date 1784, execution, debt, file #1796

GLOVER Jonathan, esquire, of Marblehead MA, vs MITCHELL Francis, yeoman, of Dunbarton, rec date 1783, civil litigious, debt, file #2947

GLOVER Jonathan, esquire, of Marblehead MA, vs MITCHELL Francis, yeoman, of Dunbarton, rec date 1783, execution, debt, file #3250

GLOVER William, carpenter, of Greenfield, vs DARRAH William, husbandman, of Greenfield, doc date 1799, writ, debt, file #316

GLOVER William, carpenter, of Greenfield, vs KINGSBURY Nathaniel, trader, of Grafton ma, doc date 1799, debt, file #338

GODFRED John, husbandman, of Hollis, vs BOYNTON Joshua, clock maker, of Hollis, rec date 1784, judgment, debt, file #4216

GOFF John, esquire, of Bedford, vs DALTON Michael, yeoman, of Merrimack, doc date 1778, writ, debt, file #2047

GOFF Samuel, yeoman, of Bedford, vs NEWMAN Thomas, yeoman, of Bedford, doc date 1773, execution, debt, file #1215

GOFFE John, esquire, of Derryfield, vs RAND John & Sarah, of Derryfield, rec date 1777, writ & land deed, debt, file #2193

GOFFE John, esquire, of Bedford, vs LEACH James, yeoman, of Bedford, doc date 1786, rec date 1787, deed, land transfer, file #2489

GOFFE John, of Deerfield, vs BAYLEY Jacob, of Newbury NY, rec date 1783, judgment, debt, file #3058, fragile

GOFFE John, esquire, of Bedford, vs CALDWELL William, husbandman, of Francestown, rec date 1785, judgment, debt, file #5220

GOFFE John G, esquire, of Bedford, vs SANDERS Joseph, housewright, of Deerfield, doc date 1784, deed, land transfer, file #2000

GOFFE Samuel, yeoman, of Bedford, vs NEWMAN Thomas, yeoman, of Bedford, doc date 1773, execution, debt, file #1471

GOFFE Samuel, husbandman, of Bedford, vs PATTERSON William, husbandman, of Goffstown, rec date 1785, writ, debt, file #5370

GOING Asahel, trader, of Hillsborough, vs RICHARDSON Timothy, blacksmith, of Greenfield, doc date 1799, judgment, debt, file #291

GOOCH William, merchant, of Boston MA, vs WAIT Nathan, tanner, of Pembroke, rec date 1783, civil litigious, debt, file #3060

GOOCH William, merchant, of Boston MA, vs WAIT Nathan, trader, of Pembroke, rec date 1783, civil litigation, debt, file #3060

GOOCH William, merchant, of Boston MA, vs WAIT Nathan, trader, of Pembroke, rec date 1783, execution, debt, file #3275

GOODALE Bartholomew, husbandman, of Weare, vs FERRIN Enos, husbandman, of Alexandria, rec date 1783, writ, debt, file #3808

GOODALE Bartholomew, husbandman, of Weare, vs FERRIN Enos, husbandman, of Alexandria, rec date 1783, execution, debt, file #3829

GOODALE Job, trader, of Marlborough MA, vs TAYLOR Nathan, yeoman, of Antrim, doc date 1784, execution, debt, file #1817

GOODGRIDGE Philip, innholder, of Lunenburg MA, vs PARKER Abel, yeoman, of Peterborough, rec date 1783, judgment, debt, file #4314

GOODHUE John, yeoman, of Ipswich MA, vs PORTER Francis, husbandman, of Peterborough, rec date 1785, judgment, debt, file #5330

GOODHUE John, husbandman, of Cockermouth, vs KENDRICK Daniel Jr, cooper, of Hollis, rec date 1787, writ, debt, file #2422

GOODHUE John, husbandman, of Cockermouth, vs POOL William W, wheelwright, of Hollis, rec date 1787, judgment, debt, file #2465

GOODHUE John, husbandman, of Cockermouth, vs ATWELL John, joiner, of Hollis, rec date 1783, writ, damages to woodland, file #2762

GOODHUE John & Samuel, husbandman, of Cockermouth, vs PIERCE William, husbandman, of Wilton, rec date 1787, writ, debt, file #2425

GOODHUE Samuel, husbandman, of Stratham, vs KENDRICK Daniel Jr, cooper, of Hollis, rec date 1787, writ, debt, file #2422

GOODHUE Samuel, husbandman, of Hollis, vs ATWELL John, joiner, of Hollis, rec date 1783, writ, debt, file #2760

GOODHUE Samuel, husbandman, of Hollis, vs WHITTEMORE Samuel, gentleman, of Cambridge, rec date 1785, judgment, land dispute, file #5358

GOODHUE Samuel & John, husbandman, of Stratham, vs HOLT Timothy, husbandman, of Wilton, rec date 1787, judgment, debt, file #2474

GOODHUE Samuel Jr, husbandman, of Cockermouth, vs POOL William W, wheelwright, of Hollis, rec date 1787, judgment, debt, file #2473

GOODNOW Ebenezer, yeoman, of Henniker, vs ANDREWS Molly, single woman, of Henniker, rec date 1785, various, assault, file #4747

GOODNOW John, yeoman, of Henniker, vs ANDREWS Molly, single woman, of Henniker, rec date 1785, various, assault, file #4747

GOODNOW John, husbandman, of Henniker, vs WADWORTH Samuel, husbandman, of Henniker, rec date 1785, writ, debt, file #5406

GOODNOW John, husbandman, of Henniker, vs HOW Peter, husbandman, of Henniker, rec date 1785, writ, debt, file #5406

GOODRIDGE Lemuel, clerk, of Lyndeborough, vs DUNCKLE Joseph, yeoman, of Amherst, rec date 1783, judgment, debt, file #3728

GOODRIDGE Levi, cordwainer, of Andover, vs GOULD James, gentleman, of Hanover, doc date 1784, execution, debt, file #1876

GOODRIDGE Levi, cordwainer, of Andover MA, vs GOOLD James, gentleman, of Hanover, rec date 1783, writ, debt, file #3420

GOODRIDGE Levi, cordwainer, of Andover MA, vs POWERS Joseph, husbandman, of Charlestown, rec date 1784, writ, debt, file #4858, bail for James GOULD

GOODRIDGE Philip, gentleman, of Lunenburg MA, vs KELLEY Moses, esquire, of Goffstown, rec date 1787, various, debt, file #2533

GOODRIDGE Philip, gentleman, of Lunenburg MA, vs PARKER Abel, husbandman, of Peterborough, rec date 1785, judgment, debt, file #5181

GOODRIDGE Philip, gentleman, of Lunenburg MA, vs KELLY Moses, esquire/sheriff, of Goffstown, rec date 1785, judgment, debt, file #6360

GOODRIDGE Sewall, clerk, of Lyndeborough, vs GREGG David, yeoman, of Francestown, rec date 1783, civil litigious, debt, file #2932

GOODRIDGE Sewall, husbandman, of Lyndeborough, vs CAMPBELL James, husbandman, of Lyndeborough, rec date 1784, various, debt, file #4178

GOODRIDGE Thomas, housewright, of Boxford MA, vs TAGGART Archibald, gentleman, of Hillsborough, rec date 1784, appeal, debt, file #4139

GOODWIN James & Margaret, yeoman, of Berwick Me, vs QUIMBY Joseph, yeoman, of Weare, doc date 1775, rec date 1778, deed, land transfer, file #2160

GOODWIN Jesse, husbandman, of Petersham MA, vs WIGGIN Mark, esquire, of Stratham, rec date 1785, judgment, debt, file #6424

GOODWIN John, gentleman, of Reading MA, vs PEARSON Amos, husbandman, of Lyndeborough, rec date 1784, writ, debt, file #4674

GOOL Lois, widow, of Salem MA, vs WILKINS John, gentleman, of Francestown, rec date 1782, judgment, debt, file #3132

GOOLD Benjamin, blacksmith, of Hillsborough, vs ATHERTON Joshua, esquire, of Amherst, doc date 1772, writ, debt, file #1416

GOOLD Benjamin, blacksmith, of Marlborough MA, vs GOOLD Elijah, schoolmaster, of Marlborough MA, rec date 1786, confession, debt, file #2324

GOOLD John, yeoman, of Lyndeborough, vs CARLTON Osgood, yeoman, of Lyndeborough, doc date 1772, judgment, debt, file #665, fragile

GOOLL John, merchant, of Salem MA, vs WILKINS John, gentleman, of Amherst, doc date 1774, judgment, debt, file #1155

GORDON Cosmo, yeoman, of Dunstable MA, vs PIKE Daniel, husbandman, of Dunstable, rec date 1784, various, debt, file #4598, estate of Wm GORDON

GORDON Cosmo, yeoman, of Groton MA, vs BALLARD Uriah, yeoman, of Wilton, rec date 1784, judgment, debt, file #4649, estate of Wm GORDON

GORDON Cosmo, yeoman, of Dunstable MA, vs McALLISTER Daniel, yeoman, of New Boston, rec date 1784, judgment, debt, file #4662

GORDON Cosmo, husbandman, of Dunstable MA, vs DICKERMAN Samuel, blacksmith, of Francestown, rec date 1786, judgment, debt, file #5758

GORDON Cosmo, husbandman, of Dunstable MA, vs DICKERMAN Samuel, blacksmith, of Francestown, rec date 1786, execution, debt, file #5880

GORDON Cozmo, merchant, of Dunstable MA, vs CLARK Timothy, yeoman, of Amherst, rec date 1783, judgment, debt, file #3719

GORDON James, yeoman, of Deerfield, vs HALL John, gentleman, of Deerfield, doc date 1772, writ, debt, file #1049

GORDON James, gentleman, of Dunstable MA, vs WOOD Ebenezer, yeoman, of Goffstown, doc date 1784, execution, debt, file #1551

GORDON James, merchant, of Dunstable MA, vs MacMURPHY Robert, husbandman, of Londonderry, rec date 1783, judgment, debt, file #2620

GORDON James, gentleman, of Dunstable MA, vs TRUEL Amos, yeoman, of Amherst, rec date 1783, judgment, debt, file #3719

GORDON James, gentleman, of Dunstable MA, vs PIKE Daniel, husbandman, of Dunstable, rec date 1784, various, debt, file #4598, estate of Wm GORDON

GORDON James, gentleman, of Dunstable MA, vs BARRETT Moses, gentleman, of Nottingham-West, rec date 1783, various, debt, file #4518, kinship GORDON and Cosmo

GORDON James, gentleman, of Dunstable MA, vs GORDON Cosmo, merchant, of Nottingham-West, rec date 1783, various, debt, file #4518, kinship GORDON and Cosmo

GORDON James, gentleman, of Dunstable MA, vs McALLISTER Archibald, yeoman, of New Boston, rec date 1784, judgment, debt, file #4662

GORDON James, gentleman, of Groton MA, vs BALLARD Uriah, yeoman, of Wilton, rec date 1784, judgment, debt, file #4649, estate of Wm GORDON

GORDON James & Cosmo, merchants, of Dunstable MA, vs HERRICK Joseph, husbandman, of Lyndeborough, rec date 1782, writ, debt, file #2714, kinship in file

GORDON James & Cosmo, gentleman, of Dunstable MA, vs TAYLOR James, gentleman, of Merrimack, rec date 1783, execution, debt, file #2977

GORDON James & Cosmo, gentleman, of Dunstable MA, vs WOOD Ebenezer, yeoman, of Goffstown, rec date 1783, judgment, debt, file #4320, estate of Wm GORDON

GORDON James & Cosmo, gentleman, of Dunstable MA, vs WALKER Silas, yeoman, of Goffstown, rec date 1783, judgment, debt, file #4308, estate of Wm GORDON

GORDON James & Cosmo, yeoman, of Dunstable, vs McALLISTER Archibald, yeoman, of New Boston, rec date 1785, judgment, debt, file #5117

GORDON James & Cosmo, yeoman, of Dunstable MA, vs PARKER John, yeoman, of Bedford, rec date 1785, judgment, debt, file #5053, estate of Wm GORDON

GORDON James & Cosmo, gentleman, of Dunstable, vs ANDREWS Ammi, husbandman, of Hillsborough, rec date 1788, writ, debt, file #6626

GORDON James & Cosmo, merchants, of Dunstable MA, vs GILLMORE James, yeoman, of Merrimack, rec date 1783, writ, debt, file #3922, estate of William GORDON

GORDON James & Cozmo, of Dunstable MA, vs McMURPHY Robert, husbandman, of Londonderry, rec date 1784, various, debt, file #4774

GORDON John, tailor, of Campbells Gore, vs TAYLOR Nathan, yeoman, of Antrim, doc date 1779, writ, debt, file #2098

GORDON John, yeoman, of Campbells Gore, vs PATTEN John, yeoman, of Bedford, rec date 1782, writ, debt, file #2847

GORDON John, taylor, of Campbells Gore, vs McLAUGHLIN John Jr, innkeeper, of New BOSTON, rec date 1783, writ, debt, file #3223

GORDON Samuel, carpenter, of Hancock, vs AMES David, trader, of Hancock, doc date 1799, various, debt, file #530

GORDON William, trader, of Amherst, vs PITTS John, esquire, of Tyngsboro, doc date 1798, execution, debt, file #197

GORDON William, esquire, of Amherst, vs KELLEY Joseph, gentleman, of Nottingham, doc date 1798, judgment, debt, file #563

GORDON William, merchant, of Dunstable MA, vs KILLICUT Thomas Jr, yeoman, of Dunstable, doc date 1774, judgment, debt, file #740

GORDON William, esquire, of Amherst, vs BROOKS William, gentleman, of Hollis, doc date 1798, execution, debt, file #80

GORDON William, merchant, of Dunstable MA, vs SPAULDING Stephen, yeoman, of Lyndeborough, doc date 1774, judgment, debt, file #726

GORDON William, merchant, of Dunstable MA, vs ABBOTT Josiah, yeoman, of Lyndeborough, doc date 1774, writ, debt, file #1116

GORDON William, merchant, of Dunstable MA, vs BUTTERFIELD Josiah, yeoman, of Dunstable, doc date 1774, execution, file #1005

GORDON William, of Dunstable MA, vs LUND Phineas, yeoman, of Lyndeborough, doc date 1774, execution, file #941

GORDON William, merchant, of Dunstable MA, vs KILLICUT Thomas Jr, yeoman, of Dunstable, doc date 1774, writ, debt, file #1115

GORDON William, merchant, of Dunstable MA, vs JEWELL Nathaniel, yeoman, of Dunstable, doc date 1773, execution, debt, file #1465

GORDON William, merchant, of Dunstable, vs RAMSEY Hugh, yeoman, of Merrimack, doc date 1773, execution, debt, file #1483

GORDON William, merchant, of Dunstable MA, vs CLAGSTONE John, yeoman, of Dunstable, rec date 1774, writ, debt, file #2178

GORMAN James, yeoman, of Derryfield, vs PIERCE Joshua, yeoman, of Derryfield, rec date 1782, judgment, debt, file #2730

GORMAN James, yeoman, of Derryfield, vs GILMORE James, yeoman, of Merrimack, rec date 1783, writ, debt, file #3342

GORMAN James, yeoman, of Deerfield, vs PIERCE Joshua, yeoman, of Derryfield, rec date 1783, execution, debt, file #3258

GORMAN James, yeoman, of Derryfield, vs COX Charles Jr, yeoman, of Londonderry, rec date 1784, writ, debt, file #4782

GORMAN James, yeoman, of Derryfield, vs COX Charles Jr, yeoman, of Londonderry, rec date 1786, various, debt, file #6081

GORMAN James, wheelwright, of Derryfield, vs ROBBINS Jonas, husbandman, of Westmoreland, rec date 1788, writ, debt, file #7003

GOSS Ebenezer Harden, esquire, of Concord, vs HILLS David, trader, of New Ipswich, rec date 1783, various, debt, file #3942

GOSS Ebenezer Harden, esquire, of Concord, vs HILLS David, trader, of New Ipswich, rec date 1788, various, debt, file #6582

GOSS James, cabinetmaker, of Hampstead, vs WHITING Timothy, cordwainer, of Billerica MA, doc date 1772, writ, debt, file #902

GOSS John, husbandman, of Derryfield, vs STARK John, esquire, of Derryfield, rec date 1788, writ, debt, file #2545

GOSS John, esquire, of Bedford, vs SANDERS Joseph, gentleman, of Derryfield, rec date 1784, judgment, debt, file #4614

GOSS Thomas, clerk, of Bolton MA, vs DAVIS William, yeoman, of Putney NY, doc date 1773, execution, debt, file #1220

GOULD Christopher, husbandman, of Hopkinton, vs ALEXANDER Jabez Jr, husbandman, of Acworth, rec date 1786, writ, debt, file #6315

GOULD Daniel, yeoman, of Amherst, vs HOBART Joel, husbandman, of Mile Slip, doc date 1784, execution, debt, file #1533

GOULD Daniel, innholder, of Lyndeborough, vs LUND Phineas, yeoman, of Lyndeborough, doc date 1784, execution, debt, file #1934

GOULD Daniel, innholder, of Lyndeborough, vs LUND Phineas, yeoman, of Lyndeborough, rec date 1783, writ, debt, file #3577

GOULD Daniel, husbandman, of Amherst, vs HOBART Joel, husbandman, of Mile Slip, rec date 1784, judgment, debt, file #4293

GOULD Daniel, innholder, of Lyndeborough, vs GREGG David, wheelwright, of Francestown, rec date 1784, judgment, debt, file #4369

GOULD Daniel, yeoman, of Amherst, vs BALLARD Joseph, yeoman, of Amherst, rec date 1786, execution, debt, file #5881

GOULD Daniel, yeoman, of Amherst, vs COLE John, yeoman, of Amherst, rec date 1786, writ, debt, file #6884

GOULD Ebenezer, gentleman, of Chelmsford MA, vs McCLENCHE John, yeoman, of Merrimack, doc date 1774, execution, file #996

GOULD Ebenezer, yeoman, of Chelmsford MA, vs McCLENCHE John, yeoman, of Merrimack, doc date 1774, writ, debt, file #1122

GOULD Ebenezer, executor, of Chelmsford MA, vs McCLENCHE John, yeoman, of Merrimack, doc date 1773, execution, debt, file #1469

GOULD Jacob, yeoman, of Rindge, vs MORRISON John, yeoman, of Peterborough, doc date 1773, execution, debt, file #1457

GOULD Jacob, yeoman, of Rindge, vs TAGGART James, yeoman, of Peterborough, doc date 1784, execution, debt, file #1457

GOULD John, husbandman, of Merrimack, vs HUTCHINSON David, husbandman, of Merrimack, doc date 1799, writ, debt, file #384

GOULD John, yeoman, of Sutton MA, vs THORNTON Matthew, esquire, of Merrimack, rec date 1785, various, debt, file #6253, estate of Robert BOYCE

GOULD Mary, rec date NONE, loose pieces, bill, file #7017

GOULD Noah M, yeoman, of Dunstable MA, vs LUND Jesse, yeoman, of Lyndeborough, doc date 1786, rec date 1787, deed, land transfer, file #2485

GOULD Richard, yeoman, of Greenfield, vs WILSON James, husbandman, of Peterborough, doc date 1799, judgment, debt, file #302

GOULE Ezekiel, gentleman, of Nottingham-West, vs POLLARD Timothy, yeoman, of Nottingham-West, rec date 1783, execution, debt, file #2976

GOULT Samuel, husbandman, of Chester, vs CHAMPNEY Ebenezer, esquire, of Groton MA, rec date 1785, writ, debt, file #5391

GOVE Abraham, yeoman, of Deering, vs GRIMES James, gentleman, of Deering, rec date 1783, civil litigious, debt, file #2912

GOVE Jonathan, gentleman, of New Boston, vs CUMMINGS Silas, blacksmith, of New Boston, rec date 1783, execution, debt, file #3667

GOVE Jonathan, esquire, of Goffstown, vs WILSON Alexander, husbandman, of New Boston, doc date 1798, judgment, debt, file #563

GOVE Jonathan, gentleman, of New Boston, vs CUMMINGS Silas, blacksmith, of New Boston, doc date 1784, execution, debt, file #1812

GOVE Jonathan, physician, of New Boston, vs BALDWIN Nahum, esquire, of Amherst, rec date 1782, writ, debt, file #2673, estate of Zacheus CUTLER

GOVE Jonathan, physician, of New Boston, vs GRIMES James, gentleman, of Deering, rec date 1782, execution, debt, file #3535

GOVE Jonathan, physician, of New Boston, vs GRIMES James, gentleman, of Deering, rec date 1783, execution, debt, file #3682

GOVE Jonathan, gentleman, of New Boston, vs CUMMINGS Silas, blacksmith, of New Boston, rec date 1782, execution, debt, file #3509

GOVE Jonathan, gentleman, of New Boston, vs JONES Samuel, yeoman, of Hillsborough, rec date 1783, writ, debt, file #3894

GOVE Jonathan, physician, of New Boston, vs GREEN David, yeoman, of Hillsborough, rec date 1783, judgment, debt, file #3803

GOVE Jonathan, physician, of New Boston, vs ABBOTT Samuel, yeoman, of Hollis, rec date 1783, execution, debt, file #3822

GOVE Jonathan, physician, of New Boston, vs GILMORE John, husbandman, of Antrim, rec date 1783, judgment, debt, file #4467

GOVE Jonathan, physician, of New Boston, vs GREEN David, yeoman, of Hillsborough, rec date 1785, judgment, debt, file #4963

GOVE Jonathan, physician, of New Boston, vs TAYLOR John, yeoman, of Amherst, rec date 1785, judgment, debt, file #5586

GOVE Jonathan, physician, of New Boston, vs GREEN David, yeoman, of Hillsborough, rec date 1785, judgment, debt, file #6423

GOVE Jonathan, physician, of New Boston, vs BARNARD Jeremiah, clerk, of Amherst, doc date 1787, rec date 1788, deed, land transfer, file #6830

GOVE Jonathan, of New Boston, vs GREGG Alexander, administrator of estate, of New Boston, rec date 1788, deposition, debt, file #6976

GOVE Nathan, yeoman, of Hampton, vs HALE John Jr, husbandman, of Boscawen, rec date 1784, judgment, debt, file #4274

GOWEN John, husbandman, of New Ipswich, vs PRENTICE Nathaniel, clothier, of New Ipswich, rec date 1784, judgment, debt, file #5291

GRAGG David, yeoman, of Francestown, vs GOODRIDGE Sewall, city clerk, of Lyndeborough, rec date 1783, writ, debt, file #3054

GRAGG Jacob, husbandman, of Peterborough, vs ROBBE Alexander, gentleman, of Peterborough, rec date 1783, writ, debt, file #3201

GRAGG John Jr, yeoman, of Colrain MA, vs COCHRAN George, husbandman, of Goffstown, rec date 1783, writ, debt, file #3467

GRAGG Samuel, yeoman, of Peterborough, vs BACON Retire, yeoman, of New Ipswich, rec date 1785, judgment, debt, file #5522

GRAGG Samuel, husbandman, of Peterborough, vs MOSHER James, husbandman, of Hollis, rec date 1783, writ, debt, file #2753

GRAGG Samuel, of Peterborough Slip, vs FULLER Samuel, husbandman, of Walpole, rec date 1783, execution, debt, file #2885

GRAGG Samuel, yeoman, of Peterborough Slip, vs CUNNINGHAM Moses, husbandman, of Peterborough, rec date 1783, writ, debt, file #3308

GRAGG Samuel, yeoman, of Peterborough Slip, vs MOSHER James, husbandman, of Hollis, rec date 1782, execution, debt, file #3525

GRAGG Samuel, yeoman, of Peterborough Slip, vs LASLEY Joseph, husbandman, of Hollis, rec date 1782, execution, debt, file #3525

GRAGG Samuel, yeoman, of Peterborough Slip, vs APPLETON Isaac, gentleman, of New Ipswich, rec date 1783, various, debt, file #3562

GRAGG Samuel, yeoman, of Peterborough Slip, vs HOW Isaac, gentleman, of New Ipswich, rec date 1783, various, debt, file #3562

GRAGG Samuel, yeoman, of Peterborough Slip, vs MOSHER James, husbandman, of Hollis, rec date 1783, execution, debt, file #3665

GRAGG Samuel, yeoman, of Peterborough Slip, vs HOAR Benjamin, gentleman, of New Ipswich, rec date 1783, various, debt, file #3562

GRAGG Samuel, yeoman, of Peterborough Slip, vs CHAMPNEY Ebenezer, esquire, of Groton MA, rec date 1783, various, debt, file #3940

GRAGG Samuel, yeoman, of Peterborough Slip, vs LASLEY Joseph, husbandman, of Hollis, rec date 1783, execution, debt, file #3665

GRAGG Samuel, yeoman, of Peterborough Slip, vs HOAR Benjamin, gentleman, of New Ipswich, rec date 1783, various, debt, file #3940

GRAGG Samuel, yeoman, of Peterborough Slip, vs APPLETON Isaac, gentleman, of New Ipswich, rec date 1783, various, debt, file #3940

GRAGG Samuel, innkeeper, of Peterborough Slip, vs BARKER David Jr, yeoman, of Temple, rec date 1784, appeal, debt, file #4113

GRAGG Samuel, innholder, of Peterborough Slip, vs ROBBE Alexander, gentleman, of Hillsborough, rec date 1783, writ, debt, file #3964

GRAGG Samuel, yeoman, of Peterborough Slip, vs HOW Isaac, gentleman, of New Ipswich, rec date 1783, various, debt, file #3940

GRAGG Samuel, innholder, of Peterborough Slip, vs QUINTON David, husbandman, of Walpole, rec date 1785, various, debt, file #4601

GRAGG Samuel, yeoman, of Peterborough Slip, vs COSTELOE John, yeoman, of Effingham, rec date 1784, judgment, debt, file #4594

GRAGG Samuel, yeoman, of Peterborough Slip, vs COSTELLOE John, yeoman, of Effingham, rec date 1785, judgment, debt, file #5107

GRAGG Samuel, gentleman, of Peterborough, vs CRAM Joseph, yeoman, of Society Land, rec date 1785, judgment, debt, file #5104

GRAGG Samuel, yeoman, of Peterborough Slip, vs CUNNINGHAM Moses, husbandman, of Peterborough, rec date 1785, various, debt, file #5249

GRAGG Samuel, yeoman, of Peterborough Slip, vs CONANT John, of Townsend MA, rec date 1783, writ, debt, file #3939

GRAGG Samuel, yeoman, of Peterborough Slip, vs YOUNG John, physician, of Peterborough, rec date 1785, judgment, debt, file #5836

GRAGG Samuel, innholder, of Peterborough Slip, vs HORSEY James, gentleman, of New Ipswich, rec date 1785, writ, debt, file #6369

GRAGG Samuel Jr, yeoman, of Peterborough, vs YOUNG John, physician, of Peterborough, doc date 1772, judgment, debt, file #686

GRAGG William, husbandman, of Colerain, vs ROBERTSON Silas, gentleman, of Bennington NY, rec date 1785, various, debt, file #6251

GRAGZ Samuel, gentleman, of Peterborough, vs GRAY Abigail, widow, of Boston MA, doc date 1799, land dispute, debt, file #195

GRAGZ Samuel, gentleman, of Peterborough, vs GRINDLEY Jeremiah, esquire, of Boston MA, doc date 1797, land dispute, land, file #195

GRAGZ Samuel, gentleman, of Peterborough, vs BRIDGE Rebecca, widow, of Boston MA, doc date 1797, land dispute, debt, file #195

GRAGZ Samuel, gentleman, of Peterborough, vs SCOTT Moses & Sarah, widow, of Nova Scotia, doc date 1797, land dispute, debt, file #195

GRAHAM Samuel, yeoman, of Hancock, vs HOPKINS Ebenezer, husbandman, of Amherst, rec date 1783, writ, debt, file #3466

GRAHAM William, husbandman, of Raby, vs GIBSON Esimon, gentleman, of Pepperell MA, doc date 1798, judgment, debt, file #563

GRANT Isaac, blacksmith, of Weare, vs MITCHEL Hugh, yeoman, of Francestown, doc date 1799, writ, debt, file #418

GRANTHAM John, gentleman, of Hillsborough, vs GRIMES James, gentleman, of Deering, rec date 1782, writ, debt, file #2680

GRATHAM John, yeoman, of Society Land, vs KIDDER Reuben, esquire, of New Ipswich, doc date 1772, writ, debt, file #883

GRAVES Ebenezer, innholder, of Boston MA, vs ROCHE John Jr, yeoman, of Campbells Gore, rec date 1785, writ, debt, file #6238

GRAY John, yeoman, of Peterborough, vs BROWNE Aaron, trader, of Groton MA, doc date 1783, writ, debt, file #1262

GRAY John, yeoman, of Rindge, vs ABBOTT Joseph, yeoman, of Wilton, doc date 1776, rec date 1779, deed, land transfer, file #2145

GRAY Joseph, physician, of Nottingham-West, vs REED Abijah, husbandman, of Nottingham-West, rec date 1784, writ, debt, file #4199

GRAY Matthew, of Peterborough, vs TREADWELL Samuel, yeoman, of Peterborough, rec date 1787, deed, land transfer, file #2487

GRAY Matthew, husbandman, of Peterborough, vs STEEL David Jr, husbandman, of Peterborough, rec date 1788, writ, debt, file #6633

GRAY Robert, gentleman, of Peterborough, vs YOUNG John, physician, of Peterborough, rec date 1785, judgment, debt, file #5506

GRAY Robert, innholder, of Peterborough, vs STEEL Jonathan, yeoman, of Peterborough, doc date 1784, writ, debt, file #1628

GRAY Robert, yeoman, of Peterborough, rec date 1779, deposition, land dispute, file #2236B

GRAY Robert, gentleman, of Peterborough, vs STEEL David, gentleman, of Peterborough, rec date 1782, writ, debt, file #2825

GRAY Robert, innkeeper, of Peterborough, vs TAGGART James, of Peterborough, rec date 1785, writ, debt, file #5378

GRAY Robert, gentleman, of Peterborough, vs YOUNG John, physician, of Peterborough, rec date 1785, writ, debt, file #5935

GRAY Robert, gentleman, of Peterborough, vs ALLD John, laborer, of Peterborough, rec date 1786, various, debt, file #6297

GREELE Ezekiel, gentleman, of Nottingham-West, vs KILLICUTT Reuben, yeoman, of Dunstable, doc date 1779, writ, debt, file #2100

GREELE Ezekiel, gentleman, of Nottingham-West, vs MOOR Daniel, husbandman, of Bedford, rec date 1788, writ, debt, file #6609

GREELE Jonathan, husbandman, of Wilton, vs BALLARD Nathan, gentleman, of Wilton, rec date 1785, writ, debt, file #5538

GREELE Joseph, gentleman, of Nottingham-West, vs BLODGETT Jonathan, husbandman, of Rumney, rec date 1788, writ, debt, file #6904

GREELE Zacheus, yeoman, of Londonderry, vs ORDWAY Nehemiah, of Londonderry, doc date 1784, rec date 1786, deed, land transfer, file #5015

GREELEY Ezekiel, gentleman, of Londonderry, vs KELLEY Joseph, gentleman, of Nottingham, doc date 1772, writ, debt, file #915

GREELEY Ezekiel, gentleman, of Londonderry, vs KELLEY Joseph, gentleman, of Nottingham-West, doc date 1772, writ, assault, file #932

GREELEY Ezekiel, gentleman, of Londonderry, vs KELLEY Joseph, gentleman, of Nottingham, doc date 1773, execution, debt, file #1479

GREELEY Ezekiel, gentleman, of Londonderry, vs KELLEY Joseph, gentleman, of Nottingham-West, doc date 1773, execution, debt, file #1490

GREELEY Ezekiel, gentleman, of Londonderry, vs KELLEY Joseph, gentleman, of Nottingham, doc date 1773, execution, debt, file #1461

GREELEY Ezekiel, gentleman, of Londonderry, vs KELLEY Joseph, gentleman, of Nottingham, doc date 1773, execution, debt, file #1462

GREELEY Jonathan, esquire, of Kingston, vs SWEATT Benjamin, shipwright, of Boscawen, doc date 1775, judgment, debt, file #2042

GREELEY Jonathan, husbandman, of Wilton, vs GRIMES John, husbandman, of Amherst, rec date 1783, writ, debt, file #3327

GREELEY Joseph, husbandman, of Nottingham-West, vs SMITH Edward, husbandman, of Peterborough, rec date 1788, writ, debt, file #2546

GREELEY Nathaniel, husbandman, of Wilton, vs DODGE William, husbandman, of Mason, doc date 1784, civil litigation, debt, file #1644

GREELEY Nathaniel, husbandman, of Wilton, vs DODGE William, husbandman, of Mason, rec date 1783, judgment, debt, file #4500

GREEN Amos, yeoman, of Amherst, vs FISH Jonathan, blacksmith, of Francestown, rec date 1786, writ, debt, file #6886

GREEN Benjamin, physician, of Worcester MA, vs ROGERS John, physician, of Plymouth, rec date 1785, judgment, debt, file #5182

GREEN Benjamin, physician, of Worcester MA, vs ROGERS John, physician, of Plymouth, rec date 1785, judgment, debt, file #5981

GREEN David, yeoman, of Hollis, vs HALE William, physician, of Hollis, doc date 1798, execution, debt, file #135

GREEN David, yeoman, of Groton MA, vs HOBART Jeremiah, yeoman, of Raby, rec date 1785, execution, debt, file #5491

GREEN David, yeoman, of Amherst, vs HUTCHINS James, yeoman, of Amherst, doc date 1773, writ, debt, file #1359

GREEN David, husbandman, of Groton MA, vs FISK Thomas, husbandman, of Jaffrey, rec date 1786, judgment, debt, file #2309

GREEN David, yeoman, of Hillsborough, vs GOVE Jonathan, physician, of New Boston, rec date 1782, writ, debt, file #2784

GREEN David, yeoman, of Hillsborough, vs PEADBODY William, gentleman, of Amherst, rec date 1782, writ, debt, file #2797

GREEN David, yeoman, of Hillsborough, vs BISHOP George, innkeeper, of Hillsborough, rec date 1783, writ, debt, file #3072

GREEN David, yeoman, of Hillsborough, vs WYLEY John, yeoman, of Amherst, rec date 1783, writ, debt, file #3047

GREEN David, yeoman, of Hillsborough, vs DODGE Samuel, yeoman, of Amherst, rec date 1783, writ, debt, file #3056

GREEN David, yeoman, of Hillsborough, vs DUNBAR Asa, gentleman, of Harvard MA, rec date 1783, execution, debt, file #2998

GREEN David, yeoman, of Hillsborough, vs ROCH John, yeoman, of Campbells Gore, rec date 1782, debt, debt, file #3145

GREEN David, yeoman, of Hillsborough, vs McCLUER Robert, yeoman, of Acworth, rec date 1783, summons, ejectment, file #3321

GREEN David, husbandman, of Hillsborough, vs SHANNON Richard Cutts, esquire, of Hollis, rec date 1784, judgment, debt, file #4391

GREEN David, husbandman, of Hillsborough, vs MEANS Robert, trader, of Amherst, rec date 1784, judgment, debt, file #4355

GREEN David, yeoman, of Hillsborough, vs COSTON Ebenezer, yeoman, of Society Land, rec date 1784, appeal, debt, file #4148

GREEN David, yeoman, of Hillsborough, vs TAGGART Archibald, gentleman, of Hillsborough, rec date 1784, judgment, debt, file #4357

GREEN David, yeoman, of Groton MA, vs FRENCH Theodore, yeoman, of Dunstable, rec date 1784, judgment, debt, file #4663

GREEN David, yeoman, of Groton MA, vs SANDERSON Benjamin, husbandman, of Hollis, rec date 1785, judgment, debt, file #5088

GREEN David, husbandman, of Groton MA, vs KIDDER Reuben, esquire, of New Ipswich, rec date 1785, judgment, debt, file #5333

GREEN David, husbandman, of Groton MA, vs WRIGHT Uriah, gentleman, of Hollis, rec date 1785, judgment, debt, file #5334

GREEN David, yeoman, of Groton MA, vs FRENCH Theodore, husbandman, of Dunstable, rec date 1785, judgment, debt, file #5398

GREEN David, yeoman, of Groton, vs SPAULDING William, yeoman, of Raby, rec date 1785, judgment, debt, file #5329

GREEN David, husbandman, of Groton MA, vs QUEEN John, physician, of Bedford, rec date 1785, execution, debt, file #5934

GREEN David, of Groton MA, vs WRIGHT Uriah, gentleman, of Hollis, rec date 1786, various, debt, file #6067

GREEN David, husbandman, of Groton MA, vs KELLEY Moses, esquire/sheriff, of Goffstown, rec date 1785, writ, debt, file #6263

GREEN David, husbandman, of Groton MA, vs WRIGHT Uriah, gentleman, of Hollis, rec date 1785, judgment, debt, file #6215

GREEN Elijah, cordwainer, of Campbells Gore, vs SWEET Jonathan Jr, husbandman, of Campbells Gore, rec date 1786, writ, debt, file #6320

GREEN Jabez, gentleman, of Roby, vs CAMPBELL Benjamin, gentleman, of Roby, doc date 1798, execution, debt, file #139

GREEN John, physician, of Worcester MA, vs MARSTEN John, physician, of Newmarket, rec date 1783, writ, debt, file #4553

GREEN Nathaniel, esquire, of Boscawen, vs COOPER Stephen, yeoman, of Boscawen, doc date 1799, execution, debt, file #174

GREEN Nathaniel, esquire, of Boscawen, vs CORSER Samuel, gentleman, of Boscawen, doc date 1798, execution, debt, file #127

GREEN Nathaniel, gentleman, of Concord, vs PEMERY Medad, physician, of MA, doc date 1784, writ, debt, file #1624

GREEN Nathaniel, gentleman, of Concord, vs HALL John, physician, of Warner, rec date 1785, judgment, debt, file #5200

GREEN Peter, esquire, of Concord, vs EMERSON James, husbandman, of Hopkinton, doc date 1784, execution, debt, file #1698

GREEN Peter, esquire, of Concord, vs REED Zadock, yeoman, of New Boston, doc date 1784, execution, debt, file #1988

GREEN Peter, esquire, of Concord, vs REED Zadock, yeoman, of New Boston, rec date 1783, execution, debt, file #2992

GREEN Peter, esquire, of Concord, vs WILSON John, husbandman, of New Boston, rec date 1783, civil litigious, debt, file #2928

GREEN Peter, esquire, of Concord, vs FRENCH Daniel, blacksmith, of Hopkinton, rec date 1783, civil litigious, debt, file #2906

GREEN Peter, esquire, of Concord, vs NICHOLS John, blacksmith, of Hopkinton, rec date 1783, civil litigious, debt, file #2906

GREEN Peter, of Concord, vs GREENOUGH Richard, husbandman, of Salisbury, rec date 1783, writ, debt, file #3379

GREEN Peter, esquire, of Concord, vs WILSON John, husbandman, of New Boston, rec date 1783, writ, debt, file #3382

GREEN Peter, esquire, of Concord, vs TAYLOR Nathan, yeoman, of Antrim, rec date 1782, execution, debt, file #3473

GREEN Peter, esquire, of Concord, vs GREENOUGH Richard, husbandman, of Salisbury, rec date 1783, execution, debt, file #3697

GREEN Peter, esquire, of Concord, vs FRENCH Daniel, blacksmith, of Hopkinton, rec date 1783, execution, debt, file #3827

GREEN Peter, esquire, of Concord, vs NICKOLS John, blacksmith, of Hopkinton, rec date 1783, writ, debt, file #3807

GREEN Peter, esquire, of Concord, vs FRENCH Daniel, blacksmith, of Hopkinton, rec date 1783, writ, debt, file #3807

GREEN Peter, esquire, of Concord, vs EMERSON James, husbandman, of Hopkinton, rec date 1783, judgment, debt, file #4079

GREEN Peter, esquire, of Concord, vs NICHOLS John, blacksmith, of Hopkinton, rec date 1783, execution, debt, file #3827

GREEN Peter, esquire, of Concord, vs ANDREWS Israel, esquire, of Hillsborough, rec date 1783, writ, debt, file #4561

GREEN Peter, esquire, of Concord, vs FLANDERS Philip, husbandman, of Warner (Gore), rec date 1785, judgment, debt, file #5044

GREEN Peter, esquire, of Concord, vs TYLOR Nathan, yeoman, of Antrim, rec date 1783, execution, debt, file #4918

GREEN Peter, esquire, of Concord, vs TUXBURY Jacob, husbandman, of Weare, rec date 1783, writ, debt, file #4854

GREEN Peter, esquire, of Concord, vs GARVIN Samuel, husbandman, of Dunbarton, rec date 1785, judgment, debt, file #5827

GREEN Peter, esquire, of Concord, vs MAXWELL Thomas, gentleman, of Amherst, rec date 1785, writ, debt, file #6348

GREEN Peter, esquire, of Concord, vs DICKEY James, gentleman, of Raby, rec date 1787, various, debt, file #6210

GREEN Peter, esquire, of Concord, vs NICHOLS Moses, esquire, of Amherst, rec date 1786, various, debt, file #6316

GREEN Peter, esquire, of Concord, vs READ Zadock, yeoman, of New Boston, rec date 1786, judgment, debt, file #4929

GREEN William, gentleman, of Pepperell MA, vs RAHAM William, husbandman, of Raby, rec date 1786, writ, debt, file #2412

GREEN William, husbandman, of Pepperell MA, vs MOSHER James, husbandman, of Hollis, rec date 1784, judgment, debt, file #4992

GREEN William & Hannah, witness, of Hollis, vs ELIOTT Jeremiah, husbandman, of Pepperell MA, doc date 1772, rec date 1772, deed, land transfer, file #6844

GREENFIELD Nathaniel, husbandman, of Merrimack, vs LOWELL John & Rebecca, of Boston MA, rec date 1783, writ, debt, file #3108, estate of James TYNG

GREENWOOD Nathaniel, yeoman, of Dublin, vs BLANCHARD Jothan, gentleman, of Peterborough, rec date 1784, judgment, debt, file #4276

GREENWOOD Nathaniel, yeoman, of Dublin, vs MORRISON Thomas, yeoman, of Peterborough, rec date 1784, judgment, debt, file #4276

GREGG Benjamin, yeoman, of Peterborough, vs GREGG John, of Peterborough, doc date 1788, rec date 1788, deed, land transfer, file #6821

GREGG David, wheelwright, of Londonderry, vs BLASSDELL Samuel, esquire, of Goffstown, doc date 1774, writ, debt, file #1125, fragile

GREGG David, yeoman, of Francestown, vs GLOVER William, yeoman, of Nottingham-West, doc date 1784, writ, debt, file #1625

GREGG David, yeoman, of Francestown, vs TAYLOR Timothy, innkeeper, of Merrimack, rec date 1783, writ, debt, file #3015

GREGG David, yeoman, of Francestown, vs BALDWIN Nahum, esquire, of Amherst, rec date 1782, writ, debt, file #2818, estate of Zacheus CUTLER

GREGG James (estate), weaver, yeoman, rec date 1788, various, debt, file #6976

GREGG James Jr, yeoman, of New Boston, vs BALDWIN Nathan, esquire, of Amherst, rec date 1782, writ, debt, file #2665

GREGG John, gentleman, of Peterborough, vs SWAN John Jr, gentleman, of Peterborough, doc date 1772, civil litigation, debt, file #647

GREGG John, husbandman, of Peterborough, vs PARKER Alexander, husbandman, of Society Land, rec date 1783, judgment, debt, file #4465

GREGG John Jr, yeoman, of Colrain MA, vs COCHRAN George, husbandman, of Goffstown, rec date 1783, execution, debt, file #3224

GREGG Lesley, husbandman, of New Boston, vs CRAWFORD James, husbandman, of New Boston, doc date 1799, judgment, debt, file #250

GREGG Nancy, widow, of Merrimack, vs COCHRAN Elijah, administrator of estate, of Londonderry, rec date 1785, writ, debt, file #6224

GREGG Nancy, widow, of Merrimack, vs GREGG James (estate), deceased, of Londonderry, rec date 1785, writ, debt, file #6224

GREGG Samuel, trader, of Peterborough, vs PRENTICE John, gentleman, of Londonderry, doc date 1772, writ, debt, file #1052

GREGG Samuel, housewright, of New Boston, vs GREGG Alexander, yeoman, of New Boston, rec date 1788, writ, debt, file #2385

GREGG Samuel, of Peterborough Slip, vs MOSHER James, husbandman, of Hollis, rec date 1783, execution, debt, file #3852

GREGG Samuel, of Peterborough Slip, vs LIDY Joseph, husbandman, of Hollis, rec date 1783, execution, debt, file #3852

GREGG Samuel, gentleman, of Peterborough, vs INHABITANTS of Peterborough, rec date 1785, writ, debt, file #5420

GREGG Samuel, esquire, of Peterborough, vs RAMSEY William, yeoman, of Londonderry, rec date 1786, deed, land transfer, file #5549

GREGG Samuel, trader, of Peterborough Slip, vs GILCREST William, trader, of Shrewsbury MA, rec date 1788, writ, debt, file #6630

GREGG Samuel, deceased, of Londonderry, rec date 1785, debt, file #6998

GRELE Ezekiel, gentleman, of Nottingham-West, doc date 1781, capias, speaking in public, file #768, fine for speaking in public

GRELE Ezekiel, gentleman, of Nottingham-West, vs ANDREWS Asa, yeoman, of Londonderry, rec date 1784, judgment, debt, file #4864

GRELL Ezekiel, gentleman, of Nottingham-West, vs ROBY Silas, yeoman, of Merrimack, rec date 1788, writ, debt, file #6719

GRIDLEY Samuel, gentleman, of Hollis, vs POWERS Jonathan, gentleman, of Hillsborough, doc date 1774, recognizance, debt, file #1158

GRIDLEY Samuel, gentleman, of Boston MA, vs BAGLEY Timothy, laborer, of Hollis, rec date 1786, writ, debt, file #2415

GRIDLEY Samuel, gentleman, of Boston MA, vs BROWN Joseph, husbandman, of Hollis, rec date 1786, judgment, debt, file #2451

GRIDLEY Samuel, blacksmith, of Hollis, vs LAWRENCE Zachariah, yeoman, of Hollis, rec date 1774, writ, debt, file #2203

GRIDLEY Samuel, gentleman, of Boston MA, vs BOYNTON Joshua, clockmaker, of Hollis, rec date 1786, judgment, debt, file #2452

GRIDLEY Samuel, gentleman, of Boston MA, vs McDANIELS James, husbandman, of Raby, rec date 1786, writ, debt, file #2416

GRIDLEY Samuel, gentleman, of Boston MA, vs CUMINGS Philip, joiner, of Peterborough, rec date 1786, writ, debt, file #2418

GRIDLEY Samuel, gentleman, of Boston MA, vs GILSON Ebenezer, husbandman, of Hollis, rec date 1786, judgment, debt, file #2453

GRIDLEY Samuel, gentleman, of Boston MA, vs PRATT Thomas, feltmaker, of Hollis, rec date 1786, judgment, debt, file #2450

GRIFFIN Daniel, husbandman, of Hillsborough, vs JONES Nehemiah, husbandman, of Hillsborough, doc date 1799, debt, file #327

GRIFFIN J, yeoman, of Derryfield, vs SANDERS Joseph, gentleman, of Derryfield, doc date 1784, deed, land transfer, file #2008

GRIFFIN Mary, rec date 1781, deposition, debt, file #2241, for J DWINELL & A ANDREWS

GRIFFITH Nathaniel S, watchmaker, of Portsmouth, vs EUSTIS Jacob, merchant, of Boston MA, doc date 1799, judgment, debt, file #219

GRIMES Francis, yeoman, of Deering, vs WILEY John, husbandman, of Hillsborough, doc date 1797, various, debt, file #545

GRIMES Francis, yeoman, of Deering, vs WILSON James, yeoman, of New Boston, doc date 1798, judgment, debt, file #563

GRIMES Francis, yeoman, of Deering, vs BALDWIN Nahum, esquire, of Amherst, rec date 1782, appeal, debt, file #3989

GRIMES Francis, gentleman, of Deering, vs ANDREWS Ammi, gentleman, of Hillsborough, rec date 1785, judgment, debt, file #6446

GRIMES Francis Sr, yeoman, of Deering, vs McKEEN James, yeoman, of Amherst, rec date 1783, civil litigious, debt, file #2955

GRIMES George, of Derryfield, vs SANDERS Joseph, housewright, of Derryfield, doc date 1784, deed, land transfer, file #2001

GRIMES James, husbandman, of Deering, vs NELSON Moses, husbandman, of Hillsborough, doc date 1798, execution, debt, file #59

GRIMES James, gentleman, of Deering, vs CALL John, innkeeper, of New Boston, doc date 1782, execution, file #1020

GRIMES James, yeoman, of Deering, vs FLANDERS Thomason, gentleman, of Deering, doc date 1782, execution, file #1011

GRIMES James, gentleman, of Deering, vs WILSON David, gentleman, of Deering, rec date 1783, writ, debt, file #2756

GRIMES James, gentleman, of Deering, vs DOW Evan, yeoman, of Deering, rec date 1783, writ, debt, file #3025

GRIMES James, gentleman, of Deering, vs ALCOCK Robert, gentleman, of Deering, rec date 1783, writ, debt, file #3059

GRIMES James, gentleman, of Deering, vs GRAHAM John, gentleman, of Hillsborough, rec date 1783, civil litigious, debt, file #2964, John Graham (deceased)

GRIMES James, gentleman, of Deering, vs WHITIKER James, yeoman, of Deering, rec date 1783, writ, debt, file #3025

GRIMES James, gentleman, of Deering, vs GOVE Abraham, yeoman, of Deering, rec date 1783, writ, debt, file #3025

GRIMES James, gentleman, of Deering, vs STEVENS Samuel, physician, of Amherst, rec date 1783, writ, debt, file #3195

GRIMES James, gentleman, of Deering, vs WILKINS Jonathan, yeoman, of Amherst, rec date 1783, execution, debt, file #3274

GRIMES James, gentleman, of Deering, vs BUTTERFIELD John, gentleman, of Goffstown, rec date 1783, writ, debt, file #3338

GRIMES James, gentleman, of Deering, vs HOYT Moses, yeoman, of Society Land, rec date 1783, execution, debt, file #3231

GRIMES James, gentleman, of Deering, vs HOYT Moses, yeoman, of Society Land, rec date 1782, execution, debt, file #3524

GRIMES James, gentleman, of Deering, vs TAYLOR John, yeoman, of Antrim, rec date 1783, judgment, debt, file #3723

GRIMES James, gentleman, of Deering, vs HOYT Moses, yeoman, of Society Land, rec date 1783, execution, debt, file #3660

GRIMES James, gentleman, of Deering, vs HOGG John, yeoman, of Deering, rec date 1784, judgment, debt, file #4628

GRIMES James, gentleman, of Deering, vs ROBINSON William, yeoman, of Deering, rec date 1785, judgment, debt, file #5160

GRIMES James, gentleman, of Deering, vs RICHARDSON Zachariah, yeoman, of Francestown, rec date 1785, judgment, debt, file #5570

GRIMES James, gentleman, of Deering, vs LITTLE Bond, yeoman, of Deering, rec date 1785, judgment, debt, file #6428

GRIMES Jonathan, yeoman, of Amherst, vs TAYLOR James, husbandman, of Merrimack, doc date 1784, execution, debt, file #1523

GRIMES Jonathan, yeoman, of Amherst, vs TAYLOR James, husbandman, of Merrimack, doc date 1784, execution, debt, file #1685

GRIMES Jonathan, yeoman, of Amherst, vs GIBSON James, husbandman, of Merrimack, doc date 1784, execution, debt, file #1523

GRIMES Jonathan, yeoman, of Amherst, vs GIBSON James, husbandman, of Merrimack, doc date 1779, execution, debt, file #1685

GRIMES Jonathan, yeoman, of Amherst, vs TAYLOR James, husbandman, of Merrimack, rec date 1783, execution, debt, file #4917

GRIMES Jonathan, yeoman, of Amherst, vs GIBSON James, husbandman, of Merrimack, rec date 1783, execution, debt, file #4917

GRIMES Moses, gentleman, of Londonderry, vs MILLS Daniel, yeoman, of Windham, doc date 1772, writ, debt, file #1389

GRIMES Thaddeus, yeoman, of Amherst, vs RUSSELL James, gentleman, of Litchfield, doc date 1784, execution, debt, file #1920

GRIMES Thaddeus, yeoman, of Amherst, vs CLARK Joshua, yeoman, of Amherst, rec date 1783, writ, debt, file #3092

GRIMES Thaddeus, yeoman, of Amherst, vs GILMAN James, yeoman, of Amherst, rec date 1783, writ, debt, file #3347

GRIMES Thaddeus, yeoman, of Amherst, vs RUSSELL James, gentleman, of Litchfield, rec date 1783, execution, debt, file #4914

GRIMES Thaddeus, yeoman, of Hillsborough, vs RUSSELL James, gentleman, of Litchfield, rec date 1782, execution, debt, file #4898

GRIMES Thaddeus & John, yeoman, of Amherst, vs HOBART Joel, yeoman, of Pepperell MA, rec date 1783, writ, debt, file #3349

GROSVENOR Samuel, esquire, of Pomfret CT, vs HALE William, physician, of Hollis, doc date 1799, debt, file #531

GROUT Jehosaphat, yeoman, of Charlestown, vs BLANCHARD Joseph, esquire, of Amherst, rec date 1783, judgment, debt, file #2855

GUILD Dana, gentleman, of Keene, vs SMITH John, yeoman, of Goffstown, rec date 1787, various, debt, file #2537

HAARRINGTON Robert, esquire, of Lexington MA, vs SWAN Robert, gentleman, of Peterborough, rec date 1788, writ, debt, file #6932

HACKET Ebenezer, husbandman, of Dunbarton, vs SAUNDERS James, innkeeper, of Salem, doc date 1798, execution, debt, file #107

HACKET Ebenezer, husbandman, of Dunbarton, vs CHURCH John, yeoman, of Dunbarton, rec date 1783, writ, debt, file #3100

HACKLEY James, husbandman, of Sharon, vs BOYNTON Abel, esquire, of Westford MA, doc date 1795, petition, release of debit, file #21

HADLEY Abijah, husbandman, of Antrim, vs SPAULDING Edward, husbandman, of Hancock, rec date 1792, judgment, debt, file #2578

HADLEY Eliphalet, yeoman, of Nottingham-West, vs BOYD Thomas, husbandman, of Londonderry, rec date 1785, writ, debt, file #6007

HADLEY Eliphalet, yeoman, of Nottingham-West, vs BOID Thomas, husbandman, of Londonderry, rec date 1785, judgment, debt, file #5995

HADLEY Enos, husbandman, of Nottingham-West, vs HADLEY Seth, husbandman, of Nottingham-West, doc date 1784, execution, debt, file #1862

HADLEY George, gentleman, of Weare, vs SAWYER Enoch, husbandman, of Goffstown, doc date 1784, execution, debt, file #1869

HADLEY Nehemiah, yeoman, of Hollis, vs PETTINGILL Abbit, gentleman, of Salem, rec date 1782, judgment, debt, file #2625

HADLEY Nehemiah, yeoman, of Hollis, vs PETTINGILL Abbit, gentleman, of Salem, rec date 1783, various, debt, file #3612

HADLEY Nehemiah, deceased, of Newbury VT, rec date 1788, writ, debt, file #6621

HADLEY Plumer, husbandman, of Goffstown, vs PERKINS Philemon, tailor, of New Boston, rec date 1783, judgment, debt, file #4073

HADLEY Samuel, husbandman, of Newbury NY, vs COPPS Joshua, husbandman, of Hampstead, doc date 1772, judgment, debt, file #688

HADLEY Seth, gentleman, of Hancock, vs MITCHEL Germet, yeoman, of Francestown, doc date 1799, writ, debt, file #420

HAGGET John, blacksmith, of Lyndeborough, vs HARWOOD Andrew, husbandman, of Lyndeborough, doc date 1799, writ, debt, file #573

HAINES Joshua, of Temple, vs BENNETT Abraham, of Ashby MA, doc date 1785, petition, release of debit, file #12

HAKLEY James, laborer, of Peterborough, vs SMITH William, gentleman, of Peterborough, rec date 1784, writ, debt, file #4608

HAKLEY James, laborer, of Peterborough, vs WALLACE Matthew, gentleman, of Peterborough, rec date 1784, writ, debt, file #4608

HALE Abigail, widow, of Rindge, vs RUSSELL Joel Jr, yeoman, of Hancock, rec date 1783, writ, debt, file #3455

HALE David, husbandman, of Goffstown, vs ROWELL Samuel, husbandman, of Weare, doc date 1784, execution, debt, file #1958

HALE David, husbandman, of Goffstown, vs ROWELL Samuel, husbandman, of Weare, rec date 1783, writ, debt, file #3215

HALE Enoch, vs MARCH Clement, rec date 1773, letter, file #7009

HALE John, esquire, of Hollis, vs KENNEY Stephen, husbandman, of Nottingham-West, doc date 1774, writ, debt, file #1100

HALE John, taylor, of Boscawen, vs GERRISH Moses, gentleman, of Canterbury, doc date 1773, writ, debt, file #1337

HALE John, esquire, of Hollis, vs DODGE William, husbandman, of Mason, doc date 1784, civil litigation, debt, file #1827

HALE John, gentleman, of Hollis, vs COBURN James, cordwainer, of Hollis, doc date 1777, deed, land transfer, file #2015

HALE John, esquire, of Hollis, vs LOVEJOY Francis, feltmaker, of Amherst, rec date 1783, execution, debt, file #2894

HALE John, esquire, of Hollis, vs LOVEJOY Francis, feltmaker, of Amherst, rec date 1782, judgment, debt, file #3129

HALE John, husbandman, of Cockermouth, vs ATKINSON Samuel, gentleman, of Boscawen, rec date 1782, debt, debt, file #3148

HALE John, esquire, of Hollis, vs DODGE William, husbandman, of Mason, rec date 1783, judgment, debt, file #4090

HALE John, husbandman, of Nottingham-West, vs BRADLEY Jonathan, husbandman, of Nottingham-West, rec date 1783, judgment, debt, file #4714

HALE John, of Boscawen, vs GREENFIELD Thomas, yeoman, of Boscawen, rec date 1785, writ, land dispute, file #4804

HALE John, physician, of Hollis, vs BAYLEY Daniel, housewright, of Hollis, rec date 1785, judgment, debt, file #5215

HALE John, tailor, of Boscawen, vs GREENFIELD Thomas, yeoman, of Boscawen, rec date 1785, various, debt, file #5883

HALE John, tailor, of Boscawen, vs HALE Richard, of Newbury MA, rec date 1785, deed, land transfer, file #5883, deed to John from father

HALE Joseph, husbandman, of Dunstable, vs CHASE Stephen Jr, yeoman, of Nottingham, doc date 1782, execution, file #1012

HALE Paul, gentleman, of Peterborough, vs COCKRAN John, yeoman, of Amherst, doc date 1784, execution, debt, file #1664

HALE Paul, blacksmith, of Amherst, vs HOBSON Jeremiah, gentleman, of Amherst, rec date 1795, jury decision, assault, file #4066

HALE Paul, gentleman, of Peterborough, vs COCHRAN John, yeoman, of Amherst, rec date 1786, judgment, debt, file #6508

HALE Richard, yeoman, of Merrimack, vs THORNTON James, yeoman, of Merrimack, doc date 1796, various, military dispute, file #509

HALE Samuel, physician, of Pepperell MA, vs SAWYER Edmund, apothecary, of Newbury MA, rec date 1782, appeal, debt, file #3982

HALE Thomas, husbandman, of Merrimack, vs WINN Nathan, husbandman, of Nottingham, doc date 1798, judgment, debt, file #564

HALES David Jr, husbandman, of Goffstown, vs SHIPLE Oliver, cordwainer, of New Boston, rec date 1786, writ, debt, file #6100

HALL Benjamin, merchant, of Medford MA, vs GOVE Jonathan, physician, of Goffstown, doc date 1798, judgment, debt, file #564

HALL Benjamin, merchant, of Medford MA, vs McLAUGHLIN John, gentleman, of New Boston, doc date 1798, judgment, debt, file #564

HALL Benjamin, merchant, of Medford MA, vs TUTTLE Charles, physician, of New Boston, doc date 1798, judgment, debt, file #564

HALL Benjamin, esquire, of Medford MA, vs ABBOTT Samuel, yeoman, of Hollis, doc date 1784, execution, debt, file #1946

HALL Benjamin, esquire, of Medford MA, vs ABBOT Samuel, yeoman, of Hollis, rec date 1783, writ, debt, file #3441

HALL Benjamin, esquire, of Medford MA, vs BALDWIN Jesse, husbandman, of Amherst, rec date 1783, writ, debt, file #3440

HALL Benjamin, esquire, of Medford MA, vs LAWRENCE Zachariah, yeoman, of Hollis, rec date 1783, writ, debt, file #3441

HALL Benjamin, esquire, of Medford MA, vs McGAA Robert, shopkeeper, of Hollis, rec date 1783, judgment, debt, file #3709

HALL Benjamin, distiller, of Medford MA, vs CHAMBERS William, husbandman, of Mason, rec date 1786, judgment, debt, file #6475

HALL Benjamin, distiller, of Medford MA, vs LOVEWELL Jonathan, esquire, of Dunstable, rec date 1785, judgment, debt, file #6489

HALL Benjamin, distiller, of Medford MA, vs LOVEWELL Jonathan, esquire, of Dunstable, rec date 1788, judgment, debt, file #7015

HALL Daniel, husbandman, of Deerfield, vs GILE Ebenezer, husbandman, of Henniker, doc date 1772, judgment, debt, file #689

HALL David, yeoman, of Mason, vs CHAMBERS William, trader, of Mason, rec date 1783, execution, debt, file #3842

HALL John, gentleman, of Deerfield, vs HALL Thomas, yeoman, of Goffstown, doc date 1772, writ, debt, file #911

HALL John, physician, of Warner, vs ORDWAY Bradshaw, husbandman, of Warner, doc date 1784, deed, land transfer, file #2005

HALL John, gentleman, of Deerfield, vs GILMAN Daniel, gentleman, of Kingston, doc date 1776, rec date 1779, deed, land transfer, file #2124

HALL John, gentleman, of Deerfield, vs SHIRLEY Samuel, husbandman, of Goffstown, rec date 1782, writ, debt, file #2663

HALL John, yeoman, of Derryfield, vs FARMER Hannah, wife, of Derryfield, rec date 1795, judgment, assault, file #4056

HALL Joseph, merchant, of Wilton, vs ABBOTT George, tanner, of Wilton, doc date 1798, execution, debt, file #78

HALL Nathan, yeoman, of Mason, vs HALL David, yeoman, doc date 1799, debt, file #431

HALL Stephen, husbandman, of Antrim, vs HARMAN Martin, gentleman, of Whitetowns N y, doc date 1799, judgment, debt, file #248

HALL William, clerk, of Salem, vs HOW Mark, husbandman, of Merrimack, rec date 1788, writ, debt, file #6942

HALL Willis, merchant, of Medford MA, vs McKEEN Samuel, gentleman, of Windham, doc date 1784, execution, debt, file #1672

HALL Willis, merchant, of Medford MA, vs McKEEN Samuel, gentleman, of Windham, rec date 1783, writ, debt, file #3402

HALL Willis, saddler, of Westford MA, vs LITTLE William, physician, of Hillsborough, rec date 1785, judgment, debt, file #5078

HAMBLET Hezekiah, yeoman, of Litchfield, vs HUTCHINSON Samuel, husbandman, of Lyndeborough, rec date 1782, execution, debt, file #4891

HAMILTON James, laborer, of Londonderry, vs WALLACE Robert, husbandman, of Londonderry, doc date 1773, writ, debt, file #1436

HAMMILL Joseph, yeoman, of Peterborough, vs WHITE Patrick, yeoman, of Peterborough, rec date 1783, writ, debt, file #3040

HAMMOND Ephraim, husbandman, of Lexington MA, vs AMES Simon, husbandman, of Mason, doc date 1784, execution, debt, file #1511

HAMMOND Ephraim, esquire, of Lexington MA, vs AMES Simeon, husbandman, of Mason, rec date 1783, judgment, debt, file #4299

HARDEN Ebenezer, physician, of Goffstown, vs BLOOD Robert, of Groton MA, rec date 1782, writ, debt, file #2808

HARDEN Ebenezer, esquire, of Concord, vs HILLS David, trader, of New Ipswich, rec date 1783, various, debt, file #3617

HARDEN Samuel, husbandman, of Hollis, vs WARNER Daniel, gentleman, of Amherst, rec date 1783, writ, debt, file #3216

HARDEY Nehemiah, yeoman, of Hollis, vs STEARNS John, yeoman, of Amherst, rec date 1786, judgment, debt, file #2460

HARDY Daniel, gentleman, of Lyndeborough, vs SPAULDING Henry, yeoman, of Amherst, doc date 1799, writ, debt, file #575

HARDY Daniel, cordwainer, of Nottingham, vs PERREY Ebenezer, cordwainer, of Nottingham, doc date 177819, rec date 1779, deed, land transfer, file #2121

HARDY Daniel, gentleman, of Nottingham-West, vs ALEXANDER John, yeoman, of Londonderry, doc date 1784, execution, debt, file #1936

HARDY Daniel, gentleman, of Nottingham-West, vs McKEEN Samuel, gentleman, of Amherst, doc date 1779, writ, debt, file #2102

HARDY Daniel, gentleman, of Nottingham-West, vs ALEXANDER John, yeoman, of Londonderry, rec date 1783, civil litigious, debt, file #2923

HARDY Daniel, vs POLLARD Tim, husbandman, of Nottingham-West, rec date 1786, indictment, debt, file #6511

HARDY Daniel, gentleman, of Lyndeborough, vs KELLY Joseph, gentleman, of Nottingham-West, rec date 1787, various, debt, file #6696

HARDY Jesse, husbandman, of Hollis, vs HOW Joel, husbandman, of Peterborough, doc date 1798, judgment, debt, file #564

HARDY Jonathan, yeoman, of Nottingham-West, vs MERRILL William, yeoman, of Nottingham-West, rec date 1783, writ, debt, file #3314

HARDY Jonathan, yeoman, of Nottingham-West, vs GLYNN John, yeoman, of Hillsborough, rec date 1782, execution, debt, file #3491

HARDY Moody, yeoman, of Goffstown, vs POLLARD Samuel, husbandman, of Nottingham-West, rec date 1783, writ, debt, file #3206

HARDY Nehemiah, husbandman, of Hollis, vs HALE William, physician, of Hollis, doc date 1799, debt, file #217

HARDY Phinehas & Martha, husbandman, of Hollis, vs CHASE Henry & Mercy, husbandman, of Nottingham-West, rec date 1787, various, estate dispute, file #2532

HARKLIFF William, physician, of Bolton MA, vs BLOOD Thomas, of Peterborough, doc date 1799, judgment, debt, file #306

HARNDEN Ebenezer, physician, of Concord, vs RUSSELL Joel, husbandman, of Hancock, rec date 1783, writ, debt, file #3446

HARRIAM Stephen, gentleman, of Hopkinton, vs STORY David, husbandman, of Dunbarton, rec date 1785, writ, debt, file #6223

HARRIAM Stephen, gentleman, of Hopkinton, vs PAGE Jeremiah, esquire, of Dunbarton, rec date 1785, writ, debt, file #6223

HARRIS Abel, gentleman, of Concord, vs BURBANK Moses Jr, husbandman, of Boscawen, rec date 1786, judgment, debt, file #2296

HARRIS Abel, gentleman, of Concord, vs SANBORN Benjamin, husbandman, of Salisbury, rec date 1785, judgment, debt, file #5834

HARRIS Ellen C, vs HARRIS George W, doc date 1890, appellee's brief, supreme court, file #622

HARRIS Peter, yeoman, of Methuen MA, vs LINSDAY John, yeoman, of New Boston, rec date 1784, writ, debt, file #5158

HARRIS Robert, merchant, of Concord, vs WRIGHT Uriah, of Hollis, doc date 1798, judgment, debt, file #564

HARRIS Robert, merchant, of Boston MA, vs HOW Isaac, gentleman, of New Ipswich, rec date 1785, judgment, debt, file #5496

HARRIS Robert, merchant, of Boston MA, vs TAYLOR Isaiah, innholder, of Peterborough, rec date 1785, judgment, debt, file #5510

HARRIS Robert, merchant, of Littleton MA, vs YOUNG John, physician, of Peterborough, doc date 1774, execution, file #986

HARRIS Robert, merchant, of Boston MA, vs GRAGG Robert, innholder, of Peterborough, rec date 1785, judgment, debt, file #5510

HARRIS Robert, of Littleton MA, vs SPENCER William, yeoman, of Peterborough, doc date 1773, execution, debt, file #1451

HARRIS Robert, of Littleton MA, vs YOUNG John, physician, of Peterborough, doc date 1773, execution, debt, file #1451

HARRIS Robert, trader, of Concord, vs WRIGHT Uriah, gentleman, of Hollis, doc date 1784, civil litigation, debt, file #1633

HARRIS Robert, trader, of Concord, vs JEWETT Jacob Jr, trader, of Hollis, doc date 1784, civil litigation, debt, file #1633

HARRIS Robert, merchant, of Concord, vs BROWN Peter, husbandman, of Temple, rec date 1783, writ, debt, file #3450

HARRIS Robert, shopkeeper, of Concord, vs GRAGG Samuel, yeoman, of Peterborough Slip, rec date 1783, writ, debt, file #3934

HARRIS Robert, merchant, of Concord, vs HOUSTON William, yeoman, of Peterborough, rec date 1783, writ, debt, file #3634

HARRIS Robert, merchant, of Concord, vs YOUNG Duncan, yeoman, of Society Land, rec date 1783, writ, debt, file #3634

HARRIS Robert, merchant, of Boston MA, vs BLANCHARD Jotham, merchant, of Peterborough, rec date 1784, judgment, debt, file #4335

HARRIS Robert, merchant, of Boston MA, vs POWERS David, laborer, of Rutland VT, rec date 1785, complaint, counterfeiting, file #4753

HARRIS Robert, merchant, of Boston MA, vs KIMBALL George, trader, of Charlestown, rec date 1785, writ, debt, file #4817

HARRIS Robert, merchant, of Boston MA, vs GOLDSMITH Josiah, gentleman, of Walpole, rec date 1785, writ, debt, file #4815

HARRIS Robert, merchant, of Boston MA, vs ATKINSON Samuel, gentleman, of Boscawen, rec date 1785, writ, debt, file #4814

HARRIS Robert, merchant, of Boston MA, vs FLETCHER Francis, gentleman, of New Ipswich, rec date 1785, judgment, debt, file #5515

HARRIS Robert, merchant, of Boston MA, vs HEYWOOD Samuel, innholder, of New Ipswich, rec date 1785, judgment, debt, file #5833

HARRIS Robert, merchant, of Boston MA, vs BURBANK David, blacksmith, of Boscawen, rec date 1785, judgment, debt, file #5843

HARRIS Robert, merchant, of Boston MA, vs HOAR Benjamin, gentleman, of New Ipswich, rec date 1785, judgment, debt, file #5835

HARRIS Robert, merchant, of Boston MA, vs HOUSTON William, yeoman, of Peterborough, rec date 1785, writ, debt, file #6023

HARRIS Robert, merchant, of Boston MA, vs MOOR Samuel Jr, yeoman, of Peterborough, rec date 1785, writ, debt, file #6016

HARRIS Stephen, yeoman, of Hollis, vs TARBELL Thomas, esquire, of Mason, doc date 1774, judgment, trespass, file #706

HART John, blacksmith, of Hopkinton, vs CHADWICK John, husbandman, of Hopkinton, doc date 1799, debt, file #475

HART John, yeoman, of Charlestown, vs DICKEY James, gentleman, of Raby, rec date 1783, execution, debt, file #3652

HART Seth, yeoman, of Francestown, vs GRIMES James, husbandman, of Deering, doc date 1798, judgment, debt, file #564

HART Thomas, physician, of Boston MA, vs CLUFF James, yeoman, of Hopkinton, doc date 1784, execution, debt, file #1787

HARTHORN Nathaniel, husbandman, of Henniker, vs SWAN Caleb, trader, of Charlestown, doc date 1799, judgment, debt, file #226

HARTWELL Ephraim, shopkeeper, of New Ipswich, vs WHEELER Uriah, husbandman, of Packersfield, doc date 1784, execution, debt, file #1680

HARTWELL Ephraim, gentleman, of New Ipswich, vs CUTLER Solomon, gentleman, of Rindge, rec date 1786, judgment, debt, file #2299

HARTWELL Ephraim, of New Ipswich, vs ALLEN Abijah, yeoman, of Mason, rec date 1785, judgment, debt, file #5061

HARTWELL Ephraim, shopkeeper, of New Ipswich, vs BACON Retire, yeoman, of New Ipswich, rec date 1785, writ, debt, file #6038

HARTWELL Ephraim, shopkeeper, of New Ipswich, vs HALE John, esquire, of Hollis, rec date 1785, various, debt, file #6258

HARTWELL Ephraim, trader, of New Ipswich, vs TARBELL John, husbandman, of MA, rec date 1787, writ, debt, file #6707

HARTWELL Ephraim, gentleman, of New Ipswich, vs ROBE William Jr, yeoman, of Peterborough, rec date 1788, writ, debt, file #6918

HARTWELL Ephraim, gentleman, of New Ipswich, vs DIX Nathan, gentleman, of Peterborough, rec date 1788, writ, debt, file #6926

HARTWELL Ephraim Capt, doc date 1787, license, tavern license, file #872

HARVEY John, gentleman, of Northwood, vs WALLACE Matthew, esquire, of Peterborough, rec date 1784, writ, debt, file #4208

HARVEY John, gentleman, of Northwood, vs SMITH William, esquire, of Peterborough, rec date 1784, writ, debt, file #4208

HARVEY John, gentleman, of Northwood, vs WILLS Samuel, gentleman, of Peterborough, rec date 1786, judgment, debt, file #6384

HARVEY John (Lt), gentleman, of Northwood, vs WELLS Samuel, gentleman, of Peterborough, rec date 1784, judgment, debt, file #4331

HARWOOD Andrew, husbandman, of Lyndeborough, vs SEWELL Rachell, tailor, of Londonderry, doc date 1799, various, debt, file #536

HARWOOD James, yeoman, of Dunstable, vs KILLICUT Reuben, yeoman, of Dunstable, doc date 1772, writ, debt, file #900

HARWOOD Mary, widow, of Dunstable, vs HILDRETH John, yeoman, of Litchfield, rec date 1783, judgment, debt, file #4489

HARWOOD Thomas, gentleman, of Dunstable, vs POLLARD Samuel, yeoman, of Nottingham-West, rec date 1783, judgment, debt, file #3730

HARWOOD Thomas, gentleman, of Dunstable, vs CALDWELL John, yeoman, of Nottingham-West, rec date 1783, judgment, debt, file #3730

HASELTINE Nathan, yeoman, of Salem, vs EATON John, yeoman, of Haverhill, doc date 1763, judgment, debt, file #787

HASELTON Stephen, yeoman, of Hollis, vs DICKEY James, gentleman, of Raby, rec date 1785, judgment, debt, file #5352

HASSALL Benjamin & Eliz, vs HASALL Abel, yeoman, doc date 1777, deed, land transfer, file #2059

HAVEN John, esquire, of Exeter, vs MOOR William, husbandman, of Dunbarton, rec date 1785, judgment, debt, file #5810

HAVEN John, esquire, of Exeter, vs MOOR William, husbandman, of Dunbarton, rec date 1785, execution, debt, file #5940

HAVEN Samuel, clerk, of Portsmouth, vs BURNS John, husbandman, of Francestown, rec date 1788, judgment, debt, file #7012

HAWKINS William A, gentleman, of Wilton, vs PUTNAM John, husbandman, of Lyndeborough, rec date 1786, writ, debt, file #6292

HAWKINS William A, gentleman, of Wilton, vs HUDSON Elisha, husbandman, of Wilton, rec date 1786, writ, debt, file #6106

HAWKINS William A, gentleman, of Wilton, vs BARRON Mijiah, husbandman, of Lyndeborough, rec date 1786, writ, debt, file #6292

HAWKINS William Adrian, gentleman, of Wilton, vs FLETCHER Oliver, husbandman, of Wilton, rec date 1784, judgment, debt, file #4655

HAWKINS William Adrian, esquire, of Wilton, vs PUTNAM Jacob, husbandman, of Temple, rec date 1785, judgment, debt, file #5501

HAWKINS William Adrian, gentleman, of Wilton, vs FLETCHER Oliver, husbandman, of Wilton, rec date 1785, judgment, debt, file #5147

HAWKINS William Adrian, esquire, of Wilton, vs PUTNAM Jacob, husbandman, of Temple, rec date 1785, judgment, debt, file #5988

HAWSE David, yeoman, of Townsend MA, vs GRAGG Samuel, innkeeper, of Peterborough Slip, rec date 1783, writ, debt, file #3452

HAYNES Tristram, hatter, of Litchfield, vs FRENCH Benjamin, merchant, of Charlestown, doc date 1799, execution, debt, file #177

HAYNES Tristram, hatter, of Litchfield, vs SENTER Samuel, merchant, of Charlestown, doc date 1799, execution, debt, file #177

HAYNES Tristram, hatter, of Litchfield, vs GIBSON John, trader, of Francestown, doc date 1799, debt, file #347

HAYWOOD Josiah, yeoman, of Nottingham-West, vs READ William, yeoman, of Nottingham-West, rec date 1787, various, debt, file #2540

HAYWOOD Josiah, yeoman, of Nottingham-West, vs KELLEY Joseph, gentleman, of Nottingham-West, rec date 1787, various, debt, file #2540

HAYWOOD Josiah, of Westford MA, rec date 1788, deposition, land dispute, file #6583

HAYWOOD Josiah, yeoman, of Nottingham-West, vs KELLEY Joseph, gentleman, of Nottingham-West, rec date 1786, various, debt, file #6363

HAYWOOD Samuel, gentleman, of New Ipswich, vs DODGE William, husbandman, of Mason, doc date 1784, civil litigation, debt, file #1641

HAYWOOD Samuel, yeoman, of Nottingham-West, vs KELLEY Joseph, gentleman, of Nottingham-West, rec date 1782, writ, debt, file #2689

HAYWOOD Samuel, tanner, of New Ipswich, vs MITCHELL William, yeoman, of Acworth, rec date 1783, writ, debt, file #4556

HAYWOOD Samuel Smith, yeoman, of Nottingham, vs DARRAH William, yeoman, of Litchfield, doc date 1784, writ, debt, file #1630

HAZELTINE Nathaniel, tanner, of Methuen MA, vs BAYLEY Phineas, gentleman, of Dunbarton, rec date 1788, writ, debt, file #6680

HAZELTON Ebenezer, gentleman, of Hollis, vs HAZELTON Stephen, yeoman, of Hollis, doc date 1773, execution, debt, file #1467

HAZELTON Samuel, husbandman, of Cockermouth, vs JONES Samuel, husbandman, of Hillsborough, rec date 1782, execution, debt, file #5742

HAZELTON Stephen, husbandman, of Hollis, vs HAZELTON Samuel, gentleman, of Cockermouth, rec date 1785, judgment, debt, file #5350

HAZEN William, merchant, of Newburyport MA, vs BEDEL Timothy, esquire, of Bath, doc date 1774, writ, debt, file #743

HEAILL Joseph, yeoman, of Dunstable, vs PEABODY Hannah*, widow, of Amherst, rec date 1782, writ, debt, file #2831, husband Stephen PEABODY*

HEALD George F, of Manchester, vs CONCORD & Montreal Rail, doc date 1892, injuries to plaintiff, supreme court, file #596, a Manchester railroad yard diagram

HEALD Joseph, yeoman, of Temple, vs HEALD Joseph Jr, trader, of Temple, doc date 1792, rec date 1792, deed, land transfer, file #6574

HEALD Thomas, esquire, of New Ipswich, vs MORRISON John, husbandman, of Peterborough, rec date 1785, judgment, debt, file #5512

HEALD Thomas, esquire, of New Ipswich, vs CUNNINGHAM James, gentleman, of Peterborough, doc date 1784, execution, debt, file #1778

HEALD Thomas, esquire, of New Ipswich, vs CUMMINGHAM James, gentleman, of Peterborough, rec date 1784, judgment, debt, file #4342

HEALD Thomas, esquire, of New Ipswich, vs CHAMBERS William, gentleman, of Mason, rec date 1784, judgment, debt, file #4332

HEARD David, yeoman, of Raby, vs WORSTER Noah, esquire, of Hollis, rec date 1784, judgment, debt, file #4258

HEARTWELL Ephraim, trader, of New Ipswich, vs BANCROFT Benjamin, yeoman, of Rindge, rec date 1783, judgment, debt, file #3297

HEARTWELL Ephraim, trader, of New Ipswich, vs BROWN Aaron, trader, of Groton MA, rec date 1783, judgment, debt, file #3297

HEARTWELL Ephraim, shopkeeper, of New Ipswich, vs WHEELER Uriah, husbandman, of Packersfield, rec date 1783, judgment, debt, file #4499

HEARTWELL Stephen, husbandman, of Bedford MA, vs HAGG Elijah, yeoman, of New Ipswich, rec date 1782, writ, debt, file #2678

HEATH Amos, husbandman, of Sandown, vs HARD James, gentleman, of Haverhill MA, doc date 1773, writ, debt, file #1331

HEATH Joanna, widow, of Deering, vs CLOUGH David, husbandman, of Dracut MA, doc date 1784, execution, debt, file #1822, description of land attachment

HEATH Joanna, widow, of Deering, vs CLOUGH David, husbandman, of Dracut MA, rec date 1784, judgment, debt, file #4343

HEATH Samuel, gentleman, of Roxbury MA, vs McNEIL John Caldwell, husbandman, of New Boston, doc date 1784, civil litigation, debt, file #1851

HEATH Samuel, gentleman, of Roxbury MA, vs McNEIL John Caldwell, husbandman, of New Boston, rec date 1783, judgment, debt, file #4468

HEATH Samuel, gentleman, of Roxbury MA, vs McNEIL James Caldwell, of Weare, rec date 1785, writ, debt, file #4846, fragile

HEBERT Israel, esquire, of Groton MA, vs WRIGHT Josiah, laborer, of Raby, doc date 1788, rec date 1788, deed, land transfer, file #6818

HEBRON Jeremiah, gentleman, of Amherst, vs SMITH Moses, husbandman, of Henniker, doc date 1799, execution, debt, file #201

HECKMAN Nathaniel, physician, of Amherst, vs QUEEN John, physician, of Bedford, rec date 1786, judgment, debt, file #5774

HEICHMAN Nathaniel, physician, of Amherst, vs HOUSTON James, blacksmith, of Bedford, rec date 1788, judgment, debt, file #6906

HENCHMAN Nathaniel, physician, of Amherst, vs QUEEN John, physician, of Bedford, rec date 1785, execution, debt, file #5900

HENCHMAN Nathaniel, physician, of Amherst, vs HOUSTON James, blacksmith, of Bedford, rec date 1786, writ, debt, file #6050

HENDERSON, vs WILLIAMS, doc date 1890, plaintiff's counsel argument, supreme court, file #626, oral arguments

HENDERSON Daniel R, vs WILLIAMS Charles, doc date 1890, court arguments, supreme court, file #576

HENDERSON Joshua, distiller, of Boston MA, vs TAGGART James, husbandman, of Hillsborough, doc date 1784, civil litigation, debt, file #1853

HENICHMAN Nathaniel, physician, of Amherst, vs BROWN John, blacksmith, of Amherst, doc date 1798, execution, debt, file #88

HENRY John, husbandman, of Dunstable, vs McCLURE William, husbandman, rec date 1769, writ, debt, file #2229

HENRY Joseph, yeoman, of Merrimack, vs PATTERSON John, yeoman, of Boston MA, rec date 1783, judgment, debt, file #4493

HENRY Joseph, yeoman, of Merrimack, vs DUTY Mark, yeoman, of Windham, rec date 1783, judgment, debt, file #4493

HENRY Samuel, yeoman, of Merrimack, vs HENRY Joseph, yeoman, of Merrimack, doc date 1783, rec date 1783, deed, land transfer, file #2647

HENRY Samuel, husbandman, of Merrimack, vs CHAMBERLIN Thomas, husbandman, of Merrimack, doc date 1785, rec date 1786, deed, land transfer, file #5025

HENRY William, groom, of Marlborough MA, vs HAYDE Persi, bride, of Marlborough MA, rec date 1787, marriage license, license, file #6158, part of Samuel CURTIS file

HENRY William, of Bennington VT, rec date 1788, various, debt, file #6972

HENSHAW Joshua, gentleman, of Boston MA, vs BLANCHARD Jotham, gentleman, of Peterborough, rec date 1783, land dispute, court case, file #3285

HENSHAW Joshua, esquire, of Boston MA, vs McCALLEY John, gentleman, of Hillsborough, rec date 1785, judgment, debt, file #5585, estate of John HILL

HENSHAW Joshua, esquire, of Boston MA, vs McCALLEY John, gentleman, of Hillsborough, rec date 1785, judgment, debt, file #6396

HERON John, husbandman, of Hampton, vs HALL John, innkeeper, of Derryfield, rec date 1785, writ, debt, file #5395

HERRICK Daniel, yeoman, of Hollis, vs RUSS James, yeoman, of Chester, doc date 1773, judgment, debt, file #1317

HERRICK Joseph, husbandman, of Mason, vs BALLARD Nathan, gentleman, of Wilton, rec date 1785, judgment, debt, file #5519

HERRICK Joseph, gentleman, of Lyndeborough, vs JONES Nathan, husbandman, of Amherst, rec date 1785, judgment, debt, file #4690

HERRICK Joseph, husbandman, of Lyndeborough, vs PUTNAM William, esquire, of Sterling MA, rec date 1785, judgment, debt, file #5351

HERRICK Joseph, husbandman, of Mason, vs BALLARD Nathan, gentleman, of Wilton, rec date 1785, execution, debt, file #5947

HERRICK Josiah, yeoman, of Amherst, vs DENNIS Arthur, yeoman, of New Boston, doc date 1788, petition, debt, file #513

HEYWAY Samuel, yeoman, of New Ipswich, vs GOLDSMITH Josiah, gentleman, of Walpole, rec date 1785, judgment, debt, file #5114

HEYWOOD Jeame, yeoman, of Dunstable, rec date 1772, letter, escape from prison, file #7018

HEYWOOD Joseph, gentleman, of Concord, vs HOSMER Nathaniel, yeoman, of Mason, rec date 1787, writ, debt, file #6957

HEYWOOD Joshua, clerk, of Dunstable MA, vs PARKER Alexander, housewright, of Hillsborough, doc date 1810, rec date 1814, deed, land transfer, file #5698

HEYWOOD Nathaniel, husbandman, of Hillsborough, vs CROSBY Jonah, yeoman, of Billerica MA, rec date 1786, various, debt, file #6065

HEYWOOD Samuel, turner, of New Ipswich, vs MITCHELL William, yeoman, of Acworth, doc date 1784, court case, debt, file #1610

HEYWOOD Samuel, vs BROWN Seth, rec date 1777, deposition, file #2202

HEYWOOD Samuel, gentleman, of New Ipswich, vs BROWN Seth Ingerson, yeoman, of Cambridge MA, rec date 1783, court case, debt, file #2874

HEYWOOD Samuel, innholder, of New Ipswich, vs GOLDSMITH Josiah, gentleman, of Walpole, rec date 1784, judgment, debt, file #4657

HEYWOOD Samuel, gentleman, of New Ipswich, vs DODGE William, husbandman, of Mason, rec date 1783, judgment, debt, file #4502

HEYWOOD Samuel, husbandman, of New Ipswich, vs WALLACE Matthew, gentleman, of Peterborough, rec date 1785, writ, debt, file #5415

HEYWOOD Samuel, gentleman, of New Ipswich, vs LAWRENCE Stephen, husbandman, of Mason, rec date 1785, writ, debt, file #5957

HICHMAN Nathaniel, physician, of Amherst, vs QUEEN John, physician, of Bedford, rec date 1785, writ, debt, file #6858

HICKEY John, yeoman, of Portsmouth, vs ELLERY Harris, physician, of Boston MA, doc date 1773, writ, debt, file #1228

HICKMAN Nathaniel, physician, of Amherst, vs HUSTON James, blacksmith, of Bedford, rec date 1786, judgment, debt, file #5261

HICKS Sarah, widow, of Madbury, vs RICHARDSON James, esquire, of Leominster MA, rec date 1783, writ, debt, file #3203

HIDDEN James, yeoman, of Chester, vs WILSON Thomas, husbandman, of New Boston, doc date 1773, writ, debt, file #1339

HILDRETH David, yeoman, of Amherst, vs ATHERTON Joshua, esquire, of Amherst, rec date 1784, judgment, debt, file #4238

HILDRETH Ephraim, gentleman, of Amherst, vs STEARNS John, yeoman, of Amherst, rec date 1786, writ, debt, file #6881

HILDRETH Ephraim, gentleman, of Amherst, vs PERWIDY Elizabeth, laboring woman, of Amherst, doc date 1778, rec date 1779, deed, land transfer, file #2133

HILDRETH Ephraim, gentleman, of Amherst, vs KEEF Michael, yeoman, of Amherst, rec date 1786, judgment, debt, file #2301

HILDRETH Ephraim, esquire, of Amherst, vs BRADFORD Samuel, gentleman, of Lyndeborough, rec date 1783, writ, debt, file #3500

HILDRETH Ephraim, esquire, of Amherst, vs BRADFORD Samuel, gentleman, of Lyndeborough, rec date 1782, execution, debt, file #3506

HILDRETH Ephraim, gentleman, of Amherst, vs CALDWELL Joseph, yeoman, of Nottingham-West, rec date 1785, judgment, debt, file #5083

HILDRETH Ephraim, gentleman, of Amherst, vs LOVEJOY Francis, feltmaker, of Amherst, rec date 1785, execution, debt, file #5903

HILDRETH Ephraim Jr, yeoman, of Amherst, vs LOVEJOY Francis Jr, yeoman, of Amherst, rec date 1787, writ, debt, file #6971

HILDRETH Esther, singlewoman, of Hollis, vs FARMER Benjamin Jr, husbandman, of Hollis, doc date 1772, judgment, fornication, file #692

HILDRETH Esther, singlewoman, of Hollis, vs FARMER Benjamin Jr, husbandman, of Hollis, doc date 1773, complaint, fornication, file #1222

HILDRETH Jacob, yeoman, of Amherst, vs STEARNS Samuel, yeoman, of Amherst, rec date 1783, execution, debt, file #2871

HILDRETH Jacob, yeoman, of Amherst, vs STEARNS Samuel, yeoman, of Amherst, rec date 1782, judgment, debt, file #3138

HILDRETH Jacob, yeoman, of Amherst, vs STEARNS Samuel Jr, yeoman, of Amherst, rec date 1782, appeal, debt, file #4025

HILDRETH James, yeoman, of Pepperell MA, vs BLANCHARD Jotham, merchant, of Peterborough, rec date 1783, execution, debt, file #4916

HILDRETH John, yeoman, of Litchfield, vs LUND Stephen, yeoman, of Merrimack, rec date 1783, writ, debt, file #3005

HILDRETH John, husbandman, of Litchfield, vs PRINTICE William, yeoman, of Cambridge MA, rec date 1783, writ, debt, file #3169

HILDRETH Simeon, husbandman, of Bradford, vs JONES Phinehas, cordwainer, of Amherst, doc date 1799, writ, debt, file #574

HILDRETH William, blacksmith, of Amherst, vs SERGEANT Moses, gentleman, of Londonderry, rec date 1782, writ, debt, file #2622

HILL Aaron, bricklayer, of Cambridge MA, vs COTTON Samuel, clerk, of Litchfield, rec date 1783, judgment, debt, file #4711

HILL David, yeoman, of New Ipswich, vs LAWRENCE Stephen, yeoman, of Mason, doc date 1782, judgment, debt, file #1170

HILL John, of Boston MA, vs MORIN Antony, wheelwright, of Hillsborough, doc date 1769, rec date 1770, deed, land transfer, file #6836

HILL Samuel, husbandman, of Goffstown, vs PRENTICE John, esquire, of Sandown, doc date 1784, writ, debt, file #1585

HILL Samuel, yeoman, of Fitchburg MA, vs HILL William, yeoman, of Billerica MA, doc date 1785, rec date 1786, deed, land transfer, file #5024, land in Goffstown

HILL Stephen, yeoman, of Cheshire, vs ROBINSON Joseph, husbandman, of Deering, rec date 1783, execution, debt, file #3824

HILL Stephen, husbandman, of Chester, vs GRIMES James, gentleman, of Deering, rec date 1783, execution, debt, file #4912

HILL Steven, husbandman, of Chester, vs GRIMES James, gentleman, of Deering, rec date 1782, execution, debt, file #3482

HILL William, esquire, of Wilmington NC, vs BLANCHARD Jotham, gentleman, of Peterborough, rec date 1783, land dispute, court case, file #3285

HILL William, gentleman, of Wilmington NC, vs BLANCHARD Jonathan, gentleman, of Peterborough, rec date 1783, various, land dispute, file #5231, deed /09

HILL William, esquire/deceased, of Brunswich NC, vs TAGGART Archibald, husbandman, of Hillsborough, doc date 1784, civil litigation, debt, file #1853

HILLDRETH Ephraim, gentleman, of Amherst, vs TEMPLE Jonathan, husbandman, of Henniker, rec date 1785, execution, debt, file #5906

HILLS David, shopkeeper, of Wilton, vs CARLETON Jesse, clothier, of Wilton, doc date 1799, judgment, debt, file #225

HILLS David, trader, of New Ipswich, vs PARKER Obadiah, gentleman, of Mason, doc date 1784, court case, debt, file #1614

HILLS David, yeoman, of New Ipswich, vs GRAGG Adams, laborer, of Peterborough, rec date 1785, various, debt, file #5530

HILLS David, yeoman, of New Ipswich, vs SMITH Robert, yeoman, of Peterborough, rec date 1784, judgment, debt, file #4222

HILLS David, yeoman, of New Ipswich, vs HOSMER Reuben, husbandman, of Mason, rec date 1784, judgment, debt, file #5319

HILLS David, yeoman, of New Ipswich, vs CUTTER John, husbandman, of New Ipswich, rec date 1785, judgment, debt, file #5227

HILLS David, yeoman, of New Ipswich, vs CUTTER John, yeoman, of New Ipswich, rec date 1785, writ, debt, file #5409

HILLS David, yeoman, of New Ipswich, vs McCLOUD Thomas, husbandman, of Peterborough, rec date 1786, writ, debt, file #6286

HILLS David, yeoman, of New Ipswich, vs GRAY Robert, gentleman, of Peterborough, rec date 1786, writ, debt, file #6285

HILLS David, yeoman, of New Ipswich, vs HOLMS Robert, husbandman, of Peterborough, rec date 1786, writ, debt, file #6286

HILLS Moses, of Hopkinton, vs SELECTMEN of Hopkinton, of Hopkinton, rec date 1788, appointments, tavern license, file #3539

HILLS Stephen, yeoman, of Merrimack, vs SOUL Bildad, yeoman, of Goffstown, rec date 1785, judgment, debt, file #4688, land in Peeling (Woodstock)

HILTON Charles, husbandman, of Andover, vs WADLEIGH Benjamin, yeoman, of Salisbury, doc date 1784, execution, debt, file #1718

HILTON Charles, husbandman, of Andover, vs WADLEIGH Benjamin, yeoman, of Salisbury, doc date 1784, execution, debt, file #1912

HILTON Charles, husbandman, of Andover, vs WADLEIGH Benjamin, yeoman, of Salisbury, rec date 1783, writ, debt, file #3389

HINCHMAN Nathaniel, physician, of Amherst, vs LOVEJOY Francis, feltmaker, of Amherst, rec date 1786, writ, debt, file #6314

HINES Charles, yeoman, of New Ipswich, vs PARKER Samuel, yeoman, of New Ipswich, doc date 1772, judgment, debt, file #910

HINES Charles, yeoman, of New Ipswich, vs PARKER Samuel, yeoman, of New Ipswich, doc date 1774, execution, file #991

HINES Charles, yeoman, of New Ipswich, vs PARKER Samuel, yeoman, of New Ipswich, doc date 1772, execution, debt, file #1207

HITCHBORN Samuel, jewelry, of Boston MA, vs DODGE Noah & Nathaniel, yeoman, of New Boston, rec date 1783, ejectment, land dispute, file #2616

HITCHBORN Samuel, jewelry, of Boston MA, vs DODGE Noah & Nathaniel, yeoman, of New Boston, rec date 1784, various, debt, file #4165

HITCHBORN Samuel, jewelry, of Boston MA, vs WILSON James & Alexander, yeoman, of New Boston, rec date 1784, various, debt, file #4166

HITE Henry, esquire, of Boston MA, vs STONE Ezekiel, yeoman, of Fitzwilliam, rec date 1788, writ, debt, file #6988

HOAG Samuel, yeoman, of Deering, vs CODMAN Henry, physician, of Amherst, rec date 1786, judgment, debt, file #2307

HOAG Samuel, yeoman, of Deering, vs TAYLOR John, yeoman, of Amherst, rec date 1785, judgment, debt, file #5587

HOAGG James Jr, gentleman, of Weare, vs McGREGOR David, esquire, of Londonderry, rec date 1786, various, trespass, file #6080

HOAR Benjamin, laborer, of New Ipswich, vs TAGGART James, gentleman, of Peterborough, rec date 1785, judgment, debt, file #5782

HOAR Benjamin, gentleman, of New Ipswich, vs TAGGART John, gentleman, of Peterborough Slip, doc date 1784, ejectment, land dispute, file #1600

HOAR Benjamin Jr, laborer, of New Ipswich, vs TAGGART James, gentleman, of Peterborough, rec date 1785, judgment, debt, file #5990

HOAR James, cooper, of Littleton MA, vs HOAR Jotham, husbandman, of New Ipswich, rec date 1783, judgment, debt, file #4097

HOBART Benjamin, yeoman, of Townsend MA, vs GLENEY John Jr, husbandman, of Westmoreland, rec date 1783, writ, debt, file #3449

HOBART Jeremiah, cordwainer, of Amherst, vs WILKINS Isaac (alias SIMONS), yeoman, of Lyndeborough, rec date 1786, writ, debt, file #5464

HOBART Joel, of Mile Slip, vs BULLARD Joyn, clerk, of Pepperell MA, rec date 1784, writ, debt, file #4926

HOBART Jonathan Jr, of Hollis, vs DIX Jonas, trader, of Keene, doc date 1794, petition, release from jail, file #44

HOBART Jonathan Jr, yeoman, of Hollis, vs WILKINS Bray & Lucy, yeoman, of Deering, rec date 1783, judgment, debt, file #4325

HOBART Samuel, esquire, of Exeter, vs AMORY Jonathan & John, merchants, of Boston MA, doc date 1784, writ, debt, file #1268

HOBART Samuel, esquire, of Exeter, vs SCRIPTURE Samuel, of Mason, rec date 1783, writ, debt, file #3624

HOBART Samuel, esquire, of Exeter, vs KEYES Elijah, of Mason, rec date 1783, writ, debt, file #3624

HOBART Samuel, esquire, of Exeter, vs CUTLER Jonas, shopkeeper, of Groton MA, rec date 1782, appeal, debt, file #4008

HOBART Shebual, husbandman, of Hollis, vs POOLE William Welstead, wheelwright, rec date 1785, writ, debt, file #2409

HOBART William, gentleman, of Townsend MA, vs HOSMER Nathaniel, husbandman, of Mason, rec date 1788, writ, debt, file #6734

HOBBS Joseph, taylor, of Lyndeborough, vs MANNING John, physician, of Ipswich MA, doc date 1784, execution, debt, file #1930

HOBBS Joseph, taylor, of Lyndeborough, vs MANNING John Jr, physician, of Ipswich MA, rec date 1783, civil litigious, debt, file #2937

HOBBS Joseph, yeoman, of Nottingham-West, vs TARBOSC Henry, gentleman, of Nottingham-West, rec date 1786, writ, debt, file #6280

HOBBS Joseph, yeoman, of Nottingham-West, vs KIDDER Benjamin, gentleman, of Nottingham-West, rec date 1786, writ, debt, file #6280

HOBERT Lydia & Joel, widow, of Amherst, vs BARNARD Jeremiah, clerk, of Amherst, doc date 1787, rec date 1788, deed, land transfer, file #6743

HOBSON Andrew, tanner, of Amherst, vs FORSAITH Thomas, husbandman, of Husbandman, doc date 1799, writ, debt, file #574

HOBSON Jeremiah, gentleman, of Amherst, vs BARTELTT Joseph Jr, gentleman, of Amherst, doc date 1799, writ, debt, file #573

HOBSON Jeremiah, gentleman, of Amherst, vs LYNCH John, blacksmith, of New Boston, rec date 1789, execution, debt, file #5719

HOBSON Jeremiah, tanner, of Amherst, vs GREEN David, yeoman, of Hillsborough, rec date 1785, writ, debt, file #6241

HOBSON William, innholder, of Hopkinton, vs PERKINS Roger Elliot, trader, of Hopkinton, doc date 1799, execution, debt, file #42

HODGDON John, yeoman, of Weare, vs ATWOOD Joshua, husbandman, of Antrim, doc date 1799, various, land dispute, file #539

HODGDON John, yeoman, of Weare, vs NICHOLS John, yeoman, of Francestown, doc date 1799, various, land dispute, file #539

HODGE Samuel, gentleman, of Francestown, vs WILSON Thomas, yeoman, of New Boston, doc date 1798, execution, debt, file #148

HODGMAN John, yeoman, of Mason, vs WOOD Samuel, yeoman, of Mason, rec date 1782, writ, debt, file #2791

HODGMAN Zacheus, yeoman, of Raby, vs HODGMAN Joseph, yeoman, of Mason, rec date 1782, writ, debt, file #2845

HOGG Abner, of New Boston, vs GREGG Alexander, administrator of estate, of New Boston, rec date 1788, deposition, debt, file #6976

HOGG Alexander, yeoman, vs STARK Archibald, yeoman, rec date 1778, deed, land transfer, file #2162

HOGG Ebenezer, mariner, of Boston MA, vs JONES John Paul, esquire, of Portsmouth, rec date 1782, judgment, debt, file #2700, for service on ship *Bonne homme Richard*

HOGG Eleazer, housewright, of Hollis, vs LAWRENCE Thomas, husbandman, of Mason, rec date 1782, writ, debt, file #2837

HOGG George, yeoman, of Deering, vs BLOOD Ebenezer, yeoman, of Deering, rec date 1785, writ, debt, file #5190

HOGG George, yeoman, of Deering, vs HADLOCK Levi, yeoman, of Deering, rec date 1785, writ, debt, file #5190

HOGG James, husbandman, of Weare, vs FEUVOU David, husbandman, of Dunbarton, doc date 1798, execution, debt, file #113

HOGG James, gentleman, of Dunbarton, vs NEWHALL Jeremiah, yeoman, of Oxford, doc date 1798, judgment, debt, file #564

HOGG James, gentleman, of Dunbarton, vs BABROIS Isaac, gentleman, of Derryfield, doc date 1799, execution, debt, file #218

HOGG James, gentleman, of Dunbarton, vs BABSON Isaac, gentleman, of Deerfield, doc date 1798, execution, debt, file #110

HOGG James, gentleman, of Weare, vs HOGG Robert, yeoman, of Weare, doc date 1784, deed, land transfer, file #1997

HOGG James, gentleman, of Dunbarton, vs EMERSON George, yeoman, of Dunbarton, doc date 1782, rec date 1783, deed, land transfer, file #2648

HOGG James, of Weare, vs INHABITANTS of Dunbarton, rec date 1784, writ, debt, file #4639, rev soldiers list Dunbarton

HOGG James, esquire, of Weare, vs GOULD John, husbandman, of Dunbarton, rec date 1785, judgment, debt, file #5809

HOGG James, gentleman, of Weare, vs DOW Oliver, gentleman, of Hopkinton, rec date 1785, judgment, debt, file #5842

HOGG James, esquire, of Weare, vs EASTMAN Caleb, husbandman, of Goffstown, rec date 1785, judgment, debt, file #5809

HOGG James, gentleman, of Weare, vs BAGLEY Phineas, gentleman, of Dunbarton, rec date 1785, execution, debt, file #5786

HOGG John, esquire, of Dunbarton, vs STARK William, esquire, of Dunbarton, doc date 1773, writ, assault, file #826

HOGG John, esquire, of Dunbarton, vs STARK William, gentleman, of Dunbarton, doc date 1774, writ, complaint of assault, file #748

HOGG John, esquire, of Dunbarton, vs HOGG David, gentleman, of Dunbarton, doc date 1774, writ, complaint of assault, file #748

HOGG John, yeoman, of Dunbarton, vs McCARTNEY Jane, spinster, of Dunbarton, rec date 1783, indictment, perjury, file #3557

HOGG John, yeoman, of Deering, vs HOIT Philip, physician, of Weare, rec date 1783, execution, debt, file #3870

HOGG John, yeoman, of Deering, vs HOIT Philip, physician, of Weare, rec date 1783, writ, debt, file #3897

HOGG John, yeoman, of Deering, vs GRIMES James, gentleman, of Deering, rec date 1785, judgment, debt, file #5221

HOGG John, esquire, of Hampstead, vs SYMONDS Joseph, husbandman, of Derryfield, rec date 1787, writ, debt, file #6644

HOGG John, esquire, of Hampstead, vs WETHEY? Luke, husbandman, of Derryfield, rec date 1787, writ, debt, file #6644

HOGG John, vs McCARTNEY Jane, spinster, rec date 1783, indictment, file #7037

HOGG Robert, husbandman, of New Boston, vs FRENCH Ephraim, innkeeper, of Amherst, doc date 1800, writ, debt, file #574

HOGG Robert, of Deering, doc date 1787, license, tavern license, file #863

HOGG Samuel, yeoman, of Dublin, vs ROBBE Alexander, gentleman, of Peterborough, rec date 1783, writ, debt, file #3181

HOIT John, yeoman, of Hillsborough, vs SCRIBNER Iddo, gentleman, of Hillsborough, doc date 1799, various, debt, file #528

HOIT John, yeoman, of Salisbury, vs SCRIBNER Iddo, gentleman, of Salisbury, doc date 1799, various, debt, file #528

HOIT Philip, physician, of Weare, vs McGINNIS Barnabas, trader, of Nottingham-West, doc date 1784, execution, debt, file #1911

HOIT Philip, physician, of Weare, vs CLARK Ephraim, husbandman, of Deering, rec date 1783, execution, debt, file #3653

HOIT Robert, yeoman, of Amesbury MA, vs KELLY William, clerk, of Warner, rec date 1785, deed, land transfer, file #5614

HOLDEN Abel, husbandman, of Lunenburg MA, vs STONE Joseph, labourer, of Temple, doc date 1791, rec date 1791, deed, land transfer, file #2661

HOLDEN David, husbandman, of Hollis, vs POOL Jonathan, physician, of Hollis, rec date 1786, judgment, debt, file #2458

HOLDEN Isaac, yeoman, of Mason, vs CHAMPNEY Ebenezer, gentleman, of New Ipswich, rec date 1773, writ, debt, file #2176

HOLDEN Oliver, merchant, of Charlestown, vs CUMMINGS Benjamin, gentleman, of Hollis, doc date 1802, judgment, debt, file #568

HOLDEN Oliver, merchant, of Charlestown, vs CUMMINGS Benjamin, gentleman, of Hollis, doc date 1801, judgment, debt, file #568

HOLDIN Isaac, yeoman, of Mason, vs PARKER Samuel, yeoman, of Mason, doc date 1772, summons, complaint, file #1226

HOLLAND John, yeoman, of Merrimack, vs KELLEY Joseph, gentleman, of Nottingham, doc date 1772, judgment, assault, file #666

HOLLAND John, yeoman, of Merrimack, vs KELLEY Joseph, gentleman, of Nottingham-West, doc date 1772, writ, assault, file #932

HOLLAND John, yeoman, of Merrimack, vs KELLEY Joseph, doc date 1772, execution, debt, file #1196

HOLLAND John, yeoman, of Amherst, vs KELLEY Joseph, gentleman, of Nottingham-West, rec date 1773, judgment, debt, file #2336

HOLLAND John, yeoman, of Amherst, vs HOLBROOK Abigail, rec date 1777, indictment, fraud counterfeiting, file #2212

HOLLAND John, yeoman, of Amherst, vs FARNSWORTH Daniel, rec date 1777, indictment, fraud counterfeit, file #2212

HOLLAND John, yeoman, of Amherst, vs KELLY Joseph, gentleman, of Nottingham-West, rec date 1773, petition, debt, file #6510

HOLLAND Stephen, esquire, vs JONES Daniel, bill, file #811

HOLLAND Stephen, of Ireland, vs McMURPHY James (estate), deceased, of Londonderry, doc date 1799, various, debt, file #538

HOLLAND Stephen, of Ireland, vs McMURPHY Alex & Mary, husbandman, of Londonderry, doc date 1799, various, debt, file #538

HOLLAND Stephen Col, collector, vs WHITE John, rec date 1774, bill, file #7029

HOLLAND Stephen Col, serviceman, of Londonderry, rec date 1774, various, loose paper, file #7005

HOLLIS Stephen, yeoman, of Pepperell MA, vs POLLARD Joseph, yeoman, of New Ipswich, rec date 1786, writ, debt, file #6324

HOLMES Nathaniel & Mary, husbandman, of Sandown, vs WELLS Reuben, husbandman, of Sandown, doc date 1772, writ, debt, file #1396

HOLMES Nathaniel & Mary, husbandman, of Sandown, vs BACHELDER Stephan, husbandman, of Sandown, doc date 1772, writ, debt, file #1396

HOLMES Oliver, gentleman, of Francestown, vs JONES Samuel, yeoman, of Hillsborough, rec date 1782, judgment, debt, file #2741

HOLMES Oliver, gentleman, of Francestown, vs MARDEN George, yeoman, of Francestown, rec date 1786, judgment, debt, file #6385

HOLMES Robert, gentleman, of Goffstown, vs KELLEY Moses, esquire, of Goffstown, rec date 1785, judgment, debt, file #5348

HOLMES William, yeoman, of Francestown, vs STEWART Alexander, cordwainer, of Peterborough, rec date 1785, writ, debt, file #2358

HOLMES William, husbandman, of Francestown, vs MOOR John, husbandman, of Francestown, rec date 1785, judgment, debt, file #5172

HOLMES William, husbandman, of Antrim, vs MOORE John, husbandman, of Francestown, rec date 1786, writ, debt, file #6111

HOLMES William, husbandman, of Antrim, vs MORE John, husbandman, of Francestown, rec date 1786, writ, debt, file #6138

HOLMS Oliver, gentleman, of Francestown, vs CARSON John, gentleman, of Francestown, rec date 1783, civil litigious, debt, file #2907

HOLMS Oliver, gentleman, of Francestown, vs CARSON John, gentleman, of Francestown, rec date 1783, execution, debt, file #3233

HOLMS Oliver, gentleman, of Francestown, vs JONES Samuel, yeoman, of Hillsborough, rec date 1783, execution, debt, file #3835

HOLMS Oliver, gentleman, of Francestown, vs MARSDIN George, yeoman, of Francestown, rec date 1784, judgment, debt, file #5452

HOLMS William, husbandman, of Dunbarton, vs McGINNIS Barnabas, trader, of New Boston, doc date 1782, execution, debt, file #963

HOLMS William, of Dunbarton, vs McGINNIS Barnabas, trader, of New Boston, rec date 1783, execution, debt, file #3243

HOLT Ebenezer, yeoman, of Amherst, vs WHITE Andrew, yeoman, of New Boston, doc date 1784, execution, debt, file #1525

HOLT Ebenezer, yeoman, of Amherst, vs WHITE Andrew, yeoman, of New Boston, rec date 1784, judgment, debt, file #4284

HOLT Humphrey, yeoman, of Londonderry, vs SENTER John, husbandman, of Hollis, rec date 1785, judgment, debt, file #5259

HOLT Isaiah, youth, of Wilton, vs STATE of NH, rec date 1783, coroners report, inquisition, file #2597

HOLT Jacob, husbandman, of Andover MA, vs FLINT Jacob, housewright, of Hillsborough, rec date 1788, judgment, debt, file #2560

HOLT James Jr, yeoman, of Wilton, vs BROWN James, gentleman, of Moultonborough, rec date 1776, writ, debt, file #2200

HOLT Joseph, of Wilton, vs PUTNAMAN Jacob, of Wilton, rec date 1783, writ, debt, file #3602, (part of writ)

HOLT Nehemiah, husbandman, of Wilton, vs BLANCHARD Jothan, merchant, of Peterborough, rec date 1785, various, debt, file #5250

HOLT Nehemiah, husbandman, of Wilton, vs BLANCHARD Jotham, merchant, of Peterborough, rec date 1785, judgment, debt, file #4799

HOLT Oliver, yeoman, of Wilton, vs ABBOTT Joseph, yeoman, of Wilton, doc date 1776, rec date 1779, deed, land transfer, file #2137

HOLT Simeon, yeoman, of Wilton, vs CRAM Humphrey, yeoman, of Wilton, rec date 1786, execution, debt, file #5877

HOLT Simeon, yeoman, of Wilton, vs CRAM Humphrey, yeoman, of Wilton, rec date 1785, judgment, debt, file #6196

HOLT Thomas, yeoman, of Amherst, vs SHURTLEFF Jonathan, yeoman, of Merrimack, rec date 1784, appeal, debt, file #4127

HOLT Thomas, yeoman, of Amherst, vs SHURLET Jonathan, of Merrimack, rec date 1785, judgment, debt, file #6355

HOMER John, trader, of Winchendon MA, vs COLBY Samson, physician, of Hopkinton, doc date 1772, judgment, debt, file #684

HONEY Parminter, husbandman, of Hollis, vs PARKER Samuel, gentleman, of Pepperell MA, doc date 1799, writ, debt, file #377

HONEY Peter, yeoman, of Dunstable, vs CHAMPNEY Ebenezer, gentleman, of New Ipswich, doc date 1772, civil litigation, debt, file #646

HONEY Peter, yeoman, of Dunstable, vs SAWYER James, yeoman, of Dunstable, rec date 1772, execution, debt, file #4878

HOOD Joseph, mariner, of Boston MA, vs McQUAID James, husbandman, of Bedford, doc date 1798, judgment, debt, file #564

HOOKER John Jr, yeoman, of Rutland MA, vs HOW Ephraim, yeoman, of Marlborough MA, rec date 1786, statement, debt, file #6178, part of Samuel CURTIS file

HOPKINS Benjamin, husbandman, of Amherst, vs TWISS John, yeoman, of Amherst, doc date 1784, execution, debt, file #1955

HOPKINS Benjamin, husbandman, of Amherst, vs TWISS John, yeoman, of Amherst, rec date 1783, execution, debt, file #2994

HOPKINS Benjamin, gentleman, of Amherst, vs HAZELTINE Nathaniel, yeoman, of Amherst, rec date 1787, writ, debt, file #6663

HOPKINS Benjamin, yeoman, of Amherst, vs PETTINGILL William, yeoman, of Wilton, rec date 1786, writ, debt, file #6885

HOPKINS Benjamin, yeoman, of Amherst, vs PETTINGILL Samuel, yeoman, of Wilton, rec date 1786, writ, debt, file #6885

HOPKINS Benjamin Sr, yeoman, of Amherst, vs RICHARDSON Thomas, yeoman, of Lyndeborough, rec date 1786, writ, debt, file #6880

HOPKINS Hezekiah, yeoman, of Mason, vs CUMMINGS John, yeoman, of Mason, rec date 1788, summons, land dispute, file #6975

HOPKINS James, yeoman, of Francestown, vs GRIMES James, gentleman, of Deering, rec date 1782, execution, debt, file #3508

HOPKINS John, vs MILLIMORE Jean, of Londonderry, rec date 1794, recognizance, support of child, file #4150

HOPKINS Martha, widow, of Amherst, vs DUNKLE Joseph, yeoman, of Goffstown, rec date 1784, writ, debt, file #6855, husband Ebenezer (deceased)

HOPKINS Richard, yeoman, of Hollis, vs JEWET Jacob Jr, yeoman, of Hollis, doc date 1774, writ, debt, file #1086

HOPKINS Richard, yeoman, of Hollis, vs WRIGHT Joshua, esquire, of Hollis, doc date 1774, writ, debt, file #1102, fragile

HOPKINS Richard & Mary, husbandman, of Hollis, vs JAQUITH Ebenezer, yeoman, of Hollis, doc date 1774, rec date 1777, deed, land transfer, file #6553

HOPKINS Robert, yeoman, of Francestown, vs GIBSON James, yeoman, of Merrimack, rec date 1785, judgment, debt, file #5082

HOPKINSON Jonathan, husbandman, vs CUTLER Jonas & Ebenezer, yeoman, of Groton MA, doc date 1774, rec date 1775, judgment, debt, file #6963

HOPKNS Robert, yeoman, of Francestown, vs GIBSON Daniel, yeoman, of Hillsborough, rec date 1785, judgment, debt, file #5082

HOSELEY Samuel, physician, of Townsend MA, vs BARRETT Joseph, gentleman, of Mason, rec date 1785, judgment, debt, file #5056

HOSELEY Samuel, physician, of Townsend MA, vs BALL Joseph, gentleman, of Mason, rec date 1785, judgment, debt, file #5056

HOSELY Samuel, husbandman, of Pepperell MA, vs HOW Isaac, gentleman, of New Ipswich, rec date 1785, judgment, debt, file #5058

HOSMER Nathaniel, of Mason, vs HOBART William, of Townsend MA, doc date 1788, petition, release of debit, file #6

HOSMER Nathaniel, husbandman, of Mason, vs WHEELER David, gentleman, of Concord, doc date 1799, petition, debt, file #519

HOSMER Nathaniel, yeoman, of Mason, vs WILLSON Robert, gentleman, of Peterborough, doc date 1773, writ, debt, file #817

HOSMER Nathaniel, yeoman, of Mason, vs STEVENS Joseph, gentleman, of New Ipswich, doc date 1773, writ, debt, file #1447

HOSMER Nathaniel, yeoman, of Mason, vs CHAMPNEY Ebenezer, esquire, of Groton MA, rec date 1788, writ, debt, file #2547

HOSMER Nathaniel, yeoman, of Mason, vs BALL Joseph, gentleman, of Mason, rec date 1783, writ, debt, file #4538

HOSMER Nathaniel, yeoman, of Mason, vs CHRISTOPHER Oliver, yeoman, of Mason, doc date 1788, rec date 1788, deed, land transfer, file #6748

HOSMER Reuben, yeoman, of Mason, vs INHABITANTS of Mason, rec date 1785, judgment, debt, file #5065

HOUSTON James, blacksmith, of Bedford, vs POWERS Stephen, yeoman, of Mile Slip, doc date 1774, writ, debt, file #1136

HOUSTON James, blacksmith, of Bedford, vs MILLER Thomas, yeoman, of Hillsborough, rec date 1785, execution, debt, file #5904

HOUSTON Joseph, yeoman, of Bedford, vs PARKHURST John, yeoman, of Cardigan, doc date 1784, execution, debt, file #1751

HOUSTON Joseph, yeoman, of Bedford, vs PARKHURST John, yeoman, of Cardigan, doc date 1784, execution, debt, file #1550

HOUSTON Joseph, yeoman, of Bedford, vs PARKERHURST John, yeoman, of Cardigan, rec date 1783, civil litigious, debt, file #2913

HOUSTON Joseph, yeoman, of Bedford, vs PARKHURST John, yeoman, of Cardigan, rec date 1783, writ, debt, file #3391

HOUSTON Ovid, trader, of Dunstable MA, vs FARRAR Ebenezer, yeoman, of Alexandria, rec date 1785, judgment, debt, file #5573

HOUSTON Ovid, trader, of Dunstable MA, vs FARRAR Jonathan, gentleman, of Alexandria, rec date 1785, judgment, debt, file #5573

HOUSTON Samuel, yeoman, of Bedford, vs FULTON Robert, gentleman, of Francestown, rec date 1782, writ, debt, file #2823

HOW Benjamin, gentleman, of New Ipswich, vs TAGGART John, gentleman, of Peterborough Slip, rec date 1785, writ, debt, file #4682

HOW Ebenezer & William, yeoman, of Henniker, vs WILSON David, gentleman, of Deering, doc date 1799, writ, debt, file #416

HOW Eleakin & Jr, laborers, of Henniker, vs ANDREWS Molly, single woman, of Henniker, rec date 1785, various, assault, file #4747

HOW Eliakin (Capt), gentleman, of Henniker, vs HOW Ezekiel (Capt), gentleman, of Amherst, rec date 1784, judgment, debt, file #4231

HOW Ephraim, husbandman, of Hollis, vs RIDEOUT Nathaniel, husbandman, of Hollis, doc date 1784, execution, debt, file #1673

HOW Ephraim, husbandman, of Hollis, vs BALL Eleazer, husbandman, of Hollis, rec date 1783, writ, debt, file #3114

HOW Ephraim, husbandman, of Hollis, vs RIDEOUT Nathaniel, husbandman, of Hollis, rec date 1783, writ, debt, file #3410

HOW Ephraim, husbandman, of Hollis, vs ROSS Walter, husbandman, of Lyndeborough, rec date 1783, writ, debt, file #3361

HOW Ephraim, yeoman, of Hollis, vs RIDEOUT Nathaniel, of Hollis, rec date 1784, writ, debt, file #5381, fragile

HOW Ezra, husbandman, of Henniker, vs HOW Peter, husbandman, of Henniker, rec date 1783, writ, debt, file #3033

HOW Francis, yeoman, of Marlborough MA, vs WOODS John Waldo, yeoman, of Hartford CT, rec date 1786, confession, debt, file #2325

HOW Francis, yeoman, of Marlborough MA, vs RICE Daniel, yeoman, of Marlborough MA, rec date 1786, confession, debt, file #2321

HOW Francis, yeoman, of Marlborough MA, vs TEMPLE Jonas, yeoman, of Marlborough MA, rec date 1786, confession, debt, file #2321

HOW Isaac, yeoman, of Amherst, vs McCLUER William, yeoman, of Merrimack, doc date 1774, various, debt, file #1173

HOW Isaac, yeoman, of Amherst, vs STEARNS Daniel, yeoman, of Merrimack, doc date 1774, various, debt, file #1173

HOW Isaac, gentleman, of New Ipswich, vs TAGGART John, gentleman, of Peterborough Slip, doc date 1784, ejectment, land dispute, file #1600

HOW Isaac, gentleman, of New Ipswich, vs TAGGART John, gentleman, of Peterborough Slip, rec date 1785, writ, debt, file #4682

HOW Isaac, gentleman, of New Ipswich, vs MILLER Joseph, yeoman, of Peterborough Slip, rec date 1785, writ, debt, file #4682

HOW Jonathan, yeoman, of MA, vs DIX James, husbandman, of Framingham MA, rec date 1785, writ, debt, file #6157, part of Samuel CURTIS file

HOW Joseph, yeoman, of Hollis, vs HOW John, of Hollis, doc date 1778, rec date 1783, deed, land transfer, file #2637

HOW Nathan, husbandman, of Hillsborough, vs RICHARDSON Thomas, husbandman, of Billerica MA, doc date 1799, debt, file #345

HOW Otis, yeoman, of Hillsborough, vs ROBERTSON Elisha, trader, of Framingham MA, rec date 1783, execution, debt, file #3689

HOW Peter, husbandman, of Henniker, vs HOW Ezra, husbandman, of Henniker, doc date 1784, execution, debt, file #1555

HOW Peter, husbandman, of Henniker, vs HOWE Ezra, husbandman, of Henniker, rec date 1783, civil litigious, debt, file #2946

HOW Phebe, spinster, of Hollis, vs WRIGHT Lemuel, yeoman, of Hollis, doc date 1781, capias, assault, file #767

HOW Samuel, husbandman, of Henniker, vs McGREGOR David, esquire, of Londonderry, rec date 1786, various, trespass, file #6080A

HOW Samuel, husbandman, of Henniker, vs McGREGOR David, esquire, of Londonderry, rec date 1786, various, trespass, file #6080B

HOW Samuel, husbandman, of Henniker, vs McGREGOR David, esquire, of Londonderry, rec date 1786, various, trespass, file #6080

HOW Samuel, husbandman, of Henniker, vs McGREGOR David, esquire, of Londonderry, rec date 1786, various, trespass, file #6080B

HOW Theodore, husbandman, of Henniker, vs CLEMENTS John, physician, of Hopkinton, doc date 1773, writ, debt, file #1336

HOW William, yeoman, of Henniker, vs SHERMAN Miah, of Marlborough MA, doc date 1799, writ, debt, file #354

HOWARD Asa & Samuel, yeoman, of Temple, vs FARRAR Simon, gentleman, of Temple, doc date 1799, execution, debt, file #199

HOWARD Joseph, husbandman, of New Boston, vs BOSSEE Thomas, gentleman, of Medford MA, rec date 1786, writ, debt, file #6105

HOWARD Josiah (minor), laborer, of Nottingham, vs KILLY Richard, yeoman, of Weare, rec date 1785, writ, debt, file #4819

HOWARD Silas, husbandman, of Lyndeborough, vs CRAM Zebulon, husbandman, of Lyndeborough, doc date 1799, execution, debt, file #185

HOWARD William, husbandman, of Amherst, vs BOSSEE Thomas, gentleman, of Lyndeborough, doc date 1784, execution, debt, file #1935

HOWARD William, husbandman, of Amherst, vs BOFFE Thomas, gentleman, of Lyndeborough, rec date 1783, execution, debt, file #2984

HOWARD William, yeoman, of Amherst, vs WELLS John, yeoman, of New Boston, rec date 1783, judgment, debt, file #3721

HOWE John, husbandman, of Goffstown, vs DUTTON John, husbandman, of Amherst, rec date 1784, judgment, debt, file #4388

HOYT Enoch, husbandman, of Bradford, vs WILLOUGHBY Samuel, yeoman, of Hillsborough, doc date 1799, judgment, debt, file #229

HOYT John, carpenter, of Hillsborough, vs BEAN Nathaniel, husbandman, of Salisbury, doc date 1784, deed, land transfer, file #1992

HOYT Jonathan, gentleman, of Amesbury, vs SELECTMEN of Amherst, of Amherst, rec date 1783, petition, support, file #4061

HOYT Moses, cordwainer, of Henniker, vs NICHOLS Thomas, gentleman, of Antrim, rec date 1783, writ, debt, file #3071

HOYT Thomas, husbandman, of Dunbarton, vs FEUVEUR Samuel, husbandman, of Kingston, doc date 1792, petition, release from jail, file #43

HOYT Thomas, husbandman, of Dunbarton, vs KENNEY Matthew, husbandman, of Goffstown, doc date 1773, writ, debt, file #1443

HUBBARD David, husbandman, of Hancock, vs STATE of NH, rec date 1787, recognizance, counterfeiting, file #3556

HUBBARD Josiah & Lucy, yeoman, of Groton MA, vs ATWILL John, joiner, of Hollis, rec date 1786, judgment, debt, file #2302

HUBBARD Nathan, yeoman, of Groton MA, vs POLLARD Timothy, husbandman, of Nottingham-West, rec date 1788, writ, debt, file #6911

HUBBBARD Job, yeoman, of Mile Slip, vs BARNARD Jeremiah, clerk, of Amherst, doc date 1784, writ, debt, file #1594

HUDSON Elisah, yeoman, of Wilton, vs TALBORD Joshua, esquire, of Alexandria, doc date 1784, execution, debt, file #1891

HUDSON Elisha, yeoman, of Wilton, vs TOLFORD Joshua, esquire, of Alexandria, rec date 1783, writ, debt, file #3588

HUDSON Elisha, yeoman, of Wilton, vs PUTNAM Philip, gentleman, of Wilton, rec date 1785, deed, land transfer, file #5639

HUES Richard, cordwainer, of Francestown, vs TODD John, husbandman, of Temple, rec date 1784, judgment, debt, file #4588

HUEY John, yeoman, of Nottingham-West, vs KELLEY Joseph, gentleman, of Nottingham-West, rec date 1783, judgment, debt, file #3750

HUIS Richard, cordwainer, of Francestown, vs TODD John, husbandman, of Temple, rec date 1785, judgment, debt, file #5399

HULL Darius, husbandman, of Croydon, vs CHAFFIN John, husbandman, of Goffstown, doc date 1799, debt, file #503

HULL John, cordwainer, of Mason, vs WHITING Jonas, cordwainer, of Hillsborough, doc date 1784, writ, debt, file #1621

HUMBPREY Ebenezer, gentleman, of New Ipswich, vs JOHNSTON Rachel, single woman, of Lyndeborough, doc date 1773, writ, debt, file #1182

HUNT Elizabeth, widow, of Hollis, vs LONG Samuel, husbandman, of Hollis, rec date 1783, writ, debt, file #3919, widow of Josiah hunt

HUNT Josiah, yeoman, of Hollis, vs TURNER Benjamin, cooper, of Hollis, doc date 1772, writ, debt, file #922

HUNT William, yeoman, of Hancock, vs MARGERY Jona, yeoman, of Hancock, doc date 1799, execution, debt, file #98

HUNT William & Hannah, gentleman, of Dunstable, vs CUMINGS Simeon, gentleman, of Dunstable MA, rec date 1785, judgment, debt, file #5567

HUNT William & Hannah, gentleman, of Dunstable, vs DICKEY Robert, yeoman, of Londonderry, rec date 1785, judgment, debt, file #5567

HUNT William & Hannah, gentleman, of Dunstable, vs ANDREWS Asa, yeoman, of Londonderry, rec date 1785, judgment, debt, file #5567

HUNT William Deacon, of Dunstable, doc date 1786, license, tavern license, file #860

HUNTER John, husbandman, of Londonderry, vs McCLINTOCK John, gentleman, of Hillsborough, rec date 1783, judgment, debt, file #3752

HUNTINGTON Elijah, husbandman, of Amesbury MA, vs HUNTINGTON John, husbandman, of Weare, rec date 1788, writ, debt, file #6681

HURD Isaac, physician, of Billerica MA, vs DIX Nathan, gentleman, of Peterborough, rec date 1785, judgment, debt, file #5537

HURD Isaac, physician, of Billerica MA, vs DIX Nathan, gentleman, of Peterborough, rec date 1785, writ, debt, file #6151

HUSE Enoch, husbandman, of Weare, vs WILSON James, husbandman, of Londonderry, doc date 1797, various, debt, file #546

HUSE Isaac, yeoman, of Deerfield, vs WOOD Jonathan, husbandman, of Goffstown, rec date 1783, judgment, debt, file #3751

HUSE Joseph, husbandman, of Hillsborough, vs WILSON James, husbandman, of Londonderry, doc date 1799, judgment, debt, file #535

HUSE Moses, husbandman, of Henniker, vs ROBERTS Thomas, physician, of Meredith, doc date 1799, debt, file #501

HUSE Thomas, yeoman, of Dunbarton, vs HAMMOND Thomas, blockmaker, of Hopkinton, doc date 1778, rec date 1779, deed, land transfer, file #2129

HUSTON Caleb, yeoman, of Lyndeborough, vs HOLMES Jabez Jr, yeoman, of Francestown, doc date 1807, rec date 1826, deed, land transfer, file #5710

HUTCHINGS Joshiah, cordwainer, of New Boston, vs BALDWIN Nahum, esquire, of Amherst, rec date 1782, appeal, debt, file #3988

HUTCHINS Charles, husbandman, of Keene, vs DODGE John Perkins, yeoman, of Mason, rec date 1783, execution, debt, file #2883

HUTCHINS Charles, husbandman, of Keene, vs DODGE John Perkins, yeoman, of Mason, rec date 1783, judgment, debt, file #2862

HUTCHINS Ebenezer, yeoman, of Merrimack, vs VARNUM Bradley, yeoman, of Dracut MA, rec date 1783, writ, debt, file #3204

HUTCHINS John, yeoman, of Weare, vs DRURY Benjamin, physician, of Spencer MA, rec date 1783, writ, debt, file #3160

HUTCHINS Josiah, cordwainer, of New Boston, vs JONES Nathan, husbandman, of Amherst, rec date 1782, appeal, debt, file #3981

HUTCHINS Nathaniel, of Dunbarton, vs ORDWAY James, of Goffstown, doc date 1775, deed, land transfer, file #837

HUTCHINS Phinehas, gentleman, of Lunenburg MA, vs PRATT Thomas, hatter, of Hollis, doc date 1773, judgment, debt, file #1289

HUTCHINS Phinehas, gentleman, of Walpole, vs GEARFIELD Nathaniel, husbandman, of Merrimack, rec date 1784, writ, debt, file #4619

HUTCHINS Samuel, yeoman, of Temple, vs KIDDER Joseph, gentleman, of Temple, doc date 1774, execution, file #990

HUTCHINS Samuel, yeoman, of Lyndeborough, vs KELLEY Moses, esquire, of Goffstown, rec date 1783, writ, debt, file #3185

HUTCHINS Solomon, yeoman, of Merrimack, vs VARNUM Bradley, yeoman, of Dracut MA, rec date 1783, writ, debt, file #3204

HUTCHINS William, gentleman, of New London, vs SWEAT Enoch, husbandman, of Cardigan, rec date 1783, judgment, debt, file #3703

HUTCHINSON Cyrus, gentleman, of Hillsborough, vs DICKEY Joseph & Gilman, gentleman, of Hillsborough, doc date 1793, rec date 1826, deed, land transfer, file #6581

HUTCHINSON Daniel, husbandman, of Merrimack, vs McGAW Jacob, of Merrimack, doc date 1799, judgment, debt, file #311

HUTCHINSON Daniel, husbandman, of Merrimack, vs TAYLOR Timothy, esquire, of Merrimack, doc date 1799, judgment, debt, file #264

HUTCHINSON Daniel, yeoman, of Merrimack, vs HOW Mark, yeoman, of Merrimack, doc date 1800, writ, debt, file #574

HUTCHINSON Ebenezer, yeoman, of Amherst, vs WHIDDEN John, yeoman, of Merrimack, rec date 1782, writ, debt, file #2821

HUTCHINSON George, husbandman, of Wilton, vs JONES William, husbandman, of Hillsborough, rec date 1787, writ, debt, file #2368

HUTCHINSON George, yeoman, of Lyndeborough, vs BUTTERFIELD Jonathan, yeoman, of Dunstable, rec date 1785, writ, debt, file #6860

HUTCHINSON James, yeoman, of Amherst, vs GREEN David, yeoman, of Amherst, doc date 1773, judgment, debt, file #1300

HUTCHINSON James, yeoman, of Amherst, vs CLAGETT Wyseman, esquire, of Hillsborough, doc date 1773, various, debt, file #829

HUTCHINSON James, yeoman, of Amherst, vs GIBSON John, yeoman, of Hillsborough, doc date 1773, various, debt, file #829

HUTCHINSON Jonathan, yeoman, of Gilmington, vs WENTWORTH Rebecca, widow`, of Merrimack, rec date 1783, writ, debt, file #2764

HUTCHINSON Nathaniel, husbandman, of Dunbarton, vs HOGG David, of Dunbarton, doc date 1773, writ, debt, file #1338

HUTCHINSON Nathaniel, cordwainer, of Pepperell MA, vs SPAULDING William, yeoman, of Raby, rec date 1782, execution, debt, file #5746

HUTCHINSON Nehemiah, yeoman, of Lyndeborough, vs BALDWIN Nahum, esquire, of Amherst, rec date 1783, writ, debt, file #3007

HUTCHINSON Samuel, husbandman, of Lyndeborough, vs PEARSON Amos, husbandman, of Lyndeborough, rec date 1784, appeal, debt, file #4135

HUTCHINSON Solomon, husbandman, of Merrimack, vs BIXBY Daniel, of Litchfield, doc date 1799, judgment, debt, file #312

HUTCHINSON Solomon, yeoman, of Merrimack, vs BLANCHARD Joshua, merchant, of Boston MA, doc date 1772, writ, debt, file #921

HUTCHINSON Solomon, yeoman, of Merrimack, vs SPRAGUE John, esquire, of Lancaster MA, doc date 1774, writ, debt, file #1083

HUTCHINSON Solomon, yeoman, of Merrimack, vs ATHERTON John, esquire, of Amherst, doc date 1799, writ, debt, file #366

HUTCHINSON Solomon, yeoman, of Merrimack, vs SMITH John, husbandman, of Lunenburg MA, doc date 1773, writ, debt, file #1343

HUTCHINSON Solomon, yeoman, of Merrimack, vs GORDON James, merchant, of Dunstable MA, rec date 1782, writ, debt, file #2785

HUTCHINSON Solomon, yeoman, of Merrimack, vs DODGE Samuel, yeoman, of Amherst, rec date 1783, execution, debt, file #2995

HUTCHINSON Solomon, husbandman, of Merrimack, vs DODGE Samuel, husbandman, of Amherst, rec date 1785, various, debt, file #6639

HUTCHINSON Solomon Jr, husbandman, of Merrimack, vs HASSELL Jason, husbandman, of Merrimack, rec date 1786, writ, debt, file #6301

HYSLOP William, of Brookline MA, vs STEPHEN Holland, esquire, doc date 1771, judgment, power of attorney, file #569

IMBALL Thomas, yeoman, of Wenham MA, vs FARSON James & Samuel, yeoman, of Francestown, rec date 1785, writ, debt, file #4821

INGALLS Israel, clothier, of Dunstable, vs PIKE Daniel, innkeeper, of Dunstable, rec date 1784, judgment, debt, file #4394

INGALS Israel, gentleman, of Dunstable, vs BARR James, yeoman, of New Ipswich, rec date 1782, writ, debt, file #2790

J Hillard (sic), yeoman, vs HITCHINS Josiah, yeoman, of New Boston, rec date 1778, deed, land transfer, file #2116

JACK Andrew, blacksmith, of New Boston, vs BALDIWN Nathaniel, esquire, of Amherst, rec date 1782, various, debt, file #2672, estate of Zacheus CUTLER

JACKMAN Benjamin, gentleman, of Boscawen, vs CALL Silas, gentleman, of Boscawen, rec date 1788, various, gun dispute, file #6683

JACKMAN Benjamin, gentleman, of Boscawen, vs CALL Silas & David, gentleman, of Boscawen, rec date 1788, writ, debt, file #6682

JACKSON George, esquire, of Boscawen, vs BOHANAN Andrew, gentleman, of Salisbury, doc date 1798, execution, debt, file #112

JACKSON Samuel, yeoman, of MA, vs SHURTEFF Simeon, gentleman, of Dunstable, rec date 1788, writ, debt, file #6978

JACOBS John, yeoman, of Merrimack, vs DARNELEY James, labourer, doc date 1774, judgment, debt, file #719, escape from jail

JAFFREY George, esquire, of Portsmouth, vs HALL John, gentleman, of Deerfield, doc date 1784, civil litigation, debt, file #1654

JAFFREY George, esquire, of Portsmouth, vs HALL John, gentleman, of Derryfield, rec date 1783, writ, debt, file #4051

JAMESON Albert M, vs CARPENTER William H, doc date 1894, assumpsit, supreme court, file #595

JAMESON Hugh, cordwainer, of Dunbarton, vs STINSON William, gentleman, of Dunbarton, rec date 1782, debt, debt, file #3146

JAMESON Hugh Jr, laborer, of Dunbarton, vs McLAUGHLIN Thomas, gentleman, of Bedford, doc date 1784, execution, debt, file #1947

JAMESON Hugh Jr, laborer, of Dunbarton, vs VOSE Samuel, gentleman, of Bedford, doc date 1784, execution, debt, file #1947

JAMESON Hugh Jr (minor), laborer, of Dunbarton, vs McLAUGHLIN Thomas, gentleman, of Bedford, rec date 1783, civil litigious, debt, file #2948

JAMESON Hugh Jr (minor), laborer, of Dunbarton, vs VOSE Samuel Thomas, husbandman, of Bedford, rec date 1783, civil litigious, debt, file #2948

JAQUES (JAQUITH) Parker, husbandman, of Newbury MA, vs CHASE Benjamin, husbandman, of Sandown, rec date 1783, writ, debt, file #4636, agent for Moody SMITH

JAQUETH John, husbandman, of Ashby MA, vs TUCKER Moses, yeoman, of New Ipswich, doc date 1773, judgment, debt, file #1322

JAQUITH Benjamin, yeoman, of Jaffrey, vs KITTREDGE Nehemiah, gentleman, of Billerica MA, rec date 1783, writ, debt, file #3022

JAQUITH Ebenezer, miller, of Hollis, vs BLOOD Robert Jr, yeoman, of Monadnock #7, doc date 1774, judgment, debt, file #716

JARVIS Leonard, merchant, of Dartmouth, vs BEDEL Timothy, esquire, of Bath, doc date 1774, writ, debt, file #743

JEFFRIES David, merchant, of Boston MA, vs MOOR James, husbandman, of Goffstown, rec date 1783, execution, debt, file #2867

JEFFRIES David, merchant, of Boston MA, vs MOOR James, husbandman, of Goffstown, rec date 1782, judgment, debt, file #3136

JEFTS Thomas, yeoman, of Mason, vs TARBELL Samuel, husbandman, of Mason, doc date 1772, writ, debt, file #916

JENNINS Eliphalet, yeoman, of Dunstable, vs GORDON Cosmo, schoolmaster, of Goffstown, rec date 1788, writ, debt, file #6924

JEWEL James, yeoman, of Dunstable, vs BOYES William, of New Boston, rec date 1783, judgment, debt, file #3741

JEWELL Benoni, yeoman, of Dunstable, vs KELLEY Joseph, gentleman, of Nottingham-West, rec date 1778, writ, trespass, file #2234

JEWELL Jacob F, vs McQUESTEN Hannah C, doc date 1894, petition for partition, supreme court, file #612

JEWELL Jacob Jr, trader, of Hollis, vs HARRIS Robert, trader, of Concord, rec date 1783, writ, debt, file #3179

JEWELL James, yeoman, of Dunstable, vs BOYES William, esquire, of New Boston, rec date 1782, writ, debt, file #2822

JEWELL Nathan, yeoman, of Dunstable, vs GORDON William, merchant, of Dunstable MA, doc date 1774, writ, debt, file #120, fragile

JEWELL Thomas, yeoman, of Amherst, vs GRIMES James, gentleman, of Deering, rec date 1785, writ, debt, file #2346

JEWET Caleb, yeoman, of Pepperell MA, vs BATCHELDER Archibald, gentleman, of Milford, doc date 1800, judgment, debt, file #568

JEWET Jacob Jr, yeoman, of Hollis, vs DARBY Tarbox, yeoman, of Hollis, doc date 1774, writ, debt, file #1082

JEWET Jacob Jr, yeoman, of Hollis, vs WRIGHT Samuel Jr, yeoman, of Hollis, doc date 1774, writ, debt, file #1082

JEWET Jacob Jr, trader, of Hollis, vs WHEELER Lebius, yeoman, of Hollis, doc date 1774, execution, debt, file #1209

JEWET Jacob Jr, trader, of Hollis, vs TAYLOR James, gentleman, of Merrimack, doc date 1773, judgment, debt, file #1299

JEWET Jacob Jr, trader, of Hollis, vs FISK James, yeoman, of Hollis, doc date 1773, execution, debt, file #1217

JEWET Jacob Jr, trader, of Hollis, vs CARTA Edward, husbandman, of Hollis, doc date 1773, execution, debt, file #1221

JEWET Jacob Jr, husbandman, of Hollis, vs POLLARD Timothy, husbandman, of Nottingham-West, rec date 1783, execution, debt, file #3862

JEWET Jacob Jr, yeoman, of Hollis, vs DANA Samuel, gentleman, of Amherst, rec date 1783, writ, debt, file #4927

JEWET Jedidiah, yeoman, of New London, vs HUNTOON Nathaniel, gentleman, of Unity, rec date 1782, writ, debt, file #2591

JEWET John, tanner, of Hollis, vs PIKE Joseph, yeoman, of Brookline, doc date 1797, judgment, debt, file #568

JEWETT Ezekiel, yeoman, of Temple, vs FOSTER Jacoby, yeoman, of Temple, doc date 1775, deed, land transfer, file #840

JEWETT Ezra, gentleman, of Hopkinton, vs PIERCE Daniel, yeoman, of Warner, doc date 1797, execution, debt, file #202

JEWETT Ezra, gentleman, of Hopkinton, vs PIERCE Daniel, yeoman, of Warner, doc date 1798, judgment, debt, file #564

JEWETT Jacob, husbandman, of Hollis, vs STEARNS Samuel, husbandman, of Plymouth, rec date 1785, writ, debt, file #5076

JEWETT Jacob, husbandman, of Rowley MA, vs WALLINGSFORD David, gentleman, of Hollis, rec date 1785, execution, debt, file #5911

JEWETT Jacob, husbandman, of Rowley MA, vs WALLINGFORD David, gentleman, of Hollis, rec date 1785, writ, debt, file #6036

JEWETT Jacob, yeoman, of Rowley MA, vs SMITH Thomas, husbandman, of Westford MA, doc date 1771, rec date 1777, deed, land transfer, file #6546

JEWETT Jacob Jr, of Hollis, vs STEVENS Samuel, of Plymouth, doc date 1786, petition, release of debit, file #7

JEWETT Jacob Jr, yeoman, of Hollis, vs WILKINS Bray, yeoman, of Hollis, doc date 1774, judgment, debt, file #738

JEWETT Jacob Jr, trader, of Hollis, vs KILLICUT Reuben, yeoman, of Dunstable, doc date 1774, judgment, debt, file #710

JEWETT Jacob Jr, yeoman, of Hollis, vs STEVENS Isaac, yeoman, of Hollis, doc date 1774, judgment, debt, file #739

JEWETT Jacob Jr, yeoman, of Hollis, vs WILKINS Bray, yeoman, of Hollis, doc date 1774, writ, debt, file #1084

JEWETT Jacob Jr, shopkeeper, of Hollis, vs FARMER Benjamin, cooper, of Hollis, doc date 1773, execution, debt, file #1472

JEWETT Jacob Jr, shopkeeper, of Hollis, vs ADAMS Stephen, husbandman, of Hollis, doc date 1773, execution, debt, file #1472

JEWETT Jacob Jr, trader, of Hollis, vs FARLEY Ebenezer, husbandman, of Hollis, doc date 1773, judgment, debt, file #1290

JEWETT Jacob Jr, husbandman, of Hollis, vs POLLARD Timothy, husbandman, of Nottingham-West, doc date 1784, execution, debt, file #1544

JEWETT Jacob Jr, husbandman, of Hollis, vs STEARNS Samuel, husbandman, of Plymouth, rec date 1784, various, court case, file #4523, kinship Joseph STEARNS

JEWETT Jacob Jr, husbandman, of Hollis, vs STEARNS Samuel, husbandman, of Plymouth, rec date 1784, various, court case, file #4524, deposition kinships WOOSTER

JEWETT Jacob Jr, husbandman, of Hollis, vs BALDWIN Nahum, esquire, of Amherst, rec date 1788, writ, debt, file #6802

JEWETT James, yeoman, of Hollis, vs CALDWELL John, yeoman, of Nottingham-West, doc date 1774, judgment, debt, file #708

JEWETT James, yeoman, of Hollis, vs CALDWELL John, yeoman, of Nottingham, doc date 1774, writ, debt, file #1120

JEWETT John, husbandman, of Bath, vs ATKINSON Samuel, gentleman, of Boscawen, doc date 1784, writ, debt, file #1570

JOHNSON Adam, gentleman, of Lyndeborough, vs KELLEY Moses, esquire, of Goffstown, rec date 1783, writ, debt, file #3185

JOHNSON David, husbandman, of Pelham, vs HEYWOOD Samuel Smith, husbandman, of Nottingham, doc date 1784, execution, debt, file #1806

JOHNSON David, husbandman, of Pelham, vs HEDGEWOOD Samuel Smith, yeoman, of Nottingham-West, doc date 1784, execution, debt, file #1504

JOHNSON David, yeoman, of Pelham, vs RUSSELL James, gentleman, of Litchfield, rec date 1783, execution, debt, file #3695

JOHNSON David, husbandman, of Pelham, vs HAYWOOD Samuel Smith, yeoman, of Nottingham-West, rec date 1783, judgment, debt, file #4722

JOHNSON John, yeoman, of Dunstable MA, vs CLISBEE Ezekiel, yeoman, of Marlborough, doc date 1773, rec date 1773, deed, land transfer, file #6550

JOHNSON John, yeoman, of Dunstable MA, vs BARNARD Joel, yeoman, of Marlborough, doc date 1773, rec date 1773, deed, land transfer, file #6550

JOHNSON Jonathan, feltmaker, of Hollis, vs BLOOD Samuel, feltmaker, of Littleton MA, doc date 1772, writ, debt, file #919

JOHNSON Moses, of Nottingham-West, vs DURANT Samuel, blacksmith, of Nottingham-West, doc date 1778, rec date 1787, deed, land transfer, file #2498

JOHNSON Moses, husbandman, of Peterborough, vs DAVIDSON Thomas, yeoman, of Peterborough, rec date 1783, writ, debt, file #3334

JOHNSON Moses, husbandman, of Peterborough, vs CARLTON Henry, husbandman, of Cumberland NY, rec date 1783, writ, debt, file #3946

JOHNSON Moses Jr, yeoman, of Dedham MA, vs UNDERWOOD Isaac, husbandman, of Dedham MA, doc date 1784, deed, land transfer, file #2017, land in Peterborough

JOHNSON Nathaniel, merchant, of Boston MA, vs COBURN Jacob, trader, of Litchfield, doc date 1798, judgment, debt, file #564

JOHNSON William, gentleman, of Hillsborough, vs MURDOUGH Samuel, husbandman, of Hillsborough, doc date 1798, petition, release of debit, file #28

JOHNSON William, husbandman, of Hillsborough, vs GORING Asahel, yeoman, of Peterborough, doc date 1799, judgment, debt, file #233

JOHNSON William, yeoman, of Pelham, vs DICKEY James, gentleman, of Raby, rec date 1784, judgment, debt, file #5286

JOHNSON William, yeoman, of Pelham, vs DICKEY James, gentleman, of Raby, rec date 1785, judgment, debt, file #5116

JOHNSON William Pierce, merchant, of Newburyport MA, vs SANDERS Joseph, husbandman, of Derryfield, rec date 1784, judgment, debt, file #5455

JOHNSON Wm Pierce, merchant, of Newburyport MA, vs SANDERS Joseph, husbandman, of Derryfield, rec date 1786, judgment, debt, file #6390

JONES Benjamin, husbandman, of Hillsborough, vs JONES James, husbandman, of Windsor, doc date 1807, rec date 1807, deed, land transfer, file #5688

JONES Caleb, yeoman, of Mile Slip, vs PARKER Susannah, spinster, of Wilton, doc date 1784, writ, debt, file #1597

JONES Caleb, husbandman, of Amherst, vs EWINS James, yeoman, of Londonderry, rec date 1783, writ, debt, file #3397, estate of James EWINS

JONES Caleb, husbandman, of Amherst, vs McMURPHY Robert, gentleman, of Londonderry, rec date 1783, writ, debt, file #3397, estate of James EWINS

JONES Elnathan, of Concord MA, vs ALLEN Abijah, yeoman, of Mason, rec date 1786, writ, debt, file #6135

JONES Ephraim, traders, of Watertown MA, vs PORTER Francis, trader, of Peterborough, rec date 1786, writ, debt, file #6361

JONES James, yeoman, of Hillsborough, vs DANG Samuel, esquire, of Amherst, doc date 1784, execution, debt, file #1528

JONES James, yeoman, of Hillsborough, vs DODGE Samuel, yeoman, of Amherst, rec date 1782, writ, debt, file #2820

JONES James, yeoman, of Hillsborough, vs STEEL Moses, yeoman, of Hillsborough, rec date 1782, writ, debt, file #2829

JONES James, yeoman, of Hillsborough, vs PERKINS David, yeoman, of Campbells Gore, rec date 1783, writ, debt, file #3052

JONES James, husbandman, of Hillsborough, vs ANDREWS Ammi, gentleman, of Hillsborough, rec date 1783, writ, debt, file #3205

JONES James, yeoman, of Hillsborough, vs ABBOTT Josiah, yeoman, of New Boston, rec date 1783, writ, debt, file #3200

JONES James, yeoman, of Hillsborough, vs TAGGART Archibald, gentleman, of Hillsborough, rec date 1785, execution, debt, file #5956

JONES James, yeoman, of Hillsborough, vs TAGGART Archibald, gentleman, of Hillsborough, rec date 1785, judgment, debt, file #5871

JONES James, husbandman, of Hillsborough, vs BOYLES John, husbandman, of Deering, rec date 1785, execution, debt, file #5920

JONES James, husbandman, of Hillsborough, vs BAYLES John, husbandman, of Deering, rec date 1785, writ, debt, file #6020

JONES James, yeoman, of Hillsborough, vs DRESSER Asa, yeoman, of Campbells Gore, rec date 1785, writ, debt, file #6344

JONES James & William, husbandman, of Hillsborough, vs KELLEY Moses, esquire, of Goffstown, rec date 1784, various, debt, file #4371

JONES James & William, husbandman, of Hillsborough, vs KELLEY Moses, esquire, of Goffstown, rec date 1784, judgment, debt, file #4243

JONES John C, of Norton MA, vs WHITE John Jr, merchant, of Haverhill MA, rec date 1788, writ, debt, file #6737

JONES Joshua, yeoman, of Wilmington MA, vs JONES Samuel, yeoman, of Hillsborough, rec date 1783, writ, debt, file #3924

JONES Nathan, husbandman, of Amherst, vs FLINT Amos, husbandman, of Amherst, doc date 1773, civil litigation, debt, file #1377

JONES Nathan, husbandman, of Amherst, vs FLINT Amos, husbandman, of Amherst, doc date 1773, civil litigation, debt, file #1376

JONES Nathan, husbandman, of Amherst, vs WRIGHT Lemuel, yeoman, of Hollis, doc date 1784, execution, debt, file #1820

JONES Nathan, husbandman, of Amherst, vs FRENCH Ephraim, yeoman, of Amherst, doc date 1784, execution, debt, file #1809

JONES Nathan, husbandman, of Amherst, vs WARNER Daniel, gentleman, of Amherst, doc date 1784, civil litigation, debt, file #1843

JONES Nathan, husbandman, of Amherst, vs FLINT Amos, husbandman, of Amherst, rec date 1782, appeal, molasses dispute, file #2690, other family kinships

JONES Nathan, husbandman, of Amherst, vs WARNER Daniel, gentleman, of Amherst, rec date 1783, judgment, debt, file #4436

JONES Nathan, husbandman, of Amherst, vs NICHOLS Aaron, yeoman, of Amherst, rec date 1785, judgment, debt, file #5084

JONES Nathan, yeoman, of Antrim, vs LOWELL Steven Jr, yeoman, of Dunstable, rec date 1782, execution, debt, file #5726

JONES Nathan, husbandman, of Amherst, vs FORD James, gentleman, of Nottingham-West, rec date 1786, execution, debt, file #6059

JONES Nathan Jr, husbandman, of Amherst, vs FORBUSH Charles, gentleman, of Andover MA, rec date 1782, writ, debt, file #2694

JONES Nathan Jr, husbandman, of Amherst, vs FURBUSH Charles, gentleman, of Andover MA, rec date 1783, execution, debt, file #3240

JONES Nathaniel Jr, innholder, of Amherst, vs ROLLINGS Joseph, cooper, of Amherst, rec date 1788, writ, debt, file #6996

JONES Nehemiah, trader, of Hillsborough, vs DWINNELL Jonathan, husbandman, of Hillsborough, doc date 1798, execution, debt, file #62

JONES Nehemiah, husbandman, of Windsor, vs CARR Nathan, husbandman, of Hillsborough, doc date 1818, rec date 1818, deed, land transfer, file #5705

JONES Nathan, husbandman, of Amherst, vs HITCHINS Josiah, cordwainer, of New Boston, rec date 1782, judgment, debt, file #3130

JONES Philip, yeoman, of Goffstown, vs KARR James, yeoman, of Goffstown, doc date 1784, execution, debt, file #1693

JONES Philip, yeoman, of Goffstown, vs KARR James, gentleman, of Goffstown, doc date 1784, execution, debt, file #1810

JONES Philip, yeoman, of Goffstown, vs KARRY James, gentleman, of Goffstown, rec date 1783, judgment, debt, file #4089

JONES Phineas, innholder, of Amherst, vs SWEET David, gentleman, of Amherst, doc date 1799, writ, debt, file #390

JONES Phineas, yeoman, of Amherst, vs FRENCH Thomas, gentleman, of Dunstable, doc date 1799, writ, debt, file #367

JONES Phineas, husbandman, of Amherst, vs DODGE Joseph, husbandman, of Newport, doc date 1799, writ, debt, file #395

JONES Phineas, cordwainer, of Amherst, vs MINCHIN John, trader, of Boston MA, doc date 1799, writ, debt, file #564

JONES Phineas, cordwainer, of Amherst, vs MINICHIN John, trader, of Boston MA, doc date 1799, writ, debt, file #575

JONES Phineas, cordwainer, of Amherst, vs FARRAR Caleb, minor, of New Ipswich, doc date 1799, execution, debt, file #184

JONES Phineas, innholder, of Amherst, vs HUMPHREY Charles, esquire, of Amherst, doc date 1799, writ, debt, file #399

JONES Phinehas, cordwainer, of Amherst, vs MEANS Robert, esquire, of Amherst, doc date 1799, execution, debt, file #183

JONES Phinehas, cordwainer, of Amherst, vs COSTELOE John, trader, of Berwick Me, rec date 1782, execution, debt, file #3487

JONES Samuel, yeoman, of Hillsborough, vs SPOFFORD John, innkeeper, of Amherst, doc date 1784, petition, release of debit, file #14, papers very fragile & torn

JONES Samuel, vs TAGGART Archibald, gentleman, of Hillsborough, doc date 1782, judgment, debt, file #770

JONES Samuel, yeoman, of Hillsborough, doc date 1780, capias, recognizance, file #763

JONES Samuel, husbandman, of Hillsborough, vs NEWALL Asa, yeoman, of Lynn MA, doc date 1778, rec date 1778, deed, land transfer, file #2159

JONES Samuel, yeoman, of Hillsborough, vs BIREBA Andrew, yeoman, of Hillsborough, doc date 1783, rec date 1783, deed, land transfer, file #2630

JONES Samuel, yeoman, of Hillsborough, vs BIXBE Andrew, yeoman, of Hillsborough, rec date 1783, various, debt, file #3124

JONES Samuel, yeoman, of Hillsborough, vs ATHERTON Joshua, esquire, of Amherst, rec date 1783, writ, debt, file #3008

JONES Samuel, gentleman, of Concord MA, vs BROWN Peter, husbandman, of Temple, rec date 1784, judgment, debt, file #4330

JONES Timothy, of Amherst, vs STEARNS Samuel, of Amherst, doc date 1782, judgment, referee's report, file #1660

JONES Timothy, yeoman, of Amherst, vs BORDEN John, yeoman, of Deering, doc date 1784, execution, debt, file #1881

JONES Timothy, yeoman, of Amherst, vs NEWMAN Ebenezer, husbandman, of Deering, doc date 1784, execution, debt, file #1896

JONES Timothy, yeoman, of Amherst, vs STEARNS Samuel Jr, yeoman, of Amherst, rec date 1783, court case, debt, file #2878

JONES Timothy, yeoman, of Amherst, vs ATHERTON Joshua, esquire, of Amherst, rec date 1783, writ, debt, file #3081

JONES Timothy, husbandman, of Amherst, vs JONES Jonathan, husbandman, of Westford MA, rec date 1783, writ, debt, file #3121

JONES Timothy, yeoman, of Amherst, vs STEARNS Samuel, yeoman, of Amherst, rec date 1783, execution, debt, file #2896

JONES Timothy, yeoman, of Amherst, vs EVERDEN John, yeoman, of Deering, rec date 1783, writ, debt, file #3589

JONES Timothy, yeoman, of Amherst, vs NEWMAN Ebenezer, husbandman, of Deering, rec date 1783, writ, debt, file #3576

JONES Timothy, yeoman, of Amherst, vs WILKINS Benjamin, yeoman, of Amherst, rec date 1783, judgment, debt, file #3790

JONES Timothy, yeoman, of Amherst, vs WILKINS Benjamin Jr, yeoman, of Amherst, rec date 1783, judgment, debt, file #3792

JONES Timothy, yeoman, of Lyndeborough, vs WILKINS Andrew, yeoman, of Amherst, rec date 1784, appeal, debt, file #4142

JONES Timothy, yeoman, of Lyndeborough, vs DODGE Samuel, husbandman, of Amherst, rec date 1784, various, taken of oxen, file #4170

JONES Timothy, yeoman, of Lyndeborough, vs WILKINS Andrew, yeoman, of Amherst, rec date 1784, judgment, debt, file #4277

JONES Timothy, yeoman, of Lyndeborough, vs WILEY John, yeoman, of Amherst, rec date 1783, judgment, debt, file #4472

JONES Timothy, yeoman, of Lyndeborough, vs DODGE Samuel, husbandman, of Amherst, rec date 1783, judgment, debt, file #4481

JONES Timothy, yeoman, of Lyndeborough, vs FORD James, esquire, of Nottingham-West, rec date 1785, judgment, debt, file #5118

JONES Timothy, yeoman, of Lyndeborough, vs FORD James, esquire, of Nottingham-West, rec date 1784, judgment, debt, file #5287

JONES Timothy, yeoman, of Lyndeborough, vs WYLEY John, yeoman, of Amherst, rec date 1785, judgment, debt, file #6492

JONES Timothy, yeoman, of Lyndeborough, vs FOROUGH Charles, gentleman, of Andover MA, rec date 1784, writ, land dispute, file #6964

JONES Timothy & Rebeccah, gentleman, of Bedford MA, vs REED Josiah, yeoman, of Lexington MA, rec date 1788, deed, land transfer, file #6820, land in New Ipswich

JONES William, husbandman, of Amherst, vs CODMAN Henry, trader, of Amherst, doc date 1772, writ, debt, file #1420

JONES William, yeoman, of Hillsborough, vs BALDWIN Nathaniel, esquire, of Amherst, rec date 1783, various, debt, file #2769, trustee of Zachery CUTLER

JONES William, of Amherst, vs Town of Amherst, rec date 1775, grant request, file #3537

JONES William, husbandman, of Hillsborough, vs LOWELL John, esquire, of Boston MA, rec date 1783, writ, debt, file #3968

JONES William, of Amherst, rec date 1785, committee report, land claim, file #4765

JONES William, husbandman, of Hillsborough, vs DANA William, gentleman, of Hollis, rec date 1787, writ, force & assault, file #6893

JONES William, husbandman, of Hillsborough, vs DANA Samuel, esquire, of Hollis, rec date 1787, writ, force & assault, file #6893

JONES William, husbandman, of Hillsborough, vs FLETCHER Robert, gentleman, of Hollis, rec date 1787, writ, force & assault, file #6893

JONES William Jr, yeoman, of Hillsborough, vs RICHARDSON Zachariah, innkeeper, of Francestown, rec date 1782, writ, debt, file #2668

JONES William Jr, yeoman, of Hillsborough, vs DODGE Samuel, yeoman, of Amherst, rec date 1782, writ, debt, file #2687

JONES William Jr, husbandman, of Hillsborough, vs KELLEY Moses, esquire, of Hollis, rec date 1784, judgment, debt, file #4390

JONES William Jr, husbandman, of Hillsborough, vs SHANNON Richard Cutts, esquire, of Hollis, rec date 1784, judgment, debt, file #4354

JORDAN John, yeoman, of New Boston, vs BALDWIN Nahum, gentleman, of Amherst, doc date 1774, writ, debt, file #2105

JOSLYN Nathan, husbandman, of Henniker, vs BRADFORD Samuel 3rd, yeoman, of Hillsborough, doc date 1772, writ, debt, file #1415

JOSLYN Nathaniel, yeoman, of Henniker, vs ATHERTON Joshua, esquire, of Amherst, doc date 1774, writ, debt, file #1077

JUDKINS Jonathan, of Hopkinton, vs BAILEY Enock & Isaac, traders, of Hopkinton, doc date 1798, judgment, debt, file #564

JUEL John, yeoman, of Hopkinton, vs JEWELL Thomas, of Hopkinton, doc date 1770, rec date 1772, deed, land transfer, file #6852

KARR Jacob, husbandman, of Weare, vs DENSMORE James, tailor, of Londonderry, rec date 1784, summons, assault, file #4597

KARR Jacob, husbandman, of Weare, vs BELL John, esquire, of Londonderry, rec date 1784, summons, assault, file #4597

KARR Jacob, husbandman, of Weare, vs BELL John, esquire, of Londonderry, rec date 1785, various, driving on Sunday, file #4827

KARR Jacob, husbandman, of Weare, vs DINSMORE James, taylor, of Londonderry, rec date 1785, various, driving on Sunday, file #4827, fragile

KARR James, gentleman, of Goffstown, vs RANKIN Samuel, innkeeper, of Londonderry, doc date 1774, execution, file #1003

KARR James, gentleman, of Goffstown, vs GODFREY Meriam, exec of estate, of Hopkinton, rec date 1784, judgment, debt, file #2289, fragile

KARR James, gentleman, of Goffstown, vs ABBOTT Darius, gentleman, of Amherst, rec date 1783, writ, debt, file #3094

KARR James, gentleman, of Goffstown, vs GOFFE John, gentleman, of Bedford, rec date 1785, writ, debt, file #5539

KARR Jesse, of Goffstown, vs ORDWAY Joseph, of Goffstown, doc date 1775, deed, land transfer, file #836

KARR Jonathan, yeoman, of Chester, vs TRACY Patrick, esquire, of Newburyport MA, doc date 1774, writ, debt, file #1129

KARR Thomas, yeoman, of New Boston, vs EPES Francis, esquire, of Lyndeborough, doc date 1783, rec date 1785, deed, land transfer, file #5615

KARR Thomas, yeoman, of New Boston, vs EPES Francis, yeoman, of Lyndeborough, doc date 1782, rec date 1785, deed, land transfer, file #5621

KARR William, of Dunbarton, vs MARTIN Joshua, gentleman, of Goffstown, doc date 1785, petition, release of debit, file #13

KAST Thomas, physician, of Boston MA, vs CLUFF James, yeoman, of Hopkinton, doc date 1784, execution, debt, file #1976

KAST Thomas & Sally, physician, of Boston MA, vs CLUFF James, yeoman, of Hopkinton, rec date 1783, execution, debt, file #3251

KAST Thomas & Sally, physician, of Boston MA, vs CLUFF James, husbandman, of Hopkinton, rec date 1783, writ, debt, file #3927

KEAZAR Edmund, husbandman, of Hampstead, vs STEVENS Samuel, husbandman, of Sandown, doc date 1772, writ, debt, file #1409

KEEF Michael, yeoman, of Amherst, vs HUTCHINSON Samuel, yeoman, of Lyndeborough, rec date 1787, judgment, debt, file #2464

KEEF Michael, husbandman, of Londonderry, vs WESTON Ebenezer, gentleman, of Amherst, rec date 1783, execution, debt, file #3639

KEEF Michael, husbandman, of Londonderry, vs LOVEJOY Hezekiah, gentleman, of Amherst, rec date 1783, execution, debt, file #3639

KEEF Michael, husbandman, of Londonderry, vs DAVIS Benjamin, husbandman, of Amherst, rec date 1783, execution, debt, file #3639

KEEF Michael, yeoman, of Amherst, vs WATT John, yeoman, of Londonderry, rec date 1785, various, debt, file #4828, fragile

KEEF Michael, yeoman, of Amherst, vs HUCHINSON Samuel, yeoman, of Lyndeborough, rec date 1787, judgment, debt, file #6200

KEEF Michael, yeoman, of Amherst, vs GARLAND Robert, saddler, of Amherst, rec date 1786, writ, debt, file #6109

KEEF Michael, yeoman, of Amherst, vs WATT John, husbandman, of Londonderry, rec date 1786, writ, debt, file #6114

KEELER Abijah, esquire, of Temple, vs KIDDER John, yeoman, of Temple, doc date 1798, judgment, debt, file #564

KEEN Robert W, yeoman, of Antrim, vs BATCHELDER David, yeoman, of Deerfield, doc date 1799, execution, debt, file #208

KEEP Jonathan, gentleman, of Groton MA, vs DICKEY James, of Raby, rec date 1784, judgment, debt, file #4375

KEEP Jonathan, gentleman, of Groton MA, vs BIXBY Jacob, yeoman, of Wilton, rec date 1783, writ, debt, file #4532

KEEP (KEEFE?) Jonathan, gentleman, of Groton MA, vs CLAY Ephraim, gentleman, of Putney VT, rec date 1785, judgment, debt, file #5502

KELLEY Ebenezer, tailor, of Weare, vs KARR William, husbandman, of Deering, rec date 1785, execution, debt, file #5926

KELLEY Joseph, gentleman, of Nottingham, vs BADGE John, shipwright, of Almsbury, doc date 1769, judgment, debt, file #820

KELLEY Joseph, gentleman, of Nottingham, vs BAGLEY Enoch, of Almsbury MA, doc date 1769, judgment, debt, file #820

KELLEY Joseph, gentleman, of Nottingham, vs HOLLAND John, yeoman, of Merrimack, doc date 1772, writ, debt, file #912, fragile

KELLEY Joseph, gentleman, of Nottingham, vs GREELEY Ezekiel, gentleman, of Londonderry, doc date 1772, writ, debt, file #931

KELLEY Joseph, gentleman, of Nottingham-West, vs DOW Perry, yeoman, of Nottingham-West, doc date 1784, execution, debt, file #1529

KELLEY Joseph, gentleman, of Nottingham-West, vs RIDEOUT Nathaniel, yeoman, of Hollis, doc date 1784, civil litigation, debt, file #1646

KELLEY Joseph, gentleman, of Nottingham-West, rec date 1776, recognizance, counterfeiting, file #2248

KELLEY Joseph, gentleman, of Nottingham-West, vs SMITH Edward, innkeeper, of Boston MA, rec date 1787, judgment, debt, file #2314

KELLEY Joseph, gentleman, of Nottingham-West, vs SMITH Edward, innkeeper, of Boston MA, doc date 1787, rec date 1787, deed, land transfer, file #2494

KELLEY Joseph, husbandman, of Nottingham-West, vs SMITH Edward, husbandman, of Peterborough, rec date 1788, writ, debt, file #2546

KELLEY Joseph, gentleman, of Nottingham-West, vs GIBSON John, cooper, of Pelham, rec date 1783, execution, debt, file #2966

KELLEY Joseph, gentleman, of Nottingham-West, vs GIBSON John, cooper, of Pelham, rec date 1782, judgment, debt, file #3128

KELLEY Joseph, gentleman, of Nottingham-West, vs HUEY John, yeoman, of Nottingham-West, rec date 1783, writ, debt, file #3433

KELLEY Joseph, esquire, vs FORD James, gentleman, of Nottingham-West, rec date 1783, writ, debt, file #3928

KELLEY Joseph, gentleman, of Nottingham-West, vs BARRETT James Jr, yeoman, of Nottingham-West, rec date 1783, judgment, debt, file #4435

KELLEY Joseph, gentleman, of Nottingham-West, vs HALL John, physician, of Nottingham-West, rec date 1783, judgment, debt, file #4435

KELLEY Joseph, gentleman, of Nottingham-West, vs CAMPBELL David, yeoman, of Nottingham-West, rec date 1783, judgment, debt, file #4725

KELLEY Joseph, gentleman, of Nottingham-West, vs BISHOP James Prime, yeoman, of Portsmouth, rec date 1785, writ, debt, file #4580

KELLEY Joseph, gentleman, of Nottingham-West, vs BISHOP Elizabeth, of Portsmouth, rec date 1784, writ, debt, file #4580, estate of James DWYER

KELLEY Joseph, gentleman, of Nottingham-West, vs SMITH Edward, innkeeper, of Boston MA, rec date 1785, judgment, animal dispute, file #5357

KELLEY Joseph, gentleman, of Nottingham, vs SMITH Edward, innkeeper, of Boston MA, rec date 1785, judgment, debt, file #5356

KELLEY Joseph, esquire, of Nottingham-West, vs PORTER Frank, yeoman, of Peterborough, rec date 1785, writ, debt, file #5281

KELLEY Joseph, gentleman, of Nottingham-West, vs SMITH Edward, innholder, of Boston MA, rec date 1786, various, debt, file #6075

KELLEY Joseph, rec date 1772, letter, escape from prison, file #7018

KELLEY Langley, physician, of Weare, vs CLARK Ephraim, yeoman, of New Boston, doc date 1798, execution, debt, file #66

KELLEY Moses, esquire, of Goffstown, vs McNEIL John Caldwell, husbandman, of New Boston, rec date 1783, writ, debt, file #4044

KELLEY Moses, esquire/sheriff, of Goffstown, vs BLANCHARD Joseph, esquire, of Amherst, rec date 1788, various, bond, file #6997

KELLEY Moses, esquire/sheriff, of Goffstown, vs LOVEWELL Noah, esquire, of Dunstable, rec date 1788, various, bond, file #6997

KELLEY Moses, esquire/sheriff, of Goffstown, vs HEAIL Joseph, husbandman, of Dunstable, rec date 1788, various, bond, file #6997

KELLEY Richard, tailor, of Weare, vs HOWARD Samuel Smith, husbandman, of Nottingham-West, rec date 1785, writ, debt, file #2347

KELLEY Ruth, spinster, of Nottingham-West, vs SPAULDING Reuben, husbandman, of Nottingham-West, doc date 1772, judgment, trespass, file #694

KELLY Ebenezer, tailor, of Weare, vs KARR William, husbandman, of Deering, rec date 1785, judgment, debt, file #5508

KELLY Ebenezer, yeoman, of Weare, vs SHAW Ichabod, yeoman, of Marlborough, rec date 1783, writ, debt, file #4544

KELLY Joseph, gentleman, of Nottingham, vs EWINS James, husbandman, of Londonderry, doc date 1772, judgment, debt, file #667

KELLY Joseph, gentleman, of Nottingham-West, vs CALDWELL John, yeoman, of Nottingham-West, rec date 1783, judgment, debt, file #4302

KELLY Joseph, gentleman, of Nottingham-West, vs RIDEOUT Nathaniel, yeoman, of Hollis, rec date 1783, writ, debt, file #4431

KELLY Joseph, gentleman, of Nottingham-West, vs PEMBERTON James Jr, yeoman, of Nottingham-West, rec date 1783, judgment, debt, file #4715, proof of Revolutionary War service (Pemberton)

KELLY Joseph, gentleman, of Nottingham-West, vs JOHNSON David, yeoman, of Pelham, rec date 1783, judgment, debt, file #4721

KELLY Joseph, gentleman, of Nottingham-West, vs STODDARD Thomas & John, merchant, of Boston MA, rec date 1772, various, debt, file #4879

KELLY Joseph, esquire, of Nottingham-West, vs SEAVEY Nathaniel, rec date 1785, writ, debt, file #5284

KELLY Joseph, esquire, of Nottingham-West, vs WALLACE Matthew, husbandman, of Peterborough, rec date 1785, writ, debt, file #5282

KELLY Joseph, esquire, of Nottingham-West, vs CAMPBELL David, yeoman, of Nottingham-West, rec date 1785, writ, debt, file #5283

KELLY Joseph, gentleman, of Nottingham-West, vs MORSS Stephen, goldsmith, of Concord, rec date 1785, judgment, debt, file #5578

KELLY Joseph, gentleman, of Nottingham-West, vs HEYWOOD Samuel Smith, yeoman, of Nottingham-West, rec date 1786, warrant, stolen goods, file #5748

KELLY Joseph, gentleman, of Nottingham-West, vs PUTNAM David, yeoman, of Chelmsford MA, rec date 1785, execution, debt, file #5965

KELLY Joseph, esquire, of Nottingham-West, vs WICOM Thomas, yeoman, of Goffstown, rec date 1785, judgment, debt, file #5817

KELLY Joseph, esquire, of Nottingham-West, vs HARDY Moody, yeoman, of Goffstown, rec date 1785, judgment, debt, file #5817

KELLY Joseph, gentleman, of Nottingham-West, vs HAYWOOD Josiah, yeoman, of Nottingham-West, rec date 1786, various, debt, file #6365

KELLY Joseph, gentleman, of Nottingham-West, vs SMITH Samuel, yeoman, of Nottingham-West, rec date 1786, writ, debt, file #6692

KELLY Langley, physician, of Weare, vs SOUTHERICK Isaac, husbandman, of Milford, doc date 1798, judgment, debt, file #564

KELLY Moses, of Goffstown, vs CUSHMAN John, physician, of Goffstown, doc date 1782, execution, file #1018

KELLY Moses, esquire, of Goffstown, vs McGINNIS Barnabas, yeoman, of Nottingham-West, doc date 1784, civil litigation, debt, file #1652

KELLY Moses, esquire, of Goffstown, vs LOVEJOY Francis, feltmaker, of Amherst, doc date 1784, execution, debt, file #1816

KELLY Moses, sheriff, vs JONES James & William, yeoman, of Hillsborough, doc date 1784, execution, debt, file #1776

KELLY Moses, esquire, vs JONES James & William, husbandman, of Hillsborough, doc date 1784, execution, debt, file #1795

KELLY Moses, sheriff, vs COOLIDGE Nathaniel, yeoman, of Hillsborough, doc date 1784, execution, debt, file #1818

KELLY Moses, sheriff, vs JONES James & William, yeoman, of Hillsborough, doc date 1784, execution, debt, file #1818

KELLY Moses, esquire, vs JONES James & William, husbandman, of Hillsborough, doc date 1784, execution, debt, file #1784

KELLY Moses, esquire, of Goffstown, vs STEVENS Thomas, feltmaker, of Amherst, doc date 1784, execution, debt, file #1816

KELLY Moses, esquire, of Goffstown, vs BEARD Wm & Joseph, yeoman, of Nottingham-West, doc date 1784, civil litigation, debt, file #1652

KELLY Moses, esquire, of Goffstown, vs JONES William Jr, husbandman, of Hillsborough, doc date 1784, execution, debt, file #1788

KELLY Moses, sheriff, of Goffstown, vs TAGGART Archibald, gentleman, of Hillsborough, doc date 1784, execution, debt, file #1959

KELLY Moses, esquire, of Goffstown, vs PUTNAM Israel, yeoman, of Hollis, doc date 1784, civil litigation, debt, file #1842

KELLY Moses, sheriff, vs COOLIDGE Nathaniel, husbandman, of Hillsborough, doc date 1779, execution, debt, file #1795

KELLY Moses, sheriff, of Goffstown, vs ANDREWS Isaac, gentleman, of Hillsborough, doc date 1784, execution, debt, file #1959

KELLY Moses, esquire, of Goffstown, vs CLARK Timothy, yeoman, of Amherst, doc date 1784, civil litigation, debt, file #1842

KELLY Moses, sheriff, of Goffstown, vs BRADFORD Samuel, gentleman, of Hillsborough, doc date 1784, execution, debt, file #1959

KELLY Moses, esquire, of Goffstown, vs DAVIS Benjamin, yeoman, of Amherst, doc date 1784, civil litigation, debt, file #1842

KELLY Moses, esquire, of Goffstown, vs HUTCHINSON Samuel, yeoman, of Lyndeborough, doc date 1784, civil litigation, debt, file #1856

KELLY Moses, esquire, of Goffstown, vs McNEIL John C, gentleman, of Weare, doc date 1784, civil litigation, debt, file #1854

KELLY Moses, esquire, of Goffstown, vs WILKINS Amos, yeoman, of Lyndeborough, doc date 1784, civil litigation, debt, file #1856

KELLY Moses, sheriff, vs JONES James, yeoman, of Hillsborough, doc date 1784, execution, debt, file #1864

KELLY Moses, esquire, vs COOLIDGE Nathaniel, yeoman, of Hillsborough, doc date 1784, execution, debt, file #1864

KELLY Moses, esquire, of Goffstown, vs JOHNSON Adam, gentleman, of Lyndeborough, doc date 1784, civil litigation, debt, file #1856

KELLY Moses, sheriff, of Goffstown, vs RICHARDSON Samuel, esquire, of Goffstown, rec date 1783, execution, debt, file #2899

KELLY Moses, esquire, of Goffstown, vs McGINNIS Barnabas, yeoman, of Nottingham-West, rec date 1783, judgment, debt, file #3291

KELLY Moses, esquire, of Goffstown, vs CUSHING John, physician, of Goffstown, rec date 1783, writ, debt, file #3354

KELLY Moses, esquire, of Goffstown, vs BEARD Wm & Joseph, yeoman, of New Boston, rec date 1783, judgment, debt, file #3291

KELLY Moses, sheriff, of Goffstown, vs STEWARD Samuel, yeoman, of Hillsborough, rec date 1783, writ, debt, file #3587

KELLY Moses, sheriff, of Goffstown, vs BRADFORD Samuel, esquire, of Hillsborough, rec date 1783, writ, debt, file #3598

KELLY Moses, sheriff, of Goffstown, vs ANDREWS Isaac, esquire, of Hillsborough, rec date 1783, writ, debt, file #3598

KELLY Moses, esquire, of Goffstown, vs CUSHING John, physician, of Goffstown, rec date 1783, judgment, debt, file #3774

KELLY Moses, sheriff, of Goffstown, vs TAGGART Archibald, esquire, of Hillsborough, rec date 1783, writ, debt, file #3598

KELLY Moses, esquire, of Goffstown, vs BALL Eleazer, husbandman, of Berwick ME, rec date 1783, writ, debt, file #4038

KELLY Moses, esquire, of Goffstown, vs McGAA Robert, gentleman, of Hollis, rec date 1783, writ, debt, file #4038

KELLY Moses, esquire, of Goffstown, vs BLASDELL Henry, yeoman, of Goffstown, rec date 1783, writ, debt, file #3971

KELLY Moses, esquire, of Goffstown, vs CALDWELL William, yeoman, of Goffstown, rec date 1783, writ, debt, file #4044, fragile

KELLY Moses, esquire, of Goffstown, vs WORCESTER Noah, esquire, of Hollis, rec date 1783, writ, debt, file #4038

KELLY Moses, esquire, of Goffstown, vs CALDWELL Samuel, gentleman, of Weare, rec date 1783, writ, debt, file #4044

KELLY Moses, esquire, of Goffstown, vs WAIT John, yeoman, of Mason, rec date 1784, appeal, debt, file #4110

KELLY Moses, esquire, of Goffstown, vs PUTNAM Archeleaus & Jr, yeoman, of Wilton, rec date 1785, judgment, debt, file #5446

KELLY Moses, esquire, of Goffstown, vs LIVINGSTON William, gentleman, of New Boston, rec date 1783, judgment, debt, file #3788

KELLY Moses, esquire, of Goffstown, vs SCOBY David, gentleman, of Francestown, rec date 1783, judgment, debt, file #3788

KELLY Moses, esquire, of Goffstown, vs BOYES William, gentleman, of New Boston, rec date 1783, judgment, debt, file #3788

KELLY Moses, esquire, of Goffstown, vs McCLINTOCK Alexander, yeoman, of Hillsborough, rec date 1784, judgment, debt, file #4190

KELLY Moses, esquire, of Goffstown, vs McCALLEY James, gentleman, of Hillsborough, rec date 1784, judgment, debt, file #4190

KELLY Moses, esquire, of Goffstown, vs GRIMES James, gentleman, of Deering, rec date 1784, judgment, debt, file #4190

KELLY Moses, sheriff, of Goffstown, vs BARNS Asa, yeoman, of Bedford, rec date 1784, judgment, debt, file #4202

KELLY Moses, esquire, of Goffstown, vs GRAGG David, yeoman, of Francestown, rec date 1784, appeal, debt, file #4129

KELLY Moses, esquire, of Goffstown, vs HOGG James, yeoman, of Francestown, rec date 1784, appeal, debt, file #4129

KELLY Moses, esquire, of Goffstown, vs GRIMES James, gentleman, of Deering, rec date 1784, appeal, debt, file #4129

KELLY Moses, sheriff, of Goffstown, vs RICHARDSON Zechariah, yeoman, of Francestown, rec date 1784, judgment, debt, file #4202

KELLY Moses, esquire, of Goffstown, vs SHURTLEFF Jonathan, yeoman, of Merrimack, rec date 1784, judgment, debt, file #4653

KELLY Moses, esquire, of Goffstown, vs CLARK Timothy, yeoman, of Hollis, rec date 1783, judgment, debt, file #4476

KELLY Moses, esquire, of Goffstown, vs GRAGG David, yeoman, of Francestown, rec date 1784, judgment, debt, file #4642

KELLY Moses, esquire, of Goffstown, vs PUTNAM Israel, yeoman, of Hollis, rec date 1783, judgment, debt, file #4476

KELLY Moses, esquire, of Goffstown, vs WARNER Daniel, gentleman, of Amherst, rec date 1784, judgment, debt, file #4648

KELLY Moses, esquire, of Goffstown, vs SHURTLEFF Jonathan Jr, trader, of Amherst, rec date 1784, judgment, debt, file #4653

KELLY Moses, esquire, of Goffstown, vs GRIMES James, yeoman, of Deering, rec date 1784, judgment, debt, file #4642

KELLY Moses, esquire, of Goffstown, vs BIXBY Andrew, yeoman, of Hillsborough, rec date 1784, judgment, debt, file #4642

KELLY Moses, esquire, of Goffstown, vs DAVIS Benjamin, yeoman, of Hollis, rec date 1783, judgment, debt, file #4476

KELLY Moses, sheriff, of Goffstown, vs BIXBY Andrew, yeoman, of Hillsborough, rec date 1784, judgment, debt, file #4202

KELLY Moses, esquire, of Goffstown, vs PUTNAM Archelaus Sr & Jr, yeoman, of Wilton, rec date 1784, judgment, debt, file #4584

KELLY Moses, esquire, of Goffstown, vs DODGE Samuel, husbandman, of Amherst, rec date 1784, judgment, debt, file #4648

KELLY Moses, esquire, of Goffstown, vs WALKER William, gentleman, of Amherst, rec date 1784, judgment, debt, file #4648

KELLY Moses, esquire, of Goffstown, vs PUTNAM Jacob, yeoman, of Temple, rec date 1784, judgment, debt, file #4584

KELLY Moses, esquire, of Goffstown, vs WARNER Daniel, gentleman, of Amherst, rec date 1784, judgment, debt, file #4869

KELLY Moses, esquire, of Goffstown, vs STEWART Thomas, yeoman, of Peterborough, rec date 1785, writ, debt, file #4816

KELLY Moses, esquire, of Goffstown, vs ROBBE Alexander, gentleman, of Peterborough, rec date 1785, writ, debt, file #4816

KELLY Moses, esquire, of Goffstown, vs WILKINS Robert Bradford, gentleman, of Amherst, rec date 1784, judgment, debt, file #4869

KELLY Moses, sheriff, of Amherst, vs SUPERIOR Court, rec date 1785, petition, repairs to jail, file #4838

KELLY Moses, esquire, of Goffstown, vs HILDRETH Ephraim, gentleman, of Amherst, rec date 1785, writ, debt, file #4816

KELLY Moses, esquire, of Goffstown, vs DODGE Samuel, yeoman, of Amherst, rec date 1785, writ, debt, file #4816

KELLY Moses, esquire, of Goffstown, vs WALKER William, gentleman, of Amherst, rec date 1784, judgment, debt, file #4869

KELLY Moses, esquire, of Goffstown, vs MOOR William, yeoman, of New Boston, rec date 1785, judgment, debt, file #4950

KELLY Moses, esquire, of Goffstown, vs BOYES William, gentleman, of New Boston, rec date 1785, judgment, debt, file #4950

KELLY Moses, esquire, of Goffstown, vs HITCHINS Josiah, cordwainer, of New Boston, rec date 1785, judgment, debt, file #4950

KELLY Moses, esquire, of Goffstown, vs WARNER David, gentleman, of Amherst, rec date 1785, judgment, debt, file #5140

KELLY Moses, esquire, of Goffstown, vs WILKINS Amos, yeoman, of Lyndeborough, rec date 1784, judgment, debt, file #5317

KELLY Moses, esquire, of Goffstown, vs MOOR William Jr, husbandman, of Bedford, rec date 1784, judgment, debt, file #5285

KELLY Moses, esquire, of Goffstown, vs GRIMES James, gentleman, of Deering, rec date 1784, judgment, debt, file #5320

KELLY Moses, esquire, of Goffstown, vs DODGE Samuel, husbandman, of Amherst, rec date 1785, judgment, debt, file #5140

KELLY Moses, esquire, of Goffstown, vs HUTCHINSON John, yeoman, of Lyndeborough, rec date 1784, judgment, debt, file #5317

KELLY Moses, esquire, of Goffstown, vs JOHNSON Adam, gentleman, of Lyndeborough, rec date 1784, judgment, debt, file #5317

KELLY Moses, esquire, of Goffstown, vs HUTCHINSON Samuel, yeoman, of Lyndeborough, rec date 1784, judgment, debt, file #5317

KELLY Moses, esquire, of Goffstown, vs BIXBE Andrew, yeoman, of Hillsborough, rec date 1784, judgment, debt, file #5320

KELLY Moses, esquire sheriff, of Goffstown, vs COLE Eleazer, yeoman, of Amherst, rec date 1784, judgment, debt, file #4653

KELLY Moses, sheriff, of Goffstown, vs EATON John, blacksmith, of Amherst, rec date 1785, judgment, debt, file #5091

KELLY Moses, esquire, of Goffstown, vs CHASE Samuel, esquire, of Litchfield, rec date 1785, various, debt, file #5274

KELLY Moses, esquire, of Goffstown, vs GIBSON Matthew, yeoman, of Francestown, rec date 1785, various, debt, file #5275

KELLY Moses, sheriff, of Goffstown, vs MOOR James, husbandman, of Goffstown, rec date 1785, judgment, debt, file #5119

KELLY Moses, esquire, of Goffstown, vs BURNS John Jr, yeoman, of New Boston, rec date 1785, various, debt, file #5275

KELLY Moses, esquire, of Goffstown, vs HILDRETH Ephraim, gentleman, of Amherst, rec date 1785, various, debt, file #5275

KELLY Moses, esquire, of Goffstown, vs WALLINGFORD David, gentleman, of Hollis, rec date 1785, various, debt, file #5563

KELLY Moses, sheriff, of Goffstown, vs MELENDY William, yeoman, of Amherst, rec date 1785, judgment, debt, file #5091

KELLY Moses, esquire, of Goffstown, vs MOOR James, husbandman, of Goffstown, rec date 1784, judgment, debt, file #5285

KELLY Moses, esquire sheriff, of Goffstown, vs COLE Eleager, yeoman, of Merrimack, rec date 1785, judgment, debt, file #5111

KELLY Moses, esquire, of Goffstown, vs KENNEDY Samuel, husbandman, of Goffstown, rec date 1784, judgment, debt, file #5285

KELLY Moses, esquire, of Goffstown, vs CROSS John, yeoman, of Litchfield, rec date 1785, various, debt, file #5274

KELLY Moses, sheriff, of Goffstown, vs FRENCH Ephraim, yeoman, of Amherst, rec date 1785, judgment, debt, file #5091

KELLY Moses, esquire, of Goffstown, vs KELLY Joseph, esquire, of Nottingham-West, rec date 1785, various, debt, file #5274

KELLY Moses, sheriff, vs KENNEDY Samuel, husbandman, of Goffstown, rec date 1785, judgment, debt, file #5119

KELLY Moses, esquire, of Goffstown, vs ANDREWS Isaac, esquire, of Hillsborough, rec date 1785, judgment, debt, file #5068

KELLY Moses, sheriff, of Goffstown, vs LIVINGSTON William, gentleman, of New Boston, rec date 1785, judgment, debt, file #5085

KELLY Moses, esquire sheriff, of Goffstown, vs BIXBE Andrew, yeoman, of Hillsborough, rec date 1785, judgment, debt, file #5110

KELLY Moses, esquire, of Goffstown, vs SYMONDS Joseph, gentleman, of Hillsborough, rec date 1785, judgment, debt, file #5068

KELLY Moses, sheriff, of Goffstown, vs JOHNSON Adam, gentleman, of Lyndeborough, rec date 1785, judgment, debt, file #5123

KELLY Moses, esquire, of Goffstown, vs HOW Eliakim, gentleman, of Henniker, rec date 1785, judgment, debt, file #5068

KELLY Moses, esquire, of Goffstown, vs SEACOMB John, yeoman, of Amherst, rec date 1785, judgment, debt, file #5050

KELLY Moses, esquire, of Goffstown, vs CLUFF James, yeoman, of Hopkinton, rec date 1785, judgment, debt, file #5050

KELLY Moses, sheriff, of Goffstown, vs HUTCHINSON Samuel & John, yeoman, of Lyndeborough, rec date 1785, judgment, debt, file #5123

KELLY Moses, sheriff, of Goffstown, vs MOOR William Jr, husbandman, of Bedford, rec date 1785, judgment, debt, file #5119

KELLY Moses, esquire, of Goffstown, vs CAMPBELL Daniel, yeoman, of Amherst, rec date 1785, judgment, debt, file #5050

KELLY Moses, esquire sheriff, of Goffstown, vs GREGG David, yeoman, of Francestown, rec date 1785, judgment, debt, file #5110

KELLY Moses, esquire, of Goffstown, vs GRAGG David, yeoman, of Francestown, rec date 1784, judgment, debt, file #5320

KELLY Moses, esquire, of Goffstown, vs WALKER William, gentleman, of Amherst, rec date 1785, judgment, debt, file #5140

KELLY Moses, sheriff, of Goffstown, vs BOYES William, gentleman, of New Boston, rec date 1785, judgment, debt, file #5085

KELLY Moses, esquire sheriff, of Goffstown, vs SHURTLEFF Jonathan Jr, yeoman, of Merrimack, rec date 1785, judgment, debt, file #5111

KELLY Moses, sheriff, of Goffstown, vs CAIRNS Jonas, yeoman, of New Boston, rec date 1785, judgment, debt, file #5085

KELLY Moses, esquire, of Goffstown, vs SHANNON Richard Cutts, esquire, of Hollis, rec date 1785, writ, debt, file #5597

KELLY Moses, esquire sheriff, of Goffstown, vs PUTNAM Jacob, yeoman, of Temple, rec date 1785, judgment, debt, file #5446

KELLY Moses, esquire, of Goffstown, vs WALKER William, gentleman, of Amherst, rec date 1785, various, debt, file #5600

KELLY Moses, esquire, of Goffstown, vs FRENCH Nehemiah, yeoman, of Hollis, rec date 1785, various, debt, file #5563

KELLY Moses, esquire, of Goffstown, vs McCURDY John, gentleman, of Dunbarton, rec date 1785, various, debt, file #5600

KELLY Moses, sheriff, of Goffstown, vs GRIMES James, gentleman, of Deering, rec date 1785, judgment, debt, file #5112

KELLY Moses, esquire, of Goffstown, vs KELLY Joseph, gentleman, of Nottingham-West, rec date 1785, writ, debt, file #5597

KELLY Moses, sheriff, of Goffstown, vs BIXBE Andrew, yeoman, of Francestown, rec date 1785, judgment, debt, file #5112

KELLY Moses, sheriff, of Goffstown, vs WILKINS Amos, yeoman, of Lyndeborough, rec date 1785, judgment, debt, file #5123

KELLY Moses, esquire, of Goffstown, vs WILSON Jesse, husbandman, of Amherst, rec date 1785, judgment, debt, file #5565

KELLY Moses, esquire, of Goffstown, vs STEVENS Caleb, cordwainer, of Loudon, rec date 1785, judgment, debt, file #5565

KELLY Moses, esquire, of Goffstown, vs ATWILL John, innholder, of Hollis, rec date 1785, writ, debt, file #5597

KELLY Moses, esquire, of Goffstown, vs ROLF Jesse, trader, of Francestown, rec date 1785, judgment, debt, file #5590

KELLY Moses, esquire, of Goffstown, vs BRADFORD Andrew, husbandman, of Hillsborough, rec date 1785, judgment, debt, file #5590

KELLY Moses, esquire, of Goffstown, vs McCLENCHE Joseph, blacksmith, of Merrimack, rec date 1785, judgment, debt, file #5565

KELLY Moses, esquire, of Goffstown, vs HILDRETH Ephraim, gentleman, of Amherst, rec date 1785, various, debt, file #5600

KELLY Moses, esquire, of Goffstown, vs BAGLEY Richard, cordwainer, of Hollis, rec date 1785, various, debt, file #5563

KELLY Moses, esquire, of Goffstown, vs READ Zadock, yeoman, of New Boston, rec date 1785, judgment, debt, file #5872

KELLY Moses, esquire, of Goffstown, vs RICHARDS Samuel, esquire, of Goffstown, rec date 1782, execution, debt, file #5738

KELLY Moses, esquire, of Goffstown, vs MOOR James, gentleman, of Bedford, rec date 1786, writ, debt, file #6113

KELLY Moses, esquire, of Goffstown, vs POTTER James, gentleman, of Bedford, rec date 1786, writ, debt, file #6113

KELLY Moses, esquire, of Goffstown, vs GILMORE James, yeoman, of Bedford, rec date 1786, writ, debt, file #6113

KELLY Moses, sheriff, of Goffstown, vs MOOR William, husbandman, of Bedford, rec date 1785, judgment, debt, file #4796

KELLY Moses, esquire/sheriff, of Goffstown, vs GRAY Robert, husbandman, of Peterborough, rec date 1786, writ, debt, file #6322

KELLY Moses, esquire/sheriff, of Goffstown, vs CROSS John, yeoman, of Litchfield, rec date 1786, judgment, debt, file #6481

KELLY Moses, sheriff/Esquire, of Goffstown, vs CHASE Samuel, esquire, of Litchfield, rec date 1786, judgment, debt, file #6481

KELLY Moses, esquire/sheriff, of Goffstown, vs CARNES James, of New Boston, rec date 1785, judgment, debt, file #4797

KELLY Moses, sheriff, of Goffstown, vs MOOR James, husbandman, of Goffstown, rec date 1785, judgment, debt, file #4796

KELLY Moses, esquire/sheriff, of Goffstown, vs BOYES William, of New Boston, rec date 1785, judgment, debt, file #4797

KELLY Moses, esquire/sheriff, of Goffstown, vs LIVINGSTON William, of New Boston, rec date 1785, judgment, debt, file #4797

KELLY Moses, sheriff, of Goffstown, vs KENNEDY Samuel, husbandman, of Goffstown, rec date 1785, judgment, debt, file #4796

KELLY Moses, sheriff/Esquire, of Goffstown, vs KELLY Joseph, esquire, of Nottingham, rec date 1786, judgment, debt, file #6481

KELLY Moses, esquire/sheriff, of Goffstown, vs McCLURY Thomas, husbandman, of Peterborough, rec date 1786, writ, debt, file #6322

KELLY Moses, esquire/sheriff, of Goffstown, vs JONES James & Wm, husbandman, of Hillsborough, rec date 1786, judgment, debt, file #6382

KELLY Moses, sheriff, of Goffstown, vs COOLAGE Nathaniel, husbandman, of Hillsborough, rec date 1785, judgment, debt, file #6461

KELLY Moses, sheriff, of Goffstown, vs JONES William, husbandman, of Hillsborough, rec date 1785, judgment, debt, file #6461

KELLY Moses, esquire/sheriff, of Goffstown, vs COOLAGE Nathaniel, husbandman, of Hillsborough, rec date 1786, judgment, debt, file #6382

KELLY Moses, sheriff, of Goffstown, vs JONES William, husbandman, of Hillsborough, rec date 1785, judgment, debt, file #6460

KELLY Moses, sheriff, of Goffstown, vs JONES James, husbandman, of Hillsborough, rec date 1785, judgment, debt, file #6460

KELLY Moses, esquire/sheriff, of Goffstown, vs WAITE John, yeoman, of Mason, rec date 1784, judgment, debt, file #6353

KELLY Moses, esquire/sheriff, of Goffstown, vs ROBB William, husbandman, of Peterborough, rec date 1786, writ, debt, file #6322

KELLY Moses, sheriff, of Goffstown, vs WOOD Jonathan & Edward, husbandman, of Goffstown, rec date 1786, judgment, debt, file #6477

KELLY Moses, esquire/sheriff, of Goffstown, vs RICHARDS Samuel, esquire, of Goffstown, rec date 1784, judgment, debt, file #6354

KELLY Moses, sheriff, of Goffstown, vs EATON James, husbandman, of Goffstown, rec date 1786, judgment, debt, file #6477

KELLY Moses, sheriff, of Goffstown, vs COOLAGE Nathaniel, husbandman, of Hillsborough, rec date 1785, judgment, debt, file #6460

KELLY Moses, esquire, of Goffstown, vs GOVE Jonathan, physician, of New Boston, rec date 1785, various, debits, file #6808

KELLY Moses, esquire, of Goffstown, vs BLANCHARD Augustus, esquire, of Amherst, rec date 1785, various, debits, file #6808

KELLY Moses, esquire, of Goffstown, vs BLANCHARD Jotham, gentleman, of Peterborough, rec date 1785, various, debits, file #6808

KELLY Richard, taylor, of Salem, vs SARGENT Moses, yeoman, of Weare, rec date 1783, writ, debt, file #3067

KELLY Richard, tailor, of Weare, vs HOWARD Samuel Smith, yeoman, of Nottingham-West, rec date 1785, execution, debt, file #6041

KELSO Daniel, husbandman, of New Boston, vs CALDWELL James, husbandman, of New Boston, rec date 1784, judgment, debt, file #4223

KELSO Daniel, husbandman, of New Boston, vs CHRISTY Jesse, husbandman, of New Boston, rec date 1784, judgment, debt, file #4223

KELSO Daniel, husbandman, of New Boston, vs DODGE Noah & Solomon, yeoman, of New Boston, rec date 1784, judgment, debt, file #4223

KELSO Daniel, husbandman, of New Boston, vs COCHRAN John, esquire, of New Boston, rec date 1784, judgment, debt, file #4223

KEMP Benjamin, yeoman, of Ashburnham, vs BOURKETT Jacob, yeoman, of Peterborough, doc date 1772, execution, debt, file #1206

KEMP Jason, yeoman, of Henniker, vs WITHINGTON Francis, yeoman, of Henniker, rec date 1782, execution, debt, file #3527

KEMP Thomas, blacksmith, of Hollis, vs TAYLOR John, husbandman, of Amherst, rec date 1785, judgment, debt, file #5571

KEMP Thomas, blacksmith, of Hollis, vs SMITH Samuel, husbandman, of Hollis, rec date 1787, writ, debt, file #6662

KENDAL Timothy, innholder, of Litchfield, vs STEARNS Samuel, yeoman, of
Amherst, doc date 1773, judgment, debt, file #1311

KENDAL Timothy, innholder, of Litchfield, vs NICHOLS Moses, esquire, of
Amherst, doc date 1773, judgment, debt, file #1311

KENDALL ----, vs PICKARD ----, doc date 1893, plaintiffs brief, supreme court,
file #606

KENDALL Asa, gentleman, of Ashby MA, vs ATWELL John, innkeeper, of
Hollis, rec date 1783, writ, debt, file #3463

KENDALL Asa, executor, of Ashby MA, vs ATWELL John, joiner, of Hollis, rec
date 1786, various, debt, file #6085

KENDALL Daniel, gentleman, of Litchfield, vs LITTLE Thomas, husbandman, of
Hillsborough, rec date 1786, writ, debt, file #6137

KENDALL David, gentleman, of Litchfield, vs BARNES Joseph, physician, of
Litchfield, doc date 1772, writ, debt, file #1047, fragile

KENDALL Josiah, yeoman, of New Salem ma, vs WALDREN John, esquire, of
Dover, doc date 1784, execution, debt, file #1871

KENDALL Josiah, yeoman, of Sterling ma, vs WATKINS John, esquire, of
Dover, rec date 1784, judgment, debt, file #4374

KENDALL Nathan, yeoman, of Amherst, vs HUTCHINSON Solomon,
husbandman, of Merrimack, doc date 1779, rec date 1779, deed, land transfer,
file #2131

KENDALL Nathan, esquire, of Amherst, vs WESTON Jesse & Daniel, of
Amherst, doc date 1814, rec date 1814, deed, land transfer, file #6580

KENDALL Nathan Jr, yeoman, of Amherst, vs HUTCHINSON Solomon,
husbandman, of Merrimack, doc date 1779, rec date 1779, deed, land transfer,
file #2131

KENDALL Nathan Jr, husbandman, of Amherst, vs TAGGART John,
husbandman, of Goffstown, rec date 1787, writ, debt, file #2365

KENDALL Nathan Jr, yeoman, of Amherst, vs BRADFORD William, yeoman, of
Deering, rec date 1784, appeal, debt, file #4138

KENDALL Nathan Jr, yeoman, of Amherst, vs BRADFORD William, yeoman, of
Deering, rec date 1784, judgment, debt, file #4288

KENDALL Nathan Jr, yeoman, of Amherst, vs RICHARDSON Zechariah,
yeoman, of Francestown, rec date 1785, deed, land transfer, file #5617

KENDALL Nathan Jr, yeoman, of Amherst, vs TAYLOR James, husbandman, of
Merrimack, rec date 1782, execution, debt, file #5722

KENDALL Samuel, yeoman, of New Salem ma, vs WALDREN John, esquire, of
Dover, doc date 1784, execution, debt, file #1871

KENDALL Samuel, yeoman, of New Salem ma, vs WATKINS John, esquire, of
Dover, rec date 1784, judgment, debt, file #4374

KENDALL Thaddeus, trader, of Manchester, vs WARD William, blacksmith, of
New Boston, doc date 1805, execution, file #1029

KENDALL (CUMMINGS) Lucy, widow, vs MERRILL Daniel, deed, land
transfer, file #6566

KENDRICK Daniel Jr, husbandman, of Hollis, vs HOW Isaac, husbandman, of
Amherst, rec date 1787, judgment, debt, file #2475

KENDRICK John, husbandman, of Newton MA, vs MANN Benjamin, esquire, of Mason, rec date 1786, judgment, debt, file #5756

KENDRICK John, husbandman, of Newton MA, vs MANN Benjamin, esquire, of Mason, rec date 1787, judgment, debt, file #6189

KENDRICK Stephen, yeoman, of Amherst, vs HUNT Elizabeth, widow, of Hollis, rec date 1782, judgment, debt, file #2744

KENDRICK Stephen, yeoman, of Amherst, vs HUNT Elizabeth, widow, of Hollis, rec date 1783, execution, debt, file #3235

KENNARD John, of Manchester, vs CITY of Manchester, doc date 1894, appeal tax dispute, supreme court, file #581

KENNEDY Jane, widow, of Goffstown, vs BELL Joseph, yeoman, of Bedford, rec date 1783, judgment, debt, file #3726

KENNEDY John, laborer, of Londonderry, vs MACK Robert Jr, gentleman, of Londonderry, doc date 1772, writ, debt, file #1391

KENNEDY Samuel, yeoman, of Goffstown, vs KELLY Moses, sheriff, of Goffstown, rec date 1783, judgment, theft of oxen, file #2619

KENNEY Hannah, spinster, of Nottingham, vs STEWART Francis, husbandman, of Nottingham, doc date 1799, judgment, debt, file #315

KENNEY Israel, yeoman, of Hollis, vs STEARNS Samuel, yeoman, of Amherst, doc date 1773, writ, debt, file #1367

KENNEY Israel, yeoman, of Hollis, vs RIDEOUT James & Nathaniel, yeoman, of Hollis, doc date 1773, writ, debt, file #1340

KENNEY Israel, yeoman, of Hollis, vs CARSON William, husbandman, of Lyndeborough, doc date 1772, writ, debt, file #1417

KENNEY Israel, husbandman, of Hollis, vs McGAA Robert, trader, of Hollis, rec date 1782, appeal, debt, file #3978

KENNEY John, yeoman, of Peterborough, vs THOM John, yeoman, of Peterborough Slip, doc date 1773, execution, debt, file #1474

KENNEY Mary, spinster, of Goffstown, vs ROSS John, yeoman, of Bedford, doc date 1783, rec date 1788, deed, land transfer, file #6758

KENNEY Thomas, yeoman, of Goffstown, vs BURNAM Asa, yeoman, of Dunbarton, doc date 1783, rec date 1788, deed, land transfer, file #6756

KENNEY Tivail, yeoman, of Hadley, vs BELL James, cooper, of Dunstable, doc date 1800, judgment, debt, file #568

KENNRICK John Jr, housewright, of Newton?, vs MERIAM Jonas, clerk, of MA, rec date 1783, judgment, debt, file #4470

KESTON Southwick, husbandman, of Antrim, vs FLINT Jacob, husbandman, of Hillsborough, rec date 1785, judgment, debt, file #5801

KEYES Jonathan, husbandman, of Westford MA, vs SMITH Adam, gentleman, of Bedford, rec date 1785, judgment, debt, file #5055

KEYES Stephen, husbandman, of Plymouth, vs FOWLER Samuel, esquire, of Boscawen, rec date 1784, judgment, debt, file #4250

KEYSER Timothy, yeoman, of Henniker, vs STONE Thomas, of Henniker, doc date 1784, deed, land transfer, file #1989

KEZAR John, cordwainer, of Hampstead, vs CHASE John, of Haverhill, doc date 1770, judgment, debt, file #789

KIBRIDGE Solomon, blacksmith, of Amherst, vs FARNUM Stephen, yeoman, of Amherst, rec date 1783, execution, debt, file #3061

KIDDER John Jr, yeoman, of Lyndeborough, vs BRADFORD William, husbandman, of Deering, rec date 1783, judgment, debt, file #3796

KIDDER Jonas, gentleman, of Lyndeborough, vs STILES Jonathan, yeoman, of Lyndeborough, doc date 1777, rec date 1779, deed, land transfer, file #2151

KIDDER Joseph, gentleman, of Temple, vs BUCKLEY John, gentleman, of Groton MA, doc date 1774, writ, debt, file #1134

KIDDER Reuben, of New Ipswich, vs CUTTER Nathan, housewright, of New Ipswich, doc date 1772, writ, debt, file #890, very fragile

KIDDER Reuben, esquire, of New Ipswich, vs GRAHAM John, yeoman, of Society Land, doc date 1773, execution, debt, file #1459

KIDDER Reuben, of Henniker, rec date 1794, appointment, file #3621

KIDDER Reuben, esquire, of New Ipswich, vs TARBELL Edmond, yeoman, of Mason, rec date 1785, judgment, debt, file #6442

KIDDER Reuben, esquire, of New Ipswich, vs EMERSON Nathaniel, gentleman, of Stoddard, rec date 1788, writ, debt, file #6901

KIDDER Samuel Philips, yeoman, of Deerfield, vs WILSON John, of Chelmsford MA, doc date 1799, judgment, debt, file #308

KIDER Reuben, esquire, of New Ipswich, vs GRAHAM John, yeoman, of Society Land, doc date 1772, execution, debt, file #1200

KILLICUT Charity, laborer, of Dunstable, vs WORSTER Noah, esquire, of Hollis, rec date 1784, judgment, debt, file #4254

KILLICUT Daniel, husbandman, of Dunstable, vs STATE of NH, recognizance, debt, file #2228

KILLICUT Reuben, yeoman, of Dunstable, vs JEWETT Jacob Jr, trader, of Hollis, doc date 1774, writ, debt, file #1110, fragile

KILLICUT Reuben, yeoman, of Dunstable, vs PIKE Daniel, yeoman, of Dunstable, doc date 1775, writ, debt, file #956

KILLICUT Reuben, yeoman, of Dunstable, vs FRENCH Joseph, gentleman, of Dunstable, rec date 1783, writ, debt, file #3352

KILLICUT Thomas, husbandman, of Dunstable, vs EMERSON Parker, yeoman, of Litchfield, doc date 1774, writ, debt, file #1126

KILLICUTT Reuben, yeoman, of Dunstable, vs COMBS Midad, yeoman, of Hollis, rec date 1782, execution, debt, file #4901

KILY Caleb?, husbandman, of Lyndeborough, vs PRENTICE Henry, of Littleton MA, rec date 1784, judgment, debt, file #4214

KIMBALL Abraham, husbandman, of Hopkinton, vs MERRILL Nehemiah, blacksmith, of Dunbarton, doc date 1798, judgment, debt, file #564

KIMBALL Amherst, gentleman, of Grafton, vs BURBANK Daniel, husbandman, of Boscawen, doc date 1799, debt, file #461

KIMBALL Caleb, husbandman, of Sutton, vs STEVENS Jonathan, husbandman, of Sutton, doc date 1798, execution, debt, file #190

KIMBALL Carriage Co, vs CITY of Manchester, doc date 1893, defendants brief, supreme court, file #609

KIMBALL Daniel, husbandman, of Bradford, vs ADAMS David, husbandman, of Dunstable, rec date 1774, execution, debt, file #4884

KIMBALL Daniel Jr, husbandman, of Bradford, vs ADAMS Daniel, husbandman, of Dunstable, doc date 1774, judgment, debt, file #703

KIMBALL Ebenezer, husbandman, of Amherst, vs HOLT Thomas, yeoman, of Lyndeborough, doc date 1798, judgment, debt, file #564

KIMBALL Ebenezer, gentleman, of Hollis, vs CHAMPNEY Ebenezer, gentleman, of New Ipswich, doc date 1773, writ, debt, file #1446

KIMBALL Edmond, yeoman, of Bradford, vs RICE Jacob, clerk, of Henniker, doc date 1798, judgment, debt, file #564

KIMBALL Henry, hatter, of Amherst, vs MINICHIN John, trader, of Boston MA, doc date 1799, writ, debt, file #575

KIMBALL Henry, hatter, of Amherst, vs CUTTLEY Zacheus, esquire, rec date 1777, misc, file #2220

KIMBALL Isaac, yeoman, of Temple, vs MOOR John, yeoman, of Peterborough, rec date 1783, writ, debt, file #4557

KIMBALL John, husbandman, of Hopkinton, vs DARLING Benjamin & Ruth, of Hopkinton, doc date 1796, deed, land transfer, file #1996

KIMBALL Joseph, of Henniker, rec date 1773, appointments, file #3620

KIMBALL Joseph, yeoman, of Weare, vs SHAW Ichabod, yeoman, of Marlborough, rec date 1783, writ, debt, file #4544

KIMBALL Joshua, cordwainer, of Amherst, vs WILKINS Robert B, gentleman, of Hillsborough, doc date 1787, rec date 1787, deed, land transfer, file #2499

KIMBALL Moses, blacksmith, of Hopkinton, vs COLBY Nathan, yeoman, of Alexandria, doc date 1784, execution, debt, file #1800

KIMBALL Moses, blacksmith, of Hopkinton, vs COLBY Nathan, yeoman, of Alexandria, rec date 1786, judgment, debt, file #5292

KIMBALL Nathan, laborer, of Hopkinton, vs DARLING John, gentleman, of Hopkinton, doc date 1778, rec date 1779, deed, land transfer, file #2141

KIMBALL Reuben, joiner, of Hopkinton, vs SANBORN Peter, joiner, of Enfield, doc date 1799, debt, file #460

KIMBALL Reuben Jr, gentleman, of Rindge, vs DENNIS Moses, yeoman, of Hancock, rec date 1783, writ, debt, file #3196

KIMBALL Samuel, yeoman, of Henniker, vs ANDREWS Molly, single woman, of Henniker, rec date 1785, various, assault, file #4747

KIMBALL Thomas, cooper, of Wenham MA, vs BUSWELL John, cordwainer, of Goffstown, rec date 1787, judgment, debt, file #2310

KIMBALL Thomas, yeoman, of Wenham MA, vs GRIMES James, gentleman, of Deering, rec date 1784, judgment, debt, file #4585

KIMBALL Thomas, yeoman, of Wenham MA, vs GRIMES James, gentleman, of Deering, rec date 1785, judgment, debt, file #5121

KIMBALL Timothy, yeoman, of Goffstown, vs DUSTON John Jr, yeoman, of Haverhill MA, doc date 1777, rec date 1779, deed, land transfer, file #2136

KIMBALL Timothy, yeoman, of Goffstown, vs DUSTON John, yeoman, of Goffstown, doc date 1779, rec date 1779, deed, land transfer, file #2130

KIMBALL Timothy, husbandman, of Goffstown, vs CUSHING John, physician, of Goffstown, rec date 1785, writ, debt, file #5434

KIMBALL William, husbandman, of Henniker, vs BRADFORD Samuel 3rd, yeoman, of Hillsborough, doc date 1772, writ, debt, file #1415

KIMBLE Ebenezer, of Lyndeborough, doc date 1787, license, tavern license, file #869

KINDRICK Daniel (Capt), of Hollis, rec date 1784, bill, debt, file #4742

KINDRICK David, yeoman, of Hollis, vs DICKEY James, rec date 1784, writ, stealing cattle, file #4746

KING James, yeoman, of Bradford, vs HART Charles Walker, yeoman, of Bradford, doc date 1798, judgment, debt, file #564

KING Sarah, widow/spinster, of Bedford, vs MORREL Robert, yeoman, of Bedford, rec date 1784, various, debt, file #4985

KING William, blacksmith, of Amherst, vs MOOR John, husbandman, of Francestown, rec date 1786, writ, debt, file #6102

KING William Jr, husbandman, of Londonderry, vs BLANCHARD Augustus, gentleman, of Amherst, doc date 1784, petition, release of debit, file #1

KING William Jr, husbandman, of Londonderry, vs BLANCHARD Augustus, gentleman, of Amherst, rec date 1783, writ, debt, file #3078

KINNEY Stephen, yeoman, of Nottingham-West, vs BRADBURY Sanders, yeoman, of Nottingham-West, doc date 1774, judgment, debt, file #709

KINSLEY Daniel, yeoman, of Bennington NY, vs HUTCHINS Samuel, clerk, of Lee, rec date 1783, execution, debt, file #3267

KINSMAN Aaron, esquire, of Concord, vs DOW Oliver, gentleman, of Hopkinton, rec date 1785, judgment, debt, file #5561

KINSMAN Aaron, esquire, of Concord, vs CHADWICK Joseph, yeoman, of Henniker, rec date 1786, writ, debt, file #6284

KINSMAN Aaron, esquire, of Concord, vs CHADWICK Joseph, yeoman, of Henniker, rec date 1786, judgment, debt, file #6466

KINSMOR Aaron, esquire, of Concord, vs DOW Oliver, gentleman, of Hopkinton, rec date 1785, judgment, debt, file #6394

KITRIDGE Ebenezer, gentleman, of Goffstown, vs FRENCH Thomas, yeoman, of Tewksbury MA, rec date 1783, writ, debt, file #3959

KITRIDGE Zephaniah, surgeon, of Amherst, vs BOUTELL Amos, yeoman, of Amherst, rec date 1786, judgment, debt, file #5757

KITTREDGE Asa, yeoman, of Francestown, vs CAMPBELL Henry, trader, of Antrim, doc date 1799, writ, debt, file #321

KITTREDGE Asa, yeoman, of Deering, vs GIBSON John, trader, of Francestown, doc date 1799, debt, file #341

KITTREDGE Ella E F, vs HODGMAN James C F, doc date 1892, brief for plaintiff, supreme court, file #617

KITTREDGE Nehemiah, gentleman, of Billerica MA, vs KITTREDGE James, yeoman, of Goffstown, doc date 1784, execution, debt, file #1554

KITTREDGE Nehemiah, gentleman, of Billerica MA, vs KITTREDGE Ebenezer, yeoman, of Chester, doc date 1784, execution, debt, file #1554

KITTREDGE Nehemiah, gentleman, of Billerica MA, vs KITTRIDGE Ebenezer, yeoman, of Chester, rec date 1783, judgment, debt, file #4311

KITTREDGE Nehemiah, gentleman, of Billerica MA, vs KITTRIDGE James, yeoman, of Goffstown, rec date 1783, judgment, debt, file #4311

KITTRIDGE Asa, yeoman, of Deering, vs LAWTON Michael, of Francestown, doc date 1799, judgment, debt, file #240

KITTRIDGE James, husbandman, of Goffstown, vs DUTY William, cooper, of Salem, doc date 1784, petition, release of debit, file #4

KITTRIDGE Nehemiah, husbandman, of Billerica MA, vs FRENCH Nehemiah, husbandman, of Hollis, rec date 1793, judgment, debt, file #2587 B

KITTRIDGE Nehemiah, husbandman, of Billerica MA, vs FRENCH Nehemiah, husbandman, of Hollis, rec date 1793, judgment, debt, file #2587 B

KITTRIDGE Nehemiah, husbandman, of Billerica MA, vs FRENCH Nehemiah, husbandman, of Hollis, rec date 1793, judgment, debt, file #2587 A

KITTRIDGE Nehemiah, gentleman, of Billerica MA, vs JAQUITH Benjamin, yeoman, of Jaffrey, rec date 1783, civil litigious, debt, file #2911

KITTRIDGE Nehemiah, gentleman, of Billerica MA, vs KITTRIDGE Ebenezer, yeoman, of Chester, rec date 1783, judgment, debt, file #4716

KITTRIDGE Nehemiah, gentleman, of Billerica MA, vs FROST Jonathan Jr, yeoman, of Moultonborough, rec date 1785, judgment, debt, file #4693

KITTRIDGE Nehemiah, gentleman, of Billerica MA, vs WRIGHT Uriah, gentleman, of Hollis, rec date 1785, judgment, debt, file #5346

KITTRIDGE Solomon, blacksmith, of Amherst, vs FARNUM Stephen, yeoman, of Amherst, rec date 1783, court case, debt, file #2877, KITTRIDGE kinship

KITTRIDGE Solomon, blacksmith, of Amherst, vs FARNUM Stephen, yeoman, of Amherst, rec date 1782, appeal, debt, file #4022, kinship of KITTRIDGE also

KNIGHT Enos, yeoman, of Hillsborough, vs BALL Joseph, yeoman, of Mason, doc date 1784, civil litigation, debt, file #1650

KNIGHT Enos, yeoman, of New Ipswich, vs BALL Joseph, gentleman, of Mason, rec date 1783, writ, debt, file #3178

KNIGHT Enos, husbandman, of Hancock, vs PRESTON Abner, husbandman, of Hancock, rec date 1785, judgment, debt, file #5589

KNIGHT Joseph, mariner, of Newburyport MA, vs BLODGETT Benjamin, merchant, of Goffstown, doc date 1798, judgment, debt, file #564

KNIGHT Margaret, spinster, of Litchfield, vs THORNTON Ming, laborer, of Merrimack, rec date 1782, various, assault, file #3551

LADD Edward, yeoman, of Andover, vs TRUE William, husbandman, of Andover, rec date 1792, judgment, debt, file #2580

LADD Edward, yeoman, of Andover, vs BLAKE Samuel, husbandman, of Andover, rec date 1792, judgment, debt, file #2580

LADD Edward, yeoman, of Andover, vs FULLER David, husbandman, of Andover, rec date 1792, judgment, debt, file #2580

LADD Edward, yeoman, of Andover, vs STATE of NH, rec date 1792, indictment, road dispute, file #4158

LADD James, yeoman, of Plainfield, vs ALEXANDER Samuel, husbandman, of Salisbury, doc date 1798, execution, debt, file #111

LADD Nathaniel, laborer, of Sandown, vs SANBORN John, yeoman, of Sandown, doc date 1768, rec date 1788, deed, land transfer, file #6752

LADD Nathaniel Jr, yeoman, of Alexandria, vs RUSSELL James, yeoman, of Litchfield, rec date 1782, appeal, debt, file #3979

LAFRANCE Frank, of Manchester, vs SIMON Edward & Eugene, of Raymond, doc date 1894, misc, supreme court, file #631

LAIN John, yeoman, of Fisherfield, vs STANLEY John, husbandman, of Fisherfield, rec date 1785, writ, debt, file #4803

LAKIN David, husbandman, of Groton, vs WRIGHT Josiah, husbandman, of Hollis, rec date 1788, writ, debt, file #6720

LAKIN Samuel, gentleman, of Hancock, vs CARLTON Samuel, yeoman, of Greenfield, doc date 1798, execution, debt, file #147

LAMARSH Edmund, of Nashua, vs LUNION St Jean Baptiste, of Nashua, doc date 1894, assumpsit, supreme court, file #591

LAMB Benjamin, yeoman, of Framingham MA, vs RICE Daniel, gentleman, of Marlborough MA, rec date 1786, confession, debt, file #2322

LAMBERT Thomas, yeoman, of Rowley MA, vs EAGERS Joseph, yeoman, of Merrimack, doc date 1784, execution, debt, file #1757

LAMON Jonathan, husbandman, of Middleton MA, vs WILKINS Daniel, husbandman, of Amherst, rec date 1785, judgment, debt, file #6445

LAMON Jothan, husbandman, of Middleton MA, vs WILKINS Daniel, husbandman, of Amherst, rec date 1785, writ, debt, file #5969

LAMPRON William, innholder, of Amherst, vs JONES Samuel, yeoman, of Hillsborough, rec date 1783, execution, debt, file #3874

LAMPSON William, innholder, of Amherst, vs JONES Samuel, yeoman, of Hillsborough, rec date 1783, writ, debt, file #3909

LAMSON Joseph Jr, stone cutter, of Charleston MA, vs WARNER Daniel, gentleman, of Amherst, rec date 1784, judgment, debt, file #4592

LANCEY Samuel, yeoman, of Chelmsford MA, vs KARR Thomas, yeoman, of New Boston, rec date 1785, judgment, debt, file #4970

LANCEY Thomas, yeoman, of Bradford, vs COLE Benjamin, yeoman, of Society Land, doc date 1773, writ, debt, file #1233

LANCEY Thomas, yeoman, of Bedford, vs SPAULDING Reuben, gentleman, of Nottingham-West, rec date 1783, writ, debt, file #2767

LANDEN Oliver, husbandman, of Hollis, vs PEABODY William, gentleman, of Amherst, rec date 1782, writ, debt, file #2783

LANE John, husbandman, of Fisherfield, vs PHILBRICK Benjamin, yeoman, of Sutton, rec date 1785, judgment, debt, file #5166

LANGDON John, esquire, of Portsmouth, vs BLANCHARD Jotham, merchant, of Peterborough, rec date 1784, writ, debt, file #4673

LANGDON Wobury, of Portsmouth, vs ANDERSON James, cordwainer, of Boxford MA, doc date 1781, rec date 1781, deed, land transfer, file #6803

LANGDON Woodbury, esquire, of Portsmouth, vs LORD Mark, merchant, of Berwick Me, rec date 1788, writ, debt, file #6635

LANGLEY Joshua, gentleman, of Shirley MA, vs WHITCOMB Jonathan, gentleman, of Swanzey, rec date 1783, writ, debt, file #3920

LANQUETTE Joseph F A, vs LAPLANTE Louis M, defendants brief, supreme court, file #627

LAUGHLIN Samuel, husbandman, of Goffstown, vs SMITH Robinson, husbandman, of Gilmanton, doc date 1798, judgment, debt, file #564

LAUGHLIN Samuel, husbandman, of Hillsborough, vs SMITH Robinson, husbandman, of Gilmanton, doc date 1799, debt, file #467

LAVIN Jon Clarke, license, tavern license, file #876

LAWRANCE Peleg, blacksmith, of Hollis, vs HASKELL Joseph, miller, of Hollis, rec date 1787, writ, debt, file #2424, theft corn

LAWRANCE Peter, yeoman, of Hollis, vs PARK Thomas, stone cutter, of Shirley MA, rec date 1782, writ, debt, file #2806

LAWRENCE Abel, distiller, of Salem MA, vs BUTLERS John Jr, husbandman, of Jaffrey, rec date 1788, judgment, debt, file #2567

LAWRENCE Abel, distiller, of Salem MA, vs SMITH Reuben, yeoman, of New Boston, rec date 1783, judgment, debt, file #3794

LAWRENCE Abel, distiller, of Salem MA, vs WILKINS John, gentleman, of Amherst, rec date 1783, various, debt, file #4315

LAWRENCE Abel, esquire, of Salem, vs WILKINS John, gentleman, of Amherst, rec date 1785, various, debt, file #4829

LAWRENCE Abel, distiller, of Salem MA, vs BRADFORD Samuel, gentleman, of Hillsborough, rec date 1786, writ, debt, file #6120

LAWRENCE Amos, yeoman, of Wilton, vs ATHERTON Joshua, esquire, of Amherst, doc date 1799, writ, debt, file #400

LAWRENCE Benjamin, gentleman, of Pepperell MA, vs MOSHER James, husbandman, of Hollis, rec date 1784, judgment, debt, file #4994

LAWRENCE Daniel, yeoman, of Hollis, vs CUMMINGS Benjamin, gentleman, of Hollis, doc date 1801, judgment, debt, file #568

LAWRENCE David, gentleman, of Nottingham-West, vs STEEL Joseph, yeoman, of Nottingham-West, doc date 1781, capias, debt, file #769

LAWRENCE David, yeoman, of Londonderry, vs STEEL Joseph, rec date 1777, various, debt, file #2231

LAWRENCE David, yeoman, of Littleton MA, vs SMITH Edward, gentleman, of Peterborough Slip, rec date 1787, writ, debt, file #6645

LAWRENCE Enos, yeoman, of Mason, vs BLANCHARD Jonathan, esquire, of Merrimack, rec date 1775, civil litigation, debt, file #2222

LAWRENCE Ephraim, physician, of Pepperell MA, vs WRIGHT David, yeoman, of Hollis, rec date 1785, judgment, debt, file #5514

LAWRENCE Ephraim, physician, of Pepperell MA, vs FLAGG Eleazer, housewright, of Hollis, doc date 1784, execution, debt, file #1821

LAWRENCE Ephraim, physician, of Pepperell MA, vs FLAGG Eleazer, carpenter, of Hollis, doc date 1784, various, debt, file #1598

LAWRENCE Ephraim, physician, of Pepperell MA, vs ABBOTT Samuel, yeoman, of Hollis, rec date 1782, judgment, debt, file #3131

LAWRENCE Ephraim, physician, of Pepperell MA, vs ABBOTT Samuel, yeoman, of Hollis, rec date 1783, execution, debt, file #2900

LAWRENCE Ephraim, physician, of Pepperell MA, vs FLAGG Eleazer, housewright, of Hollis, rec date 1784, judgment, debt, file #4377

LAWRENCE Ephraim, physician, of Pepperell MA, vs FELT Benjamin, blacksmith, of Temple, rec date 1785, writ, debt, file #6009

LAWRENCE Ezekiel, laborer, of Hollis, vs DICKEY James, gentleman, of Raby, rec date 1785, writ, debt, file #2403

LAWRENCE James Jr, husbandman, of Pepperell MA, vs GRAHAM William, husbandman, of Raby, rec date 1788, writ, debt, file #2429

LAWRENCE James Jr, husbandman, of Pepperell MA, vs LEE Abigail, spinster, of Hollis, rec date 1788, writ, debt, file #2432

LAWRENCE Jonathan, husbandman, of Nottingham-West, vs BRADLEY Ithmar, innkeeper, of Hollis, rec date 1784, judgment, debt, file #5451

LAWRENCE Love & William, clerk, of Lincoln MA, vs FARWELL Oliver, gentleman, of Chesterfield, rec date 1785, judgment, debt, file #5178

LAWRENCE Love & William, executors, of Lincoln MA, vs FARWELL Oliver, gentleman, of Chesterfield, rec date 1785, judgment, debt, file #5979

LAWRENCE Obel, distiller, of Boston MA, vs COCHRAN John, husbandman, of New Boston, rec date 1785, judgment, debt, file #5169

LAWRENCE Obel, distiller, of Boston MA, vs BOYES William, husbandman, of New Boston, rec date 1785, judgment, debt, file #5169

LAWRENCE Obel, distiller, of Boston MA, vs McNEIL John C, husbandman, of Derryfield, rec date 1785, judgment, debt, file #5169

LAWRENCE Oliver, husbandman, of Hollis, vs CUMMINGS Benjamin, gentleman, of Hollis, rec date 1792, judgment, debt, file #2579

LAWRENCE Oliver, husbandman, of Pepperell MA, vs PATTEN Matthew, esquire, of Bedford, rec date 1783, writ, debt, file #3107

LAWRENCE Oliver, husbandman, of Derryfield, vs EMERSON George, husbandman, of Dunbarton, rec date 1783, writ, debt, file #4565

LAWRENCE Oliver, husbandman, of Hollis, vs SHANNON Richard Cutts, esquire, of Hollis, rec date 1786, writ, debt, file #6334, /

LAWRENCE Oliver, husbandman, of Hollis, vs CUMMINGS Benjamin, gentleman, of Hollis, rec date 1786, writ, debt, file #6334, /

LAWRENCE Peter, husbandman, of Hollis, vs HARD Phinehas, husbandman, of Hollis, rec date 1782, debt, debt, file #3159

LAWRENCE Peter, husbandman, of Hollis, vs GIBSON Simeon, gentleman, of Pepperell MA, rec date 1782, appeal, debt, file #3977

LAWRENCE Stephen, yeoman, of Mason, vs HILL David, of New Ipswich, doc date 1782, judgment, file #1163

LAWRENCE Thomas, husbandman, of Mason, vs FLAGG Eleazer, of Hollis, rec date 1783, judgment, debt, file #3714

LAWRENCE Zachariah, yeoman, of Hollis, vs FLAGG Eleazer, housewright, of Hollis, rec date 1784, judgment, debt, file #4242

LAWRENCE Zachariah, trader, of Hollis, vs ROGERS Solomon, gentleman, of Hollis, doc date 1781, rec date 1781, deed, land transfer, file #6569

LAWRENCE Zachariah Jr, trader, of Hollis, vs SAWYER Abel Jr, trader, of Newbury MA, rec date 1782, judgment, debt, file #2713

LEACH Robert, shopkeeper, of Salem, vs WALKER John, shopkeeper, of Salem, rec date 1783, execution, debt, file #3698

LEALAND Simeon, yeoman, of Shelburn MA, vs MILLS John, gentleman, of Amherst, rec date 1786, writ, debt, file #6112

LEE Joseph, esquire, of Cambridge MA, vs HOAR Timothy, gentleman, of Concord, rec date 1787, judgment, file #7049

LEE Joseph, esquire, of Cambridge MA, vs WHITTAKER David, yeoman, of Concord, rec date 1787, judgment, file #7049

LEE Joseph, esquire, of Cambridge MA, vs BARRETT James, of Concord, rec date 1787, judgment, debt, file #7047

LEE Joseph, esquire, of Cambridge MA, vs MILES Charles, gentleman, of Concord, rec date 1787, judgment, file #7049

LEE William, yeoman, of Lyndeborough, vs STEEL William, yeoman, of Campdon, doc date 1774, writ, debt, file #1096

LEE William, of Lyndeborough, vs THOMPSON Andrew, doc date 1775, writ, dispute of oxen, file #962

LEGATE Thomas, esquire, of Leominster MA, vs MOULTON Jonathan, esquire, of Hampton, rec date 1786, judgment, debt, file #6494

LEGATE Thomas, esquire, of Leominster MA, vs ROGERS John Jur, physician, of Plymouth, rec date 1788, writ, debt, file #6941

LEILY Jonas, cooper, of Brookline, vs LAWRENCE Timothy, gentleman, of Lawrence MA, doc date 1799, execution, debt, file #170

LEROY Stephen, vs LUTWEYTHE Sarah, deceased, rec date 1778, civil litigation, land dispute, file #2217

LESLEY Jonas, cooper, of Hollis, vs PARKER Oliver, husbandman, of Hollis, rec date 1783, writ, debt, file #3110

LESLEY Joseph, husbandman, of Hollis, vs MOSHER James, husbandman, of Hollis, rec date 1784, judgment, debt, file #4991

LEWIS Aaron, yeoman, of Lyndeborough, vs SMITH David, husbandman, of Lyndeborough, rec date 1785, execution, debt, file #5908

LEWIS Aaron, yeoman, of Lyndeborough, vs SMITH David, husbandman, of Lyndeborough, rec date 1785, writ, debt, file #6865

LEWIS Benjamin, yeoman, of Deering, vs JONES Caleb, husbandman, of Mile Slip, doc date 1774, writ, debt, file #1099

LEWIS Jonathan, merchant, of Groton MA, vs MORRISON Moses, yeoman, of Society Land, doc date 1774, execution, file #985

LEWIS Jonathan, cordwainer, of Harvard MA, vs EVERETT Edward, gentleman, of Rumney, rec date 1784, judgment, debt, file #4999

LEWIS Joseph, gentleman, of Henniker, vs GIBSON Timothy Jr, yeoman, of Henniker, doc date 1779, rec date NOT GIVEN, deed, land transfer, file #5657

LEWIS Reuben, of MA, vs GREEN David, yeoman, of NH, rec date 1782, execution, debt, file #4904, missing torn pieces

LEWIS Samuel, husbandman, of Chelmsford MA, vs ELLINGWOOD Benjamin, husbandman, of Amherst, doc date 1772, writ, debt, file #881

LEWIS Samuel, husbandman, of Washington, vs WARNER Daniel, gentleman, of Amherst, rec date 1783, judgment, debt, file #3771

LEWIS Samuel, husbandman, of Washington, vs KELLY Moses, esquire, of Goffstown, rec date 1785, judgment, debt, file #4870

LIERCE Levi, yeoman, of Temple, vs BOYNTON John, yeoman, of Hollis, doc date 1778, rec date 1781, deed, land transfer, file #5659

LINCOLN Elisha, husbandman, of Bedford, vs DANA Anna, widow, of Amherst, doc date 1799, judgment, debt, file #246

LINTON Michael, yeoman, of Francestown, vs ROLLAND Nathaniel, yeoman, of Greenfield, doc date 1799, execution, debt, file #157

LITTLE Bond, yeoman, of Deering, vs GRIMES James, yeoman, of Deering, doc date 1784, writ, debt, file #1620

LITTLE Bond, husbandman, of Deering, vs CLOUGH David, husbandman, of Dracut MA, rec date 1784, judgment, debt, file #4344

LITTLE Bond, husbandman, of Deering, vs BLAISDELL Jonathan, blacksmith, of Weare, rec date 1784, judgment, debt, file #4226

LITTLE Caleb, husbandman, of Goffstown, vs SHIPLE Oliver, cordwainer, of New Boston, rec date 1786, writ, debt, file #6100

LITTLE Elizabeth, singlewoman, of Peterborough Slip, vs HOLMES Robert, husbandman, of Peterborough, rec date 1784, appeal, debt, file #4105

LITTLE Enoch, esquire, of Boscawen, vs BOHANAN Andrew, gentleman, of Salisbury, doc date 1798, execution, debt, file #112

LITTLE John, gentleman, of Deerfield, vs STINSON William, gentleman, of Dunbarton, rec date 1782, debt, debt, file #3147

LITTLE John, husbandman, of Derryfield, vs THORNTON Matthew, esquire, of Merrimack, rec date 1785, judgment, debt, file #5354

LITTLE John, gentleman, of Derryfield, vs McNEILL John Caldwell, husbandman, of Derryfield, rec date 1785, judgment, debt, file #5579

LITTLE John, gentleman, of Lunenburg MA, vs WOOD Barnabas, husbandman, of Jaffrey, rec date 1785, writ, debt, file #6144

LITTLE John, gentleman, of Derryfield, vs LITTLE Lattice, spinster, rec date 1788, deed, land transfer, file #6824

LITTLE Joseph, laborer, of Peterborough, vs BLACHARD Jothan, merchant, of Peterborough, doc date 1784, execution, debt, file #1745

LITTLE Joseph, laborer, of Peterborough, vs BLANCHARD Jotham, merchant, of Peterborough, rec date 1782, judgment, debt, file #2722, 108

LITTLE Joseph, laborer, of Peterborough, vs BLANCHARD Jotham, merchant, of Peterborough, rec date 1783, civil litigious, debt, file #2959

LITTLE Joseph, laborer, of Peterborough, vs BLANCHARD Jonathan, merchant, of Peterborough, rec date 1786, writ, debt, file #6337

LITTLE Moses, esquire, of Goffstown, vs WOOD Jonathan, husbandman, of Goffstown, rec date 1783, writ, debt, file #3362

LITTLE Moses, esquire, of Goffstown, vs INHABITANTS of Goffstown, rec date 1782, various, debit for beef, file #3613

LITTLE Moses, gentleman, of Goffstown, vs INHABITANTS of Goffstown, rec date 1782, appeal, debt, file #4027, beef debit for army

LITTLE Moses, esquire, of Goffstown, vs DUSTON Paul, yeoman, rec date 1782, execution, debt, file #5745

LITTLE Moses, esquire, of Goffstown, vs EASTMAN Benjamin, tanner, of Canterbury, doc date 1787, rec date 1787, various, debits, file #6806

LITTLE Moses, esquire, of Goffstown, vs EASTMAN Benjamin, tanner, of Canterbury, rec date 1788, writ, debt, file #6784

LITTLE Richard, yeoman, of Newbury MA, vs WOOD Samuel, clerk, of Boscawen, doc date 1781, rec date 1783, deed, land transfer, file #2656

LITTLE Sampson, gentleman, of Littleton MA, vs WOOD Samuel, yeoman, of Mason, rec date 1784, appeal, debt, file #4109

LITTLE Thomas, husbandman, of Peterborough, vs BIGELOW Timothy, esquire, of Groton MA, doc date 1799, writ, debt, file #405

LITTLE Thomas, yeoman, of Litchfield, vs SAUNDERS James, yeoman, of Salem, doc date 1784, civil litigation, debt, file #1639

LITTLE Thomas, rec date 1779, deposition, land dispute, file #2236B

LITTLE Thomas, yeoman, of Peterborough, vs SCOTT Benjamin & Jenne, yeoman, of Peterborough, rec date 1783, writ, debt, file #2768

LITTLE Thomas, husbandman, of Peterborough, vs PATTERSON Adam, husbandman, of Hancock, rec date 1788, judgment, debt, file #2561

LITTLE Thomas, yeoman, of Peterborough, vs SCOTT William, esquire, of Groton MA, rec date 1784, appeal, debt, file #4114

LITTLE Thomas, yeoman, of Peterborough, vs TAYLOR Ezra, esquire, of MA, rec date 1784, judgment, debt, file #4233

LITTLE Thomas, husbandman, of Peterborough, vs INHABITANTS of Peterborough, rec date 1786, writ, debt, file #6640

LITTLE Wallis, gentleman, of Shirley MA, vs McELLASTER Peter, yeoman, of Peterborough, rec date 1782, execution, debt, file #5727

LITTLE William, physician, of Hillsborough, vs STEWARD Samuel, husbandman, of Lyndeborough, rec date 1786, writ, debt, file #6326

LIVERMORE Edward, gentleman, of Concord, vs FOX John, husbandman, of Packersfield, rec date 1784, judgment, debt, file #5300

LIVERMORE Edward S, gentleman, of Concord, vs CUTTER John, husbandman, of New Ipswich, rec date 1788, writ, debt, file #6955

LIVERMORE Jonathan, gentleman, of New Ipswich, vs HOLT William, yeoman, of Wilton, doc date 1799, judgment, debt, file #224

LIVERMORE Jonathan, clerk, of Wilton, vs INHABITANTS of Stoddard, doc date 1784, execution, debt, file #1539

LIVERMORE Jonathan, clerk, of Wilton, vs RUSSELL Thomas, yeoman, of Wilton, rec date 1783, writ, debt, file #3602

LIVERMORE Jonathan, clerk, of Wilton, vs INHABITANTS of Stoddard, rec date 1783, writ, debt, file #3579

LIVERMORE Samuel, esquire, of Londonderry, vs RICHARDSON Thomas, husbandman, of Pelham, doc date 1772, writ, debt, file #1402

LIVINGSTON John, yeoman, of New Boston, vs WILSON Samuel, husbandman, doc date 1798, execution, debt, file #52

LIVINGSTON William, blacksmith, of New Boston, vs GORDON William, esquire, of Amherst, doc date 1799, debt, file #348

LIVINGSTON William, of New Boston, vs Town of New Boston, rec date 1778, license, tavern license, file #2233

LIVINGSTON William, gentleman, of New Boston, vs BALDWIN Nahum, esquire, of Amherst, rec date 1782, writ, debt, file #2849, estate Zacheus CUTLER

LIVINGSTON William, gentleman, of New Boston, vs KELLY Moses, esquire, of Goffstown, rec date 1783, writ, debt, file #3957

LIVINGSTON William, gentleman, of New Boston, vs McGINNIS Barnabas, yeoman, of New Boston, rec date 1782, appeal, debt, file #3994

LIVINGSTON William, of New Boston, vs GREGG Alexander, administrator of estate, of New Boston, rec date 1788, deposition, debt, file #6976

LIVINGSTON William, gentleman, of New Boston, vs McGAA Robert, trader, of Hollis, rec date 1782, writ, debt, file #2782

LOCKE Daniel, husbandman, of Stoddard, vs KITTREDGE Nathaniel, yeoman, of Deering, doc date 1798, execution, debt, file #61

LOCKE Daniel, esquire, of Rindge, vs PARKER Benjamin, laborer, of New Ipswich, rec date 1782, writ, assault, file #3559

LOCKE Jonathan, of Ashby MA, vs HERRICK Amos, laborer, of Mason, rec date 1785, judgment, debt, file #6373

LOCKE Thomas, gentleman, of Cambridge MA, vs BENSON Isaac, gentleman, of Richmond, rec date 1793, judgment, debt, file #2585

LORING John, apothecary, of Boston MA, vs GIBSON James, husbandman, of Merrimack, rec date 1783, execution, debt, file #3232

LORING John, apothecary, of Boston MA, vs GIBSON James, husbandman, of Merrimack, rec date 1782, execution, debt, file #3480

LOVE William, yeoman, of Hillsborough, vs STARET William, husbandman, of Francestown, doc date 1788, rec date 1788, deed, land transfer, file #6817

LOVEJOY Benjamin, yeoman, of Hillsborough, vs STEEL John, yeoman, of Hillsborough, doc date 1772, civil litigation, debt, file #662

LOVEJOY Francis, feltmaker, of Amherst, vs STEVENS Samuel, physician, of Amherst, doc date 1784, writ, debt, file #1588

LOVEJOY Francis, feltmaker, of Amherst, vs LOVEJOY Francis Jr, yeoman, of Amherst, rec date 1787, judgment, debt, file #2468

LOVEJOY Francis, feltmaker, of Amherst, vs DODGE Samuel, esquire, of Amherst, rec date 1783, writ, debt, file #3312

LOVEJOY Francis, hatter, of Amherst, vs KELLEY Moses, esquire, of Goffstown, rec date 1783, bond, debt, file #3358

LOVEJOY Francis, feltmaker, of Amherst, vs KELLEY Moses, esquire, of Goffstown, rec date 1783, writ, debt, file #3184

LOVEJOY Francis, feltmaker, of Amherst, vs ATHERTON Joshua, esquire, of Amherst, rec date 1783, writ, debt, file #3312

LOVEJOY Francis, husbandman, of Amherst, vs KELLY Moses, esquire, of Goffstown, rec date 1783, writ, debt, file #3351

LOVEJOY Francis, feltmaker, of Amherst, vs LOVEJOY John, yeoman, of Amherst, rec date 1783, execution, debt, file #3814

LOVEJOY Francis, feltmaker, of Amherst, vs PIKE Zachariah, yeoman, of Bedford, rec date 1783, execution, debt, file #3814

LOVEJOY Francis, feltmaker, of Amherst, vs HOIT John, esquire, of Hollis, rec date 1782, appeal, debt, file #3984

LOVEJOY Francis, feltmaker, of Amherst, vs FARNUM Stephen, yeoman, of Lyndeborough, rec date 1784, judgment, debt, file #4237

LOVEJOY Francis, feltmaker, of Amherst, vs PIKE Zachariah, yeoman, of Bedford, rec date 1784, judgment, debt, file #4387

LOVEJOY Francis, feltmaker, of Amherst, vs LOVEJOY John, yeoman, of Bedford, rec date 1784, judgment, debt, file #4387

LOVEJOY Francis, feltmaker, of Amherst, vs LOVEJOY John, yeoman, of Amherst, rec date 1785, various, debt, file #4841

LOVEJOY Francis, feltmaker, of Amherst, vs PIKE Zachariah, yeoman, of Bedford, rec date 1785, various, debt, file #4841, fragile

LOVEJOY Francis, feltmaker, of Amherst, vs BROWN William Jr, yeoman, of Amherst, rec date 1786, writ, debt, file #6099

LOVEJOY Hezekiah, gentleman, of Amherst, vs KELLY Moses, esquire, of Goffstown, rec date 1783, writ, debt, file #3351

LOVEJOY John, yeoman, of Amherst, vs BISHOP George, husbandman, of Hillsborough, rec date 1782, execution, debt, file #3516

LOVEJOY John, yeoman, of Amherst, vs BISHOP George, husbandman, of Hillsborough, rec date 1783, writ, debt, file #3501

LOVEJOY John, yeoman, of Amherst, vs GLYNN John, yeoman, of Hillsborough, rec date 1783, execution, debt, file #3501

LOVEJOY John, yeoman, of Amherst, vs BISHOP George, husbandman, of Hillsborough, rec date 1783, execution, debt, file #3813

LOVEJOY Jonathan Jr, husbandman, of Hollis, vs CUMINGS Samuel, esquire, of Hollis, rec date 1777, writ, debt, file #2191

LOVEJOY Joseph & Patricia, yeoman, of Amherst, vs LAMSON William, yeoman, of Amherst, doc date 1786, rec date 1786, deed, land transfer, file #5031

LOVEJOY Samuel, husbandman, of Wilton, vs GREEN ----, doc date 1799, writ, debt, file #573

LOVELL Nehemiah, esquire, of Newbury NY, vs VICKERY Hannah, spinster, of Merrimack, doc date 1772, writ, debt, file #1062

LOVEWELL Jonathan, esquire, of Dunstable, vs HARRIS Lois, widow, of Dunstable, doc date 1777, rec date 1778, deed, land transfer, file #2164

LOVEWELL Jonathan, esquire, of Dunstable, vs HALL Benjamin, distiller, of Medford MA, rec date 1785, writ, debt, file #5416

LOVEWELL Noah, esquire, of Dunstable, vs BALLARD Uriah, yeoman, of Wilton, rec date 1783, judgment, debt, file #4432

LOVEWELL Noah, esquire, of Dunstable, vs BUTTERFIELD Jonathan, yeoman, of Dunstable, rec date 1786, execution, debt, file #5783

LOVEWELL Noah, esquire, of Dunstable, vs BUTTERFIELD Jonathan, yeoman, of Dunstable, rec date 1785, judgment, debt, file #5865

LOVEWELL Noah, esquire, of Dunstable, vs BUTTERFIELD Jonathan, yeoman, of Dunstable, rec date 1786, judgment, debt, file #6411

LOVWELL Noah, esquire, of Dunstable, vs CARSON John, gentleman, of Francestown, rec date 1783, civil litigious, debt, file #2926

LOW William, husbandman, of Chelsea MA, vs MOOR Samuel, husbandman, of Bedford, doc date 1784, judgment, debt, file #1601

LOW William, husbandman, of Chelsea MA, vs LITTLE Moses, esquire, of Goffstown, doc date 1784, judgment, debt, file #1601

LOW William, husbandman, of Chelsea MA, vs BOYD Samuel, gentleman, of Goffstown, doc date 1784, judgment, debt, file #1601

LOW William, husbandman, of Chelsea MA, vs LITTLE Moses, esquire, of Goffstown, rec date 1783, judgment, debt, file #4036

LOW William, husbandman, of Chelsea MA, vs MOOR Samuel, husbandman, of Bedford, rec date 1783, judgment, debt, file #4036

LOW William, husbandman, of Chelsea MA, vs BOYD Samuel, gentleman, of Goffstown, rec date 1783, judgment, debt, file #4036

LOW William, husbandman, of Chelsea MA, vs MOORE Samuel, husbandman, of Bedford, rec date 1784, judgment, debt, file #6352

LOW William, husbandman, of Chelsea MA, vs BOYDON Samuel, gentleman, of Goffstown, rec date 1784, judgment, debt, file #6352

LOW William, husbandman, of Chelsea MA, vs LITTLE Moses, esquire, of Bedford, rec date 1784, judgment, debt, file #6352

LOWEL David, yeoman, of Mason, vs JOHNSON Noah, husbandman, of Dunstable, doc date 1773, writ, debt, file #1441

LOWEL Moses, yeoman, of Mason, vs JOHNSON Noah, husbandman, of Dunstable, doc date 1772, writ, debt, file #1414

LOWELL ----, esquire, of Boston MA, vs McCALLEY John, husbandman, of Hillsborough, rec date 1783, judgment, debt, file #3713

LOWELL John, esquire, of Merrimack, vs USHER Robert, husbandman, of Merrimack, doc date 1799, debt, file #491

LOWELL John, yeoman, of Boston MA, vs CLARK Benjamin, yeoman, of Amherst, doc date 1782, execution, file #1024

LOWELL John, esquire, of Boston MA, vs POLLARD John, husbandman, of Nottingham-West, rec date 1783, judgment, debt, file #3288

LOWELL John, esquire, of Boston MA, vs MERRILL Nathaniel, husbandman, of Nottingham-West, rec date 1783, judgment, debt, file #3288

LOWELL John, esquire, of Boston MA, vs BRADFORD Andrew, gentleman, of Amherst, rec date 1783, writ, debt, file #3447

LOWELL John, esquire, of Boston MA, vs HOWARD William, husbandman, of Amherst, rec date 1783, writ, debt, file #3447

LOWELL John, esquire, of Boston MA, vs GIBSON James, yeoman, of Merrimack, rec date 1783, execution, debt, file #3645

LOWELL John, esquire, of Boston MA, vs DODGE Josiah, husbandman, of Amherst, rec date 1783, writ, debt, file #3630

LOWELL John, esquire, of Boston MA, vs ABBOTT Benjamin, yeoman, of Hollis, rec date 1783, writ, debt, file #3464

LOWELL John, esquire, of Boston MA, vs JONES William, husbandman, of Hillsborough, rec date 1783, judgment, debt, file #3713

LOWELL John, esquire, of Boston MA, vs AIKEN James, gentleman, of Londonderry, rec date 1783, judgment, debt, file #4451, note of Nathaniel GEARFIELD

LOWELL John, esquire, of Boston MA, vs GIBSON James, yeoman, of Merrimack, rec date 1782, execution, debt, file #4894

LOWELL John & Rebecca, of Boston MA, vs HARDY Jonathan, husbandman, of Nottingham, rec date 1782, judgment, debt, file #3127, widow Rebecca THYNG

LOWELL John & Rebecca, esquire, of Boston MA, vs HARDY Jonathan, husbandman, of Nottingham-West, rec date 1783, execution, debt, file #2890

LOWELL John & Rebecca, esquire, of Boston MA, vs GEARFIELD Nathaniel, husbandman, of Merrimack, rec date 1783, judgment, debt, file #3725

LOWELL John & Rebecca, esquire, of Boston MA, vs READ Robert, yeoman, of Amherst, rec date 1783, execution, debt, file #3670

LOWELL John & Rebecca, esquire, of Boston MA, vs SMALL Joseph, yeoman, of Amherst, rec date 1782, execution, debt, file #3519

LOWELL John & Rebecca, esquire, of Boston MA, vs SMALL Joseph, yeoman, of Amherst, rec date 1783, execution, debt, file #3670

LOWELL John & Rebecca, esquire, of Boston MA, vs HARDY Jonathan Jr, husbandman, of Nottingham-West, rec date 1782, appeal, debt, file #4029

LOWELL John & Rebecca, esquire, of Boston MA, vs SMALL Joseph, yeoman, of Amherst, rec date 1783, execution, debt, file #3875

LOWELL John & Rebecca, esquire, of Boston MA, vs WILKINS John, gentleman, of Amherst, rec date 1783, writ, debt, file #4554

LOWELL John & Rebecca, of Boston MA, vs NICHOLS Moses, esquire, of Goffstown, rec date 1786, writ, debt, file #6323

LOWELL Joseph, yeoman, of Pelham, vs CHAMPNEY Ebenezer, gentleman, of New Ipswich, doc date 1772, civil litigation, debt, file #649

LULL Sarah, spinster, of Derryfield, vs TOWN of Derryfield, doc date 1782, indictment, fornication, file #771

LUND Augusta, minor, of Dunstable, vs STEARNS Jotham, yeoman, of Goffstown, rec date 1784, judgment, debt, file #4367

LUND Augustas, laborer, of Dunstable, vs STEARNS Jonathan, yeoman, of Goffstown, doc date 1784, execution, debt, file #1774

LUND Charity, gentleman, of Merrimack, vs BRADFORD Samuel 3rd, yeoman, of Hillsborough, doc date 1774, judgment, debt, file #712

LUND Charity, gentleman, of Merrimack, vs BRADFORD Samuel Jr, gentleman, of Hillsborough, rec date 1782, execution, debt, file #3534

LUND Charity, gentleman, of Merrimack, vs BRADFORD Samuel Jr, gentleman, of Hillsborough, rec date 1785, writ, debt, file #4778

LUND Charity, gentleman, of Merrimack, vs BALDWIN Isaac, deceased, of Hillsborough, rec date 1785, judgment, debt, file #4875

LUND Charity, gentleman, of Merrimack, vs BADFORD Samuel Jr, gentleman, of Hillsborough, rec date 1785, writ, debt, file #4952

LUND Charity, gentleman, of Merrimack, vs BRADFORD Andrew, gentleman, of Hillsborough, rec date 1785, judgment, debt, file #5909

LUND Charity, esquire, of Merrimack, vs ANDREWS Isaac, esquire, of Hillsborough, rec date 1786, judgment, debt, file #6480

LUND Jesse, yeoman, of Goffstown, vs MARSH Samuel Jr, yeoman, of Nottingham-West, doc date 1784, civil litigation, debt, file #1636

LUND Jesse, yeoman, of Lyndeborough, vs McMASTERS Samuel, husbandman, of Lyndeborough, doc date 1784, execution, debt, file #1662

LUND Jesse, yeoman, of Lyndeborough, vs MILLER Thomas, yeoman, of Society Land, doc date 1784, execution, debt, file #1879

LUND Jesse, yeoman, of Lyndeborough, vs DUNCAN Robert, gentleman, of Hancock, rec date 1783, writ, debt, file #3570

LUND Jesse, yeoman, of Lyndeborough, vs MELLEN Thomas, yeoman, of Society Land, rec date 1783, writ, debt, file #3590

LUND Jesse, yeoman, of Lyndeborough, vs McMASTER Samuel, husbandman, of Lyndeborough, rec date 1783, writ, debt, file #3591

LUND Jesse, yeoman, of Lyndeborough, vs RUSSELL James, gentleman, of Litchfield, rec date 1784, judgment, debt, file #4400

LUND Jesse, husbandman, of Lyndeborough, vs ABBOTT Joseph, husbandman, of New Boston, rec date 1783, judgment, debt, file #4480

LUND Jesse, yeoman, of Lyndeborough, vs MERRILL Roger, husbandman, of Goffstown, rec date 1783, judgment, debt, file #4484

LUND Jesse, yeoman, of Hillsborough, vs RICHARDS Eliphalet, yeoman, of Goffstown, doc date 1783, rec date 1786, deed, land transfer, file #5011

LUND Jesse, yeoman, of Hillsborough, vs KITTRIDGE Daniel, yeoman, of Goffstown, rec date 1785, writ, debt, file #4761

LUND Jesse, yeoman, of Lyndeborough, vs FARNUM Stephen, husbandman, of Lyndeborough, rec date 1788, writ, debt, file #6929

LUND John, gentleman, of Dunstable, vs PATTERSON William, yeoman, of Goffstown, doc date 1784, execution, debt, file #1865

LUND John, gentleman, of Dunstable, vs LOVEWELL Noah, esquire, of Dunstable, rec date 1785, judgment, debt, file #4956

LUND John, gentleman, of Dunstable, vs BAKER Robert, yeoman, of Marlborough MA, rec date 1785, judgment, debt, file #4956

LUND John, gentleman, of Dunstable, vs FLETCHER Robert, esquire, of Dunstable, rec date 1785, judgment, debt, file #4956

LUND John, gentleman, of Dunstable, vs LOWELL Jonathan, esquire, of Dunstable, rec date 1785, judgment, debt, file #4956

LUND John, gentleman, of Dunstable, vs HARWOOD Thomas, esquire, of Dunstable, rec date 1785, judgment, debt, file #4956

LUND John & James, of Merrimack, vs LUND Phineas, husbandman, of Greenfield, doc date 1798, judgment, debt, file #564

LUND Jonathan, husbandman, of Dunstable, vs RUSSELL James, gentleman, of Goffstown, rec date 1785, judgment, debt, file #5268

LUND Phinehas, yeoman, of Lyndeborough, vs PEADBODY William, gentleman, of Amherst, rec date 1783, writ, debt, file #3174

LUND Phineas, yeoman, of Lyndeborough, vs ATHERTON Joshua, esquire, of Merrimack, doc date 1772, writ, debt, file #880

LUND Phinehas, husbandman, of Lyndeborough, vs GOODRIDGE Sewall, clerk, of Lyndeborough, rec date 1784, judgment, debt, file #4217

LUND Phinehas, husbandman, of Lyndeborough, vs DUTTON Asa, yeoman, of Lyndeborough, rec date 1786, writ, debt, file #5460

LUND Phinehas, yeoman, of Lyndeborough, vs CHAMBERLAIN Samuel, yeoman, of Lyndeborough, rec date 1785, writ, debt, file #6866

LUND Simeon P, yeoman, of Lyndeborough, vs FULLER Betty & Children, of Middleton MA, doc date 1779, various, land dispute, file #2067

LUNT Jonathan, husbandman, of Dunstable, vs ADAMS Richard, husbandman, of Hollis, rec date 1785, writ, debt, file #6149

LUNT Joseph, shoemaker, of Boscawen, vs CLARK Joseph, gentleman, of Sanbornton, rec date 1786, writ, debt, file #6134

LUNT Phinehas, yeoman, of Lyndeborough, vs FULLER Hannah & Children, yeoman, of Middleton MA, doc date 1778, various, land dispute, file #2050

LUTWYCKE Edward, of Merrimack, vs SCOTT Alexander, yeoman, of Monadnock #7, doc date 1773, execution, debt, file #1374

LUTWYCKE Edward, esquire, of Merrimack, vs BOYNTON Thomas, yeoman, of Hollis, doc date 1772, judgment, debt, file #671

LUTWYCKE Edward G, esquire, of Merrimack, vs SCOTT Alexander, gentleman, of Monadnock #1, doc date 1772, judgment, debt, file #676

LUTWYCKE Edward G, esquire, of Merrimack, vs FARLEY Ebenezer, husbandman, of Hollis, doc date 1782, judgment, debt, file #671

LUTWYCKE Edward G, esquire, of Merrimack, vs HALL John, gentleman, of Deerfield, doc date 1773, judgment, debt, file #1310

LYNCH Catharine, widow, of New Boston, vs GILMAN James, yeoman, of Bedford, rec date 1785, judgment, debt, file #5124

LYNDE Benjamin, cordwainer, of Salem, vs HUTCHINSON John, of Lyndeborough, doc date 1766, rec date 1778, deed, land transfer, file #2113

LYNDE Mary, widow, of Salem MA, vs BLANCHARD Joseph, esquire, of Amherst, rec date 1785, writ, debt, file #4775, estate of Benjamin LYNDE

LYON John, yeoman, of Deering, vs MILLS John, gentleman, of Amherst, rec date 1784, writ, debt, file #4637

MACARTY Thaddeus, physician, of Boston MA, vs RALSTON Alexander, esquire, of Keene, doc date 1799, various, debt, file #529

MACARTY Thaddeus, physician, of Boston MA, vs RALSTON Eliah, esquire, of Keene, doc date 1799, various, debt, file #529

MACE Eliphalet, esquire, of Moultonborough, vs HOLT Barachias, husbandman, of Wilton, rec date 1784, appeal, debt, file #4101

MACE Eliphalet, esquire, of Stafford, vs HOLT Barachias, husbandman, of Wilton, rec date 1784, judgment, debt, file #4423

MacFERSON James, yeoman, of Francestown, vs KIMBALL Thomas, yeoman, of Wenham MA, doc date 1783, rec date 1785, deed, land transfer, file #5645

MacGAA Robert, of Hollis, vs McNEIL John Calwell, trader, of New Boston, rec date 1785, judgment, debt, file #4794

MacGAA Robert, of Hollis, vs CALDWELL James, husbandman, of Weare, rec date 1785, judgment, debt, file #4794

MacGREGOR James, of Dunbarton, doc date 1772, application, tavern license, file #855

MacGREGOR Robert, esquire, of Goffstown, vs MOORE John 3rd, husbandman, of Bedford, doc date 1798, judgment, debt, file #565

MacGREGOR Robert, esquire, of Goffstown, vs WOOD Jonathan, husbandman, of Hopkinton, doc date 1798, judgment, debt, file #565

MacINTIRE Timothy, husbandman, of Goffstown, vs BARRON Micah, husbandman, of Lyndeborough, rec date 1786, writ, debt, file #6874

MACK Margaret, widow, of Litchfield, vs EWINS Ann, singlewoman, of Londonderry, rec date 1785, judgment, debt, file #5503

MACK Margaret, widow, of Litchfield, vs NAHOR James, husbandman, of Litchfield, rec date 1785, petition, guardians, file #5235

MACK Margaret, widow, of Litchfield, vs EWINS Ann, singlewoman, of Londonderry, rec date 1785, execution, debt, file #5936

MACK Robert, blacksmith, of Londonderry, vs LOWELL John, esquire, of Newburyport MA, rec date 1772, judgment, debt, file #4881

MACK Robert Jr, blacksmith, of Londonderry, vs BOYNTON Thomas, husbandman, of Hollis, doc date 1772, judgment, debt, file #691

MACK Robert Jr, blacksmith, of Londonderry, vs BOYNTON Thomas, husbandman, of Hollis, doc date 1773, execution, debt, file #1375

MacKNIGHT Margaret, vs MINGO (Negroman), laborer, of Merrimack, rec date 1788, warrant, assault, file #7061

MacLAUGHLIN John, gentleman, of New Boston, vs WATERS Samuel, husbandman, doc date 1798, judgment, debt, file #565

MacQUESTON William, esquire, of Litchfield, vs GORMAN James, wheelwright, of Derryfield, rec date 1788, writ, debt, file #6979

MAGAA Robert, trader, of Hollis, vs PATTERSON Robert Jr, yeoman, of New Boston, doc date 1779, writ, theft, file #2095

MAGAA Robert, trader, of Hollis, vs PATTEN John, husbandman, of Merrimack, rec date 1783, judgment, debt, file #4473

MAGOON Joseph & Ephraim, husbandman, of Thornton, vs CHAMPNEY Ebenezer, esquire, of Groton MA, rec date 1785, writ, debt, file #5388

MAKEPEACE George, of Boston MA, vs COLLEDGE Nathaniel, yeoman, of Hillsborough, doc date 1783, rec date 1783, deed, land transfer, file #2633

MANAHAN Adam, husbandman, of Deering, vs EATON Thomas, physician, of Francestown, doc date 1799, judgment, debt, file #230

MANAHAN John, yeoman, of Francestown, vs MANAHAN Adam, yeoman, of Deering, doc date 1798, judgment, debt, file #565

MANAHAN John, yeoman, of Francestown, vs TUTTLE Stephen, yeoman, of Goffstown, rec date 1785, execution, debt, file #5925

MANN Benjamin, cordwainer, of Mason, vs POLLARD Solomon, tanner, of Billerica MA, doc date 1772, writ, debt, file #884

MANN Benjamin, esquire, of Mason, vs BATTERS John, yeoman, of Jaffrey, doc date 1784, execution, debt, file #1558

MANN Benjamin, esquire, of Mason, vs BUTTERS John, yeoman, of Jaffrey, rec date 1783, writ, debt, file #3306

MANN Nathan, yeoman, of Holden MA, vs BRADFORD Samuel, gentleman, of Hillsborough, rec date 1786, judgment, debt, file #2305

MANN Nathan, yeoman, of Dedham MA, vs BRADFORD Samuel Jr, gentleman, of Hillsborough, rec date 1783, execution, debt, file #3498

MANN Nathan, yeoman, of Holden MA, vs BRADFORD Samuel Jr, gentleman, of Hillsborough, rec date 1786, writ, debt, file #6119

MANNAHAN John, yeoman, of Francestown, vs TUTTLE Stephen, yeoman, of Goffstown, rec date 1785, writ, debt, file #5819

MANNING John Jr, physician, of Ipswich MA, vs HOBBS Joseph, tailor, of Lyndeborough, rec date 1782, writ, debt, file #2683

MANSFIELD Elijah, blacksmith, of New Ipswich, vs WHEAT Jonathan, joiner, of New Ipswich, doc date 1772, rec date 1773, deed, land transfer, file #6551

MANSFIELD Rebecca, of New Ipswich, vs WHEAT Jonathan, joiner, of New Ipswich, doc date 1772, rec date 1773, deed, land transfer, file #6551

MANSFIELD Rebeckah, widow, of Temple, vs FELT Benjamin, blacksmith, of Temple, rec date 1784, appeal, debt, file #4143

MANSIS Cornelius, esquire, of Haverhill MA, vs COPPS Joshua, husbandman, of Hampstead, doc date 1772, judgment, debt, file #690

MARBLE Ephraim, of Bennington VT, rec date 1788, various, debt, file #6972

MARCH Samuel Jr, yeoman, of Nottingham-West, vs FORD James, esquire, of Nottingham-West, doc date 1784, execution, debt, file #1497

MARK William, esquire, of Dunbarton, vs STATE of NH, doc date 1779, writ, debt, file #2065

MARSDEN George & Wife, of Perrystown, vs TOWN of Francestown, doc date 1784, warning out of town, warning to leave, file #1562

MARSH J Cutting & Ruth, cordwainer, of Methuen MA, vs CHENEY Enoch, cordwainer, of Methuen MA, doc date 1779, rec date 1779, deed, land transfer, file #2148, land in Perrystown

MARSH Samuel, yeoman, of Nottingham-West, vs LUND Jesse, yeoman, of Goffstown, rec date 1783, writ, debt, file #3209

MARSHAL David, yeoman, of Packersfield, vs BLANCHARD James, yeoman, of Dunstable, doc date 1774, judgment, debt, file #722

MARSHALL Aaron & Esther, yeoman, of Temple, vs ALLARD Andrew, of Framingham MA, doc date 1775, deed, land transfer, file #844

MARSHALL David, gentleman, of Hillsborough, vs WILSON James, trader, of Deering, doc date 1799, judgment, debt, file #257

MARSHALL David, gentleman, of Hillsborough, vs JONES Nehemiah, trader, of Stoddard, doc date 1799, judgment, debt, file #251

MARSHALL David, gentleman, of Hillsborough, vs JONES Joel, husbandman, of Hillsborough, doc date 1799, writ, debt, file #406

MARSHALL Jesse, husbandman, of Westford MA, vs HUTCHINSON Solomon Jr, husbandman, of Merrimack, rec date 1784, appeal, debt, file #4145

MARSHALL Jesse, husbandman, of Westford MA, vs HUTCHINSON Solomon & Jr, husbandman, of Merrimack, rec date 1784, judgment, debt, file #4427

MARSHALL Jesse, husbandman, of Westford MA, vs HUTCHINSON Solomon & Jr, husbandman, of Merrimack, rec date 1784, judgment, debt, file #4645

MARSHALL Jesse, husbandman, of Westford MA, vs HUTCHINSON Solomon, husbandman, of Merrimack, rec date 1784, judgment, debt, file #4645

MARSHALL Jesse, husbandman, of Westford MA, vs HUTCHINS Solomon & Jr, husbandman, of Merrimack, rec date 1785, judgment, debt, file #5141

MARSHALL Jesse, husbandman, of Westford MA, vs HUTCHINSON Solomon Jr, husbandman, of Merrimack, rec date 1787, writ, debt, file #6678

MARSHALL John, yeoman, of Goffstown, vs MARSHALL David, yeoman, of Hillsborough, rec date 1787, judgment, debt, file #2315

MARSHALL John, husbandman, of Londonderry, vs SESSIONS David, husbandman, of Derryfield, rec date 1785, writ, debt, file #4818

MARSHALL John, husbandman, of Londonderry, vs BUTTERFIELD Jonathan, husbandman, of Dunstable, rec date 1785, judgment, debt, file #5049

MARSHALL John, yeoman, rec date 1788, deed, land dispute, file #7001

MARSHALL John Pierce, of Portsmouth, vs ANDERSON James, cordwainer, of Boxford MA, doc date 1781, rec date 1781, deed, land transfer, file #6803

MARSHALL Jonas, physician, of Fitchburg MA, vs PARKER Benjamin, husbandman, of Hollis, rec date 1784, writ, debt, file #4587, estate of Benjamin PARKER

MARSHALL Jonas, husbandman, of Fitchburg MA, vs PARKER Benjamin, husbandman, of Hollis, rec date 1785, judgment, debt, file #5150, estate of Benjamin PARKER

MARSHALL Jonas, of Fitchburg MA, vs PARKER Benjamin, of Hollis, rec date 1785, judgment, debt, file #4795

MARSHALL Joseph, husbandman, of Fisherfield, vs CHENEY James, yeoman, of Londonderry, doc date 1798, execution, debt, file #124

MARSHALL Nathaniel, gentleman, of Nottingham, vs BUCKLEY Lawrence, yeoman, of Derryfield, doc date 1798, judgment, debt, file #565

MARSHALL Samuel, trader, of Chelmsford MA, vs CONNER James, trader, of Lyndeborough, doc date 1799, debt, file #451

MARSHALL Samuel Jr, yeoman, of Nottingham-West, vs DAVIDSON Francis, yeoman, of Merrimack, rec date 1783, writ, debt, file #3975

MARSHALL Samuel & Wm, trader, of Chelmsford MA, vs CONNER James, trader, of Lyndeborough, doc date 1798, judgment, debt, file #565

MARSHALL Samuel & Wm, traders, of Chelmsford MA, vs CORNER James, trader, of Lyndeborough, doc date 1798, judgment, debt, file #565

MARSHALL Thomas, husbandman, of Chelmsford MA, vs BOWER Oliver, husbandman, of Hollis, rec date 1785, judgment, debt, file #5149

MARSHALL Thomas, husbandman, of Chelmsford MA, vs BOWERS Oliver, husbandman, of Hollis, rec date 1784, judgment, debt, file #5324

MARSHALL William, trader, of Chelmsford MA, vs CONNER James, trader, of Lyndeborough, doc date 1799, debt, file #451

MARTIN Jacob, gentleman, of Boscawen, vs MORRISON Samuel, gentleman, of Amherst, doc date 1799, writ, debt, file #398

MARTIN Jacob, gentleman, of Londonderry, vs McDANIELS James Jr, yeoman, of Hollis, rec date 1784, judgment, debt, file #4191

MARTIN Jacob, gentleman, of Londonderry, vs FOLBURT Philo, yeoman, of Amherst, rec date 1785, judgment, debt, file #5165

MARTIN Jacob, gentleman, of Londonderry, vs McDANIELS James Jr, yeoman, of Hollis, rec date 1785, judgment, debt, file #5439

MARTIN Jacob, gentleman, of Londonderry, vs McDANIEL James, yeoman, of Hollis, rec date 1786, various, debt, file #6061

MARTIN James, gentleman, of Bedford, vs DALTON Michael, yeoman, of Merrimack, doc date 1778, writ, debt, file #2047

MARTIN Jonathan, gentleman, of Wilton, vs SARGENT Paul Dudley, esquire, of Sullivan, doc date 1799, writ, debt, file #575

MARTIN Jonathan, husbandman, of Wilton, vs BROWN James, gentleman, of Moultonborough, rec date 1776, writ, debt, file #2197

MARTIN Jonathan, husbandman, of Wilton, vs BROWN James, gentleman, of Moultonborough, rec date 1776, writ, debt, file #2199

MARTIN Jonathan, husbandman, of Wilton, vs PATTERSON William, yeoman, of Goffstown, rec date 1784, appeal, debt, file #4147

MARTIN Jonathan, gentleman, of Wilton, vs COLE Eleazer, yeoman, of Amherst, rec date 1785, judgment, debt, file #5193

MARTIN Joshua, gentleman, of Goffstown, vs KARR William, yeoman, of Dunbarton, doc date 1784, execution, debt, file #1691

MARTIN Joshua, gentleman, of Goffstown, vs KARR William, yeoman, of Dunbarton, doc date 1784, execution, debt, file #1505

MARTIN Joshua, gentleman, of Goffstown, vs KARR William, yeoman, of Goffstown?, rec date 1783, judgment, debt, file #4076

MARTIN Samuel, husbandman, of Lyndeborough, vs WRIGHT Uriah, gentleman, of Hollis, rec date 1785, writ, debt, file #4749

MARTIN William, husbandman, of Salem, vs PIERCE John, rec date 1785, indictment, debt, file #4729

MASTEN Benjamin, yeoman, of Litchfield, vs JEWET Jacob Jr, yeoman, of Hollis, doc date 1773, writ, debt, file #1341

MASTON Isaac, yeoman, of Salisbury, vs BAKER Benjamin, yeoman, of Deerfield, doc date 1777, deed, land transfer, file #2061

MATHES Joseph, yeoman, of Bedford, vs MOOR William, husbandman, of Dunbarton, rec date 1785, judgment, debt, file #5594

MATHES Joseph, yeoman, of Bedford, vs GILLMOR James, husbandman, of Bedford, rec date 1785, judgment, debt, file #5594

MATHES Joseph, yeoman, of Bedford, vs GILMORE James, husbandman, of Bedford, rec date 1786, judgment, debt, file #6409

MATHES Joseph, yeoman, of Bedford, vs MOOR William, husbandman, of Dunbarton, rec date 1786, judgment, debt, file #6409

MATHEW Robert & Elizabeth, husbandman, of Bedford, vs O'NEIL John, of Society Land, doc date 1778, rec date 1778, deed, land transfer, file #2155

MATHEWS Joseph, husbandman, of Bedford, vs PATTEN John, husbandman, of Bedford, rec date 1785, writ, dispute over delivery of boards, file #4763

MAXFIELD Joshua, yeoman, of Bradford, vs DANA Anna, widow, of Amherst, doc date 1799, judgment, debt, file #236

MAXWELL William, yeoman, of Dublin, vs HEALD Thomas, esquire, of New Ipswich, doc date 1784, writ, debt, file #1265

MAY John, cordwainer, of Francestown, vs BALCH Israel, gentleman, of Francestown, doc date 1799, writ, debt, file #421

MAY John, cordwainer, of Francestown, vs MORSE Jacob, cordwainer, of Francestown, doc date 1799, writ, debt, file #318

MAYBERRY Jonathan, yeoman, of Hancock, vs CUBURN Parthenia, seamstress, of Peterborough, doc date 1799, judgment, debt, file #305

MAYNARD Hezekiah, yeoman, of Marlborough MA, vs DEXTER Betty, widow, of Marlborough M, rec date 1786, confession, debt, file #2326

McALEASTER Benjamin, yeoman, of Amherst, vs TAYLOR Timothy, gentleman, of Merrimack, rec date 1782, writ, debt, file #2832

McALISTER William, yeoman, of Peterboro Slip, vs THOM John, yeoman, of Peterboro Slip, doc date 1772, judgment, trespass, file #680

McALLASTER Archibald, yeoman, of Amherst, vs GORDON James, merchant, of Dunstable MA, rec date 1782, writ, debt, file #2848

McALLESTER Alexander, of Londonderry, vs McKAY Gilbert, weaver, of Peterborough Slip, doc date 1771, debt, file #1384

McALLESTER Peter, yeoman, of Monadnock #2, vs THOMPSON John, yeoman, of Peterborough, rec date 1771, various, debt, file #4876

McALLESTER William, yeoman, of Peterboro Slip, vs THOM John, of Peterboro Slip, doc date 1772, judgment, debt, file #823

McALLISTER Archibald, yeoman, of Francestown, vs BALCH Israel, gentleman, of Francestown, doc date 1799, debt, file #336

McALLISTER John, yeoman, of Sharon, vs CUNNINGHAM Thomas, yeoman, of Peterborough, doc date 1797, various, debt, file #507

McALLISTER Robert, yeoman, of Francestown, vs BALCH Israel, gentleman, of Francestown, doc date 1799, debt, file #336

McALPINE Joseph, of Amherst, vs COUNTY of Hillsborough, rec date 1788, convection to jail, file #3545

McCALLASTER Jerusha, spinster, of Bedford, vs GORDON William, esquire, of Amherst, doc date 1799, writ, debt, file #352

McCALLEY James, husbandman, of Hillsborough, vs JONES Joel, husbandman, of Hillsborough, doc date 1799, judgment, debt, file #241

McCALLEY John, husbandman, of Hillsborough, vs LOWELL John, esquire, of Boston MA, rec date 1783, writ, debt, file #3968

McCALLEY John, gentleman, of Hillsborough, vs McCLINTOCK John, husbandman, of Hillsborough, rec date 1785, judgment, debt, file #6430

McCALLISTER John, of Peterboro Slip, vs MITCHEL Isaac, husbandman, of Peterborough, rec date 1786, judgment, debt, file #6387

McCALOM Alexander, yeoman, of Londonderry, vs WALLACE Robert, husbandman, of Londonderry, doc date 1777, rec date 1779, deed, land transfer, file #6559

McCARLOSTIN James, husbandman, of Antrim, vs TAGGART Robert, physician, of Merrimack, rec date 1782, debt, debt, file #3158

McCAY William, husbandman, of Peterborough, vs CLARK Samuel, husbandman, of Peterborough, rec date 1785, writ, debt, file #5413

McCLARY Andrew, gentleman, of Epsom, vs BLODGETT Samuel, esquire, of Goffstown, doc date 1771, writ, debt, file #796

McCLAUGHLIN John Jr, innholder, of New Boston, vs McCOLLOM Thomas, yeoman, of New Boston, doc date 1784, execution, debt, file #1970

McCLEARY David, husbandman, of Goffstown, vs PATTERSON William Jr, yeoman, of Litchfield, rec date 1782, writ, debt, file #2846

McCLEARY David, yeoman, of Bedford, vs GILMORE Mary, widow, of Goffstown, rec date 1783, writ, debt, file #3331

McCLEARY William, yeoman, of Antrim, vs TAGGART Archibald, gentleman, of Hillsborough, rec date 1785, judgment, debt, file #5090

McCLENCHE John, yeoman, of Merrimack, vs PEABODY William, gentleman, of Amherst, doc date 1773, writ, debt, file #1354

McCLENCHE John, yeoman, of Boston MA, vs SHURTHEFF Jonathan, yeoman, of Merrimack, doc date 1784, civil litigation, debt, file #1830

McCLENCHE John, yeoman, of Boston MA, vs CLARK Lydian, widow, of Merrimack, rec date 1784, judgment, debt, file #4428, kinship to Hugh CLARK

McCLENCHE John, yeoman, of Boston MA, vs SHURTLEFF Jonathan, yeoman, of Merrimack, rec date 1783, judgment, debt, file #4440

McCLENCHE John, yeoman, of Merrimack, vs MERRILL Benjamin, husbandman, of Amherst, rec date 1785, writ, debt, file #6260

McCLENCHE Joseph, blacksmith, of Merrimack, vs MEANS Robert, esquire, of Amherst, doc date 1799, judgment, debt, file #285

McCLENCHE Joseph, cardmaker, of Boston MA, vs USHER Robert, yeoman, of Merrimack, rec date 1787, various, debit/stealing, file #2541

McCLENCHE Joseph, yeoman, of Merrimack, vs SCOTT William, yeoman, of Peterborough, rec date 1783, writ, debt, file #2757

McCLENCHE Joseph, yeoman, of Merrimack, vs BALDWIN Jesse, yeoman, of Amherst, rec date 1784, appeal, debt, file #4119

McCLINCOCK John, husbandman, of Hillsborough, vs BRADFORD John, gentleman, of Hillsborough, rec date 1785, various, service committee, file #4831

McCLINCOCK John, husbandman, of Hillsborough, vs McCALLEY John, gentleman, of Hillsborough, rec date 1785, judgment, service committee, file #4831

McCLINTOCK Alexander, yeoman, of Hillsborough, vs MOORE Samuel, of Bedford, rec date 1783, judgment, debt, file #3761

McCLINTOCK Alexander, yeoman, of Hillsborough, vs MOORE James, of Bedford, rec date 1783, judgment, debt, file #3761

McCLINTOCK John, yeoman, of Hillsborough, vs TAGGART Robert, physician, of Merrimack, doc date 1784, execution, debt, file #1948

McCLINTOCK John, yeoman, of Hillsborough, vs DICKEY Joseph, yeoman, of Hollis, doc date 1784, execution, debt, file #1894

McCLINTOCK John, gentleman, of Hillsborough, vs HUNTER John, husbandman, of Londonderry, rec date 1782, debt, debt, file #3140

McCLINTOCK John, yeoman, of Hillsborough, vs TAGGART Robert, physician, of Merrimack, rec date 1783, writ, debt, file #3582

McCLINTOCK John, husbandman, of Hillsborough, vs McCALLEY John, gentleman, of Hillsborough, rec date 1784, judgment, debt, file #4275

McCLINTOCK John, husbandman, of Hillsborough, vs BRADFORD Samuel, gentleman, of Hillsborough, rec date 1784, judgment, debt, file #4275

McCLINTOCK John, gentleman, of Hillsborough, vs DICKEY Joseph, yeoman, of Hollis, rec date 1782, execution, debt, file #4893

McCLINTOCK John, husbandman, of Hillsborough, vs RICHARDSON Zechariah, husbandman, of Francestown, rec date 1785, judgment, debt, file #4962

McCLINTOCK John, yeoman, of Hillsborough, vs DICKEY Joseph, yeoman, of Hollis, rec date 1783, execution, debt, file #4915

McCLINTOCK John, husbandman, of Hillsborough, vs BRADFORD Samuel, gentleman, of Hillsborough, rec date 1784, writ, debt, file #4860

McCLINTOCK John, husbandman, of Hillsborough, vs McCALLEY John, gentleman, of Hillsborough, rec date 1784, writ, debt, file #4860

McCLOUD Samuel, yeoman, of Society Land, vs BARRET Jonathan, yeoman, of Society Land, doc date 1778, rec date 1778, deed, land transfer, file #6796, f 267

McCLOUD Thomas, yeoman, of Peterborough, vs KELLEY Moses, esquire, of Goffstown, rec date 1785, writ, debt, file #5348

McCLUER Robert, yeoman, of Acworth, vs GREEN David, yeoman, of Hillsborough, rec date 1784, various, land dispute, file #4172, kinships

McCLURE James, yeoman, of Merrimack, vs FOSTER Samuel, gentleman, of Merrimack, doc date 1784, appeal, guardianship, file #1599, over 40 signatures from residents of Merrimack

McCLURGE Samuel, husbandman, of Stoddard, vs GRAHAM Samuel, husbandman, of Hancock, rec date 1784, judgment, debt, file #4998

McCLURY David, yeoman, of Bedford, vs McCLENCHE Joseph, yeoman, of Londonderry, rec date 1783, writ, debt, file #3926

McCOLLINS Thomas, yeoman, of New Boston, vs McLAUGHLIN John Jr, innkeeper, of New Boston, rec date 1783, writ, debt, file #3161

McCOLLY James, yeoman, of Dunbarton, vs GOODWIN Theophelius, yeoman, of Hampstead, doc date 1775, deed, land transfer, file #847

McCORMACK John, husbandman, of Londonderry, vs WOODMAN John, husbandman, of New London, doc date 1799, debt, file #331

McCOTTON Thomas, husbandman, of New Boston, vs WILSON James, husbandman, of New Boston, rec date 1783, writ, debt, file #3180

McCOY John, yeoman, of Antrim, vs NUTT Samuel, gentleman, of Francestown, doc date 1783, execution, debt, file #1679

McCOY John, yeoman, of Antrim, vs NUTT Samuel, gentleman, of Francestown, rec date 1783, writ, debt, file #3396

McCOY William, yeoman, of Hillsborough, vs CUNNINGHAM Moses, yeoman, of Peterborough, doc date 1783, writ, debt, file #1257

McCURDY John, husbandman, of Tunbridge VT, vs LASLEY Alexander, yeoman, of Dunbarton, doc date 1799, debt, file #481

McCURDY John, gentleman, of Dunbarton, vs TAGGART John, husbandman, of Goffstown, rec date 1784, writ, debt, file #4676

McCURDY John, husbandman, of Goffstown, vs TAGGART John, gentleman, of Dunbarton, rec date 1785, various, ejectment, file #4844, fragile

McCURDY Robert, husbandman, of Dunbarton, vs TAGGART John, rec date 1783, various, assault, file #3604

McCURDY Robert, husbandman, of Dunbarton, vs KITTRIDGE Nathaniel, yeoman, of Goffstown, rec date 1784, appeal, debt, file #4146

McCURDY Robert, husbandman, of Dunbarton, vs KITTRIDGE Nathaniel, yeoman, of Goffstown, rec date 1784, judgment, debt, file #4401

McCURTY Robert, husbandman, of Dunbarton, vs TAGGART John, yeoman, of Goffstown, rec date 1787, indictment, assault, file #3553

McDOEL William, husbandman, of Goffstown, vs DOW Job, husbandman, of Goffstown, doc date 1773, judgment, debt, file #1180

McDOEL William, husbandman, of Goffstown, vs MARTIN Jonathan, husbandman, of Goffstown, doc date 1773, judgment, debt, file #1180

McDOEL William, husbandman, of Goffstown, vs SALTMARSH Thomas, husbandman, of Goffstown, doc date 1773, judgment, debt, file #1180

McDONELL Randel Capt, of Weare, vs Town of Raby (Weare), doc date 1787, license, tavern license, file #867

McDOUGALL William, yeoman, of Goffstown, vs MORRISON John, yeoman, of Bedford, rec date 1784, judgment, debt, file #4617

McFARLAND Ann (Mrs), wife, of Dunbarton, vs STINSON John, of Dunbarton, doc date 1783, charge, rape, file #1252

McFARLAND Daniel, yeoman, of Goffstown, vs FERREN Philip, yeoman, of Goffstown, doc date 1770, rec date 1786, deed, land transfer, file #5029

McFARLAND John, attorney, of Hillsborough, vs BURNAM John, of Hillsborough, doc date 1819, rec date 1819, deed, land transfer, file #5707

McFARLAND Moses, trader, of Antrim, vs HADLEY Seth, yeoman, of Antrim, doc date 1772, civil litigations, debt, file #156

McFARLAND Moses, trader, of Antrim, vs STARRET William, tanner, of Antrim, doc date 1772, civil litigations, debt, file #156

McFARLAND Samuel, yeoman, of Goffstown, vs PALMER William, husbandman, of Goffstown, doc date 1774, writ, debt, file #1119

McFARLAND Samuel, husbandman, of Londonderry, vs KARR James, gentleman, of Goffstown, rec date 1785, writ, debt, file #5379

McFARLAND Samuel, husbandman, of Londonderry, vs KENNEDY Samuel, of Goffstown, doc date 1788, rec date 1788, deed, land transfer, file #6828, ?

McGAA Jacob, trader, of Merrimack, vs CALDWELL William, husbandman, of Goffstown, rec date 1783, civil litigious, debt, file #2956

McGAA Jacob, trader, of Merrimack, vs CALDWELL William, husbandman, of Goffstown, rec date 1783, execution, debt, file #3869

McGAA Jacob, trader, of Merrimack, vs GEARFIELD Nathaniel, husbandman, of Merrimack, rec date 1785, various, debt, file #5233

McGAA Robert, trader, of Hollis, vs SMITH Manasseh, gentleman, of Hollis, doc date 1784, court case, debt, file #1612

McGAA Robert, trader, of Hollis, vs McNEIL John Caldwell, trader, of New Boston, doc date 1784, civil litigation, debt, file #1844

McGAA Robert, gentleman, of New Boston, vs STATE of NH, rec date 1776, recognizance, debt, file #2249

McGAA Robert, trader, of Hollis, vs ROBERTSON Peter, tailor, of Amherst, rec date 1782, judgment, debt, file #2705

McGAA Robert, trader, of Hollis, vs McMURPHY John, husbandman, of Alexandria, rec date 1782, writ, debt, file #2698

McGAA Robert, trader, of Hollis, vs ROBERTON Peter, tailor, of Amherst, rec date 1783, execution, debt, file #3280

McGAA Robert, trader, of Hollis, vs McNEIL John Caldwell, husbandman, of New Boston, rec date 1783, writ, debt, file #3369

McGAA Robert, trader, of Hollis, vs McGINIS Barnabas, husbandman, of New Boston, rec date 1782, execution, debt, file #3521

McGAA Robert, trader, of Hollis, vs LIVINGSTON William, gentleman, of New Boston, rec date 1783, judgment, debt, file #3787

McGAA Robert, trader, of Hollis, vs McGINNIS Barnabas, husbandman, of New Boston, rec date 1783, execution, debt, file #3642

McGAA Robert, trader, of Hollis, vs SMITH Manasseh, gentleman, of Hollis, rec date 1783, writ, debt, file #4039

McGAA Robert, shopkeeper, of Hollis, vs HALL Benjamin, esquire, of Medford MA, rec date 1783, writ, debt, file #3951

McGAA Robert, trader, of Hollis, vs SMITH Manasseh, gentleman, of Hollis, rec date 1784, various, debt, file #4168

McGAA Robert, trader, of Hollis, vs PUTNAM John, husbandman, of Alexandria, rec date 1783, execution, debt, file #4727

McGAA Robert, trader, of Hollis, vs McNEIL John Caldwell, trader, of New Boston, rec date 1783, judgment, debt, file #4474

McGAA Robert, trader, of New Boston, vs BAILEY Timothy, husbandman, of Hollis, rec date 1784, various, debt, file #4740A, 2 folders

McGAA Robert, trader, of New Boston, vs BAILEY Timothy, husbandman, of Hollis, rec date 1784, various, debt, file #4740

McGAA Robert, trader, of Hillsborough, vs PUTNAM Israel & John, husbandman, of Alexandria, rec date 1782, execution, debt, file #4903

McGAA Robert, trader, of Hollis, vs PUTNAM Israel, husbandman, of Alexandria, rec date 1783, judgment, debt, file #4727

McGAA Robert, husbandman, of New Boston, vs BOGES William, gentleman, of New Boston, rec date 1785, execution, debt, file #5910

McGAA Robert, husbandman, of New Boston, vs BOYES William, gentleman, of New Boston, rec date 1785, writ, debt, file #6003

McGAA Robert, trader, of Hollis, vs WHITE Robert, yeoman, of New Boston, rec date 1782, execution, debt, file #5721

McGAA Robert, trader, of New Boston, vs BAYLES John, yeoman, of Deering, rec date 1785, execution, debt, file #5919

McGAA Robert, trader, of New Boston, vs BAYLES John, yeoman, of Deering, rec date 1785, writ, debt, file #6014

McGAUGLIN Thomas, gentleman, of Bedford, vs FLAGG Samuel, esquire, of Worcester MA, rec date 1785, writ, debt, file #5392

McGAW Jacob, esquire, of Merrimack, vs CUMMINGS James, gentleman, of Merrimack, doc date 1798, execution, debt, file #109

McGAW Jacob, esquire, of Merrimack, vs GAMAN James, yeoman, of Plymouth, doc date 1799, debt, file #455

McGAW Jacob, trader, of Merrimack, vs RICHARDSON Zechariah, yeoman, of Francestown, doc date 1784, civil litigation, debt, file #1635

McGAW Jacob, trader, of Merrimack, vs CALDWELL William, husbandman, of Goffstown, doc date 1784, execution, debt, file #1937

McGAW Jacob, trader, of Merrimack, vs CALDWELL William, husbandman, of Goffstown, rec date 1783, writ, debt, file #3921

McGAW Jacob, trader, of Merrimack, vs RICHARDSON Zachariah, husbandman, of Francestown, rec date 1783, judgment, debt, file #4072

McGAW Jacob, trader, of Merrimack, vs GEARFIELD Nathaniel, husbandman, of Merrimack, rec date 1784, writ, debt, file #4675

McGAW Jacob, esquire, of Merrimack, vs INHABITANTS of Merrimack, rec date 1788, writ, debits, file #6810

McGAW John, trader, of Merrimack, vs MOORE John, husbandman, of Bedford, doc date 1798, execution, debt, file #129

McGAW John, gentleman, of Merrimack, vs MORRISON John, husbandman, of Bedford, doc date 1798, execution, debt, file #130

McGAW John, gentleman, of Merrimack, vs BARNS Cornelius, husbandman, of Merrimack, doc date 1798, judgment, debt, file #565

McGAW John, gentleman, of Merrimack, vs McCLENCKE Joseph, blacksmith, of Merrimack, doc date 1798, judgment, debt, file #565

McGAW John, gentleman, of Merrimack, vs HUTCHINSON Solomon, husbandman, of Merrimack, doc date 1798, judgment, debt, file #565

McGAW John, trader, of Merrimack, vs ROBY Silas, husbandman, of Merrimack, doc date 1798, judgment, debt, file #565

McGAW John, gentleman, of Merrimack, vs CUMMINGS Simeon, esquire, of Merrimack, doc date 1798, judgment, debt, file #565

McGAW John, gentleman, of Merrimack, vs LONZEA William, husbandman, of Merrimack, doc date 1798, judgment, debt, file #565

McGAW John, trader, of Merrimack, vs HENRY Samuel, husbandman, of Amherst, doc date 1798, judgment, debt, file #565

McGAW John, trader, of Merrimack, vs BARNS Reuben, gentleman, of Merrimack, doc date 1798, judgment, debt, file #565

McGAW John, gentleman, of Merrimack, vs HASKELL Jason, husbandman, of Merrimack, doc date 1798, judgment, debt, file #565

McGAW Rebecca, trader, of Hollis, vs TOURTETTELL Abraham, gentleman, of New Boston, doc date 1782, execution, file #1017

McGAW Robert, trader, of Hollis, vs MELLEN Thomas, husbandman, of Francestown, doc date 1782, execution, debt, file #965

McGAW Robert, trader, of Hollis, vs JONES Samuel, husbandman, of Hillsborough, doc date 1782, execution, file #1010

McGILVERAY John, husbandman, of Merrimack, vs LIBBY Joseph, husbandman, of Merrimack, doc date 1799, writ, debt, file #371

McGINNIS Barnabas, trader, of Nottingham-West, vs DANA Samuel, esquire, of Amherst, doc date 1784, writ, debt, file #1596

McGINNIS Barnabas, yeoman, of New Boston, vs LIVINGSTON William, gentleman, of New Boston, rec date 1783, execution, debt, file #2868

McGINNIS Barnabas, yeoman, of New Boston, vs LIVINGSTON William, gentleman, of New Boston, rec date 1782, judgment, debt, file #3133

McGINNIS Barnabas, trader, of Nottingham-West, vs HOIT Philip, physician, of Weare, rec date 1783, writ, debt, file #3186

McGINNIS Barnabas, yeoman, of Nottingham-West, vs BARKER William, physician, of Francestown, rec date 1783, writ, debt, file #3191

McGINNIS Barnabas, yeoman, of Nottingham-West, vs PARKER Jonathan, physician, of Litchfield, rec date 1783, writ, debt, file #3336

McGINNIS Barnabas, husbandman, of Nottingham-West, vs McINTOSH John, yeoman, of Bedford, rec date 1783, various, debt, file #3965

McGINNIS Barnabas, yeoman, of Nottingham-West, vs BOWIE Thomas, husbandman, of Bedford, rec date 1783, writ, debt, file #3950

McGINNIS Barnabas, yeoman, of New Boston, vs DAVIS Joseph, yeoman, of New Boston, rec date 1783, judgment, debt, file #4513

McGINNIS Barnabas, vs DEAN Thaddeus, rec date 1785, misc, debt, file #5396

McGINNIS Barnabas, yeoman, of New Boston, vs McINTOSH John, yeoman, of Bedford, rec date 1783, writ, debt, file #3925

McGIVERAY John, yeoman, of Merrimack, vs BIXBY Daniel, gentleman, of Litchfield, doc date 1799, judgment, debt, file #313

McGRAW Jacob, of Merrimack, doc date 1777, license, tavern license, file #856

McGREGOR David, esquire, of Dunbarton, vs BURNSIDE Thomas, esquire, of Northumberland, rec date 1788, writ, debt, file #6617

McGREGOR James, esquire, of Londonderry, vs LITTLE Bond, esquire, of Fisherfield, doc date 1798, execution, debt, file #71

McGREGOR James, esquire, of Londonderry, vs ALLISON Samuel, husbandman, of Dunbarton, doc date 1798, execution, debt, file #134

McGREGOR Robert, esquire, of Goffstown, vs GREEN Nathaniel, esquire, of Boscawen, doc date 1799, execution, debt, file #205

McGREGOR Robert, esquire, of Goffstown, vs FARMER William, gentleman, of Derryfield, doc date 1799, debt, file #496

McGREGOR Robert, esquire, of Goffstown, vs ROWELL David, husbandman, of Derryfield, rec date 1787, writ, debt, file #6711

McGREGOR Robert, esquire, of Goffstown, vs KELLY Moses, esquire, of Goffstown, rec date 1787, writ, debt, file #6709

McGREGORE Daniel, esquire, of Londonderry, vs HOGG James, gentleman, of Weare, rec date 1785, various, debt, file #5328

McGREGORE David, esquire, of Londonderry, vs COLBY Isaac, husbandman, of Weare, rec date 1785, writ, debt, file #5328

McGREGORE David, esquire, of Londonderry, vs HOW Samuel, husbandman, of Henniker, rec date 1785, writ, debt, file #5328

McGREGORE Robert, esquire, of Goffstown, vs CLOGSTON William, husbandman, of Goffstown, doc date 1798, execution, debt, file #53

McGREGORE Robert, esquire, of Goffstown, vs GRIFFIN Theophilus, husbandman, of Deerfield, doc date 1799, debt, file #447

McGREGORE Robert, esquire, of Goffstown, vs GREEN Nathaniel, esquire, of Boscawen, doc date 1798, judgment, debt, file #565

McGREGORE Robert, esquire, of Goffstown, vs BOIES John, husbandman, of Bedford, doc date 1798, judgment, debt, file #565

McGREGORE Robert, esquire, of Goffstown, vs READ Zadock, husbandman, of Antrim, doc date 1799, debt, file #456, fragile

McGREGORE Robert, esquire, of Goffstown, vs CARR David, trader, of Boscawen, rec date 1786, writ, debt, file #6317

McGREGORY James, doc date 1772, license, tavern license, file #850

McHARD James, gentleman, of Haverhill MA, vs KIMBALL Timothy, yeoman, of Goffstown, doc date 1777, rec date 1779, deed, land transfer, file #2122

McHARD James, gentleman, of Haverhill MA, vs McKILLIPS David, husbandman, of Henniker, rec date 1785, writ, debt, file #5340

McILVERAY John, yeoman, of Merrimack, vs BELL Joseph, yeoman, of Bedford, rec date 1788, writ, debt, file #6721

McINTIRE Jacob, husbandman, of Lyndeborough, vs SAWYER Nathaniel, trader, of Wilton, doc date 1799, writ, debt, file #575

McINTOSH Alexander, gentleman, of Raby, vs HEALD Thomas, esquire, of New Ipswich, doc date 1784, writ, debt, file #1274

McINTOSH James, yeoman, of Raby, vs CUTLER Thomas, yeoman, of Nottingham-West, doc date 1784, execution, debt, file #1772

McINTOSH James, yeoman, of Raby, vs CUTLER Thomas, yeoman, of Nottingham-West, rec date 1782, judgment, debt, file #2709

McINTOSH James, yeoman, of Raby, vs CUTLER Thomas, yeoman, of Nottingham-West, rec date 1783, execution, debt, file #3811

McINTOSH John, yeoman, of Society Land, vs HODGE Samuel, gentleman, of Francestown, doc date 1799, judgment, debt, file #249

McINTOSH John, yeoman, of Society Land, vs GIBSON John, husbandman, of Francestown, doc date 1799, judgment, debt, file #254

McINTOSH John, yeoman, of Bedford, vs McCLAY William, yeoman, of Francestown, rec date 1783, writ, debt, file #2775

McINTOSH John, yeoman, of Bedford, vs McGINNIS Barnabas, yeoman, of New Boston, rec date 1783, execution, debt, file #3264

McINTOSH John, yeoman, of Bedford, vs McGINNIS Barnabas, yeoman, of New Boston, rec date 1783, execution, debt, file #3686

McINTOSH John, husbandman, of Bedford, vs SHANNON Richard Cutt, esquire, of Hollis, rec date 1784, judgment, debt, file #4353

McINTOSH John, vs ORR John, justice of pea, rec date 1788, convection, file #7016

McIVERAY John, yeoman, of Merrimack, vs BELL Joseph, husbandman, of Bedford, rec date 1785, writ, debt, file #4790

McKANE Samuel, yeoman, of Amherst, vs LOVEJOY Benjamin, gentleman, of Hillsborough, doc date 1774, execution, file #945

McKEEN James, yeoman, of Amherst, vs GRIMES Francis, yeoman, of Deering, rec date 1783, writ, debt, file #3032

McKEEN James, yeoman, of Amherst, vs MITCHELL John, yeoman, of Amherst, rec date 1783, execution, debt, file #2892

McKEEN James, yeoman, of Amherst, vs MITCHEL John, yeoman, of Amherst, rec date 1783, judgment, debt, file #2859

McKEEN James, yeoman, of Amherst, vs MITCHEL John, yeoman, of Amherst, rec date 1782, appeal, debt, file #4012

McKEEN Levi, minor, of Peterborough, vs SMITH James, husbandman, of Peterborough, rec date 1785, various, debt, file #5039

McKEEN Martha, singlewoman, of New Boston, vs NOT Known, doc date 1774, jury foreman statement, illegitimate child, file #749

McKEEN James, yeoman, of Amherst, vs WILKINS Jonathan, yeoman, of Amherst, doc date 1783, rec date 1785, deed, land transfer, file #5606

McKEEN Samuel, yeoman, of Amherst, vs LOVEJOY Benjamin, yeoman, of Hillsborough, doc date 1774, execution, file #983, executor of estate of Joshua ABB

McKEEN Samuel, husbandman, of Amherst, vs EMERSON John, of Amherst, doc date 1776, deed, land transfer, file #1172

McKEEN Samuel, gentleman, of Windham, vs KARR James, yeoman, of Hillsborough, rec date 1783, execution, debt, file #3273

McKEEN Samuel, husbandman, of Windham, vs STEVENS Bimsley, yeoman, of Salem MA, rec date 1782, debt, debt, file #3141

McKEEN Samuel, gentleman, of Windham, vs KARR William, yeoman, of Goffstown, rec date 1783, writ, debt, file #3898

McKEEN Samuel, gentleman, of Windham, vs KARR James, yeoman, of Hillsborough, rec date 1783, writ, debt, file #3898

McKEEN Samuel, gentleman, of Windham, vs KARR James, yeoman, of Hillsborough, rec date 1785, writ, debt, file #6252

McLAUGHLIN John Jr, husbandman, of New Boston, vs McLAUGHLIN John, husbandman, of New Boston, doc date 1778, writ, debt, file #2106

McLAUGHLIN John, gentleman, of New Boston, vs WOODBURY Jesse, trader, of Weare, doc date 1796, judgment, breaking & entry, file #29, a deed of Woodbury property

McLAUGHLIN John, yeoman, of New Boston, vs McFERSON James, of New Boston, rec date 1779, writ, counterfeiting, file #2238

McLAUGHLIN John, husbandman, of Deering, vs UNDERWOOD James, gentleman, of Goffstown, rec date 1787, various, debt, file #2374

McLAUGHLIN John, innholder, of New Boston, vs ABBOTT Benjamin, yeoman, of Hollis, rec date 1783, judgment, debt, file #3700

McLAUGHLIN John, innholder, of New Boston, vs GRAGG David, yeoman, of Francestown, rec date 1782, execution, debt, file #3492

McLAUGHLIN John, innholder, of New Boston, vs McNEIL John Caldwell, yeoman, of Derryfield, rec date 1784, judgment, debt, file #4268

McLAUGHLIN John, innholder, of New Boston, vs BRADFORD Samuel Jr, gentleman, of Hillsborough, rec date 1785, judgment, debt, file #5576

McLAUGHLIN John, gentleman, of New Boston, vs SMITH Thomas, yeoman, of New Boston, rec date 1787, writ, debt, file #6710

McLAUGHLIN John, yeoman, of Deering, vs UNDERWOOD James, gentleman, of Goffstown, rec date 1788, writ, debt, file #6930

McLAUGHLIN John & James, yeoman, of New Boston, vs STATE of NH, rec date 1779, writ, counterfeiting, file #2238

McLAUGHLIN John Jr, innholder, of New Boston, vs PATTERSON Isaac, yeoman, of Antrim, rec date 1783, writ, debt, file #4048

McLAUGHLIN John Jr, innholder, of New Boston, vs DAVIS Joseph, cooper, of Goffstown, rec date 1784, judgment, debt, file #4286

McLAUGHLIN John Jr, innholder, of New Boston, vs ROGERS Roger, yeoman, of Society Land, rec date 1784, judgment, debt, file #4654

McLAUGHLIN John Jr, innholder, of New Boston, vs ROGERS Robert, yeoman, of Society Land, rec date 1785, judgment, debt, file #5129

McLAUGHLIN Thomas, yeoman, of Francestown, vs BALDWIN Nahum, esquire, of Boston MA, rec date 1782, appeal, debt, file #4014, estate of z CUTLER

McLAUGHLIN Thomas, gentleman, of Bedford, vs BACON Samuel, gentleman, of Merrimack, rec date 1784, judgment, debt, file #4227

McLAUGHLIN Thomas, husbandman, of Bedford, vs CUSHING John, physician, of Goffstown, rec date 1785, judgment, debt, file #5353

McLUER James, husbandman, of Acworth, vs MILLER James, yeoman, of Merrimack, doc date 1799, judgment, debt, file #309

McMASTER Alexander, weaver, of Windham, vs WALLACE John, cordwainer, of Londonderry, doc date 1772, writ, debt, file #830

McMASTER John, yeoman, of Antrim, vs WOODBURY Mark, trader, of Antrim, doc date 1799, judgment, debt, file #238

McMELLAN Archibald, husbandman, of New Boston, vs WILSON Thomas, husbandman, of New Boston, rec date 1783, writ, debt, file #3346

McMILLAN Andrew, esquire, of Concord, vs CHADWICK John, husbandman, of Hopkinton, doc date 1774, execution, file #1001

McMILLAN Archibald, husbandman, of New Boston, vs CALDWELL James, husbandman, of New Boston, rec date 1782, writ, debt, file #2779

McMILLAN Archibald, husbandman, of New Boston, vs PATTERSON William, husbandman, of Goffstown, rec date 1784, appeal, debt, file #4133

McMILLAN John Jr, yeoman, of New Boston, vs BALDWIN Nahum, esquire, of Amherst, rec date 1782, appeal, debt, file #3987

McMILLEN ----, yeoman, of New Boston, vs WILSON James, husbandman, of New Boston, doc date 1799, judgment, debt, file #259

McMILLEN Daniel Jr, yeoman, of New Boston, vs TAGGART James, yeoman, of Hillsborough, doc date 1774, recognizance, debt, file #1157

McMILLIAN Daniel, husbandman, of New Boston, vs GOOLL John, doc date 1773, writ, debt, file #1351

McMULLIN Andrew, esquire, of Conway, vs GOFFE John, esquire, of Derryfield, rec date 1785, judgment, debt, file #5072

McMURPHY Daniel, yeoman, of Alexandria, vs McNEAL Daniel, gentleman, of Hillsborough, doc date 1773, judgment, debt, file #1327

McMURPHY Daniel, gentleman, of Alexandria, vs WILKINS John, gentleman, of Francestown, rec date 1783, writ, debt, file #3960

McMURPHY Robert, husbandman, of Londonderry, vs MOOR Samuel, esquire, of Nottingham-West, rec date 1786, writ, debt, file #6321, Mary MOOR widow

McMURPHY Robert, gentleman, of Londonderry, vs THORNTON Matthew, esquire, of Merrimack, rec date 1785, writ, debt, file #6998

McMURPHY Robert, gentleman, of Londonderry, vs GREGG Mary, widow, of New Boston, rec date 1785, writ, debt, file #6998

McNEAL Daniel, gentleman, of Hillsborough, vs McGAW Jacob, shopkeeper, of Merrimack, doc date 1774, writ, debt, file #1118

McNEAL Daniel, gentleman, of Hillsborough, vs McMURPHY Daniel, yeoman, of Alexandria, doc date 1773, writ, debt, file #1445

McNEAL Daniel, yeoman, of Hillsborough, vs KARR James, esquire, of Goffstown, doc date 1774, summons, file #1141

McNEE William, husbandman, of Peterborough, vs STEWART Alexander, cordwainer, of Peterborough, rec date 1788, writ, debt, file #6922

McNEIL Daniel, husbandman, of New Boston, vs SERGEANT Asa, yeoman, of Weare, doc date 1799, debt, file #334

McNEIL John C, husbandman, of Derryfield, vs CLARK Joseph, yeoman, of Antrim, rec date 1785, various, debt, file #6340

McNEIL John Caldwell, yeoman, of Derryfield, vs TERRILL Joseph, merchant, of Lynn MA, rec date 1785, writ, debt, file #4762

McNEIL John Caldwell, innholder, of New Boston, vs GRIMES James, gentleman, of Deering, rec date 1782, execution, debt, file #3533

McNEIL John Caldwell, innholder, of New Boston, vs GRIMES James, gentleman, of Deering, rec date 1782, execution, debt, file #3505

McNEIL John Caldwell, innholder, of New Boston, vs GRIMES James, gentleman, of Deering, rec date 1783, execution, debt, file #4911

McNEIL John Caldwell, innholder, of New Boston, vs GRIMES James, gentleman, of Deering, rec date 1783, execution, debt, file #4913

McNEIL John Caldwell, yeoman, of Derryfield, vs HUPSEY Silvan?, merchant, of Lynn MA, rec date 1785, writ, debt, file #4762

McNEIL John Calwell, yeoman, of New Boston, vs RAMSEY Hugh, yeoman, of New Boston, rec date 1783, writ, land title dispute, file #4547

McNEIL John Calwell, farmer, of Derryfield, vs LITTLE John, gentleman, of Derryfield, rec date 1786, writ, debt, file #6130

McQUAID Jacob, yeoman, of Bedford, vs LEOBY David, gentleman, of Francestown, doc date 1784, execution, debt, file #1556

McQUAID Jacob, yeoman, of Bedford, vs McQUESTEN William, yeoman, of Litchfield, rec date 1782, writ, debt, file #2778

McQUAID Jacob, yeoman, of Bedford, vs DANFORTH Samuel, yeoman, of Andover MA, rec date 1782, writ, debt, file #2814

McQUAID Jacob, yeoman, of Bedford, vs SCOBY David, gentleman, of Francestown, rec date 1783, judgment, debt, file #3299

McQUAID Jacob, yeoman, of Bedford, vs SCOBY David, gentleman, of Francestown, rec date 1785, judgment, debt, file #5983

McQUESTEN William, esquire, of Litchfield, vs HALL John, of Derryfield, rec date 1785, judgment, debt, file #5520

McQUESTEN William, esquire, of Litchfield, vs LITTLE John (Lt), gentleman, of Derryfield, rec date 1785, judgment, debt, file #5500

McQUESTEN William, esquire, of Litchfield, vs ROGERS Jonathan, husbandman, of Acworth, rec date 1785, writ, debt, file #5814

McQUESTEN William, esquire, of Litchfield, vs HALL John, gentleman, of Derryfield, rec date 1785, judgment, debt, file #5996

McQUESTIN William, esquire, of Litchfield, vs McQUAID Jacob, yeoman, of Bedford, rec date 1783, judgment, debt, file #3778

McQUESTION Simon, husbandman, of Litchfield, vs McCLURG Thomas, husbandman, of Peterborough, rec date 1785, judgment, debt, file #5791

McQUESTION William, esquire/agent, of Litchfield, vs WALKER Zacheus, gentleman, of Merrimack, rec date 1788, writ, debt, file #6982

McQUESTON William, gentleman, of Litchfield, vs BARNES Joseph, physician, of Litchfield, doc date 1772, writ, debt, file #1047, fragile

McQUESTON William, esquire, of Litchfield, vs CARR Timothy, husbandman, of Thornton, rec date 1785, judgment, debt, file #5581

McQUIG David, yeoman, of Litchfield, vs GREER David, yeoman, of Goffstown, rec date 1785, various, debt, file #5822

McQUIG David, gentleman, of Litchfield, vs GREER David, yeoman, of Goffstown, rec date 1785, execution, debt, file #5915

McQUITIM William, esquire, of Litchfield, vs LITTLE John, gentleman, of Derryfield, rec date 1785, judgment, debt, file #5991

McSHILLINGS David & Ann, yeoman, of Henniker, vs CHAMPNEY Ebenezer, gentleman, of New Ipswich, doc date 1772, writ, debt, file #1063

MEAD Zadock, yeoman, of New Boston, vs McQUESTION Simon, husbandman, of Litchfield, doc date 1783, writ, debt, file #1165

MEANS Robert, esquire, of Amherst, vs BLANCHARD Joseph, esquire, of Thornton, doc date 1799, debt, file #486

MEANS Robert, esquire, of Amherst, vs TAYLOR James Jr, clothier, of Antrim, doc date 1798, judgment, debt, file #565

MEANS Robert, esquire, of Amherst, vs TAYLOR James Jr, clothier, of Antrim, doc date 1798, judgment, debt, file #565

MEANS Robert, esquire, of Amherst, vs BLANCHARD Joseph, esquire, of Thornton, doc date 1798, judgment, debt, file #565

MEANS Robert, esquire, of Amherst, vs BLANCHARD Joseph, esquire, of Thornton, doc date 1798, judgment, debt, file #565

MEANS Robert, trader, of Amherst, vs GREEN David, husbandman, of Hillsborough, doc date 1784, execution, debt, file #1763

MEANS Robert, trader, of Amherst, vs BRADFORD William, gentleman, of Deering, rec date 1783, execution, debt, file #2978

MEANS Robert, trader, of Amherst, vs BRADFORD Andrew, gentleman, of Amherst, rec date 1783, execution, debt, file #2990

MEANS Robert, trader, of Amherst, vs CORVIN Thomas, yeoman, of Merrimack, rec date 1783, civil litigious, debt, file #2936

MEANS Robert, trader, of Amherst, vs JONES Samuel, yeoman, of Hillsborough, rec date 1783, settlement, debt, file #3168

MEANS Robert, city treas, rec date 1788, report, file #3552

MEANS Robert, gentleman, of Amherst, vs CARLETON Thomas, yeoman, of Lyndeborough, rec date 1784, judgment, debt, file #4205

MEANS Robert, gentleman, of Amherst, vs CUSHING John, physician, of Goffstown, rec date 1784, judgment, debt, file #5449

MEANS Robert, gentleman, of Amherst, vs LITTLE John, gentleman, of Derryfield, rec date 1785, judgment, debt, file #4687

MEANS Robert, gentleman, of Amherst, vs CUSHING John, physician, of Goffstown, rec date 1785, judgment, debt, file #5109

MEANS Robert, esquire, of Amherst, vs ROBINSON Silas, husbandman, of Bennington VT, rec date 1785, judgment, debt, file #5599

MEANS Robert, esquire, of Amherst, vs HEALL Joseph, of Dunstable, rec date 1790, writ, debt, file #5257

MEANS Robert, esquire, of Amherst, vs PEMBERTON James, husbandman, of Nottingham-West, rec date 1785, judgment, debt, file #5795

MEANS Robert, trader, of Amherst, vs McNEIL Daniel, yeoman, of Hillsborough, rec date 1782, execution, debt, file #5744

MEANS Robert, trader, of Amherst, vs JOHNSON Zedadiah, yeoman, of Hillsborough, rec date 1782, execution, debt, file #5744

MEANS Robert, esquire, of Amherst, vs ROBINSON Silas, husbandman, of Bennington, rec date 1785, judgment, debt, file #6402

MEARS Daniel, husbandman, of Deering, vs McLAUGHLIN John, husbandman, of Deering, doc date 1798, judgment, debt, file #565

MELLEN Thomas, yeoman, of Society Land, vs MONTGOMERY William, yeoman, of Francestown, rec date 1782, judgment, debt, file #2746

MELLEN Thomas, yeoman, of Society Land, vs MONTGOMERY Hugh, husbandman, of Francestown, rec date 1783, writ, debt, file #3304

MELLEN Thomas, yeoman, of Society Land, vs RICHARDSON Zechariah, innkeeper, of Francestown, rec date 1783, writ, debt, file #3304

MELLEN Thomas, cordwainer, of Francestown, vs BRADFORD Samuel Jr, gentleman, of Hillsborough, rec date 1783, execution, debt, file #3276

MELLEN Thomas, cordwainer, of Society Land, vs DUSTON Paul, yeoman, of New Boston, rec date 1782, appeal, debt, file #4009

MELLEN Thomas, yeoman, of Society Land, vs MONTGOMERY William, yeoman, of Francestown, rec date 1783, execution, debt, file #3861

MELLENDY Thomas, yeoman, of Amherst, vs BALDWIN Jesse, yeoman, of Amherst, rec date 1783, writ, debt, file #3083

MELLENDY William, cordwainer, of Amherst, vs WRIGHT Uriah, gentleman, of Hollis, doc date 1798, execution, debt, file #116

MELLENDY William Jr, yeoman, of Amherst, vs BALDWIN Jesse, yeoman, of Amherst, rec date 1783, writ, debt, file #3083

MELVIN Ebenezer, gentleman, of Cockermouth, vs HAZELTON Stephen, yeoman, of Hollis, doc date 1774, writ, debt, file #1121

MELVIN Ebenezer, gentleman, of Cockermouth, vs PROPRIETORS of Cockermouth, of Grafton County, rec date 1788, writ, debt, file #2574

MELVIN Isaac, husbandman, of Concord MA, vs WARNER Daniel, gentleman, of Amherst, doc date 1784, execution, debt, file #1941

MELVIN Isaac, husbandman, of Concord MA, vs WARNER Daniel, gentleman, of Amherst, rec date 1783, writ, debt, file #3459

MELVIN John, yeoman, of New Ipswich, vs HILLS David, yeoman, of New Ipswich, rec date 1786, deed, land transfer, file #4825

MELVIN Martha, spinster, of Nottingham-West, vs CUTLER Thomas, yeoman, of Nottingham-West, rec date 1782, judgment, debt, file #2727

MELVIN Martha, spinster, of Nottingham-West, vs CUTTER Thomas, yeoman, of Nottingham-West, rec date 1783, execution, debt, file #3849

MELVIN Nathaniel, husbandman, of Ashby MA, vs TUCKER Moses, yeoman, of New Ipswich, doc date 1773, judgment, debt, file #1322

MERIAM Nathan, yeoman, of New Ipswich, vs DEAN Benjamin, yeoman, of Francestown, rec date 1782, writ, debt, file #2839

MERRIAM Benjamin, of Mason, vs PARKMAN Samuel, merchant, of Boston MA, doc date 1799, judgment, debt, file #282

MERRIAM Ezra, yeoman, of Mason, vs CHAMPNEY Benjamin, doc date 1799, judgment, debt, file #222

MERRILL Benjamin, yeoman, of Amherst, vs HUTCHINSON Solomon, yeoman, of Merrimack, rec date 1785, writ, debt, file #6139

MERRILL Daniel, yeoman, of Hollis, vs GORDON William, merchant, of Dunstable MA, doc date 1774, writ, debt, file #1114, fragile

MERRILL Daniel, husbandman, of Hollis, vs AMES Jeremiah, gentleman, of Hollis, rec date 1783, writ, debt, file #3427

MERRILL Hugh, yeoman, of Buckland MA, vs BUTLER Jesse, yeoman, of Nottingham-West, rec date 1785, judgment, debt, file #4960

MERRILL William, gentleman, of Warner, vs CUMMINGS Ephraim, yeoman, of Swansey, doc date 1784, writ, debt, file #1627

MILLEN Robert, yeoman, of Holliston MA, vs LESLEY Joseph, husbandman, of Hollis, rec date 1786, writ, debt, file #6332

MILLER Farrea, yeoman, of Amherst, vs COCHRAN Eliah, administrator of estate, of Francestown, rec date 1785, judgment, debt, file #5365, estate of James GREGG

MILLER James, yeoman, of Hillsborough, vs HUBBARD Hatch, yeoman, of Winsor VT, doc date 1799, writ, debt, file #439

MILLER James, yeoman, of Hillsborough, vs ALLISTER Richard & Francis, yeoman, of Acworth, doc date 1798, execution, debt, file #79

MILLER John, yeoman, of Hancock, vs SPEARE Robert, yeoman, of Goffstown, doc date 1785, rec date 1786, deed, land transfer, file #5020

MILLER Matthew, yeoman, of Bedford, vs MORRISON John, yeoman, of Bedford, rec date 1783, various, debt, file #4298

MILLER Robert, yeoman, of Holliston MA, vs SEALY Joseph?, husbandman, of Hollis, rec date 1786, judgment, debt, file #6497

MILLER Samuel, husbandman, of Peterborough, vs COOK Ebenezer, husbandman, of Keene, rec date 1784, appeal, debt, file #4103

MILLER Samuel, husbandman, of Peterborough, vs WHITNEY David, husbandman, of Peterborough, rec date 1786, various, debt, file #6346

MILLER Samuel, husbandman, of Peterborough, vs WHITNEY David, husbandman, of Peterborough, rec date 1786, appeal, debt, file #6374

MILLER Samuel Jr, of Londonderry, vs WILSON James Jr, yeoman, of Peterborough, doc date 1774, writ, debt, file #1117, fragile

MILLIKEN James, husbandman, of Peterboro Slip, vs GREEN Thomas, husbandman, of Swanzey, rec date 1788, writ, debt, file #6688

MILLS John, yeoman, of Amherst, vs BREDFORD Henry, yeoman, of Hillsborough, doc date 1773, judgment, debt, file #1306

MILLS John, yeoman, of Amherst, vs BREDFORD Samuel 3rd, yeoman, of Hillsborough, doc date 1773, judgment, debt, file #1306

MILLS John, gentleman, of Amherst, vs BULLARD Benjamin, gentleman, of Sherburne MA, rec date 1787, judgment, debt, file #2316

MILLS John, yeoman, of Dunbarton, vs BEARD William, yeoman, of New Salem, doc date 1782, rec date 1786, deed, land transfer, file #5013

MILLS Samuel, yeoman, of Londonderry, vs WILSON James, yeoman, of Peterborough, doc date 1773, execution, debt, file #1468

MINCHIN John, trader, of Amherst, vs LANE Tiba, gentleman, of Amherst, doc date 1798, execution, debt, file #76

MINOT John, esquire, of Chelmsford MA, vs MILTIMOR John, yeoman, of Antrim, rec date 1784, rule of court, file #4202

MINOT John, esquire, of Chelmsford MA, vs PARKER William, husbandman, of Hillsborough, rec date 1784, judgment, debt, file #4626

MINOT John, esquire, of Chelmsford MA, vs MILTEMOR John, yeoman, of Antrim, doc date 1783, rec date 1783, deed, land transfer, file #5661

MINOT Jonas, gentleman, of Concord MA, vs KELLEY Timothy, physician, of Bridgewater, doc date 1798, judgment, debt, file #565

MINOT Jonas, gentleman, of Concord, vs SMITH John, esquire, of Bridgewater, doc date 1798, judgment, debt, file #565

MINOT Jonas, gentleman, of Concord MA, vs APPLETON Isaac, gentleman, of New Ipswich, doc date 1784, execution, debt, file #1801

MINOT Jonas, gentleman, of Concord MA, vs CHAMPNEY Ebenezer, esquire, of Groton MA, doc date 1784, execution, debt, file #1801

MINOT Jonas, gentleman, of Concord MA, vs LOVEJOY Henry, yeoman, of Wilton, rec date 1785, judgment, debt, file #5052

MINOT Jonas, gentleman, of Concord MA, vs BOYNTON Thomas, joiner, of Amherst, rec date 1785, judgment, debt, file #5064

MINOT Jonas, gentleman, of Concord MA, vs ABBOT Joseph Jr, cordwainer, of Wilton, rec date 1785, judgment, debt, file #5051

MINOT Jonas, gentleman, of Concord MA, vs EVERETT Nathaniel, yeoman, of New London, rec date 1785, judgment, debt, file #5183

MINOT Jonas, gentleman, of Concord MA, vs BALDWIN Ezra, yeoman, of Amherst, rec date 1785, judgment, debt, file #5269

MINOT Jonas, gentleman, of Concord MA, vs PRATT Ebenezer, laborer, of Sliptown, doc date 1770, rec date 1772, deed, land transfer, file #6841

MINOTT John, esquire, of Chelmsford MA, vs BOWEN Oliver, husbandman, of Hollis, doc date 1784, civil litigation, debt, file #1826

MINOTT John, esquire, of Chelmsford MA, vs MILLER Samuel Jr, husbandman, of Peterborough, doc date 1784, execution, debt, file #1811

MINOTT John, esquire, of Chelmsford MA, vs BOWERS Oliver, husbandman, of Hollis, rec date 1783, judgment, debt, file #4092

MINOTT John, esquire, of Chelmsford MA, vs MILLER Samuel Jr, husbandman, of Peterborough, rec date 1783, judgment, debt, file #4091

MINOTT John, gentleman, of Chelmsford MA, vs FARRAR Ebenezer, husbandman, of Alexandria, rec date 1784, judgment, debt, file #5001

MIRELL Joseph, joiner, of Hampstead, vs PARKER Samuel, yeoman, of Rindge, rec date 1786, writ, debt, file #6290

MITCHEL Isaac, yeoman, of Peterborough, vs PEABODY William, gentleman, of Amherst, doc date 1773, writ, debt, file #1360

MITCHEL Isaac, yeoman, of Peterborough, vs MORRISON John, clerk, of Peterborough, doc date 1772, bond, file #1194

MITCHEL Isaac, husbandman, of Peterborough, vs BRADLEY Stephen, esquire, of Westminster MA, rec date 1785, writ, debt, file #5412

MITCHEL Samuel, yeoman, of Peterborough, vs WHITE John, yeoman, of Peterborough, rec date 1785, writ, debt, file #6004

MITCHELL Francis, husbandman, of Campbells Gore, vs GLOVER Daniel, of MA, rec date 1782, writ, debt, file #2811

MITCHELL Isaac, yeoman, of Peterborough, vs CUTLER Jonas, shopkeeper, of Groton MA, doc date 1774, writ, debt, file #1283

MITCHELL Isaac, yeoman, vs GRAY Robert, rec date 1779, land deed, land dispute, file #2236B

MITCHELL John, planter, of Charleston SC, vs MITCHELL Isaac, of Peterborough, rec date 1774, lawyer appointment, to sell land, file #2179

MITCHELL John, esquire, of Charlestown SC, vs MORRISON John, clerk, of Peterborough, rec date 1779, various, land dispute, file #2236

MITCHELL John, yeoman, of Hancock, vs TAYLOR Isaiah, yeoman, of Peterborough, rec date 1783, writ, debt, file #3082

MITCHELL John, vs MORRISON John, of Hillsborough, rec date 1778, civil litigation, file #2168, papers very fragile

MITCHELL Margaret, of Francestown, vs MITCHELL John, yeoman, rec date 1794, warrant, assault, file #4152

MITCHELL Samuel, gentleman, of Peterborough, vs MOOR Ebenezer, yeoman, of Peterborough, doc date 1799, judgment, debt, file #290

MONRO Josiah, gentleman, of Amherst, vs LEWIS Jonathan Clark, shopkeeper, of Groton MA, doc date 1778, writ, debt, file #2034

MONTGOMERY Hugh, yeoman, of Francestown, vs McLAUGHLIN John Jr, innkeeper, of New Boston, rec date 1783, writ, debt, file #3177

MONTGOMERY Hugh, husbandman, of Francestown, vs CORSON William, husbandman, of Lyndeborough, doc date 1778, rec date 1784, deed, land transfer, file #6832

MOODY William, shipwright, of Newbury MA, vs CARLTON Moses, gentleman, of New Town, doc date 1774, execution, file #1007

MOOR Hugh, tailor, of Merrimack, vs UPHAM George B, esquire, of Claremont, doc date 1799, writ, debt, file #355

MOOR Hugh, tailor, of Merrimack, vs CHAFFIN John, of Claremont, doc date 1799, writ, debt, file #376

MOOR James, yeoman, of Bedford, vs PATTEN Matthew, esquire, of Bedford, doc date 1779, writ, assault, file #2068

MOOR James, husbandman, of Goffstown, vs ADDISON George, yeoman, of Goffstown, rec date 1782, writ, debt, file #2828

MOOR James, husbandman, of Goffstown, vs GEORGE Austin, husbandman, of Dunbarton, rec date 1783, writ, debt, file #3098

MOOR James, husbandman, of Goffstown, vs JEFFERIES David, merchant, of Boston MA, rec date 1782, appeal, debt, file #3995

MOOR James & Samuel, yeoman, of Goffstown, vs McCLINTOK Alexander, administrator of estate, of Hillsborough, rec date 1782, writ, debt, file #2794

MOOR John, gentleman, of Londonderry, vs NORRIS Benjamin, gentleman, of Pembroke, doc date 1773, writ, debt, file #1380

MOOR John, yeoman, of Bedford, vs ALLD John Jr, yeoman, of Merrimack, doc date 1784, writ, debt, file #1592

MOOR John, yeoman, of Londonderry, vs WILSON Thomas, gentleman, of New Boston, rec date 1783, writ, debt, file #3197

MOOR John, yeoman, of Francestown, vs PATTERSON Robert, yeoman, of Antrim, rec date 1785, judgment, debt, file #5204

MOOR John, wheelwright, of Walpole, vs WHITE Robert, husbandman, of New Boston, rec date 1785, judgment, debt, file #5846

MOOR John, esquire, of Derryfield, vs COSTEN Ebenezer, laborer, of Derryfield, doc date 1777, rec date 1777, deed, land transfer, file #6558

MOOR John, wheelwright, of Londonderry, vs MacGREGORCHIS James, merchant, of Londonderry, doc date 1788, rec date 1788, deed, land transfer, file #6798, ? pg 506

MOOR John Jr, yeoman, of Bedford, vs PARKER Jonathan, physician, of Litchfield, rec date 1782, writ, debt, file #2834

MOOR Joseph, esquire, of Groton MA, vs STONE Abel, yeoman, of Plainfield, rec date 1786, judgment, debt, file #6472

MOOR Joseph, esquire, of Groton MA, vs HALE Enoch, yeoman, of Rindge, rec date 1785, judgment, debt, file #6472

MOOR Robert, esquire, of Londonderry, vs HOUSTON James, blacksmith, of Bedford, doc date 1778, rec date 1778, deed, land transfer, file #2158

MOOR Robert, esquire, of Londonderry, vs MOOR John, yeoman, of Bedford, doc date 1772, rec date 1779, deed, land transfer, file #2126

MOOR Robert, esquire, of Londonderry, vs HICKINGS Josiah, cordwainer, of New Boston, doc date 1775, rec date 1786, deed, land transfer, file #5035

MOOR Samuel, esquire, of Canterbury, vs BROWN Jeremiah, yeoman, of Dunbarton, doc date 1774, execution, debt, file #756

MOOR Samuel, esquire, of Canterbury, vs BOWEN Jeremiah, yeoman, of Dunbarton, doc date 1774, execution, file #999

MOOR Samuel, miller, of Bedford, vs CASTON Ebenezer, yeoman, of Society Land, rec date 1783, writ, debt, file #2774

MOOR Samuel, miller, of Bedford, vs DICKEY Adams, husbandman, of Bedford, rec date 1783, writ, debt, file #3938

MOOR Samuel, gentleman, of Bedford, vs SAWYER Enoch, of Goffstown, rec date 1785, various, debt, file #5276

MOOR William, yeoman, of Pembroke, doc date 1763, note, debt, file #1611, 1

MOOR William, yeoman, of Bedford, vs PATTEN Matthew, esquire, of Bedford, doc date 1779, writ, assault, file #2068

MOOR William, husbandman, of New Boston, vs STATE of NH, rec date 1777, recognizance, forgery, file #2211

MOOR William, gentleman, of Londonderry, vs CHASE Jacob, yeoman, of Londonderry, rec date 1785, judgment, debt, file #5171

MOOR William Jr, husbandman, of Bedford, vs WALTON William, of Amherst, rec date 1785, writ, debt, file #6242

MOOR Witter Davidson, deceased, of New Boston, vs STATE of NH, rec date 1780, death inquiry, inquiry, file #2219

MOORE Benjamin, shopkeeper, of Littleton MA, vs JOHNSON Moses, husbandman, of Peterborough, rec date 1784, judgment, debt, file #4381

MOORE Daniel, trader, of Hopkinton, vs JOHNSON Jonas, of Lancaster MA, doc date 1798, execution, debt, file #97

MOORE Daniel, esquire, of Bedford, vs BELL John, yeoman, of Bedford, doc date 1774, writ, debt, file #1140, fragile

MOORE Daniel, esquire, of Bedford, vs AKIN James, yeoman, of Bedford, doc date 1774, writ, debt, file #1140

MOORE Daniel, esquire, of Bedford, vs CASWELL James, yeoman, of Bedford, doc date 1774, writ, debt, file #1140, fragile

MOORE Daniel, gentleman, of Bedford, vs ALLD Wm (Capt), gentleman, of Peterborough, rec date 1782, writ, debt, file #2777

MOORE Ebenezer, yeoman, of Peterborough, vs TAYLOR Charles, yeoman, of Peterborough, doc date 1799, judgment, debt, file #292

MOORE James, husbandman, of Goffstown, vs GEORGE Austin, yeoman, of Dunbarton, doc date 1784, writ, debt, file #1571

MOORE John, yeoman, of Bedford, vs TYLER John, laborer, of Goffstown, rec date 1771, various, debt, file #2170

MOORE John, yeoman, of Peterborough, vs MITCHELL Benjamin, yeoman, of Peterborough, rec date 1782, appeal, debt, file #4007

MOORE John, husbandman, of Dublin, vs PORTER Francis, husbandman, of Peterborough, rec date 1785, writ, debt, file #6218

MOORE Martha, seamstress, of Southboro MA, vs WEEKS William, husbandman, of Southboro MA, rec date 1788, writ, debt, file #6166, part of Samuel CURTIS file

MOORE Martha, seamstress, of Southboro MA, vs ALLEN Stephen, husbandman, of Marlborough MA, rec date 1788, writ, debt, file #6166

MOORE Samuel, yeoman, of Antrim, vs WOODMAN John, trader, of New London, doc date 1799, execution, debt, file #162

MOORE Samuel, gentleman, of Canterbury, vs BOVEN Jeremiah, yeoman, of Dunbarton, doc date 1770, judgment, debt, file #782

MOORE Samuel, miller, of Bedford, vs DICKEY Adam, husbandman, of Bedford, rec date 1783, various, debt, file #3616

MOORE Samuel Jr, husbandman, of Peterborough, vs MITCHEL Benjamin, yeoman, of Peterborough, doc date 1783, writ, debt, file #1259

MOORE William, gentleman, of Bedford, vs PARKER Ebenezer, husbandman, of Merrimack, doc date 1797, debt, file #553

MOORS Joseph, esquire, of Groton MA, vs STONE Abel, yeoman, of Plainfield, rec date 1785, judgment, debt, file #5224

MOORS Joseph, esquire, of Groton MA, vs HALE Enoch, esquire, of Rindge, rec date 1785, judgment, debt, file #5224

MOORS Joseph, husbandman, of Rindge, vs CUMMINGS John, yeoman, of Mason, rec date 1788, summons, land dispute, file #6975

MORE William, of New Boston, vs BOYES William, gentleman, of New Boston, rec date 1785, writ, debt, file #4785

MORELAND William, in jail, of Nottingham-West, vs RICE Joseph, innkeeper, of Weymouth MA, doc date 1795, petition, release of debit, file #17

MORGAN John, yeoman, of Weare, vs TAYLOR Anthony, husbandman, of Alexandria, rec date 1783, judgment, debt, file #4418

MORIN Anthony, yeoman, of Hillsborough, vs BRADFORD William, yeoman, of Amherst, doc date 1773, writ, debt, file #1355

MORIN Anthony, yeoman, of Hillsborough, vs SARGENT Paul Dudley, merchant, of Amherst, doc date 1773, writ, debt, file #1350

MORISON David, husbandman, of Windsor, vs GILBERT Josiah, husbandman, of Washington, doc date 1799, debt, file #333

MORISON Moses, gentleman, of Hancock, vs HEALD Thomas, esquire, of New Ipswich, doc date 1784, writ, debt, file #1271

MORREL Hugh, yeoman, of Francestown, vs STEARNS Samuel Jr, yeoman, of Amherst, rec date 1783, judgment, debt, file #3773

MORREL Hugh, yeoman, of Francestown, vs MELLEN Thomas, yeoman, of Society Land, rec date 1783, execution, debt, file #3848

MORREL John, yeoman, of Warner, vs BELL John, husbandman, of Bedford, rec date 1786, writ, debt, file #6275

MORREL Robert, yeoman, of Bedford, vs UNDERWOOD James, gentleman, of Bedford, rec date 1781, appeal, land dispute, file #3976

MORREL Robert, yeoman, of Bedford, vs INHABITANTS of Bedford, rec date 1785, writ, debt, file #6043

MORRELL Hugh, yeoman, of Francestown, vs MELLEN Thomas, yeoman, of Society Land, rec date 1782, judgment, debt, file #2725

MORRELL Hugh, husbandman, of Francestown, vs STEARNS Samuel & Jr, husbandman, of Amherst, rec date 1785, complaint, debt, file #5437

MORRILL Abraham, trader, of Boscawen, vs CALL John, husbandman, of Andover, rec date 1785, judgment, debt, file #5823

MORRILL Abraham, husbandman, of Derryfield, vs MERRILL David, husbandman, of Derryfield, doc date 1774, rec date 1774, deed, land transfer, file #6554

MORRILL Ephraim, husbandman, of Henniker, vs ANDREWS Abraham, husbandman, of Hillsborough, doc date 1799, debt, file #499

MORRILL Hugh, yeoman, of Francestown, vs BALDWIN Nathan, esquire, of Amherst, rec date 1782, various, debt, file #2669

MORRILL Hugh, husbandman, of Francestown, vs STEARNS Samuel & Jr, husbandman, of Amherst, rec date 1784, judgment, debt, file #5298

MORRILL John, yeoman, of Warner, vs BEVES John?, husbandman, of Bedford, rec date 1786, judgment, debt, file #6503

MORRILL Paul, husbandman, of Loudon, vs FOSTER Andrew, yeoman, of Bradford, rec date 1785, writ, debt, file #5404

MORRILL Robert, of New Boston, vs INHABITANTS of Bedford, doc date 1787, petition, release from jail, file #46

MORRILL Robert, yeoman, of Francestown, vs NICHOL Alexander, husbandman, of Londonderry, rec date 1782, writ, debt, file #2810

MORRILL Robert, yeoman, of Bedford, vs UNDERWOOD James, gentleman, of Bedford, rec date 1783, execution, debt, file #3062

MORRILL Robert, yeoman, of Bedford, vs CURRIER Jonathan, yeoman, of Bedford, rec date 1772, various, debt, file #4880

MORRILL Robert, yeoman, of Bedford, vs MARTIN James, husbandman, of Bedford, rec date 1785, writ, debt, file #4779

MORRILL Robert, yeoman, of Bedford, vs BEARD William, yeoman, of New Boston, rec date 1784, judgment, debt, file #5299

MORRILL Robert, yeoman, of Bedford, vs BEARD William, yeoman, of New Boston, rec date 1785, judgment, debt, file #5440

MORRILL Robert, weaver, of New Boston, vs PATTERSON Robert, husbandman, of New Boston, rec date 1786, writ, debt, file #6098

MORRILL Robert, weaver, of Bedford, vs INHB of Bedford, of Bedford, rec date 1788, various, debits, file #6813

MORRILL Robert, yeoman, of New Boston, vs GRAGG Alexander, yeoman, of New Boston, rec date 1787, writ, debt, file #6647

MORRILL Robert, of Warner, vs INHABITANTS of Bedford, rec date 1788, writ, debt, file #6736

MORRISON David, husbandman, of Campbells Gore, vs HOPKINS James, yeoman, of Antrim, doc date 1799, writ, debt, file #425

MORRISON Ezekiel, husbandman, of Peterborough, vs BANCOTT Charles, of Peterborough, rec date 1784, bond, debt, file #6351

MORRISON John, yeoman, of Peterborough, vs GOULD Jacob, yeoman, of Rindge, doc date 1772, writ, debt, file #1066

MORRISON John, yeoman, of Peterborough, vs MITCHEL Isaac, yeoman, of Peterborough, doc date 1774, judgment, debt, file #1147

MORRISON John Jr, yeoman, of Peterborough, vs HEALD Thomas, esquire, of New Ipswich, doc date 1784, writ, debt, file #1269

MORRISON Jonathan, physician, of Rindge, vs PALMER Stephen, yeoman, of Dunbarton, doc date 1773, writ, debt, file #1365

MORRISON Robert, tax collector, of Peterborough, vs TREADWELL Samuel, yeoman, of Peterborough, doc date 1779, rec date 1787, deed, land transfer, file #2481

MORRISON Robert, husbandman, of Windham, vs POLLARD Timothy, husbandman, of Nottingham-West, rec date 1783, judgment, debt, file #3757

MORRISON Robert, husbandman, of Peterborough, vs HOAR Benjamin, of Peterborough, rec date 1784, bond, debt, file #6351

MORRISON Robert, tax collector, of Peterborough, vs WHITE John, yeoman, of Peterborough, doc date 1780, rec date 1788, deed, land transfer, file #6833

MORRISON Samuel, husbandman, of Windham, vs SOUL Bildad, husbandman, of Goffstown, rec date 1783, judgment, debt, file #3756

MORRISON Samuel, husbandman, of Peterborough, vs WHITTEMORE Nathaniel, husbandman, of Peterborough, rec date 1785, various, debt, file #6230

MORRISON Samuel, husbandman, of Peterborough, vs WIER Robert, gentleman, of Walpole, rec date 1786, judgment, debt, file #6212

MORRISON Samuel, gentleman, of Peterborough, vs HOAR Benjamin, of Peterborough, rec date 1784, bond, debt, file #6351

MORRISON Samuel, husbandman, of Peterborough, vs WIER Robert, gentleman, of Walpole, rec date 1785, writ, debt, file #6341

MORRISON Sarah, widow, of Peterborough, vs WILLSON James, husbandman, of Uxbridge MA, rec date 1785, writ, debt, file #5096

MORRISON Sarah, widow, of Peterborough, vs WILLSON James, husbandman, of Oxbridge MA, rec date 1786, various, debt, file #6078

MORRISON Thomas, gentleman, of Peterborough, vs HOLMS Robert, husbandman, of Peterborough, rec date 1785, judgment, debt, file #5217

MORRISON Thomas, gentleman, of Peterborough, vs WHITE John, yeoman, of Peterborough, rec date 1785, writ, debt, file #6004

MORRISON Thomas, of Peterborough, vs WALES Thomas Jr, esquire, of Londonderry, rec date 1788, writ, debt, file #6615

MORRISON Thomas, of Peterborough, vs BETT James, esquire, of Windham, rec date 1788, writ, debt, file #6615

MORROW James, vs MORROW Robert, deed, land transfer, file #6563

MORROW Mary, single, of Bedford, vs MORROW Robert, yeoman, of Londonderry, doc date 1777, rec date 1777, deed, land transfer, file #6563

MORSE Aaron, groom, of Marlborough MA, vs FELTON Sarah, bride, of Marlborough MA, rec date 1788, marriage license, license, file #6159, part of Samuel CURTIS file

MORSE Edmond, carpenter, of Newbury MA, vs COFIN David, husbandman, of Boscawen, rec date 1787, writ, debt, file #6787

MORSE Eliakim, physician, of Boston MA, vs WEBSTER Amos, hatter, of Hampstead, doc date 1798, judgment, debt, file #565

MORSE Henry, joiner, of Loudon, vs FAULKNER Enoch, trader, of Haverhill MA, doc date 1799, judgment, debt, file #278

MORSE Jacob, yeoman, of Francestown, vs CRAM Joseph, yeoman, of Francestown, doc date 1806, rec date 1806, deed, land transfer, file #5684

MORSE John, yeoman, of Newbury MA, vs QUIMBE William, husbandman, of Weare, doc date 1782, rec date 1783, deed, land transfer, file #2653

MOSCHER James, vs TENNEY William, rec date 1784, rule of court, file #4184

MOSHEN James, husbandman, of Hollis, vs PATCH Timothy, husbandman, of Nottingham-West, rec date 1783, execution, debt, file #3844

MOSHER Daniel, of Hollis, vs POWERS Stephen, of Hollis, rec date 1783, deposition, deposition/deed, file #6800

MOSHER James, husbandman, of Hollis, vs SAWTELL Nathaniel, husbandman, of Pepperell MA, doc date 1784, writ, debt, file #1584

MOSHER James, husbandman, of Hollis, vs CARTER Edward, husbandman, of Hollis, rec date 1784, judgment, debt, file #4263

MOSHER James, cooper, of Hollis, vs LAWRENCE Zachariah, of Majorbigwaduce MA, doc date 1786, rec date 1786, deed, land transfer, file #5014

MOSHER James & Joshiah, of Hollis, vs POWERS Stephen, of Hollis, rec date 1783, deposition, deposition/deed, file #6800

MOSHER John, gentleman, of Pepperell MA, vs MOSHER James, husbandman, of Hollis, rec date 1784, judgment, debt, file #4603

MOSHER Lydia, widow, of Hollis, vs POWERS Stephen, of Hollis, rec date
1783, deposition, deposition/deed, file #6800
MOULTON Jonathan, esquire, of Hampton, vs JOHNSON Moses, husbandman,
of Peterborough, rec date 1783, judgment, debt, file #3707
MOULTON Jonathan, of Hampton, vs JOHNSON Moses, rec date 1783, writ,
debt, file #3945
MOULTON Jonathan, esquire, of Hampton, vs LEGHATE Thomas, esquire, of
Leominster MA, rec date 1785, writ, debt, file #6219
MUDGET Miriam, widow, rec date 1787, writ, file #6665
MUDGET William, husbandman, of Weare, vs SMITH Thomas, husbandman, of
New Boston, doc date 1798, execution, debt, file #90
MULLEN Thomas, cordwainer, of Francestown, vs BRADFORD Samuel Jr,
gentleman, of Hillsborough, doc date 1784, execution, debt, file #1928
MUMOC Stephen, yeoman, of Groton MA, vs CHAFMAN Jeremiah,
husbandman, of Rindge, rec date 1782, judgment, debt, file #4889
MUNN Nathan, yeoman, of Holden MA, vs BRADFORD Samuel, gentleman, of
Hillsborough, rec date 1786, judgment, debt, file #6468
MUNROE Ephraim, physician, of Harvard MA, vs McCOY William, yeoman, of
New Boston, doc date 1784, execution, debt, file #1922
MUNROE Ephraim, physician, of Harvard MA, vs LIVINGSTON John, yeoman,
of New Boston, doc date 1784, execution, debt, file #1922
MUNROE Ephraim, physician, of Harvard MA, vs McCAY William, yeoman, of
New Boston, rec date 1783, execution, debt, file #2980
MUNROE Ephraim, physician, of Harvard MA, vs LIVINGSTON John, yeoman,
of New Boston, rec date 1783, execution, debt, file #2980
MUNROE Ephraim, physician, of Harvard MA, vs LIVINGSTON John, yeoman,
of New Boston, rec date 1783, execution, debt, file #3255
MUNROE Ephraim, physician, of Harvard MA, vs McCOY William, yeoman, of
New Boston, rec date 1783, execution, debt, file #3255
MUNROE Isaac, housewright, of Lincoln, vs BARRETT Charles, trustee, of New
Ipswich, rec date 1788, writ, debt, file #6730
MUNROE Josiah, esquire, of Amherst, vs BIRD George, esquire, of Londonderry,
rec date 1785, writ, debt, file #4802
MURDOUGH Samuel, husbandman, of Hillsborough, vs TOLBUSH William,
husbandman, of Hillsborough, rec date 1786, writ, debt, file #6307
MURDOUGH Samuel, husbandman, of Hillsborough, vs TOLBART William,
husbandman, of Hillsborough, rec date 1786, judgment, debt, file #6500
MURDOUGH Thomas, husbandman, of Hillsborough, vs MARSHALL David,
husbandman, of Hillsborough, rec date 1785, judgment, debt, file #5213
MURPHY Reuben, husbandman, of Amherst, vs WESTON Thomas, yeoman, of
Amherst, doc date 1782, execution, file #1013
MURPHY Robert, husbandman, of Londonderry, vs GREGG Samuel,
husbandman, of Antrim, doc date 1798, judgment, debt, file #565
MURPHY Robert, husbandman, of Londonderry, vs GRAGG Samuel,
husbandman, of Antrim, doc date 1799, debt, file #448
NAHAN James Jr, husbandman, of Litchfield, vs PAIGE Abraham, gentleman, of
Nottingham-West, rec date 1782, writ, trespass of land, file #2682

NAHOR James Jr, yeoman, of Litchfield, vs MACK Margaret, widow, of Litchfield, rec date 1785, writ, assault, file #5410

NEAL John, yeoman, of Merrimack, vs RAND Nathaniel, gentleman, of Rye, doc date 1772, writ, debt, file #914, fragile

NEAL John, yeoman, of Merrimack, vs MOOR Samuel, yeoman, of Merrimack, doc date 1773, execution, debt, file #1458

NEAL John, of Merrimack, vs RAND Nathaniel, yeoman, of Rye, doc date 1773, execution, debt, file #1473

NEAL John, of Merrimack, vs MOOR Samuel, yeoman, of Merrimack, doc date 1772, execution, debt, file #1433

NEAL John, yeoman, of Merrimack, vs MOORE Samuel, yeoman, of Merrimack, doc date 1773, execution, debt, file #1488

NEAL John, yeoman, of Hillsborough, vs MOOR Samuel, yeoman, of Merrimack, doc date 1773, execution, debt, file #1480

NEAL John, esquire, of Londonderry, vs NEEDHAM Benjamin, husbandman, of Billerica MA, rec date 1788, writ, debt, file #6676

NEAL John, esquire, of Londonderry, vs HERRICK Josiah, husbandman, of New Boston, rec date 1788, writ, debt, file #6917

NEAL William, yeoman, of Londonderry, vs GORMAN James, wheelwright, of Londonderry, doc date 1772, writ, debt, file #1407

NELSON Moses, yeoman, of Hillsborough, vs WILSON David, gentleman, of Deering, doc date 1799, writ, debt, file #319

NELSON Stephen, husbandman, of Salisbury, vs PAGE Moses, husbandman, of Sanbornton, doc date 1799, debt, file #485

NENT John, esquire, of Londonderry, vs ADAMS Gideon, yeoman, of Henniker, rec date 1787, writ, debt, file #6653

NESMITH John, gentleman, of Londonderry, vs PUTNAM Francis, gentleman, of Walpole, doc date 1779, writ, debt, file #2091

NESMITH John, yeoman, of Londonderry, vs WILSON Thomas, gentleman, of New Boston, rec date 1783, writ, debt, file #3197

NESMITH Jonathan, husbandman, of Antrim, vs MOOR John, husbandman, of Francestown, rec date 1785, writ, debt, file #6010

NESMITH Jonathan, husbandman, of Antrim, vs MOOR John, husbandman, of Francestown, rec date 1785, judgment, debt, file #6444

NEVINS Joseph, husbandman, of Hollis, vs DAKIN Justus, husbandman, of Nottingham-West, rec date 1783, execution, debt, file #3640

NEVINS Joseph, husbandman, of Hollis, vs DAKIN Justus, husbandman, of Nottingham-West, rec date 1782, execution, debt, file #3472

NEVINS Joseph, husbandman, of Hollis, vs ABBOTT Samuel, yeoman, of Hollis, rec date 1782, execution, debt, file #3471

NEWALL Jeremiah, yeoman, of Dunbarton, vs LINSAY Samuel, husbandman, of Rumney, rec date 1786, writ, debt, file #6131

NEWCOMB Daniel, esquire, of Keene, vs BREWSTER Isaac, yeoman, of Francestown, rec date 1786, writ, debt, file #6107

NEWCOMB Daniel, esquire, of Keene, vs BREWSTER Isaac, yeoman, of Francestown, rec date 1786, writ, debt, file #6052

NEWELL Asa, yeoman, of Lynn MA, vs ANDREWS Ammi, gentleman, of Hillsborough, rec date 1783, execution, debt, file #3855

NEWELL Asa, yeoman, of Lynn MA, vs ANDREWS Ammi, gentleman, of Hillsborough, rec date 1783, writ, debt, file #3905

NEWELL Asa, husbandman, of Lynn MA, vs JONES James & William, of Hillsborough, rec date 1785, judgment, debt, file #6490

NEWELL John, of Hancock, vs TOWN of Hancock, doc date 1891, defendants brief, supreme court, file #633

NEWELL Oliver, yeoman, of Pepperell MA, vs LAWRENCE Zachariah, yeoman, of Hollis, doc date 1775, writ, debt, file #954

NEWHALL Asa, husbandman, of Lynn MA, vs JONES William & James, gentleman, of Hillsborough, rec date 1785, judgment, debt, file #5584

NEWHALL Josiah, yeoman, of Chesterfield, vs MOORS David, husbandman, of Groton MA, doc date 1799, judgment, debt, file #274

NEWHALL Josiah, yeoman, of Chesterfield, vs MORSE Joseph, esquire, of Groton, doc date 1799, judgment, debt, file #270

NEWHALL Josiah, blacksmith, of Pepperell MA, vs MOSHER James, husbandman, of Hollis, rec date 1784, judgment, debt, file #4989

NEWHALL Oliver, husbandman, of Pepperell MA, vs HASELTON Stephen, yeoman, of Hollis, doc date 1787, judgment, debt, file #510

NEWHALL Oliver, blacksmith, of Pepperell MA, vs HASELTON Stephen, yeoman, of Hollis, doc date 1779, writ, debt, file #2094

NEWHALL Oliver, husbandman, of Pepperell MA, vs HESELTON Stephen, husbandman, of Hollis, rec date 1787, judgment, debt, file #2472

NEWHALL Oliver, husbandman, of Pepperell MA, vs BROOK William Jr, blacksmith, of Hollis, rec date 1787, writ, debt, file #2426, defendant deceased

NEWHALL Oliver, husbandman, of Hollis, vs KELLY Joseph, gentleman, of Nottingham-West, rec date 1785, writ, debt, file #5041

NEWMAN Ebenezer, yeoman, of Deering, vs ABBOTT James, trader, of Billerica MA, doc date 1799, writ, debt, file #372

NEWMAN Ebenezer, husbandman, of Deering, vs BROWN Francis, yeoman, of Antrim, doc date 1799, debt, file #344

NEWMAN Ebenezer, yeoman, of Deering, vs FORSAITH William, esquire, of Deering, doc date 1799, judgment, debt, file #227

NEWMAN Ebenezer, yeoman, of Deering, vs WILSON Alexander, husbandman, of Wilton, doc date 1799, debt, file #340

NEWMAN Ebenezer, husbandman, of Deering, vs GIBSON John, trader, of Francestown, doc date 1799, judgment, debt, file #258

NEWMAN Ebenezer, yeoman, of Deering, vs VASEL Derby, yeoman, of Boston MA, doc date 1799, judgment, debt, file #235

NEWMAN Josiah, husbandman, of Deering, vs AIKEN James Jr, husbandman, of Antrim, rec date 1806, deed, land transfer, file #5685

NEWMAN Thomas, yeoman, of Bedford, vs MOOR James, husbandman, of Goffstown, doc date 1772, writ, debt, file #898

NEWMAN Thomas, yeoman, of Bedford, vs PARKER Samuel, yeoman, of Amherst, doc date 1772, writ, debt, file #1423

NEWMAN Thomas, yeoman, of Bedford, vs SARGENT Paul Dudley, merchant, of Amherst, doc date 1773, writ, debt, file #1227

NEWTON Joseph, groom, of Marlborough MA, vs JOSLIN Lucy, bride, of Marlborough MA, rec date 1787, marriage license, license, file #6161, part of Samuel CURTIS file

NICHOLAS Adam, yeoman, of Antrim, vs MARTIN Jesse, yeoman, of Francestown, doc date 1784, execution, debt, file #1722

NICHOLAS John, yeoman, of Corlisle MA, vs SWALLOW John, yeoman, of Mason, doc date 1799, debt, file #478

NICHOLAS John, yeoman, of Corlisle MA, vs LAWRENCE Stephen, yeoman, of Mason, doc date 1799, debt, file #478

NICHOLAS John, yeoman, of Corlisle MA, vs LAWRENCE John, yeoman, of Mason, doc date 1799, debt, file #478

NICHOLAS John, blacksmith, of Boscawen, vs MOODY Elisha, of New Boston, rec date 1783, writ, debt, file #3954

NICHOLAS John, yeoman, of Redding MA, vs PEARSON Elizabeth, widow, of Lyndeborough, rec date 1785, writ, land dispute, file #6140, /

NICHOLAS John, yeoman, of Reading MA, vs PEARSON Elizabeth, widow, of Lyndeborough, rec date 1786, writ, debt, file #6486

NICHOLAS Moses, of Amherst, vs HILLSBORO County, doc date 1783 9, bond, registration of deed bond, file #806, years 1783 1789

NICHOLAS William, laborer, of Londonderry, vs STEVENS Peter, husbandman, of Sandown, doc date 1772, writ, debt, file #1387

NICHOLS Aaron, yeoman, of Amherst, vs CRAM Nathan, yeoman, of Lyndeborough, rec date 1785, execution, debt, file #5902

NICHOLS Adam, yeoman, of Antrim, vs MARTIN Jesse, yeoman, of Francestown, rec date 1782, judgment, debt, file #2728

NICHOLS Adam, yeoman, of Antrim, vs MARTIN Jesse, yeoman, of Francestown, rec date 1783, execution, debt, file #3266

NICHOLS Daniel, husbandman, of Antrim, vs MOOR John, husbandman, of Francestown, rec date 1785, writ, debt, file #6010

NICHOLS Daniel, yeoman, of Antrim, vs EASTMAN Samuel, yeoman, of Henniker, rec date 1785, writ, debt, file #6216

NICHOLS Daniel, husbandman, of Antrim, vs MOOR John, husbandman, of Francestown, rec date 1785, judgment, debt, file #6444

NICHOLS Ebenezer, esquire, of Merrimack, vs TOWNSEND William B, esquire, of Boston MA, doc date 1774, writ, debt, file #1123

NICHOLS Ebenezer, esquire, of Merrimack, vs FAYERWEATHER Thomas, esquire, of Boston MA, doc date 1774, writ, debt, file #1123

NICHOLS James, husbandman, of Litchfield, vs BREED Allen, yeoman, of Merrimack, rec date 1784, judgment, debt, file #4399

NICHOLS John, husbandman, of Hillsborough, vs McKEEN John, yeoman, of Deering, doc date 1799, writ, debt, file #412

NICHOLS John, husbandman, of Hillsborough, vs WILSON David, gentleman, of Deering, doc date 1799, writ, debt, file #325

NICHOLS John, husbandman, of Francestown, vs TREAT Robert, esquire, of Boston MA, doc date 1799, judgment, debt, file #244

NICHOLS John, yeoman, of Hillsborough, vs BRADFORD Andrew, husbandman, of Hillsborough, rec date 1785, judgment, debt, file #2435

NICHOLS John, husbandman, of Hillsborough, vs STEVENS Calvin, husbandman, of Hillsborough, rec date 1785, writ, debt, file #2408

NICHOLS John, yeoman, of Billerica MA, vs ASTEN Timothy, yeoman, of Temple, rec date 1783, judgment, debt, file #3716

NICHOLS John, yeoman, of Hillsborough, vs BRADFORD Samuel, gentleman, of Hillsborough, doc date 1784, rec date 1785, deed, land transfer, file #5641

NICHOLS John, tax collector, of Hillsborough, vs DUTTON James, yeoman, of Hillsborough, doc date 1784, rec date 1785, deed, land transfer, file #5643

NICHOLS John, husbandman, of Reading MA, vs WRIGHT David, husbandman, of Hillsborough, rec date 1785, execution, debt, file #5946

NICHOLS John, husbandman, of Reading MA, vs WRIGHT David, husbandman, of Hillsborough, rec date 1785, writ, debt, file #6021

NICHOLS Moses, physician, of Amherst, doc date 1779, journal book & papers, various papers, file #2031

NICHOLS Moses, physician, of Amherst, doc date 1779, journal book & papers, various papers, file #2031

NICHOLS Moses, physician, of Amherst, doc date 1779, journal book & papers, various papers, file #2031

NICHOLS Moses, esquire, of Amherst, vs COCHRAN John, yeoman, of Amherst, doc date 1784, execution, land value, file #1859

NICHOLS Moses, physician, of Amherst, doc date 1779, journal book & papers, various papers, file #2031

NICHOLS Moses, esquire, of Amherst, vs BOUTELL Lydia & Amos, widow/yeoman, of Amherst, rec date 1785, execution, debt, file #5938

NICHOLS Moses, esquire, of Amherst, vs BOUTELL Lydia, widow, of Amherst, rec date 1785, judgment, debt, file #5845

NICHOLS Moses, esquire, of Amherst, vs WHITE Robert, husbandman, of New Boston, rec date 1786, writ, debt, file #6122

NICHOLS Perkins, merchant, of Boston MA, vs NICHOLS Joseph, gentleman, of Amherst, doc date 1798, judgment, debt, file #565

NICHOLS Samuel, yeoman, of Francestown, vs CARSON John, gentleman, of Francestown, rec date 1784, appeal, debt, file #4123

NICHOLS Samuel, yeoman, of Hillsborough, vs ANDREWS Ammi, yeoman, of Hillsborough, rec date 1785, writ, debt, file #6232

NICHOLS Thomas, husbandman, of Weare, vs HADLEY Enoch, of Deering, doc date 1799, judgment, debt, file #228

NICHOLS Thomas, yeoman, of Weare, vs MOULTON David, yeoman, of Weare, rec date 1783, civil litigious, debt, file #2965

NICHOLS Thomas, yeoman, of Weare, vs MOULTON David, yeoman, of Weare, rec date 1783, writ, debt, file #3888

NICKELS Alexander & Margaret, yeoman, of Londonderry, vs BOYD Arthur, yeoman, of Londonderry, doc date 1766, writ, debt, file #819

NORWOOD David, physician, of Londonderry, vs FREEMAN Cesar, yeoman, of Lyndeborough, rec date 1782, judgment, debt, file #2732

NORWOOD David, physician, of Londonderry, vs FELT Peter, yeoman, of Temple, rec date 1783, execution, debt, file #2997

NORWOOD David, physician, of Londonderry, vs RICHARDSON Zachariah, yeoman, of Francestown, rec date 1784, judgment, debt, file #4249

NOWEL Rachel, of Berwick ME, vs COSTALE John, yeoman, of Berwick Me, doc date 1778, rec date 1787, deed, land transfer, file #2500

NOYES Benjamin, gentleman, of Bow, vs MITCHELL Francis, yeoman, of Dunbarton, doc date 1799, deed, land transfer, file #1995

NOYES Cuter, husbandman, of Boscawen, vs CORSER Samuel, yeoman, of Concord, rec date 1785, judgment, debt, file #5844

NOYES Cuter, husbandman, of Boscawen, vs PAGE Daniel, tanner, of Concord, rec date 1785, judgment, debt, file #5844

NOYES Daniel, husbandman, of Hopkinton, vs BARNS Silas, husbandman, of Henniker, doc date 1772, judgment, debt, file #1287

NOYES Nathaniel, merchant, of Salisbury, vs CUSHING Caleb, blacksmith, of Salisbury, doc date 1798, execution, debt, file #68

NOYES Nathaniel, trader, of Salisbury, vs ELKINS Abel, innkeeper, of Salisbury, doc date 1798, judgment, debt, file #565

NOYES Nathaniel, trader, of Salisbury, vs ELKINS Abel, innkeeper, of Salisbury, doc date 1798, judgment, debt, file #565

NOYES Nathaniel, trader, of Salisbury, vs PAGE Timothy, taylor, of Rumney, doc date 1798, execution, debt, file #150

NOYES Nathaniel, trader, of Salisbury, vs ELKINS Abel, innkeeper, of Salisbury, doc date 1799, debt, file #450

NOYES Sarah, single, of Hollis, vs FARLEY Ebenezer, yeoman, of Hollis, doc date 1770, rec date 1774, deed, land transfer, file #6545

NOYES Stephen, cordwainer, of Hampstead, vs MANSIS Cornelius, merchant, of Haverhill MA, doc date 1772, writ, debt, file #1054

NUTT Samuel, gentleman, of Francestown, vs WASON Thomas, gentleman, of Nottingham-West, rec date 1783, writ, debt, file #3329

NUTT Wm & Samuel, yeoman, of Francestown, vs MORRILL Hugh, yeoman, of Francestown, doc date 1783, recognizance, assault & batter, file #778

NUTTING Elizabeth, widow, of New Ipswich, vs NUTTING Amos, yeoman, of Hollis, doc date 1772, writ, debt, file #1282

NUTTING Jacob, laborer, of Hollis, vs HADLEY Nehemiah, yeoman, of Dunstable, rec date 1783, writ, debt, file #3423

NUTTING John, gentleman, of Pepperell MA, vs WOOD William, husbandman, of Hollis, rec date 1785, judgment, debt, file #5167

NUTTING John, gentleman, of Pepperell MA, vs WRIGHT Uriah, gentleman, of Hollis, rec date 1785, judgment, debt, file #5167

NUTTING John, gentleman, of Pepperell MA, vs WRIGHT Lemuel, husbandman, of Hollis, rec date 1785, judgment, debt, file #5167

NUTTING John, gentleman, of Pepperell MA, vs WRIGHT Uriah, gentleman, of Hollis, rec date 1786, judgment, debt, file #6479

NUTTING John, gentleman, of Pepperell MA, vs WRIGHT Samuel, husbandman, of Hollis, rec date 1786, judgment, debt, file #6479

NUTTING John, sheriff, of Pepperell MA, vs WOOD William, husbandman, of Hollis, rec date 1786, judgment, debt, file #6479

NUTTING Jonathan, yeoman, of Raby, vs GREEN William, husbandman, of Pepperell MA, doc date 1772, writ, debt, file #907

NUTTING Peter, cabinetmaker, of Hillsborough, vs CAMPBELL Benjamin, gentleman, of Roby, doc date 1798, execution, debt, file #149

NUTTING Thomas, of Westford MA, vs LITTLE William, physician, of Hillsborough, rec date 1788, writ, debt, file #6980

NUTTING William, husbandman, of Groton MA, vs BENNET Benjamin, cordwainer, of Amherst, rec date 1783, judgment, debt, file #3789

O'DELL William, husbandman, of Amherst, vs COCHRAN John, husbandman, of Amherst, doc date 1776, rec date 1779, deed, land transfer, file #2138

OATHOUT Abraham, merchant, of Albany NY, vs RANKIN Samuel, innkeeper, of Londonderry, doc date 1774, execution, file #1003

OBER Samuel, husbandman, of Wenmham MA, vs RAMSEY William, husbandman, of Londonderry, rec date 1787, writ, debt, file #6648

ODEL Ebenezer, gentleman, of Amherst, vs JONES Samuel, husbandman, of Campbells Gore, rec date 1788, writ, debt, file #6801

ODELL Ebenezer, gentleman, of Amherst, vs STEARNS John, yeoman, of Amherst, rec date 1783, judgment, debt, file #4443

ODELL William Jr, yeoman, of Amherst, vs WILKINS Benjamin, yeoman, of Amherst, rec date 1783, writ, debt, file #3085

ODIONNE George, trader, of Boston MA, vs WILSON James, trader, of Windham, doc date 1798, execution, debt, file #64

OLCOTT Simeon, of Charlestown, vs HOLLAND Stephen, of Londonderry, rec date 1772, letter, file #7027

OLIVER Andrew, esquire, of Salem MA, vs STONE Watson, of Raby, doc date 1780, rec date 1783, deed, land transfer, file #2632

OLIVER Andrew, esquire, of Salem MA, vs CROSS Peter, gentleman, of Nottingham-West, rec date 1784, various, land dispute, file #4180

OLIVER Andrew & Mary Ann, of Salem MA, vs GIBSON William, housewright, of Nottingham-West, doc date 1778, deed, land transfer, file #2014, fragile

OLIVER Andrew & Mary Ann, of Salem MA, vs PAGE Abraham, gentleman, of Nottingham-West, doc date 1778, deed, land transfer, file #2014

OLIVER Andrew & Mary Ann, of Salem MA, vs STUCKLIN John, gentleman, of Nottingham-West, doc date 1778, deed, land transfer, file #2014

ORDWAY James, cordwainer, of Lyndeborough, vs CRAM Zebulon, yeoman, of Lyndeborough, doc date 1799, writ, debt, file #373

ORDWAY John, yeoman, of Lyndeborough, vs WHITNEY Samuel, merchant, of Amherst, doc date 1799, judgment, debt, file #262

ORDWAY Samuel, husbandman, of Hopkinton, vs WEBSTER Benjamin, husbandman, of Boscawen, doc date 1798, execution, debt, file #94

ORDWAY Samuel, husbandman, of Goffstown, vs EATON Enoch, husbandman, of Atkinson, rec date 1783, writ, debt, file #3319

ORR Alexander, yeoman, of Merrimack, vs CURRIER Jonathan, yeoman, of Bedford, rec date 1772, various, debt, file #4880

OSGOOD Isaac, yeoman, of Haverhill MA, vs DOW Joseph Jr, yeoman, of Goffstown, doc date 1774, recognizance, debt, file #1154

OSGOOD Isaac, merchant, of Haverhill MA, vs DOW Joseph, yeoman, of Goffstown, rec date 1774, execution, debt, file #4885

OSGOOD Joseph, blacksmith, of Raby, vs BARRETT Abigail, of Mason, doc date 1779, rec date 1783, pre nuptial agreement, land transfer, file #2657

OSGOOD Joshua, gentleman, of Andover MA, vs BUXTON Benjamin, yeoman, of Merrimack, rec date 1785, judgment, debt, file #5798

OTIS Joseph, gentleman, of Scituate MA, vs McLAUGHLIN John Jr, innkeeper, of New Boston, rec date 1785, writ, debt, file #4776

PAGE Abraham, captain, of Nottingham-West, vs DAKIN Justus, husbandman, of Nottingham-West, doc date 1779, various, land dispute, file #2107

PAGE Abraham, captain, of Nottingham-West, vs BARRETT Simeon, husbandman, of Nottingham-West, doc date 1779, various, land dispute, file #2107

PAGE Abraham, captain, of Nottingham-West, vs BARRETT Moses Jr, husbandman, of Nottingham-West, doc date 1779, various, land dispute, file #2107

PAGE Abraham, esquire, of New Boston, vs WILSON Thomas, gentleman, of New Boston, doc date 1777, writ, debt, file #2071

PAGE Abraham, gentleman, of Nottingham-West, vs BROWN Samuel, husbandman, of Nottingham-West, rec date 1782, appeal, debt, file #4004

PAGE Abraham (Capt), of Nottingham-West, vs BARRETT Simeon, husbandman, of Nottingham-West, doc date 1778, writ, breaking & entry, file #2021, fragile

PAGE Caleb, gentleman, of Dunbarton, vs WILLARD Josiah, esquire, of Winchester, rec date 1783, execution, debt, file #3681

PAGE Caleb, gentleman, of Dunbarton, vs WILLARD Josiah, esquire, of Winchester, rec date 1782, execution, debt, file #4900

PAGE Enoch, husbandman, of Goffstown, vs CUSHING John, physician, of Goffstown, rec date 1783, writ, debt, file #3309

PAGE Isaac, yeoman, of Nottingham-West, vs STEEL Joseph, yeoman, of Nottingham-West, doc date 1781, capias, file #765

PAGE Jeremiah, esquire, of Dunbarton, vs CALDWELL William, husbandman, of Francestown, rec date 1787, writ, debt, file #2364

PAGE John, merchant, of Salem MA, vs ATKINSON Samuel, gentleman, of Boscawen, rec date 1785, judgment, debt, file #5054

PAGE John Jr, esquire, of Dover, vs DAVIS Samuel (estate), of Madbury, doc date 1771, civil litigations, debt, file #571

PAGE Moses, gentleman, of Weare, vs FLANDERS Philip, gentleman, of Warner, rec date 1783, writ, debt, file #3394

PAGE Samuel, husbandman, of Henniker, vs ARCHER Michael, husbandman, of Henniker, doc date 1799, petition, release of debit, file #22

PAGE Sargent, yeoman, of Merrimack, vs NICHOLS Ebenezer, of Merrimack, doc date 1774, judgment, debt, file #713

PAGE Silas, gentleman, of Rindge, vs KELLEY Joseph, esquire, of Nottingham-West, rec date 1785, recognizance, debt, file #7042

PAINE Nathaniel, esquire, of Groton MA, vs RUSSELL Nathaniel, gentleman, of Rindge, rec date 1785, judgment, debt, file #5499

PAINE Nathaniel, esquire, of Groton MA, vs FELT Benjamin, blacksmith, of Temple, rec date 1784, judgment, debt, file #4379

PAINE Nathaniel, esquire, of Groton MA, vs SLOAN David, husbandman, of Mason, rec date 1785, judgment, debt, file #5225

PAINE Nathaniel, esquire, of Worcester MA, vs BALL Joseph, yeoman, of Mason, rec date 1788, writ, debt, file #6716

PALMER William, cooper, of Goffstown, vs EATON Enoch, husbandman, of Atkinson, rec date 1782, writ, debt, file #2840

PARKER Abel, yeoman, of Peterborough, vs TAYLOR John, yeoman, of Uxbridge MA, doc date 1784, petition, release from jail, file #47

PARKER Abel, yeoman, of Peterborough, vs TEMPLETON James, yeoman, of Peterboro Slip, doc date 1779, writ, debt, file #2092

PARKER Abel, yeoman, of Peterborough, vs DANA Samuel, gentleman, of Amherst, rec date 1783, writ, debt, file #2772

PARKER Alexander, husbandman, of Society Land, vs GREGG John, husbandman, of Peterborough, doc date 1784, execution, debt, file #1741

PARKER Alexander, yeoman, of Society Land, vs BALDWIN Nahum, esquire, of Amherst, rec date 1782, writ, debt, file #2686, estate of Zacheus CUTLER

PARKER Benjamin, laborer, of Rindge, vs KELLEY Joseph, esquire, of Nottingham-West, rec date 1785, recognizance, debt, file #7042

PARKER Benjamin, yeoman, of Temple, vs LEE Joseph, physician, of Roylston MA, doc date 1799, judgment, debt, file #271

PARKER Benjamin, yeoman, of Clarendon NY, vs PAGE Leme, husbandman, of Rindge, rec date 1782, judgment, debt, file #2731

PARKER Benjamin, yeoman, of Clarendon NY, vs DEMARY John, husbandman, of Rindge, rec date 1782, judgment, debt, file #2731

PARKER Benjamin, yeoman, of Clarendon NY, vs DEMARY John, husbandman, of Rindge, rec date 1783, civil litigious, debt, file #2925

PARKER Benjamin, yeoman, of Clarendon NY, vs PAGE Leme, husbandman, of Rindge, rec date 1783, civil litigious, debt, file #2925

PARKER Benjamin, yeoman, of Clarendon NY, vs DEMARY John, husbandman, of Rindge, rec date 1783, execution, debt, file #3253

PARKER Benjamin, yeoman, of Clarendon NY, vs PAGE Leme, husbandman, of Rindge, rec date 1783, execution, debt, file #3253

PARKER Benjamin, husbandman, of Rindge, vs BELLOWS John, of Walpole, rec date 1785, judgment, false statement, file #3558

PARKER Benjamin, housewright, of Sutton MA, vs PARKER Samuel & Jonathan, yeoman, of Rindge, rec date 1784, writ, debt, file #6048

PARKER Benjamin Woods, shopkeeper, of Hollis, vs SHATTUCK Daniel, yeoman, of Hollis, doc date 1798, execution, debt, file #138

PARKER Benjamin Woods, shopkeeper, of Hollis, vs HALE William, physician, of Hollis, doc date 1798, execution, debt, file #55

PARKER Benjamin Woods, gentleman, of Hollis, vs BENNET Phinehas Jr, cooper, of Brookline, doc date 1799, judgment, debt, file #568

PARKER Benjamin Woods, shopkeeper, of Hollis, vs BELL James, yeoman, of Dunstable, doc date 1798, execution, debt, file #104

PARKER David, yeoman, of Peterborough, vs PARKER Samuel, yeoman, of Peterborough, doc date 1773, execution, debt, file #1373

PARKER Deborah, spinster, of Amherst, vs AVERHILL Moses, yeoman, of Amherst, rec date 1785, appeal, marriage refusal, file #4801

PARKER Ebenezer, husbandman, of Goffstown, vs BARRON William, esquire, of Goffstown, doc date 1799, execution, debt, file #198

PARKER Henry, yeoman, of Wilton, vs FRYE Isaac, yeoman, of Wilton, doc date 1773, judgment, debt, file #1303

PARKER John, gentleman, of Litchfield, vs McCAY Gilbert, weaver, of Peterboro Slip, doc date 1774, execution, file #1006

PARKER John, gentleman, of Litchfield, vs THOMPSON Benjamin, cordwainer, of Concord, doc date 1772, writ, debt, file #1390

PARKER John, gentleman, of Litchfield, vs WHITING John, husbandman, of Amherst, rec date 1782, writ, debt, file #2674

PARKER John, gentleman, of Billerica MA, vs STILES Caleb, cordwainer, of Lyndeborough, rec date 1786, execution, debt, file #5463

PARKER John, gentleman, of Billerica MA, vs STILES Caleb, cordwainer, of Lyndeborough, rec date 1785, writ, debt, file #6857

PARKER John Jr, husbandman, of Litchfield, vs GEARFIELD Nathaniel, husbandman, of Merrimack, doc date 1772, judgment, debt, file #675

PARKER Jonathan, physician, of Litchfield, vs McGINNIS Barnabas, yeoman, of Nottingham-West, doc date 1784, execution, debt, file #1915

PARKER Jonathan, physician, of Litchfield, vs TAYLOR James, gentleman, of Merrimack, doc date 1784, execution, debt, file #1983

PARKER Jonathan, husbandman, of New Ipswich, vs FLETCHER Joshua, husbandman, of Plymouth, rec date 1786, judgment, debt, file #2293

PARKER Jonathan, physician, of Litchfield, vs TAYLOR James, gentleman, of Merrimack, rec date 1782, judgment, debt, file #2726

PARKER Jonathan, physician, of Litchfield, vs TAYLOR James, gentleman, of Merrimack, rec date 1783, execution, debt, file #3279

PARKER Jonathan, physician, of Litchfield, vs MOORE John, yeoman, of Bedford, rec date 1783, judgment, debt, file #3780

PARKER Jonathan, physician, of Litchfield, vs TUTTLE Stephen, yeoman, of Goffstown, rec date 1783, judgment, debt, file #3776

PARKER Jonathan, physician, of Litchfield, vs UNDERWILL James, esquire, of Litchfield, rec date 1788, various, assaults, file #6812

PARKER Jonathan, physician, of Litchfield, vs UNDERWOOD James, esquire, of Litchfield, rec date 1787, writ, debt, file #6785

PARKER Jonathan, rec date 1778, deposition, file #7057

PARKER Joseph, husbandman, of New Ipswich, vs WRIGHT Thomas, husbandman, of Westford MA, doc date 1773, writ, debt, file #1239

PARKER Joseph, husbandman, of New Ipswich, vs CLARK Isaac, gentleman, of Chelmsford MA, rec date 1788, writ, debt, file #6949

PARKER Josiah, yeoman, of Wilton, vs ADAMS Jacob, yeoman, of Wilton, doc date 1777, rec date 1779, deed, land transfer, file #2150

PARKER Lemuel, cooper, of Pepperell MA, vs COOMBS Medad, husbandman, of Dunstable, rec date 1784, appeal, debt, file #4102

PARKER Lemuel, cooper, of Pepperell MA, vs COMBS Medad, husbandman, of Dunstable, rec date 1784, judgment, debt, file #4420, kinship to combs

PARKER Lemuel, cooper, of Pepperell MA, vs AMES David, husbandman, of Dublin, rec date 1784, judgment, debt, file #4422

PARKER Lucle, of Peterborough, vs CALDWELL Thomas, yeoman, of Peterborough, doc date 1799, judgment, debt, file #304

PARKER Mary, widow, of Litchfield, vs SCOTT Alexander, gentleman, of Monadnock #1, doc date 1772, judgment, debt, file #676

PARKER Mary, widow, of Litchfield, vs BLANCHARD Joseph, esquire, of Amherst, rec date 1785, judgment, debt, file #5205

PARKER Mary, widow/administrator of estate, of Litchfield, vs BLANCHARD Joseph, esquire, of Amherst, rec date 1785, judgment, debt, file #5977, estate of John PARKER

PARKER Matthew, husbandman, of Litchfield, vs CLEMENT Moses, husbandman, of Warner, rec date 1785, judgment, debt, file #5812

PARKER Nathaniel, cordwainer, of Pepperell MA, vs WHEAT Solomon, cordwainer, of Hollis, doc date 1799, judgment, debt, file #568

PARKER Nathaniel, gentleman, of Groton MA, vs WARNER Joseph, of Pepperell MA, doc date 1777, deed, land transfer, file #2072

PARKER Obadiah, gentleman, of Mason, vs HILLS David, trader, of New Ipswich, rec date 1783, execution, debt, file #3230

PARKER Obadiah, gentleman, of Mason, vs HILL David, yeoman, of New Ipswich, rec date 1783, writ, debt, file #3320

PARKER Oliver, gentleman, of Hollis, vs BENNETT Jonathan, husbandman, of Hancock, doc date 1784, civil litigation, debt, file #1634

PARKER Oliver, gentleman, of Groton MA, vs HALL James, husbandman, of Mason, doc date 1769, rec date 1778, deed, land transfer, file #2153

PARKER Oliver, husbandman, of Hollis, vs TAYLOR Jacob, laborer, of Hopkinton, rec date 1788, writ, debt, file #2430

PARKER Oliver, labourer, of Hollis, vs STATE of NH, rec date 1782, recognizance, debt, file #2606

PARKER Oliver, gentleman, of Penobscot Me, vs AMES Phineas, husbandman, of Hancock, rec date 1783, writ, debt, file #4049

PARKER Oliver, gentleman, of Penobscot Me, vs KENNEY Moses, gentleman, of Stoddard, rec date 1783, judgment, debt, file #4310

PARKER Oliver, esquire, of Penobscott Me, vs BENNETT Jonathan, husbandman, of Hancock, rec date 1783, judgment, debt, file #4710

PARKER Oliver, gentleman, of Penobscott Me, vs PARKS Samuel, gentleman, of Stoddard, rec date 1783, judgment, debt, file #4709

PARKER Oliver, gentleman, of Penobscott MA, vs WIER David, gentleman, of Walpole, rec date 1785, execution, debt, file #5963

PARKER Oliver, gentleman, of MA, vs WIER Robert, gentleman, of Walpole, rec date 1786, judgment, debt, file #6506

PARKER Oliver (Capt), gentleman, of Penobscott Me, vs PARKS Samuel, husbandman, of Stoddard, rec date 1784, judgment, debt, file #5453

PARKER Penelope, single, of Amherst, vs HEYWOOD William, husbandman, of Amherst, rec date 1788, warrant, fornication, file #6537

PARKER Phebe, widow, of Wilton, vs BROWN Isaac, husbandman, of Wilton, doc date 1777, rec date 1778, deed, land transfer, file #2109

PARKER Phinehas, yeoman, of Groton, vs BROOKS William, gentleman, of Hancock, doc date 1798, execution, debt, file #54

PARKER Robert, esquire, of Lytchfield, vs McQUESTONES Hugh, husbandman, of Lytchfield, doc date 1799, writ, debt, file #573

PARKER Robert, labourer, vs STATE of NH, rec date 1782, recognizance, debt, file #2611

PARKER Robert, yeoman, of Litchfield, vs DICKERMAN Samuel, yeoman, of Francestown, rec date 1783, writ, debt, file #3400

PARKER Robert Sr & Jr, yeoman, of Amherst, vs COSTON Ebenezer, yeoman, of Society Land, rec date 1783, writ, debt, file #3039

PARKER Samuel, trader, of Pepperell MA, vs PRATT Thomas, husbandman, of Hollis, doc date 1799, execution, debt, file #211

PARKER Samuel, of Rindge, vs BROWN Reuben & Jesse, saddlers, of Concord, doc date 1785, petition, jail release, file #50

PARKER Samuel, gentleman, of Pepperell MA, vs GILLSON Nathan, cooper, of Roby, doc date 1798, execution, debt, file #142

PARKER Samuel, gentleman, of Pepperell MA, vs WHITCOMB Rupas, yeoman, of Roby, doc date 1800, judgment, file #511

PARKER Samuel, gentleman, of Pepperell MA, vs CAMPBELL Benjamin, cooper, of Roby, doc date 1798, judgment, debt, file #565

PARKER Samuel, gentleman, of Pepperell MA, vs FOSTER Caleb, gentleman, of Roby, doc date 1799, judgment, debt, file #568

PARKER Samuel, gentleman, of Pepperell MA, vs FOSTER Caleb, gentleman, of Roby, doc date 1799, judgment, debt, file #568

PARKER Samuel, gentleman, of Pepperell MA, vs WARREN Benjamin, gentleman, of Roby, doc date 1799, judgment, debt, file #568

PARKER Samuel, yeoman, of Greenfield, vs WILSON James, esquire, of Peterborough, doc date 1799, judgment, debt, file #298

PARKER Samuel, gentleman, of Pepperell MA, vs WHITCOMB Rupas, yeoman, of Roby, doc date 1799, judgment, debt, file #568

PARKER Samuel, gentleman, of Mason, vs CHAPMAN Samuel, yeoman, of Mason, doc date 1798, execution, debt, file #137

PARKER Samuel, gentleman, of Pepperell MA, vs LAWRENCE Ezekiel, of Roby, doc date 1797, judgment, debt, file #568

PARKER Samuel, gentleman, of Pepperell MA, vs AUSTIN Jacob, husbandman, of Roby, doc date 1798, execution, debt, file #140

PARKER Samuel, yeoman, of Peterborough, vs CUTTER Nathan, gentleman, of New Ipswich, doc date 1772, writ, debt, file #1069

PARKER Samuel, gentleman, of New Ipswich, vs HINES Charles, yeoman, of New Ipswich, doc date 1772, writ, debt, file #927

PARKER Samuel, yeoman, of New Ipswich, vs GREGG Samuel, yeoman, of Peterborough, doc date 1772, writ, debt, file #925

PARKER Samuel, yeoman, of New Ipswich, vs THOMPSON John, yeoman, of Peterboro Slip, doc date 1772, writ, debt, file #926

PARKER Samuel, gentleman, of New Ipswich, vs COBURN Robert, gentleman, of Hollis, doc date 1773, judgment, debt, file #1325

PARKER Samuel, gentleman, of New Ipswich, vs KENDALL Ebenezer, yeoman, of Hollis, doc date 1773, judgment, debt, file #1325

PARKER Samuel, yeoman, of Pepperell MA, vs KENNEY Israel, husbandman, of Hollis, rec date 1786, writ, debt, file #2417

PARKER Samuel, yeoman, of Greenfield, vs CRESSEY Jabez, yeoman, of Hopkinton, doc date 1799, various, debt, file #550

PARKER Samuel, trader, of Pepperell MA, vs PRATT Thomas, husbandman, of Hollis, doc date 1799, debt, file #211

PARKER Samuel, husbandman, of Rindge, vs PHILLIPS Samuel, esquire, of Andover MA, rec date 1785, indictment, debt, file #7019

PARKER Stephen, husbandman, of Groton MA, vs MOSHER James, husbandman, of Hollis, rec date 1784, judgment, debt, file #4982

PARKER William, husbandman, of Hillsborough, vs JONES Nehemiah, husbandman, of Hillsborough, doc date 1799, debt, file #328

PARKER William, trader, of Bedford, vs GILROY Robert, yeoman, of Goffstown, doc date 1798, judgment, debt, file #180

PARKER William, husbandman, of Exeter, vs STATE of NH, rec date 1777, recognizance, forgery, file #2211

PARKER William, cordwainer, of Bedford, vs SAWYER Enoch, esquire, of Goffstown, rec date 1787, judgment, debt, file #2317

PARKER William, husbandman, of Lyndeborough, vs CLAGETE Lethie Clifton, gentleman, of Litchfield, rec date 1785, writ, debt, file #5389, estate of Wyseman CLAGETE

PARKER William, esquire, of Exeter, vs NEWTON William, yeoman, of Salisbury, doc date 1773, rec date 1787, deed, land transfer, file #6790

PARKER Winslow, yeoman, of Groton MA, vs ABBOTT Benjamin, yeoman, of Hollis, rec date 1783, writ, debt, file #3465

PARKHURST John, yeoman, of Lexington MA, vs HOSMER Nathaniel, husbandman, of Mason, rec date 1784, various, court case, file #4525

PARKHURST John, yeoman, of Lexington MA, vs HOSMER Nathaniel, husbandman, of Mason, rec date 1785, various, debt, file #5447, very fragile

PARKHURST Joseph, husbandman, of Dunstable MA, vs WYMAN Timothy, husbandman, of Deering, rec date 1785, judgment, debt, file #5228

PARKHURST Nathan, yeoman, of Needham MA, vs MILLS Luke, yeoman, of Needham MA, rec date 1785, judgment, debt, file #5364

PARKHURST Touch?, husbandman, of Dunstable MA, vs WYMAN Timothy, husbandman, of Deering, rec date 1785, judgment, debt, file #5980

PARKINSON Henry, gentleman, of Pembroke, vs CONEY John, yeoman, of Lyndeborough, rec date 1783, execution, debt, file #3858

PARKINSON Henry, gentleman, of Pembrooke, vs CONEY John, yeoman, of Lyndeborough, rec date 1783, writ, debt, file #3885

PARKINSON Henry, yeoman, of Concord, vs CUSHING John, physician, of Goffstown, rec date 1784, judgment, debt, file #4867

PARSON William, yeoman, of Duxbury School, vs HUTCHINSON Benjamin, gentleman, of Amherst, doc date 1784, execution, debt, file #1878

PARSON William, yeoman, of Duxbury School, vs HUTCHINSON Benjamin, gentleman, of Amherst, rec date 1783, execution, debt, file #3816

PATCH Benjamin, yeoman, of Otisfield MA, vs HOUSE John, esquire, of Hanover, rec date 1783, writ, debt, file #3442

PATCH Isaac, husbandman, of Westford MA, vs GLYNN John, yeoman, of Hillsborough, rec date 1782, execution, debt, file #3475

PATCH Isaac, husbandman, of Westford MA, vs GLYNN John, yeoman, of Hillsborough, rec date 1783, execution, debt, file #3650

PATCH Isaac, husbandman, of Westford MA, vs GLYNN John, yeoman, of Hillsborough, rec date 1783, execution, debt, file #3234

PATCH Nancy, of New Boston, vs GREGG Alexander, administrator of estate, of New Boston, rec date 1788, deposition, debt, file #6976

PATEE Asa, gentleman, of Goffstown, vs AYRE Joseph, blacksmith, of Londonderry, doc date 1771, writ, debt, file #1382

PATEE Asa, gentleman, of Enfield, vs KELLY Moses, esquire, of Goffstown, rec date 1784, judgment, debt, file #4224

PATEN Stephen, trader, of Townsend MA, vs SHATTUCK Jonas, husbandman, of Raby, doc date 1787, rec date 1788, deed, transfer of land, file #6835

PATERSON James, gentleman, of Bedford, vs ALLD Wm (Capt), gentleman, of Peterborough, rec date 1782, writ, debt, file #2777

PATTEN John, yeoman, of Merrimack, vs WILKINS Jonathan, yeoman, of Amherst, doc date 1772, judgment, debt, file #664

PATTEN John, of Merrimack, vs WILKINS Jonathan, yeoman, doc date 1774, execution, file #1161, very fragile

PATTEN John, husbandman, of Merrimack, vs BLANCHARD Stephen, husbandman, of Duxbury MA, rec date 1782, writ, debt, file #2780

PATTEN John, husbandman, of Bedford, vs GORDON John, yeoman, of Campbells Gore, rec date 1783, judgment, debt, file #3759

PATTEN John, yeoman, of Merrimack, vs BOUTALL Amos, yeoman, of Amherst, rec date 1782, appeal, debt, file #4015

PATTEN John, yeoman, of Merrimack, vs BALDWIN Nahum, esquire, of Amherst, rec date 1782, appeal, debt, file #3993

PATTEN John, yeoman, of Bedford, vs DICKERMAN Samuel, yeoman, of Francestown, rec date 1783, judgment, debt, file #4312

PATTEN John, yeoman, of Bedford, vs DICKERMAN Samuel, yeoman, of Francestown, rec date 1784, various, debt, file #4163

PATTEN John, husbandman, of Merrimack, vs BLANCHARD Stephen, husbandman, of Mile Slip, rec date 1782, judgment, debt, file #4512, kinship BLANCHARD

PATTEN John, husbandman, of Bedford, vs MATTHEWS Joseph, husbandman, of Bedford, rec date 1785, judgment, debt, file #5992

PATTEN Matthew, esquire, of Bedford, vs NEWMAN William, blacksmith, of Bedford, rec date 1783, execution, debt, file #3694

PATTEN Matthew, esquire, of Bedford, vs MOORE William, husbandman, of Bedford, rec date 1783, various, trespass, file #3615

PATTEN Matthew, esquire, of Bedford, vs MOORE James, husbandman, of Bedford, rec date 1783, writ, debt, file #3615

PATTEN Matthew, esquire, of Bedford, vs MOORE Wm 3rd, husbandman, of Bedford, rec date 1783, writ, debt, file #3615

PATTEN Matthew, esquire, of Bedford, vs NEWMAN William, blacksmith, of Bedford, rec date 1783, execution, debt, file #3851

PATTEN Matthew, esquire, of Bedford, vs NEWMAN William, yeoman, of Bedford, rec date 1783, writ, debt, file #3917

PATTEN Matthew, esquire, of Bedford, vs BALDWIN Nahum, esquire, of Amherst, rec date 1783, writ, debt, file #4045, estate of Z CUTLER (Loyalist)

PATTEN Matthew, esquire, of Bedford, vs SMITH James, gentleman, of Bedford, rec date 1784, judgment, debt, file #4426

PATTEN Matthew, esquire, of Bedford, vs GLOVER Martha, wife, of Nottingham-West, rec date 1784, writ, debt, file #4863

PATTEN Matthew, esquire, of Bedford, vs PORTER David, yeoman, of Nottingham-West, rec date 1784, writ, debt, file #4863

PATTEN Matthew, esquire, of Bedford, vs GLOVER William, yeoman, of Nottingham-West, rec date 1784, writ, debt, file #4863

PATTEN Matthew, esquire, of Bedford, vs GRELE Ezekiel, yeoman, of Nottingham-West, rec date 1784, writ, debt, file #4863

PATTEN Matthew, esquire, of Bedford, vs SHIRLA Thomas, yeoman, of Goffstown, doc date 1785, rec date 1786, deed, land transfer, file #5030

PATTEN Robert, husbandman, of Chester, vs HARD James, gentleman, of Haverhill, doc date 1773, writ, debt, file #1330

PATTEN William, yeoman, of Amherst, vs GEARFIELD Nathaniel, husbandman, of Merrimack, doc date 1784, execution, debt, file #1899

PATTEN William Jr, yeoman, of Merrimack, vs GEARFIELD Nathaniel, husbandman, of Merrimack, rec date 1783, civil litigious, debt, file #2933

PATTERSON David, yeoman, of Temple, vs McGREGORE James, esquire, of Loudon, doc date 1799, debt, file #453

PATTERSON James, yeoman, of Bedford, vs ARROWIN William, yeoman, of Bedford, rec date 1772, recognizance, debt, file #2173

PATTERSON Nicholas, husbandman, of Harvard MA, vs DICKEY James, gentleman, of Raby, rec date 1783, execution, debt, file #3831

PATTERSON Peter, gentleman, of Goffstown, vs THORN Isaac, esquire, of Londonderry, doc date 1798, judgment, debt, file #565

PATTERSON Peter, gentleman, of Goffstown, vs HUNTER John, gentleman, of Londonderry, doc date 1798, judgment, debt, file #565

PATTERSON Robert, yeoman, of New Boston, vs MORRILL Robert, weaver, of New Boston, rec date 1787, judgment, debt, file #6194

PATTERSON Samuel, esquire, of Bradford, vs GORDON William, esquire, of Amherst, doc date 1799, writ, debt, file #402

PATTERSON Samuel, yeoman, of Francestown, vs RUSSELL James, of Litchfield, rec date 1782, execution, debt, file #3518

PATTERSON Samuel, yeoman, of Francestown, vs RUSSELL James, gentleman, of Litchfield, rec date 1783, execution, debt, file #3657

PATTERSON Samuel, yeoman, of Deering, vs GREGG John, yeoman, of Deering, rec date 1785, judgment, debt, file #5192

PATTERSON William, yeoman, of Goffstown, vs LUND John, gentleman, of Dunstable, doc date 1784, writ, debt, file #1574

PATTERSON William, husbandman, of Litchfield, vs DODGE Bartholomew, husbandman, of Amherst, doc date 1779, deed, land transfer, file #2019

PATTERSON William, husbandman, of Litchfield, vs WAIT Nathan, yeoman, of Pembroke, rec date 1777, writ, debt, file #2186

PATTERSON William, husbandman, of Goffstown, vs RICE Benjamin, husbandman, of Grafton, rec date 1783, writ, debt, file #3384

PATTERSON William, yeoman, of Goffstown, vs LOW Jonathan, tanner, of Goffstown, doc date 1785, rec date 1786, deed, land transfer, file #5023

PATTERSON William Jr, yeoman, of New Boston, vs DAMON Daniel, yeoman, of Amherst, doc date 1799, writ, debt, file #573

PATTERSON William Jr, yeoman, of Litchfield, vs McMURPHY John, husbandman, of Alexandria, rec date 1782, writ, debt, file #2699

PATTON William, yeoman, of Amherst, vs GEARFIELD Nathaniel, yeoman, of Merrimack, doc date 1784, execution, debt, file #1742

PAYSON Phillip, yeoman, of Charlestown MA, vs BLAKE William W, merchant, of Keene, doc date 1798, execution, debt, file #65

PEABODY Benjamin, esquire, of Middleton MA, vs WILKINS Ralph, gentleman, of Hillsborough, doc date 1799, debt, file #480

PEABODY Ephraim, yeoman, of Wilton, vs BROWN James, gentleman, of Moultonborough, rec date 1776, writ, debt, file #2196

PEABODY Isaac, yeoman, of Wilton, vs BUTTERFIELD Isaac, husbandman, of Barlards Farm, doc date 1779, writ, debt, file #2090

PEABODY Isaac, taylor, of Londonderry, vs LYON Jonathan Jr, yeoman, of Amherst, doc date 1778, rec date 1778, deed, land transfer, file #2163

PEABODY Nathaniel, physician, of Atkinson, vs YOUNG Robert, yeoman, of Londonderry, doc date 1768, writ, debt, file #816

PEABODY Oliver, gentleman, of Andover MA, vs HOW Joseph Jr, shipwright, of Goffstown, doc date 1774, recognizance, debt, file #1146

PEABODY Oliver, gentleman, of Andover, vs DOW Joseph, shipwright, of Goffstown, rec date 1774, execution, debt, file #4887

PEABODY William, gentleman, of Amherst, vs WILKINS Jonathan, husbandman, of Amherst, rec date 1785, judgment, debt, file #5504

PEABODY William, gentleman, of Soughean West, vs HUTCHINSON Abner, yeoman, of Amherst, doc date 1775, deed, land transfer, file #839

PEABODY William, gentleman, of Amherst, vs MacINTIRE Timothy, husbandman, of Amherst, doc date 1773, judgment, debt, file #1302

PEABODY William, gentleman, of Amherst, vs MITCHEL Israel, yeoman, of Peterborough, doc date 1773, judgment, debt, file #1292

PEABODY William, gentleman, of Amherst, vs WILKINS Daniel 3rd, yeoman, of Amherst, doc date 1773, judgment, debt, file #1301

PEABODY William, gentleman, of Amherst, vs WILKINS Daniel, clerk, of Amherst, doc date 1773, judgment, debt, file #1301

PEABODY William, gentleman, of Amherst, vs AVERILL Ebenezer, yeoman, of Amherst, doc date 1773, judgment, debt, file #1309

PEABODY William, gentleman, of Amherst, vs MORRISON Thomas, yeoman, of Peterborough, doc date 1773, judgment, debt, file #1292

PEABODY William, husbandman, of Amherst, vs SAUNDERS Oliver, husbandman, of Alexandria, doc date 1784, execution, debt, file #1767

PEABODY William, gentleman, of Amherst, vs LUND Phineas, yeoman, of Lyndeborough, doc date 1784, execution, debt, file #1960

PEABODY William, gentleman, of Amherst, vs FULLER Timothy, of Middleton MA, doc date 1784, deed, land transfer, file #2003

PEABODY William, gentleman, of Amherst, vs SHEPARD John, esquire, of Amherst, rec date 1787, judgment, debt, file #2319

PEABODY William, gentleman, of Amherst, vs PROPRIETORS of Amherst, of Amherst, rec date 1782, writ, debt, file #2623

PEABODY William, gentleman, of Amherst, vs SANDERS Oliver, husbandman, of Hollis, rec date 1783, judgment, debt, file #3784

PEABODY William, gentleman, of Amherst, vs GILMORE James, husbandman, of Bedford, doc date 1788, rec date 1788, deed, land transfer, file #6819

PEABODY William (Capt), gentleman, of Amherst, vs GILMORE James, husbandman, of Bedford, rec date 1785, judgment, debt, file #5511

PEABODY William (Capt), gentleman, of Amherst, vs MURREY Robert, husbandman, of Alexandria, rec date 1785, judgment, debt, file #5511

PEABODY William Jr, yeoman, of Amherst, vs SMALL William Jr, yeoman, of Amherst, doc date 1770, rec date 1786, deed, land transfer, file #5004

PEADBODY Hannah, of Amherst, vs HALE Joseph, yeoman, of Dunstable, rec date 1783, judgment, debt, file #3779

PEADBODY William, gentleman, of Amherst, vs HARWOOD John, yeoman, of Amherst, rec date 1786, writ, debt, file #6095

PEARNE William & Mary, merchant, of Portsmouth, vs COSTELLOE John & Lidia, of Berwick Me, doc date 1780, rec date 1795, deed, land transfer, file #5668

PEARSE James, cordwainer, of Chester, vs CALCORD Samuel, husbandman, of Candia, doc date 1773, writ, debt, file #827

PEARSON Amos, yeoman, of Lyndeborough, vs UPTON Hezekiah, gentleman, of Reading MA, rec date 1783, writ, debt, file #3013

PEARSON Amos, husbandman, of Lyndeborough, vs GOODWIN John, gentleman, of Reading MA, rec date 1784, writ, debt, file #4739

PEARSON Joseph, yeoman, of Sutton, vs HUTCHINS William, gentleman, of Sutton, doc date 1800, rec date 1802, deed, land transfer, file #5678

PEARSON Noah, yeoman, of Hopkinton, vs WEST Mary, widow, of Haverhill MA, rec date 1783, writ, debt, file #3105, administrator of Thomas WEST estate

PEASLEY Ebenezer, husbandman, of Weare, vs ABBOTT Henry, tanner, of Concord, doc date 1799, debt, file #504

PEASLEY Ebenezer, husbandman, of Weare, vs CURRIER John, brickmaker, of Concord, doc date 1799, debt, file #504

PEASLEY Ebenezer, husbandman, of Weare, vs FIFIELD Wilhiem, husbandman, of Concord, doc date 1799, debt, file #504

PEASLEY James, yeoman, of Fisherfield, vs FAVOUR Reuben, yeoman, of Dunbarton, doc date 1801, rec date 1801, deed, land transfer, file #6578

PEMBERTON James, husbandman, of Nottingham-West, vs CUTTER Richard, husbandman, of Nottingham-West, rec date 1783, writ, debt, file #3915

PEMBERTON James, cordwainer, of Nottingham-West, vs ROBY James, yeoman, of Nottingham-West, rec date 1788, writ, debt, file #6943

PERKINS David, yeoman, of Campbells Gore, vs COLLAGE Silas, yeoman, of Hillsborough, doc date 1784, execution, debt, file #1560

PERKINS David, yeoman, of Campbells Gore, vs JONES James, yeoman, of Hillsborough, doc date 1784, execution, debt, file #1885

PERKINS David, yeoman, of Campbells Gore, vs JONES James, yeoman, of Hillsborough, rec date 1783, execution, debt, file #2983

PERKINS David, yeoman, of Campbells Gore, vs COOLEDGE Silas, yeoman, of Hillsborough, rec date 1783, judgment, debt, file #4317

PERKINS Dorothy, spinster, of Dunstable, vs PIKE Thomas, laborer, of Dunstable, rec date 1785, various, debt, file #5531

PERKINS James, of Northfield, vs MORRILL Levi, of Northfield, doc date 1797, petition, debt, file #34

PERKINS Jeremiah, gentleman, of New Ipswich, vs APPLETON Isaac, yeoman, of New Ipswich, doc date 1775, deed, land transfer, file #843

PERKINS Joseph, yeoman, of Weare, vs PERKINS Simeon, yeoman, of Weare, rec date 1784, judgment, debt, file #4386

PERKINS Simon, husbandman, of Weare, vs COOLEDGE Nathaniel, husbandman, of Hillsborough, rec date 1786, writ, debt, file #6325

PERKINS William, husbandman, of New Boston, vs SERGANT Asa, yeoman, of Weare, doc date 1799, debt, file #334

PERRY Ebenezer, cordwainer, of Nottingham-West, vs BARRETT James Jr, yeoman, of Nottingham-West, rec date 1783, judgment, debt, file #4435

PERRY Ebenezer, physician, of Wilton, vs BROWN Isaac & Hannah, yeoman, of Wilton, rec date 1782, writ, debt, file #4549

PERRY James, saddler, of Temple, vs BROWN Peter, yeoman, of Temple, rec date 1783, judgment, debt, file #3294

PERRY James, saddler, of Temple, vs EATON Joseph, yeoman, of Dublin, rec date 1784, judgment, debt, file #5322

PERRY James, saddler, of Temple, vs EATON Joseph, yeoman, of Dublin, rec date 1785, judgment, debt, file #5401

PERRY James, saddler, of Temple, vs MORRISON Ezekiel, captain, of Peterborough, rec date 1785, writ, debt, file #6367

PERSIDY Elizabeth, labouring, of Amherst, vs FREEMAN Cezar, husbandman, of Amherst, doc date 1778, rec date 1779, deed, land transfer, file #2149

PETER John, husbandman, of Andover MA, vs LAUNDEN Samuel, wheelwright, of Goffstown, doc date 1773, execution, debt, file #1494

PETERS John, husbandman, of Andover, vs SANDERS Samuel, wheelwright, of Goffstown, doc date 1772, execution, debt, file #1204

PETERS William, of Henniker, vs STATE of NH, rec date 1775, inquisition, death inquiry, file #2258

PETERSON Daniel, physician, of Boscawen, vs CLOUGH Davis, yeoman, of Gilmanton, doc date 1798, judgment, debt, file #565

PETERSON Daniel, physician, of Boscawen, vs CARR David, gentleman, of Boscawen, doc date 1786, rec date 1787, deed, land transfer, file #2492

PETERSON Daniel, physician, of Boscawen, vs SHATTUCK William, husbandman, of New Ipswich, rec date 1783, writ, debt, file #3370

PETERSON Willet, yeoman, of Salisbury, vs CHANDLER Joseph, gentleman, of Andover, rec date 1783, execution, debt, file #3244

PETERSON Willet, yeoman, of Salisbury, vs SELECTMEN of Salisbury, of Salisbury, rec date 1799, petition, land dispute, file #4063

PETTINGILL Jonathan, blacksmith, of Salisbury, vs BUSH Deseth Ira, husbandman, of Boston MA, doc date 1799, judgment, debt, file #276

PETTINGILL Jonathan, yeoman, of Pelham, vs FORD James, esquire, of Nottingham-West, rec date 1783, writ, debt, file #3332

PETTINGILL Joseph, yeoman, of Salisbury, vs GALE John Collins, husbandman, of Salisbury, rec date 1784, judgment, debt, file #4215, fragile

PETTINGILL Matthew, gentleman, of Salisbury, vs CHAMPNEY John, husbandman, of Alexandria, doc date 1779, writ, debt, file #2099

PETTINGILL Nathaniel Jr, cooper, of Methuen MA, vs BOYNTON Moses, cordwainer, of Andover MA, doc date 1780, rec date 1783, deed, land transfer, file #2649

PHELPS Levi, Edward, yeoman, of Leominster, vs CUMMINGS John, yeoman, of Mason, rec date 1788, summons, land dispute, file #6975

PHELPS Peter, yeoman, of Leominster MA, vs CUMMINGS John, yeoman, of Mason, rec date 1788, summons, land dispute, file #6975

PHILBRICK Benjamin, yeoman, of Sutton, vs ANDREW Samuel, yeoman, of Sutton, doc date 1781, rec date 1787, deed, land transfer, file #2508

PHILBRICK Jonathan, husbandman, of Weare, vs SPAULDING Edward, husbandman, of Hollis, rec date 1785, writ, debt, file #6039

PHILIPS Ebenezer, husbandman, of Henniker, vs MORRISON Samuel, husbandman, of Henniker, doc date 1799, deed, land transfer, file #1993

PHILLIPS Amos, miller, of Greenfield, vs McCAY Samuel, husbandman, of Peterborough, doc date 1799, judgment, debt, file #299

PICKMAN Benjamin, esquire, of Salem MA, vs RAND John, of Bedford, doc date 1788, petition, debt, file #2

PICKMAN Benjamin, of Salem MA, vs RAND John, esquire, of Bedford, rec date 1787, writ, debt, file #6960

PICKMAN William, gentleman, of Salem MA, vs LEE William, yeoman, of Peterborough, doc date 1778, rec date 1778, deed, land transfer, file #2157

PIERCE Benjamin, yeoman, of Westford MA, vs HALE David, husbandman, of Cockermouth, doc date 1784, execution, debt, file #1521

PIERCE Benjamin, husbandman, of Westford MA, vs HALE David, husbandman, of Cockermouth, rec date 1786, judgment, debt, file #2308

PIERCE Benjamin, yeoman, of Westford MA, vs HALE David, husbandman, of Cockermouth, rec date 1782, execution, debt, file #3479

PIERCE Benjamin, yeoman, of Westford MA, vs LAPHAM Benjamin, gentleman, of Rindge, rec date 1782, execution, debt, file #4906

PIERCE Benjamin, gentleman, of Hillsborough, vs DICKEY William, gentleman, of Hillsborough, doc date 1826, rec date 1826, deed, land transfer, file #5709

PIERCE Benjamin, esquire, of Amherst, vs WESTON Jesse & Daniel, of Amherst, doc date 1814, rec date 1814, deed, land transfer, file #6580

PIERCE Ephraim, laborer, of Hollis, vs BATCHELDER Bruce, esquire, of Packersfield, rec date 1778, writ, debt, file #2216

PIERCE George, yeoman, of Otisfield MA, vs CHAMBERLIN Isaac, gentleman, of Westmoreland, rec date 1783, execution, debt, file #2905

PIERCE George & Deborah, esquire, of Groton MA, vs CUMMINGS John, yeoman, of Mason, rec date 1788, summons, land dispute, file #6975

PIERCE Joseph, yeoman, of Westmoreland, vs WHEELER Joseph, gentleman, of Harvard MA, doc date 1772, civil litigation, debt, file #659

PIERCE Joseph, yeoman, of Westmoreland, vs ZWIEAR Daniel, yeoman, of Lancaster MA, doc date 1772, civil litigation, debt, file #657

PIERCE Joshua, deceased, of Portsmouth, rec date 1787, various, land dispute, file #6807

PIERCE Merrill, prisoner, of Hillsborough, vs MURRY Ralph, of St Johnsbury VT, doc date 1799, petition, release from jail, file #35

PIERCE Nehemiah, labourer, vs STATE of NH, rec date 1782, recognizance, debt, file #2611

PIERCE Richard, husbandman, of Hollis, vs RUSSELL James, gentleman, of Goffstown, rec date 1788, writ, debt, file #2387

PIERCE Silas, shopkeeper, of Peterborough, vs LAKIN William, yeoman, of Peterborough, rec date 1785, judgment, debt, file #5222

PIERCE Silas, shopkeeper, of Peterborough, vs HOCKLEY James, husbandman, of Peterborough, rec date 1785, judgment, debt, file #5527

PIERCE William & Wm Jr, yeoman, of Wilton, vs ABBOTT Joseph (Lt), gentleman, of Wilton, doc date 1784, rec date 1785, deed, land transfer, file #5629

PIEVER Merrill, tanner, of Hillsborough, vs JONES Nehemiah, trader, of Hillsborough, doc date 1799, writ, debt, file #317

PIKE Benjamin, blacksmith, of Hampton Falls, vs LOWELL John & Elizabeth, of Roxbury MA, doc date 1799, judgment, debt, file #281

PIKE Benjamin, housewright, of Amherst, vs WESSON Isaac, yeoman, of Amherst, rec date 1785, writ, debt, file #4680

PIKE Daniel, yeoman, of Dunstable, vs KILLICUT Reuben, yeoman, of Dunstable, doc date 1775, judgment, debt, file #2037

PIKE Daniel, innholder, of Dunstable, vs EAYERS Joseph, husbandman, of Merrimack, rec date 1783, judgment, debt, file #3785

PIKE Daniel, yeoman, of Dunstable, vs PIKE Zachariah, yeoman, of Bedford, rec date 1782, appeal, debt, file #3998

PIKE Daniel, husbandman, of Dunstable, vs McGAA Robert, trader, of Hollis, rec date 1783, writ, debt, file #4041, son Daniel kinship

PIKE Daniel, husbandman, of Dunstable, vs EAYRES Joseph, husbandman, of Merrimack, rec date 1785, writ, debt, file #2341

PIKE Enoch, husbandman, of Amherst, vs BAILEY John, husbandman, of Dunbarton, doc date 1782, execution, file #1022

PIKE James, husbandman, of Westford MA, vs KILLICUT Reuben, husbandman, of Dunstable, rec date 1787, judgment, debt, file #2469

PIKE Joseph, of Dunstable MA, vs ADAMS Thomas, of Dunstable, rec date 1775, deposition, land boundary, file #2230

PIKE Joseph, yeoman, of Hollis, vs STEVENS Joseph, yeoman, of Hollis, rec date 1784, recognizance, assault, file #4177

PIKE Perkins, husbandman, of Northfield, vs DUNCAN James, esquire, of Haverhill MA, doc date 1799, judgment, debt, file #279

PIKE Samuel P, vs N H Trust Co, doc date 1892, argument for defendant, supreme court, file #619

PIKE Zachariah, yeoman, of Bedford, vs PIKE Daniel, of Dunstable, rec date 1783, execution, debt, file #2895

PIKE Zachariah, yeoman, of Bedford, vs LOVEJOY Francis, feltmaker, of Amherst, rec date 1785, writ, debt, file #5189

PIKE Zechariah, yeoman, of Bedford, vs PIKE Daniel, husbandman, of Dunstable, rec date 1783, judgment, debt, file #2854

PINGREE John, trader, of Boston MA, vs GREEEN Thomas, yeoman, of Salem, doc date 1798, judgment, debt, file #565

PINGREE John, trader, of Boston MA, vs WEDDLETON John, yeoman, of Salem, doc date 1798, judgment, debt, file #565

PINKERTON John, husbandman, of Londonderry, vs McCLINTOCKE Alexander, husbandman, of Hillsborough, doc date 1784, execution, debt, file #1527

PINKERTON John, esquire, of Londonderry, vs McCLINTOCK Alexander, husbandman, of Hillsborough, rec date 1783, judgment, debt, file #4463

PINKERTON John, trader, of Londonderry, vs TAGGART John, husbandman, of Dunbarton, rec date 1785, writ, debt, file #5816

PLATTS Abel Jr, husbandman, of Rindge, vs CHOPLIN David Jr, husbandman, of Lunenburg MA, doc date 1773, writ, debt, file #1342

POLLARD Amos, husbandman, of Nottingham-West, vs WASSON Samuel, husbandman, of Nottingham-West, rec date 1772, various, assault, file #2174

POLLARD Amaziah, yeoman, of New Boston, vs GOSSE John, of Deerfield, doc date 1782, writ, debt, file #893

POLLARD Amaziah, yeoman, of Goffstown, vs PHILBRICK Samuel, yeoman, of Weare, doc date 1773, execution, debt, file #1487

POLLARD Amaziah, husbandman, of New Boston, vs LUTWYCHE Edward, esquire, of Merrimack, doc date 1772, writ, debt, file #1030

POLLARD John, husbandman, of Nottingham-West, vs KELLY Joseph, gentleman, of Nottingham-West, doc date 1784, deed, land transfer, file #1999

POLLARD John, husbandman, of Nottingham-West, vs SMITH Edward, innkeeper, of Boston MA, doc date 1787, rec date 1787, deed, land transfer, file #2493

POLLARD John, husbandman, of Nottingham-West, vs SMITH Edward, husbandman, of Peterborough, rec date 1788, writ, debt, file #2546

POLLARD John, gentleman, of Nottingham-West, vs BURROUGH Josiah, cordwainer, of Londonderry, doc date 1763, rec date 1785, deed, land transfer, file #5665

POLLARD Samuel, husbandman, of Nottingham-West, vs HARY Moody, yeoman, of Goffstown, doc date 1784, civil litigation, debt, file #1638

POLLARD Samuel, husbandman, of Nottingham-West, vs WICOM Thomas, yeoman, of Goffstown, doc date 1784, civil litigation, debt, file #1638

POLLARD Samuel, yeoman, of Nottingham-West, vs HARWOOD Thomas, gentleman, of Dunstable, rec date 1782, execution, debt, file #2827

POLLARD Samuel, yeoman, of Nottingham-West, vs SHEPARD John Sr, esquire, of Amherst, rec date 1783, writ, debt, file #3030

POLLARD Samuel, yeoman, of Nottingham-West, vs CALDWELL John, yeoman, of Nottingham-West, rec date 1783, writ, debt, file #4530

POLLARD Samuel, yeoman, of Nottingham-West, vs DICKEY John, yeoman, of Francestown, rec date 1785, judgment, debt, file #5069

POLLARD Samuel, yeoman, of Nottingham-West, vs DICKEY John, yeoman, of Francestown, rec date 1785, judgment, debt, file #6414

POLLARD Solomon, gentleman, of Billerica MA, vs LUND Phineas, husbandman, of Lyndeborough, rec date 1783, execution, debt, file #3226

POLLARD Solomon, gentleman, of Billerica MA, vs LUND Phineas, husbandman, of Lyndeborough, rec date 1782, judgment, debt, file #2743

POLLARD Solomon, gentleman, of Billerica MA, vs FARMER Jonas, husbandman, of Goffstown, rec date 1783, execution, debt, file #3857

POLLARD Solomon, gentleman, of Billerica MA, vs FARMER Jonas, husbandman, of Hillsborough, rec date 1783, writ, debt, file #3932

POLLARD Solomon, gentleman, of Billerica MA, vs KENNY Israel, yeoman, of Hollis, rec date 1785, judgment, debt, file #5170

POLLARD Timothy, husbandman, of Nottingham-West, vs PAGE Reuben, gentleman, of Londonderry, doc date 1772, writ, debt, file #1395

POLLARD Timothy, husbandman, of Nottingham-West, vs TUTTLE William, husbandman, of Littleton MA, rec date 1782, writ, debt, file #2795

POLLARD Timothy, yeoman, of Nottingham-West, vs ALLAD David, gentleman, of Dunstable, doc date 1786, rec date 1787, deed, land transfer, file #2506

POLLARD Timothy, yeoman, of Nottingham-West, vs GRUB Ezekiel, husbandman, of Nottingham-West, rec date 1783, writ, debt, file #2759

POLLARD Timothy, yeoman, of Nottingham-West, vs LOWELL Jan Jr, gentleman, of Dunstable, doc date 1786, rec date 1787, deed, land transfer, file #2506

POLLARD Timothy, husbandman, of Nottingham-West, vs RIDEOUT Nathaniel, husbandman, of Hollis, rec date 1783, writ, debt, file #3116

POLLARD Timothy, husbandman, of Nottingham-West, vs MORISON Robert, husbandman, of Windham, rec date 1782, debt, debt, file #3142

POLLARD Timothy, yeoman, of Nottingham-West, vs DAVIDSON Francis, yeoman, of Merrimack, rec date 1782, writ, debt, file #3975

POLOOD Solomon, vs POLOOD Elnathan, yeoman, of Merrimack, doc date 1774, execution, file #948

POND John, husbandman, of Brooklyn MA, vs DIX Nathan, esquire, of Peterborough, rec date 1787, writ, debt, file #6668

POOL James, trader, of Hollis, vs MARTIN Zirah, cordwainer, of Hollis, rec date 1785, writ, debt, file #2411

POOL Jonathan, physician, of Hollis, vs SMITH Phinehas, of Salem MA, rec date 1783, writ, debt, file #3118

POOL Rufus, yeoman, of Hollis, vs SPAULDING Isaac, farmer, of New Ipswich, doc date 1799, judgment, debt, file #220

POOL William, trader, of Hollis, vs LIMAN Nathaniel, yeoman, of Hollis, doc date 1796, judgment, debt, file #568

POOL William Welstead, wheelwright, of Hollis, vs CUMINGS Benjamin, gentleman, of Hollis, rec date 1789, judgment, debt, file #2576

POOR Andrew, prisoner, of Peterborough, vs WARD Samuel, of Lancaster MA, doc date 1798, petition, release of debit, file #27

POOR Daniel, gentleman, of Atkinson, vs MOOR Daniel, gentleman, of Bedford, doc date 1773, writ, debt, file #1370

POOR Timothy, trader, of Haverhill MA, vs STEVENS Daniel Jr, husbandman, of Amherst, doc date 1798, judgment, debt, file #565

POOR Timothy, trader, of Haverhill MA, vs STEVENS Daniel, husbandman, of Amherst, doc date 1798, judgment, debt, file #565

POPE Samuel, gentleman, of Hillsborough, vs NICHOLS Thomas, gentleman, of Antrim, doc date 1799, writ, debt, file #434

POPE Thomas, yeoman, of Henniker, vs PEASLE Benjamin, yeoman, of New Salem, rec date 1777, writ, debt, file #2192

POPE William, yeoman, of Hillsborough, vs SARGENT Paul Dudley, merchant, of Amherst, doc date 1773, writ, debt, file #1352

POPE William, gentleman, of Hillsborough, vs TAYLOR John, yeoman, of Amherst, doc date 1784, execution, debt, file #1987

PORTER Ezekiel, gentleman, of Hallowell MA, vs WYMAN Ashabel, trader, of Lincoln MA, rec date 1787, writ, debt, file #6895

PORTER Francis, trader, of Peterborough, vs GOLDSMITH Josiah, esquire, of Walpole, rec date 1788, writ, debt, file #6631

PORTER John, physician, of Hampstead, vs KELLEY Moses, gentleman, of Atkinson, doc date 1773, writ, debt, file #818

PORTER John, esquire, of Littleton MA, vs DUDLEY Stephen, innkeeper, of New Ipswich, rec date 1784, judgment, debt, file #4633

PORTER John, physician, of Hampstead, vs KELLY Moses, gentleman, of Atkinson, doc date 1773, writ, debt, file #1438

PORTER John, esquire, of Littleton MA, vs DUDLEY Stephen, yeoman, of New Ipswich, rec date 1785, judgment, debt, file #6427

PORTER Roger W, vs BALDWIN Lucy & Joseph, of Nashua, doc date 1890, plaintiffs brief, supreme court, file #621

PORTER Tyler, esquire, of Wenham MA, vs MORRILL Paul, husbandman, of Loudon, rec date 1784, judgment, debt, file #5289

PORTER Tyler, esquire, of Wenham MA, vs MORRILL Paul, husbandman, of Loudon, rec date 1785, judgment, debt, file #5135

POTTER Stephen, trader, of Townsend MA, vs TARBELL John, yeoman, of Mason, rec date 1787, writ, debt, file #6654

POWER Samson, trader, of Hollis, vs BROWN Eliphelet, laborer, of Amherst, doc date 1803, judgment, debt, file #568

POWER Samson, trader, of Hollis, vs KENNEY Aaron, laborer, of Amherst, doc date 1802, judgment, debt, file #568

POWERS Alice, singleman, of Hollis, vs AMES Burpee, husbandman, of Hollis, rec date 1786, writ, debt, file #2414

POWERS David, feltmaker, of Rutland VT, vs KELLLEY Joseph, esquire, of Nottingham-West, rec date 1785, recognizance, debt, file #7022

POWERS Francis, cordwainer, of Hollis, vs SPAULDING Joseph, husbandman, of Henniker, rec date 1785, writ, debt, file #2407

POWERS Francis, cordwainer, of Hollis, vs WHITTEMORE Samuel, gentleman, of Cambridge, rec date 1785, judgment, land dispute, file #5358

POWERS Francis, cordwainer, of Hollis, vs READ William, gentleman, of Hollis, rec date 1787, writ, debt, file #2423

POWERS Jonas & John, husbandman, of Dunbarton, vs FARLEY Thomas, husbandman, of Hollis, doc date 1799, execution, debt, file #182

POWERS Jonathan, yeoman, of Dunstable, vs KELLEY Joseph, gentleman, of Nottingham-West, rec date 1778, writ, trespass, file #2234

POWERS Jonathan, yeoman, of Hollis, vs JAQUITH Ebenezer, husbandman, of Dunstable, doc date 1771, rec date 1777, deed, land transfer, file #6547

POWERS Peter, gentleman, of Hollis, vs BLOOD Josiah, yeoman, of Hollis, doc date 1750, rec date 1787, deed, land transfer, file #6789

POWERS William, clothier, of Peterborough, vs WHITE John Sr, yeoman, of Peterborough, doc date 1784, court case, theft of crops, file #1605

POWERS William, clothier, of Peterborough, vs WHITE John Sr, yeoman, of Peterborough, rec date 1785, various, debt, file #5248

PRATT Ebenezer, blacksmith, of Shirley MA, vs BLOOD Samuel, husbandman, of Mason, rec date 1786, writ, debt, file #6294

PRATT John, husbandman, of New Ipswich, vs BROWN Aaron, shopkeeper, of Groton MA, rec date 1783, writ, debt, file #3952

PRATT Thomas, feltmaker, of Hollis, vs BENNETT Aaron, cordwainer, of Groton MA, doc date 1772, writ, debt, file #1073

PRATT Thomas, feltmaker, of Hollis, vs NEWHALL Oliver, yeoman, of Hollis, rec date 1785, writ, debt, file #4683

PRENTICE Henry, gentleman, of Littleton MA, vs DUDLEY Stephen, innkeeper, of New Ipswich, rec date 1785, judgment, debt, file #6426

PRENTICE John, esquire, of Marblehead MA, vs EATON John, yeoman, of Hampstead, doc date 1774, judgment, debt, file #718

PRENTICE John, gentleman, of Londonderry, vs GRAGG Samuel Jr, trader, of Peterborough, doc date 1772, judgment, debt, file #687

PRENTICE John, gentleman, of Londonderry, vs LADD Trueworth, gentleman, of Goffstown, doc date 1770, execution, debt, file #828

PRENTICE John, gentleman, vs SHIRLEY Thomas, yeoman, doc date 1772, writ, debt, file #1397

PRENTICE John, gentleman, of Londonderry, vs FOSTER John, husbandman, of Pelham, doc date 1773, writ, debt, file #1435

PRENTICE John, esquire, of Londonderry, vs TUTTLE Stephen, husbandman, of Goffstown, rec date 1786, writ, debt, file #6274

PRENTICE John, esquire, of Londonderry, vs FORD James, esquire, of Nottingham-West, rec date 1786, writ, debt, file #6121

PRENTICE John, esquire, of Londonderry, vs WOOD Jonathan, husbandman, of Goffstown, rec date 1786, writ, debt, file #6274

PRENTICE John, esquire, of Londonderry, vs KELLY Moses, esquire, of Goffstown, rec date 1787, writ, debt, file #6698

PRENTICE John, esquire, of Londonderry, vs BIXBEE Andrew, husbandman, of Hillsborough, rec date 1788, writ, debt, file #6995

PRENTICE William, yeoman, of Marblehead MA, vs BLASDELL Henry & Jonathan, of Kingston, doc date 1772, execution, debt, file #1201

PRENTICE William, yeoman, of Cambridge MA, vs BOYES James Jr, yeoman, of Londonderry, rec date 1783, judgment, debt, file #4305

PRENTICE William Henry, gentleman, of Littleton MA, vs DUDLEY Stephen, innkeeper, of New Ipswich, rec date 1784, judgment, debt, file #4624

PRESBURY William, yeoman, of Bradford, vs PIERCE John & Mary, of Fisherfield, doc date 1799, deed, land transfer, file #2018, land in Fisherfield

PRESCOTT Abijah, yeoman, of Groton MA, vs ATWILL John, innholder, of Hollis, rec date 1785, judgment, debt, file #6440

PRESCOTT Abijah, yeoman, of Groton MA, vs ATTWILL John, innholder, of Hollis, rec date 1785, judgment, debt, file #5548

PRESCOTT James, esquire, of Groton, vs ROSS Walter, yeoman, of Lyndeborough, doc date 1797, various, debt, file #551

PRESCOTT Oliver, esquire, of Marlborough MA, vs BARNS Edward, esquire, of Marlborough MA, rec date 1787?, declaration, debt, file #6170, part of Samuel CURTIS file

PRESTON John, physician, of New Ipswich, vs MARSHALL Thomas, gentleman, of Temple, rec date 1782, appeal, debt, file #4026

PRESTON Samuel, yeoman, of Deering, vs WILLEY John, yeoman, of Amherst, rec date 1783, writ, debt, file #3016

PRESTON Samuel Jr, yeoman, of Hillsborough, vs STEWARD Samuel, yeoman, of Lyndeborough, rec date 1785, writ, debt, file #2354

PRICHARD Jeremiah, gentleman, of New Ipswich, vs CUNNINGHAM Samuel, gentleman, of Peterborough, rec date 1787, writ, debt, file #6660

PRINCE Abel, yeoman, of Amherst, vs COWAN Thomas Jr, yeoman, of Merrimack, rec date 1784, appeal, debt, file #4121

PRINCE Abel, yeoman, of Amherst, vs COWAN Thomas Jr, yeoman, of Merrimack, rec date 1784, appeal, debt, file #4121

PRINCE Asa, gentleman, of Danvers MA, vs LAWRENCE Zachariah, trader, of Hollis, rec date 1783, various, debit on land, file #4563

PRINCE Berry, esquire, of Hillsborough, vs BOARDMAN Aaron, husbandman, of Hillsborough, doc date 1811, rec date 1823, deed, land transfer, file #6579

PRINCE? Abel, husbandman, of Amherst, vs McQUAID Jacob, yeoman, of Bedford, rec date 1783, writ, debt, file #3340

PRITCHARD Jeremiah, husbandman, of Hollis, vs SMITH Moses, husbandman, of Deering, rec date 1784, judgment, debt, file #4260

PROCTER Moses, yeoman, of Hollis, vs DICKEY James, gentleman, of Raby, rec date 1783, judgment, debt, file #4316

PROCTOR Ezekiel, husbandman, of Hollis, vs TRUEL David, taylor, of Merrimack, doc date 1784, execution, debt, file #1793

PROCTOR Ezekiel, husbandman, of Hollis, vs TRUCE David, tailor, of Merrimack, rec date 1783, appeal, debt, file #2750

PROCTOR Ezekiel, husbandman, of Hollis, vs TRUEL David, of Merrimack, rec date 1783, execution, debt, file #3859

PROCTOR Jonas, yeoman, of Westford MA, vs MANOR Benjamin, yeoman, of Mason, doc date 1773, judgment, debt, file #1312

PROCTOR Jonas, yeoman, of Westford MA, vs AMES Simon, cordwainer, of Mason, doc date 1773, judgment, debt, file #1312

PROCTOR Jonathan, husbandman, of Hopkinton, vs BAILEY Isaac, cordwainer, of Hopkinton, doc date 1799, execution, debt, file #168

PROCTOR Moses, esquire, of Hollis, vs WHITE David, husbandman, of Hollis, rec date 1785, various, stealing cattle, file #4570

PROCTOR Moses, esquire, of Hollis, vs McDANIEL James Jr, husbandman, of Hollis, rec date 1785, various, stealing cattle, file #4570

PROCTOR Moses, esquire, of Hollis, vs DICKEY James, husbandman, of Raby, rec date 1785, various, stealing cattle, file #4570

PROCTOR Moses, yeoman, of Hollis, vs DICKEY James, rec date 1784, writ, stealing cattle, file #4746

PROCTOR Nathaniel, husbandman, of Littleton MA, vs BALL Joseph, husbandman, of Mason, rec date 1788, writ, debt, file #6947

PUFFER Ephraim, yeoman, of Ashby MA, vs BOYNTON Amos, husbandman, of Jaffrey, rec date 1783, writ, debt, file #4551

PUFFER Mathais, husbandman, of Society Land, vs McFARLAND Moses, trader, of Antrim, doc date 1799, judgment, debt, file #247

PUFFER Mathais, husbandman, of Society Land, vs MOOR Samuel, trader, of Windsor, doc date 1799, judgment, debt, file #247

PUFFER Mathais, yeoman, of Society Land, vs GRIMES Francis, husbandman, of Deering, doc date 1799, writ, debt, file #326

PUNCHARD James, innholder, of Lyndeborough, vs TEMPLE Benjamin, husbandman, of Amherst, rec date 1786, judgment, debt, file #5371

PURMORT Richard, yeoman, of Enfield, vs PETTINGIL Matthew, captain, of Salisbury, doc date 1784, rec date 1785, deed, land transfer, file #5611

PURPLE John, laborer, of Amherst, vs LITTLE William, physician, of Hillsborough, rec date 1786, judgment, debt, file #5770

PURPLE John, laborer, of Amherst, vs LITTLE William, physician, of Hillsborough, rec date 1786, writ, debt, file #6104

PUTMAN Jacob, husbandman, of Alstead, vs BOSSEE Thomas, gentleman, of Lyndeborough, rec date 1788, writ, debt, file #6907

PUTNAM Aaron, merchant, of Charlestown, vs FISHER Daniel, esquire, of Newport, doc date 1798, execution, debt, file #89

PUTNAM Aaron, physician, of Medford MA, vs YOUNG John, physician, of Peterborough, rec date 1785, judgment, debt, file #5191

PUTNAM Aaron, physician, of Medford MA, vs RUSSELL Daniel, physician, of Lyndeborough, rec date 1786, writ, debt, file #6333

PUTNAM Archelaus Jr, yeoman, of Wilton, vs RUSSELL Jacob, yeoman, of Wilton, doc date 1784, execution, debt, file #1949

PUTNAM Benaijah, housewright, of Sutton MA, vs PARKER Samuel & Jona, yeoman, of Rindge, rec date 1784, various, debt, file #4181

PUTNAM Benjamin, housewright, of Sutton MA, vs PARKER Samuel, yeoman, of Rindge, rec date 1784, judgment, debt, file #4385

PUTNAM Benjamin, housewright, of Sutton MA, vs PARKER Jonathan, esquire, of Rindge, rec date 1784, judgment, debt, file #4385

PUTNAM Jacob, husbandman, of Temple, vs WHITING Oliver, gentleman, of Temple, doc date 1787, rec date 1787, deed, land transfer, file #2502

PUTNAM Jacob, yeoman, of Temple, vs RICHARDSON Joseph, husbandman, of Temple, rec date 1786, various, debt, file #6377

PUTNAM John & Olive, yeoman, of Lyndeborough, vs DAMONE Ebenezer, gentleman, of Reading MA, doc date 1788, rec date 1788, deed, land transfer, file #6744

PUTNAM Lisa?, widow, of Chelmsford MA, vs WARNER Daniel, gentleman, of Amherst, rec date 1786, writ, debt, file #6642

PUTNAM Philip, gentleman, of Wilton, vs GOLDSMITH Josiah, gentleman, of Walpole, rec date 1784, judgment, debt, file #4657

PUTNAM Philip, innholder, of Wilton, vs GOLDSMITH Josiah, gentleman, of Walpole, rec date 1785, judgment, debt, file #5114

PUTNAM William, gentleman, of Sterling MA, vs STILES Joshua, yeoman, of Lyndeborough, doc date 1783, rec date 1783, deed, land transfer, file #2645

PUTNAM William, esquire, of Sterling MA, vs SAVAGE John, husbandman, of Lyndeborough, rec date 1785, judgment, debt, file #5559

PUTNAM William, esquire, of Sterling MA, vs ABBOTT Ephraim, husbandman, of Lyndeborough, rec date 1785, judgment, debt, file #5596

PUTNAM William, esquire, of Sterling MA, vs STEVENS Samuel, husbandman, of Lyndeborough, rec date 1785, judgment, debt, file #5569

PUTNAM William, esquire, of Sterling MA, vs STILES Joshua, husbandman, of Lyndeborough, rec date 1785, judgment, debt, file #5572

PUTNAM William, gentleman, of Salem, vs GOODRIDGE Sewall, clerk, of Lyndeborough, rec date 1788, various, land dispute, file #6598

PUTNEY Isaac, yeoman, of Henniker, vs ANDREWS Molly, single woman, of Henniker, rec date 1785, various, assault, file #4747

PUTNEY James, yeoman, of Dunbarton, vs FOSTER David, husbandman, of Bedford, rec date 1785, judgment, debt, file #6403

PUTNEY John, gentleman, of Hopkinton, vs HOW Prota Jr, yeoman, of Hopkinton, doc date 1778, rec date 1778, deed, land transfer, file #2166

PUTNEY John, husbandman, of Henniker, vs FOSTER David, husbandman, of Dunbarton, rec date 1784, various, debt, file #4187

PUTNEY John, husbandman, of Henniker, vs FOSTER David, husbandman, of Dunbarton, rec date 1784, writ, debt, file #4424

PUTNEY Nathan, yeoman, of Henniker, vs ANDREWS Molly, single woman, of Henniker, rec date 1785, various, assault, file #4747

PYNEHOW William, esquire, of Salem MA, vs WILKINS Aquilla, yeoman, of Hillsborough, rec date 1783, judgment, debt, file #4212

QUEEN John, yeoman, of Bedford, vs PIKE Zachariah, yeoman, of Hopkinton, rec date 1785, execution, debt, file #5476

QUESTEN William, husbandman, of Londonderry, vs DIKE Stephen, blacksmith, of Francestown, doc date 1798, execution, debt, file #96

QUIGLEY John, yeoman, of Francestown, vs Town of Francestown, rec date 1775, various, meeting house?, file #2180

QUIMBE Moses, yeoman, of Weare, vs QUIMBE William Jr, yeoman, of Weare, doc date 1768, rec date 1783, deed, land transfer, file #2652

QUIMBY Jeremiah, husbandman, of Springfield, vs PATCH Benjamin, yeoman, of Francestown, doc date 1799, writ, debt, file #410

QUIMBY John, husbandman, of Hawke, vs BRADBURY Barnabas, trader, of Amesbury MA, doc date 1772, civil litigation, debt, file #654

QUINTON Agnes, widow, of Sheensboro NY, vs HOLMS Robert, husbandman, of Peterborough, rec date 1785, judgment, debt, file #5145

QUINTON Agnes, widow, of Skeensboro NY, vs HOLMS Robert, husbandman, of Peterborough, rec date 1784, judgment, debt, file #5303

RAMSEY Hugh, yeoman, of Hillsborough, vs SAMPSON Samuel Jr, yeoman, of Amherst, doc date 1773, execution, debt, file #1452

RAMSEY Hugh, yeoman, of New Boston, vs BALDWIN Nahum, esquire, of Amherst, rec date 1782, writ, debt, file #2801, estate of Zacheus CUTLER

RAMSEY James, yeoman, of Londonderry, vs McNEAL Josiah, yeoman, of New Boston, doc date 1774, writ, debt, file #1133

RAMSEY John, husbandman, of Society Land, vs McWILLIAM Thomas, husbandman, of Fisherfield, doc date 1782, rec date 1785, deed, land transfer, file #5648

RAMSEY Jonathan, yeoman, of New Boston, vs RAMSY Hugh, yeoman, of New Boston, doc date 1783, rec date 1783, deed, land transfer, file #2662

RAMSEY William, yeoman, of Londonderry, vs BROWN Nathaniel, yeoman, of Londonderry, doc date 1786, rec date 1786, deed, land transfer, file #5021

RAND John, esquire, of Deerfield, vs GOFFE John, esquire, of Derryfield, rec date 1777, various, land dispute, file #2215

RAND John, of MA, vs WALKER Joshua, of Rindge, rec date 1786, various, care of children, file #6213

RAND John, esquire, of Worcester MA, vs WALKER Joshua, husbandman, of Rindge, rec date 1785, various, debt, file #6347

RANDAL Joseph, yeoman, of Sharon MA, vs CRAFT Abner, of Watertown MA, rec date 1788, appointments, file #6154, part of Samuel CURTIS file

RANKIN Samuel, innholder, of Londonderry, vs ARCHIBALD Arthur, husbandman, of Londonderry, doc date 1765, writ, debt, file #1378

RANKIN Sussanah, single, of Hollis, vs FARLEY Ebenezer, yeoman, of Hollis, doc date 1770, rec date 1774, deed, land transfer, file #6545

RANO Samuel, husbandman, of Andover, vs SCRIBNER Samuel, husbandman, of Salisbury, rec date 1785, writ, debt, file #5394

RAWLIN John, deceased, of Amherst, rec date 1767, administrator notice, estate, file #7026

RAWSON Jonathan, gentleman, of Nottingham, vs READ Zadock, husbandman, of New Boston, rec date 1785, judgment, debt, file #5195

RAY ---- et al, of Nashua, vs SCRIPTURE ---- et al, doc date 1892, plaintiffs brief, land dispute, file #579

RAY James, esquire, of Amherst, vs BURNS John, husbandman, of Fisherfield, doc date 1798, execution, debt, file #58

REA Caleb, physician, of Ipswich MA, vs SYMONDS Joseph, husbandman, of Derryfield, rec date 1782, judgment, debt, file #2710

REA Caleb, physician, of Ipswich MA, vs SYMONDS Joseph, husbandman, of Deerfield, rec date 3237, execution, debt, file #3237

REA Roger, yeoman, of Dracut MA, vs DICKEY James, gentleman, of Raby, rec date 1784, execution, debt, file #5887

READ Abiel, gentleman, of Hollis, vs BIGELOW Timothy, esquire, of Groton MA, doc date 1799, writ, debt, file #361

READ Abijah, yeoman, of Nottingham-West, vs WILKINS Benjamin, yeoman, of Amherst, rec date 1782, appeal, debt, file #3999

READ Eleazer, husbandman, of Dunstable MA, vs BAILEY David Jr, husbandman, of Jaffrey, rec date 1784, judgment, debt, file #5308

READ Eleazer, husbandman, of Dunstable MA, vs PRATT Thomas, feltmaker, of Hollis, rec date 1785, judgment, debt, file #2444

READ Eleazer, husbandman, of Dunstable, vs BAILEY David Jr, husbandman, of Jaffrey, rec date 1785, judgment, debt, file #5153

READ Joseph, laborer, of Bedford, vs DICKEY Adam, husbandman, of Bedford, doc date 1792, petition, release of debit, file #23

READ Joseph, of Westford MA, rec date 1788, deposition, land dispute, file #6583

READ Joshua, tailor, of Hollis, vs SPAULDING Jacob, yeoman, of Hollis, rec date 1786, judgment, debt, file #2454

READ Joshua, tailor, of Hollis, vs FRANCH William Jr, yeoman, of Hollis, rec date 1786, judgment, debt, file #2456

READ Lucy, widow, of Litchfield, vs KARR James, esquire, of Goffstown, doc date 1774, writ, debt, file #747

READ Lucy, widow, of Litchfield, vs KARR James, esquire, of Goffstown, rec date 1783, writ, debt, file #4043

READ Robert, esquire, of Amherst, vs BIXBE Andrew, yeoman, of Hillsborough, rec date 1786, judgment, debt, file #6180

READ Samuel, gentleman, of Westford MA, vs ADAMS Stephen & Silas, yeomen, of Hollis, doc date 1775, writ, debt, file #759

READ Thomas, yeoman, of Littleton MA, vs DUDLEY Stephen, yeoman, of New Ipswich, rec date 1785, judgment, debt, file #6425

READ Timothy Jr, husbandman, of Dunstable MA, vs WHITNEY Silvanus, husbandman, of Dunstable, rec date 1783, writ, debt, file #3363

READ William, gentleman, of Hollis, vs PATTEN Nathaniel, husbandman, of Brooklin, doc date 1800, judgment, debt, file #568

READ William, husbandman, of Amherst, vs BLANCHARD Augustus, esquire, of Amherst, rec date 1788, writ, taking furniture, file #2551

READ William, gentleman, of Hollis, vs FRENCH William Jr, husbandman, of Hollis, rec date 1784, judgment, debt, file #4264

READ William, yeoman, of Hollis, vs BLOOD Francis, yeoman, of Hollis, doc date 1798, judgment, debt, file #566

READ William, gentleman, of Amherst, vs SMITH Jonathan, esquire, of Amherst, doc date 1802, rec date 1802, deed, land transfer, file #5676

READ William, yeoman, of Amherst, vs GRIMES James, gentleman, of Deering, rec date 1785, judgment, debt, file #6412

READ William, husbandman, of Amherst, vs JONES Timothy, yeoman, of Lyndeborough, rec date 1788, writ, debt, file #6731

READ William Jr, yeoman, of Hollis, vs BLOAD Seth, husbandman, of Temple, doc date 1799, writ, debt, file #437

READ William, yeoman, of Amherst, vs GRIMES James, gentleman, of Deering, rec date 1785, judgment, debt, file #6422

READY Jeremiah, vs MANCHESTER Gas Lite Co, doc date 1891, defendants brief, supreme court, file #630

REED Ebenezer, mariner, of Marblehead MA, vs CLENDINNIN James, yeoman, of Londonderry, doc date 1784, execution, debt, file #1797

REED Ebenezer, mariner, of Marblehead MA, vs CLENDENIN James, yeoman, of Londonderry, rec date 1782, judgment, debt, file #2712

REED Ebenezer, yeoman, of Marblehead MA, vs CLENDENIN James, yeoman, of Londonderry, rec date 1783, civil litigious, debt, file #2909

REED Ebenezer, mariner, of Marblehead MA, vs CLENDENIN James, yeoman, of Londonderry, rec date 1783, execution, debt, file #3252

REED Ebenezer, mariner, of Marblehead MA, vs SANDERS Oliver, gentleman, of Londonderry, rec date 1783, judgment, debt, file #4724

REED Hammon, husbandman, of Lexington MA, vs NEWMAN Ebenezer, yeoman, of Deering, doc date 1784, execution, debt, file #1887

REED Hammond, husbandman, of Lexington MA, vs NEWMAN Ebenezer & Josiah, husbandman, of Deering, rec date 1783, writ, debt, file #3573

REED Israel, innholder, of Littleton MA, vs SLOAN David, husbandman, of Mason, rec date 1785, judgment, debt, file #5226

REED Jacob, yeoman, of Dunstable, vs STATE of NH, recognizance, debt, file #2228

REED Jonathan, cordwainer, of Londonderry, vs BAGLEY Phinehas, gentleman, of Dunbarton, rec date 1783, judgment, debt, file #3289

REED Jonathan, husbandman, rec date 1785, indictment, perjury, file #4751

REED Jonathan, husbandman, of Woburn MA, vs POOL Jonathan, physician, of Hollis, rec date 1787, writ, debt, file #6671

REED Thomas, yeoman, of Littleton MA, vs DUDLEY Stephen, innkeeper, of New Ipswich, rec date 1784, judgment, debt, file #4618

REED Zadork, yeoman, of New Boston, vs GREEN Peter, esquire, of Concord, rec date 1783, writ, debt, file #3363

REID George, esquire, of Londonderry, vs MUNROE Josiah, esquire, of Amherst, rec date 1785, writ, debt, file #5967

REID James, esquire, of Fitzwilliam, vs GARY Thomas, brickmaker, of Amherst, doc date 1774, judgment, debt, file #721

REID Joel, husbandman, of Antrim, vs GIBSON John, gentleman, of Francestown, doc date 1799, judgment, debt, file #255

REID Matthew, yeoman, of Londonderry, vs CHAMPNEY Ebenezer, esquire, of Groton MA, doc date 1784, writ, debt, file #1626

RENKIN Samuel, innholder, of Londonderry, vs McDUFFEE Hugh, yeoman, of Chester, doc date 1773, writ, debt, file #1437

RENKIN Samuel, innholder, of Londonderry, vs WALLACE John, cordwainer, of Londonderry, doc date 1772, writ, debt, file #1400

RENKIN William, husbandman, of Londonderry, vs BLUNT Samuel, husbandman, of Chester, doc date 1773, writ, debt, file #1439

RICE Eleazor, yeoman, of Marlborough MA, vs WOODS Alpheus, gentleman, of Marlborough MA, rec date 1786, confession, debt, file #2323

RICE Ezekiel Jr, husbandman, of E Sudbury ma, vs RICE Daniel, gentleman, of Marlborough MA, rec date 1786, confession, debt, file #2322

RICE Jonah, yeoman, of Marlborough MA, vs HADSON Elisha, yeoman, of Wilton, rec date 1785, judgment, debt, file #5272

RICE Josiah, innholder, of Weymouth, vs MORELAND William, laborer, of Nottingham, doc date 1791, rec date 1793, various, stealing horse, file #2530, other names dyer HOLBROOK

RICHARD Thomas, husbandman, of Temple, vs RUSSELL Jason, yeoman, of Mason, doc date 1799, writ, debt, file #434

RICHARDS Daniel, of Newbury MA, vs CLARK Daniel, cordwainer, of Boscawen, doc date 1775, deed, land transfer, file #848

RICHARDS Eliphalet, gentleman, of Goffstown, vs HOGG William, husbandman, of Deering, doc date 1799, debt, file #458

RICHARDS Joel & Prudance, husbandman, of Campbells Gore, vs SWEET Benjamin, husbandman, of Claremont, doc date 1794, rec date 1794, deed, land transfer, file #6793, pg 333

RICHARDS Joseph, of Temple, vs COBB Seth & Cate, of Temple, doc date 1775, deed, land transfer, file #834

RICHARDS Samuel, gentleman, of Goffstown, vs KELLEY Moses, esquire, of Goffstown, rec date 1783, indictment, assault, file #2605

RICHARDSON Abel, yeoman, of Woburn MA, vs BOFFE Thomas, gentleman, of Lyndeborough, rec date 1785, deed, land transfer, file #5608

RICHARDSON Elizabeth, spinster, of Temple, vs STEVENS William, husbandman, of Townsend MA, rec date 1787, various, debt, file #6700

RICHARDSON James, esquire, of Dover, vs PATTERSON Joseph, trader, of Temple, doc date 1774, execution, file #1002

RICHARDSON James, esquire, of Dover, vs DRURY Zedekiah Jr, yeoman, of Temple, doc date 1774, writ, debt, file #1139

RICHARDSON James, esquire, of Leominster MA, vs HICKS Sarah, widow, of Madbury, doc date 1784, execution, debt, file #1748

RICHARDSON James, esquire, of Leominster MA, vs HICKS Sarah, widow, of Madbury, doc date 1784, execution, debt, file #1951

RICHARDSON Jepthah, innkeeper, of Groton MA, vs HENDERSON John, husbandman, of Rindge, rec date 1784, judgment, debt, file #4200

RICHARDSON Jepthah, innholder, of Groton MA, vs BALLARD Nathan, gentleman, of Wilton, rec date 1786, various, debt, file #6370

RICHARDSON Josiah, trader, of Hillsborough, vs RICHARDSON Timothy, blacksmith, doc date 1799, judgment, debt, file #291

RICHARDSON Nathaniel, of Salem MA, vs JONES Timothy, yeoman, of Lyndeborough, rec date 1783, various, debt, file #4717

RICHARDSON Samuel, vs BLODGET Samuel, doc date 1782, subpoena, bridge repair, file #1159

RICHARDSON Sarah, wife, of Francestown, vs FISK Jonathan, blacksmith, of Francestown, doc date 1787, rec date 1788, deed, land transfer, file #6751

RICHARDSON Stephen, yeoman, of Warner, vs INHABITANTS of Hollis, rec date 1785, various, debt, file #4845, fragile

RICHARDSON Stephen, yeoman, of Warner, vs INHABITANTS of Hollis, rec date 1784, writ, debt, file #5295

RICHARDSON Thomas, yeoman, of Temple, vs BALLARD Joseph, yeoman, of Amherst, rec date 1786, execution, debt, file #5879

RICHARDSON Thomas, yeoman, of Temple, vs BALLARD Joseph, yeoman, of Amherst, rec date 1786, writ, debt, file #6056

RICHARDSON Tilly, husbandman, of Jaffrey, vs SMITH Samuel, gentleman, of Peterborough, doc date 1792, rec date 1796, deed, land transfer, file #5669

RICHARDSON Zachariah, innholder, of Francestown, vs FISK Jonathan, blacksmith, of Amherst, doc date 1783, deed, land transfer, file #2016

RICHARDSON Zachariah, innholder, of Francestown, vs JONES Samuel, yeoman, of Hillsborough, rec date 1782, judgment, debt, file #2723

RICHARDSON Zachariah, innholder, of Francestown, vs JONES William Jr, yeoman, of Hillsborough, rec date 1783, civil litigious, debt, file #2962

RICHARDSON Zachariah, yeoman, of Francestown, vs JONES Samuel, yeoman, of Hillsborough, rec date 1783, execution, debt, file #3868

RICHARDSON Zachariah, husbandman, of Francestown, vs WINCHESTER Lemuel, yeoman, of Amherst, rec date 1784, judgment, debt, file #4652

RICHARDSON Zachariah, yeoman, of Francestown, vs GREEN David, yeoman, of Hillsborough, rec date 1783, judgment, debt, file #4508

RICHARDSON Zachariah, husbandman, of Francestown, vs WINCHESTER Lemuel, yeoman, of Amherst, rec date 1785, judgment, debt, file #5131

RICHARDSON Zachariah, yeoman, of Francestown, vs BARRETT Charles, gentleman, of New Ipswich, rec date 1785, deed, land transfer, file #5610

RICHARDSON Zachariah, yeoman, of Francestown, vs FISHER James, yeoman, of Francestown, doc date 1787, rec date 1788, deed, land transfer, file #6750

RICHARDSON Zachariah, yeoman, of Francestown, vs FISK Jonathan, blacksmith, of Francestown, doc date 1787, rec date 1788, deed, land transfer, file #6751

RICHARDSON Zachariah, innholder, of Francestown, vs STEVENS Samuel, physician, of Amherst, rec date 1783, writ, debt, file #3192

RICHARDSON Zechariah, innholder, of Francestown, vs PALMER Jonathan, innkeeper, of Litchfield, rec date 1784, judgment, debt, file #4613

RICKMAN William, gentleman, of Salem MA, vs GOODRIDGE Sewall, of Lyndeborough, rec date 1788, power of attorney, file #6638

RIDDLE Isaac, husbandman, of Bedford, vs MOOR Samuel, of Bedford, rec date 1788, writ, debt, file #6636

RIDDLE John, gentleman, of Bedford, vs PATTERSON James, gentleman, of Bedford, rec date 1782, writ, debt, file #2666

RIDEOUT David, husbandman, of Wilton, vs SAWYER Nathaniel, trader, of Wilton, doc date 1799, writ, debt, file #575

RIDEOUT James, yeoman, of Hollis, vs KENNEY Israel, yeoman, of Hollis, doc date 1773, judgment, debt, file #1295

RIDEOUT James, yeoman, of Hollis, vs GRIFFIN David, husbandman, of Alstead, rec date 1783, execution, debt, file #3810

RIDEOUT Nathaniel, yeoman, of Hollis, vs BLOOD Josiah, yeoman, of Hollis, doc date 1773, judgment, debt, file #1295

RIDEOUT Nathaniel, yeoman, of Hollis, vs KENNEY Israel, yeoman, of Hollis, doc date 1773, judgment, debt, file #1295

RIDEOUT Nathaniel, yeoman, of Hollis, vs CUMMINGS Simeon, gentleman, of Dunstable, rec date 1783, writ, debt, file #3326

RIDEOUT Nathaniel, yeoman, of Hollis, vs SHATTUCK William, husbandman, of Deering, rec date 1783, writ, debt, file #3323

RIDEOUT Nathaniel, husbandman, of Hollis, vs POLLARAD Timothy, yeoman, of Nottingham-West, rec date 1783, judgment, debt, file #3772

RIDEOUT Nathaniel, yeoman, of Hollis, vs FARNSWORTH Samuel, yeoman, of Stoddard, rec date 1783, execution, debt, file #3812

RIDEOUT Nathaniel, yeoman, of Hollis, vs HOW Ephraim, yeoman, of Hollis, rec date 1785, writ, debt, file #5385

RIDEOUT Nathaniel, husbandman, of Hollis, vs WILKINS Bray, husbandman, of Deering, rec date 1782, execution, debt, file #5734

RIDER Ebenezer, husbandman, of Amherst, vs HINCHMAN Nathaniel, physician, of Amherst, doc date 1799, writ, debt, file #574

RIDGOUT Nathaniel, yeoman, of Hollis, vs FARNSWORTH Samuel, yeoman, of Stoddard, doc date 1784, execution, debt, file #1711

RILEY Major, yeoman, of Antrim, vs GIBSON John, trader, of Francestown, rec date 1807, deed, land transfer, file #5692

RILEY Major & Mary, yeoman, of Hillsborough, vs CHANEY Elias, yeoman, of Antrim, doc date 1785, rec date 1788, deed, land transfer, file #6742

RITTER Moses, cordwainer, of Shirley MA, vs PARKER Abel, husbandman, of Peterborough, rec date 1785, judgment, debt, file #5797

ROBBE Alexander, gentleman, of Peterborough, vs ELLINWOOD Joseph, yeoman, of Greenfield, doc date 1796, various, trespass, file #560

ROBBE Alexander, gentleman, of Peterborough, vs DORMAN Ephraim, gentleman, of Keene, doc date 1784, execution, debt, file #1690

ROBBE Alexander, gentleman, of Peterborough, vs TUCKER Benjamin, gentleman, of Marlborough, doc date 1784, execution, debt, file #1690

ROBBE Alexander, gentleman, of Peterborough, vs DORMAN Ephraim, gentleman, of Keene, doc date 1784, execution, debt, file #1978

ROBBE Alexander, gentleman, of Peterborough, vs HOGG Samuel, yeoman, of Dublin, doc date 1784, execution, debt, file #1917

ROBBE Alexander, gentleman, of Peterborough, vs TUCKER Benjamin, gentleman, of Marlborough, doc date 1784, execution, debt, file #1978

ROBBE Alexander, gentleman, of Peterborough, vs SMITH John, husbandman, of Peterborough, rec date 1778, civil litigation, road lay out, file #2167

ROBBE Alexander, gentleman, of Peterborough, vs STEEL David, gentleman, of Peterborough, rec date 1783, court case, debt, file #2880, 2 folders

ROBBE Alexander, gentleman, of Peterborough, vs STEEL David, gentleman, of Peterborough, rec date 1783, court case, debt, file #2881, 2 folders

ROBBE Alexander, gentleman, of Peterborough, vs DORMAN Ephraim, gentleman, of Keene, rec date 1783, writ, debt, file #3421

ROBBE Alexander, gentleman, of Peterborough, vs TUCKER Benjamin, gentleman, of Marlborough, rec date 1783, writ, debt, file #3421

ROBBE Alexander, gentleman, of Peterborough, vs STEEL David, gentleman, of Peterborough, rec date 1783, various, debt, file #3611

ROBBE Alexander, gentleman, of Peterborough, vs AMES David, miller, of Peterborough, rec date 1783, writ, debt, file #3623

ROBBE Alexander, gentleman, of Peterborough, vs WALACE Matthew, gentleman, of Peterborough, rec date 1785, writ, debt, file #6259, estate of Norman MIRIAMA Jr

ROBBE Alexander, gentleman, of Peterborough, vs STUART Charles, gentleman, of Peterborough, rec date 1787, writ, debt, file #6740

ROBBE Alexander, gentleman, of Peterborough, vs FERGUSON Henry, gentleman, of Peterborough, rec date 1787, writ, debt, file #6740

ROBBE Alexander, gentleman, of Peterborough, vs CUNNINGHAM Samuel, gentleman, of Peterborough, rec date 1787, writ, debt, file #6740

ROBBE Andrew, husbandman, of Stoddard, vs SMITH William, esquire, of Peterborough, rec date 1786, writ, debt, file #6293

ROBBE Samuel, yeoman, of Peterborough, vs WHITTERMORE Nathaniel, yeoman, of Peterborough, doc date 1797, fraud, debt, file #505

ROBBE Samuel, gentleman, of Goffstown, vs INHABITANTS of Goffstown, rec date 1782, various, debit for beef, file #3613

ROBBE William, husbandman, of Hancock, vs STATE of NH, rec date 1787, recognizance, counterfeiting, file #3556

ROBBE William, gentleman, of Peterborough, vs MORRISON Ezekiel, yeoman, of Peterborough, rec date 1785, judgment, debt, file #5059

ROBBE William Jr, yeoman, of Peterborough, vs BLODGETT Jacob, yeoman, of Temple, rec date 1783, judgment, debt, file #4430

ROBBE William Jr, yeoman, of Peterborough, vs BUTTERFIELD Isaac, blacksmith, of Temple, rec date 1784, judgment, debt, file #4656

ROBBE William Jr, yeoman, of Peterborough, vs SMITH John, yeoman, of Peterborough, rec date 1784, writ, debt, file #4577

ROBBE William Jr, yeoman, of Peterborough, vs McDONALD James Jr, yeoman, of Hollis, rec date 1785, writ, debt, file #4955

ROBBE William Jr, yeoman, of Peterborough, vs HOCKLEY James, laborer, of Peterborough, rec date 1785, judgment, debt, file #5523

ROBBE William Jr, husbandman, of Peterborough, vs PARKHURST Jonathan, husbandman, of Wilton, rec date 1785, judgment, debt, file #5562

ROBBE William Jr, gentleman, of Peterborough, vs ROBBE Alexander, husbandman, of Dublin, rec date 1788, various, assault, file #6541, see also prisoner list 6541

ROBBE William Jr, yeoman, of Peterborough, vs HOCKLEY James, laborer, of Peterborough, rec date 1786, judgment, debt, file #6501

ROBBIE William, yeoman, of Peterborough, vs SMITH John, yeoman, of Peterborough, rec date 1786, various, debt, file #6074

ROBBINS John, yeoman, of Littleton MA, vs BROOKS Joseph, yeoman, of Jaffrey, rec date 1782, judgment, debt, file #2718

ROBBINS Jonathan, yeoman, of New Ipswich, vs WHITEMORE Patrick, yeoman, of New Ipswich, doc date 1772, writ, debt, file #1074

ROBBINS Josiah, husbandman, of Mason, vs SLOAN David, husbandman, of Groton, doc date 1773, writ, debt, file #1238

ROBBINS Josiah, yeoman, of Pepperell, vs ASTIN Timothy, yeoman, of Temple, doc date 1773, judgment, debt, file #1319

ROBBINS Josiah, husbandman, of New Ipswich, vs SCRIPTER Samuel, husbandman, of Mason, rec date 1785, judgment, debt, file #5271

ROBEE Andrew, husbandman, of Stoddard, vs McCOY Thomas, husbandman, of Peterborough, rec date 1785, writ, debt, file #6141

ROBERSON Joseph, yeoman, of Deering, vs BAYL William, husbandman, of Wilton, doc date 1780, rec date 1783, deed, land transfer, file #2641

ROBERTS Jeremiah, husbandman, of Salisbury, vs ELKINS Abil, husbandman, of Salisbury, rec date 1788, writ, debt, file #6987

ROBERTSON Robert, wharfinger, of Boston MA, vs OSBORN Samuel, husbandman, of Fitzwilliam, rec date 1785, judgment, debt, file #5184

ROBESON William, yeoman, of Deering, vs GRIMES James, gentleman, of Deering, doc date 1786, rec date 1786, deed, land transfer, file #5028

ROBIE Jonathan, husbandman, of Perrystown, vs PEARSON Daniel, husbandman, of Weare, rec date 1783, writ, debt, file #3366

ROBINS Jonathan & Mary, yeoman, of New Ipswich, vs MEED David, husbandman, of Lynn MA, doc date 1775, rec date 1788, deed, land transfer, file #6829

ROBINSON Alexander, yeoman, of Society Land, vs SMALL Jonathan, yeoman, of Amherst, doc date 1774, writ, debt, file #815

ROBINSON Alexander, yeoman, of Society Land, vs SMALL Nathan, husbandman, of Dunstable, doc date 1772, writ, debt, file #892

ROBINSON Alexander, yeoman, of Deering, vs McCALLEY James, yeoman, of Hillsborough, doc date 1784, writ, debt, file #1616

ROBINSON Eliazer, husbandman, of Lebanon, vs WEARE Peter, of Andover, doc date 1782, execution, file #1025

ROBINSON Elisha, gentleman, of Amherst, vs PATTERSON Adam, gentleman, of Amherst, rec date 1778, recognizance, memorandum, file #1041

ROBINSON Joseph, yeoman, of Deering, vs DODGE Samuel, yeoman, of Amherst, doc date 1784, writ, debt, file #1573

ROBINSON Joseph, yeoman, of Deering, vs ATHERTON Joshua, esquire, of Amherst, rec date 1783, writ, debt, file #3012

ROBINSON Joseph, yeoman, of Deering, vs BAYLES William, yeoman, of Wilton, rec date 1782, execution, debt, file #3520

ROBINSON Thomas, yeoman, of Pembroke, vs MELVILE John, merchant, of Grenada, doc date 1772, civil litigation, debt, file #1034

ROBINSON William, yeoman, of Deering, vs ATHERTON Joshua, esquire, of Amherst, rec date 1783, writ, debt, file #3038

ROBINSON William, yeoman, of Deering, vs WHILEY John, yeoman, of Amherst, rec date 1783, writ, debt, file #3368

ROBINSON William, yeoman, of Deering, vs McFERSON James, yeoman, of Francestown, rec date 1783, judgment, debt, file #4450

ROBISON Alexander, yeoman, of Society Land, vs SMALL Jonathan, yeoman, of Amherst, doc date 1774, judgment, debt, file #717

ROBY James, husbandman, of Amherst, vs SPAULDING Hesakiah, widow, of Chelmsford MA, doc date 1799, execution, debt, file #167

ROBY James, prisoner, of Amherst, vs STATE of NH, rec date 1776, confession, counterfeiting, file #2254

ROBY James, husbandman, of Nottingham-West, vs BLODGETT Jonathan, husbandman, of Rumney, rec date 1788, writ, debt, file #6905

ROBY James, yeoman, of Nottingham, vs HADLEY Moses, yeoman, of Nottingham, rec date 1785, indictment, debt, file #7021

ROBY Samuel, cordwainer, of Dunstable MA, vs DICKEY James, gentleman, of Raby, rec date 1783, judgment, debt, file #3800

ROBY Samuel, cordwainer, of Dunstable MA, vs McALLISTER Archibald, husbandman, of New Boston, rec date 1785, judgment, debt, file #5327

ROBY Samuel, yeoman, of Dunstable, vs KEYS John, yeoman, of Hollis, rec date 1785, execution, debt, file #5901

ROBY Silas, husbandman, of Merrimack, vs KITTREDGE Nehemiah, gentleman, of Billerica MA, doc date 1799, writ, debt, file #391

ROBY Silas, yeoman, of Merrimack, vs BARRON William, gentleman, of Merrimack, rec date 1783, writ, debt, file #3356

ROBY William, yeoman, of Dunstable, vs DARRAH Robert, yeoman, of Litchfield, doc date 1774, writ, debt, file #1090, fragile

ROCHE John, yeoman, of Windsor, vs DANA Anna, widow, of Amherst, doc date 1799, judgment, debt, file #261

ROCK John, of Dunbarton, vs GLOVER Jonathan, of MA, rec date 1782, writ, debt, file #2812

ROCKWOOD Timothy, of Holliston MA, vs COBB Stephen, husbandman, of Holliston MA, doc date 1768, rec date 1778, deed, land transfer, file #2118

RODGERS Solomon, trader, of Hollis, vs FORD James, esquire, of Nottingham-West, doc date 1784, execution, debt, file #1974

RODGERS Solomon, esquire, of Hollis, vs GILSON Ebenezer, husbandman, of Hollis, rec date 1785, judgment, debt, file #2449

ROGER Charles, husbandman, of Rutland MA, vs ESTERBROOK John, husbandman, of Packersfield, doc date 1784, execution, debt, file #1908

ROGER Charles, husbandman, of Rutland MA, vs EASTBROOK John, husbandman, of Packersfield, rec date 1783, writ, debt, file #3444

ROGER John (Rev), minister, of Leominster MA, vs ROGERS John Jur, physician, of Plymouth, rec date 1788, writ, debt, file #6985

ROGER Solomon, trader, of Hillsborough, vs FORD James, esquire, of Nottingham-West, doc date 1784, execution, debt, file #1531

ROGERS James, wheelwright, of Acworth, vs CHAMPNEY Ebenezer, esquire, of Groton MA, rec date 1787, writ, debt, file #6659

ROGERS James, yeoman/deceased, of Dunbarton, of Dunbarton, doc date 1787, rec date 1788, deed, land transfer, file #6823

ROGERS John, clerk, of Leominster MA, vs ERVING Henry, trader, of New Holderness, rec date 1785, judgment, debt, file #5805

ROGERS Josiah, yeoman, of Petersham MA, vs BATCHELDER Samuel, yeoman, of Jaffrey, rec date 1782, judgment, debt, file #2734

ROGERS Josiah, yeoman, of Petersham MA, vs BATCHELDER Samuel, yeoman, of Jaffrey, rec date 1783, execution, debt, file #3254

ROGERS Josiah, trader, of New Ipswich, vs MILLER Samuel Jr, husbandman, of Peterborough, rec date 1785, judgment, debt, file #5505

ROGERS Robert, yeoman, of Society Land, vs NICHOLS Thomas, gentleman, of Antrim, rec date 1783, writ, debt, file #3071

ROGERS Samuel, husbandman, of Newbury NY, vs FOSTER David, husbandman, of Dunbarton, doc date 1784, execution, debt, file #1699

ROGERS Samuel, husbandman, of Newbury NY, vs PORTER David, husbandman, of Dunbarton, doc date 1784, execution, debt, file #1508

ROGERS Samuel, husbandman, of Newbury NY, vs FOSTER David, husbandman, of Dunbarton, rec date 1783, judgment, debt, file #4080

ROGERS Solomon, trader, of Hollis, vs FORD James, esquire, of Nottingham-West, doc date 1784, execution, debt, file #1726

ROGERS Solomon, husbandman, of Hollis, vs BLANCHARD William, housewright, of Jaffrey, doc date 1784, execution, debt, file #1900

ROGERS Solomon, esquire, of Hollis, vs LESLEY Joseph, husbandman, of Hollis, rec date 1785, judgment, debt, file #2445

ROGERS Solomon, gentleman, of Hollis, vs MOSHER Abijah, husbandman, of Pepperell MA, rec date 1783, execution, debt, file #3666

ROGERS Solomon, gentleman, of Hollis, vs McGAA Robert, trader, of Hollis, rec date 1783, execution, debt, file #3666

ROGERS Solomon, gentleman, of Hollis, vs BLANCHARD William, housewright, of Jaffrey, rec date 1783, writ, debt, file #3601

ROGERS Solomon, trader, of Hollis, vs WALLINGSFORD David, gentleman, of Hollis, rec date 1784, judgment, debt, file #4658

ROGERS Solomon, gentleman, of Hollis, vs WHITTIMORE Samuel, gentleman, of Cambridge, rec date 1785, judgment, land dispute, file #5358

ROGERS William, yeoman, of Weare, vs TUXBURY Jacob, doc date 1787, rec date 1787, deed, land transfer, file #2507

ROGERS William, cooper, of Goffstown, vs UNDERWOOD James, gentleman, of Goffstown, doc date 1786, rec date 1786, deed, land transfer, file #5016

ROGERS William, innholder, of Goffstown, vs WOOD Jonathan, yeoman, of Goffstown, rec date 1786, writ, debt, file #6288

ROGERS William, innholder, of Goffstown, vs WOOD Jonathan, yeoman, of Goffstown, rec date 1786, summons, debt, file #6118

ROGERS William, husbandman, of Weare, vs MUDGET Ezra, husbandman, of Weare, rec date 1787, writ, trespass of land, file #6665

ROGERS William, yeoman, of Weare, vs PATTERSON William, yeoman, of Goffstown, rec date 1787, writ, debt, file #6652

ROGERS William, husbandman, of Weare, vs WELLS Timothy, blacksmith, of Goffstown, rec date 1788, writ, debt, file #6679

ROLF Jesse, trader, of Francestown, vs WILKINS Andrew, yeoman, of Amherst, doc date 1784, execution, debt, file #1743

ROLF Jesse, trader, of Francestown, vs JONES Samuel, yeoman, of Hillsborough, rec date 1782, judgment, debt, file #2742

ROLF Jesse, trader, of Francestown, vs SHANNON Richard C, esquire, of Hollis, rec date 1785, writ, debt, file #5384, fragile

ROLFE Benjamin, yeoman, of Deering, vs WILLEY John, yeoman, of Amherst, rec date 1783, writ, debt, file #3016

ROLFE Benjamin, husbandman, of Boscawen, vs BURBANK Moses, husbandman, of Boscawen, rec date 1788, writ, debt, file #6925

ROLFE Enoch, yeoman, of Newbury MA, vs BURBANK Moses, gentleman, of Boscawen, rec date 1772, judgment, debt, file #4883

ROLFE Enoch, yeoman, of Newbury MA, vs SWEET Benjamin, carpenter, of Boscawen, rec date 1772, judgment, debt, file #4883

ROLFE Jesse, trader, of Francestown, vs JONES Samuel, yeoman, of Hillsborough, rec date 1783, execution, debt, file #3834

ROLFE Stephen, husbandman, of Hillsborough, vs RICHARDSON Josiah, yeoman, doc date 1799, judgment, debt, file #232

ROLFE Stephen, husbandman, of Hillsborough, vs GORING Asahel, yeoman, of Peterborough, doc date 1799, judgment, debt, file #232

ROLLINS John, yeoman, of Londonderry, vs WOODNBURY William, yeoman, of Amherst, rec date 1783, various, debt, file #3563

ROLLINS Joseph, cooper, of Amherst, vs DUTTON Jesse, blacksmith, of Dunstable MA, rec date 1779, writ, land dispute, file #2243

ROLSTON Jesse, trader, of Francestown, vs WILKINS Andrew, yeoman, of Amherst, rec date 1783, judgment, debt, file #4461

ROSS Jonathan, yeoman, of Henniker, vs GILCHRIST Alexander, yeoman, of Goffstown, rec date 1783, writ, debt, file #3048

ROWE John, yeoman, of Salisbury, vs EASTMAN Benjamin, husbandman, of Salisbury, rec date 1782, writ, debt, file #4850

ROWE Josiah, cordwainer, of Warner, vs HALL John, physician, of Warner, rec date 1783, writ, debt, file #3213

ROWE Nathan, yeoman, of Andover, vs ELKINS Abel, husbandman, of Salisbury, rec date 1784, writ, debt, file #4425, kinship to John ROWE

ROWELL Jonathan, yeoman, of Goffstown, vs FOWLER Nathaniel, yeoman, of Goffstown, doc date 1777, rec date 1782, deed, land transfer, file #6562

ROWELL Moses, blacksmith, of Temple, vs HOUSTON William, joiner, of Peterborough, rec date 1788, writ, debt, file #6685

RUE Benjamin, of Marlborough MA, vs ARNOLD Joseph, yeoman, of Henniker, doc date 1787, rec date 1787, deed, land transfer, file #2490

RUMSEY William, yeoman, of Londonderry, vs McLAUGHLIN William, yeoman, of Bedford, doc date 1786, rec date 1786, deed, land transfer, file #5017

RUNELS Ebenezer, yeoman, of Hollis, vs BALL Eleazer, yeoman, of Hollis, rec date 1783, writ, debt, file #3335

RUNILS Stephan, blacksmith, of Hollis, vs RIDEOUT Nathaniel, yeoman, of Hollis, rec date 1785, judgment, debt, file #2447

RUNNELLS Fletcher, husbandman, of Durham, vs SULLIVAN John, esquire, of Amherst, rec date 1785, indictment, debt, file #7020

RUNNELS Daniel, joiner, of Londonderry, vs MORRILL Micajah, blacksmith, of Atkinson, doc date 1772, writ, debt, file #1404

RUSS James, innholder, of Deerfield, vs BLAIR William, husbandman, of New Holderness, doc date 1771, writ, debt, file #1386

RUSS Thomas, yeoman, of Derryfield, vs KARR William, yeoman, of Goffstown, doc date 1763, writ, debt, file #1379

RUSSELL Andrew, labourer, of Raby, vs STATE of NH, rec date 1782, recognizance, debt, file #2609

RUSSELL Ephraim, gentleman, of Groton MA, vs NEWHALL Oliver, yeoman, of Hollis, rec date 1785, various, debt, file #6368

RUSSELL George, yeoman, of Raby, vs LAWRENCE Enoch, gentleman, of Mason, doc date 1775, judgment, debt, file #2036

RUSSELL Jacob, yeoman, of Wilton, vs PUTNAM Archelaus, yeoman, of Wilton, rec date 1783, writ, debt, file #3318

RUSSELL Jacob, yeoman, of Wilton, vs HOLT Joseph Jr, yeoman, of Wilton, rec date 1784, judgment, debt, file #4230

RUSSELL James, gentleman, of Litchfield, vs SAWYER Jonathan, yeoman, of Hancock, doc date 1784, execution, debt, file #1938

RUSSELL James, gentleman, of Litchfield, vs JOHNSTON David, yeoman, of Pelham, rec date 1783, writ, debt, file #3337

RUSSELL James, gentleman, of Litchfield, vs DUNLAP Thomas, of Society Land, rec date 1782, execution, debt, file #5736

RUSSELL Joel & Mary, yeoman, of Hancock, vs BROOKS William, blacksmith, of Hollis, doc date 1784, deed, land transfer, file #2009

RUSSELL John, yeoman, of Mason, vs STICKNEY Joseph, yeoman, of New Ipswich, doc date 1799, writ, debt, file #433

RUSSELL Joseph, merchant, of Boston MA, vs PORTER Jonathan, husbandman, of Deerfield, doc date 1784, civil litigation, debt, file #1651

RUSSELL Joseph, merchant, of Boston MA, vs PORTER Jonathan Jr, husbandman, of Derryfield, rec date 1783, judgment, debt, file #3303

RUSSELL Joseph, merchant, of Boston MA, vs BOYES James Jr, husbandman, of Londonderry, rec date 1783, judgment, debt, file #4309, estate of James BOYES

RUSSELL Nathaniel, gentleman, of Rindge, vs BLOOD Robert, yeoman, of
    Peterborough, doc date 1784, civil litigation, debt, file #1649
RUSSELL Nehemiah, gentleman, of Rindge, vs BLOOD Robert, yeoman, of
    Peterborough, rec date 1783, writ, debt, file #4559
RUSSELL Peter, husbandman, of Lyndeborough, vs LUND Phineas, yeoman, of
    Lyndeborough, doc date 1778, writ, debt, file #2054
RUSSELL Thomas, merchant, of Boston MA, vs GIBSON James, husbandman, of
    Merrimack, rec date 1783, execution, debt, file #3232
RUSSELL Thomas, merchant, of Boston MA, vs GIBSON James, husbandman, of
    Merrimack, rec date 1782, execution, debt, file #3480
RUSSELL Thomas, husbandman, of Wilton, vs LEARNARD John, husbandman,
    of Dublin, rec date 1784, judgment, debt, file #4977
RYAN Samuel, yeoman, of Sharon, vs BLAKE Joseph, merchant, of Boston MA,
    doc date 1798, writ, debt, file #436
RYAN Samuel, yeoman, of Sharon, vs PARKMAN Samuel, merchant, of Boston
    MA, doc date 1798, writ, debt, file #436
SABINE Elizabeth, vs MERRILL William T, doc date 1892, defendants brief,
    supreme court, file #620
SADDLERY Hdw Manufacturing Co, vs HILLSBOROUGH Mills, doc date 1894,
    assumpsit, supreme court, file #614
SAFFORD John, innholder, of Ipswich MA, vs JONES Samuel, yeoman, of
    Hillsborough, rec date 1783, writ, debt, file #3916
SAFFORD John, innholder, of Ipswich MA, vs JONES Samuel, yeoman, of
    Hillsborough, rec date 1783, execution, debt, file #3836
SAFFORD Samuel, cordwainer, of Ipswich MA, vs McNEIL John Caldwell,
    innkeeper, of New Boston, rec date 1783, court case, break & enter, file
    #2876
SAFFORD Samuel, cordwainer, of Ipswich MA, vs RAMSEY Hugh, yeoman, of
    New Boston, rec date 1783, execution, debt, file #2901
SAMMPLE Samuel, vs McCARTNEY Jane, spinster, rec date 1783, indictment,
    false testimony, file #7037
SAMON Jonathan, of Acton MA, vs HUTCHINSON Ebenezer, yeoman, of
    Amherst, rec date 1786, writ, debt, file #6298
SANBORN Benjamin, yeoman, of Salisbury, vs WILLSON Thomas, husbandman,
    of Candia, rec date 1787, various, debt, file #2543 B, 2 folders
SANBORN Benjamin, yeoman, of Salisbury, vs WILLSON Thomas, husbandman,
    of Candia, rec date 1787, various, debt, file #2543 A, 2 folders
SANBORN Benjamin, administrator of estate, of Salisbury, vs THOMAS Wilson,
    husbandman, of Candia, rec date 1786, various, debt, file #6349
SANBORN Benjamin, administrator of estate, of Salisbury, vs HALL Obed'm,
    husbandman, of Candia, rec date 1786, various, debt, file #6349
SANBORN John, yeoman, of Salisbury, vs PERKINS Robert, esquire, of
    Northfield, doc date 1798, execution, debt, file #122
SANBORN John, gentleman, of Salisbury, vs WEBSTER David, administrator of
    estate, of Plymouth, rec date 1785, writ, debt, file #6236
SANDERS James, yeoman, of Salem, vs GOOLD John, husbandman, of
    Dunbarton, rec date 1785, writ, debt, file #5277

SANDERS James, yeoman, of Salem, vs CLEMENTS Jonathan, husbandman, of Bow, rec date 1785, writ, debt, file #5277

SANDERS James, yeoman, of Salem, vs STEARNS Jotham, husbandman, of Goffstown, rec date 1785, writ, debt, file #5277

SANDERS Samuel, wheelwright, of Goffstown, vs PETERS John, husbandman, of Andover MA, doc date 1772, writ, debt, file #1058

SANDERSON Aaron, husbandman, of Hillsborough, vs CHAMPANY Ebenezer, esquire, of New Ipswich, doc date 1799, judgment, debt, file #223

SANDERSON Jonathan, cordwainer, of Hollis, vs POOL William, wheelwright, of Hollis, doc date 1798, execution, debt, file #152

SANDERSON Jonathan, cordwainer, of Hollis, vs HALE William, physician, of Hollis, doc date 1805, judgment, debt, file #568

SARGENT James, yeoman, of Goffstown, vs RUSSELL James, yeoman, of Goffstown, rec date 1788, writ, debt, file #6919

SARGENT Joshua, yeoman, of Lyndeborough, vs WILSON James, yeoman, of Peterborough, doc date 1799, judgment, debt, file #294

SARGENT Nathaniel Peaslee, yeoman, of Haverhill MA, vs PINGREY Moses & Hannah, cordwainer, of Methuen MA, doc date 1770, recognizance, debt, file #781

SARGENT Nathaniel S, esquire, of Haverhill MA, vs DOW Joseph, yeoman, of Goffstown, doc date 1774, judgment, debt, file #704

SARGENT Paul Dudley, of Amherst, doc date 1772, license, tavern license, file #851

SARGENT Paul Dudley, esquire, of Sullivan, vs TUTTLE Nathan, yeoman, of Lyndeborough, doc date 1799, debt, file #493

SARGENT Paul Dudley, merchant, of Amherst, vs FRYE Israel, yeoman, of Wilton, doc date 1774, writ, debt, file #1075

SARGENT Paul Dudley, merchant, of Amherst, vs ABBOTT Ephraim, yeoman, of Deering, doc date 1774, writ, debt, file #1075

SARGENT Paul Dudley, merchant, of Amherst, vs FRYE Isaac, yeoman, of Wilton, doc date 1774, execution, file #980

SARGENT Paul Dudley, merchant, of Amherst, vs POPE William, yeoman, of Hillsborough, doc date 1773, judgment, debt, file #1296

SARGENT Paul Dudley, merchant, of Amherst, vs TUTTLE Nathan, yeoman, of Amherst, rec date 1784, judgment, debt, file #4267

SARGENT Paul Dudley, merchant, of Amherst, vs FRY Isaac, esquire, of Wilton, rec date 1784, writ, debt, file #4638

SARGENT Paul Dudley, esquire, of Salem, vs ODELL Ebenezer, gentleman, of Amherst, doc date 1780, rec date 1781, deed, land transfer, file #6567

SARTEL Ephraim, gentleman, of Townsend MA, vs CHAMBERS William, gentleman, of Mason, doc date 1784, execution, debt, file #1667

SARTEL Ephraim, gentleman, of Townsend MA, vs CHAMBERS William, gentleman, of Mason, doc date 1784, execution, debt, file #1731

SARTELL Ephraim, gentleman, of MA, vs CHAMBERS Will, of Mason, doc date 1784, writ, debt, file #1273

SAUNDERS James, husbandman, of Salem, vs HILL Samuel, yeoman, of Goffstown, doc date 1784, execution, debt, file #1863

SAUNDERS James, of Salem, vs WHITTLE Thomas Jr, yeoman, of Litchfield, rec date 1783, writ, debt, file #3956

SAUNDERS James, husbandman, of Salem, vs HAZELTINE Asa, husbandman, of Derryfield, rec date 1785, writ, debt, file #4789

SAUNDERS Joshua & Sarah, of Fisherfield, vs AYERS William, yeoman, of Hillsborough, doc date 1799, deed, land transfer, file #1990

SAUNDERS Oliver, husbandman, of Alexandria, vs PEABODY William, husbandman, of Amherst, rec date 1784, judgment, debt, file #4362

SAVAGE John, yeoman, of Lyndeborough, vs HERRICK Joseph, yeoman, of Lyndeborough, rec date 1783, judgment, debt, file #4319

SAWLAW David, yeoman, of Litchfield, vs HERVEY Joseph, yeoman, of Londonderry, rec date 1784, writ, debt, file #4783, 1

SAWTELL Nathaniel, husbandman, of Pepperell MA, vs MOSHERS James, husbandman, of Hollis, doc date 1784, execution, debt, file #1819

SAWTELL Obadiah, gentleman, of Shirley MA, vs PRATT Thomas, feltmaker, of Hollis, rec date 1784, judgment, debt, file #5315

SAWTELL Obadiah, gentleman, of Shirley MA, vs PRATT Thomas, feltmaker, of Hollis, rec date 1785, judgment, debt, file #5442

SAWYER David, trader, of Goffstown, vs McCLURE Joseph, yeoman, of Francestown, rec date 1789, judgment, debt, file #2577

SAWYER David, trader, of Goffstown, vs BOYES William, gentleman, of New Boston, rec date 1787, writ, debt, file #6670

SAWYER David, trader, of Goffstown, vs GILMORE James, yeoman, of Bedford, rec date 1788, writ, debt, file #6687

SAWYER David, of Goffstown, vs RUSSELL James, yeoman, of Hillsborough, rec date 1788, writ, debt, file #6919

SAWYER Ebenezer, husbandman, of Nottingham, vs GLOVER Robert, cordwainer, of Nottingham, doc date 1799, debt, file #492

SAWYER Edmund, apothecary, of Newbury MA, vs HALE Samuel, physician, of Pepperell MA, rec date 1783, judgment, debt, file #2858

SAWYER Edmund, apothecary, of Newbury MA, vs HALE Samuel, of Pepperell MA, rec date 1783, execution, debt, file #3063

SAWYER Enoch, husbandman, of Goffstown, vs HADLEY George, gentleman, of Weare, rec date 1783, writ, debt, file #3343

SAWYER Enoch, gentleman, of Goffstown, vs ROLF Stephen, yeoman, of Reading MA, rec date 1785, judgment, debt, file #5984

SAWYER Enoch, gentleman, of Goffstown, vs ROAFF Stephen, yeoman, of Reading MA, rec date 1785, writ, debt, file #6026

SAWYER James, yeoman, of Dunstable, vs READ Timothy, husbandman, of Dunstable, doc date 1771, judgment, assault, file #699

SAWYER James, yeoman, of Dunstable, vs KIMBALL Samuel, yeoman, of Boxford MA, doc date 1773, writ, land dispute, file #1241

SAWYER James, yeoman, of Dunstable, vs BLANCHARD Thomas, husbandman, of Dunstable, doc date 1772, writ, debt, file #1411

SAWYER John, shopkeeper, of Haverhill MA, vs SMITH William Jr, husbandman, of Salem, doc date 1774, judgment, debt, file #702

SAWYER John (Capt), gentleman, of Almsbury MA, vs HOGG James, yeoman, of Dunbarton, doc date 1778, rec date 1779, deed, land transfer, file #2144

SAWYER Jonathan, yeoman, of Hancock, vs STEARNS John, yeoman, of Amherst, rec date 1785, execution, debt, file #5483

SAWYER Jonathan, yeoman, of Hancock, vs RUSSELL James, gentleman, of Litchfield, rec date 1783, execution, debt, file #3883

SAWYER Jonathan, yeoman, of Hancock, vs BUSSEL James, gentleman, of Litchfield, rec date 1782, execution, debt, file #4892

SAWYER Jonathan, yeoman, of Hancock, vs HADLEY Seth, gentleman, of Hancock, doc date 1796, various, debt, file #555

SAWYER Jonathan, husbandman, of Hancock, vs ASTEN Thomas, husbandman, of Raby, rec date 1785, writ, debt, file #5831

SAWYER Nathaniel, yeoman, of Milton, vs BOUTEL Amos, yeoman, of Amherst, doc date 1782, execution, file #1021

SAWYER Nathaniel, yeoman, of Wilton, vs MEANS Robert, trader, of Amherst, doc date 1784, court case, debt, file #1606

SAWYER Nathaniel, yeoman, of Wilton, vs PATTERSON Adam, yeoman, of Hancock, doc date 1784, court case, debt, file #1606

SAWYER Nathaniel, yeoman, of Wilton, vs MEANS Robert, yeoman, of Hancock, rec date 1783, writ, debt, file #2337, trustee of Adam PATTERSON

SAWYER Nathaniel, yeoman, of Wilton, vs MEANS Robert, trader, of Amherst, rec date 1784, various, debt, file #4600

SAWYER Nathaniel, yeoman, of Wilton, vs MEANS Robert, trader, of Amherst, rec date 1785, various, debt, file #4840, trustee of Adam PATTERSON

SAWYER Samuel, husbandman, of Antrim, vs STARK John Jr, esquire, of Derryfield, doc date 1798, judgment, debt, file #566

SAYER Nathaniel Peaslee, esquire, of Haverhill MA, vs DOW Joseph, yeoman, of Goffstown, doc date 1774, execution, file #1149

SCOBEY David, husbandman, of Francestown, vs BARTLETT Jacob, yeoman, of Deering, doc date 1799, writ, debt, file #407

SCOBY David, yeoman, of Francestown, vs BALDWIN Nahum, esquire, of Amherst, rec date 1782, appeal, debt, file #3986

SCOBY Joseph, of Merrimack, vs INHABITANTS of Merrimack, rec date 1783, execution, debt, file #3064

SCOTT Alexander, yeoman, of Monadnock #1, vs LUTWYCHE Edward Y, esquire, of Merrimack, doc date 1772, civil litigation, debt, file #658

SCOTT Alexander Jr, husbandman, of Stoddard, vs WHITCOMB Samuel, husbandman, of Peterborough, rec date 1785, judgment, debt, file #5528

SCOTT Rosanna, spinster, of Peterborough, vs LITTLE Thomas, yeoman, of Peterborough, doc date 1784, execution, debt, file #1961

SCOTT William, of Amherst, vs PARKER Samuel, trader, of Pepperell MA, doc date 1799, petition, release of debit, file #26

SCOTT William, yeoman, of Peterborough, vs McCLENCHE Joseph, yeoman, of Londonderry, doc date 1784, execution, debt, file #1715

SCOTT William, yeoman, of Peterborough, vs McCLENCHE Joseph, yeoman, of Londonderry, doc date 1784, execution, debt, file #1496

SCOTT William, esquire, of Groton MA, vs HALE Paul, gentleman, of Peterborough, doc date 1784, execution, debt, file #1733

SCOTT William, yeoman, of Peterborough, vs BLANCHARD Joseph, esquire, of Amherst, rec date 1785, judgment, debt, file #2443

SCOTT William, of Amherst?, vs FERGUSON Sarah, rec date 1777, deposition, debt, file #2223

SCOTT William, rec date 1779, deposition, land dispute, file #2236B

SCOTT William, yeoman, of Peterborough, vs BLANCHARD Joseph, esquire, of Amherst, rec date 1787, judgment, debt, file #2318

SCOTT William, of Amherst?, vs MORRISON John, rec date 1777, deposition, debt, file #2223

SCOTT William, esquire, of Groton MA, vs HALE Paul, gentleman, of Peterborough, rec date 1783, writ, debt, file #4070

SCOTT William, yeoman, of Peterborough, vs BLANCHARD Jotham, gentleman, of Peterborough, rec date 1784, writ, debt, file #4575

SCOTT William, yeoman, of Peterborough, vs CUNNINGHAM Samuel, gentleman, of Peterborough, rec date 1786, execution, debt, file #5878

SCOTT William, esquire, of Groton MA, vs BLUNT Samuel, yeoman, of Chester, rec date 1785, writ, debt, file #6250

SCOTT William, husbandman, of Peterborough, vs MOORE John, gentleman, of Peterborough, rec date 1788, writ, debt, file #6921

SCOTT William, husbandman, of Peterborough, vs LITTLE Thomas, husbandman, of Peterborough, rec date 1788, writ, debt, file #6920

SCOTT William Jr, yeoman, of Peterborough, vs BLANCHARD Jotham, gentleman, of Peterborough, rec date 1785, various, debt, file #4830

SCRIBNER Samuel, husbandman, of Salisbury, vs WEBSTER Benjamin, husbandman, of Boscawen, rec date 1785, judgment, debt, file #5196

SCRIPTURE John, laborer, of Mason, vs WHITE Hannah, single woman, of Mason, rec date 1788, various, illegitimate child, file #3554

SCRIPTURE Samuel, yeoman, of Mason, vs SPRAGUE John, of Lancaster MA, doc date 1774, writ, debt, file #1079, very fragile

SCRIPTURE Samuel, yeoman, of Mason, vs SMITH Nathaniel, yeoman, of Mason, doc date 1772, execution, file #1195

SCRIPTURE Samuel, yeoman, of Mason, vs FARMER Benjamin, cooper, of Hollis, doc date 1773, writ, debt, file #1440

SCRIPTURE Samuel, yeoman, of Mason, vs CUTLER James, shopkeeper, of Groton MA, doc date 1772, writ, debt, file #1430

SEARLESS John, yeoman, of Dunstable, vs DAVIDSON Francis, yeoman, of Dunstable, rec date 1783, writ, debt, file #3328

SEARS John, trader, of Chester, vs CALDWELL Thomas, gentleman, of Dunbarton, rec date 1783, judgment, imprisonment, file #2863

SEATON Andrew, carpenter, of Hancock, vs AMES David, trader, of Hancock, doc date 1799, various, debt, file #430

SEATON Andrew, yeoman, of Amherst, vs HILDRETH William, yeoman, of Litchfield, rec date 1786, judgment, debt, file #5462

SEAVEY John, cordwainer, of Nottingham-West, vs CALDWELL John, yeoman, of Nottingham-West, doc date 1784, execution, debt, file #1977

SEIRSE James, yeoman, of Deerfield, vs BAYES James, yeoman, of Londonderry, rec date 1782, writ, delivery question, file #2807

SENTER John, husbandman, of Litchfield, vs SMITH John, yeoman, of Lyndeborough, doc date 1772, writ, debt, file #899

SENTER Levi, yeoman, doc date 1782, judgment, for profanity, file #1659

SENTER Moses, gentleman, of Deerfield, vs LUTWYCHE Edward, esquire, of Merrimack, doc date 1772, writ, debt, file #887

SENTER Moses, husbandman, of Litchfield, vs McNEIL Daniel, gentleman, of Derryfield, doc date 1771, writ, debt, file #794

SENTER Samuel, husbandman, of Londonderry, vs STATE of NH, rec date 1777, recognizance, counterfeiting, file #2253

SENTER Samuel, yeoman, of Litchfield, vs MONTGOMERY Hugh, innkeeper, of Francestown, rec date 1783, judgment, debt, file #4434

SENTER Simeon, yeoman, doc date 1782, judgment, for profanity, file #1659

SENTER Simeon, yeoman, doc date 1782, judgment, for profanity, file #1659

SENTER Simeon, yeoman, of Litchfield, vs SENTER Abel, husbandman, of Litchfield, doc date 1781, rec date 1786, deed, land transfer, file #5555

SENTER Thomas, yeoman, of Dunstable, vs PEOPLE of NH, doc date 1776, rec date 1777, jurors verdict, debt, file #2206

SENTER Thomas, husbandman, of Londonderry, vs STATE of NH, rec date 1776, recognizance, counterfeiting, file #2247

SERNED Ebenezer, physician, of Hopkinton, vs MARCH Moses, physician, of Gilmanton, doc date 1798, execution, debt, file #151

SERVICE Robert, mariner, of Boston MA, vs HASKELL Abel, yeoman, of Merrimack, rec date 1785, judgment, debt, file #4951

SERVICE Robert, mariner, of Boston MA, vs McCLENCHE John, blacksmith, of Merrimack, rec date 1785, judgment, debt, file #4972

SERVICE Robert, merchant, of Boston MA, vs WINCHESTER Lemuel, yeoman, of Amherst, rec date 1785, judgment, debt, file #6491

SERVICE Robert, mariner, of Boston MA, vs McCLENCHE John, blacksmith, of Merrimack, rec date 1785, judgment, debt, file #6408

SERVICE Robert, merchant, of Boston MA, vs BRADFORD Samuel Jr, gentleman, of Hillsborough, rec date 1785, judgment, debt, file #6400

SESSIONS David, cordwainer, of Derryfield, vs YOUNG Israel, yeoman, of Derryfield, rec date 1788, writ, land deed?, file #2566, d session deceased

SEVERANCE Benjamin, yeoman, of Boscawen, vs HARVEY John, husbandman, of Fisherfield, rec date 1786, writ, debt, file #6287

SEVERANCE Caleb, yeoman, of Francestown, vs ROLF Jesse, trader, of Francestown, doc date 1783, rec date 1783, deed, land transfer, file #2646

SEWALL John, prisoner, of Peterborough, rec date 1786, recognizance, prison break, file #7044

SEWALL Rachel, of Amherst, vs SEWALL Thomas, yeoman, of Amherst, rec date 1786, petition, divorce, file #6070

SEWEL Rachel, seamstress, of Lyndeborough, vs JONES Jeremiah, of Lyndeborough, doc date 1788, rec date 1788, deed, land transfer, file #6760

SEWELL Thomas, yeoman, of Amherst, vs GRIMES James, yeoman, of Deering, rec date 1785, execution, debt, file #5479

SEWELL Thomas, laborer, of Amherst, vs ROBERTSON Alexander, yeoman, of Deering, rec date 1785, judgment, debt, file #5067

SHAMMON Richard C, esquire, of Raby, vs NEWHALL Oliver, husbandman, of Pepperell MA, doc date 1792, various, trespass, file #552

SHAMMON Richard Cutts, esquire, of Hollis, vs BIXBE Andrew, husbandman, of Hillsborough, rec date 1785, judgment, debt, file #5154

SHANNON Richard C, husbandman, of Hollis, vs STATE of NH, rec date 1777, recognizance, forgery, file #2211

SHANNON Richard C, esquire, of Hollis, vs DICKEY Elias, husbandman, of Raby, rec date 1783, execution, debt, file #3847

SHANNON Richard C, esquire, of Hollis, vs WHITTEMORE Samuel, gentleman, of Cambridge, rec date 1785, judgment, land dispute, file #5358

SHANNON Richard C, esquire, of Hollis, vs DICKEY Rosanna, widow, of Raby, rec date 1785, writ, debt, file #5433

SHANNON Richard C, esquire, of Hollis, vs HUTCHINSON Samuel, husbandman, of Lyndeborough, rec date 1785, judgment, debt, file #6047

SHANNON Richard C, esquire, of Hollis, vs GOULD Jacob, husbandman, of Rindge, rec date 1786, writ, debt, file #6129

SHANNON Richard Cutts, esquire, of Hollis, vs HOGG Alexander, husbandman, of Deering, rec date 1783, writ, debt, file #3413

SHANNON Richard Cutt, esquire, of Hollis, vs SEARLE John, yeoman, of Dunstable, rec date 1787, writ, debt, file #6651

SHANNON Richard Cutts, esquire, of Hollis, vs HOGG Alexander, husbandman, of Deering, doc date 1784, execution, debt, file #1775

SHANNON Richard Cutts, esquire, of Hollis, vs GREEN David, husbandman, of Hillsborough, doc date 1784, execution, debt, file #1764

SHANNON Richard Cutts, esquire, of Hollis, vs McINTOCH John, husbandman, of Bedford, doc date 1784, execution, debt, file #1759

SHANNON Richard Cutts, esquire, of Hollis, vs ATWILL John, joiner, of Hollis, rec date 1786, judgment, debt, file #2303

SHANNON Richard Cutts, esquire, of Hollis, vs HODGMAN John, husbandman, of Mason, rec date 1782, judgment, debt, file #2708

SHANNON Richard Cutts, esquire, of Hollis, vs DICKEY Elias, husbandman, of Raby, rec date 1782, writ, debt, file #2693

SHANNON Richard Cutts, esquire, of Hollis, vs TARBOX James, tailor, of Dunstable MA, rec date 1783, judgment, debt, file #3767

SHANNON Richard Cutts, esquire, of Hollis, vs DAKIN Justus, husbandman, of Nottingham-West, rec date 1783, judgment, debt, file #3766

SHANNON Richard Cutts, esquire, of Hollis, vs JONES Timothy, husbandman, of Lyndeborough, rec date 1783, judgment, debt, file #4037

SHANNON Richard Cutts, esquire, of Hollis, vs FLAGG Eleazer, carpenter, of Hollis, rec date 1784, judgment, debt, file #4209

SHANNON Richard Cutts, esquire, of Hollis, vs BIXBE Andrew, husbandman, of Hillsborough, rec date 1783, writ, debt, file #4528

SHANNON Richard Cutts, esquire, of Hollis, vs DONOVAN Matthew, schoolmaster, of Canterbury, rec date 1784, judgment, debt, file #4620

SHANNON Richard Cutts, esquire, of Hollis, vs STEVENS Calvin, husbandman, of Hillsborough, rec date 1783, writ, debt, file #4526

SHANNON Richard Cutts, esquire, of Hollis, vs KILLICUT Reuben, husbandman, of Dunstable, rec date 1783, writ, debt, file #4529

SHANNON Richard Cutts, esquire, of Hollis, vs TAGGART Archibald, gentleman, of Hillsborough, rec date 1783, writ, debt, file #4527

SHANNON Richard Cutts, esquire, of Hollis, vs MOSHER James, husbandman, of Hollis, rec date 1784, judgment, debt, file #5002

SHANNON Richard Cutts, esquire, of Hollis, vs WAITE John, husbandman, of Mason, rec date 1785, execution, debt, file #5949

SHANNON Richard Cutts, esquire, of Hollis, vs HUTCHINSON Samuel, husbandman, of Lyndeborough, rec date 1785, judgment, debt, file #5818

SHANNON Richard Cutts, esquire, of Hollis, vs BOYTON Isaac, cordwainer, of Hollis, rec date 1785, execution, debt, file #5950

SHANNON Richard Cutts, esquire, of Hollis, vs BOYNTON Isaac, cordwainer, of Hollis, rec date 1785, writ, debt, file #6030

SHANNON Richard Cutts, esquire, of Raby, vs BLOOD Francis, husbandman, of Hollis, rec date 1788, writ, debt, file #6675

SHANNON Richard Cutts, esquire, of Raby, vs JEWETT Benoni, husbandman, of Dunstable, rec date 1788, writ, debt, file #6621

SHANNON Richard Cutts, esquire, of Raby, vs CUNNINGHAM Samuel, yeoman, of Peterborough, rec date 1788, writ, debt, file #6913

SHANNON Richard Cutts, esquire, of Raby, vs KENNY Israel, husbandman, of Hollis, rec date 1788, writ, debt, file #6912

SHANNOPN Richard Cutts, esquire, of Raby, vs LOVE William, husbandman, of Hillsborough, rec date 1787, writ, debt, file #2372

SHATTUCK Edmund, husbandman, of Cockermouth, vs WRIGHT David, cordwainer, of Hollis, rec date 1783, judgment, debt, file #3769

SHATTUCK Edmund, gentleman, of Cockermouth, vs McDANIEL James Jr, laborer, of Hollis, rec date 1784, writ, debt, file #4974

SHATTUCK Job, gentleman, of Groton MA, vs TARBELL Edmund, husbandman, of Mason, rec date 1784, judgment, debt, file #4659

SHATTUCK William, husbandman, of Deering, vs RIDEOUT Nathaniel, yeoman, of Hollis, doc date 1784, execution, debt, file #1982

SHATTUCK William, husbandman, of Deering, vs RIDEOUT Nathaniel, yeoman, of Hollis, doc date 1784, execution, debt, file #1872

SHATTUCK William, husbandman, of Deering, vs WRIGHT David, cordwainer, of Hollis, rec date 1783, judgment, debt, file #3763

SHAW Benjamin, gentleman, of Pembroke, vs MOOR Samuel, yeoman, of Bedford, rec date 1784, writ, debt, file #4582

SHAW Jonathan, gentleman, of Hopkinton, vs CHASE Wells, husbandman, of Hopkinton, rec date 1783, judgment, debt, file #3746

SHEA William, cordwainer, of Mason, vs LAWRENCE Isaac Jr, blacksmith, of Dunstable MA, rec date 1784, judgment, debt, file #4235

SHEBURN Samuel, husbandman, of Greenfield, vs PARKER Samuel, yeoman, of Greenfield, doc date 1800, writ, debt, file #575

SHED Daniel, husbandman, of Hollis, vs GRAHAM William, husbandman, of
   Amherst, rec date 1783, writ, debt, file #3417
SHED James, yeoman, of Antrim, vs MANIS Simon, miner, of Haverhill MA, rec
   date 1785, writ, debt, file #5431, estate of Jonathan WEBSTER
SHED John, yeoman, of Hollis, vs COBBET Isaac, clothier, of Hollis, doc date
   1800, judgment, debt, file #568
SHED Joseph, gentleman, of Groton MA, vs BROWN William, husbandman, of
   Hollis, rec date 1785, judgment, debt, file #5168
SHEDD Albert, of Nashua, vs CITY of Nashua, doc date 1893, plaintiff brief,
   supreme court, file #608
SHELDEN Abraham, yeoman, of Temple, vs ABBOTT Joseph, shopkeeper, of
   Wilton, rec date 1783, judgment, debt, file #4054
SHELDEN Jeremiah, trader, of Danvers MA, vs ABBOTT Benjamin, yeoman, of
   Hollis, rec date 1783, writ, debt, file #3633
SHELDON Ezra, husbandman, of Temple, vs FELT Benjamin, husbandman, of
   Temple, rec date 1785, judgment, debt, file #5093
SHELDON Jeremiah, trader, of Danvers MA, vs ABBOTT Benjamin, yeoman, of
   Hollis, doc date 1784, execution, debt, file #1942
SHELDON John, yeoman, of Danvers MA, vs WEBSTER Joseph, husbandman,
   of Atkinson, rec date 1783, judgment, debt, file #4713
SHEPARD Benjamin, yeoman, of Amherst, vs STRATTON Lewis, joiner, of
   Amherst, doc date 1799, writ, debt, file #575
SHEPARD Daniel, husbandman, of Boscawen, vs FLANDERS John Jr,
   husbandman, of Boscawen, rec date 1783, writ, debt, file #4536
SHEPARD Daniel, husbandman, of Northfield, vs CARR David, husbandman, of
   Boscawen, rec date 1786, writ, debt, file #6276
SHEPARD Daniel & Mary, of Boscawen, vs SHEPARD Thomas, of Boscawen,
   doc date 1774, rec date 1788, deed, land transfer, file #6745
SHEPARD John, esquire, of Nottingham, vs NEAL John, yeoman, of Merrimack,
   doc date 1772, writ, debt, file #913
SHEPARD John, esquire, of Amherst, vs KARR James, esquire, of Goffstown,
   doc date 1774, recognizance, debt, file #1153
SHEPARD John, of Portsmouth, doc date 1770, deposition, file #1186
SHEPARD John, esquire, of Soughean West, vs FULLER Timothy, of Middleton
   MA, doc date 1784, deed, land transfer, file #2003
SHEPARD John, esquire, of Amherst, vs POLLARD Samuel, yeoman, of
   Nottingham-West, rec date 1783, execution, debt, file #2982
SHEPARD John, esquire, of Amherst, vs WILKINS Bray, yeoman, of Hollis, doc
   date 1774, judgment, debt, file #737
SHEPARD John, esquire/deceased, of Amherst, rec date 1787, writ, debt, file
   #6658
SHEPARD John, esquire, of Amherst, rec date 1788, writ, debt, file #6622
SHEPARD John, esquire, of Amherst, vs MURDOUGH Samuel, yeoman, of
   Hillsborough, rec date 1788, writ, debt, file #6628
SHEPARD John, esquire, of Amherst, vs WHITE John & Charles, yeoman, of
   Peterborough, rec date 1787, writ, debt, file #6897

SHEPARD John, esquire, of Amherst, vs WHITE John, yeoman, of Peterborough, rec date 1786, writ, debt, file #6883

SHEPARD John, esquire, of Amherst, vs JONES Caleb, yeoman, of Mile Slip, rec date 1786, writ, debt, file #6879

SHEPARD John, esquire, of Amherst, vs GEARFIELD Nathaniel, gentleman, of Merrimack, rec date 1785, writ, debt, file #6859

SHEPARD John, esquire, of Amherst, vs BRADFORD William, yeoman, of Deering, rec date 1786, writ, debt, file #6878

SHEPARD John, esquire, of Amherst, vs BETTEY William, yeoman, of Wilton, rec date 1786, writ, debt, file #6879

SHEPARD John Jr, esquire, of Salem MA, vs GARDNER Samuel & Benjamin, yeoman, of Amherst, doc date 1773, judgment, debt, file #822

SHEPARD John Jr, esquire, of Amherst, vs STEARNS Samuel, yeoman, of Amherst, doc date 1773, writ, debt, file #1176

SHEPARD John Jr, yeoman, of New Boston, vs BROWN Alexander, peddler, of Amherst, doc date 1773, writ, debt, file #1175

SHEPARD John Jr, esquire, of Amherst, vs GREEN David, yeoman, of Hillsborough, doc date 1784, execution, debt, file #1753

SHEPARD John Jr, esquire, of Amherst, vs BRADFORD Joseph, husbandman, of Amherst, doc date 1771, rec date 1779, deed, land transfer, file #2125

SHEPARD John Jr, esquire, of Amherst, vs TAGGART Archibald, yeoman, of Hillsborough, rec date 1785, writ, debt, file #6862

SHEPARD Jonathan, yeoman, of Amherst, vs STEPHENSON John, husbandman, of Lyndeborough, doc date 1799, writ, debt, file #575

SHEPARD Joseph, gentleman, of New Holderness, vs GREGG David, husbandman, of Francestown, rec date 1785, judgment, debt, file #5164

SHEPARD Joseph, gentleman, of New Holderness, vs GREGG David, husbandman, of Francestown, rec date 1785, judgment, debt, file #5363

SHEPARD Jotham, yeoman, of Amherst, vs RICHARDSON Zachariah, yeoman, of Francestown, rec date 1786, judgment, debt, file #5752

SHEPARD Samuel, husbandman, of Amherst, vs KELLEY Joseph, husbandman, of Nottingham, doc date 1784, court case, salt delivery, file #1858

SHEPARD Samuel, husbandman, of Amherst, vs KELLEY Joseph, gentleman, of Nottingham-West, rec date 1783, various, debt, file #4515, fragile

SHEPARD Samuel Lt, of Amherst, license, tavern license, file #875

SHEPARD Sarah, widow/administrator of estate, of Amherst, vs RICHARDSON Thomas, yeoman, of Peterborough, rec date 1786, writ, debt, file #6889

SHEPARD Sarah, widow/administrator of estate, of Amherst, vs LYON John, husbandman, of Deering, rec date 1786, writ, debt, file #6876, estate of John SHEPARD (deceased)

SHEPARD Sarah, widow, of Amherst, vs FRENCH William, yeoman, of Hollis, rec date 1786, writ, debt, file #6873

SHEPARD Sarah, widow, of Amherst, vs JONES Caleb, yeoman, of Mile Slip, rec date 1787, writ, debt, file #6658

SHEPARD Sarah, widow, of Amherst, vs BETTEY William, yeoman, of Wilton, rec date 1787, writ, debt, file #6658

SHEPARD Thomas, yeoman, of Boscawen, vs SHEPARD Daniel, yeoman, of Boscawen, doc date 1774, rec date 1788, deed, land transfer, file #6759

SHEPLE Mussey, husbandman, of Hollis, vs MUSSEY John, physician, of Amherst, doc date 1799, writ, debt, file #573

SHERBURN John, esquire, of Portsmouth, vs GOFFE John, esquire, of Derryfield, rec date 1785, writ, debt, file #4811

SHERBURN Samuel, esquire, of Portsmouth, vs MITCHELL Isaac, husbandman, of Peterborough, rec date 1788, deed, transfer of land, file #6722

SHERBURNE John, esquire, of Portsmouth, vs GOODELL David, husbandman, of Hillsborough, rec date 1786, judgment, debt, file #2304

SHERTLEFT Simeon Lt, of Dunstable, doc date 1787, license, tavern license, file #870

SHEWS Thimbly, yeoman, of Hillsborough, vs TOWN of Hillsborough, rec date 1783, petition, abatement of tax, file #3502

SHIELS Obner, yeoman, of Wilton, vs BROWN James, gentleman, of Moultonborough, rec date 1776, writ, debt, file #2197

SHIPLE Oliver, cordwainer, of New Boston, vs HALE Caleb Jr, husbandman, of Goffstown, rec date 1786, judgment, debt, file #6202

SHIPLE Oliver, cordwainer, of New Boston, vs LITTLE David, husbandman, of Goffstown, rec date 1786, judgment, debt, file #6202

SHIPLEY Jonathan, yeoman, of Peterborough, vs BLANCHARD Jotham, merchant, of Peterborough, rec date 1784, judgment, debt, file #4409

SHIRLA Thomas, yeoman, of Goffstown, vs DUSTON Paul, yeoman, of New Boston, doc date 1779, writ, debt, file #2097

SHIRLA Thomas, husbandman, of Goffstown, vs CRAIGE David, gentleman, of Londonderry, rec date 1785, judgment, debt, file #5101

SHIRLA Thomas, husbandman, of Goffstown, vs CHAPMAN John, husbandman, of Londonderry, rec date 1785, judgment, debt, file #5101

SHIRLEY Samuel, husbandman, of Goffstown, vs HALL John, gentleman, of Deerfield, rec date 1783, execution, debt, file #3696

SHIRLEY Samuel, yeoman, of Goffstown, vs WOOD Jonathan, husbandman, of Goffstown, rec date 1783, judgment, debt, file #3722

SHURTLEFF Jonathan, gentleman, of Merrimack, vs MARTIN Peter, husbandman, of Andover MA, rec date 1784, writ, debt, file #4413, kinship to Simeon SHURTLEFF

SHURTLEFF Jonathan, gentleman, of Merrimack, vs FISHER Samuel, yeoman, of Londonderry, rec date 1783, writ, debt, file #3967

SHURTLEFF Jonathan Jr, trader, of Merrimack, vs DUTTON John, yeoman, of Amherst, rec date 1785, execution, debt, file #5778

SHURTLEFF Simeon, trader, of Dunstable, vs HOBART Jacob, laborer, of Hollis, rec date 1786, writ, debt, file #2413

SHURTLEFF Simeon, trader, of Dunstable, vs BROWN Joseph, laborer, of Hollis, rec date 1787, judgment, debt, file #2477

SHURTLEFF Simeon, gentleman, of Merrimack, vs FISHER Samuel, yeoman, of Londonderry, rec date 1783, writ, debt, file #3967

SHURTLETT Simeon, trader, of Dunstable, vs SHURTLETT Jotham, trader, of Merrimack, rec date 1786, writ, debt, file #6132

SILLY John, husbandman, of Andover, vs CHANDLER Joseph, gentleman, of Andover, rec date 1783, writ, debt, file #3218

SILVER David, husbandman, of Dunbarton, vs STARK James, husbandman, of Dunbarton, doc date 1797, various, debt, file #556

SIMONDS Daniel, cordwainer, of Francestown, vs BALCH William, tanner, of Francestown, doc date 1816, rec date 1816, judgment, debt, file #5702

SIMONDS Daniel, cordwainer, of Francestown, vs DOWNS Amasa, tanner, of Francestown, doc date 1816, rec date 1816, deed, land transfer, file #5702

SIMONDS Daniel Jr, yeoman, of Amherst, vs BELL John, cooper, of Billerica MA, doc date 1780, rec date 1785, deed, land transfer, file #5631

SIMONDS Josiah, yeoman, of Chelmsford MA, vs WILSON Jesse, yeoman, of Amherst, rec date 1784, judgment, debt, file #4329

SIMONDS Josiah, yeoman, of Chelmsford MA, vs HAYWOOD Samuel Smith, husbandman, of Nottingham-West, rec date 1782, judgment, debt, file #2745

SIMPSON Alexander, husbandman, of Bow, vs DRESSER Asa, husbandman, of Campbells Gore, rec date 1785, writ, debt, file #6033

SKIFFINGTON John, yeoman, of Albany NY, vs POLLARD John Jr, husbandman, of Nottingham-West, doc date 1784, execution, debt, file #1904

SKIFFINGTON John, yeoman, of Albany NY, vs POLLARD John Jr, husbandman, of Nottingham-West, rec date 1783, writ, debt, file #3595

SLEEPER Benjamin, gentleman, of Francestown, vs HUTCHASON Samuel, husbandman, of Lyndeborough, rec date 1787, judgment, debt, file #2313

SLEEPER Samuel, vs WEST Nathaniel, blacksmith, of Hallestown, doc date 1761, rec date 1779, deed, land transfer, file #2128

SLEEPER Thomas, yeoman, of Andover, vs CHANDLER Joseph, gentleman, of Andover, doc date 1784, execution, debt, file #1704

SLEEPER Thomas, yeoman, of Andover, vs CHANDLER Joseph, gentleman, of Andover, rec date 1783, judgment, debt, file #4087

SLOAN David, husbandman, of Mason, vs HOSLEY Samuel, physician, of Townsend MA, doc date 1784, writ, debt, file #1578

SMALL Jonathan, yeoman, of Goffstown, vs LOW Jonathan, yeoman, of Goffstown, rec date 1787, writ, debt, file #6788

SMALL Joseph, yeoman, of Amherst, vs SPRAGUE John, esquire, of Lancaster MA, doc date 1774, writ, debt, file #1093

SMALL Joseph, husbandman, of Amherst, vs CUTLER Jemima, widow, of Groton MA, rec date 1783, writ, debt, file #3947, kinship Jonas CUTLER

SMALL Joseph, husbandman, of Amherst, vs PATTINGILL Moses, yeoman, of Lyndeborough, rec date 1784, search warrant, stolen goods, file #5716

SMITH Abijah, gentleman, of New Ipswich, vs WHITING Jonas, yeoman, of New Ipswich, rec date 1785, judgment, debt, file #5097

SMITH Asa, yeoman, of MA, vs BURT Simeon, yeoman, of Jaffrey, rec date 1783, writ, debt, file #4539

SMITH Asa, yeoman, of MA, vs SPOFFORD Eleazer, yeoman, of Jaffrey, rec date 1783, writ, debt, file #4539

SMITH Benjamin, yeoman, of Bedford, vs BURNS John, yeoman, of Amherst, rec date 1782, writ, debt, file #2793

SMITH David, housewright, of Hollis, vs BLOOD William, yeoman, of Dunstable, doc date 1801, judgment, debt, file #568

SMITH David, yeoman, of Lyndeborough, vs ATWELL John, innkeeper, of Hollis, doc date 1784, execution, debt, file #1676

SMITH David, yeoman, of Lyndeborough, vs ATWELL John, innkeeper, of Hollis, doc date 1784, execution, debt, file #1713

SMITH David, yeoman, of Lyndeborough, vs LOWELL John, innkeeper, of Hollis, rec date 1783, execution, debt, file #3693

SMITH David, yeoman, of Lyndeborough, vs ATWELL John, innkeeper, of Hollis, doc date 1784, execution, debt, file #1495

SMITH Edward, yeoman, of Sharon, vs PRESCOTT Abel, yeoman, of Westford MA, doc date 1799, writ, debt, file #403

SMITH Edward, gentleman, of Sharon, vs APPLETON Samuel, merchants, of Boston MA, doc date 1798, execution, debt, file #169

SMITH Edward, yeoman, of Kingston, vs AMES Joseph, esquire, of Newbury MA, doc date 1773, writ, debt, file #1444

SMITH Edward, innkeeper, of Boston MA, vs KELLEY Joseph, gentleman, of Nottingham-West, rec date 1785, various, land dispute, file #4781, very fragile

SMITH Edward, innholder, of Boston MA, vs KELLY Joseph, gentleman, of Nottingham-West, rec date 1785, judgment, debt, file #5367

SMITH Edward, innholder, of Boston MA, vs KELLEY Joseph, gentleman, of Nottingham-West, rec date 1785, court case, debt, file #5244

SMITH Edward, innholder, of Boston MA, vs EATON Joshua, merchant, of Boston MA, rec date 1785, various, debt, file #5246, part of 5244 &5245

SMITH Edward, husbandman, of Boston MA, vs KELLY Joseph, gentleman, of Nottingham-West, rec date 1785, various, debt, file #5245

SMITH Edward, innholder, of Boston MA, vs KELLEY Joseph, husbandman, of Litchfield, rec date 1786, various, debt, file #6077

SMITH Edward, innholder, of Boston MA, vs KELLEY Joseph, gentleman, of Nottingham-West, rec date 1785, various, debt, file #6265

SMITH Edward, of Boston MA, vs DAVIDSON Francis, yeoman, of Dunstable, rec date 1786, writ, debt, file #6279

SMITH Edward, innholder, of Boston MA, vs CLAGETT Wentworth, gentleman, of Litchfield, rec date 1786, various, taking of animal, file #6077

SMITH Edward, gentleman, of Peterboro Slip, vs KELLY Joseph, gentleman, of Nottingham-West, rec date 1787, writ, debt, file #6694

SMITH Edward, rec date 1785, various, file #7040

SMITH Edward, innholder, of Boston MA, vs KELLY Joseph, gentleman, of Nottingham-West, rec date 1785, writ, debt, file #6965

SMITH Elias, clerk, of Middleton MA, vs HALE Enoch, esquire, of Walpole, rec date 1785, writ, debt, file #5344

SMITH Elias, husbandman, of Moultonborough MA, vs STEVENS Asa, of Deighton MA, rec date 1786, judgment, debt, file #6499

SMITH Elias, clerk, of Middleton MA, vs HALE Enoch, esquire, of Walpole, rec date 1788, various, land transfers, file #6587, three folders

SMITH Emerson, gentleman, of Hollis, vs CHAMBERS David, husbandman, of Hollis, rec date 1787, judgment, debt, file #2471

SMITH Hugh, gentleman, of Nottingham-West, vs BUTLER Gideon, yeoman, of Nottingham-West, rec date 1785, judgment, debt, file #5089

SMITH Ichabod, yeoman, of E Sudbury ma, vs NEAL John, trader, of Londonderry, rec date 1785, various, debt, file #4777

SMITH Ichabod, yeoman, of Sudbury MA, vs TRAVIS Asa, yeoman, of Sudbury MA, doc date 1781, rec date 1781, deed, land transfer, file #6799, land Deering

SMITH Isaac, yeoman, of Amherst, vs TUCK Joseph, yeoman, of Amherst, rec date 1785, deed, land transfer, file #5634

SMITH Jacob, yeoman, of Amherst, vs FURBUSH Charles, gentleman, of Andover MA, rec date 1785, judgment, debt, file #5799

SMITH Jacob, yeoman, of Amherst, vs FURBUSH Charles, gentleman, of Andover MA, rec date 1785, judgment, debt, file #5986

SMITH James, taylor, of Hopkinton, vs MITCHEL James, housewright, of Concord, doc date 1777, rec date 1778, deed, land transfer, file #6561

SMITH Jeremiah, gentleman, of Peterborough, vs MELLEN Thomas, husbandman, of Society Land, rec date 1783, judgment, debt, file #2861

SMITH Jeremiah, gentleman, of Peterborough, vs MELLEN Thomas, husbandman, of Society Land, rec date 1783, execution, debt, file #2903

SMITH Jeremiah, gentleman, of Peterborough, vs MELLEN Thomas, husbandman, of Society Land, rec date 1782, appeal, debt, file #4018

SMITH Jeremiah, yeoman, of Nottingham-West, vs CUTTER James, cordwainer, of Nottingham-West, doc date 1814, rec date 1815, deed, land transfer, file #5699

SMITH Joel, yeoman, of Cumberland NY, vs LAWRENCE Zachariah, yeoman, of Hollis, rec date 1783, execution, debt, file #2897

SMITH John, of Amherst, vs HILLSBORO County, doc date 1772, deed, land transfer, file #807, fold 215

SMITH John, yeoman, of Francestown, vs LUND Jesse, yeoman, of Greenfield, doc date 1797, various, debt, file #557

SMITH John, esquire, of Peterborough, vs GRAY William, wheelwright, of Peterborough, doc date 1798, execution, debt, file #75

SMITH John, husbandman, of Lyndeborough, vs HUTCHINS Solomon, yeoman, of Merrimack, doc date 1773, judgment, debt, file #1304

SMITH John, husbandman, of Lyndeborough, vs USHER Robert, yeoman, of Merrimack, doc date 1773, judgment, debt, file #1304

SMITH John, husbandman, of Lyndeborough, vs PEADBODY William, gentleman, of Amherst, rec date 1782, appeal, debt, file #4013

SMITH John, yeoman, of Goffstown, vs GOLDSMITH Josiah, gentleman, of Walpole, rec date 1784, judgment, debt, file #4591

SMITH John, yeoman, of Exeter, vs PRESTON Abner, yeoman, of Hancock, rec date 1785, judgment, debt, file #5267

SMITH John, yeoman, of Goffstown, vs GOLDSMITH Josiah, gentleman, of Walpole, rec date 1785, judgment, debt, file #5113

SMITH John, yeoman, of Goffstown, vs GUILD Daniel, gentleman, of Keene, rec date 1785, writ, debt, file #5335

SMITH John, yeoman, of Exeter, vs PRESTON Abner, yeoman, of Hancock, rec date 1785, judgment, debt, file #6002

SMITH John, husbandman, of New Chester, vs CALL John, husbandman, of Andover, rec date 1785, judgment, debt, file #5811

SMITH John, yeoman, of Peterborough, vs CHENEY Samuel, gentleman, of Londonderry, rec date 1786, writ, debt, file #6306

SMITH John, husbandman, of Peterborough, vs CUNNINGHAM Samuel, gentleman, of Peterborough, rec date 1788, writ, debt, file #6632

SMITH Jonathan, innholder, of Amherst, vs TAGGART James, husbandman, of Hillsborough, rec date 1788, writ, debt, file #2395

SMITH Jonathan, innholder, of Amherst, vs JONES Samuel, husbandman, of Campbells Gore, rec date 1788, writ, debt, file #2396

SMITH Jonathan, innholder, of Amherst, vs BIXBE Andrew, husbandman, of Campbells Gore, rec date 1788, writ, debt, file #2394

SMITH Jonathan, innholder, of Amherst, vs TAGGART Archibald, gentleman, of Hillsborough, rec date 1788, writ, debt, file #2393

SMITH Jonathan, innholder, of Amherst, vs ATHERTON Joshua, esquire, of Amherst, doc date 1774, rec date 1785, deed, land transfer, file #5625

SMITH Jonathan, innholder, of Amherst, vs JONES Samuel, husbandman, of Campbells Gore, rec date 1788, execution, debt, file #5465

SMITH Jonathan, innholder, of Amherst, vs TAGGART Archibald, gentleman, of Hillsborough, rec date 1788, writ, debt, file #5899

SMITH Jonathan, innholder, of Amherst, vs BIXBE Andrew, husbandman, of Campbell Gore, rec date 1788, writ, debt, file #5898

SMITH Jonathan, innholder, of Amherst, vs TAGGART James, husbandman, of Hillsborough, rec date 1788, writ, debt, file #7051

SMITH Jonathan Jr, gentleman, of Amherst, vs HILLSBORO County, bond, deed clerks bond, file #805, years 1790 1796

SMITH Joshua, tanner, of Rulland MA, vs HOLDEN David, husbandman, of Hollis, rec date 1788, writ, debt, file #2553

SMITH Manassah, gentleman, of Hollis, vs BURT Simeon, yeoman, of Jaffrey, doc date 1784, execution, debt, file #1888

SMITH Manassah, gentleman, of Hollis, vs SPAFFORD Eleazer, husbandman, of Jaffrey, rec date 1783, judgment, debt, file #3295

SMITH Manassah, gentleman, of Hollis, vs MOOR Stephen, feltmaker, of Charlestown, rec date 1783, execution, debt, file #3242

SMITH Manassah, gentleman, of Hollis, vs BURT Simeon, yeoman, of Jaffrey, rec date 1783, writ, debt, file #3404

SMITH Manassah, gentleman, of Hollis, vs BURT Simeon, husbandman, of Jaffrey, rec date 1783, judgment, debt, file #3295

SMITH Manassah, gentleman, of Hollis, vs WHITE Jotham, gentleman, of Charlestown, rec date 1783, execution, debt, file #3672

SMITH Manassah, gentleman, of Hollis, vs SPENCER John, yeoman, of Claremont, rec date 1783, execution, debt, file #3655

SMITH Moody, cooper, of Londonderry, vs FOLLANSBEE Moody, husbandman, of Newbury MA, rec date 1782, writ, debt, file #2813

SMITH Moses, husbandman, of Hollis, vs CUMMINGS Philip, joiner, of Peterborough, doc date 1784, execution, debt, file #1790

SMITH Manasseh, gentleman, of Hollis, vs SPAFFORD Eleazer, gentleman, of Hollis, doc date 1784, execution, debt, file #1884

SMITH Mannasseh, gentleman, of Hollis, vs BURT Simon, gentleman, of Hollis, doc date 1784, execution, debt, file #1884

SMITH Nathaniel, yeoman, of Mason, vs SECIPTURE Samuel, yeoman, of Mason, doc date 1772, writ, debt, file #934

SMITH Nathaniel, yeoman, of Mason, vs CHAMPNEY Ebenezer, gentleman, of New Ipswich, doc date 1772, writ, debt, file #928

SMITH Phineas, mariner, of Salem MA, vs HALE David, husbandman, of Cockermouth, rec date 1783, writ, debt, file #3419

SMITH Phineas, mariner, of Salem MA, vs POOL Jonathan, physician, of Hollis, rec date 1783, judgment, debt, file #3768

SMITH Reuben, husbandman, of New Boston, vs WILKINS John, gentleman, of Amherst, doc date 1784, civil litigation, debt, file #1852

SMITH Reuben, husbandman, of New Boston, vs STATE of NH, rec date 1777, recognizance, forgery, file #2211

SMITH Reuben, yeoman, of New Boston, vs STATE of NH, rec date 1779, writ, counterfeiting, file #2238

SMITH Reuben, yeoman, of New Boston, vs LAWRANCE Abel, esquire, of Salem MA, rec date 1782, writ, debt, file #2781

SMITH Reuben, yeoman, of New Boston, vs WALKER Andrew, yeoman, doc date 1777, rec date 1783, deed, land transfer, file #2631

SMITH Reuben, yeoman, of New Boston, vs BALDWIN Nahum, esquire, of Amherst, rec date 1782, various, debt, file #2691, estate of Zacheus CUTLER

SMITH Reuben, yeoman, of New Boston, vs McNEIL Daniel, yeoman, of New Boston, rec date 1782, writ, debt, file #2805

SMITH Reuben, yeoman, of New Boston, vs DUSTIN Paul, yeoman, of New Boston, rec date 1782, execution, debt, file #3481

SMITH Reuben, husbandman, of New Boston, vs WILKINS John, gentleman, of Amherst, rec date 1783, judgment, debt, file #4471

SMITH Robert, yeoman, of Londonderry, vs KELLSO William & Agnis, yeoman, of New Boston, doc date 1774, writ, debt, file #1133

SMITH Robert, yeoman, of Londonderry, vs BURNS John, yeoman, of Amherst, rec date 1782, writ, debt, file #2793

SMITH Robert, yeoman, of Peterborough, vs BERRY Jonathan, yeoman, of Jaffrey, rec date 1783, writ, debt, file #3439

SMITH Robert, yeoman, of Peterborough, vs YOUNG John, physician, of Peterborough, rec date 1784, judgment, debt, file #5304

SMITH Robert, yeoman, of Peterborough, vs YOUNG John, physician, of Peterborough, rec date 1785, judgment, debt, file #5139

SMITH Samuel, gentleman, of Peterborough, vs FREEMAN Caesar, husbandman, of Dublin, doc date 1798, execution, debt, file #125

SMITH Samuel, gentleman, of Peterborough, vs RICHARDSON John, husbandman, of Dublin, doc date 1798, judgment, debt, file #566

SMITH Samuel, schoolmaster, of Plainfield, vs ELKINS Abel, husbandman, of Salisbury, rec date 1786, writ, debt, file #6272

SMITH Simeon, of Walpole, rec date 1788, various, trespass/cattle, file #6585

SMITH Stephen, yeoman, of Surry, vs CHAMPNEY Benjamin, husbandman, of New Ipswich, doc date 1799, judgment, debt, file #283

SMITH Stephen, husbandman, of Hopkinton, vs AMES Stephen, husbandman, of Cockermouth, rec date 1785, judgment, debt, file #5820

SMITH Thomas, yeoman, of New Boston, vs WILKINS Jonathan, yeoman, of Amherst, rec date 1783, writ, debt, file #3029

SMITH Thomas, gentleman, of Nottingham-West, vs PATTEN Robert, gentleman, of Hillsborough, rec date 1788, various, assault, file #3550

SMITH Thomas, husbandman, of New Boston, vs SMITH Reuben, husbandman, of New Boston, rec date 1786, writ, debt, file #6329

SMITH Thomas & John, yeoman, of Peterborough, vs TURNER Joseph, yeoman, of Jaffrey, doc date 1783, recognizance, debt, file #777

SMITH Timothy, yeoman, of Nottingham-West, vs MERRILL William, gentleman, of Warner, rec date 1784, judgment, debt, file #4398

SMITH Uriah, yeoman, of Wilton, vs MORGAN Jonathan, yeoman, of Wilton, rec date 1787, judgment, debt, file #2312

SMITH William, gentleman, of Peterborough, vs INHABITANTS of Peterborough, doc date 1784, writ, debt, file #1603

SMITH William, esquire, of Peterborough, vs INHABITANTS of Peterborough, rec date 1784, writ, debt, file #4579

SMITH William, esquire, of Peterborough, vs INHABITANTS of Peterborough, rec date 1785, judgment, debt, file #4694

SMITH William, esquire, of Peterborough, vs INHABITANTS of Peterborough, rec date 1785, various, debt, file #4832, 1777 (two folders)

SMITH William, esquire, of Peterborough, vs INHABITANTS of Peterborough, rec date 1786, writ, debt, file #6308

SMITHNS Brinsley, yeoman, of Salem MA, vs WAKFIELD Thomas, housewright, of Amherst, rec date 1786, writ, debt, file #6271

SNOW John, yeoman, of Dunstable, vs KELLEY Joseph, gentleman, of Nottingham-West, rec date 1778, writ, trespass, file #2234

SNOW Joseph, yeoman, of Wilton, vs BROWN James, gentleman, of Moultonborough, rec date 1776, writ, debt, file #2195

SOUL Bildad, husbandman, of Goffstown, vs MORISON Samuel, husbandman, of Windham, rec date 1782, debt, debt, file #3144

SOULE Bildad, yeoman, of Goffstown, vs BUTTERFIELD William, yeoman, of Merrimack, rec date 1783, writ, debt, file #3042

SOUTHER Jonathan, saddler, of Concord, vs BURBANK David, blacksmith, of Boscawen, rec date 1783, civil litigious, debt, file #2930

SOUTHER Jonathan, saddler, of Concord, vs BURBANK David, husbandman, of Boscawen, rec date 1783, writ, debt, file #3381

SOUTHERN Jonathan, saddler, of Haverhill MA, vs McFARLAND Samuel, husbandman, of Londonderry, rec date 1788, writ, debt, file #6923

SOUTHWICK Nathaniel, husbandman, of Milford, vs GREEN Peter, trader, of Milford, doc date 1799, writ, debt, file #574

SPARHAWH Thomas, esquire, of Raby, vs SHANNON Richard Cutts, esquire, of Raby, rec date 1788, writ, debt, file #6733

SPARHAWK Nathaniel, merchant, of Salem MA, vs STEARNS Joseph, yeoman, of Hollis, rec date 1784, judgment, debt, file #4266

SPARHAWK Nathaniel Jr, merchant, of Salem MA, vs WARNER Daniel, trader, of Westmoreland, doc date 1773, judgment, debt, file #1291

SPAULDING Edward, husbandman, of Hancock, vs LEWIS Aaron, gentleman, of Lyndeborough, rec date 1789, writ, debt, file #2572

SPAULDING Edward Jr, husbandman, of Lyndeborough, vs LEAMON Nathaniel, husbandman, of Hollis, rec date 1786, writ, debt, file #2361

SPAULDING Henry, of Lyndeborough, vs MEANARD Robert, esquire, of Amherst, doc date 1799, judgment, debt, file #272

SPAULDING Jacob, husbandman, of Hollis, vs RIDEOUT Nathaniel, husbandman, of Hollis, rec date 1787, judgment, debt, file #2470

SPAULDING Jeptha, husbandman, of Chelmsford MA, vs CLARK Timothy, husbandman, of Amherst, rec date 1788, writ, debt, file #2381

SPAULDING Lemuel, yeoman, of Pepperell MA, vs SHATTUCK Nehemiah, husbandman, of Mason, rec date 1788, writ, debt, file #7002

SPAULDING Levi, yeoman, of Lyndeborough, vs SPAULDING John, yeoman, of Hancock, doc date 1799, writ, debt, file #413

SPAULDING Levi, gentleman, of Lyndeborough, vs SPAULDING Stephen, husbandman, of Henniker, rec date 1785, judgment, debt, file #4969

SPAULDING Levi, gentleman, of Lyndeborough, vs TUTTLE Stephen, yeoman, of Goffstown, rec date 1785, judgment, debt, file #5601

SPAULDING Levi, esquire, of Lyndeborough, vs LUND Phineas, husbandman, of Lyndeborough, rec date 1788, various, debt, file #6589, 458

SPAULDING Levi, gentleman, of Lyndeborough, vs TUTTLE Stephen, yeoman, of Goffstown, rec date 1786, judgment, debt, file #6391

SPAULDING Reuben, gentleman, of Nottingham-West, vs STEARNS Daniel, yeoman, of Merrimack, doc date 1784, court case, debt, file #1658

SPAULDING Reuben, gentleman, of Londonderry, vs KELLEY Joseph, gentleman, of Nottingham-West, doc date 1772, writ, assault, file #932

SPAULDING Reuben, gentleman, of Nottingham-West, vs MACK Robert, blacksmith, of Charlestown, doc date 1775, execution, file #1004

SPAULDING Reuben, gentleman, of Nottingham-West, vs STEARNS Daniel, yeoman, of Merrimack, rec date 1783, various, debt, file #3286

SPAULDING Reuben, blacksmith, of Nottingham-West, vs McCLENCHE Joseph, blacksmith, of Merrimack, rec date 1786, judgment, debt, file #6115

SPAULDING Reuben, blacksmith, of Nottingham-West, vs McCLENCHE John, blacksmith, of Merrimack, rec date 1786, judgment, debt, file #6115

SPAULDING Silas, husbandman, of Merrimack, vs HILL Benjamin, husbandman, doc date 1798, execution, debt, file #194

SPAULDING Stephen, yeoman, of Lyndeborough, vs GORDON William, merchant, of Dunstable MA, doc date 1774, writ, debt, file #1113

SPAULDING Stephen, husbandman, of Henniker, vs ATHERTON Joshua, esquire, of Amherst, rec date 1784, judgment, debt, file #4359

SPAULDING Thomas, gentleman, of Pepperell MA, vs SHATTUCK Nehemiah, husbandman, of Mason, rec date 1788, writ, debt, file #6725

SPAULDING William, husbandman, of Raby, vs MASTERS Benjamin, husbandman, of Raby, doc date 1784, writ, debt, file #1615

SPAULDING William, of Raby, vs GREEN Mary (SPAULDING), wife, of Lincoln MA, rec date 1785, petition, divorce, file #5234

SPEAR Samuel, cordwainer, of New Ipswich, vs CROMBIE John, husbandman, of Londonderry, rec date 1784, judgment, debt, file #4920

SPEAR? Jonathan, yeoman, of Peterborough, vs COVEL Joseph, of Plymouth, doc date 1778, rec date 1778, deed, land transfer, file #2165

SPEER Samuel, yeoman, of Peterborough, vs STEWART Alexander, cordwainer, of Peterborough, rec date 1788, writ, ejectment, file #2554

SPEER William, yeoman, of Peterboro, vs HARRIS Robert, merchant, of Littleton MA, doc date 1772, writ, debt, file #1071

SPOFFERD Amos, husbandman, of Peterborough, vs INHABITANTS of Peterborough, of Peterborough, rec date 1786, judgment, debt, file #6495

SPOFFORD Eleazer, husbandman, of Jaffrey, vs SMITH Manasseh, gentleman, of Hollis, rec date 1783, writ, debt, file #3183

SPRAGUE John, esquire, of Lancaster MA, vs SIMONS Daniel, yeoman, of Amherst, doc date 1774, writ, debt, file #1088, fragile

SPRAGUE John, esquire, of Lancaster MA, vs SMALL Joseph, yeoman, of Amherst, doc date 1774, execution, file #947

SPRAGUE John, esquire, of Lancaster MA, vs BRADFORD Samuel Jr, gentleman, of Hillsborough, rec date 1785, execution, debt, file #5943

SPRAGUE John, esquire, of Lancaster MA, vs CODMAN Henry, physician, of Amherst, rec date 1785, judgment, debt, file #5868

SPRAGUE Joseph, esquire, of Lancaster MA, vs HUTCHINSON James, yeoman, of Amherst, doc date 1774, execution, file #949

SPRAQUE John, esquire, of Lancaster MA, vs HUTCHINSON James, yeoman, of Amherst, doc date 1774, execution, file #982

SPRAQUE John, esquire, of Lancaster MA, vs SMALL Joseph, yeoman, of Amherst, doc date 1774, execution, file #984

SPRAQUE John, esquire, of Lancaster MA, vs KIDDER John, yeoman, of New Chester, rec date 1785, writ, debt, file #4681

STACEY William, blacksmith, of Litchfield, vs ABBOTT Jerusha, widow, of Hopkinton, doc date 1771, writ, debt, file #797

STACEY William, blacksmith, of Litchfield, vs NUTT John, husbandman, of Hopkinton, doc date 1771, writ, debt, file #797

STACK John, esquire, of Deerfield, vs HOYT George, husbandman, of Hillsborough, doc date 1799, debt, file #482

STACY William, blacksmith, of Litchfield, vs SMITH John, yeoman, of Lyndeborough, doc date 1772, writ, debt, file #899

STAN?Eliphalet, husbandman, of Francestown, vs WILLIAM ----, husbandman, doc date 1782, execution, debt, file #974, fragile

STANDWOOD Ebenezer, barber, of Ipswich MA, vs McCLARY Andrew, captain, of Epsom, doc date 1775, writ, debt, file #813

STANLEY Matthew, husbandman, of Hopkinton, vs EATON Ebenezer, husbandman, of New Bradford, rec date 1783, writ, debt, file #3395

STANLEY Samuel, vs STANLEY Samuel, husbandman, of Hopkinton, rec date 1785, presentment, file #4576

STANLEY Samuel, husbandman, of Hopkinton, vs CHOATE Jacob, husbandman, of Enfield, rec date 1792, judgment, debt, file #2586

STANLEY Samuel, husbandman, of Hopkinton, vs KIMBALL Reuben, gentleman, of Concord, rec date 1783, complaint, debt, file #3167

STANLEY Theophilus, cordwainer, of Hopkinton, vs CLEMENT Paltiah, currier, of Hopkinton, doc date 1798, judgment, debt, file #566

STANWOOD Ebenezer, vs McCLARY Andrew (Capt), of Portsmouth, doc date 1774, misc, lost of salt, file #757, tide cause lost of salt

STANWOOD Ebenezer, esquire, of MA, vs MacLARY Andrew, gentleman, of Epsom, doc date 1775, judgment, debt, file #1171

STARK Caleb, merchant, of Dunbarton, vs HOGG James, gentleman, of Dunbarton, doc date 1798, judgment, debt, file #566

STARK Caleb, trader, of Dunbarton, vs McGREGORE Robert, esquire, of Goffstown, rec date 1788, judgment, debt, file #2562

STARK Caleb, gentleman, of Dunbarton, vs McGREGORE Robert, esquire, of Goffstown, rec date 1789, writ, debt, file #2573

STARK Caleb, esquire, of Dunbarton, vs BLODGETT Samuel, esquire, of Haverhill, rec date 1785, various, debt, file #6338

STARK George, yeoman, of New Ipswich, vs HUDSON Elisha, yeoman, of Wilton, rec date 1784, judgment, debt, file #4861

STARK John, esquire, of Derryfield, vs COOK Noah, gentleman, of New Ipswich, rec date 1785, various, debt, file #5232

STARK John, esquire, of Derryfield, vs MOOR Samuel, gentleman, of Derryfield, rec date 1788, writ, debt, file #6950

STARK John, esquire, of Derryfield, vs STEVENS Ebenezer, gentleman, of Derryfield, rec date 1787, writ, debt, file #6959

STARK Joseph, yeoman, of Killingsly CT, vs GILDS Abraham, gentleman, of Warner, doc date 1796, various, debt, file #549

STARK Thomas, gentleman, of New Boston, vs HOLLAND Samuel, esquire, of Quebec Canada, doc date 1799, various, debt, file #537

STARK William, doc date 1776, recognizance default, file #760

STARK William, esquire, of Dunbarton, vs HOGG John, esquire, of Dunbarton, doc date 1778, writ, assault, file #2032

STARK William, yeoman, of Dunbarton, vs STATE of NH, rec date 1777, indictment, debt, file #2207

STARK William, esquire, of Dunbarton, vs STATE of NH, rec date 1776, indictment, counterfeiting, file #2246

STARR Ebenezer, physician, of Dunstable MA, vs CRISTY Jesse, blacksmith, of New Boston, rec date 1784, judgment, debt, file #4192

STARR Ebenezer, physician, of Dunstable MA, vs CRISTY George & Joseph, blacksmith, of New Boston, rec date 1785, writ, debt, file #6234

STARRAT David, gentleman, of Derryfield, vs WOODBURY Hezekiah, yeoman, of Dunbarton, doc date 1778, rec date 1779, deed, land transfer, file #2142

STARRETT David, guardian, of Francestown, vs MESSEY Elizabeth, of Derryfield, rec date 1779, petition, guardianship, file #2237

STEARN Jotham, husbandman, vs DANS Samuel, esquire, of Amherst, rec date 1786, writ, debt, file #6101

STEARN Jotham, husbandman, vs DANA Samuel, esquire, of Amherst, rec date 1786, writ, debt, file #6101

STEARN Samuel, yeoman, of Amherst, vs CUTTER Zacheus, esquire, of Amherst, doc date 1774, writ, debt, file #1097

STEARNS Benjamin, yeoman, of Lexington MA, vs WELLINGTON George, yeoman, of Jaffrey, doc date 1799, various, debt, file #558

STEARNS David, yeoman, of Charlestown MA, vs BLAKE William W, merchant, of Keene, doc date 1798, execution, debt, file #65

STEARNS Eleaser, yeoman, of Amherst, vs MOAR Jacob, yeoman, of Hollis, doc date 1799, judgment, debt, file #267

STEARNS John, yeoman, of Amherst, vs TOWNE Israel, esquire, of Stoddard, rec date 1783, writ, debt, file #3050

STEARNS Joseph & Mary, yeoman, of Hollis, vs TYNG James, merchant, of Dunstable MA, doc date 1772, writ, debt, file #1419

STEARNS Jotham, yeoman, of Dunbarton, vs SANDERS James, innholder, of Salem, rec date 1786, writ, debt, file #6282

STEARNS Nathaniel, yeoman, of Carlisle Canada, vs SHEPARD Sarah, widow, of Amherst, rec date 1788, writ, debt, file #6622

STEARNS Samuel, yeoman, of Amherst, vs KENNY Israel, yeoman, of Hollis, doc date 1773, judgment, debt, file #1297

STEARNS Samuel, yeoman, of Amherst, vs BUTTERFIELD Charles, yeoman, of Dunstable, doc date 1773, writ, debt, file #1364

STEARNS Samuel, husbandman, of Plymouth, vs JEWETT Jacob Jr, husbandman, of Hollis, rec date 1785, judgment, debt, file #6001

STEARNS Samuel, yeoman, of Amherst, rec date 1784, writ, land dispute , file #6964

STEARNS Samuel Jr, yeoman, of Hollis, vs WHEELER James, yeoman, of Amherst, doc date 1772, writ, debt, file #906

STEARNS Samuel Jr, yeoman, of Hollis, vs WYMAN Timothy, husbandman, of Hollis, doc date 1772, writ, debt, file #1412

STEARNS Samuel Jr, yeoman, of Amherst, vs CODMAN Henry, physician, of Amherst, rec date 1782, writ, debt, file #2697

STEARNS Samuel Jr, yeoman, of Amherst, vs WILKINS John, gentleman, of Francestown, rec date 1782, execution, debt, file #3531

STEARNS Samuel Jr, yeoman, of Amherst, vs WILKINS Benjamin Jr, yeoman, of Amherst, rec date 1784, various, debt, file #4211

STEARNS Samuel Jr, yeoman, of Amherst, vs MORRELL Hugh, yeoman, of Francestown, rec date 1782, writ, debt, file #2789

STEARNS Timothy, yeoman, of New Ipswich, vs WRIGHT Joseph, yeoman, of New Ipswich, rec date 1772, deed, land transfer, file #4882, ?

STEARNS William, apothecary, of Salem MA, vs YOUNG John, physician, of Peterborough, doc date 1784, civil litigation, debt, file #1828

STEARNS William, apothecary, of Salem MA, vs YOUNG John, physician, of Peterborough, rec date 1783, judgment, debt, file #4453, note of Samuel STEVENS

STEARNS William, apothecary, of Salem MA, vs PHELPS Nathan, yeoman, of Amherst, rec date 1783, judgment, debt, file #4534

STEARNS William, apothecary, of Salem MA, vs PIKE Zachariah, yeoman, of Bedford, rec date 1785, various, debt, file #6037

STEEL David, yeoman, of Peterborough, vs PARKER Samuel, yeoman, of Peterborough, doc date 1772, judgment, debt, file #683

STEEL David, yeoman, of Peterborough, vs PARKER Samuel, yeoman, of Peterborough, doc date 1772, writ, debt, file #1032, fragile

STEEL David, gentleman, of Peterborough, vs ROBBE Alexander, gentleman, of Peterborough, rec date 1783, execution, debt, file #2891

STEEL David, gentleman, of Peterborough, vs JOHNSON Moses, husbandman, of Peterborough, rec date 1782, execution, debt, file #3494

STEEL David, gentleman, of Peterborough, vs GRAY Robert, gentleman, of Peterborough, rec date 1783, execution, debt, file #3679

STEEL David, yeoman, of Peterborough, vs GRAY Robert, gentleman, of Peterborough, rec date 1783, judgment, debt, file #3733

STEEL David, gentleman, of Peterborough, vs HOLMES Robert, husbandman, of Peterborough, rec date 1783, writ, debt, file #3572

STEEL David, gentleman, of Peterborough, vs GRAY Robert, gentleman, of Peterborough, rec date 1782, execution, debt, file #3517

STEEL David, gentleman, of Peterborough, vs JOHNSON Moses, husbandman, of Peterborough, rec date 1783, civil litigation, debt, file #3882

STEEL David, gentleman, of Peterborough, vs ROBBE Alexander, gentleman, of Peterborough, rec date 1783, writ, debt, file #3972

STEEL David, gentleman, of Peterborough, vs WIER Robert, gentleman, of Walpole, rec date 1786, various, debt, file #6066

STEEL Davis, gentleman, of Peterborough, vs JOHNSON Moses, husbandman, of Peterborough, rec date 1783, execution, debt, file #3683

STEEL James, of Antrim, vs DICKEY Adam, husbandman, of Bedford, rec date 1784, various, debt, file #4185

STEEL James, husbandman, of Antrim, vs MOOR Samuel, miller, of Bedford, rec date 1784, judgment, debt, file #5318

STEEL James, of Antrim, vs MOOR Samuel, miller, of Bedford, rec date 1785, judgment, debt, file #5142

STEEL John, of Camden, vs BRADFORD Enos, husbandman, of Amherst, doc date 1775, writ, debt, file #953

STEEL John, yeoman, of Hillsborough, vs HILL John, esquire, of Boston MA, doc date 1773, writ, debt, file #1246

STEEL John, of Hillsborough, vs LOVEJOY Benjamin Jr, yeoman, of Hillsborough, doc date 1773, execution, debt, file #1470

STEEL Joseph, yeoman, of Amherst, vs HALE Paul, husbandman, of Peterborough, doc date 1784, execution, debt, file #1732

STEEL Joseph, husbandman, of Nottingham-West, vs STATE of NH, esquire, rec date 1779, various, debt, file #2225

STEEL Joseph, yeoman, of Amherst, vs HALE Paul, husbandman, of Peterborough, rec date 1783, writ, debt, file #3574

STEEL Joseph, yeoman, of Amherst, vs CAMPBELL Daniel, husbandman, of Amherst, rec date 1785, judgment, debt, file #5148

STEEL Joseph, yeoman, of Amherst, vs LOVEJOY Francis, feltmaker, of Amherst, rec date 1785, judgment, debt, file #5148

STEEL Joseph, yeoman, of Amherst, vs CAMPBELL Daniel, husbandman, of Amherst, rec date 1784, judgment, debt, file #5301

STEEL Joseph, yeoman, of Amherst, vs LOVEJOY Francis, feltmaker, of Amherst, rec date 1784, judgment, debt, file #5301

STEEL Moses, yeoman, of Hillsborough, vs JONES James, yeoman, of Hillsborough, rec date 1783, execution, debt, file #3260

STEEL Moses, yeoman, of Hillsborough, vs COOLEDGE Silas, yeoman, of Hillsborough, rec date 1783, judgment, debt, file #3744

STEEL Moses, yeoman, of Hillsborough, vs JONES James, yeoman, of Hillsborough, rec date 1783, judgment, debt, file #3744

STEEL Moses, of Hillsborough, vs JONES James, yeoman, of Hillsborough, rec date 1783, execution, debt, file #3692

STEEL Moses, yeoman, of Hillsborough, vs JONES James, yeoman, of Hillsborough, rec date 1783, writ, debt, file #3896

STEEL Moses, yeoman, of Hillsborough, vs JONES Joel, yeoman, of Hillsborough, doc date 1783, rec date 1784, deed, land transfer, file #5005

STEEL Samuel, yeoman, of Dunstable MA, vs WASHER Stephen, yeoman, of Wilton, rec date 1785, writ, debt, file #2340

STEEL Samuel, yeoman, of Dunstable MA, vs WASHE Stephen, yeoman, of Wilton, rec date 1785, judgment, debt, file #6204

STEEL Thomas, yeoman, of Hillsborough, vs ROGERS John, yeoman, of Keene, rec date 1784, judgment, file #4983

STEEL Thomas, yeoman, of Peterborough, vs SCOTT William, esquire, of Groton MA, rec date 1784, judgment, debt, file #6045

STEEL William, husbandman, of Nottingham-West, vs JOHNSON David, husbandman, of Pelham, rec date 1785, writ, debt, file #5279

STEEL William, yeoman, of Campden, vs LEE William, yeoman, of Lyndeborough, doc date 1774, judgment, debt, file #732

STEEL William, yeoman, of Nottingham-West, vs HILLDRETH Reuben, yeoman, of Dunstable, doc date 1784, execution, debt, file #1499

STEEL William, yeoman, of Nottingham-West, vs POLLARD Timothy, yeoman, of Nottingham-West, rec date 1783, writ, debt, file #3408

STEEL William, yeoman, of Nottingham, vs JOHNSON David, yeoman, of Nottingham-West, rec date 1783, judgment, debt, file #4483

STEEL William, yeoman, of Nottingham, vs POLLARD Timothy, yeoman, of Nottingham, rec date 1783, judgment, debt, file #4483

STEEL William, yeoman, of Nottingham-West, vs KILLICUT Reuben, yeoman, of Dunstable, rec date 1783, judgment, debt, file #4494

STEELE David Jr, gentleman, of Peterborough, vs BUTMAN Asa, yeoman, of Greenfield, doc date 1797, various, debt, file #559

STEELE David Jr, gentleman, of Peterborough, vs PARKER Samuel, yeoman, of Greenfield, doc date 1797, various, debt, file #559

STEELE David Jr, yeoman, of Peterborough, vs HOLMS Robert, yeoman, of Peterborough, rec date 1785, judgment, debt, file #5341

STEELE Thomas, yeoman, of Peterborough, vs SCOTT William, esquire, of Groton MA, rec date 1784, appeal, debt, file #4112

STEPHEN Samuel, husbandman, of Lyndeborough, vs LEAMAN Nathaniel, husbandman, of Lyndeborough, rec date 1784, appeal, debt, file #4134

STEPHENS Samuel, apothecary, of Amherst, vs CUSHING John, physician, of Goffstown, rec date 1785, judgment, debt, file #5162

STERNS John, husbandman, of Milford, vs GREEN Peter, trader, of Milford, doc date 1799, writ, debt, file #574

STEVEN Birniley, gentleman, of Salem MA, vs STEVENS Samuel Jr, yeoman, of Amherst, rec date 1783, civil litigation, debt, file #3879

STEVEN Samuel, physician, of Amherst, vs HUNT Elizabeth, widow, of Hollis, doc date 1784, execution, debt, file #1530

STEVEN Samuel, vs MORRISON Sarah, rec date 1784, bill, court bill, file #4823

STEVENS Benjamin, yeoman, of Goffstown, vs KARR James, gentleman, of Goffstown, rec date 1777, civil litigation, debt, file #2182

STEVENS Birnsly, yeoman, of Salem MA, vs McKEEN Samuel, husbandman, of Windham, rec date 1783, judgment, debt, file #3754

STEVENS Brinsley, yeoman, of Salem MA, vs WILKINS Samuel, esquire, of Amherst, rec date 1786, writ, debt, file #6271

STEVENS Brinsley, yeoman, of Salem MA, vs LOVEJOY Joshua, gentleman, of Amherst, rec date 1786, writ, debt, file #6271

STEVENS Cain, husbandman, of Hillsborough, vs BIXBE Andrew, esquire, of Hillsborough, rec date 1785, writ, debt, file #6246

STEVENS Caleb, cordwainer, of Merrimack, vs WILSON Prudance, spinster, of Merrimack, doc date 1775, deed, land transfer, file #1040

STEVENS Calvin, husbandman, of Hillsborough, vs RICHARDSON Zechariah, innkeeper, of Francestown, doc date 1784, execution, debt, file #1874

STEVENS Calvin, yeoman, of Hillsborough, vs ATHERTON Joshua, esquire, of Amherst, rec date 1783, writ, debt, file #3035

STEVENS Calvin, husbandman, of Hillsborough, vs INHABITANTS of Deering, of Deering, rec date 1783, execution, debt, file #3228

STEVENS Calvin, husbandman, of Hillsborough, vs RICHARDSON Zechariah, innkeeper, of Francestown, rec date 1783, writ, debt, file #3600

STEVENS Calvin, yeoman, of Hillsborough, vs JONES Samuel, yeoman, of Hillsborough, rec date 1783, civil litigation, debt, file #3881

STEVENS Calvin, husbandman, of Hillsborough, vs INHABITANTS of Deering, of Deering, rec date 1783, writ, debt, file #3904

STEVENS Daniel, yeoman, of Amherst, vs BOUTWELL Amos, yeoman, of Amherst, rec date 1783, civil litigious, debt, file #2951

STEVENS David & Jona, husbandman, of Temple, vs HILL David, yeoman, of New Ipswich, rec date 1788, writ, debt, file #6937

STEVENS Isaac, yeoman, of Hollis, vs JEWET Jacob Jr, yeoman, of Hollis, doc date 1774, writ, debt, file #1081

STEVENS Isaac, yeoman, of Hollis, vs FARMER Benjamin, cooper, of Hollis, doc date 1772, writ, debt, file #1410

STEVENS James Jr, rec date 1787, writ, debt, file #6700

STEVENS John, yeoman, of Mason, vs WOODS Joseph, yeoman, of Mason, doc date 1786, rec date 1786, deed, land transfer, file #5019

STEVENS Jonathan, yeoman, of New Ipswich, vs STEVENS Peter, gentleman, of Groton MA, doc date 1772, writ, debt, file #1064

STEVENS Joseph, gentleman, of New Ipswich, vs ROBERTS Josiah, yeoman, of Mason, doc date 1772, writ, debt, file #1431

STEVENS Joseph, gentleman, of New Ipswich, vs ROBINS Josiah, yeoman, of Mason, doc date 1773, judgment, debt, file #1320

STEVENS Peter, gentleman, of Groton MA, vs STEVENS Jonathan, yeoman, of New Ipswich, doc date 1772, judgment, debt, file #678

STEVENS Peter, gentleman, of Groton MA, vs STEVENS Jonathan, yeoman, of New Ipswich, doc date 1773, execution, debt, file #1371

STEVENS Samuel, husbandman, of Lyndeborough, vs ANDREWS James, gentleman, of Boxford MA, doc date 1773, trial, damage to fence, file #1286

STEVENS Samuel, physician, of Amherst, vs GREEN David, yeoman, of Hillsborough, doc date 1784, execution, debt, file #1769

STEVENS Samuel, physician, of Amherst, vs WYMAN Stephen, yeoman, of Deering, doc date 1784, execution, debt, file #1770

STEVENS Samuel, physician, of Amherst, vs GREEN David, yeoman, of Hillsborough, doc date 1784, writ, debt, file #1618

STEVENS Samuel, yeoman, of Lyndeborough, vs BOSSEE Thomas, gentleman, of Lyndeborough, doc date 1784, execution, debt, file #1814

STEVENS Samuel, physician, of Amherst, vs STEWART Samuel, yeoman, of Hillsborough, doc date 1784, civil litigation, debt, file #1839

STEVENS Samuel, physician, of Amherst, vs RICHARDSON Zachariah, innkeeper, of Francestown, doc date 1784, civil litigation, debt, file #1836

STEVENS Samuel, physician, of Amherst, vs GRIMES James, gentleman, of Deering, doc date 1784, execution, debt, file #1919

STEVENS Samuel, husbandman, of Lyndeborough, vs CRAM Benjamin, husbandman, of Lyndeborough, doc date 1784, civil litigation, debt, file #1848

STEVENS Samuel, physician, of Amherst, vs TAGGART Robert, physician, of Merrimack, doc date 1784, execution, debt, file #1903

STEVENS Samuel, physician, of Amherst, vs MORRISON Sarah, widow, of Peterborough, rec date 1785, judgment, debt, file #2292, son James mention

STEVENS Samuel, physician, of Amherst, vs WILKINS Jonathan Sr, yeoman, of Amherst, rec date 1782, judgment, debt, file #2724

STEVENS Samuel, physician, of Amherst, vs WILKINS Andrew, yeoman, of Amherst, rec date 1783, judgment, debt, file #3290

STEVENS Samuel, physician, of Amherst, vs FURBUSH Charles, gentleman, of Andover MA, rec date 1783, execution, debt, file #3241

STEVENS Samuel, physician, of Amherst, vs CODMAN Henry, physician, of Amherst, rec date 1782, execution, debt, file #3523

STEVENS Samuel, physician, of Amherst, vs CODMAN Henry, physician, of Amherst, rec date 1783, execution, debt, file #3673

STEVENS Samuel, physician, of Amherst, vs JONES Samuel, yeoman, of Hillsborough, rec date 1783, writ, debt, file #3923

STEVENS Samuel, apothecary, of Amherst, vs ROGERS Thomas, physician, of Plymouth, rec date 1782, judgment, debt, file #4034

STEVENS Samuel, yeoman, of Hillsborough, vs JONES Samuel, yeoman, of Hillsborough, rec date 1783, execution, debt, file #3840

STEVENS Samuel, apothecary, of Amherst, vs HALE Samuel, physician, of Pepperell MA, rec date 1783, execution, debt, file #3820

STEVENS Samuel, physician, of Amherst, vs HUNT Elizabeth, widow, of Hollis, rec date 1783, judgment, debt, file #4433, note of Joshua ATHERTON

STEVENS Samuel, husbandman, of Lyndeborough, vs CRAM Benjamin, husbandman, of Lyndeborough, rec date 1783, judgment, debt, file #4459

STEVENS Samuel, physician, of Amherst, vs YOUNG John, physician, of Peterborough, rec date 1784, writ, debt, file #5556

STEVENS Samuel, physician, of Amherst, vs BRADFORD Samuel Jr, gentleman, of Hillsborough, rec date 1785, judgment, debt, file #4957

STEVENS Samuel, physician, of Amherst, vs COSTON Ebenezer, yeoman, of Society Land, rec date 1785, judgment, debt, file #4949

STEVENS Samuel, physician, of Amherst, vs COCHRAN John, yeoman, of Amherst, rec date 1785, writ, debt, file #5402, fragile

STEVENS Samuel, physician, of Amherst, vs HALL John, physician, of Canterbury, rec date 1782, execution, debt, file #5741

STEVENS Samuel, physician, of Amherst, vs GREEN David, yeoman, of Hillsborough, rec date 1785, writ, debt, file #6239

STEVENS Samuel, physician, of Amherst, vs CUSHING John, physician, of Goffstown, rec date 1785, judgment, debt, file #6435

STEVENS Samuel, physician, of Amherst, vs FORBUSH Charles, gentleman, of Andover MA, rec date 1785, judgment, debt, file #2439, plaintiff deceased

STEVENS Simeon & Samuel, husbandman, of Chelmsford MA, rec date 1788, various, land dispute, file #6583

STEVENS Theodore, yeoman, of Wilton, vs SMITH Josiah, tanner, of Wilton, doc date 1778, writ, debt, file #2052

STEVENS Theodore, yeoman, of Wilton, vs HAWKINS William A, gentleman, of Wilton, doc date 1778, writ, debt, file #2048

STEVENS Theodore, yeoman, of Wilton, vs BAYL William, yeoman, of Wilton, doc date 1778, writ, debt, file #2051

STEVENS Theodore Jr, yeoman, of Wilton, vs BALLARD Uriah & Eliz, yeoman, of Wilton, rec date 1778, various, debt, file #2235

STEVENS Thomas, whitesmith, of Amherst, vs WRIGHT Uriah, husbandman, of Hollis, rec date 1788, writ, debt, file #2382

STEVENS Thomas, blacksmith, of Amherst, vs BUTLER Joseph, gentleman, of Pelham, rec date 1787, various, damages, file #2544

STEVENS Thomas, whitesmith, of Amherst, vs KELLEY Moses, esquire, of Goffstown, rec date 1783, writ, debt, file #3184

STEVENS Thomas, blacksmith, of Amherst, vs LOW William, cabinetmaker, of Amherst, rec date 1785, various, assault, file #4567

STEVENS Thomas, gentleman, of Goffstown, vs ROLF Stephen, yeoman, of Reading MA, rec date 1785, judgment, debt, file #5985

STEVENS Thomas, blacksmith, of Amherst, vs PEABODY John, of Amherst, rec date 1785, execution, debt, file #6060

STEVENS Thomas, gentleman, of Goffstown, vs ROAFF Stephen, yeoman, of Reading MA, rec date 1785, writ, debt, file #6028

STEVENS Thomas, blacksmith, of Amherst, vs PEABODY John, yeoman, of Amherst, rec date 1786, writ, debt, file #6055

STEVENS Thomas, whitesmith, of Weare, vs WRIGHT Uriah, husbandman, rec date 1788, judgment, debt, file #7052

STEVENS William, cordwainer, of Salem, vs McCLINTOCK John, gentleman, of Hillsborough, rec date 1785, writ, debt, file #6256

STEWARD Francis, yeoman, of Antrim, vs HOVEY David, yeoman, of Peterborough, rec date 1785, judgment, debt, file #2438

STEWART Alexander, yeoman, of Peterborough, vs TAYLOR Isaiah, yeoman, of Peterborough, doc date 1778, writ, debt, file #2013

STEWART Alexander, husbandman, of Peterborough, vs WHEELOCK Jonathan Jr, husbandman, of Townsend MA, rec date 1782, debt, debt, file #3153

STEWART Alexander, cordwainer, of Peterborough, vs BENNETT Jonathan Jr, husbandman, of Hancock, rec date 1784, appeal, debt, file #4104

STEWART Alexander, cordwainer, of Peterborough, vs BENNETT Jonathan Jr, husbandman, of Hancock, rec date 1784, judgment, debt, file #4412, note of Abner PRESTON

STEWART Charles, husbandman, of Peterborough, vs McCLOUD Thomas, husbandman, of Peterborough, doc date 1784, execution, debt, file #1963

STEWART David, yeoman, of Amherst, vs WILKINS Benjamin, yeoman, of Amherst, rec date 1783, judgment, debt, file #3801

STEWART James, husbandman, of Dunbarton, vs EATON Jothan, husbandman, of Weare, rec date 1783, writ, debt, file #3214

STEWART James, gentleman, of Dunbarton, vs WEBSTER John, gentleman, of Salisbury, rec date 1784, judgment, debt, file #4247

STEWART John, of Amherst, vs BARKER Nathan, yeoman, of Andover MA, doc date 1785, petition, release of debit, file #3

STEWART John & Mary, joiner, of Amherst, vs HENRY Joseph, yeoman, of Merrimack, doc date 1781, rec date 1783, deed, land transfer, file #2658

STEWART Robert, husbandman, of Nottingham-West, vs GILES John, yeoman, of Londonderry, rec date 1783, judgment, debt, file #3775

STEWART Samuel, yeoman, of Dunbarton, vs CARR Moses, laborer, of Dunbarton, doc date 1782, recognizance, assault & batter, file #774

STEWART Samuel, yeoman, of Hillsborough, vs STEVENS Samuel, physician, of Amherst, rec date 1783, writ, debt, file #3193

STEWART Samuel, yeoman, of Dunbarton, vs McCARTNEY Jane, spinster, of Dunbarton, rec date 1783, indictment, perjury, file #3557

STEWART Samuel, yeoman, of Hillsborough, vs SEWALL Thomas, yeoman, of Deering, rec date 1784, judgment, debt, file #4360

STEWART Samuel, rec date 1785, recognizance, file #7043

STEWART Thomas, husbandman, of Hillsborough, vs STEWART Francis, husbandman, of Nottingham, doc date 1799, execution, debt, file #176

STEWART Thomas, yeoman, of Henniker, vs FORSAITH James, physician, of Deering, doc date 1799, writ, debt, file #322

STEWART Thomas, yeoman, of Henniker, vs STEWART Adam, yeoman, of Lyndeborough, doc date 1798, execution, debt, file #193

STICKEY Thomas, yeoman, of Campbells Gore, vs JONES Joshua, yeoman, of Hillsborough, rec date 1785, judgment, debt, file #5098

STICKNEY Jonathan, yeoman, of Billerica MA, vs GIPSON Timothy, esquire, of Henniker, rec date 1785, deed, land transfer, file #5632

STICKNEY Richard, husbandman, of Newbury MA, vs CHASE Wells Jr, husbandman, of Hopkinton, rec date 1783, judgment, debt, file #3755

STICKNEY Samuel, housewright, of New Boston, vs WOOD Jonathan, yeoman, of Goffstown, rec date 1784, appeal, debt, file #4131

STICKNEY Samuel, housewright, of New Boston, vs WOOD Jonathan, yeoman, of Goffstown, rec date 1784, various, court case, file #4522

STILES Caleb, cordwainer, of Lyndeborough, vs PARKER John, gentleman, of Billerica MA, doc date 1786, petition, release of debit, file #9

STILES Caleb, yeoman, of Amherst, vs RODING Robert, yeoman, of New Ipswich, doc date 1772, civil litigations, debt, file #637

STILES Moses, yeoman, of Lyndeborough, vs WILSON James, husbandman, of Peterborough, doc date 1799, judgment, debt, file #301

STIMSON Benjamin, yeoman, of Groton MA, vs HAWOOD Samuel, yeoman, of Nottingham-West, rec date 1786, execution, debt, file #5890

STIMSON John, yeoman, of Dunbarton, vs STATE of NH, doc date 1779, writ, debt, file #2065

STINSON David, husbandman, of New Boston, vs EWINS Ann, spinster, of Londonderry, rec date 1786, judgment, debt, file #2298

STINSON James, husbandman, of Dunbarton, vs STATE of NH, rec date 1783, capias, to report as jur, file #2613

STINSON John, yeoman, of Dunbarton, vs STATE of NH, rec date 1777, indictment, debt, file #2207

STINSON William, gentleman, of Dunbarton, vs BEARD William, yeoman, of New Boston, rec date 1783, judgment, debt, file #3706

STINSON William, gentleman, of Dunbarton, vs JAMESON Hugh, of Dunbarton, rec date 1783, judgment, debt, file #3748

STINSON William, gentleman, of Dunbarton, vs LITTLE John, gentleman, of Derryfield, rec date 1783, judgment, debt, file #3747

STINSON William, gentleman, of Dunbarton, vs MURRAY Robert, husbandman, of Alexandria, rec date 1784, judgment, debt, file #4337

STITSON John, yeoman, of Dunbarton, vs FIFIELD Nathaniel, gentleman, of Weare, doc date 1778, writ, debt, file #2055

STOADDARD Margaret, widow, of Chelmsford MA, vs BOWERS Sarah, widow, of Merrimack, rec date 1785, judgment, debt, file #5444

STODDARD Margaret, widow, of Chelmsford MA, vs STODDARD Joseph, of Amherst, doc date 1783, writ, debt, file #1258, estate of Sampson STODDARD

STODDARD Margaret, administrator of estate, of Chelmsford MA, vs BOWERS Sarah, administrator of estate, of Merrimack, rec date 1784, judgment, debt, file #5311

STODDARD Sampson, esquire, of Chelmsford MA, vs BIXBY Andrew, yeoman, of Amherst, doc date 1774, execution, file #993

STODDARD Sampson, esquire, of Chelmsford MA, vs PARKER Samuel, yeoman, of Amherst, doc date 1773, writ, debt, file #1185

STODDARD Sampson, esquire, of Chelmsford MA, vs BIXBY Andrew, yeoman, of Amherst, rec date 1774, execution, debt, file #3497

STODDARD Sampson, of Chelmsford MA, vs SWALLOW John, gentleman, of Mason, rec date 1785, deed, land transfer, file #4728

STONE Ebenezer, of Cavendish VT, vs CAMPBELL John, yeoman, of Cavendish VT, doc date 1781, rec date 1783, deed, land transfer, file #2638

STONE Nathaniel, gentleman, of Alstead, vs CUTLER Rachel, single woman, of New Ipswich, rec date 1783, writ, debt, file #3120

STONE Nathaniel, rec date 1788, deposition, debt, file #6937

STRAW Jacob Jr, husbandman, of Hopkinton, vs BAILEY Enoch, yeoman, of Hopkinton, doc date 1799, execution, debt, file #163

STRAW Jacob Jr, husbandman, of Hopkinton, vs BAILEY Isaac, cordwainer, of Hopkinton, doc date 1799, execution, debt, file #164

STRAW Jonathan Capt, of Hopkinton, doc date 1786, license, tavern license, file #861

STRICKLAND John, of Nottingham-West, vs GREELE Joseph, gentleman, of Nottingham-West, rec date 1788, writ, debt, file #6899

STRUTHERS Robert, trader, of Boston MA, vs HARRIMAN Jaziel, husbandman, of Chester, doc date 1773, writ, debt, file #1178

STUART Alexander, cordwainer, of Peterborough, vs GORDEN John, husbandman, of New Boston, rec date 1788, writ, debt, file #6909

STUART Alexander, husbandman, of Peterborough, vs DICKEY Adam, husbandman, of Chester, rec date 1788, writ, debt, file #6910

STUART Charles, yeoman, of Peterborough, vs McCLOUD Thomas, husbandman, of Peterborough, rec date 1783, writ, debt, file #3632

STUART John, yeoman, of Amherst, vs BARKER Nathan, yeoman, of Andover MA, doc date 1799?, petition, release from jail, file #45

STUART John, husbandman, of Antrim, vs STURART Frances, husbandman, of Antrim, doc date 1796, rec date 1801, deed, land transfer, file #5671

STUART Samuel, yeoman, of Dunbarton, vs JOGG John, esquire, of Dunbarton, rec date 1782, writ, debt, file #2664B, 2 folders

STUART Samuel, yeoman, of Dunbarton, vs JOGG John, esquire, of Dunbarton, rec date 1782, writ, debt, file #2664A, 2 folders

STUART Thomas, gentleman, of Antrim, vs STEEL James, yeoman, of Antrim, doc date 1793, rec date 1794, deed, land transfer, file #6575

SUILLIVAN John, esquire, of Durham, vs BLANCHARD Jotham, gentleman, of Amherst, rec date 1788, writ, debt, file #6728

SULLIVAN Hepzibah, widow, of Boston MA, vs ROBERS William, husbandman, of Weare, rec date 1788, recognizance, debits, file #6811

SULLIVAN John, esquire, of Durham, vs KAM James, gentleman, of Goffstown, doc date 1784, execution, debt, file #1813

SULLIVAN John, esquire, of Durham, vs KARR James, gentleman, of Goffstown, rec date 1782, judgment, debt, file #4509

SULLIVAN John, esquire, of Durham, vs BISBEE Andrew, husbandman, of Campbell Gore, rec date 1788, writ, debt, file #6994

SULLIVAN Valentine, taylor, of Londonderry, vs JEFFERIES David, merchant, of Boston MA, doc date 1771, writ, debt, file #795

SUMMERS Porter, gentleman, of Milford, vs MAY Naptali, husbandman, of Milford, doc date 1798, execution, debt, file #95

SUPREME Court Docket Books, doc date 1894, docket books 2 terms, supreme court, file #635

SWAN Caleb, merchant, of Charlestown, vs FISHER Daniel, esquire, of Newport, doc date 1798, execution, debt, file #89

SWAN John, husbandman, of Peterboro Slip, vs MONROE Josiah, yeoman, of Peterborough, doc date 1774, judgment, debt, file #730

SWAN John, yeoman, of Peterboro Slip, vs HEALD Thomas, esquire, of New Ipswich, doc date 1784, writ, debt, file #1264

SWAN John, yeoman, of Peterborough, vs MITCHEL Isaac, husbandman, of Peterborough, rec date 1785, writ, debt, file #4583

SWAN John, yeoman, of Peterborough, vs MITCHEL Isaac, of Peterborough, rec date 1785, judgment, debt, file #5136

SWAN John, yeoman, of Peterborough, vs MITCHELL Isaac, of Peterborough, rec date 1785, judgment, debt, file #4793

SWAN Robert, yeoman, of Peterborough, vs AMES Samuel, yeoman, of Hancock, rec date 1783, judgment, debt, file #4096

SWAN Robert, yeoman, of Peterborough, vs AMES Phineas, yeoman, of Hancock, rec date 1783, judgment, debt, file #4096

SWAN Robert, yeoman, of Peterborough, vs EWINS James, yeoman, of Londonderry, rec date 1783, judgment, debt, file #4304

SWAN William, esquire, of Groton MA, vs YOUNG John, physician, of Peterborough, doc date 1784, execution, debt, file #1762

SWAN William, esquire, of Groton MA, vs YOUNG John, physician, of Peterborough, rec date 1784, judgment, debt, file #4347

SWAN William, esquire, of Groton MA, vs YOUNG John, physician, of Peterborough, rec date 1787, various, land dispute, file #6804

SWAN William administrator of estate, of Groton, vs YOUNG John, physician, of Peterborough, rec date 1784, judgment, debt, file #4372

SWEAT Enoch, husbandman, of Cardigan, vs HUTCHINS William, gentleman, of New London, rec date 1783, writ, debt, file #3099

SWEATT John, joiner, of Salisbury, vs BOWEN John, husbandman, of Salisbury, rec date 1785, judgment, debt, file #5849

SWEATTE Benjamin, shipwright, of Boscawen, vs GREELEY Jonathan, esquire, of Kingston, doc date 1775, writ, debt, file #952

SWEATTE Benjamin, yeoman, of Boscawen, vs MORRILL Samuel, yeoman, of Boscawen, rec date 1783, writ, debt, file #3109

SWEET Moses, gentleman, of Salisbury, vs MARACH Nehemiah, joiner, of Canterbury, doc date 1799, writ, debt, file #432

SWETT Abraham, yeoman, of Haverhill MA, vs FOSTER James, husbandman, of Pelham, doc date 1773, writ, debt, file #1434

SWETT David, yeoman, of Amherst, vs PARKER Aaron, gentleman, of Hancock, doc date 1799, judgment, debt, file #288

SWETT Josiah, yeoman, of Windham, vs DODGE Ebenezer, husbandman, of Peterborough, doc date 1784, execution, debt, file #1520

SWETT Josiah, yeoman, of Windham, vs DODGE Robert, husbandman, of Peterborough, doc date 1784, execution, debt, file #1520

SWETT Josiah, yeoman, of Wenham MA, vs DODGE Ebenezer & Robert, husbandman, of Peterborough, rec date 1784, judgment, debt, file #4281

SWETT Josiah, husbandman, of Campbells Gore, vs GORDON John, yeoman, of Campbells Gore, rec date 1788, writ, debt, file #6944

SYMONDS Elizabeth, rec date 1787, deed, witness to deed, file #6644

SYMONDS James, cordwainer, of Ashby MA, vs PEARSON Amos, husbandman, of Lyndeborough, rec date 1785, judgment, debt, file #5546

SYMONDS James, cordwainer, of Ashby MA, vs PEARSON Amos, husbandman, of Lyndeborough, rec date 1785, judgment, debt, file #5999

TABELL Thomas, gentleman, of Mason, vs LAWRENCE Enoch, gentleman, of Mason, rec date 1785, writ, debt, file #5336, estate of Enoch LAWRENCE

TABS Frederick, husbandman, of Washington, vs DEAN Benjamin, husbandman, of Francestown, rec date 1783, writ, debt, file #3173

TAGGARAT Archibald, gentleman, of Hillsborough, vs JONES Samuel, yeoman, of Hillsborough, rec date 1783, civil litigation, debt, file #3881

TAGGART Archibald, gentleman, of Hillsborough, vs ABBOTT Darius, gentleman, of Hillsborough, rec date 1788, writ, debt, file #6673

TAGGART Archibald, gentleman, of Hillsborough, vs JOHNSON Zebodiah, yeoman, of Hillsborough, rec date 1782, judgment, debt, file #2706

TAGGART Archibald, gentleman, of Hillsborough, vs CHANDLER Isaac, yeoman, of Concord, doc date 1798, execution, debt, file #121

TAGGART Archibald, gentleman, of Hillsborough, vs HOGG Moses, yeoman, of Amherst, doc date 1799, judgment, debt, file #284

TAGGART Archibald, gentleman, of Hillsborough, vs TWISS John, husbandman, of Amherst, doc date 1784, execution, debt, file #1786

TAGGART Archibald, gentleman, of Hillsborough, vs BELCHER Larson, feltmaker, of Boston MA, rec date 1793, judgment, debt, file #2584

TAGGART Archibald, gentleman, of Hillsborough, vs DANA Samuel, gentleman, of Amherst, rec date 1783, writ, debt, file #3087

TAGGART Archibald, gentleman, of Hillsborough, vs BALDWIN Nahum, esquire, of Amherst, rec date 1782, appeal, debt, file #3985

TAGGART Archibald, gentleman, of Hillsborough, vs GRIMES James, gentleman, of Deering, rec date 1784, judgment, debt, file #4269

TAGGART Archibald, of Hillsborough, vs GOODALE Job, yeoman, of Marlborough MA, rec date 1784, judgment, debt, file #4623

TAGGART Archibald, gentleman, of Hillsborough, vs BIXBE Andrew, esquire, of Hillsborough, rec date 1785, writ, debt, file #6246

TAGGART Archibald, gentleman, of Hillsborough, vs GOODRIDGE Thomas, housewright, of Boxford MA, doc date 1784, writ, debt, file #1582

TAGGART Archibald, gentleman, of Hillsborough, vs GREEN David, yeoman, of Hillsborough, doc date 1784, execution, debt, file #1860

TAGGART Archibald, gentleman, of Hillsborough, vs NICHOLS James, yeoman, of New Worcester ma, rec date 1782, writ, debt, file #2804

TAGGART Archibald, gentleman, of Hillsborough, vs TWISS John, husbandman, of Amherst, rec date 1784, judgment, debt, file #4346

TAGGART Archibald, gentleman, of Hillsborough, vs SHANNON Richard C, esquire, of Hollis, rec date 1785, judgment, debt, file #5355

TAGGART Archibald, of Goffstown, vs INHABITANTS of Goffstown, of Goffstown, rec date 1786, writ, debt, file #6763

TAGGART Christian, spinster, of Goffstown, vs McCURDY John, gentleman, of Dunbarton, rec date 1785, indictment, force and assault, file #7039

TAGGART James, yeoman, of Peterborough, vs GOULD Jacob, yeoman, of Rindge, doc date 1772, writ, debt, file #1066

TAGGART James, yeoman, of Hill, vs DRESSER Asa, yeoman, of Campbells Gore, rec date 1783, writ, debt, file #3028

TAGGART John, husbandman, of Goffstown, vs FULTON Robert, husbandman, of Londonderry, doc date 1772, writ, debt, file #1394

TAGGART John, housewright, of Hillsborough, vs HILL John, esquire, of Boston MA, doc date 1773, writ, debt, file #1244

TAGGART John, yeoman, of Hillsborough, vs McCLENTOCK John, husbandman, of Hillsborough, rec date 1783, writ, debt, file #2999

TAGGART John, gentleman, of Peterboro Slip, vs HOW Isaac, yeoman, of New Ipswich, rec date 1783, judgment, debt, file #4213

TAGGART John, gentleman, of Peterboro Slip, vs APPLETON Isaac, gentleman, of New Ipswich, rec date 1783, judgment, debt, file #4213

TAGGART John, gentleman, of Peterboro Slip, vs CHAMPNEY Ebenezer, gentleman, of Groton MA, rec date 1783, judgment, debt, file #4213

TAGGART John, gentleman, of Peterboro Slip, vs HOAR Benjamin, gentleman, of New Ipswich, rec date 1783, judgment, debt, file #4213

TAGGART John, gentleman, of Dunbarton, vs McCURDY John (Lt), husbandman, of Goffstown, rec date 1785, various, land dispute, file #4843, fragile

TAGGART John, gentleman, of Dunbarton, vs COLLINS Moses, yeoman, of Goffstown, rec date 1785, various, land dispute, file #4843, fragile

TAGGART John, gentleman, of Dunbarton, vs McCURDY Matthew Scoby, minor, of Dunbarton, rec date 1785, various, land dispute, file #4843, fragile

TAGGART John, gentleman, of Dunbarton, vs DUTTON Roger, yeoman, of Goffstown, rec date 1785, various, land dispute, file #4843, fragile

TAGGART John, gentleman, of Dunbarton, vs McCURDY Robert, yeoman, of Dunbarton, rec date 1785, various, land dispute, file #4843, fragile

TAGGART John, gentleman, of Dunbarton, vs McCURDY Daniel Jr, minor, of Dunbarton, rec date 1785, various, land dispute, file #4843, fragile

TAGGART John, yeoman, of Goffstown, vs McCURDY Matthew Scoby, minor, of Dunbarton, rec date 1784, court case, debt, file #5313

TAGGART John, yeoman, of Goffstown, vs DUTTON Robert, yeoman, of Goffstown, rec date 1784, court case, debt, file #5313

TAGGART John, yeoman, of Goffstown, vs COLLINS Moses, yeoman, of Goffstown, rec date 1784, court case, debt, file #5313

TAGGART John, yeoman, of Goffstown, vs McCURDY Daniel Jr, minor, of Goffstown, rec date 1784, court case, debt, file #5313

TAGGART John, yeoman, of Goffstown, vs McCURDY Robert, yeoman, of Dunbarton, rec date 1784, court case, debt, file #5313

TAGGART John & Eliz, husbandman, of Goffstown, vs McCURDY John, gentleman, of Dunbarton, rec date 1786, various, debt, file #6064

TAGGART John & Elizabeth, husbandman, of Goffstown, vs McCURDY John, gentleman, of Dunbarton, rec date 1785, indictment, force and assault, file #7039

TAGGART John James, laborer, of Goffstown, vs McCURDY John, gentleman, of Dunbarton, rec date 1785, indictment, force and assault, file #7039

TAGGART John & Elizabeth, husbandman, of Goffstown, vs McCURDY John, gentleman, of Dunbarton, rec date 1785, writ, assault, file #5337

TAGGART Martha, widow, rec date 1788, deposition, debt, file #6583

TAGGART Peggy, spinster, of Goffstown, vs McCURDY John, gentleman, of Dunbarton, rec date 1785, indictment, force and assault, file #7039

TAGGART Robert, physician, of Merrimack, vs ATHERTON Peter, gentleman, of Harvard MA, doc date 1784, writ, debt, file #1589

TAGGART Rose, spinster, of Goffstown, vs McCURDY John, gentleman, of Dunbarton, rec date 1785, indictment, force and assault, file #7039

TAGGART Samuel, cordwainer, of Peterborough, vs STEWART Charles, yeoman, of Peterborough, doc date 1799, judgment, debt, file #289

TAGGART William, husbandman, of Peterboro Slip, vs GRAGG Hugh, husbandman, of Peterborough, rec date 1786, writ, debt, file #6305

TAGGARTY John 2nd, husbandman, of Peterborough, vs STEEL David, husbandman, of Peterborough, doc date 1778, rec date 1778, deed, land transfer, file #2154

TAGGERT Archibald, yeoman, of Hillsborough, vs POPE William, doc date 1773, judgment, debt, file #1179

TAGGERT Robert, physician, of Merrimack, vs STEVEN Samuel, physician, of Amherst, rec date 1783, writ, debt, file #3190

TAGGERT William, rec date 1786, appointments, liquor license, file #6240, part of Samuel CURTIS file

TALBUTT William, yeoman, of Hillsborough, vs JONES Tim, yeoman, of Lyndeborough, rec date 1783, writ, debt, file #3325

TALLANT Hugh, yeoman, of Pelham, vs BARKER Ebenezer, husbandman, of Pelham, doc date 1772, writ, assault, file #1392

TARBEL Samuel, gentleman, of Digby N s, vs FARWELL Henry, British officer, of Groton MA, rec date 1788, writ, debt, file #6974

TARBELL Edmond, yeoman, of Mason, vs BROWN James, yeoman, of Wilton, doc date 1774, writ, debt, file #1166

TARBELL Edmund, husbandman, of Mason, vs DODGE William, husbandman, of Mason, doc date 1784, civil litigation, debt, file #1643

TARBELL Edmund, innholder, of Mason, vs KIDDER Reuben, esquire, of New Ipswich, rec date 1783, writ, debt, file #3313

TARBELL Edmund, husbandman, of Mason, vs DICKEY James, gentleman, of Raby, rec date 1783, execution, debt, file #3647

TARBELL Edmund, yeoman, of New Ipswich, vs EATON Joseph, yeoman, of Dublin, rec date 1783, writ, debt, file #4516

TARBELL Edmund, husbandman, of Mason, vs DODGE William, husbandman, of Mason, rec date 1783, judgment, debt, file #4503

TARBELL Henry & Henry Jr, gentleman, of Groton MA, vs CUMMINGS John, yeoman, of Mason, rec date 1788, summons, land dispute, file #6975

TARBELL Henry & Sarah, gentleman, of Digby NS, vs CUMMINGS John, yeoman, of Mason, rec date 1788, summons, land dispute, file #6975

TARBELL John, of Amherst, vs TARBELL Samuel, of Amherst, doc date 1772, civil litigation, debt, file #653

TARBELL John, husbandman, of Mason, vs DODGE William, husbandman, of Mason, doc date 1784, civil litigation, debt, file #1645

TARBELL John, husbandman, of Mason, vs DODGE William, husbandman, of Mason, rec date 1783, judgment, debt, file #4723

TARBELL Samuel, yeoman, of Mason, vs AMES David, yeoman, of Hollis, doc date 1772, writ, debt, file #1042

TARBELL Samuel, husbandman, of Mason, vs JEFTS Thomas, yeoman, of Mason, doc date 1773, execution, debt, file #1486

TARBELL Samuel, gentleman, of Digby NS vs PHELPS Edward, cooper, of Leominster MA, rec date 1788, various, land dispute, file #6732

TARBELL Samuel, gentleman, of Digby NS vs HOLDEN John & Sible, taylor, of Reading MA, rec date 1788, various, land dispute, file #6732

TARBELL Samuel, gentleman, of Digby NS, vs PIERCE George & Deborah, esquire, rec date 1788, various, land dispute, file #6732

TARBELL Samuel, gentleman, of Digby NS vs MOOR Jonathan, yeoman, of Oatsfield, rec date 1788, various, land dispute, file #6732

TARBELL Samuel, gentleman, of Digby NS vs BOYTON Joseph & Sarah, heirs of, of Pepperell MA, rec date 1788, various, land dispute, file #6732

TARBELL Samuel, gentleman, of Digby NS vs BARNWELL Henry & Sarah, of Groton MA, rec date 1788, various, land dispute, file #6732

TARBELL Samuel, gentleman, of Digby NS vs LAWRENCE Samuel & Susana, of Groton MA, rec date 1788, various, land dispute, file #6732

TARBELL Samuel, yeoman, of Digby NS vs HOGKINS Hezekiel, yeoman, of Mason, rec date 1788, writ, debt, file #6732

TARBELL Samuel, gentleman, of Digby NS vs PHELPS Peter, cooper, of Leominster MA, rec date 1788, various, land dispute, file #6732

TARBELL Samuel, gentleman, of Digby NS vs CUMMINGS John, yeoman, of Mason, rec date 1788, various, land dispute, file #6732

TARBELL Samuel, gentleman, of Digby NS vs PHELPS Levi, cooper, of Leominster MA, rec date 1788, various, land dispute, file #6732

TARBELL Samuel, gentleman, of Digby NS vs MOORS Joseph, husbandman, of Rindge, rec date 1788, various, land dispute, file #6732

TARBELL Samuel, gentleman, of Digby NS, vs CUMMINGS John, yeoman, of Mason, rec date 1788, various, land dispute, file #6975

TARBELL Thomas, esquire, of Mason, vs HARRIS Stephen, yeoman, of Hollis, doc date 1774, writ, debt, file #1092

TARBELL William, yeoman, of Mason, vs PERRY Ebenezer, yeoman, of Wilton, doc date 1783, writ, debt, file #1261

TARBLE John, husbandman, of Mason, vs WAKER Silas, husbandman, of Mason, rec date 1788, writ, debt, file #7004

TARBOR James, yeoman, of Dunstable MA, vs GRAVES Calvin, yeoman, of Dunstable, rec date 1783, various, debt, file #2758, family kinships in file

TARBOX James, yeoman, of Dunstable MA, vs CUMINGS Silas, blacksmith, of New Boston, rec date 1782, writ, debt, file #2688

TARBOX James, taylor, of Dunstable MA, vs SHANNON Richard Cutts, esquire, of Hollis, rec date 1783, writ, debt, file #3119

TARBOX James, taylor, of Dunstable MA, vs BOYNTON Joshua, clockmaker, of Hollis, rec date 1783, writ, debt, file #3431

TAY William, gentleman, of Woburn, vs GOULD Richard, yeoman, of Amherst, rec date 1784, judgment, debt, file #5323

TAY William, gentleman, of Woburn, vs BLASDON Samuel, yeoman, of Lyndeborough, rec date 1784, judgment, debt, file #5323

TAYLOR Amos, husbandman, of Wilmington MA, vs WAITE John, husbandman, of Mason, rec date 1784, judgment, debt, file #4193

TAYLOR Anthony, husbandman, of Alexandria, vs CHAMPNEY John, husbandman, of New Ipswich, rec date 1784, judgment, debt, file #5316

TAYLOR Anthony, husbandman, of Alexandria, vs CHAMPNEY John, husbandman, of New Ipswich, rec date 1785, judgment, debt, file #5151

TAYLOR Daniel, yeoman, of Wilton, vs FRYE Isaac, yeoman, of Wilton, doc date 1774, judgment, debt, file #727

TAYLOR Daniel, yeoman, of Washington, vs FRYE Isaac, yeoman, of Wilton, doc date 1784, execution, debt, file #1971

TAYLOR Daniel, yeoman, of Washington, vs FRYE Isaac, yeoman, of Wilton, rec date 1783, execution, debt, file #2981

TAYLOR Daniel, yeoman, of Washington, vs FRYE Isaac, yeoman, of Wilton, rec date 1783, execution, debt, file #3270

TAYLOR David, yeoman, of Peterborough, vs TAYLOR Isaiah, physician, of Peterborough, doc date 1773, execution, debt, file #1478

TAYLOR David, husbandman, of Dunstable MA, vs SEARLES John, husbandman, of Dunstable, rec date 1785, writ, debt, file #2410

TAYLOR David, yeoman, of Dunstable MA, vs FLETCHER Robert, esquire, of Amherst, rec date 1786, writ, debt, file #6270

TAYLOR David, yeoman, of Dunstable MA, vs MUNROE Josiah, gentleman, of Amherst, rec date 1786, writ, debt, file #6270

TAYLOR Eleazer, yeoman, of Merrimack, vs TRUEL David, yeoman, of Amherst, doc date 1784, execution, debt, file #1766

308 HILLSBOROUGH COUNTY, NEW HAMPSHIRE, COURT RECORDS

TAYLOR Isaiah, yeoman, of Peterborough, vs STEEL David, yeoman, of Peterborough, doc date 1772, writ, debt, file #885

TAYLOR Isaiah, yeoman, of Peterborough, vs MITHCELL John, yeoman, of Hancock, rec date 1783, judgment, debt, file #3729

TAYLOR Isaiah, husbandman, of Peterborough, vs BUTTERS John Jr, yeoman, of Wilmington MA, rec date 1782, writ, debt, file #2836

TAYLOR Jacob, yeoman, of Dunstable, vs CUMINGS Samuel Jr, yeoman, of New Ipswich, doc date 1773, judgment, debt, file #1314

TAYLOR Jacob, labourer, of Amherst, vs STATE of NH, rec date 1782, recognizance, debt, file #2611

TAYLOR Jacob, gentleman, of Dunstable, vs CUMINGS David, gentleman, of Nottingham-West, rec date 1785, judgment, debt, file #4691

TAYLOR Jacob, gentleman, of Dunstable, vs WRIGHT Uriah, gentleman, of Hollis, rec date 1783, judgment, debt, file #4507

TAYLOR Jacob, gentleman, of Dunstable, vs FORD James, esquire, of Nottingham-West, rec date 1785, judgment, debt, file #4691

TAYLOR Jacob, gentleman, of Dunstable, vs LUND Phineas, husbandman, of Lyndeborough, rec date 1785, execution, debt, file #5918

TAYLOR Jacob, gentleman, of Dunstable, vs LUND Phineas, husbandman, of Lyndeborough, rec date 1785, writ, debt, file #6017

TAYLOR Jacob, husbandman, of Dunstable, vs WHITNEY James, husbandman, of Dunstable, doc date 1773, rec date 1773, deed, land transfer, file #6549

TAYLOR James, gentleman, of Hillsborough, vs PEARSON Moses, yeoman, of Wilmington MA, doc date 1799, writ, debt, file #383

TAYLOR James, yeoman, of Antrim, vs BELL Samuel, gentleman, of Francestown, doc date 1799, judgment, debt, file #239

TAYLOR James, gentleman, of Hollis, vs HOPKINSON Jonathan, yeoman, of Monadnock 1, doc date 1772, writ, debt, file #1070

TAYLOR James, gentleman, of Merrimack, vs JEWET Jacob Jr, trader, of Hollis, doc date 1773, writ, debt, file #1369

TAYLOR James, gentleman, of Merrimack, vs STATE of NH, rec date 1788, recognizance, counterfeiting, file #2252

TAYLOR James, gentleman, of Merrimack, vs STATE of NH, rec date 1776, recognizance, counterfeiting, file #252

TAYLOR James, gentleman, of Hollis, vs PEOPLE of NH, doc date 1776, rec date 1777, jurors verdict, debt, file #2206

TAYLOR James, gentleman, of Merrimack, vs GORDON James & Cozmo, gentleman, of Dunstable MA, rec date 1783, writ, debt, file #3031

TAYLOR James, physician, of Lunenburg MA, vs YOUNG John, physician, of Peterborough, rec date 1784, judgment, debt, file #4370

TAYLOR John, physician, of Lunenburg MA, vs YOUNG John, physician, of Peterborough, doc date 1774, execution, file #988

TAYLOR John, yeoman, of Antrim, vs GRIMES James, gentleman, of Deering, rec date 1783, writ, debt, file #3103

TAYLOR John, yeoman, of Amherst, vs POPE William, gentleman, of Hillsborough, rec date 1783, writ, debt, file #3333

TAYLOR Jonathan, husbandman, of Hollis, vs FRENCH Nehemiah, yeoman, of Hollis, rec date 1785, judgment, debt, file #5800

TAYLOR Jonathan, husbandman, of Hollis, vs FRENCH Nehemiah, yeoman, of Hollis, rec date 1785, execution, debt, file #5942

TAYLOR Joseph, yeoman, of Windsor NY, vs BENNETT Jonathan, gentleman, of Hancock, rec date 1783, execution, debt, file #3643

TAYLOR Nathan, yeoman, of Antrim, vs GOODALE Job, trader, of Marlborough MA, rec date 1784, judgment, debt, file #4358

TAYLOR Nathan, yeoman, of Fitchburg MA, vs BRADFORD Mary, widow, of Hillsborough, rec date 1786, judgment, debt, file #5773

TAYLOR Oliver, yeoman, of Dunstable MA, vs BROWN Abael, joiner, of Hollis, rec date 1785, writ, debt, file #2405

TAYLOR Timothy, esquire, of Merrimack, vs HOGG Moses, yeoman, of Amherst, doc date 1799, writ, debt, file #574

TAYLOR Timothy, esquire, of Merrimack, vs HUTCHINSON Solomon, yeoman, of Merrimack, doc date 1798, judgment, debt, file #566

TAYLOR Timothy, esquire, of Merrimack, vs HUTCHINSON Solomon, yeoman, of Merrimack, doc date 1799, judgment, debt, file #566

TAYLOR Timothy, innholder, of Merrimack, vs CARTER Edward, husbandman, of Hollis, doc date 1784, execution, debt, file #1714

TAYLOR Timothy, innholder, of Merrimack, vs CARTER Edward, husbandman, of Hollis, doc date 1784, execution, debt, file #1973

TAYLOR Timothy, innholder, of Merrimack, vs CARTER Edward, husbandman, of Hollis, rec date 1783, civil litigious, debt, file #2920

TAYLOR Timothy, innholder, of Merrimack, vs GREGG David, yeoman, of Francestown, rec date 1783, civil litigious, debt, file #2931

TAYLOR Timothy, innholder, of Merrimack, vs CARTER Edward, husbandman, of Hollis, rec date 1783, execution, debt, file #3229

TAYLOR Timothy, innholder, of Merrimack, vs CARTER Edward, husbandman, of Hollis, rec date 1783, writ, debt, file #3889

TAYLOR Timothy, husbandman, of Merrimack, vs REED Jacob, yeoman, of Dunstable, rec date 1782, execution, debt, file #5739

TAYLOR Timothy, esquire, of Merrimack, vs INHABITANTS of Merrimack, of Merrimack, rec date 1788, writ, debits, file #6810

TAYLOR William, yeoman, of Antrim, vs CURTIS Samuel, yeoman, of Antrim, doc date 1784, writ, debt, file #1575

TAYLOR William, gentleman, of Woburn MA, vs BLASDELL Samuel, yeoman, of Lyndeborough, doc date 1784, execution, debt, file #1954

TEMPLE Dorothy, of Marlborough MA, vs JOSLYN Nathaniel, of Henniker, doc date 1770, rec date 1772, deed, land transfer, file #6840

TEMPLE Jonathan, yeoman, of Henniker, vs CUMMINGS Samuel, esquire, of Hollis, doc date 1774, writ, debt, file #1132

TEMPLE Jonathan, gentleman, of Marlborough MA, vs HOW Charles, husbandman, of Swanzey, doc date 1784, execution, debt, file #1729

TEMPLE Jonathan, husbandman, of Marlborough MA, vs ANDREW Isaac, esquire, of Hillsborough, doc date 1784, writ, debt, file #1622

TEMPLE Jonathan, gentleman, of Marlborough MA, vs HOW Charles, husbandman, of Swanzey, rec date 1783, writ, debt, file #3425

TEMPLE Jonathan, yeoman, of Henniker, vs ATHERTON Joshua, esquire, of Amherst, rec date 1785, writ, debt, file #5422

TEMPLE Jonathan, husbandman, of Henniker, vs CURTIS Samuel, physician, of Boston MA, rec date 1786, various, debt, file #6069

TEMPLE Jonathan, husbandman, of Henniker, vs CURTIS Samuel, physician, of Boston MA, rec date 1786, various, debt, file #6068

TEMPLE Jonathan, of Marlborough MA, vs JOSLYN Nathaniel, of Henniker, doc date 1771, rec date 1772, deed, land transfer, file #6840

TEMPLETON Adam, wheelwright, of Windham, vs HILL John, esquire, of Boston MA, doc date 1773, writ, debt, file #1245

TEMPLETON James, husbandman, of Peterborough, vs GRAGG Samuel, trader, of Peterboro Slip, rec date 1788, writ, debt, file #2555

TENNEY Jonathan, gentleman, of Salem, vs HARD Daniel, husbandman, of Nottingham-West, rec date 1784, writ, debt, file #4862

TENNEY William, yeoman, of Hollis, vs SPAULDING Thomas, gentleman, of Pepperell MA, doc date 1773, writ, debt, file #1232

TENNEY William, husbandman, of Hollis, vs BUTLER Jesse, husbandman, of Pelham, doc date 1784, execution, debt, file #1975

TENNEY William, husbandman, of Hollis, vs BUTLER Jesse, husbandman, of Pelham, rec date 1783, writ, debt, file #3415

TENNEY William, husbandman, of Hollis, vs MOSHER James, husbandman, of Hollis, rec date 1783, writ, debt, file #4040

TENNEY William, husbandman, of Hollis, vs HALE David, husbandman, of Hollis, rec date 1784, judgment, debt, file #4261

TENNEY William, husbandman, of Hollis, vs MOSHER James, husbandman, of Hollis, rec date 1784, judgment, debt, file #5000, estate of Daniel MOSHER

TENNEY Wm Jr, yeoman, of Hollis, vs STATE of NH, rec date 1782, recognizance, debt, file #2606

TENNO Ephraim, leather dresser, of Boston MA, vs KELLY Joseph, gentleman, of Nottingham, doc date 1773, execution, debt, file #1460

TERRELL John, yeoman, of Hancock, vs STONE David, joiner, of Hancock, doc date 1798, judgment, debt, file #566

THIDDER Reuben, esquire, of New Ipswich, vs TARBELL Edmund, yeoman, of Mason, rec date 1784, judgment, debt, file #4348

THOM John, yeoman, of Peterboro Slip, vs McALLARY William, of Amherst, doc date 1772, writ, assault, file #793

THOM John, yeoman, of Peterborough, vs KENNEDY John, yeoman, of Peterborough, doc date 1772, writ, debt, file #908

THOMAS Isaiah, printer, of Worcester MA, vs TUTTLE Stephen, husbandman, of Goffstown, rec date 1785, various, debt, file #4697

THOMAS Joseph, gentleman, of Merrimack, vs McFARLAND Samuel, husbandman, of Londonderry, rec date 1788, writ, debt, file #6939

THOMAS Nathaniel, yeoman, of Hinsdale, vs BUTTERFIELD Joseph, gentleman, of Wilton, rec date 1782, writ, debt, file #2681

THOMPSON Hugh, yeoman, of Derryfield, vs HALL John Jr, yeoman, of Derryfield, rec date 1782, judgment, debt, file #4033

THOMPSON Thomas, esquire, of Hollis, vs BLOOD Francis, yeoman, of Hollis, doc date 1798, execution, debt, file #103

THOMPSON Thomas, esquire, of Salisbury, vs LANG Lowell, yeoman, of Sanborntown, doc date 1798, execution, debt, file #70

THOMPSON Thomas, esquire, of Salisbury, vs THOMPSON Jonathan, yeoman, of Sanborntown, doc date 1798, judgment, debt, file #566

THOMPSON Thomas, esquire, of Salisbury, vs CLOUGH David, laborer, of Northfield, doc date 1799, debt, file #446

THOMPSON Thomas, esquire, of Salisbury, vs CLOUGH Davis, laborer, of Northfield, doc date 1798, judgment, debt, file #566

THOMPSON Thomas, esquire, of Salisbury, vs DUNCAN William, esquire, of Concord, doc date 1799, judgment, debt, file #566

THOMPSON Thomas, esquire, of Salisbury, vs LEVERENIO Ephraim, husbandman, of Sanbornton, doc date 1799, debt, file #495

THOMPSON Thomas, esquire, of Salisbury, vs SHIELDS Daniel, husbandman, of New Chester, doc date 1799, debt, file #454

THOMPSON Thomas, esquire, of Salisbury, vs SMART Dudley, husbandman, of Sandbornton, doc date 1799, debt, file #487

THOMPSON Thomas, esquire, of Salisbury, vs CAMPBELL Benjamin & James, yeoman, of Roby, doc date 1798, execution, debt, file #101

THOMS John & Mary M, cordwainer, of Nottingham, vs MELLER Charles, cordwainer, of Litchfield, doc date 1772, rec date 1772, deed, land transfer, file #6849

THOMSON Robert, esquire, of Elsham Endland, vs WALKER Zacheus, gentleman, of Merrimack, rec date 1788, writ, debt, file #6982

THORLA John, cordwainer, of Newbury MA, vs EASTMAN Benjamin, husbandman, of Contoocook, doc date 1757, rec date 1778, deed, land transfer, file #2161

THORNDIKE Israel, merchant, of Beverly MA, vs GOLDSMITH Josiah, gentleman, of Walpole, rec date 1786, writ, debt, file #6123

THORNDIKE Israel, husbandman, of Beverly MA, vs GOLDSMITH Josiah, gentleman, of Walpole, rec date 1786, judgment, debt, file #6483

THORNDIKE Joseph, esquire, of Jaffrey, vs RUSSELL Peter, husbandman, of Amherst, rec date 1785, judgment, debt, file #5216

THORNTON Matthew, esquire, of Merrimack, vs AMES Stephen, husbandman, of Dublin, doc date 1784, execution, debt, file #1898

THORNTON Matthew, esquire, of Merrimack, vs ASTEN Timothy, husbandman, of Temple, doc date 1784, execution, debt, file #1898

THORNTON Matthew, esquire, of Merrimack, vs SMITH Elias, husbandman, of Londonderry, rec date 1786, writ, debt, file #6296

THORNTON Matthew, esquire, of Merrimack, vs GREGG James (estate), deceased, of Londonderry, rec date 1785, writ, debt, file #6224

THORNTON Matthew, esquire, of Merrimack, vs MOOR Henry, gentleman, of Chester, rec date 1788, writ, debt, file #6738

THORNTON Matthew, esquire, of Newmarket, vs GOODRIDGE Sewall, clerk, of Lyndeborough, rec date 1788, writ, debt, file #6739

THORNTON Matthew, esquire, of Newmarket, vs SPAULDING Levi, esquire, of Lyndeborough, rec date 1788, writ, debt, file #6739

THORNTON Matthew, esquire, of Merrimack, vs CRAM Joseph, husbandman, of Society Land, rec date 1788, writ, debt, file #6637

THORNTON Matthew, yeoman, of Reeds Ferry, vs Town of Reeds Ferry, doc date 1784, bond, bond for clerk, file #802

THORNTON Matthew, esquire, of Merrimack, vs RAMSEY James Jr, husbandman, of Society Land, rec date 1784, judgment, debt, file #4606

THORNTON Matthew, esquire, of Merrimack, vs MOULTON Jonathan, esquire, of Hampton, rec date 1784, various, debt, file #4677

THORNTON Matthew, esquire, of Merrimack, vs BIXBE Andrew, yeoman, of Hillsborough, rec date 1785, judgment, debt, file #5179

THORNTON Matthew, esquire, of Merrimack, vs BUTTERFIELD Joseph, gentleman, of Wilton, rec date 1785, judgment, debt, file #5219

THORNTON Matthew, esquire, of Merrimack, vs WILLOUGHBY Jonas, yeoman, of Hollis, rec date 1786, writ, debt, file #6303

THORNTON Matthew, esquire, of Merrimack, vs KEMP Thomas, blacksmith, of Hollis, rec date 1786, writ, debt, file #6335

THORNTON Matthew, esquire, of Merrimack, vs WIGGIN Joseph, blacksmith, of Exeter, rec date 1788, writ, debt, file #6613

THORNTON Matthew, esquire, of Merrimack, vs McCLUER James, yeoman, of Candia, rec date 1788, writ, debt, file #7000

THORNTON Matthew, esquire, of Merrimack, vs WIER Robert, gentleman, of Walpole, rec date 1788, writ, debt, file #6999

THORNTON William, of Thornton, vs Town of Bedford, rec date 1778, deposition, road lay out, file #2226

THORTON Matthew, husbandman, of Merrimack, vs ARTEN Timothy, husbandman, of Temple, doc date 1784, execution, debt, file #1895

THORTON Matthew, esquire, of Merrimack, vs TAYLOR Timothy, selectman, of Merrimack, rec date 1788, writ, debt, file #6608

THORTON Matthew, esquire, of Merrimack, vs CUMMINGS Simeon, selectman, of Merrimack, rec date 1788, writ, debt, file #6608

THORTON Matthew, esquire, of Merrimack, vs McGAIO Jacob, selectman, of Merrimack, rec date 1788, writ, debt, file #6608

THORTON Matthew, esquire, of Merrimack, vs TAGGART Archibald, husbandman, of Hillsborough, rec date 1788, writ, debt, file #6916

THORTON Matthew, esquire, of Merrimack, vs JONES Joshua, husbandman, of Hillsborough, rec date 1788, writ, debt, file #6916

THORTON Matthew, esquire, of Merrimack, vs BIXBIE Andrew, husbandman, of Hillsborough, rec date 1788, writ, debt, file #6916

THORTON Matthew, esquire, of Merrimack, vs WHITTLE Thomas Jr, yeoman, of Litchfield, rec date 1784, writ, ferry dispute, file #4621

THURSTON Moses, feltmaker, of Hollis, vs CARTER Thomas, laborer, of Hollis, doc date 1784, execution, debt, file #1945

THURSTON Moses, hatter, of Hollis, vs TOPLIN John, esquire, of Newbury NY, rec date 1777, writ, debt, file #2189

THURSTON Moses, hatter, of Hollis, vs WHITING Benjamin, esquire, of Hollis, rec date 1777, writ, debt, file #2189

THURSTON Moses, feltmaker, of Hollis, vs CARTER Thomas, laborer, of Hollis, rec date 1783, writ, debt, file #3424

THURSTON William, gentleman, of Walpole MA, vs LORD William, yeoman, of Francestown, doc date 1798, judgment, debt, file #566

TIDDALL Samuel, husbandman, of Peterboro Slip, vs SAWYER Josiah, gentleman, of Hancock, rec date 1785, writ, debt, file #5390

TIDEL Amos, yeoman, of Rindge, vs PROCTOR Oliver, yeoman, of Townsend MA, doc date 1772, writ, debt, file #1068

TILTON Charles, yeoman, of Andover, vs WADLEIGH Simeon D, tanner, of Salisbury, rec date 1783, writ, debt, file #3101

TILTON Mary E, of Manchester, vs O'CONNOR Denis F, administrator of estate, of E Kingston, doc date 1894, probate dispute, supreme court, file #587

TILTON Philip, esquire, of Kingston, vs FIFIELD Anna, widow, of Salisbury, rec date 1786, various, debt, file #6084

TINNO Ephraim, gentleman, of Boston MA, vs KELLY Joseph, gentleman, of Nottingham-West, doc date 1784, writ, debt, file #1576

TITCOMB Benjamin, yeoman, of Hopkinton, vs TITCOMB Moses, yeoman, of Wenham MA, doc date 1784, rec date 1785, deed, land transfer, file #5662

TITCOMB Isaac, husbandman, of Newton MA, vs SWETT Benjamin, yeoman, of Boscawen, rec date 1784, judgment, debt, file #4244

TITCOMB Moses, taylor, of Wenham MA, vs FAIRFIELD Joseph, of Perrystown, doc date 1785, rec date 1788, deed, land transfer, file #6753

TIVET John, of Townsend MA, vs SHEPLE Abel, yeoman, of Hollis, doc date 1800, judgment, debt, file #568

TODD Alexander, tax collector, of Goffstown, vs FOWLER Nathaniel, yeoman, of Goffstown, doc date 1780, rec date 1782, deed, land transfer, file #6568

TODD Alexander, vs GRAGG Samuel, doc date 1773, cost sheets only, file #1344

TODD Bellridge, spinster, of Peterborough, vs TODD John, husbandman, of Peterborough, doc date 1780, rec date 1801, deed, land transfer, file #5674

TODD John, husbandman, of Temple, vs FOX Timothy, yeoman, of New Ipswich, doc date 1783, writ, debt, file #1260

TOMPSON Cleark, of Bedford, rec date 1777, application, tavern license, file #7034

TOWLE Francis, husbandman, of Chester, vs TRACY Patrick, esquire, of Newburyport MA, doc date 1774, writ, debt, file #1130

TOWNE Edmund, yeoman, of New Ipswich, vs WARNER Daniel, gentleman, of Amherst, doc date 1784, execution, debt, file #1515

TOWNE Edmund, yeoman, of New Ipswich, vs WARNER Daniel, gentleman, of Amherst, rec date 1783, writ, debt, file #3625

TOWNE Edmund, yeoman, of New Ipswich, vs WARNER Daniel, gentleman, of Amherst, doc date 1784, execution, debt, file #1738

TOWNE Enos, trader, of New Chester, vs CALL John, yeoman, of Andover, doc date 1798, execution, debt, file #153

TOWNE Ezra, gentleman, of New Ipswich, vs BALLARD Nathan, gentleman, of Wilton, rec date 1784, appeal, debt, file #4108

TOWNE Ezra, gentleman, of New Ipswich, vs STEVENS Caleb, yeoman, of Merrimack, rec date 1783, execution, debt, file #3817

TOWNE Ezra, gentleman, of New Ipswich, vs STEVENS Caleb, yeoman, of Merrimack, rec date 1783, writ, debt, file #3913

TOWNE Isaac, esquire, of Stoddard, vs STEARN John, yeoman, of Amherst, rec date 1783, execution, debt, file #2989

TOWNE Israel, gentleman, of Stoddard, vs WHITTMORE Amos, yeoman, of Lyndeborough, doc date 1784, civil litigation, debt, file #1631

TOWNE Israel, esquire, of Stoddard, vs STEARNS John, yeoman, of Amherst, doc date 1784, execution, debt, file #1981

TOWNE Israel, gentleman, of Stoddard, vs GRIFFIN Nathaniel, potter, of Temple, rec date 1783, judgment, debt, file #4094

TOWNE Israel, gentleman, of Amherst, vs JONES Samuel, yeoman, of Hillsborough, rec date 1783, execution, debt, file #3826

TOWNE Israel, gentleman, of Stoddard, vs WHITTMOR Amos, gentleman, of Lyndeborough, rec date 1783, judgment, debt, file #4093

TOWNE Joseph, gentleman, of Hopkinton, vs MORSE Jacob, yeoman, of Hollis, doc date 1798, execution, debt, file #85

TOWNE Joseph, gentleman, of Hopkinton, vs RUNNELLS Jonathan, clothier, of Concord, doc date 1799, debt, file #497

TOWNE Joseph, gentleman, of Hopkinton, vs BURNS John, gentleman, of Fisherfield, doc date 1799, debt, file #498

TOWNE Joseph, yeoman, of Amherst, vs BIXBE Andrew, yeoman, of Hillsborough, rec date 1783, writ, debt, file #4555

TOWNE Samuel, trader, of Acworth, vs COVER Samuel, gentleman, of Boscawen, doc date 1798, execution, debt, file #114

TOWNE Samuel, trader, of Francestown, vs GRAGG Samuel, trader, of Peterboro Slip, rec date 1788, writ, debt, file #6718

TOWNE Thomas, husbandman, of Lyndeborough, vs HENCHMAN Nathaniel, physician, of Amherst, doc date 1799, writ, debt, file #574

TOWNS Israel Jr, gentleman, of Stoddard, vs JONES Samuel, yeoman, of Hillsborough, rec date 1782, judgment, debt, file #2738

TOWNSEND Elizabeth, single, of Hollis?, vs KING Zachariah, yeoman, of Hollis, doc date 1775, rec date 1778, deed, land transfer, file #6557

TOWNSEND Mehitabel, single, of Hollis?, vs KING Zachariah, yeoman, of Hollis, doc date 1775, rec date 1778, deed, land transfer, file #6557

TOWNSEND Nathaniel, vs KING Zachariah, doc date 1775, rec date 1778, deed, land transfer, file #6557

TOWNSEND Susannah, single, of Hollis?, vs KING Zachariah, yeoman, of Hollis, doc date 1775, rec date 1778, deed, land transfer, file #6557

TOWNSEND Thomas, yeoman, of Bedford, vs BELL Joseph, yeoman, of Bedford, doc date 1784, execution, debt, file #1559

TOWNSEND Thomas, yeoman, of Bedford, vs BELL Joseph, yeoman, of Bedford, doc date 1784, execution, debt, file #1522

TOWNSEND William B, esquire, of Boston MA, vs NICHOLS Ebenezer, esquire, of Merrimack, doc date 1773, execution, debt, file #1466

TRACY Patrick, esquire, of Newburyport MA, vs KARR Jonathan, yeoman, of Chester, doc date 1774, writ, debt, file #821

TRACY Patrick, esquire, of Newburyport MA, vs PAIN Amos, husbandman, of Chester, doc date 1774, writ, debt, file #1131, fragile

TRACY Patrick, esquire, of Newburyport MA, vs BROWN Caleb, husbandman, of Candia, doc date 1784, civil litigation, debt, file #1653

TRACY Patrick, esquire, of Newburyport MA, vs BROWN Caleb, husbandman, of Candia, doc date 1777, judgment, debt, file #2043

TRACY Patrick, esquire, of Newburyport MA, vs BROWN Caleb, husbandman, of Candia, rec date 1783, writ, debt, file #4050

TREADWELL Robert Odiorne, merchant, of Portsmouth, vs FARMER Silas, husbandman, of Greenfield, doc date 1791, rec date 1793, deed, land transfer, file #5666

TRUEL Amos, yeoman, of Amherst, vs GORDON James, merchant, of Dunstable MA, rec date 1782, writ, debt, file #2785

TRUEL David, taylor, of Litchfield, vs FROST Joseph, yeoman, of Tewksbury MA, rec date 1783, writ, debt, file #3093

TRUMBEL Samuel, husbandman, of Warner, vs TUCKER Ebenezer, husbandman, of Warner, rec date 1786, judgment, debt, file #6467

TUCK John, yeoman, of Amherst, vs MILLER Farrar, yeoman, of Amherst, doc date 1786, rec date 1786, deed, land transfer, file #5018

TUCKER Joseph, of Halifax, rec date 1788, deposition, debt, file #6937

TUCKER Moses, gentleman, of New Ipswich, vs HODGMAN Reuben, husbandman, of Mason, rec date 1785, writ, debt, file #4679

TURNER Prime, blacksmith, of Harvard MA, vs PERRY James, saddler, of Temple, doc date 1784, execution, debt, file #1509

TURNER Prime, blacksmith, of Harvard MA, vs PERRY James, saddler, of Temple, doc date 1784, execution, debt, file #1682

TURNER Prince, blacksmith, of Harvard MA, vs AMSDEN Abraham Jr, yeoman, of Peterboro Slip, rec date 1783, writ, debt, file #3448

TURNER Prince, blacksmith, of Harvard MA, vs PERRY James, saddler, of Temple, rec date 1783, writ, debt, file #4560

TUSBERY Jacob & Hannah, yeoman, of Weare, vs TUXEBURY Timothy, of Almsbury, doc date 1772, rec date 1772, deed, land transfer, file #6846

TUTTLE John, minor (laborer), of Amherst, vs HOBSON William, cordwainer, of Amherst, rec date 1786, warrant, assault, file #5749

TUTTLE Nathan, yeoman, of Amherst, vs SARGENT Paul Dudley, merchant, of Amherst, doc date 1773, writ, debt, file #1346

TUTTLE Nathan, yeoman, of Amherst, vs SARGENT Paul Dudley, esquire, of Boston MA, rec date 1785, writ, debt, file #5423

TUTTLE Sampson, gentleman, of Littleton MA, vs FARR Levi, husbandman, of New Ipswich, rec date 1782, appeal, debt, file #4017

TUTTLE Sampson, gentleman, of Littleton MA, vs EVANS Elsey, husbandman, of Winchester, rec date 1785, execution, debt, file #5968

TUTTLE Sampson, gentleman, of Littleton MA, vs EVENS Elsey, husbandman, of Winchester, rec date 1785, judgment, debt, file #5829

TUTTLE Stephen, yeoman, of Goffstown, vs PARKER Jonathan, physician, of Litchfield, rec date 1783, writ, debt, file #3949

TUTTLE William, husbandman, of Littleton MA, vs JOHNSON David, husbandman, of Pelham, rec date 1783, judgment, debt, file #3786

TUTTLE William, gentleman, of Littleton MA, vs BRADFORD Samuel, gentleman, of Hillsborough, rec date 1785, writ, debt, file #4806

TUTTLE William, gentleman, of Littleton MA, vs TUCKER Moses, yeoman, rec date 1784, judgment, debt, file #4978

TUTTLE William, gentleman, of Littleton MA, vs BRADFORD Andrew, yeoman, of Hillsborough, rec date 1785, writ, debt, file #4806

TUXBURY Jacob & Isaac, yeoman, of Weare, vs SHAW Ichabod, yeoman, of Marlborough, rec date 1783, writ, debt, file #4544

TWISS John, yeoman, of Amherst, vs HOPKINS Benjamin, of Amherst, rec date 1783, writ, debt, file #3036

TWISS Jonathan, yeoman, of Amherst, vs TWISS John, yeoman, of Amherst, doc date 1776, rec date 1787, deed, land transfer, file #2495

TYLER Adonijah, husbandman, of Hopkinton, vs TEMPLE Jonathan, husbandman, of Henniker, doc date 1773, writ, debt, file #1174

TYLER Jeremiah, blacksmith, of Andover MA, vs WHITAKER Thomas, yeoman, of Londonderry, rec date 1786, writ, debt, file #6127

TYLER William, cordwainer, of Haverhill MA, vs McCURDY John, husbandman, of Londonderry, doc date 1772, writ, debt, file #1403

TYNG Dudley Atkins, esquire, of Tyngsboro, vs KELLEY Moses, esquire, of Goffstown, doc date 1798, execution, debt, file #115

TYNG James, merchant, of Dunstable MA, vs LUND Phineas, yeoman, of Lyndeborough, doc date 1773, execution, debt, file #1476

TYNG James, merchant, of Dunstable MA, vs RAND John, esquire, of Deerfield, doc date 1773, writ, debt, file #1345

TYNG James, merchant, of Dunstable, vs LUND Phinehas, yeoman, of Lyndeborough, doc date 1773, execution, debt, file #1214

UNDERWOOD Isaac, husbandman, of Needham MA, vs JOHNSON Moses, yeoman, of Peterborough, rec date 1785, judgment, debt, file #4968

UNDERWOOD Isaac, husbandman, of Needham MA, vs TAYLOR Isaiah, husbandman, of Peterborough, doc date 1784, rec date 1785, deed, land transfer, file #5622

UNDERWOOD Isaac, husbandman, of Needham MA, vs ROBBE William Jr, husbandman, of Peterborough, doc date 1784, rec date 1785, judgment, debt, file #5622

UNDERWOOD James, esquire, of Litchfield, vs CROMBIE John, gentleman, of Londonderry, doc date 1784, execution, debt, file #1866

UNDERWOOD James, esquire, of Litchfield, vs McQUESTION William, of Litchfield, rec date 1783, various, boundary dispute, file #2748

UNDERWOOD James, gentleman, of Bedford, vs MORRIL Robert, yeoman, of Bedford, rec date 1783, court case, debt, file #2879, PATTERSON kinship

UNDERWOOD James, esquire, of Litchfield, vs BARNET James, husbandman, of Londonderry, rec date 1786, writ, debt, file #6331

UNDERWOOD John, rec date NONE, bill list, file #7045

UPTON Elisha, cordwainer, of Meuthen MA, vs SANDERS Joseph, gentleman, of Derryfield, rec date 1784, judgment, debt, file #4376

UPTON Elisha, cordwainer, of Methuen MA, vs SANDON Joseph, gentleman, of Derryfield, rec date 1786, writ, debt, file #6318

UPTON Elisha, cordwainer, of Methuen MA, vs GOFFIN Theophilus, husbandman, of Derryfield, rec date 1786, writ, debt, file #6318

UPTON Elisha, cordwainer, of Methuen MA, vs SANDERS Joseph, gentleman, of Derryfield, rec date 1786, writ, debt, file #6136

UPTON Elisha, cordwainer, of Methuen MA, vs WILKINS Berry Jr, of Amherst, doc date 1787, rec date 1788, deed, land transfer, file #6827

UPTON Hezekiah, gentleman, of Reading MA, vs PEARSON Amos, yeoman, of Lyndeborough, doc date 1784, execution, debt, file #1972

URAN John, yeoman, of Boscawen, vs CARTER Winthrop, of Boscawen, doc date 1772?, judgment, sureties, file #693

USHER Eleazer, innholder, of Medford MA, vs KIMBALL Abraham, trader, of Amherst, doc date 1799, writ, debt, file #573

USHER Robert Jr, yeoman, of Merrimack, vs PRIEST William, yeoman, of Stoddard, rec date 1784, judgment, debt, file #4644

USHER Robert, yeoman, of Merrimack, vs BLANCHARD Joshua, merchant, of Boston MA, doc date 1772, writ, debt, file #921

USHER Robert, yeoman, of Merrimack, vs SMITH John, husbandman, of Lunenburg MA, doc date 1773, writ, debt, file #1343

USHER Robert Jr, yeoman, of Merrimack, vs EVERIT Samuel, yeoman, of Marlow, rec date 1784, judgment, debt, file #4984

USHER William, husbandman, of Merrimack, vs HUTCHINSON Solomon, husbandman, of Merrimack, doc date 1768, rec date 1786, deed, land transfer, file #5159

VANS William, merchant, of Salem MA, vs PORTER Francis, yeoman, of Peterborough, rec date 1784, judgment, debt, file #4651

VANS William & Wm Jr, merchants, of Salem, vs PORTER Francis, yeoman, of Windham, rec date 1785, judgment, debt, file #5127

VANS William Jr, merchant, of Salem MA, vs PORTER Francis, yeoman, of Peterborough, rec date 1784, judgment, debt, file #4651

VARNUM Bradley, yeoman, of Dracut MA, vs HUTCHINSON Solomon, yeoman, of Merrimack, doc date 1784, civil litigation, debt, file #1637

VARNUM Joseph Jr, husbandman, of Dracut MA, vs BELL Joseph, husbandman, of Bedford, rec date 1784, writ, debt, file #4669

VICKER Benjamin, husbandman, of Merrimack, vs MOOR William Jr, yeoman, of Bedford, doc date 1800, writ, debt, file #575

VICKER Benjamin, husbandman, of Merrimack, vs PRESTON Samuel, printer, of Amherst, doc date 1799, writ, debt, file #364

VICKERY John, yeoman, of Bedford, vs DARRAH James, yeoman, of Merrimack, rec date 1783, judgment, debt, file #3724

VICKORY Benjamin, gentleman, of Merrimack, vs McCLEARG David, yeoman, of Merrimack, rec date 1783, writ, debt, file #3566

VOSE James, husbandman, of Bedford, vs INHABITANTS of Bedford, of Bedford, rec date 1784, various, debt, file #4189, against selectmen

VOSE James, husbandman, of Bedford, vs WALLACE John, gentleman, of Bedford, rec date 1784, various, debt, file #4599

VOSE James, husbandman, of Bedford, vs RAND John, gentleman, of Bedford, rec date 1784, various, debt, file #4599

VOSE James, husbandman, of Bedford, vs WALLACE John, esquire, of Bedford, rec date 1785, various, debt, file #5243

VOSE James, gentleman, of Bedford, vs VOSE Samuel, gentleman, of Bedford, rec date 1786, writ, debt, file #6281

VOSE James, gentleman, of Bedford, vs MOORE James, gentleman, of Bedford, rec date 1786, writ, debt, file #6281

VOSE James, gentleman, of Bedford, vs CHANDLER Zechariah, gentleman, of Bedford, rec date 1786, writ, debt, file #6281

VOSE Samuel, husbandman, of Bedford, vs FLAGG Samuel, husbandman, of Worcester MA, rec date 1785, writ, debt, file #5392

WAIT Hannah, single, of Framingham MA, vs HOGG Ebenezer, schoolmaster, of Marlborough MA, rec date 1788, fornication, file #6174, part of Samuel CURTIS file

WAIT John, yeoman, of Mason, vs FRENCH William, yeoman, of Mason, rec date 1783, writ, debt, file #3931

WAIT Phinehas, gentleman, of Groton MA, vs GOULD James, gentleman, of Hanover, rec date 1785, writ, debt, file #5828

WAIT Robert P, vs the NASHUA ARMORY ASSOCIATION, corp, doc date 1890, plaintiffs brief, supreme court, file #598

WAITE John, husbandman, of Mason, vs SHANNON Richard Cutts, esquire, of Hollis, rec date 1785, writ, debt, file #4759

WAITE Nathan, victualler, of Pembroke, vs TYLER Benjamin, esquire, of Marblehead MA, doc date 1774, writ, debt, file #1127

WAKEFIELD Ebenezer, cordwainer, of Amherst, vs BLANCHARD Jotham, gentleman, of Peterborough, rec date 1785, writ, debt, file #6015

WAKEFIELD Ebenezer, cordwainer, of Amherst, vs BLANCHARD Jotham, gentleman, of Peterborough, rec date 1785, judgment, debt, file #6457

WAKEFIELD Thomas, yeoman, of Amherst, vs BRADFORD Joseph, husbandman, of Amherst, doc date 1771, rec date 1779, deed, land transfer, file #2125

WAKEFIELD Thomas, husbandman, of Amherst, vs KELLEY Moses, esquire, of Goffstown, rec date 1783, bond, debt, file #3358

WAKEFIELD Thomas, gentleman, of Amherst, vs KELLEY Moses, esquire, of Goffstown, rec date 1783, bond, in jail, file #3310

WAKEFIELD Thomas, husbandman, of Amherst, vs KELLY Moses, esquire, of Goffstown, rec date 1783, writ, debt, file #3351

WALDEN James, husbandman, of Bedford, vs PLATTS Daniel, husbandman, of Bedford, doc date 1798, judgment, debt, file #567

WALDO Samuel & Francis, yeoman, of Roxbury MA, vs KENDALL Ebenezer, of Dunstable, doc date 1768, rec date 1772, deed, land transfer, file #6839

WALDRON Isaac, husbandman, of New Almbury, vs COLLINS Benjamin, husbandman, of Weare, doc date 1774, execution, debt, file #753

WALDRON Isaac, husbandman, of New Almbury, vs COLLINS Benjamin, husbandman, of Weare, doc date 1774, execution, file #1000

WALINGSFORD David, gentleman, of Hollis, vs STEARNS John, yeoman, of Hollis, doc date 1784, execution, debt, file #1744

WALKER Alexander, esquire, of Goffstown, vs KELLEY Moses, yeoman, of Hopkinton, doc date 1799, writ, debt, file #445

WALKER Alexander, esquire, of Goffstown, vs MURDOUGH Thomas, yeoman, of Hillsborough, doc date 1784, execution, debt, file #1708

WALKER Alexander, esquire, of Goffstown, vs MURDOUGH Thomas, yeoman, of Hillsborough, rec date 1783, writ, debt, file #4540

WALKER Alexander, esquire, of Goffstown, vs CAMPBELL Hugh, taylor, of Alexandria, rec date 1788, writ, debt, file #6945

WALKER Andrew, carpenter, of New Boston, vs MAJOR Jonathan, yeoman, of New Boston, doc date 1778, rec date 1779, deed, land transfer, file #5656

WALKER Charles, esquire, of Concord, vs FLANDERS Philip, gentleman, of Warner, doc date 1798, execution, debt, file #73

WALKER Isaac, husbandman, of Warner, vs DOW Oliver, gentleman, of Hopkinton, rec date 1784, judgment, debt, file #4207

WALKER Isaac, yeoman, of Hopkinton, vs PALMER John, yeoman, of Warner, doc date 1784, rec date 1785, deed, land transfer, file #5649

WALKER James, gentleman, of Bedford, vs WALKER Silas, yeoman, of Goffstown, doc date 1783, rec date 1786, deed, land transfer, file #5032

WALKER James (Capt), deceased, of Goffstown, vs WALKER James, husbandman, of Bedford, doc date 1786, rec date 1787, deed, land transfer, file #2496

WALKER John, shopkeeper, of Salem MA, vs LEACH Robert, shopkeeper, of Salem, rec date 1783, writ, debt, file #2770

WALKER John, shopkeeper, of Salem MA, vs LEECH Robert, merchant, of Salem, rec date 1783, writ, debt, file #3026

WALKER Thomas, cooper, of Hollis, vs BAGSITOR Abel, esquire, of Westford MA, doc date 1799, writ, debt, file #356

WALKER Timothy, esquire, of Concord, vs COLBY Nathaniel, husbandman, of Andover, doc date 1798, execution, debt, file #126

WALKER Timothy, esquire, of Concord, vs FLOOD Richard, husbandman, of Boscawen, doc date 1798, judgment, debt, file #567

WALKER Timothy, esquire, of Concord, vs FLOOD Richard, husbandman, of Boscawen, doc date 1798, judgment, debt, file #567

WALKER Timothy, husbandman, of Concord, vs STATE of NH, rec date 1777, recognizance, forgery, file #2211

WALKER Zaccheus, husbandman, of Merrimack, vs SCOTT James, yeoman, of Stoddard, rec date 1785, judgment, debt, file #5524

WALKER Zaccheus, gentleman, of Merrimack, vs GILLMOR James, husbandman, of Bedford, rec date 1785, judgment, debt, file #5582

WALKER Zaccheus, husbandman, of Merrimack, vs SCOTT James, yeoman, of Stoddard, rec date 1785, execution, debt, file #5928

WALL Matthew, esquire, of Peterborough, vs INHABATIANTS of Peterboro, of Peterborough, rec date 1786, writ, debt, file #6308

WALLACE John Jr & Isabel, yeoman, of Bedford, vs CALDWELL William, yeoman, of Bedford, doc date 1778, various, debt, file #2044

WALLACE Matthew, gentleman, of Peterborough, vs GOULD Jacob, gentleman, of Rindge, doc date 1784, execution, debt, file #1681

WALLACE Matthew, gentleman, of Peterborough, vs GREEN Jacob, gentleman, of Rindge, rec date 1783, writ, debt, file #4562

WALLACE Matthew, gentleman, of Peterborough, vs INHABITANTS of Peterborough, of Peterborough, rec date 1785, writ, debt, file #5420

WALLACE Matthew, gentleman, of Peterborough, vs GOULD Jacob, gentleman, of Rindge, rec date 1785, judgment, debt, file #5982

WALLACE Matthew, esquire, of Peterborough, vs RAMSEY James & William, husbandman, of Londonderry, rec date 1788, writ, debt, file #6616

WALLACE Matthew, gentleman, of Peterborough, vs INHABITANTS of Peterborough, of Peterborough, doc date 1784, writ, debt, file #1603

WALLACE Matthew, gentleman, of Peterborough, vs GOULD Jacob, gentleman, of Rindge, doc date 1784, execution, debt, file #1805

WALLACE Matthew, gentleman, of Peterborough, vs INHABITANTS of Peterborough, of Peterborough, rec date 1784, writ, debt, file #4579

WALLACE Matthew, gentleman, of Peterborough, vs INHABITANTS of Peterborough, of Peterborough, rec date 1785, various, debt, file #4832A, 1777 (two folders)

WALLACE Matthew, gentleman, of Peterborough, vs INHABITANTS of Peterboro, of Peterborough, rec date 1785, writ, debt, file #5832

WALLACE Matthew, gentleman, of Peterborough, vs SHATTUCK William, of Peterborough, rec date 1784, bond, debt, file #6351

WALLACE Robert, wheatwright, of Henniker, vs JOSLYN Nathaniel, gentleman, of Henniker, doc date 1778, rec date 1781, deed, land transfer, file #5658

WALLEY Prince, yeoman, of Londonderry, vs GEARFIELD Nathaniel, gentleman, of Merrimack, rec date 1784, writ, debt, file #4389

WALLINGFORD David, gentleman, of Hollis, vs STEARNS John, yeoman, of Hollis, rec date 1783, writ, debt, file #3575

WALLINGFORD David, gentleman, of Hollis, vs STEARNS Jotham, husbandman, of Goffstown, rec date 1785, judgment, debt, file #4871

WALLINGS David, gentleman, of Hollis, vs STEARNS John, yeoman, of Hollis, doc date 1784, execution, debt, file #1897

WALLINGSFORD David, yeoman, of Hollis, vs HARWOOD James, yeoman, of Dunstable, doc date 1773, judgment, debt, file #1316

WALLIS Jonathan, of MA, vs SLOAN David, rec date 1785, writ, debt, file #6956, torn pieces of paper

WALTER William, esquire, of Boston MA, vs CRAM John, husbandman, of Wilton, doc date 1799, debt, file #484

WALTON Josiah, husbandman, of New Ipswich, vs SCOTT Johns, husbandman, of Lemster, rec date 1785, judgment, debt, file #5206

WALTON Josiah, husbandman, of New Ipswich, vs JENNINGS Israel, husbandman, of Lemster, rec date 1785, judgment, debt, file #5206

WARD Artimas, yeoman, of Francestown, vs KINGSBURY Benjamin, traders, of Grafton, doc date 1799, writ, debt, file #409

WARD Artimas, yeoman, of Francestown, vs KINGSBURY Benjamin, traders, of Grafton MA, doc date 1799, debt, file #409

WARD Miles Jr, merchant, of Salem MA, vs SESSION Samuel, yeoman, of Londonderry, doc date 1798, judgment, debt, file #567

WARD Samuel, gentleman, of Lancaster MA, vs MOORE Henry, gentleman, of Chester, rec date 1782, judgment, debt, file #2716

WARD Samuel, gentleman, of Lancaster MA, vs MOORE Henry, of Chester, rec date 1783, execution, debt, file #3819

WARE Ephraim, physician, of Groton MA, vs SLOAN David, yeoman, of Mason, rec date 1783, judgment, debt, file #4497

WARE Ephraim, physician, of Groton MA, vs SLOAN David, yeoman, of Mason, doc date 1784, civil litigation, debt, file #1648

WARE Peter, gentleman, of Andover, vs GALE John, gentleman, of Salisbury, rec date 1785, writ, debt, file #4820

WARNER Daniel, trader, of Westmoreland, vs WATKINS Benjamin, merchant, of Salem MA, doc date 1773, writ, debt, file #1231

WARNER Daniel, clothier, of Dunstable, vs STATE of NH, recognizance, debt, file #2228

WARNER Daniel, gentleman, of Amherst, vs KITTRIDGE Solomon, blacksmith, of Amherst, rec date 1788, writ, breaking & entry, file #2554

WARNER Daniel, gentleman, of Amherst, vs FARNUM Joseph, yeoman, of Amherst, rec date 1788, writ, breaking & entry, file #2554

WARNER Daniel, gentleman, of Amherst, vs MANSER William, yeoman, of Temple, rec date 1782, writ, debt, file #2842

WARNER Daniel, gentleman, of Amherst, vs JEWELL James, yeoman, of Dunstable, rec date 1783, writ, debt, file #3578

WARNER Daniel, gentleman, of Amherst, vs LEWIS Samuel, husbandman, of Washington, rec date 1783, writ, debt, file #3962

WARNER Daniel, gentleman, of Dunstable, vs CARLTON Thomas, yeoman, of Amherst, rec date 1785, writ, debt, file #6231

WARNER Daniel, gentleman, of Amherst, vs EATON Abijah, yeoman, of Haverhill MA, rec date 1788, various, trespass/cattle, file #6585

WARNER Daniel, gentleman, of Amherst, vs EATON Abijah, yeoman, of Haverhill MA, rec date 1787, writ, debt, file #6706

WARNER John, yeoman, of New Ipswich, vs GOLDSMITH Josiah, gentleman, of Walpole, rec date 1784, judgment, debt, file #4657

WARNER John, yeoman, of New Ipswich, vs GOLDSMITH Josiah, gentleman, of Walpole, rec date 1785, judgment, debt, file #5114

WARNER John, yeoman, of New Ipswich, vs LAWRENCE Stephen, husbandman, of Mason, rec date 1785, writ, debt, file #5957

WARNER John, yeoman, of New Ipswich, vs LOVEWELL Noah, gentleman, of Dunstable, rec date 1788, judgment, debt, file #7007

WARNER Joseph, husbandman, of Pepperell MA, vs CHAMBERLAIN Joseph, laborer, of Wilton, doc date 1770, rec date 1772, deed, land transfer, file #6847

WARREN Benjamin, saddler, of Chelmsford MA, vs CODMAN Henry, physician, of Amherst, rec date 1784, appeal, debt, file #4140

WARREN Benjamin, saddler, of Chelmsford MA, vs CODMAN Henry, physician, of Amherst, rec date 1784, judgment, debt, file #4279

WARREN Daniel, yeoman, of Peterborough, vs PRESTON Abner, yeoman, of Hancock, rec date 1784, writ, debt, file #4671

WARREN Josiah, housewright, of New Boston, vs McCALLEY John, gentleman, of Hillsborough, doc date 1784, civil litigation, debt, file #1845

WARREN Josiah, housewright, of New Boston, vs McCALLEY John, gentleman, of Hillsborough, rec date 1783, judgment, debt, file #4464

WARREN William, cooper, of Richmond, vs BRYANT Daniel Chandler, yeoman, of Richmond, doc date 1798, execution, debt, file #106

WASHER Stephen, yeoman, of Wilton, vs HUTCHINSON Solomon, yeoman, of Merrimack, rec date 1786, writ, debt, file #6877

WASHER Stephen & Sarah, yeoman, of Amherst, vs DODGE Samuel, yeoman, of Amherst, doc date 1785, rec date 1789, deed, transfer of land, file #6572

WATSON Ebenezer, gentleman, of Amherst, vs KELLEY Moses, esquire, of Goffstown, rec date 1783, bond, person in jail, file #3310

WATSON John, saddler, of Amherst, vs BLOOD William, yeoman, of Dunstable, doc date 1798, execution, debt, file #144

WATSON John, saddler, of Amherst, vs JOHNSON Adam Jr, gentleman, of Lyndeborough, rec date 1787, judgment, debt, file #2462

WATSON John, gentleman, of Brookfield MA, vs BAKER Joseph, yeoman, of Wilton, rec date 1783, judgment, debt, file #3745

WATSON John, saddler, of Amherst, vs MONTGOMERY Hugh, husbandman, of Francestown, rec date 1786, judgment, debt, file #5550

WATSON John, saddler, of Amherst, vs PARKER Jonathan, physician, of Litchfield, rec date 1786, judgment, debt, file #5266

WATSON John, saddler, of Amherst, vs JOHNSON Adam Jr, gentleman, of Lyndeborough, rec date 1787, judgment, debt, file #6199

WATSON John, saddler, of Amherst, vs JOHNSON Adam Jr, gentleman, of Lyndeborough, rec date 1787, judgment, debt, file #6192

WAUGH John, yeoman, of Society Land, vs MORRISON Samuel, yeoman, of Peterborough, rec date 1787, judgment, debt, file #2466

WAUGH John, yeoman, of Antrim, vs MORRISON Samuel, yeoman, of Peterborough, rec date 1787, judgment, debt, file #6190

WEARE Peter, gentleman, of Andover, vs ROBINSON Eleazer, husbandman, of Lebanon, doc date 1784, execution, debt, file #1916

WEARE Peter, gentleman, of Andover, vs ROBINSON Eleazer, husbandman, of Lebanon, rec date 1783, civil litigious, debt, file #2919

WEARE Peter, gentleman, of Andover, vs ROBINSON Eleazer, husbandman, of Lebanon, rec date 1783, execution, debt, file #3246

WEARE Peter, gentleman, of Andover, vs GALE John Collins, gentleman, of Salisbury, rec date 1785, various, debt, file #5237

WEARE Peter, gentleman, of Andover, vs GALE John Collins, blacksmith, of Salisbury, rec date 1785, writ, debt, file #5383

WEATHERSPOON Alexander, yeoman, of Deering, vs DRURY Benjamin, physician, of Spencer MA, rec date 1783, writ, debt, file #3187

WEBBER Mary, vs OSGOOD Joel F Jr, doc date 1894, trover for an organ, supreme court, file #634

WEBBER Nathaniel, husbandman, of Chester, vs HART Sally, widow, of Hopkinton, rec date 1787, various, debt, file #2538

WEBBER Nathaniel, husbandman, of Chester, vs KAST Sally, widow, of Hopkinton, rec date 1785, writ, debt, file #4812

WEBSTER ----, of Derryfield, vs RUSSELL ----, of Derryfield, doc date 1784, deed, land transfer, file #1998

WEBSTER Benjamin, yeoman, of Boscawen, vs PRESBY Nathaniel, of Bradford, doc date 1798, petition, release from jail, file #36

WEBSTER Ebenezer, esquire, of Salisbury, vs DANFORTH Edward, husbandman, of Andover, doc date 1798, judgment, debt, file #567

WEBSTER Ebenezer, esquire, of Salisbury, vs CALL John, husbandman, of Andover, doc date 1798, judgment, debt, file #567

WEBSTER Enos, husbandman, of Deerfield, vs PALMER William, cooper, of Deerfield, doc date 1798, judgment, debt, file #567

WEBSTER Enos, husbandman, of Derryfield, vs MUDGET John, husbandman, of Weare, rec date 1783, writ, debt, file #2761

WEBSTER Enos, husbandman, of Derryfield, vs TUTTLE Stephen, yeoman, of Goffstown, rec date 1785, judgment, debt, file #5048

WEBSTER Grant, merchant, of Boston MA, vs ABBOTT Samuel, husbandman, of Hollis, rec date 1785, judgment, debt, file #5998

WEBSTER Israel, yeoman, of Salisbury, vs MASON Russell, gentleman, of Grafton, rec date 1788, writ, debt, file #6689

WEBSTER John, gentleman, of Salisbury, vs CUSHING Caleb, blacksmith, of Salisbury, doc date 1798, execution, debt, file #67

WEBSTER John Jr, yeoman, of Haverhill MA, vs SEVERANCE Peter, husbandman, of Derryfield, doc date 1798, judgment, debt, file #567

WEBSTER Joseph, yeoman, of New Chester, vs PUTMAN Moses, gentleman, of Salisbury, doc date 1799, judgment, debt, file #277

WEBSTER Joseph, yeoman, of Andover, vs ELKINS Joseph, husbandman, of Litchfield, doc date 1798, execution, debt, file #51

WEBSTER Noah, yeoman, of Hollis, vs KILLICUT Charity, laborer, of Dunstable, rec date 1784, execution, debt, file #5886

WEED Nathaniel, of Francestown, vs DINSMORE John, husbandman, of Windham, rec date 1783, various, land trespass, file #3970, land of royal society

WEED Nathaniel, yeoman, of Weare, vs SHAW Ichabod, yeoman, of Marlborough, rec date 1783, writ, debt, file #4544

WEED Nathaniel, yeoman, of Weare, vs DINSMORE John, husbandman, of Windham, rec date 1783, various, land dispute, file #5229

WEEKS Holland, yeoman, of Hardwick MA, vs SARNDERSON Benjamin, yeoman, of Hollis, doc date 1774, judgment, debt, file #731

WEEKS Samuel, innholder, of Greenfield, vs PERRY Joseph, gentleman, of Greenfield, doc date 1798, judgment, debt, file #567

WELLINGTON Jeduthan, gentleman, of Cambridge MA, vs CUTLER Solomon, gentleman, of Rindge, rec date 1785, judgment, debt, file #5087

WELLMAN Jesse, yeoman, of Waltham MA, vs JOHNSON Adams Jr, gentleman, of Lyndeborough, rec date 1785, judgment, debt, file #4943

WELLMAN Jesse, yeoman, of Waltham, vs JOHNSON Adam Jr, gentleman, of Lyndeborough, rec date 1785, judgment, debt, file #6419

WELLMAN Jesse, yeoman, of Waltham MA, vs JOHNSON Adam, gentleman, of Lyndeborough, rec date 1785, judgment, debt, file #6439

WELLS John, husbandman, of New Boston, vs CUMMINGS Silas, blacksmith, of New Boston, rec date 1783, various, debt, file #2752

WELLS John, yeoman, of New Boston, vs BALEY Noah, yeoman, of Dracut MA, rec date 1783, writ, debt, file #3212

WELLS John, husbandman, of New Boston, vs CUMMINGS Silas, blacksmith, of New Boston, rec date 1783, various, debt, file #3614

WELLS John, blacksmith, of New Boston, vs STEWART Samuel, yeoman, of Hillsborough, rec date 1784, judgment, debt, file #4289

WELLS Jon, yeoman, of New Boston, vs WILKINS Amos, yeoman, of Lyndeborough, rec date 1783, writ, debt, file #3163

WELLS Prudence, spinster, of Goffstown, vs KITTREDGE Nathaniel, yeoman, of Goffstown, doc date 1784, rec date 1785, deed, land transfer, file #5604

WELLS Timothy, blacksmith, of Goffstown, vs WELLS Isaac, blacksmith, of Goffstown, doc date 1799, execution, debt, file #175

WELLS Timothy, blacksmith, of Goffstown, vs BADGER William, yeoman, of Goffstown, doc date 1784, rec date 1784, deed, land transfer, file #5006

WENTWORTH Rebecca, widow, of Merrimack, vs THORNTON Matthew & James, esquire, of Merrimack, doc date 1784, court case, crop damage, file #1609, land deed & map of farm

WENTWORTH Rebecca, widow, of Merrimack, vs THORNTON Matthew & James, esquire, of Merrimack, doc date 1782, rec date 1783, appeal, breaking & entry, file #2621

WEST Mary, widow, of Haverhill MA, vs CLOUGH James, yeoman, of Hopkinton, rec date 1783, judgment, debt, file #3701

WEST Mary, widow, of Haverhill MA, vs PEARSON Noah, yeoman, of Hopkinton, rec date 1783, judgment, debt, file #3701

WESTON John, saddler, of Amherst, vs TAGGART Archibald, gentleman, of Hillsborough, rec date 1788, judgment, debt, file #7008

WESTON Southwick, husbandman, of Antrim, vs FLINT Jacob, husbandman, of Hillsborough, rec date 1785, judgment, debt, file #5994

WESTON Sutherick & Molly, cooper, of Amherst, vs EATON James, doc date 1784, deed, land transfer, file #2025

WETHERBEE Jacob, husbandman, of Mason, vs SMITH Samuel, gentleman, of Mason, rec date 1788, writ, debt, file #6724

WETHERBEE Jacob, husbandman, of Mason, vs MERRIAM Joseph, gentleman, of Mason, rec date 1788, writ, debt, file #6724

WETHEREL Charles, blacksmith, of Pepperell MA, vs HALE Enoch, esquire, of Rindge, rec date 1783, judgment, debt, file #4458

WETHEREL Charles, blacksmith, of Pepperell MA, vs SCOTT James, yeoman, of Stoddard, rec date 1783, judgment, debt, file #4457

WETHEREL Charles, blacksmith, of Pepperell MA, vs SCOTT James, yeoman, of Stoddard, rec date 1782, execution, debt, file #4899

WHALER Nathaniel, groom, of Marlborough MA, vs DUNN Nabby, bride, of Marlborough MA, rec date 1787/88, marriage license, license, file #6162, part of Samuel CURTIS file

WHEAT Daniel, cooper, of Carlisle MA, vs BARRON Miah, gentleman, of Lyndeborough, rec date 1788, writ, debt, file #6634

WHEAT Daniel, cooper, of Carlisle MA, vs PUTNAM John, gentleman, of Lyndeborough, rec date 1788, writ, debt, file #6634

WHEAT Joseph, cooper, of Amherst, vs EMERSON Dearborn, stage driver, of Amherst, doc date 1799, debt, file #363

WHEAT Joseph, yeoman, of Amherst, vs GAY Ichabod, yeoman, of Francestown, doc date 1799, petition, debt, file #329

WHEAT Joseph, trader, of Amherst, vs NICHOLS Joseph, gentleman, of Amherst, doc date 1799, writ, debt, file #575

WHEAT Joseph, stage driver, of Amherst, vs AVERELL David, husbandman, of Lyndeborough, doc date 1799, writ, debt, file #380

WHEAT Joseph Jr, yeoman, of Hollis, vs WHEAT Joseph, husbandman, of Hollis, doc date 1793, rec date 1793, deed, land transfer, file #5667, ?

WHEAT Solomon, cordwainer, of Hollis, vs HOBART Jacob, yeoman, of Hollis, rec date 1786, judgment, debt, file #2459

WHEELER Abijah, esquire, of Temple, vs KIDDER John, yeoman, of Temple, doc date 1798, judgment, debt, file #567

WHEELER Abijah, esquire, of Temple, vs KIDDER John, yeoman, of Temple, doc date 1799, debt, file #452

WHEELER Antimas, trader, of Temple, vs WITHINGTON William, yeoman, of Mason, doc date 1798, execution, debt, file #154

WHEELER David, of Concord MA, vs HOSMER Nathaniel, husbandman, of Mason, rec date 1787, writ, debt, file #6708

WHEELER Elezar, yeoman, of Hollis, vs WHITE David, yeoman, of Peterborough, rec date 1784, writ, stealing cattle, file #4746

WHEELER Elezar, yeoman, of Hollis, vs MCDONALD James Jr, laborer, of Hollis, rec date 1784, writ, stealing cattle, file #4746

WHEELER James, husbandman, of Merrimack, vs GORDON William, esquire, of Amherst, doc date 1799, writ, debt, file #370

WHEELER James, labourer, of Amherst, vs CLARK Timothy, yeoman, of Amherst, doc date 1774, writ, debt, file #979

WHEELER John, husbandman, of Amherst, vs WHEAT Joseph, cooper, of Amherst, doc date 1799, writ, debt, file #359

WHEELER Joseph, gentleman, of Harvard MA, vs WHITCOMB Benjamin, gentleman, of Westmoreland, doc date 1773, execution, debt, file #1456

WHEELER Joseph, gentleman, of Harvard MA, vs WHITCOMB Benjamin, gentleman, of Westmoreland, doc date 1772, writ, debt, file #1428

WHEELER Lebbeus, yeoman, of Hollis, vs JEWETT Jacob Jr, trader, of Hollis, doc date 1774, writ, debt, file #1101

WHEELER Oliver, yeoman, of Hillsborough, vs JOHNSON Zebadiah, yeoman, of Hillsborough, rec date 1782, execution, debt, file #3488

WHEELER Plumer, husbandman, of Sutton, vs DODGE Nicholas, blacksmith, of Dunbarton, rec date 1788, writ, debt, file #6614

WHEELER Polomar, husbandman, of Dunbarton, vs ELKINS Abel, husbandman, of New Salisbury, rec date 1783, writ, debt, file #3222

WHEELER Samuel, yeoman, of Packersfield, vs BROWN Peter, yeoman, of Temple, rec date 1783, judgment, debt, file #3293

WHEELER Silas, yeoman, of Framingham MA, vs DARLING Jonas, cordwainer, of Watertown MA, rec date 1788, writ, debt, file #6177, part of Samuel CURTIS file

WHEELER Thaddeus, gentleman, of Hollis, vs GRIMES Thaddeus, husbandman, of Amherst, rec date 1784, judgment, debt, file #4421

WHEELER Thaddeus, gentleman, of Hollis, vs BOWERS Ephraim, yeoman, of Merrimack, rec date 1785, judgment, debt, file #5086

WHEELER Thaddeus, gentleman, of Hollis, vs BOWERS Elizabeth, widow, of Merrimack, rec date 1785, judgment, debt, file #5086

WHEELER Thomas, gentleman, of Hollis, vs BOWERS Ephraim, yeoman, of Merrimack, rec date 1785, judgment, debt, file #4792

WHEELER Timothy, husbandman, of Amherst, vs PROCTOR Reuben, yeoman, of Merrimack, rec date 1787, writ, debt, file #6898

WHEELER William, yeoman, of Dunbarton, vs FLAGG Samuel, esquire, of Worcester, rec date 1785, writ, debt, file #5425

WHEELOCK Jonathan, husbandman, of Raby, vs SWAN Robert, husbandman, of Peterborough, rec date 1783, execution, debt, file #3818

WHEELOCK Jonathan, husbandman, of Raby, vs STEEL Thomas, husbandman, of Peterborough, rec date 1783, execution, debt, file #3818

WHEELOCK Luces, husbandman, of Peterborough, vs AMAN David, clerk, of Peterborough, rec date 1789, writ, debt, file #2571 B

WHEELOCK Luces, husbandman, of Peterborough, vs AMAN David, clerk, of Peterborough, rec date 1789, writ, debt, file #2571 A, 2 folders

WHEELOCK Timothy & Joel, cordwainer, of Shrewsbury MA, vs BROOKS Aaron, of Grafton MA, doc date 1784, rec date 1785, deed, land transfer, file #5624

WHILEY John, yeoman, of Deering, vs TAGGART Archibald, yeoman, of Hillsborough, doc date 1774, judgment, debt, file #735

WHILSON Thomas, husbandman, of New Boston, vs WALKER Andrew, husbandman, of New Boston, doc date 1784, execution, debt, file #1548

WHIPPLE Joseph, husbandman, of Croydon, vs WIGGIN Timothy & Benjamin, traders, of Boston MA, doc date 1799, execution, debt, file #171

WHIPPLE Nathan, saddler, of Mason, vs KIDDER Reuben, esquire, of New Ipswich, rec date 1783, writ, debt, file #3313

WHIPPLE William, of Portsmouth, vs ANDERSON James, cordwainer, of Boxford MA, doc date 1781, rec date 1781, deed, land transfer, file #6803

WHITAKER Caleb, husbandman, of Weare, vs DOYNE Jacob, husbandman, of Pembroke, doc date 1772, writ, debt, file #1399

WHITCHER Moses, vs ROBINSON Elisha, trader, of Framingham MA, rec date 1783, civil litigious, debt, file #2969

WHITCOMB Abner, yeoman, of New Ipswich, vs BLANCHARD Simeon, husbandman, of New Ipswich, rec date 1783, various, debt, file #4323

WHITCOMB Benjamin, gentleman, of Westmoreland, vs WHEELER Joseph, gentleman, of Harvard MA, doc date 1773, writ, bail, file #1442

WHITCOMB Benjamin, gentleman, of Westmoreland, vs WHEELER Joseph, gentleman, of Harvard MA, doc date 1772, civil litigation, debt, file #659

WHITCOMB Benjamin, husbandman, of Henniker, vs MOOR John, husbandman, of Francestown, rec date 1785, execution, debt, file #5789

WHITCOMB Jacob, yeoman, of Henniker, vs GIBSON Tim, yeoman, of Henniker, doc date 1777, rec date 1778, deed, land transfer, file #2156

WHITCOMP Samuel, husbandman, of Hancock, vs STATE of NH, rec date 1787, recognizance, counterfeiting, file #3556

WHITE Charles, yeoman, of Peterborough, vs KINDRICK Daniel, rec date 1784, recognizance, theft, file #4737

WHITE Charles, yeoman, of Peterborough, vs WHEELER Ebenezer, rec date 1784, recognizance, theft, file #4737

WHITE Charles, yeoman, of Peterborough, vs PROCTOR Moses, rec date 1784, recognizance, theft, file #4737

WHITE Charles, yeoman, of Peterborough, vs WHITE John Sr, yeoman, of Peterborough, doc date 1786, rec date 1790, deed, land transfer, file #6576

WHITE David, yeoman, of Peterborough, vs SMITH Samuel, yeoman, of Peterborough, doc date 1799, writ, debt, file #440

WHITE David, yeoman, of Peterborough, vs KINDRICK Daniel, rec date 1784, recognizance, theft, file #4737

WHITE David, prisoner, of Peterborough, rec date 1786, recognizance, prison break, file #7044

WHITE Hannah, single, vs SCRIPTURE John, of Wilton, rec date 1788, warrant, fornication, file #6540

WHITE Hannah, single, vs SCRIPTURE Oliver, of Wilton, rec date 1788, warrant, fornication, file #6540

WHITE Hannah, single, vs SCRIPTURE James, yeoman, of Mason, rec date 1788, warrant, fornication, file #6540

WHITE Hannah, single, vs ABBOTT William, esquire, of Wilton, rec date 1788, warrant, fornication, file #6540

WHITE Hannah, single, vs ABBOTT William, esquire, of Wilton, rec date 1788, warrant, fornication, file #6540

WHITE John, merchant, of Haverhill MA, vs DUTY William, esquire, of Salem, doc date 1798, execution, debt, file #133

WHITE John, yeoman, of Peterborough, vs SPRAQUE John, of Lancaster MA, doc date 1772, civil litigation, debt, file #651

WHITE John, yeoman, of Pepperell MA, vs HODGMAN David, husbandman, of Mason, doc date 1773, rec date 1783, deed, land transfer, file #2636

WHITE John, yeoman, of Peterborough, vs KINDRICK Daniel, rec date 1784, recognizance, theft, file #4737

WHITE John, husbandman, of Hopkinton, vs STRAW Jacob, husbandman, of Mason, rec date 1786, various, debt, file #6690

WHITE John, prisoner, of Peterborough, rec date 1786, recognizance, prison break, file #7044

WHITE John Sr, yeoman, of Peterborough, vs POWERS William, clothier, of Peterborough, rec date 1783, writ, debt, file #3199

WHITE John Sr, husbandman, of Peterborough, vs ALLD Benjamin, husbandman, of Peterborough, rec date 1787, writ, debt, file #6890

WHITE Patrick, yeoman, of Peterborough, vs HAMMILL Joseph, yeoman, of Peterborough, doc date 1784, execution, debt, file #1671

WHITE Robert Jr, husbandman, of New Boston, vs TUTTLE Charles, physician, of New Boston, doc date 1799, writ, debt, file #360

WHITE Samuel, yeoman, of Goffstown, vs CLEMENT Jesse, of Weare, doc date 1787, rec date 1790, deed, land transfer, file #2503

WHITEMORE Nathaniel, yeoman, of Peterborough, vs WILSON James, husbandman, of Peterborough, doc date 1799, judgment, debt, file #300

WHITEMORE Paul, yeoman, of Peterborough, vs PRESTON Abner, husbandman, of Hancock, rec date 1785, judgment, debt, file #5529

WHITEMORE Samuel, gentleman, of Cambridge MA, vs SHANNON Richard Cutts, esquire, of Hollis, rec date 1786, various, land dispute, file #6086B

WHITEMORE Samuel, gentleman, of Cambridge MA, vs POWERS Francis, cordwainer, of Hollis, rec date 1786, various, land dispute, file #6086

WHITEMORE Samuel, gentleman, of Cambridge MA, vs ROGERS Solomon, gentleman, of Hollis, rec date 1786, various, land dispute, file #6086B

WHITEMORE Samuel, gentleman, of Cambridge MA, vs FARLEY Hannah, single, of Hollis, rec date 1786, various, land dispute, file #6086B

WHITEMORE Samuel, gentleman, of Cambridge MA, vs CUMMINGS Benjamin, gentleman, of Hollis, rec date 1786, various, land dispute, file #6086B

WHITEMORE Samuel, gentleman, of Cambridge MA, vs CUMMINGS Prudance, widow, of Hollis, rec date 1786, various, land dispute, file #6086A

WHITEMORE Samuel, gentleman, of Cambridge MA, vs GOODHUE Samuel, husbandman, of Hollis, rec date 1786, various, land dispute, file #6086

WHITEMORE Samuel, gentleman, of Cambridge MA, vs GOODHUE Samuel, esquire, of Hollis, rec date 1786, various, land dispute, file #6086B

WHITEMORE Samuel, gentleman, of Cambridge MA, vs WRIGHT David, esquire, of Hollis, rec date 1786, various, land dispute, file #6086B

WHITEWELL Mary, widow, of Roxbury MA, vs SEARLE John, of Dunstable, rec date 1782, execution, debt, file #5733

WHITIKER James, yeoman, of Deering, vs GRIMES James, gentleman, of Deering, rec date 1783, civil litigious, debt, file #2912

WHITING Benjamin, esquire, of Amherst, vs BANCROFT Benjamin, husbandman, of Groton MA, doc date 1778, writ, debt, file #2049

WHITING Benjamin, esquire, of Hollis, vs BANCROFT Benjamin, gentleman, of Groton MA, doc date 1777, writ, debt, file #2024

WHITING John, cordwainer, of Amherst, vs WORSTER Noah, esquire, of Hollis, rec date 1784, judgment, debt, file #4253

WHITING John, cordwainer, of Amherst, vs WORSTER Noah, esquire, of Hollis, rec date 1784, judgment, debt, file #4256

WHITING Jonas, cordwainer, of New Ipswich, vs BENNETT Jonathan Jr, yeoman, of Hancock, doc date 1784, execution, debt, file #1780

WHITING Jonas, yeoman, of New Ipswich, vs RICE David, husbandman, of Keene, rec date 1785, writ, debt, file #6011

WHITING Jonas, yeoman, of New Ipswich, vs TEMPLETON James, of Peterborough, rec date 1786, judgment, debt, file #6371

WHITING Joseph, yeoman, of Dunstable, vs STEARNS Jotham, yeoman, of Goffstown, rec date 1784, judgment, debt, file #4367

WHITING Leonard, gentleman, of Hollis, vs STEVENS Joseph, yeoman, of Hollis, doc date 1799, judgment, debt, file #568

WHITING Leonard, gentleman, of Hollis, vs CONREY Samuel, yeoman, of Hollis, doc date 1799, judgment, debt, file #568

WHITING Leonard, gentleman, of Hollis, vs BROWN Eliphalet, yeoman, of Hollis, doc date 1799, judgment, debt, file #568

WHITING Leonard, gentleman, of Hollis, vs TUTTLE Samuel, of Dunstable, doc date 1807, judgment, debt, file #568

WHITING Leonard, trader, of Hollis, vs BLOOD Jonathan, yeoman, of Hollis, doc date 1775, writ, debt, file #960

WHITING Leonard, esquire, of Merrimack, vs BAILEY Daniel, husbandman, of Hollis, doc date 1784, execution, debt, file #1666

WHITING Leonard, esquire, of Merrimack, vs BLOOD Francis, husbandman, of Hollis, doc date 1784, execution, debt, file #1735

WHITING Leonard, esquire, of Merrimack, vs ROBERTSON Joseph, husbandman, of Deering, doc date 1784, execution, debt, file #1771

WHITING Leonard, esquire, of Merrimack, vs ROBISON Joseph, husbandman, of Deering, doc date 1784, execution, debt, file #1730

WHITING Leonard, esquire, of Hollis, vs WHITING Benjamin, esquire, of Hollis, doc date 1777, writ, debt, file #2026

WHITING Leonard, vs STATE of NH, rec date 1777, forgery, file #2209

WHITING Leonard, esquire, of Hollis, vs PHELPS Nathan, yeoman, of Hollis, rec date 1785, judgment, debt, file #2448

WHITING Leonard, esquire, of Merrimack, vs LAWRENCE Zachariah, husbandman, of Hollis, rec date 1782, writ, debt, file #2695, other kinships

WHITING Leonard, gentleman, of Merrimack, vs PARCE Solomon & Simon, husbandman, of Hollis, rec date 1783, writ, debt, file #3409

WHITING Leonard, esquire, of Merrimack, vs BLOOD Francis, husbandman, of Hollis, rec date 1783, writ, debt, file #3411

WHITING Leonard, esquire, of Merrimack, vs ROBISON Joseph, husbandman, of Deering, rec date 1783, writ, debt, file #3412

WHITING Leonard, gentleman, of Merrimack, vs BOYNTON John, yeoman, of Hollis, rec date 1783, writ, debt, file #3365

WHITING Leonard, esquire, of Merrimack, vs AMES Jonathan, husbandman, of Hollis, rec date 1783, writ, debt, file #3407

WHITING Leonard, gentleman, of Merrimack, vs BAYLEY Daniel, husbandman, of Hillsborough, rec date 1783, writ, debt, file #3405

WHITING Leonard, gentleman, of Merrimack, vs HOBART Jonathan, yeoman, of Hollis, rec date 1783, writ, debt, file #3403

WHITING Leonard, gentleman, of Merrimack, vs MILLER Thomas, husbandman, of Hillsborough, rec date 1784, appeal, debt, file #4115

WHITING Leonard, esquire, of Merrimack, vs STEARNS Joseph, husbandman, of Hollis, rec date 1784, judgment, debt, file #4987

WHITING Leonard, esquire, of Merrimack, vs BROWN Joseph, joiner, of Hollis, rec date 1784, judgment, debt, file #4993

WHITING Leonard, esquire, of Merrimack, vs BRADFORD Samuel Jr, gentleman, of Hillsborough, rec date 1785, judgment, debt, file #5194

WHITING Leonard, esquire, of Hollis, vs CUMMINGS Samuel, esquire, of Hollis, rec date 1785, various, debt, file #6228

WHITING Leonard, esquire, of Merrimack, vs CUNNINGHAM Samuel, gentleman, of Peterborough, rec date 1785, judgment, debt, file #6463

WHITING Leonard, esquire, of Hollis, vs CUMMINGS Samuel, deceased, of Hollis, rec date 1786, judgment, debt, file #6474

WHITING Leonard Jr, trader, of Hollis, vs BROWN Eliphilet, husbandman, of Hollis, rec date 1792, judgment, debt, file #2479

WHITING Oliver, of Temple, vs SELECTMEN of Temple, of Temple, doc date 1772, application, tavern license, file #849

WHITING Oliver, husbandman, of Temple, vs POTTER Robert, husbandman, of Peterboro Slip, rec date 1784, judgment, debt, file #4294

WHITING Oliver, husbandman, of Temple, vs SEARLE William Jr, husbandman, of Temple, rec date 1783, judgment, debt, file #4475

WHITING Rebeckah, widow, of Hollis, vs PARKER Benjamin, gentleman, of Hollis, doc date 1808, rec date 1808, deed, land transfer, file #5691

WHITING Samuel, trader, of Amherst, vs ATKINSON Sarah, widow, of Boscawen, doc date 1799, debt, file #457

WHITING Samuel, innholder, of Rindge, vs CROSBY Stephen, yeoman, of Amherst, rec date 1785, writ, debt, file #5432

WHITING Timothy, cordwainer, of Billerica MA, vs GOSS James, cabinetmaker, of Hampstead, doc date 1773, execution, debt, file #1485

WHITNEY Daniel, baker, of Marlborough MA, vs CURTIS Samuel, esquire, of Marlborough MA, rec date 1785, power of attorney, file #6179, part of Samuel CURTIS file

WHITNEY James, yeoman, of Dunstable, vs CURRIER Jonathan, yeoman, of Bedford, doc date 1772, judgment, debt, file #674

WHITNEY James, husbandman, of Dunstable, vs ANDREW James, gentleman, of Boxford MA, doc date 1772, writ, debt, file #889

WHITNEY James, yeoman, of Dunstable, vs ANDREW James, gentleman, of Boxford MA, doc date 1773, execution, debt, file #1454

WHITNEY Leonard, esquire, of Merrimack, vs JEWETT Jacob Jr, husbandman, of Hollis, rec date 1782, execution, debt, file #3476

WHITNEY Levi, husbandman, of Townsend MA, vs CUMINGS Samuel, innkeeper, of Hollis, doc date 1773, judgment, debt, file #1323

WHITNEY Silas, yeoman, of Clarendon NY, vs PARKER Jonathan, esquire, of Charlotte NY, rec date 1785, judgment, debt, file #5359

WHITTAKER Thomas, prisoner, of Deerfield, vs HUGH John, doc date 1798, petition, release from jail, file #39

WHITTAKER Thomas, yeoman, of Londonderry, vs TYLER Jeremiah, blacksmith, of Andover MA, rec date 1786, judgment, debt, file #6502

WHITTEMORE Paul, yeoman, of Peterborough, vs PRESTON Abner, husbandman, of Hancock, rec date 1785, execution, debt, file #5930

WHITTEMORE Pelatiah, husbandman, of New Ipswich, vs YOUNG John, physician, of Peterborough, doc date 1775, writ, debt, file #1033

WHITTEMORE Pelatiah, husbandman, of New Ipswich, vs SMITH William, of Peterborough, doc date 1775, writ, debt, file #1033

WHITTEMORE Pelatiah Jr, husbandman, of New Ipswich, vs YOUNG John, esquire, of Peterborough, doc date 1777, judgment, debt, file #2041

WHITTEMORE Pelatiah Jr, husbandman, of New Ipswich, vs SMITH William, esquire, of Peterborough, doc date 1777, judgment, debt, file #2041

WHITTERMORE Nathaniel, husbandman, of Peterborough, vs ROBBE William Jr, of Peterborough, doc date 1798, judgment, debt, file #567

WHITTERMORE Nathaniel, husbandman, of Peterborough, vs INHABITANTS of Peterborough, of Peterborough, rec date 1788, various, debt, file #6590

WHITTING Leonard, esquire, of Merrimack, vs PARKER Benjamin, yeoman, of Hollis, rec date 1783, writ, debt, file #3360

WHITTING Leonard, esquire, of Merrimack, vs PARKER Oliver, gentleman, of Groton MA, rec date 1783, writ, debt, file #3359

WHITTLE Thomas, yeoman, of Litchfield, vs SAUNDERS James, yeoman, of Salem, rec date 1783, judgment, debt, file #4490

WHITTLE Thomas, trader, of Litchfield, vs TOOTHAKER Roger, physician, of Billerica MA, doc date 1784, rec date 1784, deed, land transfer, file #5010

WHITTLE Thomas Jr, yeoman, of Litchfield, vs PALMER Jonathan, yeoman, of Litchfield, rec date 1784, judgment, debt, file #4641

WHITTLE Thomas Jr, trader, of Litchfield, vs SHURTLETT Jonathan Jr, trader, of Merrimack, rec date 1786, writ, debt, file #6133

WHITWELL Mary, widow, of Roxbury MA, vs HILDRETH Ephraim, esquire, of Amherst, rec date 1785, judgment, debt, file #4938

WHITWELL Mary, widow, of Roxbury MA, vs WESTON Ebenezer, gentleman, of Amherst, rec date 1785, judgment, debt, file #4938

WICOM Thomas, husbandman, of Goffstown, vs KELLEY Joseph, gentleman, of Nottingham-West, doc date 1784, writ, debt, file #1583

WIER Robert, gentleman, of Walpole, vs BROWN Peter, yeoman, of Temple, rec date 1784, judgment, debt, file #4373

WIER Robert, gentleman, of Walpole, vs STEEL David, gentleman, of Peterborough, rec date 1785, judgment, debt, file #5369

WIGGIN Benjamin & Timothy, traders, of Boston MA, vs KIMBALL Abraham, schoolmaster, of Hopkinton, doc date 1798, judgment, debt, file #567

WIGGIN Benjamin, trader, of Boston MA, vs TYLER Adonijah, husbandman, of Hopkinton, doc date 1799, debt, file #469

WIGGIN Benjamin, trader, of Hopkinton, vs BEAN Benaiah, husbandman, of Salisbury, rec date 1785, judgment, debt, file #5199

WIGGIN Benjamin, innholder, of Hopkinton, vs CURRIER Sargent, husbandman, of Hopkinton, rec date 1785, judgment, debt, file #5713

WIGGIN Timothy, trader, of Boston MA, vs KIMBALL Abraham Jr, yeoman, of Hopkinton, doc date 1799, debt, file #470

WIGGIN Timothy, trader, of Boston MA, vs TYLER Adonijah, husbandman, of Hopkinton, doc date 1799, debt, file #469

WIGGINS Benjamin, esquire, of Hopkinton, vs CURRIER Edward, physician, of Hopkinton, doc date 1799, debt, file #468

WIGGINS Benjamin, esquire, of Hopkinton, vs BLANCHARD Augustus, deceased, of Hopkinton, doc date 1799, debt, file #468

WIGGINS Mark, esquire, of Stratham, vs GOODENOUGH Jesse, husbandman, of Petersham MA, rec date 1784, judgment, debt, file #4232

WILBER Levi, gentleman, of Lancaster MA, vs BARRON William, esquire, of Merrimack, doc date 1782, execution, file #1009

WILDER Levi, of Lancaster MA, vs RICHARD Samuel, gentleman, of Goffstown, doc date 1782, execution, file #1023

WILDER Levi, gentleman, of Lancaster, vs CRAM John, husbandman, of Wilton, doc date 1784, execution, debt, file #1500

WILDER Levi, gentleman, of Lancaster MA, vs CRAM John, husbandman, of Wilton, doc date 1784, execution, debt, file #1686

WILDER Levi, gentleman, of Lancaster MA, vs DIX Eason, yeoman, of Raby, doc date 1784, execution, debt, file #1965

WILDER Levi, gentleman, of Lancaster MA, vs USHER Robert, yeoman, of Merrimack, rec date 1783, writ, debt, file #3307

WILDER Levi, gentleman, of Lancaster MA, vs DIX Eason, yeoman, of Raby, rec date 1783, execution, debt, file #3278, administrator of estate Sampson STODDARD

WILDER Levi, gentleman, of Lancaster MA, vs DIX Eason, yeoman, of Raby, rec date 1783, writ, debt, file #3900, estate of Sampson STODDARD

WILDER Levi, gentleman, of Lancaster MA, vs PUTNAM Archelaus Jr, husbandman, of Wilton, rec date 1783, judgment, debt, file #4301

WILDER Levi, gentleman, of Lancaster MA, vs CRAM John, husbandman, of Wilton, rec date 1783, judgment, debt, file #4505

WILDER Levi, gentleman, of Lancaster MA, vs HOLT Jeremiah, husbandman, of Wilton, rec date 1783, judgment, debt, file #4504

WILDER Levi, gentleman, of Lancaster MA, vs KIDDER Reuben, esquire, of New Ipswich, rec date 1784, judgment, debt, file #4866, estate of Sampson STODDARD

WILDER Levi, gentleman, of Lancaster MA, vs MORRISON Abraham, husbandman, of Henniker, rec date 1785, judgment, debt, file #5057, estate of Sampson STODDARD

WILDER Luke, Capt, of Salisbury, doc date 1787, license, tavern license, file #868

WILDER Olive, of Orange MA, vs Town of Wilton, rec date 1787, warrant, debt, file #3547

WILEY John, yeoman, of Amherst, vs GREEN David, yeoman, of Hillsborough, doc date 1784, execution, debt, file #1536

WILEY Robert, cordwainer, of Amherst, vs TUTTLE Charles, physician, of New Boston, doc date 1799, writ, debt, file #382

WILEY Timothy, husbandman, of Hillsborough, vs HUSE Lemuel (Samuel), husbandman, of Hillsborough, doc date 1818, rec date 1818, deed, land transfer, file #5704

WILKINS Abijah, joiner, of Amherst, vs TRUSSELL Benjamin, joiner, of Hopkinton, doc date 1799, writ, debt, file #358

WILKINS Abijah, joiner, of Amherst, vs LAMSON William, yeoman, of Amherst, doc date 1799, writ, debt, file #573

WILKINS Abijah, joiner, of Amherst, vs WESTON Thomas, yeoman, of Amherst, doc date 1799, writ, debt, file #567

WILKINS Amos, yeoman, of Lyndeborough, vs WELLS John, yeoman, of New Boston, doc date 1784, civil litigation, debt, file #1837

WILKINS Amos, yeoman, of Lyndeborough, vs KELLEY Moses, esquire, of Goffstown, rec date 1783, writ, debt, file #3185

WILKINS Andrew, yeoman, of Amherst, vs CODMAN Henry, physician, of Amherst, rec date 1782, appeal, debt, file #4011

WILKINS Aquilla, yeoman, of Middleton MA, vs WILKINS Bray, yeoman, of Hollis, doc date 1775, rec date 1775, deed, land transfer, file #6555

WILKINS Asa, yeoman, of Windsor, vs JONES James, yeoman, of Hillsborough, rec date 1783, execution, debt, file #2904

WILKINS Asa Jr, yeoman, of Amherst, vs FORBUSH Charles, gentleman, of Andover MA, rec date 1783, writ, debt, file #3006

WILKINS Asaph, gentleman, of Hillsborough, vs JONES Nehemiah, trader, of Stoddard, doc date 1799, judgment, debt, file #252

WILKINS Benjamin, yeoman, of Amherst, vs SARGENT Paul Dudley, merchant, of Amherst, doc date 1773, writ, debt, file #1353

WILKINS Benjamin, yeoman, of Amherst, vs JONES Timothy, yeoman, of Amherst, rec date 1782, writ, debt, file #2799

WILKINS Benjamin, yeoman, of Amherst, vs SMITH Jonathan, yeoman, of Amherst, doc date 1783, rec date 1783, deed, land transfer, file #2654

WILKINS Benjamin, yeoman, of Haverhill MA, vs NICHOLS Timothy Jr, cordwainer, of Amherst, doc date 1781, rec date 1783, deed, land transfer, file #2642

WILKINS Benjamin, yeoman, of Amherst, vs STEWART David, yeoman, of Amherst, rec date 1783, writ, debt, file #3086

WILKINS Benjamin, yeoman, of Amherst, vs ODELL William Jr, yeoman, of Amherst, rec date 1783, judgment, debt, file #3718

WILKINS Benjamin Jr, yeoman, of Amherst, vs JONES Timothy, yeoman, of Amherst, rec date 1782, writ, debt, file #2800

WILKINS Benjamin Jr, yeoman, of Amherst, vs JONES Timothy, yeoman, of Amherst, rec date 1782, judgment, debt, file #2624

WILKINS Bray, yeoman, of Hollis, vs SHEPARD John, esquire, of Amherst, doc date 1774, writ, debt, file #1098

WILKINS Bray, yeoman, of Hollis, vs ALLARD William, gentleman, of Merrimack, doc date 1775, writ, debt, file #957

WILKINS Bray, yeoman, of Amherst, vs SARGENT Paul Dudley, merchant, of Amherst, doc date 1773, writ, debt, file #1366

WILKINS Bray, yeoman, of Deering, vs HOBAT Jonathan Jr, yeoman, of Hollis, rec date 1785, judgment, debt, file #5211

WILKINS Daniel, clerk, of Amherst, vs STODDARD Margaret, widow, of Chelmsford MA, doc date 1783, writ, debt, file #1263

WILKINS Daniel, yeoman, of Amherst, vs SHEPARD John, yeoman, of Amherst, rec date 1782, ejectment, land boundaries, file #2776

WILKINS Daniel, yeoman, of Amherst, vs FISK Amos, gentleman, of Plymouth, rec date 1785, writ, debt, file #5426

WILKINS Daniel, laborer, of Amherst, vs SAWYER Nathaniel, husbandman, of Wilton, rec date 1787, writ, debt, file #6669

WILKINS David, husbandman, of Greenfield, vs GRAY William Jr, merchant, of Salem MA, doc date 1799, writ, debt, file #574

WILKINS Isaac, yeoman, of Amherst, vs ODELL Ebenezer, gentleman, of Amherst, doc date 1786, rec date 1786, deed, land transfer, file #5012, ?

WILKINS Isaac, yeoman, of Amherst, vs AVERILL Ebenezer, yeoman, of Amherst, rec date 1786, deed, land transfer, file #5012

WILKINS Israel, yeoman, of Hollis, vs FARNSWORTH David, yeoman, of Hollis, doc date 1772, writ, debt, file #918

WILKINS Israel, yeoman, of Hollis, doc date 1773, indictment, murder, file #1187

WILKINS Israel, yeoman, of Hollis, vs RIDEOUT James & Nathaniel, yeoman, of Hollis, doc date 1773, writ, debt, file #1340

WILKINS John, gentleman, of Amherst, vs CLARK Ephraim, husbandman, of Hillsborough, doc date 1799, debt, file #494

WILKINS John, gentleman, of Amherst, vs GOOLL John, merchants, of Amherst, doc date 1773, writ, debt, file #1242

WILKINS John, gentleman, of Francestown, vs GEARFIELD Nathaniel, gentleman, of Merrimack, doc date 1784, execution, debt, file #1750

WILKINS John, gentleman, of Amherst, vs BIXBY Edward, yeoman, of Francestown, doc date 1784, execution, debt, file #1549

WILKINS John, gentleman, of Francestown, vs GEARFIELD Nathaniel, gentleman, of Merrimack, doc date 1784, execution, debt, file #1513

WILKINS John, gentleman, of Francestown, vs CODMAN Henry, physician, of Amherst, rec date 1782, judgment, debt, file #3134

WILKINS John, gentleman, of Francestown, vs ALLD James, yeoman, of Francestown, rec date 1783, civil litigious, debt, file #2939

WILKINS John, gentleman, of Francestown, vs EVERTON John, yeoman, of Deering, rec date 1783, civil litigious, debt, file #2950

WILKINS John, gentleman, of Francestown, vs CODMAN Henry, physician, of Amherst, rec date 1783, execution, debt, file #2865

WILKINS John, of Amherst, vs PATTEN Matthew, esquire, of Bedford, rec date 1783, writ, debt, file #3107

WILKINS John, gentleman, of Francestown, vs GEARFIELD Nathaniel, gentleman, of Merrimack, rec date 1783, execution, debt, file #3496

WILKINS John, gentleman, of Francestown, vs GEARFIELD Nathaniel, gentleman, of Merrimack, rec date 1782, execution, debt, file #3507

WILKINS John, physician, of Francestown, vs GOOL Lois, merchant, of Salem MA, rec date 1782, appeal, debt, file #4003

WILKINS John, gentleman, of Francestown, vs EVERTON John, yeoman, of Deering, rec date 1783, execution, debt, file #3877

WILKINS John, gentleman, of Francestown, vs GRAHAM John, gentleman, of Hillsborough, rec date 1783, execution, debt, file #3823

WILKINS John, gentleman, of Francestown, vs EVERDEN John, yeoman, of Deering, rec date 1783, writ, debt, file #3902

WILKINS John, gentleman, of Francestown, vs ROBINSON Joseph, yeoman, of Deering, rec date 1783, execution, debt, file #3876

WILKINS John, gentleman, of Francestown, vs GEARFIELD Nathaniel, gentleman, of Merrimack, rec date 1783, execution, debt, file #3860

WILKINS John, gentleman, of Amherst, vs BIXBY Edward, yeoman, of Francestown, rec date 1783, judgment, debt, file #4442

WILKINS John, gentleman, of Amherst, vs DAWSON Timothy, yeoman, of Francestown, rec date 1785, writ, debt, file #4807

WILKINS John, gentleman, of Francestown, vs CODMAN Henry, physician, of Amherst, rec date 1782, writ, debt, file #4849

WILKINS John, gentleman, of Amherst, vs GIBSON Daniel, yeoman, of Hillsborough, rec date 1785, various, debt, file #5254

WILKINS John, gentleman, of Amherst, vs ABBOTT Josiah, yeoman, of New Boston, rec date 1786, judgment, debt, file #5764

WILKINS John, gentleman, of Amherst, vs GIBSON Daniel, yeoman, of Hillsborough, rec date 1786, judgment, debt, file #5763

WILKINS John, gentleman, of Amherst, vs GIBSON Daniel, yeoman, of Hillsborough, rec date 1785, judgment, debt, file #6198

WILKINS Jonathan, yeoman, of Amherst, vs TAYLOR John, yeoman, of Antrim, rec date 1783, judgment, debt, file #3301

WILKINS Jonathan, yeoman, of Amherst, vs BARKER Ephraim, joiner, of Amherst, rec date 1783, writ, debt, file #3175

WILKINS Jonathan, yeoman, of Amherst, vs WILKINS Aquilla, yeoman, of Hillsborough, rec date 1783, execution, debt, file #3227

WILKINS Jonathan, yeoman, of Amherst, vs TAYLOR John, yeoman, of Antrim, rec date 1783, execution, debt, file #3872

WILKINS Jonathan, yeoman, of Amherst, vs TAYLOR John, yeoman, of Antrim, rec date 1783, writ, debt, file #3933

WILKINS Jonathan, yeoman, of Amherst, vs MONTGOMERY William, husbandman, of Francestown, rec date 1782, execution, debt, file #4902

WILKINS Jonathan, husbandman, of Middleton MA, vs BRADFORD Mary & Samuel, widow/gent, of Hillsborough, rec date 1788, writ, debt, file #6602

WILKINS Jonathan Jr, yeoman, of Amherst, vs SARGENT Paul Dudley, merchant, of Amherst, doc date 1773, writ, debt, file #1356

WILKINS Robert Bradford, gentleman, of Amherst, vs BOWERS Ephraim, yeoman, of Merrimack, rec date 1785, execution, debt, file #5475

WILKINS Samuel, gentleman, of Amherst, vs KELLEY Moses, esquire, of Goffstown, rec date 1783, bond, person in jail, file #3310

WILKINS Stephen, gentleman, of Merrimack, vs PRESTON Samuel, husbandman, of Campbells Gore, doc date 1799, debt, file #473

WILKINS Stephen, gentleman, of Merrimack, vs PRESTON Samuel, husbandman, of Campbells Gore, doc date 1798, judgment, debt, file #567

WILKINS Stephen, gentleman, of Merrimack, vs McCLEARG David, yeoman, of Merrimack, rec date 1782, execution, debt, file #3566

WILLARD Catherine, gentlewoman, of Lancaster MA, vs THURSTON Moses, feltmaker, of Hollis, rec date 1783, writ, debt, file #3470

WILLEY George, yeoman, of Amherst, vs SMITH Jonathan, yeoman, of Amherst, doc date 1779, rec date 1786, deed, land transfer, file #5033, ?

WILLEY John, yeoman, of Deering, vs CHANDLER Samuel, yeoman, of Amherst, doc date 1777, deed, land transfer, file #2060

WILLIAM John, of Amherst, vs McCARDY Robert, husbandman, of Londonderry, rec date 1788, writ, debt, file #6902

WILLIAM William, cordwainer, of Shirley MA, vs WILLIAM Thomas, husbandman, of Henniker, rec date 1788, writ, debt, file #6935

WILLIAMS David, husbandman, of Amherst, vs SHEPARD Mary, spinster, of Amherst, doc date 1799, writ, debt, file #575

WILLIAMS David, yeoman, of Amherst, vs SHATTUCK Nathaniel, yeoman, of Hollis, rec date 1783, writ, debt, file #4855

WILLIAMS Jeremiah, of Henniker, vs (see BROWN Jonathan, of Henniker), rec date 1785, capias, assault, file #4569

WILLIAMS John Capt, of Merrimack, vs McCLARY David, of Londonderry, doc date 1775, deed, land transfer, file #838

WILLIAMS Jonathan, merchant, of Chelmsford MA, vs WYMAN Timothy, husbandman, of Deering, rec date 1784, judgment, debt, file #5302

WILLIAMS Jonathan, merchant, of Chelmsford MA, vs WYMAN Stephen, husbandman, of Deering, rec date 1784, judgment, debt, file #5302

WILLIAMS Leonard, esquire, of Waltham MA, vs AMES Simon, husbandman, of Mason, doc date 1784, execution, debt, file #1511

WILLIAMS Leonard, esquire, of Waltham MA, vs AMES Simeon, husbandman, of Mason, rec date 1783, judgment, debt, file #4299

WILLIAMS William, husbandman, of Goffstown, vs PETTINGILL Jonathan, husbandman, of Pembroke, rec date 1788, writ, debt, file #6933

WILLISON James, yeoman, of Derryfield, vs PETTIERS James, yeoman, of Derryfield, doc date 1761, rec date 1789, deed, land transfer, file #5664

WILLOUGHBY John, husbandman, of Hollis, vs YOUNGMAN Ebenezer, yeoman, of Dunstable, doc date 1772, civil litigation, debt, file #656

WILLOUGHBY Jonas, husbandman, of Hollis, vs WRIGHT Uriah, gentleman, of Hollis, rec date 1787, judgment, debt, file #2476

WILLOUGHBY Jonas, husbandman, of Hollis, vs KENNEY Israel, husbandman, of Hollis, rec date 1787, judgment, debt, file #2478

WILLOUGHBY Jonas, husbandman, of Hollis, vs PEABODY William, gentleman, of Amherst, rec date 1782, writ, debt, file #2783

WILLOUGHBY Jonas, husbandman, of Hollis, vs STEARNES Joseph, husbandman, of Hollis, rec date 1783, judgment, debt, file #4720

WILLOUGHBY Josiah, yeoman, of Hollis, vs STEVENS Joseph, yeoman, of Hollis, rec date 1784, recognizance, assault, file #4177

WILLOUGHBY Samuel, gentleman, of Hollis, vs GIBSON Ebenezer, yeoman, of Brookline, doc date 1800, judgment, debt, file #568

WILLS John, yeoman, of New Boston, vs HOWARD William, yeoman, of Amherst, rec date 1783, writ, debt, file #3966

WILLSON Alexander, yeoman, of New Boston, vs DONCK James, yeoman, of Londonderry, rec date 1783, writ, debt, file #3399

WILLSON Robert, esquire, of Peterborough, vs BACON Retire, yeoman, of New Ipswich, rec date 1783, writ, debt, file #4068

WILLSON Robert, esquire, of Peterborough, vs WHITE John, husbandman, of Peterborough, rec date 1785, judgment, debt, file #5547

WILLSON Robert, esquire, of Peterborough, vs ALLD John, husbandman, of Peterborough, rec date 1785, judgment, debt, file #5547

WILLSON Robert, esquire, of Peterborough, vs MITCHELL Samuel, cabinetmaker, of Peterborough, rec date 1785, judgment, debt, file #5063

WILLSON Robert, esquire, of Peterborough, vs BLANCHARD Jotham, merchant, of Peterborough, rec date 1785, judgment, debt, file #5063

WILLSON Sarah, spinster, of Peterborough, vs WHITE Samuel, yeoman, of Peterborough, doc date 1779, summons, fornication, file #762

WILLSON Thomas, yeoman, of New Boston, vs GIDDEN James, of Chester, doc date 1773, execution, debt, file #1218

WILLSON Thomas, yeoman, of Merrimack, vs HUTCHINSON Ebenezer, yeoman, of Amherst, rec date 1783, judgment, debt, file #4429

WILLSON Thomas, gentleman, of New Boston, vs CLARKE Timothy, yeoman, of Amherst, rec date 1784, judgment, debt, file #6046

WILSON Benjamin, miller, of Londonderry, vs CAMPBELL James Jr, yeoman, of Windham, doc date 1772, writ, debt, file #1406

WILSON Daniel, gentleman, of Deering, vs GREGG Samuel, yeoman, of Antrim, rec date 1785, judgment, debt, file #4948

WILSON David, gentleman, of Deering, vs BEARD William, yeoman, of New Boston, rec date 1784, writ, debt, file #4595

WILSON David, gentleman, of Deering, vs BEAN William, yeoman, of New Boston, rec date 1785, judgment, debt, file #5133

WILSON David, gentleman, of Deering, vs STEVENS Calvin, husbandman, of Hillsborough, rec date 1785, judgment, debt, file #5100

WILSON James, of Peterborough, vs WILSON William, gentleman, of Peterborough, doc date 1799, execution, debt, file #200

WILSON James, trader, of Deering, vs HART Seth, yeoman, of Deering, doc date 1798, judgment, debt, file #567

WILSON James, esquire, of Peterborough, vs NAYS William & James, yeoman, of Peterborough, doc date 1798, judgment, debt, file #567

WILSON James, trader, of Deering, vs SPRAGUE John, husbandman, of Hillsborough, doc date 1798, judgment, debt, file #567

WILSON James, trader, of Deering, vs CUNNINGHAM Samuel, husbandman, of New Boston, doc date 1798, judgment, debt, file #567

WILSON James, husbandman, of New Boston, vs COLLOM Thomas W, husbandman, of New Boston, doc date 1784, execution, debt, file #1526

WILSON James, husbandman, of New Boston, vs McCOLLOM Thomas, husbandman, of New Boston, doc date 1784, execution, debt, file #1875

WILSON James, yeoman, of Londonderry, vs McCLAY William, yeoman, of Francestown, rec date 1783, writ, debt, file #2763

WILSON James, husbandman, of New Boston, vs SMITH Reuben, husbandman, of New Boston, rec date 1783, writ, debt, file #4548

WILSON James, husbandman, of New Boston, vs DOACK James, cordwainer, of Londonderry, rec date 1785, judgment, debt, file #5143

WILSON James, husbandman, of New Boston, vs DOACK James, cordwainer, of Londonderry, rec date 1784, judgment, debt, file #5305

WILSON James, husbandman, of Londonderry, vs DOAK James, cordwainer, of Londonderry, rec date 1785, judgment, debt, file #4791

WILSON James & Abeschand, yeoman, of New Boston, vs HITCHBORN Samuel, jewelry, of Boston MA, rec date 1783, writ, debt, file #2751

WILSON Jesse, yeoman, of Amherst, vs GIBSON Matthew, yeoman, of Francestown, rec date 1784, judgment, debt, file #4384

WILSON John, husbandman, of Lunenburg MA, vs SAWYER Josiah Jr, husbandman, of Hancock, rec date 1785, judgment, debt, file #5103

WILSON Joseph, yeoman, of Londonderry, vs TEMPLE Jonathan, of Marlborough MA, doc date 1773, civil litigations, debt, file #572

WILSON Robert, gentleman, of Peterborough, vs BACON Retire, yeoman, of New Ipswich, doc date 1772, judgment, debt, file #700

WILSON Robert, esquire, of Peterborough, vs BACON Retire, yeoman, of New Ipswich, doc date 1784, execution, debt, file #1804

WILSON Robert, gentleman, of Peterborough, vs BACON Retire, yeoman, of New Ipswich, doc date 1777, judgment, debt, file #2030

WILSON Robert, of New Boston, vs WILSON Robert, yeoman, of Coldrin MA, rec date 1785, writ, debt, file #6233

WILSON Robert, esquire, of Peterborough, vs BLANCHARD Jotham, merchant, of Amherst, rec date 1787, writ, debt, file #6650

WILSON Robert, esquire, of Peterborough, vs MORRISON Thomas Jr, husbandman, of Peterborough, rec date 1787, writ, debt, file #6649

WILSON Samuel, yeoman, of Colrain MA, vs STEELE Thomas, yeoman, of Peterborough, rec date 1784, judgment, debt, file #4234

WILSON Sarah, spinster, of Peterborough, vs WHITE John & Charles, husbandman, of Peterborough, rec date 1786, writ, debt, file #6273

WILSON Thomas, yeoman, of Merrimack, vs HUTCHINSON Ebenezer, yeoman, of Amherst, doc date 1784, execution, debt, file #1808

WILSON Thomas, gentleman, of New Boston, vs CLARK Timothy, yeoman, of Amherst, doc date 1784, civil litigation, debt, file #1831

WILSON Thomas, gentleman, of New Boston, vs MOORE John, yeoman, of Londonderry, doc date 1784, civil litigation, debt, file #1838

WILSON Thomas, husbandman, of New Boston, vs McMILLEN Archibald, husbandman, of New Boston, doc date 1784, civil litigation, debt, file #1849

WILSON Thomas, husbandman, of New Boston, vs DICKEY Adam & John, husbandman, of Francestown, doc date 1784, civil litigation, debt, file #1850

WILSON Thomas, yeoman, of New Boston, vs BALDWIN Nahum, esquire, of Amherst, rec date 1783, writ, debt, file #3317, Zacheus CUTLER estate

WILSON Thomas, yeoman, of Goffstown, vs POLLARD Samuel, husbandman, of Nottingham-West, rec date 1783, writ, debt, file #3206

WILSON Thomas, husbandman, of New Boston, vs WALKER Andrew, husbandman, of New Boston, rec date 1784, judgment, debt, file #4278

WILSON Thomas, yeoman, of Merrimack, vs HUTCHINSON Ebenezer, yeoman, of Amherst, rec date 1785, various, debt, file #6227

WILSON Thomas, gentleman, of New Boston, vs DODGE James, yeoman, of New Boston, rec date 1787, writ, trespassing, file #6703

WILSON Thomas, yeoman, of New Boston, vs INHABATITANTS of New Boston, of New Boston, rec date 1787, writ, debt, file #6969

WIMAN Elisha, of Mile Slip, vs STATE of NH, rec date 1777, inquiry, death inquire, file #2214

WINCHESTER Lemuel, yeoman, of Amherst, vs SERVICE Robert, merchant, of Boston MA, rec date 1785, writ, debt, file #5393

WINCHESTER Samuel, husbandman, of Deering, vs SUMMER George, yeoman, of Deering, doc date 1799, execution, debt, file #158

WINN Nathan, husbandman, of Nottingham-West, vs DAVIS Asa, minors, of Nottingham-West, rec date 1787, various, breaking & enter, file #6699

WINN Nathan, husbandman, of Nottingham-West, vs HADLEY Benjamin, cordwainer, of Nottingham-West, rec date 1787, various, breaking & enter, file #6699

WINN Nathan, husbandman, of Nottingham-West, vs WATSON Moses, minors, of Nottingham-West, rec date 1787, various, breaking & enter, file #6699

WINN Nathan, husbandman, of Nottingham-West, vs HAZELTINE Nathaniel, husbandman, of Nottingham-West, rec date 1787, various, breaking & enter, file #6699

WINN Nathan, husbandman, of Nottingham-West, vs WATSON Reuben, minors, of Nottingham-West, rec date 1787, various, breaking & enter, file #6699

WINN Nathan, husbandman, of Nottingham-West, vs WATSON Samuel, minors, of Nottingham-West, rec date 1787, various, breaking & enter, file #6699

WINSLOW Isaac & Lucy, of Boston MA, vs KENDALL Ebenezer, of Dunstable, doc date 1768, rec date 1768, deed, land transfer, file #6839

WINSLOW John, esquire, of Dunstable MA, vs WILLARD Abijah, esquire, of Lancaster MA, rec date 1784, judgment, debt, file #4416

WINSLOW John, esquire, of Dunstable MA, vs REED James, esquire, of Keene, rec date 1784, judgment, debt, file #4417

WINSLOW John, esquire, of Dunstable MA, vs RICHARDSON James, esquire, of Leominster MA, rec date 1784, judgment, debt, file #4416

WINSLOW John, esquire, of Dunstable MA, vs REED James, esquire, of Keene, rec date 1784, appeal, debt, file #4128

WINSLOW John, esquire, of Dunstable MA, vs REED James, esquire, of Keene, rec date 1784, judgment, debt, file #4416

WINTHROP John, deceased, of Marlborough MA, vs BARNS Edward, esquire, of Marlborough MA, rec date 1787?, declaration, debt, file #6170, part of Samuel CURTIS file

WISE Robert, husbandman, of Salisbury, vs FOGG Jonathan, husbandman, of Pittsfield, doc date 1798, execution, debt, file #128

WISE Robert, yeoman, of Salisbury, vs HUTCHINSON Jonathan, hatter, of Pembroke, doc date 1799, execution, debt, file #206

WISE Robert, husbandman, of Salisbury, vs EMERSON George, husbandman, of Concord, doc date 1798, execution, debt, file #117

WISE Robert, yeoman, of Salisbury, vs HUTCHINSON Jonathan, hatter, of Pembroke, doc date 1798, judgment, debt, file #567

WISWALL Priscilla, singlewoman, of Boston MA, vs HOW Benjamin, gentleman, of New Ipswich, doc date 1799, execution, debt, file #203

WISWALL Priscilla, singlewoman, of Boston MA, vs HOAR Benjamin Jetham, of New Ipswich, doc date 1798, judgment, debt, file #567

WISWALL Priscilla, single, of Boston MA, vs HOUS Benjamin, gentleman, of New Ipswich, rec date 1786, writ, debt, file #6871

WISWALL Priscilla, single, of Boston MA, vs SHATTACK William, yeoman, of New Ipswich, rec date 1786, writ, debt, file #6871

WISWALL Priscilla, single, of Boston MA, vs HOW Isaac, gentleman, of New Ipswich, rec date 1786, writ, debt, file #6871

WITCHER David, gentleman, of Methuen MA, vs HILDRETH John, yeoman, of Litchfield, rec date 1784, judgment, debt, file #5290

WITCHER David, gentleman, of Meuthen MA, vs HILDRETH John, yeoman, of Litchfield, rec date 1785, judgment, debt, file #5438

WOOD Benjamin, trader, of Hollis, vs CUMMINGS Benjamin, gentleman, of Hollis, doc date 1798, execution, debt, file #100

WOOD Edward, yeoman, of Goffstown, vs STICKNEY Samuel, yeoman, of New Boston, rec date 1785, writ, debt, file #4813

WOOD Edward, husbandman, of Goffstown, vs KELLY Moses, esquire, of Goffstown, rec date 1785, writ, debt, file #5429

WOOD Jonathan, yeoman, of Goffstown, vs COSTIN Ebenezer, yeoman, of Stafford, doc date 1779, rec date 1779, deed, land transfer, file #2134

WOOD Jonathan, yeoman, of Goffstown, vs WILTON Alexander, yeoman, of New Boston, rec date 1783, various, debt, file #2766

WOOD Jonathan, husbandman, of Goffstown, vs SHIRLEY Samuel, yeoman, of Goffstown, rec date 1782, writ, debt, file #2816

WOOD Jonathan, husbandman, of Goffstown, vs BLODGET Samuel, esquire, of Goffstown, rec date 1782, writ, debt, file #2819

WOOD Jonathan, husbandman, of Goffstown, vs HUSE Josiah, yeoman, of Deerfield, rec date 1782, debt, debt, file #3139

WOOD Jonathan, husbandman, of Goffstown, vs KELLY Moses, esquire, of Goffstown, rec date 1785, writ, debt, file #5429

WOOD Jonathan, yeoman, of Goffstown, vs DUNLAP Thomas, husbandman, of Litchfield, doc date 1780, rec date 1785, deed, land transfer, file #5630

WOOD Jonathan, yeoman, of Goffstown, vs ROGERS William, yeoman, of Weare, rec date 1787, writ, debt, file #6666

WOOD Peter, of Marlborough MA, vs BARNARD Josiah, of Marlborough MA, rec date 1787, complaint, debt, file #6172, part of Samuel CURTIS file

WOOD Samuel, yeoman, of Mason, vs HODGEMAN John, yeoman, of Mason, rec date 1783, judgment, debt, file #3798

WOOD Samuel, yeoman, of Mason, vs ASTIN Timothy, husbandman, of Temple, rec date 1783, judgment, debt, file #3797

WOOD Samuel, yeoman, of Mason, vs DANA Samuel, esquire, of Amherst, rec date 1785, writ, debt, file #5417

WOOD Samuel Jr, husbandman, of Mason, vs LEE Jonas, of Concord MA, doc date 1788, rec date 1788, deed, land transfer, file #6757

WOODBURY Jesse, gentleman, of Weare, vs MacLAUGHLIN, gentleman, of New Boston, doc date 1798, judgment, debt, file #567

WOODBURY Peter, trader, of Francestown, vs MOOR Edmund, goldsmith, of Francestown, doc date 1802, rec date 1802, deed, land transfer, file #5679

WOODBURY William, yeoman, of New Boston, vs RAMSAY James, husbandman, of New Boston, doc date 1794, petition, release of debit, file #16

WOODMAN John, gentleman, of New London, vs COLBY Joseph, trader, of New London, doc date 1799, execution, debt, file #160

WOODMAN John, gentleman, of New London, vs CARSON John, gentleman, of Francestown, doc date 1798, execution, debt, file #60

WOODMAN Nathaniel, yeoman, of Salem, vs PECKER James, physician, of Haverhill, doc date 1772, writ, assault, file #1061

WOODS Paul, tailor, of Dunstable MA, vs EMERSON Amos, gentleman, of Chester, rec date 1784, judgment, debt, file #4283

WOODWARD C E, vs BIXBY Lucina, doc date 1894, defendant assumpsit, supreme court, file #613

WOODWARD John, yeoman, of Lyndeborough, vs BRADFORD William, husbandman, of Deering, rec date 1782, execution, debt, file #3515

WOODWARD John, yeoman, of Lyndeborough, vs BRADFORD William, husbandman, of Deering, rec date 1783, execution, debt, file #3648

WOOLEY John, husbandman, of Marlborough MA, vs WHIPPLE Israel, gentleman, of Richmond, rec date 1783, writ, debt, file #3603

WOOLY Thomas, husbandman, of Marlborough MA, vs WHIPPLE Isquire, husbandman, of Richmond, doc date 1784, execution, debt, file #1670

WORCESTER Noah, esquire, of Hollis, vs LAKIN Isaac Jr, husbandman, of Groton MA, rec date 1787, writ, debt, file #2421

WORCESTER Noah, esquire, of Hollis, vs SHED Daniel, yeoman, of Hollis, rec date 1784, execution, debt, file #5888

WORCESTER Noah, esquire, of Hollis, vs WHITING John, cordwainer, of Hollis, rec date 1784, execution, debt, file #5889

WORCESTER Noah, of Hollis, vs HARDY David, husbandman, of Nottingham-West, rec date 1785, warrant, debt, file #7025

WORCESTER Noah, of Hollis, vs DURRER William, husbandman, of Nottingham-West, rec date 1785, warrant, debt, file #7025

WORCESTER Noah, of Hollis, vs KELLEY Joseph, husbandman, of Nottingham-West, rec date 1785, warrant, debt, file #7025

WORCESTER Noah, of Hollis, vs ROBY James, husbandman, of Nottingham-West, rec date 1785, warrant, debt, file #7025

WOTHERALL Charles, blacksmith, of Pepperell MA, vs WRIGHT David, cordwainer, of Hollis, rec date 1783, judgment, debt, file #4469

WRIGHT Benjamin, yeoman, of Hollis, vs CUMINGS Samuel, esquire, of Hollis, rec date 1777, writ, debt, file #2188

WRIGHT David, cordwainer, of Hollis, vs SHATTUCK William, husbandman, of Deering, rec date 1783, writ, debt, file #3113

WRIGHT David, cordwainer, of Hollis, vs SHATTUCK Edmund, husbandman, of Cockermouth, rec date 1783, writ, debt, file #3111

WRIGHT David, cordwainer, of Hollis, vs BENNET Benjamin, husbandman, of Amherst, rec date 1783, judgment, debt, file #3762

WRIGHT David, yeoman, of Hillsborough, vs FLINT Jacob, husbandman, of Hillsborough, rec date 1784, judgment, debt, file #4415

WRIGHT David, cordwainer, of Hollis, vs WHITTIMORE Samuel, gentleman, of Cambridge, rec date 1785, judgment, land dispute, file #5358

WRIGHT David, cordwainer, of Hollis, vs WILLIAMS Isaac, laborer, of Pepperell MA, rec date 1785, judgment, debt, file #5331

WRIGHT David, cordwainer, of Hollis, vs GILSON Simon, gentleman, of Pepperell MA, rec date 1785, judgment, debt, file #5331

WRIGHT David, cordwainer, of Hollis, vs CRAFFORD John, yeoman, of Pepperell MA, rec date 1785, judgment, debt, file #5331

WRIGHT David, cordwainer, of Hollis, vs NEWHALE Oliver, husbandman, of Hollis, rec date 1785, writ, debt, file #5419

WRIGHT David, cordwainer, of Hollis, vs CRAFFORD John, yeoman, of Pepperell MA, rec date 1786, various, trespassing, file #6079

WRIGHT David, cordwainer, of Hollis, vs WILLIAMS Isaac, laborer, of Pepperell MA, rec date 1786, various, trespassing, file #6079

WRIGHT David, cordwainer, of Hollis, vs GILSON Simon, gentleman, of Pepperell MA, rec date 1786, various, trespassing, file #6079

WRIGHT David, cordwainer, of Hollis, vs NEWHALL Oliver, husbandman, of Hollis, rec date 1785, judgment, debt, file #4959

WRIGHT David, cordwainer, of Pepperell MA, vs GILSON Simon, gentleman, of Pepperell MA, rec date 1787, various, breaking and entry, file #6970

WRIGHT David Jr, cordwainer, of Pepperell MA, vs GILSON Simeon, gentleman, of Pepperell MA, rec date 1789, various, land dispute in NH, file #2570

WRIGHT Isaiah, yeoman, of Hollis, vs PUTNAM Samuel, gentleman, of Salem MA, doc date 1793, petition, release of debit, file #15

WRIGHT Joshua, esquire, of Hollis, vs HOPKINS Richard, yeoman, of Hollis, doc date 1774, judgment, debt, file #741

WRIGHT Nathaniel, yeoman, of Pepperell MA, vs JACKMAN Abner, cordwainer, of Jaffrey, doc date 1784, execution, debt, file #1541

WRIGHT Nathaniel, yeoman, of Pepperell MA, vs JACKMAN Abner, cordwainer, of Jaffrey, rec date 1783, writ, debt, file #3305

WRIGHT Oliver, yeoman, of Packersfield, vs HUTCHINSON Samuel, husbandman, of Wilton, doc date 1784, execution, debt, file #1886

WRIGHT Oliver, yeoman, of Packersfield, vs HATCHINSON Samuel, husbandman, of Wilton, rec date 1783, writ, debt, file #3571

WRIGHT Samuel Jr, yeoman, of Hollis, vs FLAGG Samuel, esquire, of Salem MA, rec date 1783, writ, debt, file #3961

WRIGHT Thomas, husbandman, of Westford MA, vs PARKER Joseph, husbandman, of New Ipswich, doc date 1773, judgment, debt, file #701

WRIGHT Uriah, gentleman, of Hollis, vs CHAMPNEY Ebenezer, esquire, of Groton MA, doc date 1784, writ, debt, file #1580

WRIGHT Uriah, gentleman, of Hollis, vs PAINE Nathaniel, esquire, of Groton MA, doc date 1784, writ, debt, file #1580

WRIGHT Uriah, husbandman, of Hollis, vs BRADLEY Thomas, husbandman, of Hollis, rec date 1786, judgment, debt, file #5372

WRIGHT Uriah, gentleman, of Hollis, vs FOX John, laborer, of Hollis, doc date 1784, execution, debt, file #1944

WRIGHT Uriah, gentleman, of Hollis, vs HARRIS Robert, trader, of Concord, rec date 1783, writ, debt, file #3179

WRIGHT Uriah, gentleman, of Hollis, vs FOX John, laborer, of Hollis, rec date 1783, various, debt, file #3166

WRIGHT Uriah, gentleman, of Hollis, vs CAMPBELL Jonas, husbandman, of Townsend MA, rec date 1784, judgment, debt, file #4356

WRIGHT Uriah, gentleman, of Hollis, vs ABBOTT Benjamin, husbandman, of Hollis, rec date 1783, judgment, debt, file #4706

WRIGHT Uriah, gentleman, of Hollis, vs JEWET Jacob Jr, yeoman, of Hollis, rec date 1784, writ, debt, file #5156

WRIGHT Uriah, gentleman, of Hollis, vs WRIGHT Abigail, widow, of Hollis, rec date 1785, deed, land transfer, file #5623

WRIGHT Uriah, gentleman, of Hollis, vs WRIGHT Timothy, yeoman, of Hollis, rec date 1785, deed, land transfer, file #5623

WWILKINS John, gentleman, of Amherst, vs BIXBY Edward, yeoman, of Francestown, doc date 1784, execution, debt, file #1725

WYER Richard, housewright, of Townsend MA, vs BLANCHARD Joseph, esquire, of Amherst, rec date 1784, judgment, debt, file #4604

WYER Robert, of Walpole, vs BROOKS William Jr, gentleman, of Hollis, rec date 1783, various, debt, file #4558

WYETH Jonas, yeoman, of Cambridge MA, vs SANGER Jedediah, gentleman, of Jaffrey, rec date 1782, writ, debt, file #2715

WYLEY John, yeoman, of Amherst, vs GREEN David, yeoman, of Hillsborough, doc date 1784, execution, debt, file #1677

WYMAN Ashabel, blacksmith, of Groton MA, vs WYMAN Ashabel Jr, mariner, of Amherst, rec date 1787, writ, debt, file #6894

WYMAN J Seth, yeoman, of Goffstown, vs DUSTON John, of Goffstown, doc date 1779, deed, land transfer, file #2012

WYMAN John, yeoman, of Pelham, vs PHILIPS Samuel, esquire, of Andover MA, doc date 1773, writ, debt, file #1329

WYMAN Jonathan, husbandman, of Deering, vs CROSBY Josiah, yeoman, of Billerica MA, rec date 1785, deed, land transfer, file #5619

WYMAN Joseph Jr, husbandman, of Pelham, vs CULLWELL John, cordwainer, of Windham, doc date 1772, writ, debt, file #1388

WYMAN Noah, innholder, of Woburn MA, vs WAITE Nathan, trader, of Pembroke, doc date 1784, execution, debt, file #1979

WYMAN Noah, innholder, of Woburn MA, vs WAIT Nathan, trader, of Pembroke, rec date 1782, judgment, debt, file #2729

WYMAN Noah, innholder, of Woburn MA, vs WAITE Nathan, trader, of Pembroke, rec date 1783, civil litigious, debt, file #2968

WYMAN Noah, innholder, of Woburn MA, vs WAITE Nathan, trader, of Pembroke, rec date 1783, execution, debt, file #3265

WYMAN Seth, of Nottingham-West, vs Town of Nottingham-West, rec date 1777, petition, road lay out, file #2240

WYMAN Stephen, yeoman, of Deering, vs JONES Nathan, yeoman, of Amherst, rec date 1783, writ, debt, file #3088

WYMAN Stephen, yeoman, of Deering, vs BRADFORD Samuel Jr, of Hillsborough, rec date 1785, execution, debt, file #5948

WYMAN Stephen, yeoman, of Deering, vs BRADFORD Samuel Jr, gentleman, of Hillsborough, rec date 1785, writ, debt, file #6018

WYMAN Tim Jr, husbandman, of Deering, vs STEARN Samuel, husbandman, of Plymouth, rec date 1785, arbitration award, debt, file #5360

WYMAN Timothy, of Deering, doc date 1780, appointments, tavern license, file #1279

WYMAN Timothy, innholder, of Deering, vs ANDREWS Ammi, gentleman, of Hillsborough, rec date 1783, writ, debt, file #3176

WYMAN Timothy & Stephen, yeoman, of Deering, vs ALCOCK Robert, gentleman, of Deering, rec date 1783, writ, debt, file #3073

WYMAN Timothy Jr, husbandman, of Hollis, vs STEARNS Samuel Jr, yeoman, of Hollis, doc date 1773, judgment, debt, file #1307

YOUNG Daniel, yeoman, of Warner, vs HOYT Robert, of Amesbury MA, doc date 1780, rec date 1785, deed, land transfer, file #5650

YOUNG Jno, physician, of Peterborough, vs SWAN William, esquire, of Groton MA, rec date 1785, deed, land transfer, file #6804

YOUNG John, physician, of Peterborough, vs GRAGG Jeremiah Jr, yeoman, of Peterborough, doc date 1772, civil litigation, debt, file #648

YOUNG John, physician, of Peterborough, vs HARRIS Robert, merchant, of Littleton MA, doc date 1772, writ, debt, file #1071

YOUNG John, physician, of Peterborough, vs BALDWIN Nahum, gentleman, of Amherst, doc date 1773, writ, debt, file #1363

YOUNG Luke, husbandman, of Windsor, vs LOVE William, husbandman, of Hillsborough, doc date 1799, judgment, debt, file #237

YOUNGMAN Nicholas, yeoman, of Hollis, vs WRIGHT Samuel, yeoman, of Hollis, doc date 1772, writ, breaking & entry, file #936

YOUNGMAN Nicholas, yeoman, of Hollis, vs WRIGHT Samuel, yeoman, of Hollis, doc date 1772, execution, file #1198

INSTITUTIONS

AND MISCELLANEOUS

AMERICAN Legion of Honor, vs ADAMS Alice G, of Natick MA, doc date 1894, benefit fund dispute, supreme court, file #586

AMOSKEAG Manufacturing Co, vs CITY of Concord, doc date 1890, plaintiffs brief, supreme court, file #625

AMOSKEAG Savings Bank, vs ALGER George A, doc date 1890, plaintiffs 3rd brief, supreme court, file #623

APPOINTMENTS of Justice, of Hillsborough County, doc date 1771, civil litigations, debt, file #570

ATTORNEY Case Listings, doc date 1794, case listings, file #1275

ATTORNEY Case Listings, rec date 1785, list of cases, file #5468

ATTORNEY General, vs SANDS Thomas, of Nashua, doc date 1894, election to mayor's office, supreme court, file #593

ATTORNEY General, vs CITY of Nashua, doc date 1893, plaintiffs brief, supreme court, file #607

ATTORNEY General, vs VARNEY David B, of Manchester, doc date 1894, election to mayors off, supreme court, file #594

AUREAN Academy, of Amherst, doc date 1797, petition, debt, file #31

BANK vs HARTSHORN et al., (HARTSHORN Ellen M), doc date 1891, brief for administrator, supreme court, file #628

BOSTON and Maine Railroad, vs MANCHESTER-WEARE Railroad, doc date 1892, supreme court petition, supreme court, file #578

BROOK At Merrimack, of Merrimack, vs GILMORE James, yeoman, of Merrimack, doc date 1772, indictment, damming of brook, file #698

COMMITTEE Report, rec date 1774, committee report, file #6962

COMMITTEE Report, vs COUNTY of Hillsborough, rec date 1788, report, file #3548

COUNCIL Notes, rec date 1776, council notice, file #7032

COUNCIL of Assembly, vs OFFICE Holders, doc date 1776, resolution, file #808

COUNTY Treasury Bonds, vs ROBERT Means, bond, years 1784-1795, file #800

COUNTY Treasury Report, vs STATE of NH, rec date 1783, committee report, new jail, file #4053

COURT Adjournment, rec date 1783, warrant, file #3564

COURT Bills (Hillsborough), vs SARGENT Paul Dudley, doc date 1773, court bills, file #1223

COURT Case List, doc date 1795, list of court cases, file #1254

COURT Case List, of Amherst, rec date 1772, list of court cases, file #3538

DURGIN (Co), vs AMERICAN Express Co, doc date 1890, defendants brief, supreme court, file #624

FERRY Landing Dispute, of Litchfield, doc date 1779, deposition, ferry dispute, file #1255

HAMILTON National Bank, vs HORTON M D, laborer, doc date 1894, note and wage dispute, supreme court, file #588

HILLSBOROUGH Court House, vs PETITION To Build New, rec date 1785, building new Court house, file #5780

HILLSBOROUGH County Court, vs HOLLAND Stephen, clerk, doc date 1774, writ, record of court, file #750

HILLSBOROUGH County Court List, vs HILLSBOROUGH County, rec date 1794, court case list, file #4149

INHABITANTS of Amherst, vs MUNROE Josiah, Gentleman, of Amherst, rec date 1784, judgment, debt, file #4220

INHABITANTS of Antrim, vs ENGLISH Thomas, yeoman, of Antrim, rec date 1782, writ, debt, file #2703

INHABITANTS of Bedford, vs BOYES Tomas, husbandman, of Bedford, rec date 1785, judgment, debt, file #5105

INHABITANTS of Bedford, vs MORRILL Robert, yeoman, of Bedford, rec date 1786, judgment, debt, file #6476

INHABITANTS of Bedford, vs VOSE James, husbandman, of Bedford, rec date 1783, writ, debt, file #3344, guardian of Stephen WOOD

INHABITANTS of Bedford, vs VOSE James, husbandman, of Bedford, rec date 1785, judgment, debt, file #5105

INHABITANTS of Bedford, vs WHITE William, yeoman, of Pembroke, rec date 1785, judgment, debt, file #5105

INHABITANTS of Cockermouth, vs MELVIN Ebenezer, Gentleman, of Cockermouth, rec date 1788, writ, debt, file #3565

INHABITANTS of Derry, of Chester, rec date 1789, boundary line dispute, land boundary, file #2569

INHABITANTS of Derryfield, vs STATE of NH, rec date 1792, road lay outs, file #4183

INHABITANTS of Dunstable, vs FISK Eleaser, husbandman, of Dunstable, rec date 1785, judgment, debt, file #6488

INHABITANTS of Francestown, vs STATE of NH, rec date 1793, road lay out, file #4159

INHABITANTS of Goffstown, vs GOFFSTOWN Cong Society, of Goffstown, rec date 1784, judgment, debt, file #4245, purchasing house for Society

INHABITANTS of Goffstown, vs KIMBALL Andrew, husbandman, of Goffstown, rec date 1784, writ, debt, file #4206

INHABITANTS of Goffstown, vs RICHARDS Samuel, Esquire, rec date 1783, execution, debt, file #2898

INHABITANTS of Hancock, vs MOORE Time, rec date 1794, petition, road lay out, file #4058

INHABITANTS of Hill, of Hillsborough, vs STATE of NH, rec date 1793, road lay out, file #4159

INHABITANTS of Hollis, vs JEWET Jacob Jr, Gentleman, of Hollis, rec date 1784, judgment, debt, file #4265

INHABITANTS of Hollis, vs WILLOUGHBY Samuel, Gentleman, of Hollis, rec date 1784, judgment, debt, file #4265

INHABITANTS of Lyndeborough, vs EPES Francis, deceased-gentleman, of Lyndeborough, rec date 1793, judgment, debt/salt/molasses, file #2582

INHABITANTS of Lyndeborough, vs PEARSON Nathan, deceased-yeoman, of Lyndeborough, rec date 1793, judgment, debt/salt/molasses, file #2582

INHABITANTS of Lyndeborough, vs WOODBURY Jonah, housewright, of Lyndeborough, rec date 1793, judgment, debt/salt/molasses, file #2582

INHABITANTS of New Boston, vs CALDWELL James, husbandman, of New Boston, rec date 1785, writ, debt, file #4872

INHABITANTS of New Boston, vs COCHRAN John, Esquire, of New Boston, rec date 1785, writ, debt, file #4872

INHABITANTS of New Boston, vs DODGE Solomon, yeoman, of New Boston, rec date 1785, writ, debt, file #4872

INHABITANTS of New Boston, vs STATE of NH, rec date 1792, various, repairing of hwy, file #4161

INHABITANTS of New Boston, vs STATE of NH, rec date 1794, road lay outs, file #4157

INHABITANTS of Peterborough, vs GILCHRIST Richard, husbandman, of Dublin, rec date 1784, writ, debt, file #4627, estate of John SWAN

INHABITANTS of Raby, vs CHAMPNEY Ebenezer, Esquire, of New Ipswich, rec date 1782, writ, debt, file #2844

INHABITANTS of Wilton, vs CARLTON Ebenezer, laborer, of Wilton, rec date 1783, writ, debt, file #4520, illegitimate child charge

INHABITANTS of Wilton, vs PARKHURST Jonathan, husbandman, of Wilton, rec date 1785, judgment, debt, file #5188

INHABITANTS of Peterborough, vs SMITH William, Gentleman, of Peterborough, rec date 1783, writ, debt, file #3350

INHABITANTS of Peterborough, vs WALLACE Matthew, Gentleman, of Peterborough, rec date 1783, writ, debt, file #3350

INHABITANTS of Warner, vs BEAN Nathaniel, husbandman, of Warner, rec date 1783, writ, debt, file #3106

INHABITANTS of Westmoreland, vs BARNARD Jeremiah, clerk, of Amherst, rec date 1783, writ, debt, file #3019

INHABITANTS of Wilton, vs COBURN Amos, husbandman, of Wilton, rec date 1785, judgment, debt, file #5095

INSURANCE Commissioner, vs PEOPLES Fire Ins Co, of Manchester, doc date 1894, contract dispute, supreme court, file #583

INVENTORY List, doc date 1778, inventory list, file #1031

JAIL Expenses, rec date 1787, jail expenses, file #3549

JOURNAL Book, rec date 1785, journal, file #6966

JOURNAL Book, rec date 1785, journal, grand-petite jurors, file #6968

JOURNAL Book, vs GREEN David, doc date 1770, journal book, file #1162

JURORS-GRAND & PETITE, doc date 1773, appointments, jury notice, file #695

JURORS-GRAND & PETITE, doc date 1777, appointments, jury notice, file #1247

JURORS-GRAND & PETITE, doc date 1777, appointments, jury notice, file #1248

JURORS-GRAND & PETITE, doc date 1777, appointments, jury list, file #1249

JURORS-GRAND & PETITE, doc date 1795, appointments, jury notice, file #1250
JURORS-GRAND & PETITE, rec date 1773, notices, file #7058
JURORS-GRAND & PETITE, rec date 1783, appointments, jurors-petite & grand, file #3560
JURORS-GRAND, doc date 1772, appointments, jury notice, file #696
JURORS-GRAND, doc date 1777, appointments, jury notice, file #2027
JURORS-GRAND, doc date 1778, appointments, jury notice, file #2328
JURORS-GRAND, doc date 1779, appointments, jurors-grand, file #2074
JURORS-GRAND, doc date 1779, appointments, jury notice, file #2066
JURORS-GRAND, doc date 1783, appointments, jury notice, file #2328
JURORS-GRAND, doc date 1784, appointments, jury notices, file #1656
JURORS-GRAND, doc date 1785, appointments, jury notice, file #2330
JURORS-GRAND Notices, rec date 1782, appointments, jury notice, file #3126
JURORS-GRAND Notices, vs HILLSBOROUGH County, rec date 1787, appointments, jurors-grand, file #2534
JURORS-GRAND Notices, vs HILLSBOROUGH County, rec date 1793, appointments, jurors-grand, file #2588-A, 2 folders
JURORS-GRAND, of Hillsborough, rec date 1786, appointments, jury list, file #6073
JURORS-GRAND, rec date 1773, appointments, juror- grand, file #7058
JURORS-GRAND, rec date 1776, appointments, jurors-grand, file #2259
JURORS-GRAND, rec date 1785, appointments, jury notice, file #4837
JURORS-GRAND, rec date 1785, appointments, jury notice, file #5470
JURORS-GRAND, rec date 1785, execution, debt, file #3504
JURORS-GRAND, rec date 1788, appointments, jury list, file #6594
JURORS-GRAND, rec date 1788, appointments, jury list, file #6815
JURORS-GRAND, rec date 1793, appointments, jury notice, file #2588-B, 2 folders
JURORS-GRAND, rec date 1786, appointments, jury list, file #6207
JURORS-GRAND, vs HILLSBOROUGH County, rec date 1793, appointments, jurors-grand, file #2589-B, 2 folders
JURORS-PETITE, doc date 1771, appointments, jury notice, file #2075
JURORS-PETITE, doc date 1772, appointments, jury notice, file #2076
JURORS-PETITE, doc date 1772, appointments, jury notice, file #697
JURORS-PETITE, doc date 1773, appointments, jurors-list, file #1212
JURORS-PETITE, doc date 1773, appointments, jury notice, file #2077
JURORS-PETITE, doc date 1773, appointments, list of jurors, file #1224
JURORS-PETITE, doc date 1774, appointments, jury notice, file #2078
JURORS-PETITE, doc date 1775, appointments, jury notice, file #2079
JURORS-PETITE, doc date 1776, appointments, jury notice, file #2080
JURORS-PETITE, doc date 1777, appointments, jury notice, file #2028
JURORS-PETITE, doc date 1777, appointments, jury notice, file #2081
JURORS-PETITE, doc date 1778, appointments, jurors petite, file #2069
JURORS-PETITE, doc date 1778, appointments, jury notice, file #2082
JURORS-PETITE, doc date 1779, appointments, jury notice, file #2087
JURORS-PETITE, doc date 1779, appointments, jury notice, file #2103

JURORS-PETITE, doc date 1781, appointments, jury notice, file #2083
JURORS-PETITE, doc date 1782, appointments, jury notice, file #2084
JURORS-PETITE, doc date 1782, appointments, jury notice, file #2084
JURORS-PETITE, doc date 1783, appointments, jury notice, file #2329
JURORS-PETITE, doc date 1784, appointments, jury notice, file #1191
JURORS-PETITE, doc date 1784, appointments, jury notice, file #1655
JURORS-PETITE, doc date 1786, appointments, jury notice, file #2331
JURORS-PETITE, doc date 1788, appointments, jury notice, file #2332
JURORS-PETITE, doc date 1789, appointments, jury notice, file #2333
JURORS-PETITE, doc date 1792-93, appointments, jury notice, file #515
JURORS-PETITE, doc date 1795, appointments, jury notice, file #2334
JURORS-PETITE, doc date 1799, appointments, jury notice, file #512, for March session
JURORS-PETITE Notices, doc date 1772, ventures, summons, file #799
JURORS-PETITE Notices, of Amherst, vs HILLSBOROUGH County, rec date 1783, appointments, fall session, file #2601
JURORS-PETITE, of Amherst, vs HILLSBOROUGH County, rec date 1782, appointments, jurors-petite, file #3125
JURORS-PETITE, of Amherst, vs HILLSBOROUGH County, rec date 1787, appointments, jurors-petite, file #2480
JURORS-PETITE, of Amherst, vs HILLSBOROUGH County, rec date 1787, appointments, jurors-petite, file #2535
JURORS-PETITE, of Amherst, vs HILLSBOROUGH County, rec date 1793, appointments, jurors-petite, file #2589-A, 2 folders
JURORS-PETITE, rec date 1774, appointments, juror-petite, file #2177
JURORS-PETITE, rec date 1776, appointments, jury notice, file #2260
JURORS-PETITE, rec date 1778, appointments, jury notice, file #2169
JURORS-PETITE, rec date 1779, appointments, jurors-petite, file #2218
JURORS-PETITE, rec date 1783, appointments, jury notice, file #2602
JURORS-PETITE, rec date 1783, appointments, spring session, file #2600
JURORS-PETITE, rec date 1783, appointments, summer session, file #2601
JURORS-PETITE, rec date 1784, appointments, jury list, file #5492
JURORS-PETITE, rec date 1785, appointments, jury notice, file #4836
JURORS-PETITE, rec date 1785, appointments, jury notice, file #5469
JURORS-PETITE, rec date 1785, execution, debt, file #3503
JURORS-PETITE, rec date 1786, appointments, jury list, file #6208
JURORS-PETITE, rec date 1786, jurors, appointment, file #6071
JURORS-PETITE, rec date 1788, appointments, jury list, file #6593
JURORS-PETITE, rec date 1788, appointments, jury list, file #6814
JURORS-PETITE, rec date 1789, appointments, jury notice, file #4730
JURORS-PETITE, vs HILLSBOROUGH County, rec date 1784, appointments, jurors-petite, file #4701
JURY Case List, doc date 1796-97, appointments, jury case list 1796/7, file #33
JURY List, rec date 1784, appointments, jurors list, file #4171
JURY List, rec date 1788, writ, debt, file #7013
JURY-LIST Request, doc date 1797, appointments, jurors list, file #32
JUSTICE Peace, doc date 1771-9, appointments, file #1192, years 1771-1779

LAWYERS Oath, rec date 1786, newspaper clipping, file #6173, part of Samuel CURTIS file

LAY Out of Road, vs BRADFORD To Amherst, rec date 1794, road plan, file #5454

LETTER From J Wentworth, of Portsmouth, doc date 1772, letter, file #792

LIQUOR License, vs TEMPLE-Wilton, rec date 1785, license, innkeeper license, file #4774

LIQUOR License, vs AMHERST & Bedford, rec date 1785, appointments, innkeeper license, file #4767

LIQUOR Licenses, vs BOSCAWEN-FRANCESTOWN, rec date 1785, appointments, innkeeper license, file #4768

LIQUOR Licenses, vs MILE SLIP-NOTTINGHAM-WEST, rec date 1785, appointments, innkeeper license, file #4772

LIQUOR Licenses, vs GOFFSTOWN-HILLSBOROUGH, rec date 1785, appointments, innkeeper license, file #4769

LIQUOR Licenses, vs LITCHFIELD-MERRIMACK, rec date 1785, appointments, innkeeper license, file #4771

LIQUOR Licenses, vs HOLLIS/HOPKINTON, rec date 1785, application, liquor license, file #4770

LIST of Appeals, doc date 1773, list of appeals, file #1189

LIST of Appeals, rec date 1785, list of appeals, file #7038

LIST of Appeals, rec date 1787, list of appeals, file #3555

LIST of Appeals, rec date 1787, list of court appeals, file #6513

LIST of Court Appeals, of Amherst, rec date 1783, prisoner list, file #2599

LIST of Execution, rec date 1788, list, execution, file #7011

LIST of Prisoners, of Amherst, rec date 1779, writ, debt, file #2244

LIST of Prisoners, of Amherst, rec date 1784, list of prisoners, file #4156

LIST of Prisoners, of Amherst, vs AMHERST Jail, of Amherst, rec date 1794, prisoner list, file #4065

LIST of Prisoners, of Amherst, vs TOWN of Amherst, of Amherst, rec date 1793, prisoner list, file #3540

LIST of Prisoners, of Amherst, vs TOWN of Amherst, rec date 1783, prisoner list, file #2598

LIST of Rev Soldiers, of Dunbarton, rec date 1784, list, soldiers of Dunbarton, file #4639

LISTING of Court Cases For 1795, vs STATE of NH, rec date 1795, court case list, file #2221

LISTING of Court Cases, vs HILLSBOROUGH County, list of cases to hear, file #2339

LOOSE Receipts, rec date 1779-1787, loose receipts, file #3541

M D Fife & Co, vs THOMAS Ford, doc date 1893, plaintiffs brief, supreme court, file #602

MANCHESTER & Lawrence Railroad, railroad, vs CONCORD Railroad Corp, corp, brief for plaintiff, supreme court, file #600

MANCHESTER Railroad, vs MANCHESTER & North Weare Railroad, defendants brief, supreme court, file #629

MISC Broken Pieces, doc date 1775, misc loose papers, file #1160

MISC Items, doc date 1799, various, supreme court, file #514, loose papers

MISC Jury Information, of Hillsborough, rec date 1786, various, misc information, file #6083

MISC Loose Papers, rec date 1785, loose papers, file #6415

MISC Loose Papers, rec date 1785, various, debt, file #4750

MISC Loose Papers, various, file #7054

MISC Loose Papers, various, file #7056

MISC Loose Papers, various, misc loose papers, file #7006

MISC Paper & Receipts, rec date 1778, misc papers, file #2971

MISC Paper & Receipts, rec date 1779-80, misc papers, file #2972

MISC Paper & Receipts, rec date 1781-, misc papers, file #2973

MISC Paper & Receipts, rec date 1782, misc papers, file #2974

MISC Paper & Receipts, rec date 1783-86, misc papers, file #2975

NEW Boston Fire Ins Co, insurance, vs S W & G A Upton, doc date 1893, brief for plaintiff, supreme court, file #605

NEW Boston Fire Ins Co, of New Boston, vs SAUNDERS George W, doc date 1892, plaintiffs brief, supreme court, file #616

PETITION From Towns, of Londonderry, vs COUNTY of Hillsborough, doc date 1773, misc, petition, file #784, 6 towns petition to join hills county

PETITION of Resident, of Nottingham-West, vs Town of Nottingham-West, rec date 1781, various, road lay out, file #2240

PRISONER List, Amherst jail, rec date 1788, list of prisoner, file #6542

PRISONER List, of Amherst, doc date 1773, prisoner list, file #1188

PRISONER List, of Amherst Jail, doc date 1799, execution, debt, file #187

PRISONER List, of Amherst, rec date 1777, writ, debt, file #2213

PRISONER List, of Amherst, rec date 1788, prison list, file #3935

PROPRIETORS of Dunstable, vs WRIGHT David, cordwainer, of Hollis, rec date 1784, writ, debt, file #4630

PROPRIETORS of Dunstable, vs WILKINS Stephen, Gentleman, of Merrimack, rec date 1784, various, debt, file #4921

RESIDENT of Warner, vs TOWN of Warner, doc date 1797, various, lay out of road, file #554

RIOT of Weare, vs WHITING Benjamin, sheriff, of Weare, doc date 1772, judgment, riot in Weare, file #791

ROAD Lay Out, of Peterborough, doc date 1760, road lay out, file #1193

SELECTMEN of Amherst, vs KNIGHT Jonathan, pauper, of Amherst, rec date 1795, petition, support, file #4060

SELECTMEN of Deering, vs HOGG Alexander, yeoman, of Deering, doc date 1782, writ, summons, file #773

SELECTMEN of Mason, vs ROBBINS Josiah, yeoman, of Mason, doc date 1773, judgment, debt, file #1324

SELECTMEN of Sutton, vs HILLSBOROUGH County, doc date 1791, bond for town, file #804

SELECTMEN of Wilton, court order, road petition, file #7046

SOCIETY Land, of Society Land, vs STATE of NH, rec date 1794, committee report, road lay out, file #4057

STATE of NH, vs ABBOT Joseph, of Wilton, rec date 1784, recognizance, counterfeiting, file #4736

STATE of NH, vs ABBOTT Benjamin, rec date 1788, recognizance, debt, file #6533

STATE of NH, vs ABBOTT Samuel, husbandman, of Hollis, rec date 1785, warrant, counterfeiting, file #4834

STATE of NH, vs ABBOTT William Jr, husbandman, of Wilton, rec date 1788, recognizance, debt, file #6535

STATE of NH, vs ADAMS David Jr, husbandman, of Dunstable, rec date 1785, judgment, debt, file #5775

STATE of NH, vs ALLISON Samuel, husbandman, of Dunbarton, rec date 1784, recognizance, debt, file #4738

STATE of NH, vs ATHERTON Joshua, of Amherst, rec date 1785, recognizance, debt, file #4758

STATE of NH, vs ATWELL John, yeoman, rec date 1785, recognizance, debt, file #4755

STATE of NH, vs BENNET Jonathan, Gentleman, of Hancock, rec date 1784, writ, debt, file #4931

STATE of NH, vs BRADFORD Samuel Lt, of Hillsborough, rec date 1784, summons, counterfeiting, file #6856

STATE of NH, vs BURTON Jonathan, husbandman, of Wilton, rec date 1788, recognizance, debt, file #6535

STATE of NH, vs BURNAM Lucy, of Wilton, rec date 1784, inquiry, death inquiry, file #4735, died 20 Nov 1784

STATE of NH, vs CALDWELL James, of New Boston, rec date 1788, recognizance, file #6544

STATE of NH, vs CARVEL Charles, of Peterborough, rec date 1784, summons, counterfeiting, file #6856

STATE of NH, vs COCHRAN George, husbandman, of Goffstown, rec date 1778, indictment, assault, file #6512

STATE of NH, vs COMMITTEE Bill, rec date 1785, bill of cost, committee cost, file #4833

STATE of NH, vs COOPER Elcy, single woman, of Boscawen, doc date 1799, complaint, debt, file #189

STATE of NH, vs CORSER Samuel, husbandman, of Boscawen, rec date 1787, capias, brute force, file #6522

STATE of NH, vs COURT Appeals List, rec date 1785, list of court appeals, file #4826

STATE of NH, vs COURT Dates, rec date 1785, superior & inferior, court dates, file #4824

STATE of NH, vs CURRIER Moses, husbandman, of Weare, rec date 1785, capias, cutting trees, file #4568

STATE of NH, vs DAVIS Asa, Gentleman, of Nottingham, rec date 1788, recognizance, debt, file #6534

STATE of NH, vs DAVIS David, of Amherst, rec date 1784, bill, court case bill, file #4839

STATE of NH, vs DAVIS David, in jail, of Amherst, rec date 1785, recognizance, forgery, file #4756

STATE of NH, vs EATON Obidiah, yeoman, of Weare, rec date 1784, recognizance, forgery, file #4748

STATE of NH, vs FLANDERS Phebe, single, of Campbell Gore, rec date 1788, various, death of child, file #6530

STATE of NH, vs GREELEY Joseph, yeoman, of Nottingham-West, rec date 1785, recognizance, debt, file #4754

STATE of NH, vs GREEN David, prisoner, of Amherst, rec date 1788, jail report, prison escape, file #6543

STATE of NH, vs GREEN David, yeoman, of Hillsborough, rec date 1784, writ, debt, file #4933

STATE of NH, vs GREENLEAF Lydia, single woman, of Amherst, rec date 1785, warrant, fornication, file #5240

STATE of NH, vs HARDY Daniel, husbandman, of Nottingham-West, rec date 1785, warrant, counterfeiting, file #4834

STATE of NH, vs HARDY David, yeoman, of Nottingham-West, rec date 1785, recognizance, debt, file #4754

STATE of NH, vs GRIMES Samuel Smith, rec date 1788, recognizance, debt, file #6533

STATE of NH, vs GRIMES Samuel Smith Jr, rec date 1788, recognizance, debt, file #6533

STATE of NH, vs HAZELTINE John, Gentleman, of Nottingham, rec date 1788, recognizance, debt, file #6534

STATE of NH, vs HILDRETH Hannah, spinster, of New Ipswich, rec date 1784, court decision, fornication, file #5242

STATE of NH, vs HODGDON John, husbandman, of Weare, rec date 1788, recognizance, debt, file #6536

STATE of NH, vs HODGKINS Elizabeth, spinster, of New Ipswich, rec date 1785, writ, debt, file #5239

STATE of NH, vs HOGG James, Gentleman, of Weare, rec date 1784, recognizance, forgery, file #4748

STATE of NH, vs HOGG George, husbandman, of Deering, rec date 1785, presentment, to grand juror, file #4574

STATE of NH, vs HOW Phebe, single woman, of Hollis, rec date 1785, capias, fornication, file #4572

STATE of NH, vs HUNTERS Loies, single, of Antrim, rec date 1788, inquisition, death review, file #6531

STATE of NH, vs HUTCHINSON Solomon Jr, husbandman, of Merrimack, doc date 1798, judgment, debt, file #566

STATE of NH, vs INHABITANTS of Mason, doc date 1796, various, road dispute, file #508

STATE of NH, vs JOHNSON Lucy, widow, of New Ipswich, rec date 1785, warrant, fornication, file #5241

STATE of N H, vs KELLEY Joseph, Esquire, bill, file #7024

STATE of NH, vs KELLEY Joseph, Gentleman, of Hillsborough, rec date 1785, recognizance, debt, file #4757

STATE of NH, vs KELLEY Joseph, Gentleman, rec date 1785, recognizance, debt, file #4755

STATE of N H, vs KELLY Joseph, husbandman, of Nottingham-West, rec date 1785, recognizance, debt, file #7023

STATE of NH, vs LEACH William, laborer, of Dunbarton, rec date 1784, recognizance, debt, file #4738

STATE of NH, vs LEACH William, yeoman, of Dunbarton, rec date 1784, writ, debt, file #4930

STATE of NH, vs LIST of Prisoners, yeoman, rec date 1785, list of prisoners, file #4573

STATE of NH, vs LOVEJOY Daniel, husbandman, of Wilton, rec date 1788, recognizance, debt, file #6535

STATE of NH, vs MARTIN William, deceased, of Wilton, rec date 1787, inquisition, death review, file #6517

STATE of NH, vs McCAT Samuel, yeoman, rec date 1785, recognizance, debt, file #4755

STATE of NH, vs McCLARD Robert, of Society Land, rec date 1784, summons, counterfeiting, file #6856

STATE of NH, vs McCOY Thomas, husbandman, of Peterborough, rec date 1788, recognizance, debt, file #7060A

STATE of NH, vs McCURDY David, yeoman, of Dunbarton, rec date 1785, writ, debt, file #4934

STATE of NH, vs McCURDY John, Gentleman, of Dunbarton, rec date 1785, writ, debt, file #4934

STATE of NH, vs McCURDY Matthew, yeoman, of Dunbarton, rec date 1785, writ, debt, file #4934

STATE of NH, vs McCURDY Robert, yeoman, of Dunbarton, rec date 1785, writ, debt, file #4934

STATE of NH, vs MOORE Joseph C, of Manchester, doc date 1894, fraud, supreme court, file #582

STATE of NH, vs MOSES Steel, yeoman, rec date 1784, recognizance, debt, file #4154

STATE of NH, vs MULLIAN Alexander, of Wilton, rec date 1788, recognizance, debt, file #6527

STATE of NH, vs PATTEN Robert, of Hillsborough, rec date 1788, recognizance, debt, file #6527

STATE of NH, vs PEASLES Robert, husbandman, of Dover, rec date 1785, warrant, counterfeiting, file #4834

STATE of NH, vs PETTINGILL Mary, single woman, of Amherst, rec date 1785, capias, carnal sin, file #4752

STATE of NH, vs POLLARD John, yeoman, of Hillsborough, rec date 1785, recognizance, debt, file #4757

STATE of NH, vs POLLARD Timothy, husbandman, of Nottingham-West, rec date 1785, warrant, counterfeiting, file #4834

STATE of NH, vs POLLARD Timothy, yeoman, of Hillsborough, rec date 1785, recognizance, debt, file #4757

STATE of NH, vs POOL William, yeoman, of Hollis, doc date 1779, writ, debt, file #2073

STATE of NH, vs REED Jonathan, husbandman, of Dunbarton, rec date 1784, writ, debt, file #4928

STATE of NH, vs RICHARDSON Joel, husbandman, of Campbell Gore, rec date 1788, various, assault, file #6529

STATE of NH, vs RICKEY Alexander, rec date 1788, recognizance, debt, file #6533

STATE of NH, vs SMITH Abraham, yeoman, rec date 1788, recognizance, debt, file #6533

STATE of NH, vs SMITH Samuel, rec date 1788, recognizance, debt, file #6533

STATE of NH, vs SMITH Thomas, rec date 1788, recognizance, debt, file #6533

STATE of NH, vs STANLEY Samuel, of Weare?, rec date 1785, bill, court cost, file #4835

STATE of NH, vs STANLEY Samuel, yeoman, of Hopkinton, rec date 1784, recognizance, forgery, file #4748

STATE of NH, vs STEEL Moses, of Hillsborough, rec date 1788, recognizance, debt, file #6527

STATE of NH, vs STEVENS Samuel, physician, of Amherst, rec date 1785, recognizance, forgery, file #4756

STATE of NH, vs STEVENS Thomas, blacksmith, of Amherst, rec date 1785, presentment, for swearing, file #4766

STATE of NH, vs STEWART Samuel, husbandman, of Dunbarton, rec date 1784, recognizance, debt, file #4738

STATE of NH, vs STEWART Samuel, husbandman, of Dunbarton, rec date 1784, writ, debt, file #4932

STATE of NH, vs SWAN Robert, husbandman, of Peterborough, rec date 1788, recognizance, debt, file #7006

STATE of NH, vs SWEET David, yeoman, of Amherst, doc date 1798, execution, debt, file #84

STATE of NH, vs SWEET Jonathan & Josiah, husbandman, of Campbell Gore, rec date 1788, various, assault, file #6529

STATE of NH, vs SWIFT And Co, of Manchester, doc date 1893, brief by state, supreme court, file #601, oleo margarine coloring dispute

STATE of NH, vs TAGGART John & Eliz, of Amherst, rec date 1785, recognizance, debt, file #4758

STATE of NH, vs THORNTON Matthew, Esquire, of Merrimack, rec date 1788, recognizance, debt, file #6532

STATE of NH, vs TIDDER Mary, spinster, of New Ipswich, rec date 1784, warrant, fornication, file #5238

STATE of NH, vs TOWN of Amherst & Stoddard, rec date 1793, petition, road lay outs, file #4700, town road lay outs

STATE of NH, vs TOWN of Campbell Gore, of Campbells Gore, rec date 1793, petition, road lay out, file #4704

STATE of NH, vs TOWN of Deering, rec date 1795, petitions, road lay outs, file #4702

STATE of NH, vs TOWN of Derryfield, of Derryfield, rec date 1787, petition, road layout, file #6520

STATE of NH, vs TOWN of Hopkinton, of Hopkinton, rec date 1787, road petition, legal meeting, file #6515

STATE of NH, vs TOWN of New Boston, of New Boston, rec date 1787, indictment, school requirement, file #6518

STATE of NH, vs TOWN of Nottingham-West, of Nottingham-West, rec date 1787, inquisition, school requirement, file #6518

STATE of NH, vs TOWN of Peterborough, of Peterborough, rec date 1787, indictment, school requirement, file #6519

STATE of NH, vs TOWN of Weare, of Weare, rec date 1787, inquisition, school requirement, file #6521

STATE of NH, vs TOWN of Wilton, of Wilton, rec date 1787, inquisition, school requirement, file #6523

STATE of NH, vs WARREN Josiah, of New Boston, rec date 1787, recognizance, debt, file #6544

STATE of NH, vs WILKINS Robert B, Gentleman, of Amherst, rec date 1785, recognizance, forgery, file #4756

STATE of NH, vs WILSON Martha, deceased, of Deering, rec date 1788, inquisition, death verdict, file #6528

STRATHAM & Newmarket Br, vs LOTTERY Tickets, rec date 1777, lottery tickets, file #2201

TAVERN & Retailers License, doc date 1779, appointments, tavern-retailer license, file #1280

TAVERN License, doc date 1779, appointments, tavern license, file #1256

TAVERN License, doc date 1779, applications, tavern license, file #2088

TAVERN License, doc date 1779, application, tavern license, file #2085

TAVERN License, doc date 1784, application, tavern license, file #1563

TAVERN License, doc date 1784, application, tavern license, file #1564

TAVERN License, doc date 1785/6, appointment, license, file #1276

TAVERN License, doc date 1785/6, application, tavern license, file #1278

TAVERN License, rec date 1787/8, application, appointment, file #7010

TAVERN License, doc date 1787/8, rec date 1786, appointments, tavern license, file #2338

TAVERN License, doc date 1792, rec date 1786, appointments, tavern licenses, file #2338

TAVERN License, rec date 1783, application, tavern license, file #2592

TAVERN License, rec date 1783, application, tavern license, file #2592-B

TAVERN License, rec date 1783, application, tavern license, file #2592-C

TAVERN License, rec date 1783, application, tavern license, file #2850

TAVERN License, rec date 1783, application, tavern license, file #2851, second folder

TAVERN License, rec date 1783, applications, tavern license, file #3618

TAVERN License, rec date 1783, applications, tavern license, file #3619

TAVERN License, rec date 1785, application, file #6967

TAVERN License, rec date 1786, application, tavern license, file #4822

TOWN of Amherst, vs SABATEE John, British soldier, rec date 1783, petition, payments for stranger, file #3605

TOWN of Antrim, vs STATE of NH, rec date 1792, petition, road lay out, file #4059

TOWN of Bedford, doc date 1778, warrant, town warrants, file #2045

TOWN of Bedford, rec date 1782, various, road lay out, file #2242

TOWN of Dunstable, vs BURNS George, husbandman, of Amherst, rec date 1783, judgment, debt, file #6350

TOWN of Dunstable MA, vs CUMMINGS John, Gentleman, of Hollis, rec date 1783, writ, debt, file #6364

TOWN of Hillsborough County, vs HOLLAND Stephen, Esquire, doc date 1774, petition, removal of treas, file #729, signed by John STARK, chairman

TOWN of Jaffrey/New Ipswich, vs STATE of NH, rec date 1786, road petition, petition, file #6514

TOWN of Litchfield, vs COTTON Samuel (Rev), minister, of Litchfield, doc date 1772, judgment, town meeting, file #670, agreement for minister salary

TOWN of Lyndeborough, rec date 1787, charter, land dispute, file #6702

TOWN of Marlborough, rec date 1788, various, deed transfers, file #6587, three folders

TOWN of Mason, rec date 1788, appointments, file #3544

TOWN of New Boston, vs BUTLER Tobias, tutor, of New Boston, doc date 1778, rec date 1787, lease for 500 years, land transfer, file #2501, lib 19 fol 401

TOWN of New Bradford, vs HILLSBOROUGH Court, rec date 1786, petition, for corporation, file #3546

TOWN of Peterborough, vs SMITH John, yeoman, of Peterborough, doc date 1784, petition, road dispute, file #1604

TOWN of Peterborough, vs WHITE John Jr, yeoman, of Peterborough, doc date 1784, petition, road dispute, file #1604

TOWN of Stoddard, rec date 1788, list of early settlers, file #6583

TREASURES Receipt, vs HILLSBOROUGH County, rec date 1781, receipts, file #2380

TREASURES Report, rec date 1794, treasury report, file #4726

TREASURY Notes, vs HILLSBOROUGH County, rec date 1775, treasury notes, file #2204

UNITED STATES GOVERNMENT, vs ROCKWOOD Ebenezer, rec date 1784, settlement of account, debt, file #4734

WARNINGS Out, of Dearing, rec date 1772/9, warning outs, warning notices, file #7059

WARNINGS Out, of New Boston, rec date 1774, warnings out of town, warning to leave, file #2263

WARNINGS Out, of New Boston, vs HILLSBOROUGH County, rec date 1771, warning out of town, warning to leave, file #2265

WARNINGS Out, of New Boston, vs HILLSBOROUGH County, rec date 1776, warning out of town, warning to leave, file #2264

WARNINGS Out Temple, of Dearing, rec date 1772/9, warning outs, warning notices, file #7060

WARNINGS Out, vs HILLSBOROUGH County, Boston, rec date 1795, warning out of town, warning to leave, file #2288

WARNINGS Out, vs HILLSBOROUGH County, rec date 1772, warning out of town, warning to leave, file #2266

WARNINGS Out, vs HILLSBOROUGH County, rec date 1772, warning out of town, warning to leave, file #2277

WARNINGS Out, vs HILLSBOROUGH County, rec date 1773, warning out of town, warning to leave, file #2267

WARNINGS Out, vs HILLSBOROUGH County, rec date 1774, warning out of town, warning to leave, file #2268

WARNINGS Out, vs HILLSBOROUGH County, rec date 1778, warning out of town, warning to leave, file #2269

WARNINGS Out, vs HILLSBOROUGH County, rec date 1779, warning out of town, warning to leave, file #2270

WARNINGS Out, vs HILLSBOROUGH County, rec date 1780, warning out of town, warning to leave, file #2271

WARNINGS Out, vs HILLSBOROUGH County, rec date 1781, warning out of town, warning to leave, file #2272

WARNINGS Out, vs HILLSBOROUGH County, rec date 1782, warning out of town, warning to leave, file #2273

WARNINGS Out, vs HILLSBOROUGH County, rec date 1783, warning out of town, warning to leave, file #2274

WARNINGS Out, vs HILLSBOROUGH County, rec date 1784, warning out of town, warning to leave, file #2275

WARNINGS Out, vs HILLSBOROUGH County, rec date 1785, warning out of town, warning to leave, file #2276

WARNINGS Out, vs HILLSBOROUGH County, rec date 1786, warning out of town, warning to leave, file #2278

WARNINGS Out, vs HILLSBOROUGH County, rec date 1787, warning out of town, warning to leave, file #2279

WARNINGS Out, vs HILLSBOROUGH County, rec date 1788, warning out of town, warning to leave, file #2280

WARNINGS Out, vs HILLSBOROUGH County, rec date 1789, warning out of town, warning to leave, file #2281

WARNINGS Out, vs HILLSBOROUGH County, rec date 1790, warning out of town, warning to leave, file #2282

WARNINGS Out, vs HILLSBOROUGH County, rec date 1791, warning out of town, warning to leave, file #2283

WARNINGS Out, vs HILLSBOROUGH County, rec date 1792, warning out of town, warning to leave, file #2284

WARNINGS Out, vs HILLSBOROUGH County, rec date 1793, warning out of town, warning to leave, file #2285

WARNINGS Out, vs HILLSBOROUGH County, yeoman, rec date 1777, warning out of town, warning to leave, file #2287

WARNINGS Out, vs HILLSBOROUGH County, yeoman, rec date 1794, warning out of town, warning to leave, file #2286

WARNINGS Out, vs TOWN of Dunbarton, doc date 1771, rec date 1771, warning out of town, list, file #2510

WARNINGS Out, vs TOWN of Dunbarton, doc date 1772, rec date 1772, warning out of town, list, file #2511

WARNINGS Out, vs TOWN of Dunbarton, doc date 1779, rec date 1779, warning out of town, list, file #2512

WARNINGS Out, vs TOWN of Dunbarton, doc date 1780, rec date 1780, warning out of town, list, file #2513

WARNINGS Out, vs TOWN of Dunbarton, doc date 1782, rec date 1782, warning out of town, list, file #2514

WARNINGS Out, vs TOWN of Dunbarton, doc date 1782, rec date 1782, warning out of town, list, file #2515

WARNINGS Out, vs TOWN of Dunbarton, doc date 1783, rec date 1783, warning out of town, list, file #2516

WARNINGS Out, vs TOWN of Dunbarton, doc date 1784, rec date 1784, warning out of town, list, file #2517

WARNINGS Out, vs TOWN of Dunbarton, doc date 1785, rec date 1785, warning out of town, list, file #2518

WARNINGS Out, vs TOWN of Dunbarton, doc date 1786, rec date 1786, warning out of town, warning to leave, file #2519

WARNINGS Out, vs TOWN of Dunbarton, doc date 1787, rec date 1787, warning out of town, warning to leave, file #2520

WARNINGS Out, vs TOWN of Dunbarton, doc date 1788, rec date 1788, warning out of town, warning to leave, file #2521

WARNINGS Out, vs TOWN of Dunbarton, doc date 1789, rec date 1789, warning out of town, warning to leave, file #2522

WARNINGS Out, vs TOWN of Dunbarton, doc date 1790, rec date 1790, warning out of town, warning to leave, file #2523

WARNINGS Out, vs TOWN of Dunbarton, doc date 1791, rec date 1791, warning out of town, warning to leave, file #2524

WARNINGS Out, vs TOWN of Dunbarton, doc date 1792, rec date 1792, warning out of town, warning to leave, file #2525

WARNINGS Out, vs TOWN of Dunbarton, doc date 1793, rec date 1793, warning out of town, warning to leave, file #2526

WARNINGS Out, vs TOWN of Dunbarton, doc date 1794, rec date 1794, warning out of town, warning to leave, file #2527

WARNINGS Out, vs TOWN of Dunbarton, doc date 1795, rec date 1795, warning out of town, warning to leave, file #2528

WARNINGS Out, vs TOWN of Goffstown, rec date 1773/84, warning out of town, list, file #3608

WARNINGS Out, vs TOWN of Goffstown, rec date 1780/94, warning out of town, list of warning outs, file #3609

WARNINGS Out, vs TOWN of Goffstown, rec date 1783, warning out of town, list, file #3606

WARNINGS Out, vs TOWN of Goffstown, rec date 1786/95, warning out of town, list, file #3607

WARNINGS Out, vs TOWN of Wilton, rec date 1783, warning out of town, warning to leave, file #2604-B

WARNINGS Out, vs TOWN of Wilton, rec date 1783, warning out of town, warning to leave, file #2604-C

WARNINGS Out, vs TOWN of Wilton, rec date 1783, warning out of town, warning to leave, file #2604-D

WARNINGS Out, vs TOWN of Wilton, rec date 1783, warning out of town, warning to leave, file #2604-E

WARNINGS Out, vs TOWN of Wilton, rec date 1783, warning out of town, warning to leave, file #2604, very fragile

WARRANT Articles, of Bedford, vs TOWN of Bedford, rec date 1778, warrant, road lay out, file #2227

WARRANT To Adjourn, of Amherst, vs HILLSBOROUGH County, rec date 1783, petition, to repair court house, file #2593, warrant to repair court house

WHITTEN U S G, of Peterborough, vs STOCKWELL G S Co, manufacturing shoes, of Peterborough, doc date 1893, personal injuries, supreme court, file #580

WHITTEN U S G, vs G S STOCKWELL & Co, doc date 1894, plaintiff brief, supreme court, file #599

WARNINGS OUT

_____ Betty - formerly of Chelmsford MA, warned out of Wilton, 1784, file #2604-D, p2

_____ William - formerly of Chelmsford MA, warned out of Wilton, 1784, file #2604-D, p2

_____ Antimus (c) - formerly of Shewsbury MA, warned out of Wilton, 1793, file #2604-C, p3

ABBOT Anna - formerly of Andover MA, warned out of Wilton, 1782, file #2604-E, p3

ABBOT Barichias - formerly of Wilton, warned out of Temple, 1794, file #7060, p58

ABBOT Job - formerly of Andover MA, warned out of Wilton, 1782, file #2604-E, p3

ABBOT Rebeckah (c) - formerly of Billerica, warned out of Wilton, 1782, file #2604-E, p4

ABBOT Samuel (c) - formerly of Billerica, warned out of Wilton, 1782, file #2604-E, p4

ABBOT Solomon - formerly of Portsmouth, warned out of Dearing, 1786, file #7059, p24

ABBOTT Asa - warned out of New Boston, 1789, file #2281, p3

ABBOTT Daniel & Wife - warned out of New Boston, 1787, file #2279, p10

ABBOTT Docas (c) - formerly of Pelham, warned out of Wilton, 1790, file #2604-D, p3

ABBOTT Ephraim - formerly of Kingstown, warned out of Dunbarton, 1790, file #2523, p6

ABBOTT George - formerly of Billerica MA, warned out of Wilton, 1782, file #2604-E, p4

ABBOTT Hannah (c) - formerly of Pelham, warned out of Wilton, 1790, file #2604-D, p3

ABBOTT Nathaniel - formerly of Pelham, warned out of Wilton, 1790, file #2604-D, p3

ABBOTT Peter (c) - formerly of Pelham, warned out of Wilton, 1790, file #2604-D, p3

ABBOTT Phebe (c) - formerly of Pelham, warned out of Wilton, 1790, file #2604-D, p3

ABBOTT Rebeckah - formerly of Billerica MA, warned out of Wilton, 1782, file #2604-E, p4

ABBOTT Samuel - warned out of New Boston, 1789, file #2281, p3

ABBOTT Samuel Jr - warned out of New Boston, 1789, file #2281, p3

ABBOTT Sarah - formerly of Pelham, warned out of Wilton, 1790, file #2604-D, p3

ABBOTT Sarah (c) - formerly of Pelham, warned out of Wilton, 1790, file #2604-D, p3

ADAMS Beckee (c) - formerly of Packersfield, warned out of New Ipswich, 1782, file #2273, p1

ADAMS Daniel (c) - formerly of Fitzwilliam, warned out of New Ipswich, 1792, file #2284, p3

ADAMS Ephraim - formerly of Dunstable MA, warned out of Temple, 1798, file #7060, p40

ADAMS Luther (c) - formerly of Packersfield, warned out of New Ipswich, 1782, file #2273, p1

ADAMS Lyda - formerly of Fitzwilliam, warned out of New Ipswich, 1791, file #2283, p1

ADAMS Noah (a Lad) - warned out of New Ipswich, 1772, file #2266, p3

ADAMS Polly (c) - formerly of Packersfield, warned out of New Ipswich, 1782, file #2273, p1

ADAMS Sally - formerly of Ashburnham MA, warned out of New Ipswich, 1792, file #2284, p1

ADAMS Samuel (c) - formerly of Fitzwilliam, warned out of New Ipswich, 1792, file #2284, p3

ADAMS Sarah - formerly of Townsend MA, warned out of New Ipswich, 1794, file #2286, p1

ADAMS Sarah (widow) - formerly of Fitzwilliam, warned out of New Ipswich, 1792, file #2284, p3

ADAMS Silas - formerly of Packersfield, warned out of New Ipswich, 1782, file #2273, p1

ADAMS Susannah - formerly of Packersfield, warned out of New Ipswich, 1782, file #2273, p1

ADAMS Susannah (c) - formerly of Packersfield, warned out of New Ipswich, 1782, file #2273, p1

ADAMS Thankfull - formerly of Dunstable MA, warned out of Temple, 1798, file #7060, p40

AKEN Alexander (c) - formerly of Windham, warned out of Dunbarton, 1783, file #2516, p2

AKEN James (c) - formerly of Windham, warned out of Dunbarton, 1783, file #2516, p2

AKEN Mary - formerly of Windham, warned out of Dunbarton, 1783, file #2516, p2

AKEN William - formerly of Windham, warned out of Dunbarton, 1783, file #2516, p1

ALEXANDER Calvin - formerly of New Marlborough, warned out of New Ipswich, 1795, file #2288, p2

ALLEN Ebenezer - formerly of Lunenburgh MA, warned out of New Ipswich, 1792, file #2284, p1

ALLEN George - warned out of Goffstown, 1789, file #3609, p4

ALLEN Jerusha - warned out of Goffstown, 1789, file #3609, p4

ALLEN Mary (widow) - formerly of Lunenburgh MA, warned out of New Ipswich, 1789, file #2281, p6

ALLEN Polly - formerly of Lancaster MA, warned out of New Ipswich, 1794, file #2286, p1

ALLEN Thankfull - formerly of Lunenburgh MA, warned out of New Ipswich, 1792, file #2284, p1

ALLING Elizabeth (c) - formerly of Bedford, warned out of Goffstown, 1776, file #3608, p5

AMES Saly - formerly of Amherst, warned out of New Boston, 1794, file #2286, p3

AMSDEM Dorathia - formerly of Groton MA, warned out of Temple, 1782, file #7060, p23

AMSDEN Abraham - formerly of Groton MA, warned out of Temple, 1782, file #7060, p23

AMSDEN Adams - formerly of Groton MA, warned out of Temple, 1782, file #7060, p23

AMSDEN David (c) - formerly of Mason, warned out of New Ipswich, 1788, file #2280, p4

AMSDEN Hannah - formerly of Mason, warned out of New Ipswich, 1788, file #2280, p4

AMSDEN Hannah - formerly of Groton MA, warned out of Temple, 1782, file #7060, p23

AMSDEN Hannah (c) - formerly of Mason, warned out of New Ipswich, 1788, file #2280, p4

AMSDEN Jonas - formerly of Mason, warned out of New Ipswich, 1788, file #2280, p4

AMSDEN Levina (c) - formerly of Mason, warned out of New Ipswich, 1788, file #2280, p4

AMSDEN Meriam - formerly of Groton MA, warned out of Temple, 1782, file #7060, p23

AMSDEN Polly (c) - warned out of New Ipswich, 1788, file #2280, p4

ANDREW Joseph - warned out of New Boston, 1790, file #2282, p3

ANDREW Joseph (c) - warned out of New Boston, 1790, file #2282, p3

ANDREW Joseph (c) - warned out of New Boston, 1790, file #2282, p3

ANDREW Margarett - warned out of New Boston, 1790, file #2282, p3

ANDREW Ruth (c) - warned out of New Boston, 1790, file #2282, p3

APPLETON William - formerly of Lyndeborough, warned out of Temple, 1802, file #7060, p38

ASTIN Hannah - formerly of Antrim, warned out of Wilton, 1793, file #2604-C, p3

ATHERTON Abigail (c) - formerly of Groton, warned out of New Ipswich, 1789, file #2281, p2

ATHERTON Betey (c) - formerly of Groton, warned out of New Ipswich, 1789, file #2281, p2

ATHERTON Jonathan - formerly of Groton, warned out of New Ipswich, 1789, file #2281, p2

ATHERTON Phebe - formerly of Groton, warned out of New Ipswich, 1789, file #2281, p2

ATHERTON Polly (c) - formerly of Groton, warned out of New Ipswich, 1789, file #2281, p2

ATHERTON Samuel (c) - formerly of Groton, warned out of New Ipswich, 1789, file #2281, p2

AUSTEN George & Wife - formerly of Goffstown, warned out of Dunbarton, 1788, file #2521, p3

AUSTEN Rebeccah (c) - formerly of Goffstown, warned out of Dunbarton, 1788, file #2521, p3

AVERY Anna (c) - formerly of Westminster VT, warned out of New Ipswich, 1783, file #2274, p1

AVERY Molly (c) - formerly of Westminster VT, warned out of New Ipswich, 1783, file #2274, p1

AVERY Samuel - formerly of Westminster VT, warned out of New Ipswich, 1783, file #2274, p1

AVERY Samuel (c) - formerly of Westminster MA, warned out of New Ipswich, 1783, file #2274, p1

AVERY Sarah - formerly of Westminster VT, warned out of New Ipswich, 1783, file #2274, p1

AYERS James (c) - warned out of Goffstown, 1786, file #3607, p1

AYERS Joshua (c) - warned out of Goffstown, 1786, file #3607, p1

AYERS Mary - warned out of Goffstown, 1786, file #3607, p1

AYERS William - warned out of Goffstown, 1786, file #3607, p1

AYERS William (c) - warned out of Goffstown, 1786, file #3607, p1

BAB Rebecca - formerly of Portsmouth, warned out of Dunbarton, 1789, file #2522, p2

BACHELDER Elizabeth - formerly of Wenham MA, warned out of New Ipswich, 1780, file #2271, p3

BACHELDER Elizabeth (c) - formerly of Wenham MA, warned out of New Ipswich, 1780, file #2271, p3

BACHELDER John (c) - warned out of New Ipswich, 1780, file #2271, p3

BACHELDER Joseph - formerly of Wenham MA, warned out of New Ipswich, 1780, file #2271, p3

BACHELDER Joseph (c) - formerly of Wenham MA, warned out of New Ipswich, 1780, file #2271, p3

BACON Betty - formerly of Bedford, warned out of New Ipswich, 1789, file #2281, p6

BACON Betty (c) - formerly of Bedford, warned out of New Ipswich, 1789, file #2281, p6

BACON Erasmus (son)-Mary - warned out of New Ipswich, 1784, file #2275, p6

BACON Jonas - formerly of Bedford, warned out of New Ipswich, 1789, file #2281, p6

BACON Margaret - formerly of Peterboro Slip, warned out of New Ipswich, 1770, file #2265, p2

BACON Margaret - formerly of Peterboro Slip, warned out of New Ipswich, 1770, file #2265, p2

BACON Mary Or Molly - warned out of New Ipswich, 1772, file #2266, p1

BACON Nabby (c) - formerly of Bedford, warned out of New Ipswich, 1789, file #2281, p6

BACON Retire - formerly of Ipswich MA, warned out of New Ipswich, 1771, file #2265, p1

BACON Sarah - warned out of New Ipswich, 1772, file #2266, p1

BAGLEY Susanah - formerly of Boxford MA, warned out of Wilton, 1784, file #2604-E, p7

BAILEY Anna (c) - formerly of Weare, warned out of Dearing, 1788, file #7059, p22

BAILEY Elizabeth (c) - formerly of Ware, warned out of Dearing, 1795, file #7059, p9

BAILEY Elizabeth (c) - formerly of Weare, warned out of Dearing, 1788, file #7059, p22

BAILEY James-grandson - formerly of Weare, warned out of Dearing, 1788, file #7059, p22

BAILEY John - formerly of Ware, warned out of Dearing, 1795, file #7059, p9

BAILEY John - formerly of Weare, warned out of Dearing, 1788, file #7059, p22

BAILEY Margaret (c) - formerly of Peterboro Slip, warned out of New Ipswich, 1770, file #2265, p2

BAILEY Mary - formerly of Weare, warned out of Dearing, 1788, file #7059, p22

BAILEY Moly - formerly of Ware, warned out of Dearing, 1795, file #7059, p9

BAILY Elizabeth - warned out of Goffstown, 1789, file #3609, p4

BAILY Jonathan - warned out of Goffstown, 1789, file #3609, p4

BAILY Moses - warned out of New Boston, 1785, file #2276, p1

BAKER Daniel - warned out of Goffstown, 1796, file #3607, p8

BAKER Elizbeth - warned out of Goffstown, 1796, file #3607, p8

BAKER Enoch Sweet (c) - warned out of Goffstown, 1796, file #3607, p8

BAKER Ephraim - formerly of Hillsborough, warned out of Dearing, 1795, file #7059, p4

BAKER Ephraim (c) - formerly of Hillsborough, warned out of Dearing, 1786, file #7059, p4

BAKER Lese? (c) - warned out of Goffstown, 1796, file #3607, p8

BAKER Lucia (c) - formerly of Lyndeborough, warned out of Wilton, 1784, file #2604-D, p2

BAKER Lydia - formerly of Littleton, warned out of New Ipswich, 1784, file #2275, p4

BAKER Peter - formerly of Littleton, warned out of New Ipswich, 1784, file #2275, p4

BAKER Rebeckah - formerly of Hillsborough, warned out of Dearing, 1795, file #7059, p4

BAKER Rebeckah (c) - formerly of Hillsborough, warned out of Dearing, 1795, file #7059, p4

BAKER Sally - formerly of Billerica MA, warned out of Temple, 1803, file #7060, p48

BAKER Sarah (c) - formerly of Hillsborough, warned out of Dearing, 1795, file #7059, p4

BAKER Sira (c) - formerly of Lyndeborough, warned out of Wilton, 1784, file #2604-D, p2

BAKER William (c) - formerly of Hillsborough, warned out of Dearing, 1786, file #7059, p4

BALDWIN Isabel - formerly of Billerica, warned out of Wilton, 1782, file #2604-E, p3

BALDWIN John - formerly of Billerica MA, warned out of Wilton, 1782, file #2604-E, p3

BALEY John Wife & Children - warned out of New Ipswich, 1784, file #2275, p3

BALEY Judy - warned out of New Boston, 1785, file #2276, p1

BALEY Sally - warned out of New Boston, 1785, file #2276, p1

BALL Polly (c) - formerly of Concord MA, warned out of New Ipswich, 1788, file #2280, p3

BALL Rebeccah - formerly of Concord MA, warned out of New Ipswich, 1788, file #2280, p3

BALL Samuel - formerly of Concord MA, warned out of New Ipswich, 1788, file #2280, p3

BALL Samuel (c) - formerly of Concord MA, warned out of New Ipswich, 1788, file #2280, p3

BALLARD Barthalomew - formerly of Townsend MA, warned out of Temple, 1799, file #7060, p46

BALLARD Elizabeth - formerly of Wilton, warned out of Temple, 1801, file #7060, p56

BALLARD Jerusha - formerly of Townsend MA, warned out of Temple, 1799, file #7060, p46

BALLARD John - formerly of New Ipswich, warned out of Temple, 1796, file #7060, p35

BANCROFT Amos - formerly of Pepperell MA, warned out of New Ipswich, 1785, file #2276, p4

BARKER Bathshaba - formerly of Mile Slip, warned out of Wilton, 1778, file #2604-C, p7

BARKER Bathshaba (c) - formerly of Mile Slip, warned out of Wilton, 1778, file #2604-C, p7

BARKER Betty (c) - formerly of Acton MA, warned out of Temple, 1786, file #7060, p22

BARKER Daniel - formerly of Mile Slip, warned out of Wilton, 1778, file #2604-C, p7

BARKER Darkist - formerly of Pelham, warned out of Temple, 1784, file #7060, p19

BARKER David - formerly of Pelham, warned out of Temple, 1784, file #7060, p19

BARKER David Jr - formerly of Pelham, warned out of Temple, 1784, file #7060, p19

BARKER Deborah (c) - formerly of Pelham, warned out of Temple, 1784, file #7060, p19

BARKER Doras (c) - formerly of Mile Slip, warned out of Wilton, 1778, file #2604-C, p7

BARKER Epraim (c) - formerly of Pelham, warned out of Temple, 1784, file #7060, p19

BARKER Esther (c) - formerly of Acton MA, warned out of Temple, 1786, file #7060, p22

BARKER Hannah (c) - formerly of Lyndeborough, warned out of Wilton, 1794, file #2604-D, p2

BARKER Israel (c) - formerly of Lyndeborough, warned out of Wilton, 1784, file #2604-D, p2

BARKER John (c) - formerly of Pelham, warned out of Temple, 1784, file #7060, p19

BARKER Judith (c) - formerly of Pelham, warned out of Temple, 1784, file #7060, p19

BARKER Leanard (c) - formerly of Lyndeborough, warned out of Wilton, 1784, file #2604-D, p2

BARKER Louis (c) - formerly of Mile Slip, warned out of Wilton, 1778, file #2604-C, p7

BARKER Mary - formerly of Pelham, warned out of Temple, 1784, file #7060, p19

BARKER Molly (c) - formerly of Lyndeborough, warned out of Wilton, 1784, file #2604-D, p2

BARKER Phebe (c) - formerly of Mile Slip, warned out of Wilton, 1778, file #2604-C, p7

BARKER Phineas - formerly of Lyndeborough, warned out of Wilton, 1784, file #2604-D, p2

BARKER Rachel (widow) - formerly of Acton MA, warned out of Temple, 1786, file #7060, p22

BARKER Ruth - formerly of Andover MA, warned out of Wilton, 1778, file #2604-C, p7

BARKER Sarah - formerly of Lyndeborough, warned out of Wilton, 1794, file #2604-D, p2

BARKER Sarah (c) - formerly of Mile slip, warned out of Wilton, 1778, file #2604-C, p7

BARKER Sarah Jr (c) - formerly of Pelham, warned out of Temple, 1784, file #7060, p19

BARKER Trudy - formerly of Littleton MA, warned out of New Ipswich, 1789, file #2281, p6

BARKER William (c) - formerly of Lyndeborough, warned out of Wilton, 1784, file #2604-D, p2

BARKER William (c) - formerly of Pelham, warned out of Temple, 1784, file #7060, p19

BARNES Aaron - formerly of Pepperell MA, warned out of Temple, 1799, file #7060, p46

BARNES Aaron (c) - formerly of Pepperell MA, warned out of Temple, 1799, file #7060, p46

BARNES Lydia - formerly of Pepperell MA, warned out of Temple, 1799, file #7060, p46

BARNET Jno - formerly of Hancock, warned out of Temple, 1795, file #7060, p52

BARRCANN Hannah (c) - warned out of Goffstown, 1789, file #3607, p5

BARRCANN Pattee - warned out of Goffstown, 1789, file #3607, p5

BARRCANN Pattee (c) - warned out of Goffstown, 1789, file #3607, p5

BARRCANN Sally (c) - warned out of Goffstown, 1789, file #3607, p5

BARRCANN Tectum (c) - warned out of Goffstown, 1789, file #3607, p5

BARRCANN Thomas - warned out of Goffstown, 1789, file #3607, p5

BARRETT Andrew - warned out of New Ipswich, 1791, file #2283, p1

BARRETT Sarah - formerly of Peterborough, warned out of New Ipswich, 1791, file #2283, p1

BARRITTE Olive - formerly of Mason, warned out of New Ipswich, 1788, file #2280, p4

BARROW Elizabeth (c) - formerly of Westford, warned out of New Ipswich, 1785, file #2276, p6

BARROW Joseph (c) - formerly of Westford, warned out of New Ipswich, 1785, file #2276, p6

BARROW Mercy - formerly of Westford, warned out of New Ipswich, 1785, file #2276, p6

BARROW Sarah (c) - formerly of Westford, warned out of New Ipswich, 1785, file #2276, p6

BARROW William - formerly of Westford, warned out of New Ipswich, 1785, file #2276, p6

BARROW William (c) - formerly of Westford, warned out of New Ipswich, 1785, file #2276, p6

BARSTON Jane - formerly of Lyndeborough, warned out of Temple, 1792, file #7060, p39

BARTLET James - formerly of Groton MA, warned out of Temple, 1786, file #7060, p22

BARTLET Polley - formerly of New Ipswich, warned out of Temple, 1793, file #7060, p36

BASSET Betty (c) - formerly of Goffstown, warned out of Dunbarton, 1790, file #2523, p11

BASSET Jeremiah (c) - formerly of Goffstown, warned out of Dunbarton, 1790, file #2523, p11

BASSET Jesse (c) - formerly of Goffstown, warned out of Dunbarton, 1790, file #2523, p11

BASSET John - formerly of Goffstown, warned out of Dunbarton, 1790, file #2523, p11

BASSET Lucy (c) - formerly of Goffstown, warned out of Dunbarton, 1790, file #2523, p11

BASSET Mary (c) - formerly of Goffstown, warned out of Dunbarton, 1790, file #2523, p11

BASSET Nancy (c) - formerly of Goffstown, warned out of Dunbarton, 1790, file #2523, p11

BASSET Sarah - formerly of Goffstown, warned out of Dunbarton, 1790, file #2523, p11

BASSET Sarah (c) - formerly of Goffstown, warned out of Dunbarton, 1790, file #2523, p11

WARNINGS OUT 369

BASSET Thomas (c) - formerly of Goffstown, warned out of Dunbarton, 1790, file #2523, p11

BATCHELDER Abner (c) - formerly of Mile Slip, warned out of Wilton, 1784, file #2604-C, p6

BATCHELDER Hanah - warned out of New Ipswich, 1788, file #2280, p2

BATCHELDER Joseph - warned out of Wilton, 1795, file #2604-B, p2

BATCHELDER Judith - warned out of Wilton, 1795, file #2604-B, p2

BATCHELDER Molley - warned out of Wilton, 1795, file #2604-B, p2

BATCHELDER Polly (c) - formerly of Mile Slip, warned out of Wilton, 1784, file #2604-C, p6

BATCHELDER Sarah - formerly of Mile Slip, warned out of Wilton, 1784, file #2604-C, p6

BATCHELDER Sarah (c) - formerly of Mile Slip, warned out of Wilton, 1784, file #2604-C, p6

BATCHELDER Uzziel (c) - formerly of Mile Slip, warned out of Wilton, 1784, file #2604-C, p6

BATCHELDER Uzziel -sic - formerly of Mile Slip, warned out of Wilton, 1784, file #2604-C, p6

BATCHELLER Elizabeth - formerly of Jaffrey, warned out of New Ipswich, 1787, file #2279, p2

BATCHELLER Samuel Mr - formerly of Jaffrey, warned out of New Ipswich, 1787, file #2279, p2

BATCHELLER Samuel (c) - formerly of Jaffrey, warned out of New Ipswich, 1787, file #2279, p2

BATES Elizabeth (c) - formerly of Ipswich MA, warned out of Dunbarton, 1782, file #2515, p1

BATES Jacob Parker (c) - formerly of Ipswich MA, warned out of Dunbarton, 1782, file #2515, p1

BATES Martha (c) - formerly of Ipswich MA, warned out of Dunbarton, 1782, file #2515, p1

BATES Martha (widow) - formerly of Ipswich MA, warned out of Dunbarton, 1782, file #2515, p1

BATHCELER Abigail (c) - warned out of New Ipswich, 1788, file #2280, p2

BATHCELER Hanah - formerly of Wenham MA, warned out of New Ipswich, 1788, file #2280, p2

BAYLEY Jacob - formerly of Worcester MA, warned out of New Ipswich, 1794, file #2286, p1

BAYLEY Joshua - formerly of New Salem, warned out of Dunbarton, 1792, file #2525, p2

BAYLEY Joshua (c) - formerly of New Salem, warned out of Dunbarton, 1792, file #2525, p2

BAYLEY Moley - formerly of New Salem, warned out of Dunbarton, 1792, file #2525, p2

BAYLEY Phinhes (c) - formerly of New Salem, warned out of Dunbarton, 1792, file #2525, p2

BAYLEY Sarah (sister) - formerly of New Salem, warned out of Dunbarton, 1792, file #2525, p2

BEADLE Hannah - formerly of Hollis, warned out of Wilton, 1774, file #2604-C, p2

BEADLE Marcy - formerly of Hollis, warned out of Wilton, 1774, file #2604-C, p2

BECKE Gene (c) - formerly of Ipswich, warned out of Wilton, 1782, file #2604-C, p8

BECKE Mary - formerly of Ipswich, warned out of Wilton, 1782, file #2604-C, p8

BECKE Rhoda (c) - formerly of Ipswich, warned out of Wilton, 1782, file #2604-C, p8

BELL John & Wife - formerly of Duxbury MA, warned out of Goffstown, 1776, file #3606, p4

BELL Sarah - warned out of Goffstown, 1784, file #3609, p2

BENTWELL Thomas - formerly of Chelsey MA, warned out of New Ipswich, 1794, file #2286, p1

BIGELOW Daniel (c) - warned out of New Ipswich, 1789, file #2281, p1

BIGELOW Elizabeth (Mrs) - formerly of Ashby MA, warned out of New Ipswich, 1785, file #2276, p5

BIGELOW Eunis - warned out of New Ipswich, 1789, file #2281, p1

BIGELOW Joel (c) - warned out of New Ipswich, 1789, file #2281, p1

BIGELOW John - formerly of Marlborough, warned out of Temple, 1802, file #7060, p38

BIGELOW John (Mr) - warned out of New Ipswich, 1789, file #2281, p1

BIGELOW John (c) - warned out of New Ipswich, 1789, file #2281, p1

BIGELOW Rachel - formerly of Peterborough, warned out of Temple, 1783, file #7060, p8

BIGELOW Samuel (c) - warned out of New Ipswich, 1789, file #2281, p1

BIGELOW Silas & Wife - warned out of New Ipswich, 1789, file #2281, p1

BIGELOW Silas (c) - warned out of New Ipswich, 1789, file #2281, p1

BILLING Betsey - formerly of Mason, warned out of Temple, 1795, file #7060, p50

BILLINGS John - formerly of Walpole, warned out of Temple, 1801, file #7060, p56

BILLO Abner - formerly of Topsfield MA, warned out of Temple, 1794, file #7060, p57

BLAISDEL Henery - warned out of Goffstown, 1796, file #3607, p8

BLAISDEL Meriam - warned out of Goffstown, 1796, file #3607, p8

BLANCHARD Dolley (c) - formerly of Andover MA, warned out of Wilton, 1784, file #2604-E, p7

BLANCHARD Eber (c) - formerly of Andover MA, warned out of Wilton, 1784, file #2604-E, p7

BLANCHARD Elizabeth - formerly of Pepperell MA, warned out of New Ipswich, 1791, file #2283, p1

BLANCHARD George - formerly of Andover MA, warned out of Wilton, 1774, file #2604-D, p8

BLANCHARD Hannah - formerly of Andover MA, warned out of Wilton, 1774, file #2604-D, p8

BLANCHARD Jemima - formerly of Litchfield, warned out of Dunbarton, 1790, file #2523, p8

BLANCHARD Jeremiah (Lt) - formerly of Andover MA, warned out of Wilton, 1784, file #2604-E, p7

BLANCHARD Judath (c) - formerly of Andover MA, warned out of Wilton, 1784, file #2604-E, p7

BLANCHARD Lucey - formerly of Hollis, warned out of Wilton, 1777, file #2604, p3

BLANCHARD Lucy - formerly of Mile Stripe, warned out of Wilton, 1775, file #2604, p4

BLANCHARD Lucy (c) - formerly of Mile Strip, warned out of Wilton, 1775, file #2604, p4

BLANCHARD Ruth - formerly of Andover, warned out of Temple, 1790, file #7060, p2

BLANCHARD Samuel - formerly of Andover, warned out of Temple, 1790, file #7060, p2

BLANCHARD Sarah (c) - formerly of Andover MA, warned out of Wilton, 1784, file #2604-E, p7

BLANCHARD Susannah - formerly of Andover MA, warned out of Wilton, 1784, file #2604-E, p7

BLASDEL Elizabeth (c) - warned out of Goffstown, 1793, file #3609, p8

BLASDEL John - warned out of Goffstown, 1793, file #3609, p8

BLASDEL John Jr - warned out of Goffstown, 1793, file #3609, p8

BLASDEL Mary - warned out of Goffstown, 1793, file #3609, p8

BLASDEL Sarah (c) - warned out of Goffstown, 1793, file #3609, p8

BLASDEL Susanna - warned out of Goffstown, 1793, file #3609, p8

BLODGETT Isiah - formerly of Peterborough, warned out of New Ipswich, 1785, file #2276, p4

BLODGETT Rachael - formerly of Nottingham, warned out of Wilton, 1774, file #2604-C, p2

BLOOD Aby - formerly of Pepperell MA, warned out of New Ipswich, 1791, file #2282, p2

BLOOD David - warned out of New Ipswich, 1789, file #2281, p6

BLOOD David (c) - warned out of New Ipswich, 1789, file #2281, p6

BLOOD Hannah (c) - warned out of New Ipswich, 1789, file #2281, p6

BLOOD Olive - warned out of New Ipswich, 1772, file #2277, p1

BLOOD Polly (c) - warned out of New Ipswich, 1789, file #2281, p6

BLOOD Robert - warned out of New Ipswich, 1772, file #2277, p1

BLOOD Robert (c) - warned out of New Ipswich, 1772, file #2277, p1

BLOOD Samuel - formerly of Groton MA, warned out of New Ipswich, 1792, file #2284, p3

BLOOD Samuel (c) - formerly of Groton MA, warned out of New Ipswich, 1792, file #2284, p3

BLOOD Sarah - formerly of Groton MA, warned out of New Ipswich, 1792, file #2284, p3

BLOOD Sarah (c) - formerly of Groton MA, warned out of New Ipswich, 1792, file #2284, p3

BLOOD Sebel - warned out of New Ipswich, 1789, file #2281, p6

BLOOD Sebel (c) - warned out of New Ipswich, 1789, file #2281, p6

BOIN Abigail - formerly of Hopkinton, warned out of Dunbarton, 1788, file #2521, p2

BOIN Isaac - formerly of Hopkinton, warned out of Dunbarton, 1788, file #2521, p2

BOIN Sarah Barker (c) - formerly of Hopkinton, warned out of Dunbarton, 1788, file #2521, p2

BOND Samuel - formerly of Salem MA, warned out of Dunbarton, 1784, file #2517, p5

BOOTMAN Abigal - warned out of New Boston, 1781, file #2272, p2

BOOTMAN Abigal Jr - warned out of New Boston, 1781, file #2272, p2

BOOTMAN Anna (c) - warned out of Goffstown, 1789, file #3607, p5

BOOTMAN Betsy - warned out of Goffstown, 1789, file #3607, p5

BOOTMAN Hannah - warned out of New Boston, 1790, file #2282, p2

BOOTMAN Jno (c) - warned out of Goffstown, 1789, file #3607, p5

BOOTMAN Joseph (c) - warned out of Goffstown, 1789, file #3607, p5

BOOTMAN Nathaniel Wife - warned out of New Ipswich, 1784, file #2275, p3

BOOTMAN Zebulon (c) - warned out of Goffstown, 1789, file #3607, p5

BOYD Eli - warned out of Goffstown, 1778, file #3606, p5

BOYD Mary - warned out of Goffstown, 1778, file #3606, p5

BOYD Samuel - warned out of Goffstown, 1778, file #3606, p5

BOYNTON Benjamin - formerly of Ashbraham MA, warned out of New Boston, 1795, file #2288, p1

BOYNTON Deborah - formerly of Ashbraham MA, warned out of New Boston, 1795, file #2288, p1

BOYNTON Deborah Jr (c) - formerly of Ashbraham MA, warned out of New Boston, 1795, file #2288, p1

BOYNTON Hannah (c) - formerly of Ashbraham MA, warned out of New Boston, 1795, file #2288, p1

BOYNTON Mary (c) - formerly of Ashbraham MA, warned out of New Boston, 1795, file #2288, p1

BOYNTON Mathew (c) - formerly of Ashbraham MA, warned out of New Boston, 1795, file #2288, p1

BOYNTON Sarah (c) - formerly of Ashbraham MA, warned out of New Boston, 1795, file #2288, p1

BRADBERY Winthrup - warned out of Goffstown, 1790, file #3607, p6

BRADFORD Abigail (c) - formerly of Hillsborough, warned out of Dearing, 1788, file #7059, p21

BRADFORD Ada (c) - formerly of Hillsborough, warned out of Dearing, 1788, file #7059, p21

BRADFORD Adah - formerly of Hillsborough, warned out of Dearing, 1788, file #7059, p21

BRADFORD Bazabel (c) - formerly of Hillsborough, warned out of Dearing, 1788, file #7059, p21

BRADFORD Cryus (c) - formerly of Hillsborough, warned out of Dearing, 1788, file #7059, p21

BRADFORD Timothy - formerly of Hillsborough, warned out of Dearing, 1788, file #7059, p21

BRADFORD Timothy (c) - formerly of Hillsborough, warned out of Dearing, 1788, file #7059, p21

BRADSHAN Mary - formerly of Hardwick MA, warned out of Dearing, 1788, file #7059, p33

BRAGG Bridget (c) - formerly of Reading MA, warned out of Wilton, 1779, file #2604-B, p7

BRAGG Elizabeth (c) - formerly of Reading MA, warned out of Wilton, 1779, file #2604-B, p7

BRAGG John & Wife - formerly of Reading MA, warned out of Wilton, 1779, file #2604-B, p7

BRAGG Phebe (c) - formerly of Reading MA, warned out of Wilton, 1779, file #2604-B, p7

BRAGG Sarah (c) - formerly of Reading MA, warned out of Wilton, 1779, file #2604-B, p7

BREED Lydia - formerly of Lynn MA, warned out of New Ipswich, 1786, file #2278, p6

BREED Nathan (c) - formerly of Lynn MA, warned out of New Ipswich, 1786, file #2278, p6

BREWER Ebenezer - formerly of Peterborough, warned out of Temple, 1787, file #7060, p26

BREWER Isaac - formerly of Shrewsbury MA, warned out of Temple, 1787, file #7060, p26

BREWER Lucy - formerly of Shrewsbury MA, warned out of Temple, 1787, file #7060, p26

BREWER Lucy (c) - formerly of Shrewsbury MA, warned out of Temple, 1787, file #7060, p26

BREWER Sally (c) - formerly of Shrewsbury MA, warned out of Temple, 1787, file #7060, p26

BRIANT Abigal - formerly of Dartmouth, warned out of New Ipswich, 1779, file #2270, p1

BRIANT James - formerly of Reiding MA, warned out of New Ipswich, 1778, file #2269, p2

BRIANT James (son) - formerly of Reiding MA, warned out of New Ipswich, 1778, file #2269, p2

BRIANT Mary - formerly of Reiding MA, warned out of New Ipswich, 1778, file #2269, p2

BRIDE Betty - formerly of New Marlborough, warned out of New Ipswich, 1785, file #2276, p6

BRIGHAM Asa - formerly of Littleton, warned out of Temple, 1802, file #7060, p38

BRIZLER Catharine (c) - formerly of Boston MA, warned out of Temple, 1781, file #7060, p15

BRIZLER Charlotte - formerly of Boston MA, warned out of Temple, 1781, file #7060, p15

BRIZLER George - formerly of Boston MA, warned out of Temple, 1781, file #7060, p15

BRIZLER Mary (c) - formerly of Boston MA, warned out of Temple, 1781, file #7060, p15

BROOK Abigail - formerly of Woburn MA, warned out of Wilton, 1795, file #2604-D, p7

BROOK Isaac - formerly of Woburn MA, warned out of Wilton, 1795, file #2604-D, p7

BROOK Isaac (c) - formerly of Woburn MA, warned out of Wilton, 1795, file #2604-D, p7

BROOKS Ebenezer - formerly of Grafton MA, warned out of New Ipswich, 1785, file #2276, p5

BROOKS Zacheus - formerly of Walpole, warned out of New Ipswich, 1773, file #2267, p3

BROWN Amos - formerly of New Ipswich, warned out of Temple, 1795, file #7060, p50

BROWN Anna - formerly of Malden MA, warned out of Temple, 1791, file #7060, p55

BROWN Betty (c) - formerly of Were, warned out of Dearing, 1790, file #7059, p32

BROWN Elenezar & wife - formerly of Wilmington MA, warned out of Wilton, 1774, file #2604, p2

BROWN Eliphalet - warned out of New Boston, 1785, file #2276, p3

BROWN Eunas - warned out of New Boston, 1785, file #2276, p3

BROWN Grace - formerly of Concord, warned out of New Ipswich, 1790, file #2282, p1

BROWN Hannah (c) - formerly of Malden MA, warned out of Temple, 1791, file #7060, p55

BROWN Jane - formerly of Peterborough, warned out of Temple, 1786, file #7060, p5

BROWN John - formerly of Malden MA, warned out of Temple, 1791, file #7060, p55

BROWN John - formerly of Temple, warned out of New Ipswich, 1770, file #2265, p1

BROWN John (c) - warned out of Goffstown, 1792, file #3606, p2

BROWN John Jr (c) - formerly of Temple, warned out of New Ipswich, 1770, file #2265, p1

BROWN Joseph (c) - formerly of Were, warned out of Dearing, 1790, file #7059, p32

BROWN Joshua - warned out of Goffstown, 1786, file #3607, p1

BROWN Margaret - warned out of Goffstown, 1786, file #3607, p1

BROWN Mary - formerly of Metheun MA, warned out of Temple, 1782, file #7060, p6

BROWN Mary - formerly of Were, warned out of Dearing, 1790, file #7059, p32

BROWN Mary - formerly of Temple, warned out of New Ipswich, 1770, file #2265, p1

BROWN Nanne - warned out of Goffstown, 1792, file #3606, p2

BROWN Nanne (c) - warned out of Goffstown, 1792, file #3606, p2

BROWN Phebe (c) - formerly of Malden MA, warned out of Temple, 1791, file #7060, p55

BROWN Samuel - formerly of Boston MA, warned out of Temple, 1781, file #7060, p15

BROWN Samuel (c) - formerly of Were, warned out of Dearing, 1790, file #7059, p32

BROWN Samuel Jr - formerly of MA, warned out of New Boston, 1785, file #2276, p1

BROWN Sarah - warned out of New Boston, 1785, file #2276, p1

BROWN Sarah (c) - formerly of Were, warned out of Dearing, 1790, file #7059, p32

BROWN Silas - formerly of Metheun MA, warned out of Temple, 1782, file #7060, p6

BROWN Stephen - warned out of Goffstown, 1792, file #3606, p2

BROWN Susannah - formerly of Boston MA, warned out of Temple, 1781, file #7060, p15

BROWN Susannah Jr (c) - formerly of Boston MA, warned out of Temple, 1781, file #7060, p15

BROWN Will (c) - warned out of Goffstown, 1786, file #3607, p1

BROWN William - warned out of Goffstown, 1786, file #3607, p1

BROWN William - formerly of Were, warned out of Dearing, 1790, file #7059, p32

BROWNS Joah - formerly of Concord MA, warned out of Temple, 1786, file #7060, p22

BRUCE John - formerly of Marlborough MA, warned out of New Boston, 1787, file #2280, p2

BRUSE Artimeas - formerly of New Jane VT, warned out of Wilton, 1783, file #2604-E, p11

BRUSE Martha - formerly of New Jane VT, warned out of Wilton, 1783, file #2604-E, p11

BRUSE Zachariah Smith - formerly of New Jane VT, warned out of Wilton, 1783, file #2604-E, p11

BRUSE Charety - formerly of New Jane VT, warned out of Wilton, 1783, file #2604-E, p11

BUCK Betsey (c) - formerly of Weare, warned out of Dunbarton, 1789, file #2522, p3

BUCK Elphey - warned out of New Boston, 1785, file #2276, p3

BUCK Gidey - warned out of New Boston, 1785, file #2276, p3

BUCK Jonathan (c) - formerly of Weare, warned out of Dunbarton, 1789, file #2522, p3

BUCK Judah (c) - formerly of Weare, warned out of Dunbarton, 1789, file #2522, p3

BUCK Poley - warned out of New Boston, 1785, file #2276, p3

BUCK Poley (c) - formerly of Weare, warned out of Dunbarton, 1789, file #2522, p3

BUCK Saley - warned out of New Boston, 1785, file #2276, p3

BUCK Saley (c) - formerly of Weare, warned out of Dunbarton, 1789, file #2522, p3

BUCK Samuel - formerly of Weare, warned out of Dunbarton, 1789, file #2522, p3

BUCK Samuel - warned out of New Boston, 1785, file #2276, p3

BUCK Sarah - formerly of Weare, warned out of Dunbarton, 1789, file #2522, p3

BUCK Thomas (c) - formerly of Weare, warned out of Dunbarton, 1789, file #2522, p3

BUCKMAN Benomia - formerly of Malden MA, warned out of New Ipswich, 1794, file #2286, p2

BUCKMAN Benonia (c) - formerly of Malden MA, warned out of New Ipswich, 1794, file #2286, p2

BUCKMAN Elizabeth - formerly of Malden MA, warned out of New Ipswich, 1794, file #2286, p2

BURMAN Jeremiah & Wife - formerly of Amherst, warned out of Wilton, 1784, file #2604-C, p6

BURMAN Lucia (c) - formerly of Amherst, warned out of Wilton, 1784, file #2604-C, p6

BURMAN Parker (c) - formerly of Amherst, warned out of Wilton, 1784, file #2604-C, p6

BURNHAM Sally & Wife - formerly of Wilton, warned out of Temple, 1802, file #7060, p38

BURNS John -wife & children - warned out of New Ipswich, 1784, file #2275, p3

BURNUN Elizabeth - formerly of Ipswich MA, warned out of Dunbarton, 1784, file #2517, p3

BURPEE Abigail - formerly of Rowley MA, warned out of Wilton, 1783, file #2604-E, p10

BURPEE David & Wife - formerly of Rowley MA, warned out of Wilton, 1784, file #2604-C, p6

BURPEE Ebenezer (c) - formerly of Rowley MA, warned out of Wilton, 1784, file #2604-C, p6

BURPEE Elisabeth (c) - formerly of Rowley MA, warned out of Wilton, 1784, file #2604-C, p6

BURPEE Miriam (c) - formerly of Rowley MA, warned out of Wilton, 1784, file #2604-C, p6

BURPEE Nathaniel - formerly of Rowley MA, warned out of Wilton, 1783, file #2604-E, p10

BURPEE Ruth - formerly of Rowley MA, warned out of Wilton, 1783, file #2604-E, p10

BURPEE Sarah - formerly of Rowley MA, warned out of Wilton, 1783, file #2604-E, p10

BURRIS Sarah - formerly of Salem MA, warned out of New Boston, 1794, file #2286, p3

BURROW Polly - warned out of New Ipswich, 1788, file #2280, p2

BURT Daniel - formerly of Mason, warned out of New Ipswich, 1784, file #2275, p6

BUTRICK Elizabeth - formerly of Concord MA, warned out of Temple, 1794, file #7060, p51

BUTRICK William - formerly of Concord MA, warned out of Temple, 1794, file #7060, p51

BUTTERFIELD Ama - formerly of Wilton, warned out of Temple, 1796, file #7060, p35

BUTTERFIELD Anna (c) - formerly of Reading MA, warned out of Temple, 1790, file #7060, p37

BUTTERFIELD Betty - formerly of Wilton, warned out of Temple, 1792, file #7060, p39

BUTTERFIELD Mary - formerly of Reading MA, warned out of Temple, 1790, file #7060, p37

BUTTERFIELD Samuel - formerly of Reading MA, warned out of Temple, 1790, file #7060, p37

BUTTERFIELD Stephen (c) - warned out of Temple, 1790, file #7060, p49

BUXTON David - formerly of Wilton, warned out of Temple, 1799, file #7060, p45

BUZEL David - warned out of Goffstown, 1786, file #3607, p1

BUZEL Elizabeth - warned out of Goffstown, 1786, file #3607, p1

CALDWELL (widow)& Children - warned out of New Ipswich, 1784, file #2275, p3

CALDWELL Agnes - formerly of Francestown, warned out of New Boston, 1787, file #2279, p5&6

CALDWELL Anna - formerly of Lunenburgh MA, warned out of Temple, 1787, file #7060, p3

CALDWELL Margaret - formerly of Francestown, warned out of New Boston, 1787, file #2279, p3&8

CALDWELL Margaret (minor) - warned out of New Boston, 1792, file #2284, p1

CALTON Phebe - formerly of Temple, warned out of Wilton, 1783, file #2604-E, p10

CALTON Phineas - formerly of New Ipswich, warned out of Wilton, 1783, file #2604-E, p10

CAMP James - warned out of Goffstown, 1794, file #3609, p9

CAMP Milly - warned out of Goffstown, 1794, file #3609, p9

CAMP Nancy - warned out of Goffstown, 1794, file #3609, p9

CAMP Unus - warned out of Goffstown, 1794, file #3609, p9

CAREY Sarah - formerly of Rindge, warned out of New Ipswich, 1773, file #2267, p2

CAREY Zaraus - formerly of Rindge, warned out of New Ipswich, 1786, file #2278, p6

CARLETON Betsy - formerly of Lunenburgh MA, warned out of New Ipswich, 1789, file #2281, p2

CARLETON Nath'l - formerly of Lunenburgh MA, warned out of New Ipswich, 1789, file #2281, p2

CARLTON David (c) - formerly of Temple, warned out of New Ipswich, 1780, file #2271, p1

CARLTON Phineas - formerly of Temple, warned out of New Ipswich, 1780, file #2271, p1

CARLTON Sarah (widow) - formerly of Temple, warned out of New Ipswich, 1780, file #2271, p1

CARLTON Abigail - formerly of Lunenburgh MA, warned out of New Ipswich, 1792, file #2284, p1

CARLTON Abraham (c) - warned out of New Ipswich, 1772, file #2266, p2

CARLTON David (c) - warned out of New Ipswich, 1772, file #2266, p2

CARLTON David (c) - formerly of New Ipswich, warned out of Temple, 1779, file #7060, p24

CARLTON George (c) - warned out of New Ipswich, 1785, file #2276, p6

CARLTON Henry (c) - warned out of New Ipswich, 1785, file #2276, p6

CARLTON Jesse - warned out of New Ipswich, 1772, file #2266, p2

CARLTON Jesse - formerly of Temple, warned out of Wilton, 1793, file #2604-C, p5

CARLTON Jesse (c) - warned out of New Ipswich, 1772, file #2266, p2

CARLTON Moses - formerly of Billerica, warned out of New Ipswich, 1785, file #2276, p6

CARLTON Moses (c) - warned out of New Ipswich, 1785, file #2276, p6

CARLTON Nicholas (c) - warned out of New Ipswich, 1785, file #2276, p6

CARLTON Phineas (c) - formerly of New Ipswich, warned out of Temple, 1779, file #7060, p24

CARLTON Reuben (c) - warned out of New Ipswich, 1785, file #2276, p6

CARLTON Sarah - warned out of New Ipswich, 1772, file #2266, p2

CARLTON Sarah (widow) - formerly of New Ipswich, warned out of Temple, 1779, file #7060, p24

CARLTON Sybel - formerly of Carlisle, warned out of New Ipswich, 1785, file #2276, p6

CARLTON Sybel (c) - warned out of New Ipswich, 1785, file #2276, p6

CARR Mary - formerly of Goffstown, warned out of Dunbarton, 1792, file #2525, p5

CARR Richard (c) - formerly of Goffstown, warned out of Dunbarton, 1792, file #2525, p5

CARR Will'm - formerly of Goffstown, warned out of Dunbarton, 1792, file #2525, p5

CARY Barnabas - formerly of Rindge, warned out of New Ipswich, 1776, file #2287, p1

CARY Elizabeth Purmit - warned out of New Ipswich, 1772, file #2266, p3

CARY Theodore Atkinson - formerly of Rindge, warned out of New Ipswich, 1785, file #2276, p4

CASSADAY Catey - warned out of Goffstown, 1792, file #3606, p2

CHAMBERLAIN Thomas - warned out of New Boston, 1790, file #2282, p3

CHAMBERLAIN Abigail - formerly of Lyndeborough, warned out of Wilton, 1784, file #2604-D, p2

CHAMBERLAIN Asa - formerly of Hollis, warned out of Temple, 1787, file #7060, p26

CHAMBERLAIN Ephraim & Wife - formerly of Westford MA, warned out of Temple, 1786, file #7060, p22

CHAMBERLAIN Polley - formerly of Hollis, warned out of Temple, 1787, file #7060, p26

CHAMBERLAIN Polley Jr (c) - formerly of Hollis, warned out of Temple, 1787, file #7060, p26

CHAMBERLIN Ede - formerly of Pepperell MA, warned out of Wilton, 1780, file #2604-E, p6

CHAMPNEY Abigal (c) - formerly of Alexander, warned out of New Ipswich, 1784, file #2275, p6

CHAMPNEY Abigail - formerly of New Reading MA, warned out of New Ipswich, 1787, file #2279, p2

CHAMPNEY Ebenezer (c) - formerly of Alexander, warned out of New Ipswich, 1784, file #2275, p6

CHAMPNEY Elizabeth (c) - formerly of Alexander, warned out of New Ipswich, 1784, file #2275, p6

CHAMPNEY John (c) - formerly of Alexander, warned out of New Ipswich, 1784, file #2275, p6

CHAMPNEY John (Mr) - formerly of Alexander, warned out of New Ipswich, 1784, file #2275, p6

CHAMPNEY Lydia (c) - formerly of Alexander, warned out of New Ipswich, 1784, file #2275, p6

CHAMPNEY Mary (c) - formerly of Alexander, warned out of New Ipswich, 1784, file #2275, p6

CHAMPNEY Nathan (c) - formerly of Alexander, warned out of New Ipswich, 1784, file #2275, p6

CHAMPNEY Nathan Mr - formerly of New Reading MA, warned out of New Ipswich, 1787, file #2279, p2

CHAMPNEY Sarah - formerly of Alexander, warned out of New Ipswich, 1784, file #2275, p6

CHAMPNEY Sarah (c) - formerly of Alexander, warned out of New Ipswich, 1784, file #2275, p6

CHANDLER Daniel (c) - formerly of Hollis, warned out of Wilton, 1782, file #2604-C, p8

CHANDLER Dorothy - warned out of New Ipswich, 1772, file #2277, p1

CHANDLER Doras (c) - formerly of Hollis, warned out of Wilton, 1782, file #2604-C, p8

CHANDLER Dorothy - warned out of New Ipswich, 1772, file #2266, p3

CHANDLER Hannah - formerly of Hollis, warned out of Wilton, 1782, file #2604-C, p8

CHANDLER Hannah (c) - formerly of Hollis, warned out of Wilton, 1782, file #2604-C, p8

CHANDLER Samuel (c) - formerly of Hollis, warned out of Wilton, 1782, file #2604-C, p8

CHATMAN John - warned out of Goffstown, 1792, file #3606, p2

CHEAVER Israel - formerly of Marblehead MA, warned out of New Ipswich, 1792, file #2284, p3

CHEAVER Israel (c) - formerly of Marblehead MA, warned out of New Ipswich, 1792, file #2284, p3

CHEAVER Martha - formerly of Marblehead MA, warned out of New Ipswich, 1792, file #2284, p3

CHEAVER Mehitable (c) - formerly of Marblehead MA, warned out of New Ipswich, 1792, file #2284, p3

CHEAVER Patty (c) - formerly of Marblehead MA, warned out of New Ipswich, 1792, file #2284, p3

CHEAVER Sally (c) - formerly of Marblehead MA, warned out of New Ipswich, 1792, file #2284, p3

CHEAVER William (c) - formerly of Marblehead MA, warned out of New Ipswich, 1792, file #2284, p3

CHILD Abigail (c) - formerly of Wilton, warned out of Temple, 1798, file #7060, p59

CHILD Grace - formerly of Wilton, warned out of Temple, 1798, file #7060, p59

CHILD Grace (c) - formerly of Wilton, warned out of Temple, 1798, file #7060, p59

CHILD Isaac (c) - formerly of Wilton, warned out of Temple, 1798, file #7060, p59

CHILD Nehemiah (c) - formerly of Wilton, warned out of Temple, 1798, file #7060, p59

CHILD Simeon - formerly of Wilton, warned out of Temple, 1798, file #7060, p59

CHILD Simeon (c) - formerly of Wilton, warned out of Temple, 1798, file #7060, p59

CHILD Stephen (c) - formerly of Wilton, warned out of Temple, 1798, file #7060, p59

CHILDES Elisha - formerly of MA, warned out of Temple, 1798, file #7060, p40

CHILDES Isaac (c) - formerly of Groton MA, warned out of Temple, 1792, file #7060, p11

CHILDES Moses - formerly of Groton MA, warned out of Temple, 1792, file #7060, p11

CHILDES Prudence - formerly of MA, warned out of Temple, 1798, file #7060, p40

CHILDES Sally (c) - formerly of Groton MA, warned out of Temple, 1792, file #7060, p11

CHILDES Sarah (c) - formerly of Groton MA, warned out of Temple, 1792, file #7060, p11

CHILE Grace - formerly of Mason, warned out of Wilton, 1796, file #2604-D, p5

CHILE Grace Heard (c) - formerly of Mason, warned out of Wilton, 1796, file #2604-D, p5

CHILE Isaac (c) - formerly of Mason, warned out of Wilton, 1796, file #2604-D, p5

CHILE Simeon - formerly of Mason, warned out of Wilton, 1796, file #2604-D, p5

CHILE Simeon (c) - formerly of Mason, warned out of Wilton, 1796, file #2604-D, p5

CHILE Stephen (c) - formerly of Mason, warned out of Wilton, 1796, file #2604-D, p5

CLARK Edward Mr - formerly of Canterbury CT, warned out of New Ipswich, 1788, file #2279, p1

CLARK Ellimah (c) - warned out of New Boston, 1786, file #2278, p1

CLARK Ellinah - warned out of New Boston, 1786, file #2278, p1

CLARK Ephraim (c) - warned out of New Boston, 1786, file #2278, p1

CLARK Ephraim - warned out of New Boston, 1786, file #2278, p1

CLARK Jonathan (c) - warned out of New Boston, 1786, file #2278, p1

CLARK Joseph (c) - warned out of New Boston, 1786, file #2278, p1

CLARK Lydia (c) - warned out of New Boston, 1786, file #2278, p1

CLARK Mary (c) - warned out of New Boston, 1786, file #2278, p1

CLARK Pattiah (c) - warned out of New Boston, 1786, file #2278, p1

CLARK Sarah - formerly of Canterbury CT, warned out of New Ipswich, 1787, file #2279, p1

CLARK Sarah (c) - warned out of New Boston, 1786, file #2278, p1

CLARKE Bunker - formerly of Packersfield, warned out of New Ipswich, 1784, file #2275, p5

CLARKE Daniel - formerly of Townsend MA, warned out of Temple, 1794, file #7060, p58

CLARKE Daniel (c) - formerly of Townsend MA, warned out of Temple, 1794, file #7060, p58

CLARKE David - formerly of Danvers MA, warned out of Temple, 1791, file #7060, p54

CLARKE David (c) - formerly of Danvers MA, warned out of Temple, 1791, file #7060, p54

CLARKE John (c) - formerly of Townsend MA, warned out of Temple, 1794, file #7060, p58

CLARKE Moley - formerly of Danvers MA, warned out of Temple, 1791, file #7060, p54

CLARKE Polley (c) - formerly of Townsend MA, warned out of Temple, 1794, file #7060, p58

CLARKE Rebecca (c) - formerly of Townsend MA, warned out of Temple, 1794, file #7060, p58

CLARKE Sally (c) - formerly of Townsend MA, warned out of Temple, 1794, file #7060, p58

CLARKE Sarah - formerly of Townsend MA, warned out of Temple, 1794, file #7060, p58

CLARKE Susanna (c) - formerly of Townsend MA, warned out of Temple, 1794, file #7060, p58

COBB Josiah - formerly of Dublin, warned out of Temple, 1792, file #7060, p39

COCHRAN Elijah (Mr) - warned out of New Boston, 1786, file #2278, p1

COCHRAN James (c) - warned out of New Boston, 1790, file #2282, p2

COCHRAN James Gragg - warned out of New Boston, 1786, file #2278, p1

COCHRAN Jemima - warned out of New Boston, 1786, file #2278, p1

COCHRAN Lydia (c) - warned out of New Boston, 1790, file #2282, p2

COCHRAN Marcy Grant - warned out of New Boston, 1786, file #2278, p1

COCHRAN Margaret - warned out of New Boston, 1790, file #2282, p2

COCHRAN Nathaniel - warned out of New Boston, 1786, file #2278, p1

COCHRAN Thomas Jr - warned out of New Boston, 1790, file #2282, p2

COLBEY Benjamin (c) - formerly of Ware, warned out of Dearing, 1789, file #7059, p29

COLBEY Elizabeth (c) - formerly of Ware, warned out of Dearing, 1789, file #7059, p29

COLBEY Jonathan (c) - formerly of Ware, warned out of Dearing, 1789, file #7059, p29

COLBEY Joseph (c) - formerly of Ware, warned out of Dearing, 1789, file #7059, p29

COLBEY Philbrick - formerly of Ware, warned out of Dearing, 1789, file #7059, p29

COLBEY Rhoda (c) - formerly of Ware, warned out of Dearing, 1789, file #7059, p29

COLBEY Ruth - formerly of Ware, warned out of Dearing, 1789, file #7059, p29

COLBEY Sarah (c) - formerly of Ware, warned out of Dearing, 1789, file #7059, p29

COLBURN David - formerly of Ashbraham, warned out of New Boston, 1795, file #2288, p1

COLBURN Ephraim (c) - formerly of Ashbraham MA, warned out of New Boston, 1795, file #2288, p1

COLBURN Rebecah - formerly of Ashbraham MA, warned out of New Boston, 1795, file #2288, p1

COLBURN Trythene (c) - formerly of Ashbraham MA, warned out of New Boston, 1795, file #2288, p1

COLBY Batey (c) - warned out of Dunbarton, 1786, file #2519, p4

COLBY Exprance - warned out of Dunbarton, 1786, file #2519, p4

COLBY Isaac - warned out of Dunbarton, 1786, file #2519, p4

COLBY Phebe (c) - warned out of Dunbarton, 1786, file #2519, p4

COLE Abel F - formerly of Concord, warned out of Temple, 1787, file #7060, p26

COLE Daniel - formerly of Concord MA, warned out of Temple, 1795, file #7060, p52

COLE Elizabeth - formerly of Amherst, warned out of New Boston, 1794, file #2286, p3

COLE Ezra - formerly of Amherst, warned out of New Boston, 1794, file #2286, p3

COLE John Marsh - formerly of Amherst, warned out of New Boston, 1794, file #2286, p3

COLE Mehitable - formerly of Amherst, warned out of New Boston, 1794, file #2286, p3

COLE Patty - formerly of Amherst, warned out of New Boston, 1794, file #2286, p3

COLE Timothy - formerly of Concord MA, warned out of Temple, 1792, file #7060, p39

COLLINS Abigail - formerly of Weare, warned out of Goffstown, 1791, file #3607, p7

COLLINS Assa? (c) - warned out of Goffstown, 1794, file #3609, p9

COLLINS Elizabeth (c) - warned out of Goffstown, 1794, file #3609, p9

COLLINS Elizabeth (c) - warned out of New Boston, 1788, file #2280, p1

COLLINS Elizabeth (widow) - warned out of New Boston, 1788, file #2280, p1

COLLINS Hannah - warned out of Goffstown, 1794, file #3609, p9

COLLINS Moses - warned out of Goffstown, 1788, file #3608, p8

COLLINS Prudence (c) - warned out of Goffstown, 1788, file #3608, p8

COLLINS Reuben - warned out of Goffstown, 1794, file #3609, p9

COLLINS Stephen - formerly of Weare, warned out of Goffstown, 1791, file #3607, p7

COLMAN Elinor Or Nelly - warned out of New Boston, 1792, file #2284, p1

COLMAN William - warned out of New Boston, 1792, file #2284, p1

COLOILL Susanna - formerly of Road Island, warned out of Wilton, 1780, file #2604-E, p6

COMB Joanna - formerly of Kingstown, warned out of Dunbarton, 1790, file #2523, p4

COMB John - formerly of Kingstown, warned out of Dunbarton, 1790, file #2523, p4

CONANT George - warned out of Goffstown, 1791, file #3606, p3

CONANT George - formerly of Concord, warned out of Temple, 1799, file #7060, p26

CONNER? John - warned out of Goffstown, 1786, file #3607, p1

CONNER? Lydea - warned out of Goffstown, 1786, file #3607, p1

CONNER? Mary (c) - warned out of Goffstown, 1786, file #3607, p1

CONNER? Thomas - warned out of Goffstown, 1786, file #3607, p1

CONNER? William - warned out of Goffstown, 1786, file #3607, p1

CONWAY Sarah - warned out of Goffstown, 1786, file #3607, p1

COOK Elizabeth - formerly of Reding MA, warned out of New Ipswich, 1785, file #2276, p4

COOK Mary - formerly of Keene, warned out of New Ipswich, 1784, file #2275, p6

COOK Noah (Mr) - formerly of Keene, warned out of New Ipswich, 1784, file #2275, p6

COOLEDGE John - formerly of Ashburnham, warned out of New Ipswich, 1785, file #2276, p6

COOLIDGE Elisha - formerly of Ashburnham MA, warned out of New Ipswich, 1788, file #2281, p1

COOLIDGE Leslee - formerly of Ashburnham, warned out of New Ipswich, ___, file #2281, p1

COOLIDGE Lucy (c) - formerly of Ashburnham, warned out of New Ipswich, 1789, file #2281, p1

COOLIDGE Sarah - formerly of Ashburnham, warned out of New Ipswich, 1789, file #2281, p1

COOPER John - warned out of Dunbarton, 1785, file #2518, p4

COOPER Mary - warned out of Dunbarton, 1785, file #2518, p4

COOPER Mary - formerly of Mason, warned out of New Ipswich, 1780, file #2271, p4

COPP Jonathan & Son - formerly of Durham, warned out of Dunbarton, 1779, file #2512, p1

COPP Martha - formerly of Durham, warned out of Dunbarton, 1779, file #2512, p1

COPS David - warned out of Goffstown, 1787, file #3607, p2

COPS Jonathan - warned out of Goffstown, 1791, file #3606, p3

CORNISH Abraham - formerly of Weare, warned out of New Boston, 1794, file #2286, p3

CORNISH Margaret - formerly of Weare, warned out of New Boston, 1794, file #2286, p3

CORNISH Marget - formerly of Francestown, warned out of Dearing, 1786, file #7059, p1

COSTER Hipzedath (widow) - warned out of Goffstown, 1793, file #3608, p1

COUL Elipelet - formerly of Amherst, warned out of New Boston, 1794, file #2286, p3

COUL Ruth - formerly of Amherst, warned out of New Boston, 1794, file #2286, p3

CRAM Daniel (c) - formerly of Andover MA, warned out of Wilton, 1795, file #2604-D, p7

CRAM John - formerly of Andover MA, warned out of Wilton, 1795, file #2604-D, p7

CRAM Nathan - formerly of Lyndeborough, warned out of Wilton, 1779, file #2604-B, p7

CRAM Nathan (c) - formerly of Lyndeborough, warned out of Wilton, 1779, file #2604-B, p7

CRAM Olive - formerly of Andover MA, warned out of Wilton, 1795, file #2604-D, p7

CRAM Olive (c) - formerly of Andover MA, warned out of Wilton, 1795, file #2604-D, p7

CRAM Rachel - formerly of Lyndeborough, warned out of Wilton, 1779, file #2604-B, p7

CRAM Rachel (c) - formerly of Lyndeborough, warned out of Wilton, 1779, file #2604-B, p7

CRANE Polly - formerly of Westmoreland, warned out of Temple, 1792, file #7060, p39

CREAGE Anne - formerly of Londonderry, warned out of Goffstown, 1785, file #3606, p11

CREALEY Agnis - warned out of New Boston, 1787, file #2279, p10

CREE Joseph (c) - warned out of New Boston, 1790, file #2282, p3

CREE Loamme (c) - warned out of New Boston, 1790, file #2282, p3

CREE Mary - warned out of New Boston, 1790, file #2282, p3

CREE Moses (c) - warned out of New Boston, 1790, file #2282, p3

CREE Samuel - warned out of New Boston, 1790, file #2282, p3

CROSBY Betsy - formerly of Wilton, warned out of Temple, 1802, file #7060, p38

CROSBY John - formerly of Greenwich, warned out of Temple, 1790, file #7060, p37

CROSBY John - formerly of Winchendon MA, warned out of New Ipswich, 1790, file #2282, p1

CROSBY Simon - formerly of Wilton, warned out of Temple, 1802, file #7060, p38

CROSBY Solomon - formerly of Wilton, warned out of Temple, 1802, file #7060, p38

CROWELL Anna - formerly of Salem, warned out of Dunbarton, 1795, file #2528, p1

CROWELL John (c) - formerly of Salem, warned out of Dunbarton, 1795, file #2528, p1

CROWELL Jonathan - formerly of Salem, warned out of Dunbarton, 1795, file #2528, p1

CROWELL Nancy (c) - formerly of Salem, warned out of Dunbarton, 1795, file #2528, p1

CROWELL Sally (c) - formerly of Salem, warned out of Dunbarton, 1795, file #2528, p1

CROWELL Samuel (c) - formerly of Salem, warned out of Dunbarton, 1795, file #2528, p1

CUMMING Abel - warned out of New Ipswich, 1795, file #2288, p3

CUMMINGS Ebenezar - formerly of Conway, warned out of Wilton, 1783, file #2604-D, p1

CUMMINGS Mittey - formerly of Sharon, warned out of Temple, 1800, file #7060, p47

CUMMUNS John - formerly of Mason, warned out of Dearing, 1795, file #7059, p13

CUMMUNS Hannah - formerly of Mason, warned out of Dearing, 1795, file #7059, p13

CUMMUNS Isaac (c) - formerly of Mason, warned out of Dearing, 1795, file #7059, p13

CUMMUNS John (c) - formerly of Mason, warned out of Dearing, 1795, file #7059, p13

CUMMUNS Saly (c) - formerly of Mason, warned out of Dearing, 1795, file #7059, p13

CURTIS Abigail (Widow) - formerly of Milford, warned out of Wilton, 1795, file #2604-D, p7

CURTIS Davis (c) - warned out of New Boston, 1790, file #2282, p3

CURTIS Dudly - warned out of New Boston, 1790, file #2282, p3

CURTIS Levi (c) - warned out of New Boston, 1790, file #2282, p3

CURTIS Lucey (c) - warned out of New Boston, 1790, file #2282, p3

CURTIS Mary (widow) - warned out of Goffstown, 1791, file #3609, p7

CURTIS Polly (c) - warned out of New Boston, 1790, file #2282, p3

CURTIS Sally (c) - warned out of New Boston, 1790, file #2282, p3

CURTIS Sarah - warned out of New Boston, 1790, file #2282, p3

CUTTER Ebenezer - warned out of Goffstown, 1793, file #3609, p8

CUTTER Mary - warned out of Goffstown, 1793, file #3609, p8

CUTTER Rachel - formerly of New Ipswich, warned out of Temple, 1784, file #7060, p7

CUTTER Zacrick - warned out of Goffstown, 1793, file #3609, p8

DANFORD Thomas - formerly of Jaffrey, warned out of New Ipswich, 1789, file #2281, p2

DANFORTH Elizabeth - formerly of Billerica MA, warned out of Temple, 1794, file #7060, p51

DANSKLY Hannah - warned out of Goffstown, 1784, file #3608, p9

DANSKLY Hannah (c) - warned out of Goffstown, 1784, file #3608, p9

DANSKLY Jonathan (c) - warned out of Goffstown, 1784, file #3608, p9

DANSKLY Joseph - warned out of Goffstown, 1784, file #3608, p9

DANSKLY Joseph (c) - warned out of Goffstown, 1784, file #3608, p9

DANSKLY Robd (c) - warned out of Goffstown, 1784, file #3608, p9

DARLING Family - formerly of Hopkinton, warned out of Dunbarton, 1793, file #2526, p1

DAVIDSON Mary & Negro Boy - formerly of Londonderry, warned out of Goffstown, 1776, file #3608, p3

DAVIS Abigail - formerly of Holden MA, warned out of Temple, 1793, file #7060, p36

DAVIS Anna (c) - formerly of Goffstown, warned out of Dunbarton, 1785, file #2518, p1

DAVIS Danil (c) - formerly of Goffstown, warned out of Dunbarton, 1785, file #2518, p1

DAVIS Jonas - formerly of Holden MA, warned out of Temple, 1793, file #7060, p36

DAVIS Jonathan - formerly of Goffstown, warned out of Dunbarton, 1785, file #2518, p1

DAVIS Joseph - formerly of Concord, warned out of New Ipswich, 1776, file #2287, p1

DAVIS Joseph - formerly of Concord, warned out of New Ipswich, 1782, file #2273, p3

DAVIS Joshua - formerly of Mason, warned out of New Ipswich, 1793, file #2286, p1

DAVIS Luvercia - formerly of Holden MA, warned out of Temple, 1793, file #7060, p36

DAVIS Martha - formerly of Wenham MA, warned out of New Ipswich, 1784, file #2275, p2

DAVIS Mehitibal - formerly of Goffstown, warned out of Dunbarton, 1785, file #2518, p1

DAVIS Polley - formerly of Rindge, warned out of New Ipswich, 1791, file #2283, p1

DAVIS Polley (c) - formerly of Goffstown, warned out of Dunbarton, 1785, file #2518, p1

DAVIS Sibel - formerly of Rindge, warned out of New Ipswich, 1791, file #2283, p1

DAVIS Simeon - formerly of Concord, warned out of New Ipswich, 1777, file #2287, p1

DAVISON Abigail (c) - warned out of Goffstown, 1793, file #3608, p1

DAVISON James (c) - warned out of Goffstown, 1793, file #3608, p1

DAVISON Lydia (c) - warned out of Goffstown, 1793, file #3608, p1

DAVISON Lydia (widow) - warned out of Goffstown, 1793, file #3608, p1

DAVISON Polly (c) - warned out of Goffstown, 1793, file #3608, p1

DAVISON William (c) - warned out of Goffstown, 1793, file #3608, p1

DAWS Isaac Ambrose - formerly of Boston, warned out of New Ipswich, 1789, file #2281, p2

DERECK William - formerly of Middleton MA, warned out of Temple, 1787, file #7060, p26

DERRY James - formerly of Temple, warned out of New Ipswich, 1786, file #2278, p6

DICKEY Trypheny - formerly of Amherst, warned out of New Boston, 1794, file #2286, p3

DICKINSOSN Persis - formerly of Harvard MA, warned out of New Ipswich, 1795, file #2288, p3

DIGS Abigail - warned out of Goffstown, 1780, file #3609, p1

DIGS Betty (c) - warned out of Goffstown, 1780, file #3609, p1

DIGS Martha (c) - warned out of Goffstown, 1780, file #3609, p1

DIGS Polly (c) - warned out of Goffstown, 1780, file #3609, p1

DIGS William - warned out of Goffstown, 1780, file #3609, p1

DIGS William (c) - warned out of Goffstown, 1780, file #3609, p1

DIKE Stephen - warned out of Goffstown, 1790, file #3609, p5

DITSON Rebecca - warned out of Goffstown, 1793, file #3608, p1

DIX Benjamin - warned out of New Ipswich, 1789, file #2281, p6

DIXON William - formerly of Mason, warned out of Temple, 1796, file #7060, p35

DODGE Ana - formerly of New Chester, warned out of Dunbarton, 1789, file #2522, p1

DODGE David (c) - formerly of New Chester, warned out of Dunbarton, 1789, file #2522, p1

DODGE George - formerly of New Boston, warned out of Temple, 1800, file #7060, p44

DODGE James - warned out of Goffstown, 1792, file #3606, p2

DODGE James - formerly of Wenham MA, warned out of New Ipswich, 1784, file #2275, p2

DODGE Jemima - formerly of Wenham MA, warned out of New Ipswich, 1784, file #2275, p2

DODGE John (c) - warned out of Goffstown, 1792, file #3606, p2

DODGE Mary (c) - formerly of Wenham MA, warned out of New Ipswich, 1784, file #2275, p2

DODGE Pennellape - formerly of Wenham MA, warned out of New Ipswich, 1784, file #2275, p2

DODGE Polley (c) - warned out of Goffstown, 1792, file #3606, p2

DODGE Polly - warned out of Goffstown, 1792, file #3606, p2

DODGE Sarah (c) - formerly of Wenham MA, warned out of New Ipswich, 1784, file #2275, p2

DODGE William & Wife - warned out of New Boston, 1788, file #2280, p1

DOLE James - warned out of Goffstown, 1791, file #3606, p3

DORSON John - formerly of Ipswich MA, warned out of Dunbarton, 1780, file #2513, p1

DORSON John (c) - formerly of Ipswich MA, warned out of Dunbarton, 1780, file #2513, p1

DORSON Mary - formerly of Ipswich MA, warned out of Dunbarton, 1780, file #2513, p1

DRURY Mehetable (widow) - formerly of Shrewsbury MA, warned out of Temple, 1786, file #7060, p22

DUDLEY Abigal (c) - warned out of New Ipswich, 1784, file #2275, p4

DUDLEY Jonathan (c) - formerly of Littleton, warned out of New Ipswich, 1784, file #2275, p4

DUDLEY Joseph (c) - formerly of Littleton, warned out of New Ipswich, 1784, file #2275, p4

DUDLEY Lydia - formerly of Littleton, warned out of New Ipswich, 1784, file #2275, p4

DUDLEY Mary (c) - formerly of Littleton, warned out of New Ipswich, 1784, file #2275, p4

DUDLEY Peter (c) - formerly of Littleton, warned out of New Ipswich, 1784, file #2275, p4

DUDLEY Stephen - formerly of Littleton, warned out of New Ipswich, 1784, file #2275, p4

DUGAL Agnes (c) - formerly of Londonderry, warned out of Dunbarton, 1784, file #2517, p2

DUGAL Allener - formerly of Londonderry, warned out of Dunbarton, 1784, file #2517, p2

DUGAL Allener (c) - formerly of Londonderry, warned out of Dunbarton, 1784, file #2517, p2

DUGAL Catherine (c) - formerly of Londonderry, warned out of Dunbarton, 1784, file #2517, p2

DUGAL James (c) - formerly of Londonderry, warned out of Dunbarton, 1784, file #2517, p2

DUGAL Nancy (c) - formerly of Londonderry, warned out of Dunbarton, 1784, file #2517, p2

DUGAL Phebe (c) - formerly of Londonderry, warned out of Dunbarton, 1784, file #2517, p2

DUGAL William - formerly of Londonderry, warned out of Dunbarton, 1784, file #2517, p1

DUNKLEE Betty - formerly of Amherst, warned out of Wilton, 1793, file #2604-C, p3

DUNKLEE Hezekiah - formerly of Amherst, warned out of Wilton, 1793, file #2604-C, p3

DUNSTER Marthe - formerly of Mason, warned out of Wilton, 1782, file #2604-E, p8

DURANT Andrew (c) - formerly of Heniker, warned out of Dearing, 1788, file #7059, p30

DURANT Anna - formerly of Heniker, warned out of Dearing, 1788, file #7059, p30

DURANT Anna Jr (c) - formerly of Heniker, warned out of Dearing, 1788, file #7059, p30

DURANT Betty - formerly of Heniker, warned out of Dearing, 1788, file #7059, p15

DURANT Elathire - formerly of Heniker, warned out of Dearing, 1788, file #7059, p15

DURANT Jonathan - formerly of Heniker, warned out of Dearing, 1788, file #7059, p30

DURANT Jonathan Jr (c) - formerly of Heniker, warned out of Dearing, 1788, file #7059, p30

DURANT Joseph (c) - formerly of Heniker, warned out of Dearing, 1788, file #7059, p30

DURANT Sarah (c) - formerly of Heniker, warned out of Dearing, 1788, file #7059, p30

DURANT Susanna (c) - formerly of Heniker, warned out of Dearing, 1788, file #7059, p30

DURKINS Elizabeth (widow) - warned out of Goffstown, 1794, file #3609, p9

DURRANT Susanna - formerly of Littleton MA, warned out of New Ipswich, 1789, file #2281, p6

DUSTON Lidy - warned out of Goffstown, 1794, file #3609, p9

DUTTEN Abigal (widow) - warned out of Goffstown, 1784, file #3608, p9

DUTTEN Polly - warned out of Goffstown, 1790, file #3607, p6

DUTTON Betty - warned out of Goffstown, 1784, file #3609, p2

DUTTON Jonathan - warned out of Goffstown, 1784, file #3609, p2

DUTTON Jonathan (c) - warned out of Goffstown, 1784, file #3609, p2

DUTTON Robert - formerly of Greenfield, warned out of Temple, 1800, file #7060, p47

DUTTON Sarah - warned out of Goffstown, 1784, file #3609, p2

DUTTON Sarah (c) - warned out of Goffstown, 1784, file #3609, p2

EASTMAN Betsey - formerly of Bath, warned out of Temple, 1793, file #7060, p36

EASTMAN Betsey - formerly of Bath, warned out of Temple, 1793, file #7060, p36

EATON Amos - formerly of Reading MA, warned out of Wilton, 1793, file #2604-C, p3

EATON Asa - formerly of Reading MA, warned out of Wilton, 1793, file #2604-C, p5

EATON Barnabas - formerly of Reading MA, warned out of Temple, 1792, file #7060, p12

EATON Deborah (c) - warned out of Goffstown, 1789, file #3607, p5

EATON Dorothy (c) - warned out of Goffstown, 1789, file #3607, p5

EATON Enoch - warned out of Goffstown, 1789, file #3607, p5

EATON Enoch (c) - warned out of Goffstown, 1789, file #3607, p5

EATON Esther - warned out of Goffstown, 1789, file #3607, p5

EATON Marg - formerly of Reading MA, warned out of Wilton, 1793, file #2604-C, p3

EDWARD Abel - warned out of New Boston, 1785, file #2276, p2

EDWARD William John - warned out of New Boston, 1785, file #2276, p2
EDWARDS Hiram - warned out of New Boston, 1785, file #2276, p2
EDWARDS Mary Ann - warned out of New Boston, 1785, file #2276, p2
ELLESCAND Richard - formerly of Leominster MA, warned out of New Ipswich, 1774, file #2268, p1
ELY Betsy (c) - warned out of Goffstown, 1789, file #3607, p5
ELY Elizabeth - warned out of Goffstown, 1789, file #3607, p5
ELY Enos (c) - warned out of Goffstown, 1789, file #3607, p5
ELY Israel - warned out of Goffstown, 1789, file #3607, p5
ELY Israel (c) - warned out of Goffstown, 1789, file #3607, p5
ELY Jacob (c) - warned out of Goffstown, 1789, file #3607, p5
ELY Jonathan (c) - warned out of Goffstown, 1789, file #3607, p5
EMERSON Abigail - warned out of Goffstown, 1790, file #3607, p6
EMERSON Abijah - formerly of Mason, warned out of New Ipswich, 1791, file #2283, p1
EMERSON Daniel (c) - formerly of Hollis, warned out of New Ipswich, 1794, file #2286, p1
EMERSON Elizabeth - formerly of Hollis, warned out of New Ipswich, 1785, file #2276, p4
EMERSON James - formerly of Hollis, warned out of New Ipswich, 1794, file #2286, p1
EMERSON John (c) - formerly of Hollis, warned out of New Ipswich, 1794, file #2286, p1
EMERSON Lydia - formerly of Hollis, warned out of New Ipswich, 1794, file #2286, p1
EMERSON Sally (widow) - formerly of Townsend MA, warned out of Temple, 1802, file #7060, p38
EMERSON Thomas - formerly of Hollis, warned out of New Ipswich, 1794, file #2286, p1
EMERSON Thomas (c) - formerly of Hollis, warned out of New Ipswich, 1794, file #2286, p1
EMERSON William (c) - formerly of Hollis, warned out of New Ipswich, 1794, file #2286, p1
EMERY Abigail - warned out of Goffstown, 1776, file #3608, p9
EMERY Amos - warned out of Goffstown, 1784, file #3608, p9
EMERY Amos - formerly of Goffstown, warned out of Dunbarton, 1789, file #2522, p4
EMERY Amos & Wife - formerly of Goffstown, warned out of Dunbarton, 1789, file #2522, p4
EMERY Caleb - warned out of Goffstown, 1776, file #3608, p9
EMERY Caleb (c) - warned out of Goffstown, 1784, file #3608, p9
EMERY Caleb (c) - formerly of Goffstown, warned out of Dunbarton, 1789, file #2522, p4
EMERY Eliphelet - warned out of Goffstown, 1780, file #3606, p9
EMERY Louis - warned out of Goffstown, 1780, file #3606, p9
EMERY Samuel (c) - formerly of Goffstown, warned out of Dunbarton, 1789, file #2522, p4

EMES Lulvercia (maid) - formerly of Holden MA, warned out of Temple, 1793, file #7060, p36

ENGALS Sarah - warned out of Goffstown, 1796, file #3607, p8

FAIRFIELD Abraham - warned out of New Boston, 1789, file #2281, p4

FAIRFIELD Barnabas (c) - warned out of New Boston, 1789, file #2281, p4

FAIRFIELD Barnabas D - warned out of New Boston, 1789, file #2281, p4

FAIRFIELD Betsy - warned out of New Boston, 1786, file #2278, p5

FAIRFIELD Charlotte - warned out of New Boston, 1786, file #2278, p5

FAIRFIELD Elizabeth (widow) - warned out of New Boston, 1790, file #2282, p2

FAIRFIELD Hannah F - warned out of New Boston, 1786, file #2278, p5

FAIRFIELD Isaac Perkins - warned out of New Boston, 1789, file #2281, p4

FAIRFIELD John - warned out of New Boston, 1786, file #2278, p5

FAIRFIELD Joseph - warned out of New Boston, 1789, file #2281, p4

FAIRFIELD Martha - warned out of New Boston, 1789, file #2281, p4

FAIRFIELD Nathaniel - warned out of New Boston, 1789, file #2281, p4

FAIRFIELD Nathaniel Jr - warned out of New Boston, 1789, file #2281, p4

FAIRFIELD Sarah - warned out of New Boston, 1789, file #2281, p4

FAIRFIELD Sarah - warned out of New Boston, 1786, file #2278, p5

FAIRFIELD Tabitha - warned out of New Boston, 1789, file #2281, p4

FANNAN Mary - formerly of Newtown, warned out of New Ipswich, 1795, file #2288, p3

FARMER Anna - warned out of Goffstown, 1782, file #3606, p7

FARMER Anna (c) - warned out of Goffstown, 1782, file #3606, p7

FARMER Isaac - formerly of Leominster MA, warned out of Temple, 1802, file #7060, p38

FARMER John (c) - warned out of Goffstown, 1782, file #3606, p7

FARMER Jonas - warned out of Goffstown, 1782, file #3606, p7

FARMER Thomas (c) - warned out of Goffstown, 1782, file #3606, p7

FARNUM Ambros (c) - formerly of Lyndeborough, warned out of Wilton, 1796, file #2604-D, p5

FARNUM Betsey (c) - formerly of Lyndeborough, warned out of Wilton, 1796, file #2604-D, p5

FARNUM Molley - formerly of Lyndeborough, warned out of Wilton, 1796, file #2604-D, p5

FARNUM Rebecca - formerly of Andover MA, warned out of Wilton, 1784, file #2604-E, p7

FARNUM Richard - formerly of Lyndeborough, warned out of Wilton, 1796, file #2604-D, p5

FARR Abigail - formerly of Littleton, warned out of New Ipswich, 1771, file #2265, p1

FARR Betsey - formerly of Peterboro Slip, warned out of New Ipswich, 1770, file #2265, p2

FARR Eunice - formerly of Westford MA, warned out of New Ipswich, 1777, file #2287, p1

FARR Levie - formerly of Littleton MA, warned out of New Ipswich, 1777, file #2287, p1

FARR Martha (c) - formerly of Westford MA, warned out of New Ipswich, 1771, file #2265, p1

FARR Nathaniel - formerly of Littleton, warned out of New Ipswich, 1771, file #2265, p1

FARRAR Lydia (c) - formerly of Concord MA, warned out of Temple, 1786, file #7060, p22

FARRAR Oliver & Wife - formerly of Concord MA, warned out of Temple, 1786, file #7060, p22

FARRAR Oliver (c) - formerly of Concord MA, warned out of Temple, 1786, file #7060, p22

FARRAR Rebecca (c) - formerly of Concord MA, warned out of Temple, 1786, file #7060, p22

FARRAR Rebecca (widow) - formerly of Concord MA, warned out of Temple, 1786, file #7060, p22

FARRAR Simeon (c) - formerly of Concord MA, warned out of Temple, 1786, file #7060, p22

FARRINGTON Phebe - formerly of Andover MA, warned out of Wilton, 1784, file #2604-D, p2

FARRINGTON Anna (c) - formerly of Andover MA, warned out of Wilton, 1774, file #2604-C, p2

FARRINGTON Betty (c) - formerly of Andover MA, warned out of Wilton, 1784, file #2604-D, p2

FARRINGTON Daniel (c) - formerly of Andover MA, warned out of Wilton, 1774, file #2604-C, p2

FARRINGTON John - formerly of Andover MA, warned out of Wilton, 1784, file #2604-D, p2

FARRINGTON John (c) - formerly of Andover MA, warned out of Wilton, 1784, file #2604-D, p2

FARRINGTON Phebe (c) - formerly of Andover MA, warned out of Wilton, 1784, file #2604-D, p2

FARRINGTON Phineas & wife - formerly of Andover MA, warned out of Wilton, 1774, file #2604-C, p2

FARRINGTON Putnam (c) - formerly of Andover MA, warned out of Wilton, 1774, file #2604-C, p2

FARRINGTON Sally (c) - formerly of Andover MA, warned out of Wilton, 1784, file #2604-D, p2

FARWELL Levy - formerly of Washington, warned out of New Ipswich, 1789, file #2281, p2

FARWELL Abel - formerly of Shirley MA, warned out of Temple, 1801, file #7060, p56

FARWELL Darus - formerly of Shirley MA, warned out of Temple, 1803, file #7060, p48

FARWELL John - formerly of Fitsburgh MA, warned out of New Ipswich, ___, file #2286, p1

FELT Abner - formerly of Temple, warned out of Wilton, 1784, file #2604-C, p6

FELT Abner (c) - formerly of New Ipswich, warned out of Temple, 1782, file #7060, p60

FELT Edward (c) - formerly of Temple, warned out of Wilton, 1784, file #2604-C, p6

FELT Mary - formerly of Temple, warned out of Wilton, 1784, file #2604-C, p6

FELT Mary - formerly of Dedham, warned out of New Ipswich, 1780, file #2271, p2

FELT Mary (c) - formerly of New Ipswich, warned out of Temple, 1782, file #7060, p60

FELT Mary (widow) - formerly of New Ipswich, warned out of Temple, 1782, file #7060, p60

FELT Mary (widow) - formerly of Temple, warned out of Wilton, 1784, file #2604-C, p6

FELT Molley (c) - formerly of Temple, warned out of Wilton, 1784, file #2604-C, p6

FELT Moses - formerly of Dedham, warned out of New Ipswich, 1780, file #2271, p2

FELTON Rebeckah - formerly of Peterboro Slip, warned out of Temple, 1782, file #7060, p60

FIANEE Joseph & Wife - formerly of Londonderry, warned out of Goffstown, 1776, file #3608, p4

FISH Anna - formerly of Mason, warned out of Temple, 1801, file #7060, p56

FISH Levi - formerly of Mason, warned out of Temple, 1792, file #7060, p39

FISH Nathan - formerly of Lyndeborough, warned out of Temple, 1795, file #7060, p52

FISH Samuel - formerly of Mason, warned out of Temple, 1801, file #7060, p56

FISHER Levi - formerly of Ashburnham MA, warned out of New Ipswich, 1782, file #2273, p2

FISHER Rebeckah - formerly of Ashburnham MA, warned out of New Ipswich, 1782, file #2273, p2

FISHER Samuel (c) - formerly of Ashburnham MA, warned out of New Ipswich, 1782, file #2273, p2

FISK Dorothy (widow) - formerly of Peterborough, warned out of Temple, 1793, file #7060, p36

FISK Ebenr - formerly of Peterborough, warned out of Temple, 1793, file #7060, p36

FISK Sarah - formerly of Pepperell MA, warned out of Temple, 1789, file #7060, p32

FITCH Asa (c) - formerly of Littleton MA, warned out of Temple, 1801, file #7060, p56

FITCH Lot (c) - formerly of Littleton MA, warned out of Temple, 1801, file #7060, p56

FITCH Daniel (c) - formerly of Littleton MA, warned out of Temple, 1801, file #7060, p56

FITCH Eli (c) - formerly of Littleton MA, warned out of Temple, 1801, file #7060, p56

FITCH Frederick - formerly of Littleton MA, warned out of Temple, 1801, file #7060, p56

FITCH Lot - formerly of Littleton MA, warned out of Temple, 1801, file #7060, p56

FITCH Pamelia - formerly of Littleton MA, warned out of Temple, 1801, file #7060, p56

FITCH Pamelia (c) - formerly of Littleton MA, warned out of Temple, 1801, file #7060, p56

FLAGG Margaret - formerly of Marlborough, warned out of New Ipswich, 1779, file #2270, p4

FLANDERS David (c) - warned out of Goffstown, 1789, file #3607, p4

FLANDERS Ezekiel (c) - warned out of Goffstown, 1789, file #3607, p4

FLANDERS Mary (c) - warned out of Goffstown, 1789, file #3607, p4

FLANDERS Samuel (c) - warned out of Goffstown, 1789, file #3607, p4

FLANDERS Sarah - warned out of Goffstown, 1789, file #3607, p4

FLANDERS Stephen - warned out of Goffstown, 1789, file #3607, p4

FLETCHER Aaron (c) - formerly of Westford MA, warned out of New Ipswich, 1792, file #2284, p1

FLETCHER Beulah - formerly of Chelmsford MA, warned out of Temple, 1791, file #7060, p55

FLETCHER Beulah - warned out of Temple, 1790, file #7060, p49

FLETCHER Deborah - formerly of Westford MA, warned out of New Ipswich, 1792, file #2284, p1

FLETCHER Deborah (c) - formerly of Westford MA, warned out of New Ipswich, 1792, file #2284, p1

FLETCHER Ephraim (c) - warned out of Temple, 1790, file #7060, p49

FLETCHER Ephraim (c) - formerly of Chelmsford MA, warned out of Temple, 1791, file #7060, p55

FLETCHER Esther - formerly of New Ipswich, warned out of Temple, 1803, file #7060, p48

FLETCHER Henry - formerly of Westford MA, warned out of New Ipswich, 1792, file #2284, p1

FLETCHER Henry (c) - formerly of Westford MA, warned out of New Ipswich, 1792, file #2284, p1

FLETCHER Hepzbeth (c) - warned out of Temple, 1790, file #7060, p49

FLETCHER Ichabod (c) - warned out of Temple, 1790, file #7060, p49

FLETCHER Isaac (c) - formerly of Westford MA, warned out of New Ipswich, 1792, file #2284, p1

FLETCHER Jeremiah - formerly of New Canaan ME, warned out of Temple, 1800, file #7060, p44

FLETCHER John - formerly of Groton, warned out of New Ipswich, 1785, file #2276, p6

FLETCHER Mary - formerly of New Ipswich, warned out of Temple, 1802, file #7060, p38

FLETCHER Moses (c) - formerly of Westford MA, warned out of New Ipswich, 1792, file #2284, p1

FLETCHER Peter - formerly of Littleton MA, warned out of New Ipswich, 1789, file #2281, p6

FLETCHER Polly (c) - formerly of Groton, warned out of New Ipswich, 1785, file #2276, p6

FLETCHER Reuben (c) - formerly of Westford MA, warned out of New Ipswich, 1792, file #2284, p1

FLETCHER Samuel - warned out of Temple, 1790, file #7060, p49

FLETCHER Samuel - formerly of Chelmsford MA, warned out of Temple, 1791, file #7060, p55

FLETCHER Samuel (c) - formerly of Chelmsford MA, warned out of Temple, 1791, file #7060, p55

FLETCHER Timothy (c) - formerly of Groton, warned out of New Ipswich, 1785, file #2276, p6

FLETCHER William (c) - formerly of Westford MA, warned out of New Ipswich, 1792, file #2284, p1

FLINT Phebe - formerly of Reading MA, warned out of Wilton, 1784, file #2604-E, p7

FLOOD Sally - formerly of Mason, warned out of New Ipswich, 1794, file #2286, p1

FOBES Seth - formerly of Hanover, warned out of Temple, 1796, file #7060, p35

FOOT Isaac - warned out of New Boston, 1792, file #2285, p1

FOOT Merium - warned out of New Boston, 1792, file #2285, p1

FOOT Unis - warned out of New Boston, 1792, file #2285, p1

FORTIER Andrew - formerly of Bedford, warned out of Dunbarton, 1786, file #2519, p3

FORTIER James (c) - formerly of Bedford, warned out of Dunbarton, 1786, file #2519, p3

FORTIER Nathan (c) - formerly of Bedford, warned out of Dunbarton, 1786, file #2519, p3

FORTIER Sarah (c) - formerly of Bedford, warned out of Dunbarton, 1786, file #2519, p3

FORTIER Suzanah - formerly of Bedford, warned out of Dunbarton, 1786, file #2519, p3

FOSTER Abel - formerly of Raby, warned out of Temple, 1795, file #7060, p50

FOSTER Abel (c) - formerly of Raby, warned out of Temple, 1795, file #7060, p50

FOSTER Benjamin (c) - formerly of Raby, warned out of Temple, 1795, file #7060, p50

FOSTER Betty (c) - formerly of Raby, warned out of Temple, 1795, file #7060, p50

FOSTER Hannah (c) - formerly of Raby, warned out of Temple, 1795, file #7060, p50

FOSTER Hannah (widow) - formerly of Londonderry, warned out of Dunbarton, 1792, file #2525, p4

FOSTER Israel - warned out of New Boston, 1790, file #2282, p2

FOSTER Leonard (c) - formerly of Raby, warned out of Temple, 1795, file #7060, p50

FOSTER Lucy (c) - formerly of Raby, warned out of Temple, 1795, file #7060, p50

FOSTER Mary - formerly of Raby, warned out of Temple, 1795, file #7060, p50

FOSTER Polley (c) - formerly of Raby, warned out of Temple, 1795, file #7060, p50

FOUNDERLING Joseph - formerly of Dunstable, warned out of Wilton, 1774, file #2604, p2

FOWEL Esther - formerly of Greenfield, warned out of Temple, 1799, file #7060, p45

FOX Abigail (widow) - formerly of Littleton MA, warned out of New Ipswich, 1781, file #2272, p1

FRENCH Hannah C - formerly of Merrimack, warned out of Temple, 1782, file #7060, p60

FRENCH Isaac Barran - formerly of Merrimack, warned out of Temple, 1782, file #7060, p60

FRENCH James - warned out of New Ipswich, 1785, file #2276, p5

FRENCH Sarah - formerly of Acton MA, warned out of New Ipswich, 1791, file #2283, p2

FRENCH Sarah - formerly of Merrimack, warned out of Temple, 1782, file #7060, p60

FREY Nathan - formerly of Jaffrey, warned out of New Ipswich, 1785, file #2278, p6

FROST Abiel - formerly of Wilton, warned out of Temple, 1793, file #7060, p36

FROST Abiel - formerly of Tewksbury MA, warned out of Wilton, 1790, file #2604-D, p3

FROST Abigail - warned out of Goffstown, 1777, file #3608, p7

FROST Abigail (c) - formerly of Goffstown, warned out of Dunbarton, 1779, file #2512, p3

FROST Abrm (c) - warned out of Goffstown, 1777, file #3608, p7

FROST Isaac (c) - formerly of Goffstown, warned out of Dunbarton, 1779, file #2512, p3

FROST Isaac (c) - warned out of Goffstown, 1777, file #3608, p7

FROST Jacob (c) - warned out of Goffstown, 1777, file #3608, p7

FROST Jacob (c) - formerly of Goffstown, warned out of Dunbarton, 1779, file #2512, p3

FROST Joseph - formerly of Cambridge, warned out of New Ipswich, 1785, file #2276, p6

FROST Martha - formerly of Goffstown, warned out of Dunbarton, 1779, file #2512, p3

FROST Martha (c) - warned out of Goffstown, 1777, file #3608, p7

FROST Mary - formerly of Cambridge, warned out of New Ipswich, 1785, file #2276, p6

FROST Samuel - warned out of Goffstown, 1777, file #3608, p7

FROST Samuel - formerly of Goffstown, warned out of Dunbarton, 1779, file #2512, p3

FROST Samuel Jr (c) - formerly of Goffstown, warned out of Dunbarton, 1779, file #2512, p3

FULLER Ames - formerly of Ashby, warned out of New Ipswich, 1785, file #2276, p6

FULLER David - warned out of New Ipswich, 1773, file #2267, p2

FULTON James - warned out of Goffstown, 1790, file #3609, p6

FURBANKS Eph'm - formerly of Sterlin MA, warned out of New Ipswich, 1794, file #2286, p1

FURNER Ezra - formerly of Jaffrey, warned out of New Ipswich, 1785, file #2276, p6

GARDNER Aaron - warned out of Goffstown, 1793, file #3609, p8

GARDNER Seath (sic) - warned out of Goffstown, 1793, file #3609, p8

GARDNER Abel - formerly of Leominster MA, warned out of Temple, 1800, file #7060, p47

GARDNER Abel (c) - formerly of Leominster MA, warned out of Temple, 1800, file #7060, p47

GARDNER Adam (sic) - warned out of Goffstown, 1793, file #3609, p8

GARDNER Betty (c) - formerly of Leominster MA, warned out of Temple, 1800, file #7060, p47

GARDNER Bila (c) - formerly of Leominster MA, warned out of Temple, 1800, file #7060, p47

GARDNER Elizabeth - warned out of Goffstown, 1793, file #3609, p8

GARDNER Elizabeth (c) - warned out of Goffstown, 1793, file #3609, p8

GARDNER Ezekiel - warned out of Goffstown, 1793, file #3609, p8

GARDNER Joseph (sic) - warned out of Goffstown, 1793, file #3609, p8

GARDNER Louisann (c) - formerly of Leominster MA, warned out of Temple, 1800, file #7060, p47

GARDNER Nancy (c) - formerly of Leominster MA, warned out of Temple, 1800, file #7060, p47

GARDNER Penelop (c) - formerly of Leominster MA, warned out of Temple, 1800, file #7060, p47

GARDNER Polly - warned out of Goffstown, 1788, file #3608, p8

GARDNER Seath (sic) - warned out of Goffstown, 1793, file #3609, p8

GARDNER Susanna - formerly of Leominster MA, warned out of Temple, 1800, file #7060, p47

GARLING John - warned out of Goffstown, 1790, file #3609, p5

GEORGE Asa (c) - warned out of Goffstown, 1773, file #3608, p2

GEORGE Clideaas (c) - warned out of Goffstown, 1773, file #3608, p2

GEORGE Levina (c) - warned out of Goffstown, 1773, file #3608, p2

GEORGE Merrial - warned out of Goffstown, 1773, file #3608, p2

GEORGE Moses - warned out of Goffstown, 1773, file #3608, p2

GEORGE Naomah (c) - warned out of Goffstown, 1773, file #3608, p2

GEORGE Stephen - warned out of Goffstown, 1773, file #3608, p2

GEORGE Stephen (c) - warned out of Goffstown, 1773, file #3608, p2

GIBBS Daniel & Wife - formerly of MA, warned out of New Ipswich, 1792, file #2284, p1

GIBBS Abel (c) - formerly of MA, warned out of New Ipswich, 1792, file #2284, p1

GIBBS Asa (c) - formerly of MA, warned out of New Ipswich, 1792, file #2284, p1

GIBBS Polly (c) - formerly of MA, warned out of New Ipswich, 1792, file #2284, p1

GIBS Joseph - formerly of Peterboro Slip, warned out of Temple, 1782, file #7060, p60

GIBS Joseph (c) - formerly of Peterboro Slip, warned out of Temple, 1782, file #7060, p60

GIBS Roda - formerly of Peterboro Slip, warned out of Temple, 1782, file #7060, p60

GIDEON Abigal - formerly of Ashbraham MA, warned out of New Boston, 1795, file #2288, p1

GIDEON Prudence - formerly of Ashbraham MA, warned out of New Boston, 1795, file #2288, p1

GIFFIN Agnes - formerly of Bedford, warned out of Dearing, 1786, file #7059, p10

GIFFIN Robert (Mr) - formerly of Bedford, warned out of Dearing, 1786, file #7059, p10

GILBERT Mary - formerly of Littleton, warned out of New Ipswich, 1790, file #2282, p1

GILES Daniel (c) - formerly of Mason, warned out of New Ipswich, 1792, file #2284, p3

GILES Elizabeth - warned out of Dunbarton, 1792, file #2525, p3

GILES Joel (c) - formerly of Mason, warned out of New Ipswich, 1792, file #2284, p3

GILES Joseph - formerly of Mason, warned out of New Ipswich, 1792, file #2284, p3

GILES Mary - formerly of Mason, warned out of New Ipswich, 1792, file #2284, p3

GILES Mary (c) - formerly of Mason, warned out of New Ipswich, 1792, file #2284, p3

GILES Rebecah (c) - formerly of Mason, warned out of New Ipswich, 1792, file #2284, p3

GILES Rebecca - formerly of Mason, warned out of New Ipswich, 1791, file #2283, p1

GILES Sarah (c) - formerly of Mason, warned out of New Ipswich, 1792, file #2284, p3

GILLS Ebenezer - formerly of Billerica MA, warned out of Wilton, 1782, file #2604-E, p4

GLOVER Lucy - warned out of Goffstown, 1792, file #3606, p2

GOFFE Benjamin (c) - warned out of Goffstown, 1788, file #3608, p8

GOFFE Lydia (c) - warned out of Goffstown, 1788, file #3608, p8

GOFFE Marcy - warned out of Goffstown, 1788, file #3608, p8

GOFFE Samuel - warned out of Goffstown, 1788, file #3608, p8

GOFFE Sarah (c) - warned out of Goffstown, 1788, file #3608, p8

GOLDSMITH Hannah - formerly of Ipswich MA, warned out of Wilton, 1774, file #2604-C, p2

GOLDSMITH William - formerly of Ipswich MA, warned out of Wilton, 1774, file #2604-C, p2

GOODEN Mehitabel - formerly of Sudbury MA, warned out of Dearing, 1785, file #7059, p23

GOODEN Sarah (c) - formerly of Sudbury MA, warned out of Dearing, 1785, file #7059, p23

GOODEN Thaddeus - formerly of Sudbury MA, warned out of Dearing, 1785, file #7059, p23

GOODHUE Jean - warned out of Goffstown, 1793, file #3608, p1

GOODHUE Joseph - warned out of Goffstown, 1793, file #3608, p1

GOODRIDGE Rebecah - formerly of Winchendon MA, warned out of Wilton, 1784, file #2604-E, p5

GOOHUE Betsy (c) - warned out of New Boston, 1790, file #2282, p2

GOOHUE Ebenezer - warned out of New Boston, 1790, file #2282, p2

GOOHUE Ebenezer Jr (c) - warned out of New Boston, 1790, file #2282, p2

GOOHUE Samuel (c) - warned out of New Boston, 1790, file #2282, p2

GOOHUE Sarah - warned out of New Boston, 1790, file #2282, p2

GOOHUE Sarah Jr (c) - warned out of New Boston, 1790, file #2282, p2

GOSS Ebenezer H - warned out of New Ipswich, 1772, file #2266, p3

GOSS Gustavus Adolfus (c) - warned out of New Ipswich, 1772, file #2266, p3

GOSS Mary - warned out of New Ipswich, 1772, file #2266, p3

GOSS Samuel (a Poor Child) - formerly of Goffstown, warned out of Dunbarton, 1772, file #2511, p1

GOULD Sibel - formerly of Mason, warned out of Temple, 1795, file #7060, p52

GOURING Prisilla - formerly of Keene, warned out of New Ipswich, 1792, file #2284, p1

GOVE Swett - warned out of Goffstown, 1789, file #3609, p4

GRACE David (c) - formerly of Hollis, warned out of New Ipswich, 1783, file #2274, p1

GRACE Mary (c) - formerly of Hollis, warned out of New Ipswich, 1783, file #2274, p1

GRACE Mehitable - formerly of Hollis, warned out of New Ipswich, 1783, file #2274, p1

GRACE Sarah (c) - formerly of Hollis, warned out of New Ipswich, 1783, file #2274, p1

GRAGG Mary (widow) - warned out of New Boston, 1785, file #2276, p1

GRANT Baulah - formerly of Lunenburgh, warned out of Wilton, 1772, file #2604, p1

GRANT Eliphalet - formerly of Lunenburgh, warned out of Wilton, 1772, file #2604, p1

GRANT John - formerly of Lunenburgh, warned out of Wilton, 1772, file #2604, p1

GRAVES Samuel - warned out of New Boston, 1790, file #2282, p2

GRAY Amity - formerly of Fitsburg MA, warned out of New Ipswich, 1791, file #2283, p2

GREAR David - warned out of Goffstown, 1784, file #3608, p9

GREAR Ephraim (c) - warned out of Goffstown, 1784, file #3608, p9

GREAR John (c) - warned out of Goffstown, 1784, file #3608, p9

GREAR Richard (c) - warned out of Goffstown, 1784, file #3608, p9

GREAR Sarah - warned out of Goffstown, 1784, file #3608, p9

GREAR Sarah (c) - warned out of Goffstown, 1784, file #3608, p9

GREAR Thomas? (c) - warned out of Goffstown, 1784, file #3608, p9

GREELE Olive - formerly of Nottingham West, warned out of Wilton, 1783, file #2604-E, p11

GREELE Samuel Jr - formerly of Nottingham West, warned out of Wilton, 1783, file #2604-E, p11

GREELEY Samuel - formerly of Wilton, warned out of Temple, 1795, file #7060, p52

GREEN James (c) - formerly of Londonderry, warned out of Dunbarton, 1779, file #2512, p2

GREEN Martha - formerly of Londonderry, warned out of Dunbarton, 1779, file #2512, p2

GREEN Susannah - formerly of Temple, warned out of New Ipswich, 1791, file #2283, p1

GREEN Susannah - formerly of Pepperell, warned out of Temple, 1787, file #7060, p26

GREENLEAF Betty - formerly of Heniker, warned out of Dearing, 1788, file #7059, p15

GREENLEAF Daniel - formerly of Haverhill, warned out of Goffstown, 1791, file #3609, p7

GREENLEAF Elias - formerly of Heniker, warned out of Dearing, 1788, file #7059, p15

GREER Benjamin - formerly of Goffstown, warned out of New Boston, 1795, file #2288, p1

GREER David - formerly of Goffstown, warned out of New Boston, 1795, file #2288, p1

GREER Eaton - formerly of Goffstown, warned out of New Boston, 1795, file #2288, p1

GREER John - formerly of Goffstown, warned out of New Boston, 1795, file #2288, p1

GREER Rachel - formerly of Goffstown, warned out of New Boston, 1795, file #2288, p1

GREER Richard - formerly of Goffstown, warned out of New Boston, 1795, file #2288, p1

GREER Susanna - formerly of Goffstown, warned out of New Boston, 1795, file #2288, p1

GRIFFIN Elizabeth - formerly of Merrimack, warned out of Dunbarton, 1781, file #2514, p1

GRIFFIN Hannah - warned out of New Boston, 1776, file #2264, p1

GUILD Fanny - formerly of Swanzey, warned out of New Ipswich, 1788, file #2280, p3

GUN Eunas - warned out of New Boston, 1785, file #2276, p3

GUN Samuel - warned out of New Boston, 1785, file #2276, p3

HACKIT Hannah - warned out of Goffstown, 1787, file #3607, p2

HADLOCK Elizabeth - warned out of Goffstown, 1793, file #3608, p1

HAGAR Dinah - formerly of Northboro MA, warned out of Temple, 1800, file #7060, p44

HALE Hannah - formerly of Amherst, warned out of Wilton, 1790, file #2604-D, p3

HALL Butler - formerly of Ashburnham MA, warned out of New Ipswich, 1789, file #2281, p1

HALL Jennet (widow) - warned out of Dunbarton, 1788, file #2521, p5

HAM Susanna - warned out of New Ipswich, 1772, file #2266, p3

HAMBLET David - formerly of Pelham, warned out of Wilton, 1783, file #2604-D, p1

HARDY Esther - warned out of Goffstown, 1790, file #3609, p5

HARDY Joel - formerly of Mount Holley VT, warned out of Temple, 1801, file #7060, p56

HAROD Experiance - warned out of New Boston, 1787, file #2279, p9

HARRAMAN Marey - warned out of Goffstown, 1782, file #3606, p7

HARRIMAN Esther (c) - warned out of Goffstown, 1790, file #3609, p5

HARRIMAN James (c) - warned out of Goffstown, 1790, file #3609, p5

HARRIMAN Lydia - warned out of Goffstown, 1790, file #3609, p5

HARRIMAN Peter - warned out of Goffstown, 1790, file #3609, p5

HARRIMAN Peter (c) - warned out of Goffstown, 1790, file #3609, p5

HARRIMAN Sarah (c) - warned out of Goffstown, 1790, file #3609, p5

HARRIMAN Warren (c) - warned out of Goffstown, 1790, file #3609, p5

HARRIS James (grandchild) - formerly of Ware, warned out of Dearing, 1795, file #7059, p9

HARRIS Mary - formerly of Groton MA, warned out of New Ipswich, 1794, file #2286, p2

HARRIS Oliver - formerly of Groton MA, warned out of New Ipswich, 1794, file #2286, p2

HARRIS Oliver (c) - formerly of Groton MA, warned out of New Ipswich, 1794, file #2286, p2

HARRIS Ruth (c) - formerly of Groton MA, warned out of New Ipswich, 1794, file #2286, p2

HART Lewis (c) - formerly of Francestown, warned out of Dearing, 1791, file #7059, p18

HART Molly (Mary) - formerly of Francestown, warned out of Dearing, 1791, file #7059, p18

HART Seth - formerly of Francestown, warned out of Dearing, 1791, file #7059, p18

HART William - warned out of Goffstown, 1789, file #3607, p4

HARTHORN Esther - formerly of Peterboro, warned out of Temple, 1786, file #7060, p13

HARTSHORN Jonathan - formerly of Andover MA, warned out of Wilton, 1774, file #2604-C, p2

HARTSHORN Jonathan Lt - formerly of Wilton, warned out of Wilton, 1791, file #2604-D, p6

HARTSHORN Nathaniel - formerly of Marblehead MA, warned out of Wilton, 1791, file #2604-D, p6

HARTSHORN Oliver - formerly of MA, warned out of Wilton, 1780, file #2604-E, p6

HARTSHORN Polly (c) - formerly of Marblehead MA, warned out of Wilton, 1791, file #2604-D, p6

HARTSHORN Samuel - formerly of Wilton, warned out of Wilton, 1791, file #2604-D, p6

HARTSHORN Tamara (c) - formerly of Marblehead MA, warned out of Wilton, 1791, file #2604-D, p6

HARTSHORN Thomas - formerly of MA, warned out of Wilton, 1780, file #2604-E, p6

HARTWELL Sara (sic) - formerly of Lunenburgh MA, warned out of Wilton, 1774, file #2604-C, p2

HARTWICK Adam (c) - formerly of Boston MA, warned out of Temple, 1781, file #7060, p15

HARTWICK Catherine (c) - formerly of Boston MA, warned out of Temple, 1781, file #7060, p15

HARTWICK Catharine (c) - formerly of Boston MA, warned out of Temple, 1781, file #7060, p15

HARTWICK Elizabeth (c) - formerly of Boston MA, warned out of Temple, 1781, file #7060, p15

HARTWICK Elizabeth (c) - formerly of Boston MA, warned out of Temple, 1781, file #7060, p15

HARTWICK Hannah (c) - formerly of Boston MA, warned out of Temple, 1781, file #7060, p15

HARTWICK John & Wife - formerly of Boston MA, warned out of Temple, 1781, file #7060, p15

HARTWICK John Jr (c) - formerly of Boston MA, warned out of Temple, 1781, file #7060, p15

HARTWICK Lucrecia (c) - formerly of Boston MA, warned out of Temple, 1784, file #7060, p15

HARTWICK Lucrecia (c) - formerly of Boston MA, warned out of Temple, 1781, file #7060, p15

HASELTINE David (c) - formerly of Salem, warned out of Wilton, 1774, file #2604-C, p2

HASELTINE Elizabeth - formerly of Salem, warned out of Wilton, 1774, file #2604-C, p2

HASELTINE Follensbey (c) - formerly of Salem, warned out of Wilton, 1774, file #2604-C, p2

HASELTINE Hannah (c) - formerly of Salem, warned out of Wilton, 1774, file #2604-C, p2

HASELTINE John (c) - formerly of Salem, warned out of Wilton, 1774, file #2604-C, p2

HASELTINE Nathan - formerly of Salem, warned out of Wilton, 1774, file #2604-C, p2

HASELTINE Nathan Jr - formerly of New Salem, warned out of Wilton, 1774, file #2604-D, p8

HASELTINE Sarah - formerly of New Salem, warned out of Wilton, 1774, file #2604-D, p8

HASELTINE Susannah (c) - formerly of Salem, warned out of Wilton, 1774, file #2604-C, p2

HASKEL Joseph - formerly of Mason, warned out of Temple, 1799, file #7060, p46

HASKIN Abigail - formerly of Northborough MA, warned out of Wilton, 1774, file #2604-D, p8

HASKIN Abigail (c) - formerly of Northborough MA, warned out of Wilton, 1774, file #2604-D, p8

HASKIN Lewis (c) - formerly of Northborough MA, warned out of Wilton, 1774, file #2604-D, p8

HASKIN Marg (c) - formerly of Northborough MA, warned out of Wilton, 1774, file #2604-D, p8

HASKIN Martha (c) - formerly of Northborough MA, warned out of Wilton, 1774, file #2604-D, p8

HASKIN William - formerly of Northborough MA, warned out of Wilton, 1774, file #2604-D, p8

HASKIN William (c) - formerly of Northborough MA, warned out of Wilton, 1774, file #2604-D, p8

HASKINS Mary - formerly of Wilton, warned out of Temple, 1782, file #7060, p31

HASKINS Polly - formerly of Wilton, warned out of Temple, 1782, file #7060, p31

HAVEN Martin - formerly of Framingham MA, warned out of New Ipswich, 1795, file #2288, p2

HAVEN Milley - formerly of Framingham MA, warned out of New Ipswich, 1795, file #2288, p2

HAWKINS George Washington - formerly of Reading VT, warned out of Temple, 1795, file #7060, p52

HAYENS Elinor - formerly of Ashby MA, warned out of Temple, 1784, file #7060, p19

HAYENS Hepsabeth - formerly of Ashby MA, warned out of Temple, 1784, file #7060, p19

HAYENS Joshua - formerly of Ashby MA, warned out of Temple, 1784, file #7060, p19

HAZELTINE Daniel - formerly of Londonderry, warned out of Dunbarton, 1789, file #2523, p2

HAZEN Amos - formerly of Groton MA, warned out of Temple, 1794, file #7060, p58

HAZEN Benjamin - formerly of Groton MA, warned out of Temple, 1795, file #7060, p50

HAZEN Lydia - formerly of Groton MA, warned out of Temple, 1794, file #7060, p58

HEAD James - warned out of Dunbarton, 1789, file #2523, p1

HEALD Betty (c) - formerly of Sterling MA, warned out of New Ipswich, 1787, file #2279, p2

HEALD Elizabeth (c) - formerly of Sterling MA, warned out of New Ipswich, 1787, file #2279, p2

HEALD Ephraim Mr - formerly of Sterling MA, warned out of New Ipswich, 1787, file #2279, p2

HEALD Hannah - formerly of Sterling MA, warned out of New Ipswich, 1787, file #2279, p2

HEALD John (c) - formerly of Sterling MA, warned out of New Ipswich, 1787, file #2279, p2

HEALD Nathan (c) - formerly of Sterling MA, warned out of New Ipswich, 1787, file #2279, p2

HEART Abel - warned out of New Boston, 1790, file #2282, p3

HEART Betsey (c) - warned out of New Boston, 1790, file #2282, p3

HEART Charles (c) - warned out of New Boston, 1790, file #2282, p3

HEART Elizabeth (c) - warned out of New Boston, 1790, file #2282, p3

HEART Mary (c) - warned out of New Boston, 1790, file #2282, p3

HEART Sarah (c) - warned out of New Boston, 1790, file #2282, p3

HEART William - warned out of New Boston, 1790, file #2282, p3

HEART William (c) - warned out of New Boston, 1790, file #2282, p3

HEART William Jr - warned out of New Boston, 1790, file #2282, p3

HENRY Betsey - formerly of Lunenburgh MA, warned out of New Ipswich, 1794, file #2286, p2

HENRY John - warned out of New Boston, 1790, file #2282, p3

HENRY Margrett (c) - warned out of New Boston, 1790, file #2282, p3

HENRY Martha - warned out of New Boston, 1790, file #2282, p3

HENRY Martha Jr (c) - warned out of New Boston, 1790, file #2282, p3

HENRY William (c) - warned out of New Boston, 1790, file #2282, p3

HERRICK Betsy A - warned out of New Boston, 1786, file #2278, p5

HERRICK Charles - formerly of Ashby MA, warned out of New Ipswich, 1789, file #2281, p2

HERRICK Daniel - warned out of New Boston, 1786, file #2278, p5

HERRICK Hannah - warned out of New Boston, 1786, file #2278, p5

HERRICK Joanana - warned out of New Boston, 1786, file #2278, p5

HERRICK Jonathan - warned out of New Boston, 1786, file #2278, p5

HERRICK Joseph - warned out of New Boston, 1786, file #2278, p5

HERRICK Polly - warned out of New Boston, 1786, file #2278, p5

HERRICK Sarah - warned out of New Boston, 1786, file #2278, p5

HOAGE Andrew - formerly of Bow, warned out of Dunbarton, 1784, file #2517, p6

HOAGE Anna (c) - formerly of Bow, warned out of Dunbarton, 1784, file #2517, p6

HOAGE Lucy (c) - formerly of Bow, warned out of Dunbarton, 1784, file #2517, p6

HOAGE Rebeccah - formerly of Bow, warned out of Dunbarton, 1784, file #2517, p6

HOAGE Rebeccah (c) - formerly of Bow, warned out of Dunbarton, 1784, file #2517, p6

HOAGE Unnamed Child (c) - formerly of Bow, warned out of Dunbarton, 1784, file #2517, p6

HOAR Betty - formerly of Lancaster MA, warned out of New Ipswich, 1788, file #2280, p3

HODGMAN Oliver - formerly of Ashby MA, warned out of Temple, 1787, file #7060, p26

HOGG Abigail (c) - formerly of Ware, warned out of Dearing, 1786, file #7059, p2

HOGG Abigail (c) - formerly of Derring, warned out of Dunbarton, 1786, file #2519, p1

HOGG Agnes (c) - formerly of Weare, warned out of Dunbarton, 1783, file #2516, p3

HOGG Alenor (c) - formerly of Weare, warned out of Dunbarton, 1783, file #2516, p3

HOGG Alenor - formerly of Weare, warned out of Dunbarton, 1783, file #2516, p3

HOGG Betsey (c) - formerly of Weare, warned out of Dunbarton, 1783, file #2516, p3

HOGG Dilley (c) - formerly of Ware, warned out of Dearing, 1786, file #7059, p2

HOGG Easter - warned out of Dunbarton, 1783, file #2516, p1

HOGG Eleanor - warned out of Dunbarton, 1790, file #2523, p7

HOGG Eleanor (c) - warned out of Dunbarton, 1790, file #2523, p7

HOGG Elizabeth - formerly of Weare, warned out of Dunbarton, 1786, file #2519, p5

HOGG Elizabeth (c) - warned out of Dunbarton, 1790, file #2523, p7

HOGG George - formerly of Derring, warned out of Dunbarton, 1786, file #2519, p1

HOGG Hannah (c) - warned out of Dunbarton, 1790, file #2523, p7

HOGG Hannah (c) - formerly of Weare, warned out of Dunbarton, 1783, file #2516, p3

HOGG Harvey (c) - formerly of Ware, warned out of Dearing, 1786, file #7059, p2

HOGG James (c) - formerly of Weare, warned out of Dunbarton, 1783, file #2516, p3

HOGG Margaret (c) - formerly of Derring, warned out of Dunbarton, 1786, file #2519, p1

HOGG Mary - formerly of Derring, warned out of Dunbarton, 1786, file #2519, p1

HOGG Mary (c) - formerly of Derring, warned out of Dunbarton, 1786, file #2519, p1

HOGG Mary (c) - warned out of Dunbarton, 1790, file #2523, p7

HOGG Nancy - formerly of Ware, warned out of Dearing, 1786, file #7059, p2

HOGG Priscilla (c) - formerly of Ware, warned out of Dearing, 1786, file #7059, p2

HOGG Rebeccah (c) - formerly of Derring, warned out of Dunbarton, 1786, file #2519, p1

HOGG Robert Jr - formerly of Weare, warned out of Dunbarton, 1783, file #2516, p3

HOGG Robert - formerly of Weare, warned out of Dunbarton, 1786, file #2519, p5

HOGG Robert Jr - warned out of Dunbarton, 1790, file #2523, p7

HOGG Samuel - warned out of Dunbarton, 1783, file #2516, p1

HOGG Sarah (c) - warned out of Dunbarton, 1790, file #2523, p7

HOGG Sarah (c) - formerly of Weare, warned out of Dunbarton, 1783, file #2516, p3

HOGG William - formerly of Ware, warned out of Dearing, 1786, file #7059, p2

HOGG Wm - formerly of Jaffrey, warned out of New Ipswich, 1791, file #2283, p1

HOIT Bettee (c) - formerly of Heniker, warned out of Dearing, 1788, file #7059, p14

HOIT Daniel (c) - formerly of Heniker, warned out of Dearing, 1788, file #7059, p14

HOIT George - formerly of Heniker, warned out of Dearing, 1788, file #7059, p14

HOIT George - formerly of Amherst, warned out of New Boston, 1794, file #2286, p3

HOIT George Jr (c) - formerly of Heniker, warned out of Dearing, 1788, file #7059, p14

HOIT Martha (c) - formerly of Heniker, warned out of Dearing, 1788, file #7059, p14

HOIT Rhoda Jr (c) - formerly of Heniker, warned out of Dearing, 1788, file #7059, p14

HOIT Rhodae - formerly of Heniker, warned out of Dearing, 1788, file #7059, p14

HOIT Sanders (c) - formerly of Heniker, warned out of Dearing, 1788, file #7059, p14

HOLDEN Lydia - formerly of Mason, warned out of Temple, 1800, file #7060, p44

HOLLAND Nancy (c) - warned out of Wilton, 1783, file #2604-E, p11

HOLT Abigal - warned out of Wilton, 1772, file #2604, p1

HOLT Abigal Jr - warned out of Wilton, 1772, file #2604, p1

HOLT Anne (c) - warned out of Wilton, 1772, file #2604, p1

HOLT Asa - formerly of Wilton, warned out of Temple, 1802, file #7060, p38

HOLT Asa (c) - formerly of Andover MA, warned out of Wilton, 1796, file #2604-D, p5

HOLT Daniel - formerly of Lyndeborough, warned out of Wilton, 1793, file #2604-C, p3

HOLT Dorcas - formerly of Andover MA, warned out of Wilton, 1796, file #2604-D, p5

HOLT Dorothy - formerly of Lyndeborough, warned out of Wilton, 1793, file #2604-C, p3

HOLT Dorothy (c) - formerly of Lyndeborough, warned out of Wilton, 1793, file #2604-C, p3

HOLT Elisabeth - formerly of Andover MA, warned out of Wilton, 1796, file #2604-D, p5

HOLT Elisabeth (c) - formerly of Andover MA, warned out of Wilton, 1796, file #2604-D, p5

HOLT Elizabeth - formerly of Andover MA, warned out of Wilton, 1770, file #2604-C, p9

HOLT Fifield - warned out of Wilton, 1772, file #2604, p1

HOLT Joel (c) - formerly of Andover MA, warned out of Wilton, 1770, file #2604-C, p9

HOLT John - formerly of Wilton, warned out of Temple, 1795, file #7060, p30

HOLT Joseph (c) - formerly of Andover MA, warned out of Wilton, 1796, file #2604-D, p5

HOLT Lucy (c) - formerly of Lancaster MA, warned out of New Ipswich, 1743, file #2268, p1

HOLT Molly - formerly of Lancaster MA, warned out of New Ipswich, 1774, file #2268, p1

HOLT Molly (c) - formerly of Lancaster MA, warned out of New Ipswich, 1774, file #2268, p1

HOLT Philbrick - formerly of Amherst, warned out of Wilton, 1774, file #2604-D, p8

HOLT Rachael - formerly of MA, warned out of Wilton, 1774, file #2604-C, p2

HOLT Rachael (widow) - formerly of Andover MA, warned out of Wilton, 1770, file #2604-C, p9

HOLT Rachel - warned out of Wilton, 1772, file #2604, p1

HOLT Sarah - formerly of Wilton, warned out of Temple, 1795, file #7060, p52

HOLT Sarah (c) - formerly of Andover MA, warned out of Wilton, 1770, file #2604-C, p9

HOLT Stephen (c) - formerly of Andover MA, warned out of Wilton, 1796, file #2604-D, p5

HOLT Thomas - formerly of Lancaster MA, warned out of New Ipswich, 1774, file #2268, p1

HOLT Timothy Capt - formerly of Andover MA, warned out of Wilton, 1770, file #2604-C, p9

HOLT Timothy Jr - formerly of Andover MA, warned out of Wilton, 1774, file #2604-D, p8

HOLT William - formerly of Andover MA, warned out of Wilton, 1796, file #2604-D, p5

HOLT William (c) - formerly of Andover MA, warned out of Wilton, 1796, file #2604-D, p5

HONEY Ann (c) - formerly of Dunstable, warned out of Wilton, 1775, file #2604, p4

HONEY Anna - formerly of Dunstable, warned out of Temple, 1780, file #7060, p10

HONEY Hannah - formerly of Dunstable, warned out of Wilton, 1775, file #2604, p4

HONEY John? - formerly of Dunstable, warned out of Wilton, 1775, file #2604, p4

HONEY Sarah (c) - formerly of Dunstable, warned out of Wilton, 1775, file #2604, p4

HOOD Abner (c) - formerly of Topsfield MA, warned out of Wilton, 1784, file #2604-D, p2

HOOD Betsey (c) - formerly of Chelmsford MA, warned out of Wilton, 1784, file #2604-D, p2

HOOD Daniel & Wife - formerly of Topsfield MA, warned out of Wilton, 1784, file #2604-D, p2

HOOD Daniel (c) - formerly of Topsfield MA, warned out of Wilton, 1784, file #2604-D, p2

HOOD Jacob (c) - formerly of Topsfield MA, warned out of Wilton, 1784, file #2604-D, p2

HOOD Lucia (c) - formerly of Topsfield MA, warned out of Wilton, 1784, file #2604-D, p2

HOOD Molly (c) - formerly of Topsfield MA, warned out of Wilton, 1784, file #2604-D, p2

HOSILY Joseph - formerly of Hancock, warned out of Temple, 1799, file #7060, p43

HOW Aaron - warned out of New Boston, 1788, file #2280, p1

HOW Betty (c) - formerly of Goffstown, warned out of Dunbarton, 1787, file #2520, p1

HOW Calvin - formerly of Langdon MA, warned out of Temple, 1792, file #7060, p39

HOW Dolly - formerly of Hopkinton, warned out of Dunbarton, 1788, file #2521, p1

HOW Dolly (c) - formerly of Hopkinton, warned out of Dunbarton, 1788, file #2521, p1

HOW Hannah - formerly of Goffstown, warned out of Dunbarton, 1787, file #2520, p1

HOW Hannah (c) - formerly of Goffstown, warned out of Dunbarton, 1787, file #2520, p1

HOW Henry & Wife - warned out of Goffstown, 1776, file #3606, p10

HOW Isaac (c) - formerly of Hopkinton, warned out of Dunbarton, 1788, file #2521, p1

HOW John - formerly of Goffstown, warned out of Dunbarton, 1787, file #2520, p1

HOW John (c) - formerly of Goffstown, warned out of Dunbarton, 1787, file #2520, p1

HOW Jonathan (c) - formerly of Goffstown, warned out of Dunbarton, 1787, file #2520, p1

HOW Ob? - warned out of Goffstown, 1785, file #3606, p11

HOW Phebe - warned out of Goffstown, 1785, file #3606, p11

HOW Samuel - formerly of Hopkinton, warned out of Dunbarton, 1788, file #2521, p1

HOWARD Lydah - formerly of Townsend MA, warned out of Wilton, 1784, file #2604-E, p7

HOWARD Mary - formerly of Reding MA, warned out of Temple, 1782, file #7060, p25

HOWARD Mehitable - formerly of Temple, warned out of Wilton, 1790, file #2604-D, p3

HOWARD Nathaniel - formerly of Wilton, warned out of Temple, 1791, file #7060, p55

HOWARD Phebe - formerly of Wilton, warned out of Temple, 1791, file #7060, p55

HOWARD Robert - formerly of Reding MA, warned out of Temple, 1782, file #7060, p25

HOWS Abigail (c) - warned out of Goffstown, 1790, file #3607, p6

HOWS Nathan - warned out of Goffstown, 1790, file #3607, p6

HOWS Polly (c) - warned out of Goffstown, 1790, file #3607, p6

HOYT Israel - warned out of Goffstown, 1789, file #3607, p5

HUBBARD Isaac - warned out of Goffstown, 1786, file #3607, p1

HUBBARD Jacob - warned out of Goffstown, 1789, file #3607, p4

HUBBARD Lyda - warned out of Goffstown, 1786, file #3607, p1

HUBBERT Jona - warned out of Goffstown, 1788, file #3608, p8

HUBBERT Lydia - warned out of Goffstown, 1788, file #3608, p8

HUDSON Darius - formerly of Pepperell MA, warned out of Temple, 1795, file #7060, p52

HUNT Mary - formerly of Westford MA, warned out of New Ipswich, 1788, file #2280, p2

HUNT Mary - formerly of Bedford, warned out of New Ipswich, 1779, file #2270, p3

HUSTON Anna - warned out of New Boston, 1790, file #2282, p2

HUTCHINSON Lydia - formerly of Lyndeborough, warned out of Wilton, 1782, file #2604-E, p4

HUTCHINSON Ambrose (c) - formerly of Lyndeborough, warned out of Wilton, 1774, file #2604, p2

HUTCHINSON Clark (c) - formerly of Lyndeborough, warned out of Wilton, 1774, file #2604, p2

HUTCHINSON Deborah (widow) - formerly of Lyndeborough, warned out of Wilton, 1784, file #2604-E, p7

HUTCHINSON George (c) - formerly of Lyndeborough, warned out of Wilton, 1774, file #2604, p2

HUTCHINSON George - formerly of Lyndeborough, warned out of Wilton, 1774, file #2604, p2

HUTCHINSON Molley (c) - formerly of Lyndeborough, warned out of Wilton, 1774, file #2604, p2

HUTCHINSON Susannah - formerly of Lyndeborough, warned out of Wilton, 1774, file #2604, p2

JACKSON Benony (c) Negro - formerly of Ashburnham MA, warned out of New Ipswich, 1782, file #2273, p3

JACKSON Frances (Negro) - formerly of Ashburnham MA, warned out of New Ipswich, 1782, file #2273, p3

JACKSON Lydia (c) Negro - formerly of Ashburnham MA, warned out of New Ipswich, 1782, file #2273, p3

JACKSON Patty (c) Negro - formerly of Ashburnham MA, warned out of New Ipswich, 1782, file #2273, p3

JACKSON Sarah (c) Negro - warned out of New Ipswich, 1782, file #2273, p3

JAQUISH Nehemiah - formerly of Dracut MA, warned out of Dearing, 1790, file #7059, p31

JOHNO Prince (a Mulatto) - formerly of Methuen MA, warned out of Goffstown, 1776, file #3608, p6

JOHNSON Catharine - formerly of Mason, warned out of Temple, 1794, file #7060, p57

JOHNSON Desdmona - warned out of New Boston, 1790, file #2282, p3

JOHNSON Ezra - formerly of Salem MA, warned out of Wilton, 1774, file #2604-D, p8

JOHNSON Ezra (c) - formerly of Salem MA, warned out of Wilton, 1774, file #2604-D, p8

JOHNSON Hannah - formerly of Salem MA, warned out of Wilton, 1774, file #2604-D, p8

JOHNSON Hannah - warned out of New Boston, 1790, file #2282, p3

JOHNSON Hannah - warned out of Wilton, 1775, file #2604, p4

JOHNSON James (c) - formerly of Salem MA, warned out of Wilton, 1774, file #2604-D, p8

JOHNSON Josiah - formerly of Walpole, warned out of Wilton, 1772, file #2604, p1

JOHNSON Rhoda - warned out of New Boston, 1790, file #2282, p3

JOHNSON Ruth - formerly of Walpole, warned out of Wilton, 1772, file #2604-D, p4

JOHNSON Sally (c) - warned out of New Boston, 1790, file #2282, p3

JOHNSON Silva - formerly of Medford MA, warned out of Temple, 1790, file #7060, p53

JOHNSON William - warned out of New Boston, 1790, file #2282, p3

JOHNSON William Jr (c) - warned out of New Boston, 1790, file #2282, p3

JONAS Richard - warned out of New Ipswich, 1791, file #2283, p1

JONES Abigail - formerly of Lunenburgh MA, warned out of New Ipswich, 1792, file #2284, p3

JONES Ebenezer - formerly of Concord, warned out of New Ipswich, 1779, file #2270, p2

JONES Ebenezer (c) - formerly of Concord, warned out of New Ipswich, 1779, file #2270, p2

JONES Elathan (c) - formerly of Concord, warned out of New Ipswich, 1779, file #2270, p2

JONES Elvin (c) - warned out of Goffstown, 1793, file #3608, p1

JONES Hannah - warned out of Goffstown, 1793, file #3608, p1

JONES Hannah (c) - formerly of Concord, warned out of New Ipswich, 1779, file #2270, p2

JONES Henry (c) - formerly of Lunenburgh MA, warned out of New Ipswich, 1792, file #2284, p3

JONES Hepsabeth (c) - formerly of Lunenburgh MA, warned out of New Ipswich, 1792, file #2284, p3

JONES Isaac (c) - formerly of Lunenburgh MA, warned out of New Ipswich, 1792, file #2284, p3

JONES Jacob - warned out of Goffstown, 1793, file #3608, p1

JONES Jonas - formerly of Lunenburgh MA, warned out of New Ipswich, 1792, file #2284, p3

JONES Nathaniel (c) - formerly of Concord, warned out of New Ipswich, 1779, file #2270, p2

JONES Peter (c) - formerly of Lunenburgh MA, warned out of New Ipswich, 1792, file #2284, p3

JONES Salley - formerly of Packerfield, warned out of New Ipswich, 1785, file #2276, p5

JONES Sarah - formerly of Concord, warned out of New Ipswich, 1779, file #2270, p2

JONES Stephen (c) - formerly of Lunenburgh MA, warned out of New Ipswich, 1792, file #2284, p3

JONSON John - formerly of Fitchburg MA, warned out of New Ipswich, 1780, file #2271, p1

JONSON Lucy - formerly of Fitchburg MA, warned out of New Ipswich, 1780, file #2271, p1

JOYSTHYN Betty (c) - formerly of Hillsborough, warned out of Dearing, 1786, file #7059, p16

JOYSTHYN Catherine - formerly of Hillsborough, warned out of Dearing, 1786, file #7059, p16

JOYSTHYN Nathaniel (Mr) - formerly of Hillsborough, warned out of Dearing, 1786, file #7059, p16

JOYSTHYN Taylor (c) - formerly of Hillsborough, warned out of Dearing, 1786, file #7059, p16

KANN Mary - formerly of Goffstown, warned out of Dunbarton, 1784, file #2517, p4

KANN Merry (c) - formerly of Goffstown, warned out of Dunbarton, 1784, file #2517, p4

KANN Richard (c) - formerly of Goffstown, warned out of Dunbarton, 1784, file #2517, p4

KANN Sarah (c) - formerly of Goffstown, warned out of Dunbarton, 1784, file #2517, p4

KANN William - formerly of Goffstown, warned out of Dunbarton, 1784, file #2517, p4

KARR Frances (c) - formerly of Derryfield, warned out of Goffstown, 1774, file #3608, p10

KARR Nanny - formerly of Derryfield, warned out of Goffstown, 1774, file #3608, p10

KARR Nanny (c) - formerly of Derryfield, warned out of Goffstown, 1774, file #3608, p10

KARR Richa - formerly of Derryfield, warned out of Goffstown, 1774, file #3608, p10

KARR Sarah (c) - formerly of Derryfield, warned out of Goffstown, 1774, file #3608, p10

KARR William - formerly of Derryfield, warned out of Goffstown, 1774, file #3608, p10

KELLEY Abigal - formerly of Winham, warned out of Dearing, 1786, file #7059, p3

KELLEY John - formerly of Weir, warned out of Dearing, 1794, file #7059, p25

KELLEY John (c) - formerly of Winham, warned out of Dearing, 1786, file #7059, p3

KELLEY Lydia (c) - formerly of Winham, warned out of Dearing, 1786, file #7059, p3

KELLEY Richard (Mr) - formerly of Winham, warned out of Dearing, 1786, file #7059, p3

KELLY Ebenezer (c) - formerly of Ware, warned out of Dearing, 1785, file #7059, p28

KELLY Ebenezer (Mr) - formerly of Ware, warned out of Dearing, 1785, file #7059, p28

KELLY Hannah (c) - formerly of Ware, warned out of Dearing, 1785, file #7059, p28

KELLY Henry (c) - formerly of Ware, warned out of Dearing, 1785, file #7059, p28

KELLY Joshua (c) - formerly of Ware, warned out of Dearing, 1785, file #7059, p28

KELLY Mary - formerly of Ware, warned out of Dearing, 1785, file #7059, p28

KELLY Mary (c) - formerly of Ware, warned out of Dearing, 1785, file #7059, p28

KELLY Sarah (c) - formerly of Ware, warned out of Dearing, 1785, file #7059, p28

KELLY Sargent (c) - formerly of Ware, warned out of Dearing, 1785, file #7059, p28

KEMP Eunas - warned out of Goffstown, 1786, file #3607, p1

KEMP Joel - warned out of Goffstown, 1794, file #3609, p9

KEMP Joseph (c) - warned out of Goffstown, 1786, file #3607, p1

KEMP Lydia - formerly of Mason, warned out of Temple, 1800, file #7060, p47

KEMP Mary (c) - warned out of Goffstown, 1786, file #3607, p1

KEMP Reuben - warned out of Goffstown, 1786, file #3607, p1

KENDAL Abigal (c) - formerly of Fitsburg MA, warned out of New Ipswich, 1792, file #2284, p3

KENDAL Barzehal (c) - formerly of Fitsburg MA, warned out of New Ipswich, 1792, file #2284, p3

KENDAL Barzehal & Wife - formerly of Fitsburg MA, warned out of New Ipswich, 1792, file #2284, p3

KENDAL Elizabeth (c) - formerly of Fitsburg MA, warned out of New Ipswich, 1792, file #2284, p3

KENDAL Eunice (c) - formerly of Fitsburg MA, warned out of New Ipswich, 1792, file #2284, p3

KENDAL John (c) - formerly of Fitsburg MA, warned out of New Ipswich, 1792, file #2284, p3

KENDAL Mary (c) - formerly of Fitsburg MA, warned out of New Ipswich, 1792, file #2284, p3

KENDAL Ruth (c) - formerly of Fitsburg MA, warned out of New Ipswich, 1792, file #2284, p3

KENDAL Zeary (c) - formerly of Fitsburg MA, warned out of New Ipswich, 1792, file #2284, p3

KENDEL James - formerly of Mason, warned out of New Ipswich, 1791, file #2283, p1

KEYS John - formerly of Northborough MA, warned out of Wilton, 1774, file #2604-D, p8

KIDDER Elizabeth - warned out of Goffstown, 1793, file #3609, p8

KIDDER Eunice - warned out of Goffstown, 1789, file #3607, p4

KIDDER Eunice (c) - warned out of Goffstown, 1789, file #3607, p4

KIDDER Noah - warned out of Goffstown, 1789, file #3607, p4

KIDDER Noah - formerly of Goffstown, warned out of Dunbarton, 1791, file #2524, p1

KIDDER Noah Jr - warned out of Goffstown, 1793, file #3609, p8

KIDDER Salley (c) - warned out of Goffstown, 1789, file #3607, p4

KILBUN Paul - formerly of Rowley MA, warned out of Wilton, 1774, file #2604-D, p8

KILHAMA Sarah - warned out of New Boston, 1790, file #2282, p2

KILLAM Benjamin Jr - formerly of Lyndeborough, warned out of Temple, 1784, file #7060, p19

KILLAM Sibble - formerly of Lyndeborough, warned out of Temple, 1784, file #7060, p19

KILLAMI Benjamin - formerly of Temple, warned out of Wilton, 1784, file #2604-C, p6

KIMBALL Benoni Cutter (c) - formerly of Andover VT, warned out of Temple, 1803, file #7060, p48

KIMBALL David - formerly of New Ipswich, warned out of Temple, 1792, file #7060, p39

KIMBALL Ebenezer - formerly of Mason, warned out of New Ipswich, 1794, file #2286, p1

KIMBALL Edmond - formerly of Mason, warned out of New Ipswich, 1794, file #2286, p1

KIMBALL Ezra - formerly of Dorchester MA, warned out of Temple, 1781, file #7060, p21

KIMBALL Ezra (c) - formerly of Dorchester, warned out of Temple, 1781, file #7060, p21

KIMBALL Ezry Mr - formerly of Temple, warned out of New Ipswich, 1787, file #2279, p1

KIMBALL Francis (c) - formerly of Temple, warned out of New Ipswich, 1787, file #2279, p1

KIMBALL Francis (c) - formerly of Dorchester, warned out of Temple, 1781, file #7060, p21

KIMBALL Hannah (c) - formerly of Temple, warned out of New Ipswich, 1787, file #2279, p1

KIMBALL Holmes (c) - formerly of Temple, warned out of New Ipswich, 1787, file #2279, p1

KIMBALL Homer (c) - formerly of Dorchester, warned out of Temple, 1781, file #7060, p21

KIMBALL Isaac (c) - formerly of Andover VT, warned out of Temple, 1803, file #7060, p48

KIMBALL Isaac Jr - formerly of Andover VT, warned out of Temple, 1803, file #7060, p48

KIMBALL Jeremiah - formerly of Mason, warned out of New Ipswich, 1794, file #2286, p1

KIMBALL John (c) - formerly of Andover VT, warned out of Temple, 1803, file #7060, p48

KIMBALL Martha (widow) - formerly of New Ipswich, warned out of Temple, 1791, file #7060, p54

KIMBALL Mary - formerly of Mason, warned out of New Ipswich, 1794, file #2286, p1

KIMBALL Milley - formerly of New Ipswich, warned out of Temple, 1792, file #7060, p39

KIMBALL Milley (c) - formerly of New Ipswich, warned out of Temple, 1792, file #7060, p39

KIMBALL Patty (c) - formerly of Dorchester, warned out of Temple, 1781, file #7060, p21

KIMBALL Patty (c) - formerly of Temple, warned out of New Ipswich, 1787, file #2279, p1

KIMBALL Peggy (c) - formerly of New Ipswich, warned out of Temple, 1791, file #7060, p54

KIMBALL Reuben - formerly of Mason, warned out of New Ipswich, 1794, file #2286, p1

KIMBALL Sally - formerly of Andover VT, warned out of Temple, 1803, file #7060, p48

KIMBALL Sally (c) - formerly of Andover VT, warned out of Temple, 1803, file #7060, p48

KIMBALL Sarah - formerly of Mason, warned out of New Ipswich, 1794, file #2286, p1

KIMBALL Sarah - warned out of New Ipswich, 1787, file #2279, p1

KIMBALL Sarah - formerly of Dorchester MA, warned out of Temple, 1781, file #7060, p21

KIMBALL Sarah (c) - warned out of New Ipswich, 1787, file #2279, p1

KIMBALL Sarah (c) - formerly of Dorchester, warned out of Temple, 1781, file #7060, p21

KIMBALL William Baker (c) - formerly of Andover VT, warned out of Temple, 1803, file #7060, p48

KING Anna - formerly of Boston MA, warned out of Dunbarton, 1786, file #2519, p2

KING James - formerly of Boston MA, warned out of Dunbarton, 1786, file #2519, p2

KING James - warned out of Goffstown, 1788, file #3609, p3

KING Nancy - warned out of Goffstown, 1788, file #3609, p3

KIRKWOOD Arthur - formerly of Derry, warned out of Temple, 1796, file #7060, p35

KITTER Mary - formerly of Lunenburgh MA, warned out of New Ipswich, 1791, file #2283, p2

KITTERDGE Anna (c) - formerly of Goffstown, warned out of Dearing, 1795, file #7059, p12

KITTERDGE Martha - formerly of Goffstown, warned out of Dearing, 1795, file #7059, p12

KITTERDGE Martha (c) - formerly of Goffstown, warned out of Dearing, 1795, file #7059, p12

KITTERDGE Nathaniel - formerly of Goffstown, warned out of Dearing, 1795, file #7059, p12

KITTREDGE James - warned out of Goffstown, 1790, file #3609, p5

KNEAD Lydia - formerly of Townsend MA, warned out of New Ipswich, 1787, file #2279, p2

KNIGHTS Betty (c) - formerly of Harvard MA, warned out of New Ipswich, 1777, file #2287, p1

KNIGHTS Elizabeth - formerly of Harvard MA, warned out of New Ipswich, 1777, file #2287, p1

KNIGHTS John - formerly of Harvard MA, warned out of New Ipswich, 1777, file #2287, p1

KNIGHTS Lidia (c) - formerly of Harvard MA, warned out of New Ipswich, 1777, file #2287, p1

KNOWLTON Henry - formerly of Whites Gown VT, warned out of New Ipswich, 1795, file #2288, p3

LAMPSON Azubah - formerly of Walpole, warned out of Temple, 1794, file #7060, p58

LAMPSON Paul - formerly of Walpole, warned out of Temple, 1794, file #7060, p58

LANANCE Lucy - formerly of Ashby MA, warned out of Temple, 1802, file #7060, p38

LANCHLESS Isaac (c) - warned out of Goffstown, 1790, file #3607, p6

LANCHLESS Nancy (c) - warned out of Goffstown, 1790, file #3607, p6

LANCHLESS Polly - warned out of Goffstown, 1790, file #3607, p6

LANCHLESS Polly - warned out of Goffstown, 1790, file #3607, p6

LANCHLESS Polly (c) - warned out of Goffstown, 1790, file #3607, p6

LANCHLESS Samuel - warned out of Goffstown, 1790, file #3607, p6

LANCHLESS Samuel (c) - warned out of Goffstown, 1790, file #3607, p6

LANCHLESS Thomas - warned out of Goffstown, 1790, file #3607, p6

LANCHLESS William (c) - warned out of Goffstown, 1790, file #3607, p6

LANGDAFF Hannah (c) - formerly of Wilton, warned out of New Boston, 1794, file #2286, p3

LANGDAFF John (c) - formerly of Wilton, warned out of New Boston, 1794, file #2286, p3

LANGDAFF Margaret (widow) - formerly of Weare, warned out of New Boston, 1794, file #2286, p3

LAUCHLIN Allen - warned out of Goffstown, 1790, file #3609, p5

LAUGHLIN Hepzibah - warned out of Goffstown, 1789, file #3609, p4

LAUGHLIN Nathaniel - warned out of Goffstown, 1789, file #3609, p4

LAUGHLIN Samuel - warned out of Goffstown, 1789, file #3609, p4

LAUGHLIN Sarah - warned out of Goffstown, 1789, file #3609, p4

LAW Andrew - formerly of Peterboro Slip, warned out of Temple, 1784, file #7060, p61

LAW Betsey (c) - formerly of Billerica MA, warned out of Temple, 1793, file #7060, p36

LAW Daniel (c) - formerly of Peterboro Slip, warned out of Temple, 1784, file #7060, p61

LAW Ellen (c) - formerly of Billerica MA, warned out of Temple, 1793, file #7060, p36

LAW Eunice (widow) - formerly of Billerica MA, warned out of Temple, 1793, file #7060, p36

LAW Francis (c) - formerly of Billerica MA, warned out of Temple, 1793, file #7060, p36

LAW Harry (c) - formerly of Chelmsford MA, warned out of Temple, 1795, file #7060, p50

LAW Hepzbeth - formerly of Peterboro Slip, warned out of Temple, 1784, file #7060, p61

LAW Hepzibah (alias Fish) - formerly of Peterborough, warned out of Temple, 1793, file #7060, p36

LAW James (c) - formerly of Billerica MA, warned out of Temple, 1793, file #7060, p36

LAW Jno - formerly of Peterboro Slip, warned out of Temple, 1789, file #7060, p41

LAW John - formerly of Billerica MA, warned out of Temple, 1793, file #7060, p36

LAW John (c) - formerly of Chelmsford MA, warned out of Temple, 1795, file #7060, p50

LAW Lucy (c) - formerly of Peterboro Slip, warned out of Temple, 1784, file #7060, p61

LAW Lydia - formerly of Chelmsford MA, warned out of Temple, 1795, file #7060, p50

LAW Nancy (c) - formerly of Chelmsford MA, warned out of Temple, 1795, file #7060, p50

LAW Polly - formerly of Chelmsford MA, warned out of Temple, 1795, file #7060, p50

LAW Sally - formerly of Billerica MA, warned out of Temple, 1793, file #7060, p36

LAW Sally (c) - formerly of Billerica MA, warned out of Temple, 1793, file #7060, p36

LAW Sally (c) - formerly of Chelmsford MA, warned out of Temple, 1795, file #7060, p50

LAW Samuel - formerly of Sharon, warned out of Temple, 1800, file #7060, p47

LAW Stephen - formerly of Chelmsford MA, warned out of Temple, 1795, file #7060, p50

LAW Zelotza (c) - formerly of Chelmsford MA, warned out of Temple, 1795, file #7060, p50

LAWRENCE Ruth - formerly of Mason, warned out of Temple, 1800, file #7060, p47

LEACH William - formerly of Dunbarton, warned out of Goffstown, 1791, file #3607, p7

LEANEUSTEN Judah - formerly of New Boston, warned out of Wilton, 1772, file #2604, p1

LEANON Esther - formerly of Hollis, warned out of Wilton, 1780, file #2604-E, p6

LESLEY Alexander - formerly of Londonderry, warned out of Dunbarton, 1792, file #2525, p6

LESLEY Barber - warned out of New Boston, 1779, file #2270, p5

LESLEY Daniel (c) - formerly of Londonderry, warned out of Dunbarton, 1792, file #2525, p6

LESLEY Hannah (c) - formerly of Londonderry, warned out of Dunbarton, 1792, file #2525, p6

LESLEY John (c) - formerly of Londonderry, warned out of Dunbarton, 1792, file #2525, p6

LESLEY Lucy - formerly of Londonderry, warned out of Dunbarton, 1792, file #2525, p6

LESLEY Lucy (c) - formerly of Londonderry, warned out of Dunbarton, 1792, file #2525, p6

LESLEY Susanah (c) - formerly of Londonderry, warned out of Dunbarton, 1792, file #2525, p6

LIDE Rhoda - formerly of Wilton, warned out of Temple, 1802, file #7060, p38

LIE Dexter (c) - formerly of Mason, warned out of New Ipswich, 1790, file #2282, p1

LIE Henry (c) - formerly of Mason, warned out of New Ipswich, 1790, file #2282, p1

LIE Jonathan - formerly of Mason, warned out of New Ipswich, 1790, file #2282, p1

LIE Sarah - formerly of Mason, warned out of New Ipswich, 1790, file #2282, p1

LIE Sarah (c) - formerly of Mason, warned out of New Ipswich, 1790, file #2282, p1

LINDE Dolly (c) - formerly of Wilton, warned out of Temple, 1802, file #7060, p38

LINDE Solomon (c) - formerly of Wilton, warned out of Temple, 1802, file #7060, p38

LOFTY Mary - warned out of New Boston, 1786, file #2278, p1

LOVEJOY Daniel & Wife - formerly of Amherst, warned out of Wilton, 1784, file #2604-C, p6

LOVEJOY Darcas (c) - formerly of Amherst, warned out of Wilton, 1784, file #2604-C, p6

LOVEJOY Hannah (widow) - formerly of Andover MA, warned out of Wilton, 1774, file #2604, p2

LOVEJOY Martha - formerly of Amherst, warned out of Wilton, 1783, file #2604-E, p10

LOVEJOY Sarah (widow) - formerly of Andover MA, warned out of Wilton, 1774, file #2604, p2

LOWEL Hannah - formerly of Mason, warned out of New Ipswich, 1773, file #2267, p3

LOWEL Jonas - formerly of Mason, warned out of Temple, 1795, file #7060, p50

LOWELL Ammy - formerly of Brookline, warned out of Temple, 1803, file #7060, p48

LOWELL Betty (c) - formerly of Temple, warned out of Wilton, 1791, file #2604-B, p5

LOWELL Carlton (c) - formerly of Temple, warned out of Wilton, 1791, file #2604-B, p5

LOWELL Elizabeth - formerly of Temple, warned out of New Ipswich, 1795, file #2288, p2

LOWELL Jacob - formerly of Dunstable, warned out of Wilton, 1791, file #2604-B, p5

LOWELL Martha - formerly of Dunstable, warned out of Wilton, 1791, file #2604-B, p5

LOWELL Martha (widow) - formerly of Dunstable, warned out of Wilton, 1791, file #2604-B, p5

LOWELL Mehetable - formerly of Dunstable, warned out of Wilton, 1791, file #2604-B, p5

LOWELL Olive - formerly of Temple, warned out of Wilton, 1791, file #2604-B, p5

LOWELL Timothy - formerly of Temple, warned out of Wilton, 1791, file #2604-B, p5

LOWELL Timothy (c) - formerly of Temple, warned out of Wilton, 1791, file #2604-B, p5

LOWELL William (c) - formerly of Temple, warned out of Wilton, 1791, file #2604-B, p5

LYNCH Batren - warned out of New Boston, 1779, file #2270, p5

LYNDSON John & Wife - warned out of New Ipswich, 1784, file #2275, p3

MACKINGTIRE Phineas - formerly of Andover MA, warned out of Wilton, 1784, file #2604-E, p7

MAN James - warned out of New Boston, 1790, file #2282, p3

MAN Susana - warned out of New Boston, 1790, file #2282, p3

MANNING Olive - formerly of Billerica, warned out of Wilton, 1793, file #2604-C, p5

MANNING Samuel - warned out of New Ipswich, 1787, file #2279, p2

MANNING Solomon - formerly of Billerica MA, warned out of Wilton, 1793, file #2604-C, p5

MANNING William - warned out of New Ipswich, 1787, file #2279, p2

MANSFIELD (widow) - warned out of New Boston, 1792, file #2284, p1

MANSFIELD John - formerly of Linn, warned out of New Ipswich, 1773, file #2267, p2

MANSFIELD Mary - formerly of Linn, warned out of New Ipswich, 1773, file #2267, p2

MANSFIELD Rebeckah - formerly of Linn, warned out of New Ipswich, 1773, file #2267, p2

MARBLE John - formerly of Milford, warned out of Wilton, 1795, file #2604-D, p7

MARBLE Sarah - formerly of Milford, warned out of Wilton, 1795, file #2604-D, p7

MARCH Margaret - warned out of Goffstown, 1790, file #3609, p5

MARCH Mary - warned out of Goffstown, 1786, file #3607, p1

MARDEN Francis (c) - warned out of New Boston, 1786, file #2278, p3

MARDEN Greenough (c) - warned out of New Boston, 1786, file #2278, p3

MARDEN Hannah - warned out of New Boston, 1786, file #2278, p3

MARDEN Hannah (c) - warned out of New Boston, 1786, file #2278, p3

MARDEN Lemuel - warned out of New Boston, 1786, file #2278, p3

MARDEN Mehetible (c) - warned out of New Boston, 1786, file #2278, p3

MARDEN Nathaniel (c) - warned out of New Boston, 1786, file #2278, p3

MARDEN Samuel (c) - warned out of New Boston, 1786, file #2278, p3

MARDEN Solomon (c) - warned out of New Boston, 1786, file #2278, p3

MARGERRY Jonathan - formerly of Hancock, warned out of New Ipswich, 1789, file #2281, p2

MARGERRY Margaret - formerly of Hancock, warned out of New Ipswich, 1789, file #2281, p2

MARKUM Robert - warned out of Goffstown, 1792, file #3606, p2

MARSHEL John - warned out of Goffstown, 1786, file #3607, p1

MARSHEL John (c) - warned out of Goffstown, 1786, file #3607, p1

MARSHEL Sary - warned out of Goffstown, 1786, file #3607, p1

MARTIN Hannah - formerly of Andover MA, warned out of Wilton, 1784, file #2604-E, p7

MARTIN Rebecca & Child - formerly of Choss?, warned out of Goffstown, 1776, file #3606, p1

MEADS John - formerly of Lyndeborough, warned out of Wilton, 1782, file #2604-E, p4

MEADS Mary - formerly of Lyndeborough, warned out of Wilton, 1782, file #2604-E, p4

MEARS George - formerly of Boston MA, warned out of Temple, 1781, file #7060, p15

MEARS Hariata (c) - formerly of Townsend MA, warned out of New Ipswich, 1794, file #2286, p1

MEARS John - formerly of Townsend MA, warned out of New Ipswich, 1794, file #2286, p1

MEARS Sarah - formerly of Townsend MA, warned out of New Ipswich, 1794, file #2286, p1

MERRILL Anne - warned out of Goffstown, 1796, file #3607, p8

MERRILL Stephen - warned out of Goffstown, 1789, file #3607, p4

MERRYFIELD Susanah - warned out of New Boston, 1786, file #2278, p5

MILLAR John (c) - formerly of Hancock, warned out of New Boston, 1795, file #2288, p1

MILLAR Mary - formerly of Hancock, warned out of New Boston, 1795, file #2288, p1

MILLAR Robert - formerly of Hancock, warned out of New Boston, 1795, file #2288, p1

MONROE Polly - warned out of New Boston, 1790, file #2282, p3

MONROE Sarah - warned out of New Boston, 1790, file #2282, p3

MONTGOMERY Abigal - warned out of New Ipswich, 1784, file #2275, p1

MONTGOMERY David (c) - warned out of New Ipswich, 1784, file #2275, p1

MONTGOMERY Molly - warned out of New Boston, 1790, file #2282, p2

MOOR Aaron (c) - warned out of Goffstown, 1793, file #3609, p8

MOOR Abel (c) - formerly of Putney (VT?), warned out of Temple, 1787, file #7060, p26

MOOR Abraham - formerly of Andover MA, warned out of Wilton, 1784, file #2604-D, p2

MOOR Benjamin (c) - formerly of VT, warned out of Temple, 1789, file #7060, p41

MOOR Betty - warned out of Goffstown, 1793, file #3609, p8

MOOR Betty (c) - warned out of Goffstown, 1793, file #3609, p8

MOOR Caleb - formerly of VT, warned out of Temple, 1789, file #7060, p41

MOOR Catharine - formerly of VT, warned out of Temple, 1789, file #7060, p41

MOOR Daniel (c) - warned out of Goffstown, 1793, file #3609, p8

MOOR Edmon - warned out of Goffstown, 1793, file #3609, p8

MOOR Edmon (c) - warned out of Goffstown, 1793, file #3609, p8

MOOR John - formerly of Putney (VT?), warned out of Temple, 1787, file #7060, p26

MOOR Jonathan (c) - formerly of Putney (VT?), warned out of Temple, 1787, file #7060, p26

MOOR Lydia (c) - warned out of Goffstown, 1793, file #3609, p8

MOOR Robert Jr - warned out of Goffstown, 1789, file #3609, p4

MOOR Susanna - formerly of Andover MA, warned out of Wilton, 1784, file #2604-D, p2

MOOR Sussanah (c) - formerly of Putney (VT?), warned out of Temple, 1787, file #7060, p26

MOOR Unity - formerly of Putney (VT?), warned out of Temple, 1787, file #7060, p26

MOOR Unity (c) - formerly of Putney (VT?), warned out of Temple, 1787, file #7060, p26

MOORS Aaron (c) - formerly of Goffstown, warned out of New Boston, 1794, file #2286, p3

MOORS Betsy (c) - formerly of Goffstown, warned out of New Boston, 1794, file #2286, p3

MOORS Betty - formerly of Goffstown, warned out of New Boston, 1794, file #2286, p3

MOORS Daniel (c) - formerly of Goffstown, warned out of New Boston, 1794, file #2286, p3

MOORS Edmund - formerly of Goffstown, warned out of New Boston, 1794, file #2286, p3

MOORS Edmund (c) - formerly of Goffstown, warned out of New Boston, 1794, file #2286, p3

MOORS Lydia (c) - formerly of Goffstown, warned out of New Boston, 1794, file #2286, p3

MORRAL Hannah - warned out of Goffstown, 1791, file #3609, p7

MORRE Edward - warned out of New Boston, 1785, file #2276, p2

MORREL Jennett - warned out of New Boston, 1785, file #2276, p2

MORREL Jennett - warned out of New Boston, 1789, file #2281, p5

MORREL John - warned out of New Boston, 1785, file #2276, p2

MORREL Robert - warned out of New Boston, 1785, file #2276, p2

MORREL William - warned out of New Boston, 1785, file #2276, p2

MORRELL Robert - warned out of New Boston, 1789, file #2281, p5

MORRISON Daniel (c) - formerly of Weare, warned out of Dunbarton, 1794, file #2527, p1

MORRISON Isabel - formerly of Weare, warned out of Dunbarton, 1794, file #2527, p1

MORRISON John (c) - formerly of Weare, warned out of Dunbarton, 1794, file #2527, p1

MORRISON Samuel - formerly of Weare, warned out of Dunbarton, 1794, file #2527, p1

MORSE Jonathan - warned out of Temple, 1774, file #7060, p4

MORSE Phebe - warned out of Temple, 1774, file #7060, p4

MULLET Betse (c) - warned out of New Boston, 1792, file #2284, p2

MULLET Elizabeth - warned out of New Boston, 1792, file #2284, p2

MULLET Hannah (c) - warned out of New Boston, 1792, file #2284, p2

MULLET John (c) - warned out of New Boston, 1792, file #2284, p2

MULLET Mary (c) - warned out of New Boston, 1792, file #2284, p2

MULLET Thomas - warned out of New Boston, 1792, file #2284, p2

MULLICAN Benj'n - formerly of Rindge, warned out of New Ipswich, 1789, file #2281, p2

MUNROE Joseph - warned out of New Boston, 1790, file #2282, p3

MUNSON Darius Jr - formerly of Mason, warned out of Temple, 1803, file #7060, p48

MUNSON Henry (c) - formerly of Mason, warned out of Temple, 1803, file #7060, p48

MUNSON Leonard (c) - formerly of Mason, warned out of Temple, 1803, file #7060, p48

MUNSON Sibel - formerly of Mason, warned out of Temple, 1803, file #7060, p48

MURROW Elizabeth - warned out of New Ipswich, 1784, file #2275, p2

MURROW Margaret - warned out of New Ipswich, 1784, file #2275, p2

McCALEPSTO Mary - formerly of Hopkinton, warned out of Dunbarton, 1771, file #2510, p1

McCALLAH Hannah - warned out of New Boston, 1786, file #2278, p5

McCOLOM John - warned out of New Boston, 1790, file #2282, p2

McCOLOM Joseph - warned out of New Boston, 1790, file #2282, p2

McCOLOM Lydia - warned out of New Boston, 1790, file #2282, p2

McCOY Agnes (widow) - warned out of New Boston, 1787, file #2279, p10

McCOY Charles - warned out of New Boston, 1792, file #2284, p2

McCOY Mary - warned out of New Boston, 1792, file #2284, p2

McCOY Mary (c) - warned out of New Boston, 1787, file #2279, p10

McCOYS Agnes - warned out of Goffstown, 1787, file #3607, p2

McCOYS Mary - warned out of Goffstown, 1787, file #3607, p2

McCULLAM Susanna - formerly of New Boston, warned out of Dearing, 1795, file #7059, p11

McDUFFY Hiram (c) - warned out of Goffstown, 1793, file #3608, p1

McDUFFY Sarah - warned out of Goffstown, 1793, file #3608, p1

McDUFFY Sarah (c) - warned out of Goffstown, 1793, file #3608, p1

McGAA Isebella (c) - warned out of New Ipswich, 1784, file #2275, p1

McGAA John (c) - warned out of New Ipswich, 1784, file #2275, p1

McGAA Martha - warned out of New Ipswich, 1784, file #2275, p1

McGAA Rebecca - warned out of New Ipswich, 1784, file #2275, p1

McGAA Robert - warned out of New Ipswich, 1784, file #2275, p1

McGINNIS Rebecca - warned out of New Boston, 1785, file #2276, p1

McGINNIS Robert - warned out of New Boston, 1785, file #2276, p1

McGINNIS Sarah - warned out of New Boston, 1785, file #2276, p1

McGINNIS Sebre - warned out of New Boston, 1785, file #2276, p1

McGINNS Elonar - warned out of New Boston, 1785, file #2276, p1

McGINNS Sidey - warned out of New Boston, 1785, file #2276, p1

McGREGORE Betsey - formerly of Goffstown, warned out of Dunbarton, 1787, file #2520, p2

McGREGORE David (Capt) - formerly of Goffstown, warned out of Dunbarton, 1787, file #2520, p2

McGREGORE Polly (c) - formerly of Goffstown, warned out of Dunbarton, 1787, file #2520, p2

McGREGORE Stephen (c) - formerly of Goffstown, warned out of Dunbarton, 1787, file #2520, p2

McGURDY Jesse - warned out of New Boston, 1790, file #2282, p2

McINTIRE Andrew (c) - formerly of Lyndeborough, warned out of Wilton, 1788, file #2604-C, p10

McINTIRE Andrus (c) - warned out of Goffstown, 1789, file #3607, p5

McINTIRE Betsy - warned out of Goffstown, 1789, file #3607, p5

McINTIRE David (c) - warned out of Goffstown, 1786, file #3607, p1

McINTIRE Elizabeth - formerly of Lyndeborough, warned out of Wilton, 1788, file #2604-C, p10

McINTIRE Elizabeth - formerly of Goffstown, warned out of Wilton, 1791, file #2604-B, p5

McINTIRE Elizabeth (c) - formerly of Goffstown, warned out of Wilton, 1791, file #2604-B, p5

McINTIRE Hannah - formerly of Amherst, warned out of Wilton, 1796, file #2604-D, p5

McINTIRE Hannah (c) - warned out of Goffstown, 1786, file #3607, p1

McINTIRE Jno - warned out of Goffstown, 1789, file #3607, p5

McINTIRE John - formerly of Lyndeborough, warned out of Wilton, 1788, file #2604-C, p10

McINTIRE John - formerly of Goffstown, warned out of Wilton, 1791, file #2604-B, p5

McINTIRE John (c) - formerly of Goffstown, warned out of Wilton, 1791, file #2604-B, p5

McINTIRE John (c) - warned out of Goffstown, 1789, file #3607, p5

McINTIRE Magge - warned out of Wilton, 1795, file #2604-B, p2

McINTIRE Samuel (c) - warned out of Goffstown, 1786, file #3607, p1

McINTIRE Sarah - warned out of Goffstown, 1786, file #3607, p1

McINTIRE Timothy - warned out of Goffstown, 1786, file #3607, p1

McINTIRE David - formerly of Amherst, warned out of Wilton, 1793, file #2604-C, p5

McINTIRE Hannah - formerly of Amherst, warned out of Wilton, 1793, file #2604-C, p5

McKEEN Hue - formerly of Amherst, warned out of Wilton, 1780, file #2604-E, p6

McKEEN Joannah - formerly of Amherst, warned out of Wilton, 1780, file #2604-E, p6

McKINSE Charles (c) - warned out of New Ipswich, 1784, file #2275, p2

McKINSE Elizabeth - warned out of New Ipswich, 1784, file #2275, p2

McKINSE John (c) - warned out of New Ipswich, 1784, file #2275, p2

McKINSE Joseph - warned out of New Ipswich, 1784, file #2275, p2

McKINSE Joseph (c) - warned out of New Ipswich, 1784, file #2275, p2

McMURPHY Alma - formerly of Ashburnham MA, warned out of New Ipswich, 1794, file #2286, p1

McMURPHY Mary - warned out of Goffstown, 1789, file #3609, p4

McNEEL Naomi - warned out of Goffstown, 1790, file #3607, p6

McPHERSON Elizabeth - formerly of Francestown, warned out of Dearing, 1787, file #7059, p26

McPHERSON Joseph (Mr) - formerly of Francestown, warned out of Dearing, 1787, file #7059, p26

NEAL Samuel - formerly of Carlisle, warned out of Temple, 1794, file #7060, p58

NEWELL Benjamin (c) - formerly of Cockermouth, warned out of Dunbarton, 1785, file #2518, p2

NEWELL Bety - formerly of Cockermouth, warned out of Dunbarton, 1785, file #2518, p2

NEWELL Jeremiah - formerly of Cockermouth, warned out of Dunbarton, 1785, file #2518, p2

NEWELL Jeremiah (c) - formerly of Cockermouth, warned out of Dunbarton, 1785, file #2518, p2

NEWELL John (c) - formerly of Cockermouth, warned out of Dunbarton, 1785, file #2518, p2

NEWELL Joseph (c) - formerly of Cockermouth, warned out of Dunbarton, 1785, file #2518, p2

NEWELL Poley (c) - formerly of Cockermouth, warned out of Dunbarton, 1785, file #2518, p2

NEWELL Sarah (c) - formerly of Cockermouth, warned out of Dunbarton, 1785, file #2518, p2

NEWMAN Hanah (Mr) - formerly of Woburn MA, warned out of Dearing, 1785, file #7059, p27

NEWMAN Ruth - warned out of Dearing, 1780, file #7059, p34

NEWMAN Sarah (c) - warned out of Dearing, 1780, file #7059, p34

NEWMAN Thomas (Mr) - formerly of Woburn MA, warned out of Dearing, 1785, file #7059, p27

NEWMAN Thos - warned out of Dearing, 1780, file #7059, p34

NICHOLS Alexander & Family - formerly of Salisbury, warned out of Dunbarton, 1793, file #2526, p3

NICHOLS Judith - formerly of Dublin, warned out of New Ipswich, 1794, file #2286, p2

NICHOLS Philip - formerly of Andover MA, warned out of Wilton, 1795, file #2604-D, p7

NICHOLS Rob't - formerly of Boston MA, warned out of New Ipswich, 1794, file #2286, p2

NICKELS Rachel - warned out of Goffstown, 1794, file #3609, p9

NICKELS William - warned out of Goffstown, 1794, file #3609, p9

NOYES Abigail (c) - warned out of Goffstown, 1796, file #3607, p8

NOYES Ballard (c) - warned out of Goffstown, 1796, file #3607, p8

NOYES Betey - warned out of Goffstown, 1796, file #3607, p8

NOYES John - warned out of Goffstown, 1796, file #3607, p8

NOYES Steven (c) - warned out of Goffstown, 1796, file #3607, p8

NUTTER Polly - formerly of Hollis, warned out of Temple, 1795, file #7060, p50

NUTTING Abigail - formerly of Pepperell MA, warned out of Wilton, 1779, file #2604-B, p7

NUTTING John (c) - formerly of Groton MA, warned out of Temple, 1790, file #7060, p53

NUTTING Widow - formerly of Groton MA, warned out of Temple, 1790, file #7060, p53

OBEAR Josiah - formerly of Wentham MA, warned out of New Ipswich, 1788, file #2280, p3

OBEAR Sally (dughter) - formerly of Wenham MA, warned out of New Ipswich, 1788, file #2280, p3

OLIVER Aaron - formerly of Littleton, warned out of Temple, 1772, file #7060, p20

OLIVER Abigail - formerly of Littleton, warned out of Temple, 1772, file #7060, p20

OLIVER Abigail - formerly of Temple, warned out of New Ipswich, 1778, file #2269, p1

OLIVER Aaron (c) - formerly of Temple, warned out of New Ipswich, 1778, file #2269, p1

OLIVER James (c) - formerly of Mason, warned out of New Ipswich, 1795, file #2288, p3

OLIVER Jenny - formerly of Mason, warned out of New Ipswich, 1795, file #2288, p3

OLIVER Jenny (c) - formerly of Mason, warned out of New Ipswich, 1795, file #2288, p3

OLIVER Nancy (c) - formerly of Mason, warned out of New Ipswich, 1795, file #2288, p3

OLIVER Sally (c) - formerly of Mason, warned out of New Ipswich, 1795, file #2288, p3

OLIVER Scripture - formerly of Mason, warned out of New Ipswich, 1795, file #2288, p3

OLIVER Sebel (c) - formerly of Mason, warned out of New Ipswich, 1795, file #2288, p3

PDaniel - warned out of Goffstown, 1793, file #3608, p1

PDolly - warned out of Goffstown, 1793, file #3608, p1

PElisabeth - formerly of New Salem, warned out of Wilton, 1796, file #2604-D, p5

PALMER Elizabeth - formerly of Peterborough, warned out of Temple, 1799, file #7060, p45

PARKER Abigail - formerly of Rockingham VT, warned out of Temple, 1800, file #7060, p44

PARKER Abiel - formerly of Peterborough, warned out of Temple, 1784, file #7060, p7

PARKER Abigail - warned out of New Ipswich, 1772, file #2266, p3

PARKER Abigail (c) - warned out of New Ipswich, 1772, file #2266, p3

PARKER Abigail (c) - formerly of Westbury MA, warned out of Wilton, 1787, file #2604-B, p4

PARKER Anna (c) - formerly of Westbury MA, warned out of Wilton, 1787, file #2604-B, p4

PARKER Betsy - formerly of Groton MA, warned out of New Ipswich, 1794, file #2286, p2

PARKER Betsy (c) - formerly of Groton MA, warned out of New Ipswich, 1794, file #2286, p2

PARKER David - formerly of Chelmsford MA, warned out of Temple, 1801, file #7060, p56

PARKER Elizabeth - warned out of New Boston, 1786, file #2278, p5

PARKER Hannaniah & Wife - formerly of Westbury MA, warned out of Wilton, 1787, file #2604-B, p4

PARKER James (c) - formerly of Westbury MA, warned out of Wilton, 1787, file #2604-B, p4

PARKER Jonathan - warned out of Goffstown, 1792, file #3606, p2

PARKER Joseph (c) - formerly of Westbury MA, warned out of Wilton, 1787, file #2604-B, p4

PARKER Joshua - formerly of Amherst, warned out of Temple, 1800, file #7060, p47

PARKER Joshua (c) - formerly of Amherst, warned out of Temple, 1800, file #7060, p47

PARKER Mary - formerly of Pepperell MA, warned out of New Ipswich, 1791, file #2283, p2

PARKER Olive - formerly of Chelmsford MA, warned out of Temple, 1801, file #7060, p56

PARKER Pairpoint (c) - formerly of Westbury MA, warned out of Wilton, 1787, file #2604-B, p4

PARKER Phebe (c) - formerly of Westbury MA, warned out of Wilton, 1787, file #2604-B, p4

PARKER Phineas - formerly of Groton MA, warned out of New Ipswich, 1794, file #2286, p2

PARKER Polley - formerly of Amherst, warned out of Temple, 1800, file #7060, p47

PARKER Rachel - formerly of Mason, warned out of Dearing, 1795, file #7059, p13

PARKER Sam'l - formerly of Pepperell, warned out of New Ipswich, 1791, file #2283, p2

PARKER Samuel - formerly of Peterborough, warned out of Wilton, 1774, file #2604, p2

PARKER Susanna - formerly of Groton, warned out of New Ipswich, 1774, file #2268, p1

PARKER Tosha (c) - formerly of Westbury MA, warned out of Wilton, 1787, file #2604-B, p4

PARKER William - warned out of New Boston, 1786, file #2278, p5

PARKHURST Andrew - formerly of Wilton, warned out of Temple, 1791, file #7060, p55

PARKHURST Andrew (c) - formerly of Wilton, warned out of Temple, 1791, file #7060, p55

PARKHURST Anna (c) - formerly of Mason, warned out of Temple, 1798, file #7060, p40

PARKHURST Betsey (c) - formerly of Mason, warned out of Temple, 1798, file #7060, p40

PARKHURST Jonas Jr - formerly of Dracut MA, warned out of Wilton, 1782, file #2604-E, p8

PARKHURST Lydia - formerly of Wilton, warned out of Temple, 1791, file #7060, p55

PARKHURST Lydia (c) - formerly of Wilton, warned out of Temple, 1791, file #7060, p55

PARKHURST Rachael - formerly of Dracut MA, warned out of Wilton, 1782, file #2604-E, p8

PARKHURST Sally (c) - formerly of Mason, warned out of Temple, 1798, file #7060, p40

PARKHURST William - formerly of Mason, warned out of Temple, 1798, file #7060, p40

PARKHURST William (c) - formerly of Mason, warned out of Temple, 1798, file #7060, p40

PARKIN Sarah (widow) - formerly of Andover MA, warned out of Wilton, 1770, file #2604-C, p9

PARKMAN Reuses - warned out of Goffstown, 1791, file #3606, p3

PARKS Benja - formerly of Lincoln MA, warned out of Temple, 1792, file #7060, p34

PARKS Betsey - formerly of Lincoln MA, warned out of Temple, 1793, file #7060, p36

PARKS Louis (c) - formerly of Lincoln MA, warned out of Temple, 1792, file #7060, p34

PARKS Lydia - formerly of Lincoln MA, warned out of Temple, 1792, file #7060, p34

PATCH Abigail - formerly of Rouly Bay, warned out of New Ipswich, 1784, file #2275, p2

PATCH Ephraim - warned out of New Boston, 1785, file #2276, p1

PATCH Ephraim - warned out of New Boston, 1785, file #2276, p1

PATCH Nabey - warned out of New Boston, 1789, file #2281, p4

PATCH Reuben - warned out of New Boston, 1785, file #2276, p1

PATCH Ruben - warned out of New Boston, 1785, file #2276, p1

PATCH Salley (c) - formerly of Rouly Bay, warned out of New Ipswich, 1784, file #2275, p2

PATCH Samuel - formerly of Rouly Bay, warned out of New Ipswich, 1784, file #2275, p2

PATCH Stephen (c) - formerly of Rouly Bay, warned out of New Ipswich, 1784, file #2275, p2

PATRICK Nancy - formerly of Merrimack, warned out of Dearing, 1786, file #7059, p5

PATTS Betsy (c) - warned out of New Ipswich, 1789, file #2281, p2

PATTS David (c) - warned out of New Ipswich, 1789, file #2281, p2

PATTS Jonathan - formerly of Jaffrey, warned out of New Ipswich, 1789, file #2281, p2

PATTS Nancy (c) - warned out of New Ipswich, 1789, file #2281, p2

PATTS Rebecca - warned out of New Ipswich, 1789, file #2281, p2

PEABODY Isaac - formerly of Lyndeborough, warned out of Wilton, 1793, file #2604-C, p4

PEABODY Isaac - formerly of Wilton, warned out of Temple, 1782, file #7060, p18

PEABODY Isaac (c) - formerly of Wilton, warned out of Temple, 1782, file #7060, p18

PEABODY James (c) - formerly of Lyndeborough, warned out of Wilton, 1793, file #2604-C, p4

PEABODY Lucy - formerly of Lyndeborough, warned out of Wilton, 1793, file #2604-C, p4

PEABODY Lucy - formerly of Wilton, warned out of Temple, 1796, file #7060, p35

PEABODY Mehitable (c) - formerly of Lyndeborough, warned out of Wilton, 1793, file #2604-C, p4

PEABODY Putnam (c) - formerly of Wilton, warned out of Temple, 1782, file #7060, p18

PEABODY Sarah - formerly of Lyndeborough, warned out of Wilton, 1793, file #2604-C, p4

PEARSON Amos (c) - formerly of Littleton MA, warned out of Temple, 1801, file #7060, p56

PEARSON Dydenlias & Wife - formerly of Littleton MA, warned out of Temple, 1801, file #7060, p56

PEARSON Ebenezer - formerly of Lyndeborough, warned out of Wilton, 1784, file #2604-D, p2

PEARSON Hiram - formerly of Wilton, warned out of Temple, 1798, file #7060, p29

PEARSON Luther (c) - formerly of Amherst, warned out of Temple, 1801, file #7060, p56

PEARSON Solomon - formerly of Newbury, warned out of Temple, 1794, file #7060, p14

PECKIN Betty (c) - formerly of Middlesberry, warned out of Temple, 1789, file #7060, p33

PECKIN Horace (c) - formerly of Middlesberry, warned out of Temple, 1789, file #7060, p33

PECKIN Marcus (c) - formerly of Middlesberry, warned out of Temple, 1789, file #7060, p33

PECKIN Abigail (c) - formerly of Middlesberry, warned out of Temple, 1789, file #7060, p33

PECKIN John & Wife - formerly of Middlesberry MA, warned out of Temple, 1789, file #7060, p33

PERCY Margaret - formerly of Peterborough, warned out of Temple, 1787, file #7060, p26

PERKINS David - formerly of Topsfield MA, warned out of Temple, 1794, file #7060, p57

PERKINS Elizabeth - formerly of Ipswich MA, warned out of Dunbarton, 1784, file #2517, p1

PERREY Hannah - formerly of Landgon, warned out of Temple, 1793, file #7060, p36

PERRUM Jonathan (son) - formerly of Chelmsford MA, warned out of Wilton, 1787, file #2604-B, p4

PERRUM Samuel & Wife - formerly of Chelmsford MA, warned out of Wilton, 1787, file #2604-B, p4

PERRY Abigail (c) - formerly of Temple, warned out of Wilton, 1791, file #2604-E, p1

PERRY Dorcas (c) - formerly of Temple, warned out of Wilton, 1791, file #2604-E, p1

PERRY Hephizibak - formerly of Temple, warned out of Wilton, 1791, file #2604-E, p1

PERRY Huldah (c) - formerly of Temple, warned out of Wilton, 1774, file #2604-E, p3

PERRY James - formerly of Temple, warned out of Wilton, 1791, file #2604-E, p1

PERRY James - formerly of Temple, warned out of New Ipswich, 1785, file #2276, p4

PERRY Katharine - formerly of Westford MA, warned out of Wilton, 1784, file #2604-E, p5

PERRY Katharine (c) - formerly of Temple, warned out of Wilton, 1774, file #2604-E, p3

PERRY Louis (c) - formerly of Westford MA, warned out of Wilton, 1784, file #2604-E, p5

PERRY Mary - formerly of Temple, warned out of Wilton, 1774, file #2604-E, p3

PERRY Obadiah - formerly of Temple, warned out of Wilton, 1774, file #2604-E, p3

PERRY Sarah (c) - formerly of Temple, warned out of Wilton, 1774, file #2604-E, p3

PHEBE Servernt - warned out of New Boston, 1786, file #2278, p1

PHELPS Kezia - formerly of Pittsfield, warned out of Dearing, 1795, file #7059, p17

PHILLIPS Newhall Eliza (c) - formerly of Ashby MA, warned out of New Ipswich, 1795, file #2288, p2

PHILLIPS Rosanna - formerly of Ashby MA, warned out of New Ipswich, 1795, file #2288, p2

PIERCE Benja (c) - formerly of New Ipswich, warned out of Temple, 1798, file #7060, p40

PIERCE Benjamin - formerly of New Ipswich, warned out of Temple, 1798, file #7060, p40

PIERCE Benjamin - formerly of Rindge, warned out of New Ipswich, 1789, file #2281, p6

PIERCE Benjamin (c) - formerly of Rindge, warned out of New Ipswich, 1789, file #2281, p6

PIERCE Bridget (c) - formerly of New Ipswich, warned out of Temple, 1798, file #7060, p40

PIERCE Briget (c) - formerly of Rindge, warned out of New Ipswich, 1789, file #2281, p6

PIERCE Hannah - warned out of Lyndeborough, 1780, file #2327, p1

PIERCE Hannah - formerly of Fitsburg MA, warned out of New Ipswich, 1794, file #2286, p1

PIERCE Hannah (c) - warned out of Lyndeborough, 1780, file #2327, p1

PIERCE Joseph (c) - warned out of Lyndeborough, 1780, file #2327, p1

PIERCE Joseph (c) - formerly of New Ipswich, warned out of Temple, 1798, file #7060, p40

PIERCE Lydia (c) - formerly of New Ipswich, warned out of Temple, 1798, file #7060, p40

PIERCE Oliver - formerly of Fitsburg MA, warned out of New Ipswich, 1794, file #2286, p1

PIERCE Peg (c) - warned out of Lyndeborough, 1780, file #2327, p1

PIERCE Peter - warned out of Goffstown, 1789, file #3609, p4

PIERCE Polley (c) - formerly of New Ipswich, warned out of Temple, 1798, file #7060, p40

PIERCE Rebecca - formerly of New Ipswich, warned out of Temple, 1798, file #7060, p40

PIERCE Rebecca - formerly of Rindge, warned out of New Ipswich, 1789, file #2281, p6

PIERCE Rebecca (c) - formerly of Rindge, warned out of New Ipswich, 1789, file #2281, p6

PIERCE Sally - formerly of Peterborough, warned out of Temple, 1796, file #7060, p35

PIERCE Unice - formerly of Townsend MA, warned out of Temple, 1798, file #7060, p59

PIPER Francis - formerly of Sharon, warned out of Temple, 1800, file #7060, p47

PIRCE Joseph - warned out of New Boston, 1790, file #2282, p2

PIRKINS Ebenx - formerly of Peterborough, warned out of Wilton, 1774, file #2604, p2

POLLARD Abigail (c) - warned out of Goffstown, 1790, file #3609, p5

POLLARD Adam - warned out of New Boston, 1786, file #2278, p5

POLLARD Adam (c) - formerly of Goffstown, warned out of Dunbarton, 1790, file #2523, p5

POLLARD Amaziah - formerly of Goffstown, warned out of Dunbarton, 1790, file #2523, p5

POLLARD Anna (c) - formerly of Goffstown, warned out of Dunbarton, 1790, file #2523, p5

POLLARD David - warned out of New Boston, 1786, file #2278, p5

POLLARD David (c) - formerly of Goffstown, warned out of Dunbarton, 1790, file #2523, p5

POLLARD Elizabeth - warned out of Goffstown, 1790, file #3609, p5

POLLARD Emmeziah Mr - warned out of New Boston, 1786, file #2278, p5

POLLARD James - warned out of Goffstown, 1789, file #3607, p4

POLLARD Jennet - warned out of New Boston, 1786, file #2278, p5

POLLARD Jennet - formerly of Goffstown, warned out of Dunbarton, 1790, file #2523, p5

POLLARD John - warned out of Goffstown, 1790, file #3609, p5

POLLARD Margaret - warned out of New Boston, 1786, file #2278, p5

POLLARD Olive - warned out of New Boston, 1786, file #2278, p5

POLLARD Olive (c) - formerly of Goffstown, warned out of Dunbarton, 1790, file #2523, p5

POLLARD Oliver - warned out of Goffstown, 1796, file #3607, p8

POLLARD Peggey (c) - formerly of Goffstown, warned out of Dunbarton, 1790, file #2523, p5

POLLARD Sarah - warned out of Goffstown, 1796, file #3607, p8

POLLARD Thomas - warned out of Goffstown, 1796, file #3607, p8

POLLARD Thomas (c) - warned out of Goffstown, 1796, file #3607, p8

POLLLARD Anna - warned out of New Boston, 1786, file #2278, p5

POOL Mary - formerly of MA, warned out of New Ipswich, 1795, file #2288, p3

POOL Rufus - formerly of MA, warned out of New Ipswich, 1795, file #2288, p3

POOL Rufus Jr (c) - formerly of MA, warned out of New Ipswich, 1795, file #2288, p3

POOL Sary (c) - formerly of MA, warned out of New Ipswich, 1795, file #2288, p3

POOL Theadoah (sic) (c) - formerly of MA, warned out of New Ipswich, 1795, file #2288, p3

POOL William (c) - formerly of MA, warned out of New Ipswich, 1795, file #2288, p3

POOR Polly - warned out of Goffstown, 1789, file #3609, p4

POOR Polly (c) - warned out of Goffstown, 1789, file #3609, p4

POOR Timothy - warned out of Goffstown, 1789, file #3609, p4

POPE Jese (c) - formerly of Heniker, warned out of Dearing, 1788, file #7059, p14

POPE Judith - formerly of Heniker, warned out of Dearing, 1788, file #7059, p14

POPE Judith - formerly of Heniker, warned out of Dearing, 1788, file #7059, p14

POPE Sampson (c) - formerly of Heniker, warned out of Dearing, 1788, file #7059, p14

POPE Simeon - formerly of Heniker, warned out of Dearing, 1788, file #7059, p14

POPE Simeon Jr (c) - formerly of Heniker, warned out of Dearing, 1788, file #7059, p14

PORTER Ceasar - formerly of Litchfield, warned out of Dunbarton, 1787, file #2520, p3

PORTER Fortune (c) - formerly of Litchfield, warned out of Dunbarton, 1787, file #2520, p3

PORTER Nancy (c) - formerly of Litchfield, warned out of Dunbarton, 1787, file #2520, p3

PORTER Phillis - formerly of Litchfield, warned out of Dunbarton, 1787, file #2520, p3

PORTER Salvenus - formerly of Rindge, warned out of New Ipswich, 1773, file #2267, p2

POWERS Joseph (c) - formerly of Peterborough, warned out of New Ipswich, 1777, file #2287, p1

POWERS Lucy - formerly of Hollis, warned out of New Ipswich, 1777, file #2287, p1

POWERS Michael (c) - formerly of Peterborough, warned out of New Ipswich, 1777, file #2287, p1

POWERS Silance - formerly of Lindsbourg, warned out of New Ipswich, 1777, file #2287, p1

POWERS Silence - formerly of New Ipswich, warned out of Wilton, 1780, file #2604-E, p6

PRAT Sarah - warned out of Wilton, 1779, file #2604-B, p3

PRATT Lydia - formerly of Reding MA, warned out of New Ipswich, 1785, file #2276, p4

PRATT Mehitable - formerly of Reding MA, warned out of New Ipswich, 1785, file #2276, p4

PRATT Assenath & Wife - formerly of Reading MA, warned out of Temple, 1799, file #7060, p43

PRATT Assenath (c) - formerly of Reading MA, warned out of Temple, 1799, file #7060, p43

PRATT Betsy (c) - formerly of Malden MA, warned out of New Ipswich, 1789, file #2281, p6

PRATT Dorcas (c) - formerly of Reading MA, warned out of Temple, 1799, file #7060, p43

PRATT Edmund (c) - formerly of Reading MA, warned out of Temple, 1799, file #7060, p43

PRATT Edward - formerly of Reading MA, warned out of Temple, 1799, file #7060, p43

PRATT Edward (c) - formerly of Reading MA, warned out of Temple, 1799, file #7060, p43

PRATT Hannah - formerly of Reding MA, warned out of New Ipswich, 1785, file #2276, p4

PRATT Joanna - formerly of Malding MA, warned out of New Ipswich, 1787, file #2280, p2

PRATT John Jr (Mr) - formerly of Reding MA, warned out of New Ipswich, 1785, file #2276, p4

PRATT Lydia (c) - formerly of Malden MA, warned out of New Ipswich, 1789, file #2281, p6

PRATT Nathan (c) - formerly of Malden MA, warned out of New Ipswich, 1789, file #2281, p6

PRATT Nathaniel - formerly of Greenwich, warned out of Temple, 1790, file #7060, p37

PRATT Phebe - formerly of Malden MA, warned out of New Ipswich, 1789, file #2281, p6

PRATT Phineas - formerly of Malden MA, warned out of New Ipswich, 1789, file #2281, p6

PRATT Phineas Jr - formerly of Malden MA, warned out of New Ipswich, 1787, file #2280, p2

PRATT Ruth - formerly of Reading MA, warned out of Temple, 1799, file #7060, p43

PREIST Robert - formerly of Groton, warned out of New Ipswich, 1792, file #2284, p1

PRENTICE Harry - formerly of Littleton MA, warned out of New Ipswich, 1792, file #2284, p1

PRENTICE Polly - formerly of Littleton MA, warned out of New Ipswich, 1792, file #2284, p4

PRICE John (c) - formerly of Newbury MA, warned out of Temple, 1784, file #7060, p19

PRICE Lois & Wife - formerly of Newbury MA, warned out of Temple, 1784, file #7060, p19

PRICHARD Elizabeth - formerly of Hollis, warned out of New Ipswich, 1785, file #2276, p4

PRICHARD Jeremiah (Lt) - formerly of Hollis, warned out of New Ipswich, 1785, file #2276, p4

PRIST Sarah - formerly of Groton MA, warned out of New Ipswich, 1791, file #2283, p1

PROCTER Asa - formerly of Chensford MA, warned out of Dearing, 1795, file #7059, p8

PROCTER Emme - formerly of Chensford MA, warned out of Dearing, 1795, file #7059, p8

PROCTER Herbert (c) - formerly of Chelmsford MA, warned out of Temple, 1800, file #7060, p47

PROCTER Marshia (c) - formerly of Chelmsford MA, warned out of Temple, 1800, file #7060, p47

PROCTER Porter (c) - formerly of Chelmsford MA, warned out of Temple, 1800, file #7060, p47

PROCTER Sabrinia (c) - formerly of Chelmsford MA, warned out of Temple, 1800, file #7060, p47

PROCTER Samuel (c) - formerly of Chensford MA, warned out of Dearing, 1795, file #7059, p8

PROCTER Samuel - formerly of Chelmsford MA, warned out of Temple, 1800, file #7060, p47

PROCTER Sarah - formerly of Chelmsford MA, warned out of Temple, 1800, file #7060, p47

PROCTER William (c) - formerly of Chensford MA, warned out of Dearing, 1795, file #7059, p8

PULSIFER John - formerly of Walpole, warned out of Temple, 1794, file #7060, p58

PUTNAM Aaron Kimabl - formerly of Wilton, warned out of Temple, 1800, file #7060, p47

PUTNAM Abigail - formerly of Grafton MA, warned out of New Ipswich, 1787, file #2279, p1

PUTNAM Hannah - formerly of Littleton MA, warned out of New Ipswich, 1789, file #2281, p6

PUTNAM John - formerly of Sutton MA, warned out of New Ipswich, 1794, file #2286, p2

PUTNAM John - formerly of Wilton, warned out of Temple, 1795, file #7060, p30

QUIMBY Aaron - warned out of Goffstown, 1793, file #3609, p8

QUIMBY Elizabeth (c) - warned out of Goffstown, 1793, file #3609, p8

QUIMBY Esther (c) - warned out of Goffstown, 1793, file #3609, p8

QUIMBY Sarah - warned out of Goffstown, 1793, file #3609, p8

READ Betey (c) - formerly of Mason, warned out of New Ipswich, 1795, file #2288, p3

READ Lucy Jr - warned out of New Boston, 1790, file #2282, p2

READ Polly (c) - formerly of Mason, warned out of New Ipswich, 1795, file #2288, p3

READ Salley (c) - formerly of Mason, warned out of New Ipswich, 1795, file #2288, p3

READ Sally - formerly of Mason, warned out of New Ipswich, 1795, file #2288, p3

READ Thasmin (c) - formerly of Mason, warned out of New Ipswich, 1795, file #2288, p3

READ Thomas - formerly of Mason, warned out of New Ipswich, 1795, file #2288, p3

REDINGTON Anna - warned out of New Boston, 1790, file #2282, p3

REDINGTON Daniel - warned out of New Boston, 1790, file #2282, p3

REDINGTON Daniel Jr (c) - warned out of New Boston, 1790, file #2282, p3

REDINGTON Nancy (c) - warned out of New Boston, 1790, file #2282, p3

REED Josiah - formerly of Lexington MA, warned out of New Ipswich, 1792, file #2284, p3

REED Sarah - formerly of Lexington MA, warned out of New Ipswich, 1792, file #2284, p3

REED Hannah - formerly of Chelmsford MA, warned out of Wilton, 1784, file #2604-D, p2

REED Hannah (c) - formerly of Chelmsford MA, warned out of Wilton, 1784, file #2604-D, p2

REED James (Lt) - warned out of Goffstown, 1789, file #3607, p5

REED Patty (c) - formerly of Chelmsford MA, warned out of Wilton, 1784, file #2604-D, p2

REED Peter - formerly of Chelmsford MA, warned out of Wilton, 1784, file #2604-D, p2

REMAX Samuel - warned out of Goffstown, 1772, file #3606, p8

RICE Amas & Wife - formerly of Greenwich, warned out of Temple, 1790, file #7060, p37

RICHARDSON Abigail (c) - warned out of Goffstown, 1793, file #3608, p1

RICHARDSON Abigail (c) - warned out of Goffstown, 1790, file #3609, p5

RICHARDSON Alice - warned out of Goffstown, 1793, file #3608, p1

RICHARDSON Alle - warned out of Goffstown, 1790, file #3609, p5

RICHARDSON Elizabeth (c) - warned out of Goffstown, 1790, file #3609, p5

RICHARDSON Jacob - warned out of Goffstown, 1790, file #3609, p5

RICHARDSON John - warned out of Goffstown, 1793, file #3608, p1

RICHARDSON John - formerly of Lyndeborough, warned out of Temple, 1794, file #7060, p58

RICHARDSON John (c) - formerly of Lyndeborough, warned out of Temple, 1794, file #7060, p58

RICHARDSON Lydia - formerly of Lyndeborough, warned out of Temple, 1794, file #7060, p58

RICHARDSON Lydia (c) - formerly of Lyndeborough, warned out of Temple, 1794, file #7060, p58

RICHARDSON Mary - warned out of Goffstown, 1790, file #3609, p5

RICHARDSON Philip - formerly of Salem, warned out of Dunbarton, 1793, file #2526, p4

RICHARDSON William (c) - formerly of Harvard MA, warned out of New Ipswich, 1777, file #2287, p1

RITCHINSON Sarah - formerly of Andover MA, warned out of Wilton, 1784, file #2604-E, p7

RITCHISON Eleanor - formerly of Andover MA, warned out of Wilton, 1780, file #2604-E, p6

RITE John - formerly of Dunstable, warned out of Wilton, 1784, file #2604-E, p7

RITE Sarah - formerly of Dunstable, warned out of Wilton, 1784, file #2604-E, p7

RITTER Ruth - formerly of Lunenburgh MA, warned out of Wilton, 1777, file #2604-B, p6

RITTER William - formerly of Lunenburgh MA, warned out of Wilton, 1777, file #2604-B, p6

ROACH Patrick - warned out of Dunbarton, 1774, file #2529, p1

ROBERSON David - formerly of Rindge, warned out of New Ipswich, 1788, file #2280, p3

ROBERSON Jonathan (c) - formerly of Rindge, warned out of New Ipswich, 1788, file #2280, p3

ROBERSON Nathaniel (c) - formerly of Rindge, warned out of New Ipswich, 1788, file #2280, p3

ROBERSON Ruth (c) - formerly of Rindge, warned out of New Ipswich, 1788, file #2280, p3

ROBERSON Susanna - formerly of Rindge, warned out of New Ipswich, 1788, file #2280, p3

ROBERSON Susanna (c) - formerly of Rindge, warned out of New Ipswich, 1788, file #2280, p3

ROBERTSON Mary - formerly of Amherst, warned out of New Ipswich, 1784, file #2275, p2

ROBERTSON Peter - formerly of Amherst, warned out of New Ipswich, 1784, file #2275, p2

ROBINGS Daniel - formerly of Wilton, warned out of New Ipswich, 1773, file #2267, p4

ROBINGS Joseph - formerly of Wilton, warned out of New Ipswich, 1773, file #2267, p4

ROBINGS Rachel - formerly of Wilton, warned out of New Ipswich, 1773, file #2267, p4

ROBINS Daniel - formerly of Dunstable, warned out of Wilton, 1772, file #2604, p1

ROBINS Joseph - formerly of Dunstable, warned out of Wilton, 1772, file #2604, p1

ROBINS Rachael - formerly of Dunstable, warned out of Wilton, 1772, file #2604, p1

ROBINS Ruth - formerly of Lexington, warned out of New Ipswich, 1785, file #2276, p6

ROBINS Seth - formerly of Lexington, warned out of New Ipswich, 1785, file #2276, p6

ROBINSON Elizabeth - formerly of Bedford MA, warned out of New Ipswich, 1795, file #2288, p2

ROBINSON John - warned out of Goffstown, 1796, file #3607, p8

ROGER Abigail - formerly of Weare, warned out of Goffstown, 1791, file #3609, p7

ROGER Anne (c) - formerly of Weare, warned out of Goffstown, 1791, file #3609, p7

ROGER Hannah (c) - formerly of Weare, warned out of Goffstown, 1791, file #3609, p7

ROGER John (c) - formerly of Weare, warned out of Goffstown, 1791, file #3609, p7

ROGER Sarah (c) - formerly of Weare, warned out of Goffstown, 1791, file #3609, p7

ROGER William - formerly of Weare, warned out of Goffstown, 1791, file #3609, p7

ROGER William Jr (c) - formerly of Weare, warned out of Goffstown, 1791, file #3609, p7

ROLLINGS John - warned out of Goffstown, 1788, file #3608, p8

ROLLINGS March (c) - warned out of Goffstown, 1788, file #3608, p8

ROLLINGS Mehitteybil - warned out of Goffstown, 1788, file #3608, p8

ROLLINGS Moses (c) - warned out of Goffstown, 1788, file #3608, p8

ROLLINGS Polly (c) - warned out of Goffstown, 1788, file #3608, p8

ROLLINGS Rhodey (c) - warned out of Goffstown, 1788, file #3608, p8

ROPES John - warned out of Goffstown, 1791, file #3606, p3

ROWEL Ichabod - formerly of Dublin, warned out of Temple, 1799, file #7060, p46

RUSS Abigal Oliver - warned out of Goffstown, 1791, file #3609, p7

RUSS Abigail (c) - warned out of Goffstown, 1791, file #3609, p7

RUSS James (c) - warned out of Goffstown, 1791, file #3609, p7

RUSS John - warned out of Goffstown, 1791, file #3609, p7

RUSS John (c) - warned out of Goffstown, 1791, file #3609, p7

RUSS Sarah - warned out of Goffstown, 1791, file #3609, p7

RUSS Sarah Jr (c) - warned out of Goffstown, 1791, file #3609, p7

RUSSEL Abigail (c) - formerly of Harvard, warned out of New Ipswich, 1789, file #2281, p6

RUSSEL Eunice - formerly of Harvard, warned out of New Ipswich, 1789, file #2281, p6

RUSSEL Eunice - formerly of Harvard, warned out of New Ipswich, 1789, file #2281, p6

RUSSEL James - formerly of Lyndeborough, warned out of Temple, 1796, file #7060, p35

RUSSEL Polly (c) - formerly of Harvard, warned out of New Ipswich, 1789, file #2281, p6

RUSSEL Rhoda (c) - formerly of Harvard, warned out of New Ipswich, 1789, file #2281, p6

RUSSEL Ruth - formerly of Harvard, warned out of New Ipswich, 1789, file #2281, p6

RUSSEL Samuel - formerly of Harvard, warned out of New Ipswich, 1789, file #2281, p6

RUSSELL Abigal (c) - formerly of Rindge, warned out of New Ipswich, 1792, file #2284, p3

RUSSELL Billey - formerly of Lyndeborough, warned out of Temple, 1800, file #7060, p44

RUSSELL Ebeneszer (c) - formerly of Rindge, warned out of New Ipswich, 1778, file #2269, p3

RUSSELL Ezekiel - formerly of Harvard, warned out of New Ipswich, 1789, file #2281, p6

RUSSELL Hanah - formerly of Andover MA, warned out of Wilton, 1784, file #2604-E, p7

RUSSELL Jacob - formerly of Rindge, warned out of New Ipswich, 1778, file #2269, p3

RUSSELL John (c) - formerly of Lyndeborough, warned out of Wilton, 1795, file #2604-D, p7

RUSSELL John Gilman - warned out of New Boston, 1790, file #2282, p2

RUSSELL Louic? (c) - formerly of Rindge, warned out of New Ipswich, 1792, file #2284, p3

RUSSELL Louisa - formerly of Rindge, warned out of New Ipswich, 1792, file #2284, p3

RUSSELL Mary - formerly of Rindge, warned out of New Ipswich, 1778, file #2269, p3

RUSSELL Nancy (c) - formerly of Rindge, warned out of New Ipswich, 1792, file #2284, p3

RUSSELL Nathan (c) - formerly of Rindge, warned out of New Ipswich, 1792, file #2284, p3

RUSSELL Nathaniel - formerly of Rindge, warned out of New Ipswich, 1784, file #2275, p6

RUSSELL Patty (c) - formerly of Lyndeborough, warned out of Wilton, 1795, file #2604-D, p7

RUSSELL Polly (c) - formerly of Rindge, warned out of New Ipswich, 1792, file #2284, p3

RUSSELL Rebecah (c) - formerly of Rindge, warned out of New Ipswich, 1792, file #2284, p3

RUSSELL Samuel - formerly of Rindge, warned out of New Ipswich, 1792, file #2284, p3

RUSSELL Samuel (c) - formerly of Rindge, warned out of New Ipswich, 1792, file #2284, p3

RUSSELL Sarah (widow) - formerly of Lyndeborough, warned out of Wilton, 1795, file #2604-D, p7

RUSSELL William (c) - formerly of Rindge, warned out of New Ipswich, 1778, file #2269, p3

RYAN Sam'l - formerly of Sukesbury MA, warned out of New Ipswich, 1794, file #2286, p1

SAMPSON Joseph & Wife - warned out of New Boston, 1787, file #2279, p10

SANDERS Hannah (c) - warned out of New Ipswich, 1788, file #2280, p2

SANDERS Lydia (c) - warned out of New Ipswich, 1788, file #2280, p2

SANDERS Sanders (c) - warned out of New Ipswich, 1788, file #2280, p2

SANDERS Clark (c) - warned out of New Ipswich, 1788, file #2280, p2

SANDERS Clark Edward (Mrs) - warned out of New Ipswich, 1788, file #2280, p2

SANDERS Clark Edward Mr - formerly of Canterbury CT, warned out of New Ipswich, 1787, file #2279, p1

SANDERS Lucy - formerly of Temple, warned out of Wilton, 1783, file #2604-E, p10

SANDERS Stephen - formerly of Temple, warned out of Wilton, 1783, file #2604-E, p10

SARTWELL Joel - formerly of Groton MA, warned out of Temple, 1792, file #7060, p39

SAUTEL Asa (c) - formerly of New Ipswich, warned out of Dearing, 1772, file #2266, p2

SAUTEL Edmund (c) - warned out of New Ipswich, 1772, file #2266, p3

SAUTEL Hame (c) - warned out of New Ipswich, 1772, file #2266, p3

SAUTEL John - warned out of New Ipswich, 1772, file #2266, p3

SAUTEL John (c) - warned out of New Ipswich, 1772, file #2266, p3

SAUTEL Levy (c) - formerly of New Ipswich, warned out of Dearing, 1772, file #2266, p3

SAUTEL Susanna - warned out of New Ipswich, 1772, file #2266, p3

SAUTEL Susanna (c) - warned out of New Ipswich, 1772, file #2266, p3

SAVAGE Jabe - formerly of Lincoln MA, warned out of Temple, 1787, file #7060, p3

SAVAGE Juda - formerly of Lincoln MA, warned out of Temple, 1787, file #7060, p3

SAWYER Anna (c) - formerly of Amherst, warned out of Wilton, 1783, file #2604-E, p11

SAWYER Hannah (c) - formerly of Amherst, warned out of Wilton, 1783, file #2604-E, p11

SAWYER Nathaniel - formerly of Amherst, warned out of Wilton, 1783, file #2604-E, p11

SAWYER Prudance - formerly of Amherst, warned out of Wilton, 1783, file #2604-E, p11

SCARLET John - formerly of Groton MA, warned out of Temple, 1790, file #7060, p53

SCARLOT John - formerly of Townsend MA, warned out of New Ipswich, 1795, file #2288, p2

SERGANT Simon - formerly of Pittsfield, warned out of Dearing, 1795, file #7059, p17

SERGENT Enoch - warned out of Goffstown, 1788, file #3608, p8

SERGENT Enoch (c) - warned out of Goffstown, 1788, file #3608, p8

SERGENT Hannah (c) - warned out of Goffstown, 1788, file #3608, p8

SERGENT Polly (c) - warned out of Goffstown, 1788, file #3608, p8

SERGENT Sally (c) - warned out of Goffstown, 1788, file #3608, p8

SEVERANCE Abel - formerly of Washington, warned out of Temple, 1792, file #7060, p34

SEVERANCE Ephraim (c) - formerly of Washington, warned out of Temple, 1792, file #7060, p34

SEVERANCE Nabby - formerly of Washington, warned out of Temple, 1792, file #7060, p34

SEVERANCE Patty - formerly of Washington, warned out of Temple, 1792, file #7060, p34

SEVERANCE William (c) - formerly of Washington, warned out of Temple, 1792, file #7060, p34

SEVERENCE Abby - formerly of Ashby MA, warned out of Temple, 1784, file #7060, p19

SEVERENS Mary - formerly of Shrewsbury MA, warned out of Temple, 1787, file #7060, p26

SHANNON Eunice - formerly of Wilton, warned out of Temple, 1799, file #7060, p45

SHANNON William - formerly of Wilton, warned out of Temple, 1799, file #7060, p45

SHANNON William - formerly of Litchfield, warned out of Temple, 1794, file #7060, p58

SHATTUCK Abel (c) - formerly of Ashby MA, warned out of New Ipswich, 1794, file #2286, p2

SHATTUCK Asher (c) - formerly of Wilton, warned out of Temple, 1800, file #7060, p47

SHATTUCK Benjamin - formerly of Bradford, warned out of New Ipswich, 1795, file #2288, p3

SHATTUCK Betsy - formerly of Ashby MA, warned out of New Ipswich, 1794, file #2286, p2

SHATTUCK Betsy (c) - formerly of Ashby MA, warned out of New Ipswich, 1794, file #2286, p2

SHATTUCK Daniel (c) - formerly of Ashby MA, warned out of New Ipswich, 1794, file #2286, p2

SHATTUCK Daniel (c) - formerly of Wilton, warned out of Temple, 1800, file #7060, p47

SHATTUCK David - formerly of Wilton, warned out of Temple, 1800, file #7060, p47

SHATTUCK Francis (c) - formerly of Wilton, warned out of Temple, 1800, file #7060, p47

SHATTUCK Jenney (c) - formerly of Wilton, warned out of Temple, 1800, file #7060, p47

SHATTUCK John - formerly of Ashby MA, warned out of New Ipswich, 1794, file #2286, p2

SHATTUCK John (c) - formerly of Ashby MA, warned out of New Ipswich, 1794, file #2286, p2

SHATTUCK Lemuel (c) - formerly of Ashby MA, warned out of New Ipswich, 1794, file #2286, p2

SHATTUCK Polley (c) - formerly of Bradford, warned out of New Ipswich, 1795, file #2288, p3

SHATTUCK Salley - formerly of Bradford, warned out of New Ipswich, 1795, file #2288, p3

SHATTUCK Shebuel (c) - formerly of Wilton, warned out of Temple, 1800, file #7060, p47

SHATTUCK Sibbil - formerly of Wilton, warned out of Temple, 1800, file #7060, p47

SHATTUCK Washty? - formerly of Sutton MA, warned out of New Ipswich, 1789, file #2281, p6

SHEAD Joseph - warned out of Goffstown, 1793, file #3608, p1

SHED Daniel (c) - formerly of Ashby, warned out of New Ipswich, 1788, file #2280, p2

SHED Samuel - formerly of Ashby, warned out of New Ipswich, 1787, file #2280, p2

SHED Samuel (c) - formerly of Ashby, warned out of New Ipswich, 1788, file #2280, p2

SHED Susanna - formerly of Ashby, warned out of New Ipswich, 1788, file #2280, p2

SHORT Abigail Or Nabby - warned out of New Boston, 1792, file #2284, p1

SHORT Daniel - warned out of New Boston, 1792, file #2284, p1

SHORT Elizabeth - warned out of New Boston, file #2284, p1

SILLEY Jacob (c) - formerly of Bow, warned out of Dunbarton, 1785, file #2518, p5

SILLEY John (c) - formerly of Bow, warned out of Dunbarton, 1785, file #2518, p5

SILLEY John & Wife - formerly of Bow, warned out of Dunbarton, 1785, file #2518, p5

SILLEY Joseph (c) - formerly of Bow, warned out of Dunbarton, 1785, file #2518, p5

SIMOND Betty - formerly of Amherst, warned out of Wilton, 1795, file #2604-D, p7

SIMOND Damara - formerly of Amherst, warned out of Wilton, 1795, file #2604-D, p7

SIMOND Eliphalet - formerly of Amherst, warned out of Wilton, 1791, file #2604-D, p7

SIMOND John (c) - formerly of Amherst, warned out of Wilton, 1795, file #2604-D, p7

SIMSON Benjm - formerly of Stoddard, warned out of Temple, 1795, file #7060, p50

SMALL Aaron - warned out of Goffstown, 1791, file #3606, p11

SMALL Benjamin & Wife - warned out of Goffstown, 1793, file #3608, p1

SMALL Benjamin (c) - warned out of Goffstown, 1785, file #3606, p11

SMALL Benjamin Jr (c) - warned out of Goffstown, 1793, file #3608, p1

SMALL Elizabeth (c) - warned out of Goffstown, 1785, file #3606, p11

SMALL Eunus - warned out of Goffstown, 1791, file #3606, p11

SMALL Jesse (c) - warned out of Goffstown, 1785, file #3606, p11

SMALL John - warned out of Goffstown, 1791, file #3606, p11

SMALL John (c) - warned out of Goffstown, 1785, file #3606, p11

SMALL Jon'n - warned out of Goffstown, 1784, file #3608, p9

SMALL Jonathan - warned out of Goffstown, 1785, file #3606, p11

SMALL Jonathan (c) - warned out of Goffstown, 1785, file #3606, p11

SMALL Lydia - warned out of Goffstown, 1785, file #3606, p11

SMALL Mary (c) - warned out of Goffstown, 1785, file #3606, p11

SMALL Nathan (c) - warned out of Goffstown, 1785, file #3606, p11

SMALL Rachel - warned out of Goffstown, 1785, file #3606, p11

SMALL Rachel - warned out of Goffstown, 1790, file #3609, p6

SMALL Samuel (c) - warned out of Goffstown, 1785, file #3606, p11

SMALL Simeon - warned out of Goffstown, 1785, file #3606, p11

SMALL Susanne - warned out of Goffstown, 1791, file #3606, p11

SMALL Thomas (c) - warned out of Goffstown, 1785, file #3606, p11

SMITH Moses (c) - formerly of Hollis, warned out of New Ipswich, 1792, file #2284, p1

SMITH Abigail - warned out of Goffstown, 1794, file #3609, p9

SMITH Abigail (c) - formerly of Heniker, warned out of Dearing, 1787, file #7059, p6

SMITH Abigail - formerly of Pembroke, warned out of Dunbarton, 1785, file #2518, p3

SMITH Abigail (c) - formerly of Pembroke, warned out of Dunbarton, 1785, file #2288, p3

SMITH Benjamin (c) - formerly of Heniker, warned out of Dearing, 1787, file #7059, p6

SMITH Charles (c) - formerly of Heniker, warned out of Dearing, 1787, file #7059, p6

SMITH Ephraim (c) - formerly of Heniker, warned out of Dearing, 1787, file #7059, p6

SMITH Francis - formerly of Dublin, warned out of New Ipswich, 1790, file #2282, p1

SMITH Hannah - formerly of Dublin, warned out of New Ipswich, 1790, file #2282, p1

SMITH Jennet (c) - warned out of New Boston, 1790, file #2282, p2

SMITH Johnson - warned out of New Boston, 1790, file #2282, p2

SMITH Margaret - warned out of New Boston, 1786, file #2278, p5

SMITH Martha - warned out of New Boston, 1790, file #2282, p2

SMITH Mary (c) - formerly of Heniker, warned out of Dearing, 1787, file #7059, p6

SMITH Moses - formerly of Heniker, warned out of Dearing, 1787, file #7059, p6

SMITH Naby - warned out of New Boston, 1786, file #2278, p5

SMITH Oliver (c) - formerly of Heniker, warned out of Dearing, 1787, file #7059, p6

SMITH Samuel - formerly of Pembroke, warned out of Dunbarton, 1785, file #2518, p3

SMITH Samuel - warned out of Goffstown, 1794, file #3609, p9

SMITH Samuel Mr - warned out of New Boston, 1786, file #2278, p5

SMITH Samuel (c) - formerly of Pembroke, warned out of Dunbarton, 1785, file #2288, p3

SMITH Silas (c) - formerly of Dublin, warned out of New Ipswich, 1790, file #2282, p1

SMITH Susanna - formerly of Heniker, warned out of Dearing, 1787, file #7059, p6

SMITH Thomas (c) - formerly of Heniker, warned out of Dearing, 1787, file #7059, p6

SMITH Walter (c) - warned out of New Boston, 1790, file #2282, p2

SNOW Charles - formerly of Billerica MA, warned out of Temple, 1799, file #7060, p46

SNOW Isabel - formerly of Road Island, warned out of Wilton, 1780, file #2604-E, p6

SNOW Isabel (c) - formerly of Road Island, warned out of Wilton, 1780, file #2604-E, p6

SNOW John (c) - formerly of Road Island, warned out of Wilton, 1780, file #2604-E, p6

SNOW Josiah & Wife - formerly of Billerica MA, warned out of Temple, 1799, file #7060, p46

SNOW Mary - formerly of Andover MA, warned out of Wilton, 1774, file #2604-D, p8

SNOW William - formerly of Road Island, warned out of Wilton, 1780, file #2604-E, p6

SOLE Bildad - warned out of Goffstown, 1782, file #3606, p7

SPAULDING Anna (c) - formerly of Hollis, warned out of Wilton, 1795, file #2604-D, p7

SPAULDING Asaph (c) Sic - formerly of Hollis, warned out of Wilton, 1795, file #2604-D, p7

SPAULDING Clark (c) - formerly of Hollis, warned out of Wilton, 1795, file #2604-D, p7

SPAULDING Dinah - formerly of Northboro MA, warned out of Temple, 1800, file #7060, p44

SPAULDING Elisabeth - formerly of Tewksbury MA, warned out of Wilton, 1784, file #2604-C, p6

SPAULDING Elizabeth - formerly of Westminster MA, warned out of Temple, 1799, file #7060, p27

SPAULDING Elizabeth (c) - formerly of Westminster MA, warned out of Temple, 1799, file #7060, p27

SPAULDING Ephraim (c) - formerly of Westminster MA, warned out of Temple, 1799, file #7060, p27

SPAULDING Eunice - formerly of Westford MA, warned out of New Ipswich, 1787, file #2279, p1

SPAULDING Hannah (c) Sic - formerly of Hollis, warned out of Wilton, 1795, file #2604-D, p7

SPAULDING Henry - formerly of Stoddard, warned out of Temple, 1784, file #7060, p19

SPAULDING James Mr - formerly of Westford MA, warned out of New Ipswich, 1787, file #2279, p1

SPAULDING Jesse (c) - formerly of Westminster MA, warned out of Temple, 1799, file #7060, p27

SPAULDING John (c) - formerly of Hollis, warned out of Wilton, 1795, file #2604-D, p7

SPAULDING Jonathan - formerly of Hollis, warned out of Wilton, 1795, file #2604-D, p7

SPAULDING Jonathan (c) - formerly of Hollis, warned out of Wilton, 1795, file #2604-D, p7

SPAULDING Lamoni (c) - formerly of Hollis, warned out of Wilton, 1795, file #2604-D, p7

SPAULDING Mary - formerly of Hollis, warned out of Wilton, 1795, file #2604-D, p7

SPAULDING Mehitable (c) - formerly of Hollis, warned out of Wilton, 1795, file #2604-D, p7

SPAULDING Moran - formerly of Westminster MA, warned out of Temple, 1799, file #7060, p27

SPAULDING Moran Jr (c) - formerly of Westminster MA, warned out of Temple, 1799, file #7060, p27

SPAULDING Sampson (c) - formerly of Hollis, warned out of Wilton, 1795, file #2604-D, p7

SPAULDING Wm - formerly of Nariganeck MA, warned out of Temple, 1800, file #7060, p44

STARK James - warned out of Goffstown, 1791, file #3606, p3

STARK Stephen - warned out of Goffstown, 1789, file #3609, p4

STARK William - warned out of Goffstown, 1790, file #3609, p6

STEARNS Abigail - warned out of Goffstown, 1790, file #3607, p6

STEARNS Betsy (c) - warned out of Goffstown, 1790, file #3607, p6

STEARNS Elise - formerly of Billerica MA, warned out of Temple, 1793, file #7060, p36

STEARNS Elizabeth - formerly of Princetown, warned out of New Ipswich, 1788, file #2280, p2

STEARNS Isaac (c) - formerly of Billerica MA, warned out of Temple, 1793, file #7060, p36

STEARNS Joshua - formerly of Princetown, warned out of New Ipswich, 1788, file #2280, p2

STEARNS Samuel - formerly of Billerica MA, warned out of Temple, 1793, file #7060, p36

STEARNS Sarah (c) - warned out of Goffstown, 1790, file #3607, p6

STEARNS William (c) - formerly of Billerica MA, warned out of Temple, 1793, file #7060, p36

STEEL John - formerly of Boston MA, warned out of Temple, 1781, file #7060, p15

STERNS Elijah - warned out of Goffstown, 1789, file #3607, p5

STEVENS Anna - warned out of Temple, file #7060, p17

STEVENS Bettee - warned out of Goffstown, 1794, file #3609, p9

STEVENS David - formerly of Goffstown, warned out of Dunbarton, 1789, file #2515, p2

STEVENS Ephraim - warned out of New Boston, 1787, file #2279, p9

STEVENS Isaac (c) - formerly of Goffstown, warned out of Dunbarton, 1789, file #2515, p2

STEVENS John (c) - warned out of Goffstown, 1794, file #3609, p9

STEVENS Jonathan - warned out of Temple, file #7060, p17

STEVENS Lydia (c) - warned out of Temple, file #7060, p17

STEVENS Mollee (c) - warned out of Goffstown, 1794, file #3609, p9

STEVENS Phebe - formerly of Goffstown, warned out of Dunbarton, 1789, file #2515, p2

STEVENS Rachael (c) - formerly of Goffstown, warned out of Dunbarton, 1789, file #2515, p2

STEVENS Sarah - formerly of Merrimack, warned out of Wilton, 1778, file #2604-C, p7

STEVENS Sarah (c) - formerly of Merrimack, warned out of Wilton, 1778, file #2604-C, p7

STEVENS Thomas - formerly of Merrimack, warned out of Wilton, 1778, file #2604-C, p7

STEVENS Thomas (c) - formerly of Merrimack, warned out of Wilton, 1778, file #2604-C, p7

STEVENS Timothy (c) - warned out of Goffstown, 1794, file #3609, p9

STEVENS Timothy Jr - warned out of Goffstown, 1794, file #3609, p9

STICKNE Moses - formerly of Temple, warned out of New Ipswich, 1792, file #2284, p3

STICKNEY Abigail - warned out of Goffstown, 1782, file #3606, p7

STICKNEY Abraham - warned out of Goffstown, 1782, file #3606, p7

STICKNEY Benjamin (c) - warned out of Goffstown, 1782, file #3606, p7

STICKNEY Isaac (c) - warned out of Goffstown, 1782, file #3606, p7

STILE Azor (c) - formerly of Middleton MA, warned out of Wilton, 1779, file #2604-E, p9

STILE Esther (c) - formerly of Middleton MA, warned out of Wilton, 1779, file #2604-E, p9

STILE John - formerly of Middleton MA, warned out of Wilton, 1779, file #2604-E, p9

STILE John (c) - formerly of Middleton MA, warned out of Wilton, 1779, file #2604-E, p9

STILE Mary - formerly of Middleton MA, warned out of Wilton, 1779, file #2604-E, p9

STILE Mary (c) - formerly of Middleton MA, warned out of Wilton, 1779, file #2604-E, p9

STILE Samuel (c) - formerly of Middleton MA, warned out of Wilton, 1779, file #2604-E, p9

STILES Asa - formerly of Wilton, warned out of Temple, 1801, file #7060, p56

STILES Azybag - formerly of Lyndeborough, warned out of Temple, 1802, file #7060, p38

STILES Betsey - formerly of Wilton, warned out of Temple, 1801, file #7060, p56

STILES Polley - formerly of Wilton, warned out of Temple, 1801, file #7060, p56

STONE Eunice (c) - formerly of Rindge, warned out of New Ipswich, 1791, file #2283, p2

STONE Eunice - formerly of Rindge, warned out of New Ipswich, 1791, file #2283, p2

STONE Jesse - formerly of Groton MA, warned out of New Ipswich, 1792, file #2284, p3

STONE Jesse (c) - formerly of Groton MA, warned out of New Ipswich, 1792, file #2284, p3

STONE Joel - formerly of Rindge, warned out of New Ipswich, 1791, file #2283, p2

STONE Joel (c) - formerly of Rindge, warned out of New Ipswich, 1791, file #2283, p2

STONE John L - formerly of Ashby MA, warned out of New Ipswich, 1784, file #2275, p6

STONE Jonas - formerly of Groton MA, warned out of New Ipswich, 1787, file #2279, p1

STONE Luther (c) - formerly of Rindge, warned out of New Ipswich, 1791, file #2283, p2

STONE Lydia - formerly of Groton MA, warned out of New Ipswich, 1794, file #2286, p2

STONE Milley (c) - formerly of Rindge, warned out of New Ipswich, 1791, file #2283, p2

STONE Polly (c) - formerly of Rindge, warned out of New Ipswich, 1791, file #2283, p2

STONE Susannah - formerly of Groton MA, warned out of New Ipswich, 1792, file #2284, p3

STONE Tim - formerly of Groton MA, warned out of New Ipswich, 1794, file #2286, p2

STORY Bethiah - warned out of Goffstown, 1790, file #3609, p5

STORY Nehemiah - warned out of Goffstown, 1790, file #3609, p5

STORY Sarah - warned out of Goffstown, 1790, file #3609, p5

STOWEL Jeremiah (c) - warned out of Temple, 1790, file #7060, p49

STOWEL John - warned out of Temple, 1790, file #7060, p49

STOWEL Joshua (c) - warned out of Temple, 1790, file #7060, p49

STOWEL Moses (c) - warned out of Temple, 1790, file #7060, p49

STOWEL Newman (c) - warned out of Temple, 1790, file #7060, p49

STOWEL Polley (c) - warned out of Temple, 1790, file #7060, p49

STOWEL Susanna - warned out of Temple, 1790, file #7060, p49

STRATTON Lydia - formerly of Danvers MA, warned out of New Boston, 1787, file #2279, p2

STUART John - warned out of New Boston, 1787, file #2279, p9

SWAN Betty - formerly of Nottingham, warned out of Dunbarton, 1790, file #2523, p9

SWAN Betty (c) - formerly of Nottingham, warned out of Dunbarton, 1790, file #2523, p9

SWAN Joseph - formerly of Nottingham, warned out of Dunbarton, 1790, file #2523, p9

SWETT Anna (c) - formerly of Pembroke, warned out of Dunbarton, 1792, file #2525, p1

SWETT Benjamin (c) - formerly of Pembroke, warned out of Dunbarton, 1792, file #2525, p1

SWETT Betty - formerly of Pembroke, warned out of Dunbarton, 1792, file #2525, p1

SWETT Betty (c) - formerly of Pembroke, warned out of Dunbarton, 1792, file #2525, p1

SWETT Eliphlet (c) - formerly of Pembroke, warned out of Dunbarton, 1792, file #2525, p1

SWETT Joseph - formerly of Pembroke, warned out of Dunbarton, 1792, file #2525, p1

SWETT Joseph Jr (c) - formerly of Pembroke, warned out of Dunbarton, 1792, file #2525, p1

TAGGART Hannah - formerly of Goffstown, warned out of Dunbarton, 1793, file #2526, p2

TAGGART James - formerly of Goffstown, warned out of Dunbarton, 1793, file #2526, p2

TARBELL Benjamin (c) - formerly of Billerica MA, warned out of Temple, 1803, file #7060, p48

TARBELL Betsey - formerly of Billerica MA, warned out of Temple, 1803, file #7060, p48

TARBELL Betty (c) - formerly of Billerica MA, warned out of Temple, 1803, file #7060, p48

TARBELL Isaac (c) - formerly of Billerica MA, warned out of Temple, 1803, file #7060, p48

TARBELL Sally (c) - formerly of Billerica MA, warned out of Temple, 1803, file #7060, p48

TARBELL William - formerly of Billerica MA, warned out of Temple, 1803, file #7060, p48

TARBLE Ziba - formerly of Pepperell MA, warned out of New Ipswich, 1792, file #2284, p1

TAYLOR Abigail - formerly of Groton, warned out of New Ipswich, 1773, file #2267, p4

TAYLOR Joseph - formerly of Groton, warned out of New Ipswich, 1773, file #2267, p4

TAYLOR Olive (c) - warned out of New Ipswich, 1773, file #2267, p4

TAYLOR Rebeckah - formerly of Townsend MA, warned out of Temple, 1798, file #7060, p59

TAYLOR Samuel - formerly of Carlisle, warned out of New Ipswich, 1785, file #2276, p6

TEAL Aaron - warned out of Goffstown, 1790, file #3609, p5

TEAL Rebecca - warned out of Goffstown, 1790, file #3609, p5

TEAL Rebecca (c) - warned out of Goffstown, 1790, file #3609, p5

TEMPLE Besey (c) - formerly of Amherst, warned out of Wilton, 1796, file #2604-D, p5

TEMPLE John - formerly of Mason, warned out of New Ipswich, 1783, file #2274, p2

TEMPLE Juda - formerly of Mason, warned out of New Ipswich, 1783, file #2274, p2

TEMPLETON Adam (c) - formerly of Peterborough, warned out of Temple, 1789, file #7060, p41

TEMPLETON Jane (c) - formerly of Peterborough, warned out of Temple, 1789, file #7060, p41

TEMPLETON Matthew & Wife - formerly of Peterborough, warned out of Temple, 1789, file #7060, p41

TEMPLETON Matthew (c) - formerly of Peterborough, warned out of Temple, 1789, file #7060, p41

TEMPLETON Patty (c) - formerly of Peterborough, warned out of Temple, 1789, file #7060, p41

THOMAS Mehitibal (c) - warned out of New Boston, 1792, file #2284, p2

THOMAS Mehitibal (widow) - warned out of New Boston, 1792, file #2284, p2

THOMAS William - warned out of Goffstown, 1789, file #3609, p4

THOMAS William (c) - warned out of New Boston, 1792, file #2284, p2

THOMPSON John & Wife - warned out of New Boston, 1788, file #2280, p1

THORNE Eber - formerly of Sharon, warned out of Temple, 1801, file #7060, p56

TILTON Elizabeth (Mrs) - warned out of New Boston, 1786, file #2278, p1

TIPPET Alva - formerly of Salem, warned out of Wilton, 1793, file #2604-C, p3

TIPPET Elizabeth Jr - formerly of Salem, warned out of Wilton, 1793, file #2604-C, p3

TIPPET Jerusha (c) - formerly of Salem, warned out of Wilton, 1793, file #2604-C, p3

TIPPET John - formerly of Salem, warned out of Wilton, 1793, file #2604-C, p3

TIPPET John Jr - formerly of Salem, warned out of Wilton, 1793, file #2604-C, p3

TIPPET Joseph (c) - formerly of Salem, warned out of Wilton, 1793, file #2604-C, p3

TIPPET Phebe - formerly of Salem, warned out of Wilton, 1793, file #2604-C, p3

TIPPET Phebe - formerly of New Salem, warned out of Wilton, 1796, file #2604-D, p5

TODD Martha - formerly of Lyden MA, warned out of New Ipswich, 1794, file #2286, p1

TOLLANT William - warned out of Goffstown, 1791, file #3606, p3

TOMMSON David Mr - warned out of New Boston, 1786, file #2278, p5

TOMPSON Mehitable - formerly of Peterborough, warned out of Wilton, 1784, file #2604-E, p5

TOMSON Anna - warned out of New Boston, 1786, file #2278, p5

TOMSON David (c) - warned out of New Boston, 1786, file #2278, p5

TOMSON Elizabeth - warned out of New Boston, 1786, file #2278, p5

TOMSON Lewis - warned out of New Boston, 1786, file #2278, p5

TOMSON Lydia - warned out of New Boston, 1786, file #2278, p5

TOMSON Martha - warned out of New Boston, 1786, file #2278, p5

TOMSON Thomas - warned out of New Boston, 1786, file #2278, p5

TOMSON William - warned out of New Boston, 1786, file #2278, p5

TONEY Sarah - formerly of Ashburnham MA, warned out of New Ipswich, 1783, file #2274, p1

TOWN Thomas - formerly of Wilton, warned out of Temple, 1799, file #7060, p45

TOWNE Thomas (c) - formerly of Amherst, warned out of Wilton, 1776, file #2604-C, p1

TOWNE Elisha - formerly of Amherst, warned out of Wilton, 1777, file #2604-C, p2

TOWNE Elisha - formerly of Amherst, warned out of Wilton, 1776, file #2604-C, p1

TOWNE Joseph (c) - formerly of Amherst, warned out of Wilton, 1776, file #2604-C, p1

TOWNE Joseph (grand Child) - formerly of Amherst, warned out of Wilton, 1777, file #2604-C, p2

TOWNE Mercy - formerly of Amherst, warned out of Wilton, 1777, file #2604-C, p2

TOWNE Mercy - formerly of Amherst, warned out of Wilton, 1776, file #2604-C, p1

TOWNE Samuel - formerly of New Ipswich, warned out of Temple, 1798, file #7060, p59

TOWNE Sarah - formerly of New Ipswich, warned out of Temple, 1798, file #7060, p59

TOWNE Sarah (c) - formerly of Amherst, warned out of Wilton, 1776, file #2604-C, p1

TOWNE Sarah (grand Child) - formerly of Amherst, warned out of Wilton, 1777, file #2604-C, p2

TOWNE Thomas - formerly of Wilton, warned out of Temple, 1795, file #7060, p52

TOWNE Thomas - formerly of Amherst, warned out of Wilton, 1774, file #2604-D, p8

TOWNE Thomas (grand Child) - formerly of Amherst, warned out of Wilton, 1777, file #2604-C, p2

TOWNS Bartholomew - formerly of Amherst, warned out of Wilton, 1777, file #2604-B, p1

TOWNS Elisha (c) - formerly of Amherst, warned out of Wilton, 1777, file #2604-B, p1

TOWNS Joseph - warned out of New Boston, 1785, file #2276, p1

TOWNS Mary - formerly of Amherst, warned out of Wilton, 1777, file #2604-B, p1

TOWNS Mary (c) - formerly of Amherst, warned out of Wilton, 1777, file #2604-B, p1

TOWNS Samuel - warned out of New Boston, 1785, file #2276, p1

TOWNSEND Holley - formerly of Dublin, warned out of Temple, 1798, file #7060, p40

TRASK George - formerly of Lyndeborough, warned out of Wilton, 1793, file #2604-C, p3

TRASK Lydia - formerly of Lyndeborough, warned out of Wilton, 1793, file #2604-C, p3

TURILL Elizabeth (c) - warned out of New Boston, 1792, file #2284, p2

TURILL Elizabeth - warned out of New Boston, 1792, file #2284, p2

TURILL Isaac (c) - warned out of New Boston, 1792, file #2284, p2

TURILL Peter (c) - warned out of New Boston, 1792, file #2284, p2

TURILL William - warned out of New Boston, 1792, file #2284, p2

TURNER Hannah - formerly of Amherst, warned out of Wilton, 1780, file #2604-E, p6

TURNER Mehitibel (c) - formerly of Amherst, warned out of Wilton, 1780, file #2604-E, p6

TURNER William (c) - formerly of Amherst, warned out of Wilton, 1780, file #2604-E, p6

TUTTLE Betsy - formerly of Amherst, warned out of New Boston, 1794, file #2286, p3

TUTTLE Sarah Jr (c) - formerly of Salem MA, warned out of New Boston, 1794, file #2286, p3

TUTTLE William T - formerly of Salem MA, warned out of New Boston, 1794, file #2286, p3

TWEED? Mary - warned out of Goffstown, 1793, file #3609, p8

TWIST Hannah (c) - formerly of Washington, warned out of New Boston, 1794, file #2286, p3

TWIST Lydia - formerly of Washington, warned out of New Boston, 1794, file #2286, p3

TWIST Lydia Jr (c) - formerly of Washington, warned out of New Boston, 1794, file #2286, p3

TWIST Nabby (c) - formerly of Washington, warned out of New Boston, 1794, file #2286, p3

TWIST Nancy (c) - formerly of Washington, warned out of New Boston, 1794, file #2286, p3

TWIST Samuel - formerly of Washington, warned out of New Boston, 1794, file #2286, p3

TWIST Samuel J (c) - formerly of Washington, warned out of New Boston, 1794, file #2286, p3

TWIST Stephen (c) - formerly of Washington, warned out of New Boston, 1794, file #2286, p3

TYLER Dudley - warned out of Goffstown, 1790, file #3609, p6

TYLER Ruth - warned out of Goffstown, 1790, file #3609, p6

UNDERWOOD Betsey - formerly of Londonderry, warned out of Temple, 1793, file #7060, p36

UNDERWOOD John Bulkle - formerly of Litchfield, warned out of Temple, 1793, file #7060, p36

UPHAM Jacob - formerly of Amherst, warned out of Temple, 1799, file #7060, p43

UPHAM Jacob (c) - formerly of Amherst, warned out of Temple, 1799, file #7060, p43

UPHAM Ruth - formerly of Amherst, warned out of Temple, 1800, file #7060, p44

UPHAM Sarah - formerly of Amherst, warned out of Temple, 1799, file #7060, p43

UPTON Elisha - formerly of Methuen MA, warned out of Dunbarton, 1794, file #2527, p2

UPTON Elisha (c) - formerly of Methuen MA, warned out of Dunbarton, 1794, file #2527, p2

UPTON Ephraim (c) - formerly of Methuen MA, warned out of Dunbarton, 1794, file #2527, p2

UPTON Hezekial (c) - formerly of Methuen MA, warned out of Dunbarton, 1794, file #2527, p2

UPTON John (c) - formerly of Methuen MA, warned out of Dunbarton, 1794, file #2527, p2

UPTON Molly - formerly of Dublin, warned out of Temple, 1792, file #7060, p34

UPTON Phebe (widow) - formerly of Reding MA, warned out of Temple, 1794, file #7060, p58

UPTON Sarah - formerly of Methuen MA, warned out of Dunbarton, 1794, file #2527, p2

UPTON Sarah (c) - formerly of Methuen MA, warned out of Dunbarton, 1794, file #2527, p2

UPTON William - formerly of Dublin, warned out of Temple, 1792, file #7060, p34

UPTON William (c) - formerly of Dublin, warned out of Temple, 1792, file #7060, p34

VALEY Anne (so Called) - formerly of Plymouth MA, warned out of New Boston, 1786, file #2278, p2

VANCE William - formerly of Litchfield, warned out of Dunbarton, 1792, file #2525, p6

VANIE Anna - formerly of Weare, warned out of Dunbarton, 1788, file #2521, p4

VANIE Sarah (c) - formerly of Weare, warned out of Dunbarton, 1788, file #2521, p4

VICKER Saviah - formerly of Andover MA, warned out of Wilton, 1784, file #2604-E, p7

WALKER Abigail - warned out of New Ipswich, 1772, file #2266, p1

WALKER Abigail (c) - warned out of New Ipswich, 1772, file #2266, p1

WALKER Eunice (c) - formerly of Peterborough, warned out of New Ipswich, 1789, file #2281, p6

WALKER Lidia - warned out of New Ipswich, 1772, file #2266, p1

WALKER Mary - formerly of Peterborough, warned out of New Ipswich, 1789, file #2281, p6

WALKER Mary (c) - formerly of Peterborough, warned out of New Ipswich, 1789, file #2281, p6

WALKER Silas - formerly of Peterborough, warned out of New Ipswich, 1789, file #2281, p6

WALKER Tabitha - formerly of Hollis, warned out of New Ipswich, 1780, file #2271, p3

WALKER Willard (c) - formerly of Peterborough, warned out of New Ipswich, 1789, file #2281, p6

WALTON Artema (c) - formerly of Lyndeborough, warned out of Temple, 1791, file #7060, p54

WALTON Betsey (c) - formerly of Lyndeborough, warned out of Temple, 1791, file #7060, p54

WALTON Josiah Jr & Wife - formerly of New Ipswich, warned out of Temple, 1796, file #7060, p35

WALTON Reuben - formerly of Lyndeborough, warned out of Temple, 1791, file #7060, p54

WALTON Ruth - formerly of Lyndeborough, warned out of Temple, 1791, file #7060, p54

WALTON Ruth (c) - formerly of Lyndeborough, warned out of Temple, 1791, file #7060, p54

WALTON Sally (c) - formerly of Lyndeborough, warned out of Temple, 1791, file #7060, p54

WARREN Esther - warned out of Goffstown, 1790, file #3607, p6

WARREN Hastin - formerly of Framingham MA, warned out of New Ipswich, 1795, file #2288, p2

WARREN Judith - formerly of Wilton, warned out of New Ipswich, 1794, file #2286, p2

WARREN Nancy (c) - formerly of Wilton, warned out of New Ipswich, 1794, file #2286, p2

WARREN Peter - formerly of Wilton, warned out of New Ipswich, 1794, file #2286, p2

WARREN Peter (c) - formerly of Wilton, warned out of New Ipswich, 1794, file #2286, p2

WARREN Susannah (c) - formerly of Wilton, warned out of New Ipswich, 1794, file #2286, p2

WARREN Thomas (c) - formerly of Wilton, warned out of New Ipswich, 1794, file #2286, p2

WASHER Betsey (c) - formerly of Amherst, warned out of Wilton, 1784, file #2604-D, p2

WASHER Hannah (c) - formerly of Amherst, warned out of Wilton, 1784, file #2604-D, p2

WASHER John (c) - formerly of Amherst, warned out of Wilton, 1784, file #2604-D, p2

WASHER Lydia (c) - formerly of Amherst, warned out of Wilton, 1784, file #2604-D, p2

WASHER Sarah (c) - formerly of Amherst, warned out of Wilton, 1784, file #2604-D, p2

WASHER Solomon - formerly of Amherst, warned out of Wilton, 1786, file #2604-E, p2

WASHER Stephen & Wife - formerly of Amherst, warned out of Wilton, 1784, file #2604-D, p2

WASHER Stephen (c) - formerly of Amherst, warned out of Wilton, 1786, file #2604-E, p2

WASHER Susannah - formerly of Amherst, warned out of Wilton, 1786, file #2604-E, p2

WASHER Susannah (c) - formerly of Amherst, warned out of Wilton, 1786, file #2604-E, p2

WATKINS Jacob - formerly of Packersfield, warned out of Temple, 1800, file #7060, p47

WAUGH Leah (widow) - warned out of New Boston, 1792, file #2284, p1

WEBSTER David - warned out of Goffstown, 1789, file #3607, p4

WEBSTER Dolly (c) - warned out of Goffstown, 1789, file #3607, p4

WEBSTER Mary (c) - warned out of Goffstown, 1789, file #3607, p4

WEBSTER Sarah - warned out of Goffstown, 1789, file #3607, p4

WESTON Anna (c) - formerly of Mason, warned out of New Ipswich, 1794, file #2286, p1

WESTON Elizabeth - formerly of Mason, warned out of New Ipswich, 1794, file #2286, p1

WESTON Reuben - formerly of Mason, warned out of New Ipswich, 1794, file #2286, p1

WESTON Richard (c) - formerly of Mason, warned out of New Ipswich, 1794, file #2286, p1

WESTON Susannah (c) - formerly of Mason, warned out of New Ipswich, 1794, file #2286, p1

WETHERBY Hannah - formerly of Amherst, warned out of New Boston, 1794, file #2286, p3

WETHERBY Joseph - formerly of Amherst, warned out of New Boston, 1794, file #2286, p3

WHEAT Polly - formerly of New Ipswich, warned out of Temple, 1796, file #7060, p35

WHEELER Abner - warned out of New Boston, 1789, file #2281, p3

WHEELER Abner Jr - warned out of New Boston, 1789, file #2281, p3

WHEELER Amos (c) - formerly of Langdon, warned out of Temple, 1793, file #7060, p36

WHEELER Anna - formerly of Landgon, warned out of Temple, 1793, file #7060, p36

WHEELER James (c) - formerly of Langdon, warned out of Temple, 1793, file #7060, p36

WHEELER Jerediah (c) - formerly of Sutton, warned out of Dunbarton, 1790, file #2523, p10

WHEELER Levina - formerly of Sutton, warned out of Dunbarton, 1790, file #2523, p10

WHEELER Levina (c) - formerly of Sutton, warned out of Dunbarton, 1790, file #2523, p10

WHEELER Mary - warned out of New Boston, 1789, file #2281, p3

WHEELER Phebe (c) - formerly of Landgon, warned out of Temple, 1793, file #7060, p36

WHEELER Samuel - formerly of Langdon, warned out of Temple, 1793, file #7060, p36

WHEELER Sarah - formerly of Concord, warned out of New Ipswich, 1791, file #2283, p2

WHEELER Thomas (c) - formerly of Langdon, warned out of Temple, 1793, file #7060, p36

WHEELER William (c) - formerly of Sutton, warned out of Dunbarton, 1790, file #2523, p10

WHEELER William Jr - formerly of Sutton, warned out of Dunbarton, 1790, file #2523, p10

WHITAKER Tabitha - warned out of New Ipswich, 1773, file #2267, p1

WHITCOMB Eli - formerly of Hancock, warned out of New Ipswich, 1788, file #2280, p3

WHITE Abigal - warned out of Goffstown, 1791, file #3606, p3

WHITE Anne (c) - warned out of Goffstown, 1784, file #3608, p9

WHITE Betsey (c) - formerly of Lexington MA, warned out of Dearing, 1788, file #7059, p20

WHITE Debora - warned out of Goffstown, 1784, file #3608, p9

WHITE Edward (c) - warned out of Goffstown, 1784, file #3608, p9

WHITE Elizabeth (c) - warned out of Goffstown, 1784, file #3608, p9

WHITE Elizabeth (c) - warned out of Goffstown, 1791, file #3606, p3

WHITE Ester (c) - warned out of Goffstown, 1791, file #3606, p3

WHITE Henry (c) - warned out of Goffstown, 1784, file #3608, p9

WHITE Jenot (c) - warned out of Goffstown, 1791, file #3606, p3

WHITE John - formerly of Lexington MA, warned out of Dearing, 1788, file #7059, p20

WHITE Kim? (c) - warned out of Goffstown, 1791, file #3606, p3

WHITE Lydia - formerly of Lexington MA, warned out of Dearing, 1788, file #7059, p20

WHITE Mary (c) - warned out of Goffstown, 1791, file #3606, p3

WHITE Sam'l G - warned out of Goffstown, 1784, file #3608, p9

WHITE Samuel (c) - formerly of Lexington MA, warned out of Dearing, 1788, file #7059, p20

WHITE Susannah - formerly of Lexington MA, warned out of Dearing, 1788, file #7059, p20

WHITE Susannah - warned out of Goffstown, 1791, file #3606, p3

WHITE Susannah (c) - formerly of Lexington MA, warned out of Dearing, 1788, file #7059, p20

WHITE William - warned out of Goffstown, 1791, file #3606, p3

WHITE William (c) - formerly of Lexington MA, warned out of Dearing, 1788, file #7059, p20

WHITEMAN Abigail - formerly of Ashburnham MA, warned out of New Ipswich, 1795, file #2288, p3

WHITEMAN Henry - formerly of Ashburnham MA, warned out of New Ipswich, 1795, file #2288, p3

WHITEMORE Deborah - warned out of New Ipswich, 1772, file #2266, p3

WHITEMORE Elizabeth (c) - warned out of New Ipswich, 1772, file #2266, p3

WHITEMORE Peletiah - warned out of New Ipswich, 1772, file #2266, p3

WHITEMORE Phebe - warned out of New Boston, 1785, file #2276, p1

WHITEMORE Polley - formerly of Townsend MA, warned out of Temple, 1795, file #7060, p52

WHITING Dorothy - formerly of Pelham, warned out of Temple, 1779, file #7060, p10

WHITING Eleazar - formerly of Pelham, warned out of Temple, 1779, file #7060, p10

WHITNEY Alnathan - warned out of Goffstown, 1790, file #3609, p5

WHITNEY Betey (c) - warned out of Goffstown, 1790, file #3609, p5

WHITNEY Lucy - warned out of Goffstown, 1790, file #3609, p5

WHITNEY Lydia (c) - warned out of Goffstown, 1790, file #3609, p5

WHITNEY Polly (c) - warned out of Goffstown, 1790, file #3609, p5

WHITNEY Silas (c) - formerly of Lincoln, warned out of New Ipswich, 1780, file #2271, p2

WICOMB Thomas & Wife - formerly of Goffstown, warned out of Dunbarton, 1790, file #2523, p3

WILKINS Elisha - formerly of Lyndeborough, warned out of Temple, 1798, file #7060, p40

WILKINS Elisha - formerly of Lyndeborough, warned out of Dearing, 1788, file #7059, p7

WILKINS Elizabeth (c) - formerly of Heniker, warned out of Dearing, 1788, file #7059, p7

WILKINS Freda - formerly of Lyndeborough, warned out of Temple, 1798, file #7060, p40

WILKINS John (c) - formerly of Marlborough, warned out of New Ipswich, 1789, file #2281, p6

WILKINS Josiah - formerly of Marlborough, warned out of New Ipswich, 1789, file #2281, p6

WILKINS Josiah (c) - formerly of Marlborough, warned out of New Ipswich, 1789, file #2281, p6

WILKINS Judith - formerly of Heniker, warned out of Dearing, 1788, file #7059, p7

WILKINS Lavina (c) - formerly of Marlborough, warned out of New Ipswich, 1789, file #2281, p6

WILKINS Lois (c) - formerly of Marlborough, warned out of New Ipswich, 1789, file #2281, p6

WILKINS Lucy - warned out of New Boston, 1786, file #2278, p4

WILKINS Naomi (c) - formerly of Lyndeborough, warned out of Temple, 1798, file #7060, p40

WILKINS Naomi (c) - formerly of Heniker, warned out of Dearing, 1788, file #7059, p7

WILKINS Olive (c) - formerly of Lyndeborough, warned out of Temple, 1798, file #7060, p40

WILKINS Olive (c) - formerly of Heniker, warned out of Dearing, 1788, file #7059, p7

WILKINS Polly - formerly of Wilton, warned out of Temple, 1802, file #7060, p38

WILKINS Rebecca (c) - formerly of Heniker, warned out of Dearing, 1788, file #7059, p7

WILKINS William (c) - formerly of Marlborough, warned out of New Ipswich, 1789, file #2281, p6

WILLARD Sally - formerly of Temple, warned out of New Ipswich, 1787, file #2279, p2

WILLIAMS Aaron - formerly of Wooburn, warned out of New Ipswich, 1785, file #2276, p6

WILLIAMS Aaron (c) - formerly of Wooburn, warned out of New Ipswich, 1785, file #2276, p6

WILLIAMS Deborah - formerly of Wooburn, warned out of New Ipswich, 1785, file #2276, p6

WILLIAMS Deborah (c) - formerly of Wooburn, warned out of New Ipswich, 1785, file #2276, p6

WILLIAMS Eleazer - formerly of Windham CT, warned out of Wilton, 1774, file #2604-C, p2

WILLIAMS Hannah - formerly of Mason, warned out of New Ipswich, 1794, file #2286, p1

WILLIAMS Hannah - formerly of Cambridge, warned out of New Ipswich, 1783, file #2274, p1

WILLIAMS Joann - formerly of Mason, warned out of Wilton, 1782, file #2604-E, p8

WILLIAMS Joel (c) - formerly of Mason, warned out of New Ipswich, 1794, file #2286, p1

WILLIAMS Lydia - formerly of Pepperell, warned out of New Ipswich, 1773, file #2267, p1

WILLIAMS Mehitable - formerly of Mile Slip, warned out of Wilton, 1783, file #2604-E, p11

WILLIAMS Nath'l - formerly of Mason, warned out of New Ipswich, 1794, file #2286, p1

WILLIAMS Nathaniel - formerly of Cambridge, warned out of New Ipswich, 1783, file #2274, p1

WILLIAMS Polly (c) - formerly of Mason, warned out of New Ipswich, 1794, file #2286, p1

WILLIAMS Rhoda - formerly of Mile Slip, warned out of Wilton, 1783, file #2604-E, p11

WILLIAMS Samuel (c) - formerly of Mason, warned out of New Ipswich, 1794, file #2286, p1

WILLIAMS Sarah (c) - formerly of Cambridge, warned out of New Ipswich, 1783, file #2274, p1

WILLIAMS Sarah (c) - formerly of Wooburn, warned out of New Ipswich, 1785, file #2276, p6

WILSON Betty (c) - formerly of Dublin, warned out of Temple, 1799, file #7060, p43

WILSON Edward - formerly of Dublin, warned out of Temple, 1799, file #7060, p43

WILSON Edward (c) - formerly of Dublin, warned out of Temple, 1799, file #7060, p43

WILSON Hugh - formerly of Peterborough, warned out of New Ipswich, 1789, file #2281, p6

WILSON Lydia - formerly of Dublin, warned out of Temple, 1799, file #7060, p43

WILSON Lydia (c) - formerly of Dublin, warned out of Temple, 1799, file #7060, p43

WILSON Martha - formerly of Duxbery School, warned out of Wilton, 1780, file #2604-E, p6

WILSON Mrs James (Sr) - warned out of New Boston, 1780, file #2271, p5

WILSON Polly (c) - formerly of Dublin, warned out of Temple, 1799, file #7060, p43

WILSON Sally (c) - formerly of Dublin, warned out of Temple, 1799, file #7060, p43

WIMON Hannah - warned out of Goffstown, 1788, file #3607, p3

WINCHESTER Adam (c) - warned out of New Boston, 1787, file #2279, p4

WINCHESTER Betty (c) - warned out of New Boston, 1787, file #2279, p4

WINCHESTER Deborah (c) - warned out of New Boston, 1787, file #2279, p4

WINCHESTER Isaac (c) - warned out of New Boston, 1787, file #2279, p4

WINCHESTER Lemuel - warned out of New Boston, 1787, file #2279, p4

WINCHESTER Lydia (c) - warned out of New Boston, 1787, file #2279, p4

WINCHESTER Silas (c) - warned out of New Boston, 1787, file #2279, p4

WITHEREL Jno Longley - formerly of Mason, warned out of Temple, 1795, file #7060, p52

WITTCOM Eliz - formerly of Hancock, warned out of New Ipswich, 1787, file #2279, p1

WOOD Hannah - formerly of Raby, warned out of Temple, 1795, file #7060, p50

WOODARD Hannah - formerly of Ashburnham MA, warned out of New Ipswich, 1786, file #2281, p1

WOODBURY Amery (c) - warned out of New Boston, 1787, file #2279, p4

WOODBURY Benjamin (c) - warned out of New Boston, 1787, file #2279, p4

WOODBURY Hannah (c) - warned out of New Boston, 1787, file #2279, p4

WOODBURY William & Wife - warned out of New Boston, 1787, file #2279, p4

WOODMAN Hepesibah - formerly of Dunstable, warned out of New Ipswich, 1789, file #2281, p6

WOODS Sibbel - formerly of Groton, warned out of New Ipswich, 1774, file #2268, p1

WORCHESTER Tohabud? - formerly of Westford MA, warned out of New Ipswich, 1791, file #2283, p1

WOTTON Isabel - formerly of Beverly MA, warned out of New Ipswich, 1786, file #2279, p2

WRIGHT Aaron - formerly of Concord MA, warned out of Temple, 1800, file #7060, p47

WRIGHT Betsey (c) - formerly of Concord MA, warned out of Temple, 1800, file #7060, p47

WRIGHT Betty (c) - warned out of Goffstown, 1792, file #3606, p2

WRIGHT Deaby (c) - warned out of Goffstown, 1792, file #3606, p2

WRIGHT Elizabeth - warned out of Goffstown, 1792, file #3606, p2

WRIGHT Elizabeth (c) - formerly of Ashby MA, warned out of New Ipswich, 1794, file #2286, p1

WRIGHT Hannah (c) - formerly of Ashby MA, warned out of New Ipswich, 1794, file #2286, p1

WRIGHT Hepzebeth (c) - formerly of Concord MA, warned out of Temple, 1800, file #7060, p47

WRIGHT James (c) - warned out of Goffstown, 1792, file #3606, p2

WRIGHT John - warned out of Goffstown, 1792, file #3606, p2

WRIGHT Joseph (c) - formerly of Concord MA, warned out of Temple, 1800, file #7060, p47

WRIGHT Love (c) - formerly of Ashby MA, warned out of New Ipswich, 1794, file #2286, p1

WRIGHT Martin (c) - warned out of Goffstown, 1792, file #3606, p2

WRIGHT Mary - formerly of Ashby MA, warned out of New Ipswich, 1794, file #2286, p1

WRIGHT Rachael - warned out of Goffstown, 1780, file #3606, p6

WRIGHT Rebecca (c) - warned out of Goffstown, 1792, file #3606, p2

WRIGHT Sarah - formerly of Concord MA, warned out of Temple, 1800, file #7060, p47

WRIGHT Sarah (c) - formerly of Ashby MA, warned out of New Ipswich, 1794, file #2286, p1

WRIGHT Susannah (c) - warned out of Goffstown, 1792, file #3606, p2

WRIGHT Thomas (c) - formerly of Ashby MA, warned out of New Ipswich, 1794, file #2286, p1

WYMAN Abel (c) - formerly of Wilton, warned out of Temple, 1803, file #7060, p48

WYMAN David (c) - formerly of Wilton, warned out of Temple, 1803, file #7060, p48

WYMAN Henery - warned out of Goffstown, 1793, file #3608, p1

WYMAN Henery - warned out of Goffstown, 1790, file #3609, p6

WYMAN James - formerly of Wilton, warned out of Temple, 1803, file #7060, p48

WYMAN Nathaniel - warned out of New Boston, 1793, file #2285, p1

WYMAN Nathaniel - warned out of Goffstown, 1789, file #3607, p5

WYMAN Rhoda - formerly of Wilton, warned out of Temple, 1803, file #7060, p48

WYMAN Sarah - warned out of New Boston, 1793, file #2285, p1

WYMAN Washington - formerly of Wilton, warned out of Temple, 1803, file #7060, p48

YEULIN Joshua Pool - formerly of Fitchburg MA, warned out of New Ipswich, 1785, file #2276, p5

YOUNG Hugs - warned out of New Boston, 1790, file #2282, p2

SURNAME INDEX

BELL (continued)
314 317
BELLOWS, 242
BENNET, 57 240 242 342 352
BENNETT, 15 42 48 147 244 257
299 309 329
BENSON, 203
BERRY, 288
BETT, 233
BETTEY, 10 115 282
BEVES, 231
BEVIN, 2
BEVINS, 1 2
BICKFORD, 113
BIGELOW, 8 202 262
BIRD, 234
BIREBA, 177
BISBEE, 302
BISHOP, 2 34 47 141 181 204
BIXBE, 10 14 15 87 178 187 188
262 279 287 296 304 312 314
BIXBEE, 258
BIXBIE, 312
BIXBY, 55 98 102 114 171 181
185 219 301 334 335 341 343
BLACHARD, 201
BLACKMAN, 10
BLAIR, 24 30 272
BLAISDELL, 120 201
BLAKE, 196 249 273 293
BLANCHARD, 1 3 4 7 20 30 32
33 36-40 45 50 52 53 75 120
143 147 152 156 158 164 171
182 190 195 197 198 201 208
210 224 244 247 263 270 275
277 283 301 317 318 327 332
337 338 343
BLANEY, 53
BLASDELL, 59 113 184 258 309
BLASDON, 307
BLASSDELL, 143
BLOAD, 78 263

BLODGET, 35 85 117 265 340
BLODGETT, 118 140 196 213
267 269 292
BLOOD, 26 41 55 104 111 116
117 130 150 151 161 172 175
257 263 266 273 280 285 311
322 329
BLUNT, 264 277
BOARDMAN, 258
BOFFE, 43 78 89 168 264
BOFFEE, 90
BOGES, 217
BOHANAN, 128 172 201
BOID, 147
BOIES, 219
BOIL, 33
BOLTER, 96
BOND, 5 106
BONNEY, 31
BOOTMAN, 57 92
BORDEN, 178
BOSSEE, 12 69 168 259 297
BOURKETT, 190
BOUTALL, 247
BOUTEL, 276
BOUTELL, 4 195 238
BOUTWELL, 12 296
BOVEN, 230
BOWEN, 6 8 17 79 227 229 302
BOWER, 211
BOWERS, 44 46 54 55 211 227
300 301 326 335
BOWIE, 219
BOWIN, 52 53
BOWMAN, 6
BOWTELL, 12
BOYCE, 136
BOYD, 8 147 204 205 238
BOYDON, 205
BOYES, 3 100 108 121 127 173
185 186 188 189 199 217 230
258 272 275 346

480

SWALLOW, 237 301
SWAN, 19 144 147 152 326 344
    347 355
SWEAT, 76 99 170
SWEATT, 128 140
SWEET, 142 177 264 271 355
SWETT, 313
SWIFT, 355
SYMONDS, 162 187 262
TAGGART, 2 10 11 16 32 34 46
    52 60 62 64 66 71 79 87 93 97
    98 99 102 119 133 136 140 141
    156 158 160 166 167 176 177
    183 184 191 213-215 222 254
    280 282 287 297 312 324 326
    355
TALBERT, 96
TALBORD, 169
TALBURT, 44
TARBEL, 106
TARBELL, 37 39 49 50 64 88 95
    115 152 153 172 193 257 280
    306 310
TARBOSC, 160
TARBOX, 45 80 279
TAYLOR, 12 14 20 34 36 37 54
    62-64 82 120 126 130 132 134
    135 137 142 144 146 151 160
    170 173 190 191 202 212 224
    228 230 231 242-244 256 299
    307 312 316 335
TEMPLE, 28 79 83 121 159 167
    259 316 338 350
TEMPLETON, 242 329
TENNEY, 233
TERRILL, 223
THING, 96
THOM, 192 213
THOMAS, 273 350
THOMPSON, 90 125 200 213 243
    246 311
THORN, 248

THORNTON, 130 136 148 196
    201 222 324 355
THORTON, 8 10
THURSTON, 31 336
TIDDER, 355
TILTON, 44 79
TITCOMB, 112 313
TODD, 83 112 169 313
TOLBART, 234
TOLBERT, 126
TOLBUSH, 234
TOLFORD, 114 169
TOLLBURT, 79
TON, 122
TOOTHAKER, 331
TOPLIN, 313
TOURTETTELL, 218
TOWAN, 46
TOWN, 206
TOWNE, 13 14 35 48 293
TOWNSEND, 33 80 237
TRACY, 37 180 313
TRAVIS, 286
TREADWELL, 139 232
TREAT, 237
TRICKEY, 66
TRUCE, 259
TRUE, 196
TRUEL, 125 134 259 307
TRUELE, 44
TRUSSELL, 333
TUCK, 286
TUCKER, 79 96 107 113 172 225
    266 267 315 316
TURNER, 169 289
TUTTLE, 25 67 91 111 121 149
    209 243 255 258 274 290 310
    323 328 329 333
TUXBURY, 143 270
TUXEBURY, 315
TWISS, 165 303 304 316
TYLER, 122 230 318 331 332

.

www.ingramcontent.com/pod-product-compliance
Lightning Source LLC
Chambersburg PA
CBHW060126280326
41932CB00012B/1438